WESTERN
CIVILIZATIONS

Winkel Tripel Projection

NORTH POLAR REGION

NORTH AMERICA

ARCTIC OCEAN

ASIA

East Siberian Sea

New Siberian Islands

Laptev Sea

Victoria Island

North Magnetic Pole

North Pole ·

Novaya Zemlya

Svalbard

Franz Josef Land

Baffin Bay

GREENLAND

Iceland

ARCTIC CIRCLE

ARCTIC

QUEEN ELIZABETH ISLANDS

GREENLAND

Iceland

Baffin Bay

ARCTIC CIRCLE

NORTH AMERICA

Hudson Bay

Lake Superior

Lake Huron

Lake Michigan

L. Ontario

L. Erie

Gulf of St. Lawrence

Island of Newfoundland

NORTH PACIFIC OCEAN

TROPIC OF CANCER

Hawaii

GULF OF MEXICO

CENTRAL AMERICA

CARIBBEAN SEA

WEST INDIES

NORTH ATLANTIC OCEAN

MID ATLANTIC RIDGE

ALEUTIAN TRENCH

EQUATOR

Samoa Islands

Tahiti

Amazon Basin

SOUTH AMERICA

SOUTH ATLANTIC OCEAN

TROPIC OF CAPRICORN

SOUTH PACIFIC OCEAN

Falkland Islands

Cape Horn

Drake Passage

ANTARCTIC CIRCLE

ANTARCTIC PENINSULA

Alexander Island

WEDDELL SEA

Ellsworth Land

Marie Byrd Land

ANTARCTICA

POLYNESIA

GLOBAL SATELLITE MOSAIC

The beauty and complexity of Earth's landscapes—above and below the oceans—is revealed with the Global Satellite Mosaic. The mosaic was produced for the National Geographic Society by NASA's Jet Propulsion Laboratory, using more than 500 satellite images from the National Oceanic and Atmospheric Administration. The cloud-free images show Earth in its natural colors as it might be seen from space. One can easily identify the world's major glaciers, deserts, mountain ranges, and rain forests. For example, follow the green ribbon of lush vegetation along the Nile into the stark, dry Sahara. The mountain ranges seem to rise off the map thanks to digital elevation databases from the Department of Defense. The deepest areas of the ocean realm are colored dark blue in contrast to the light blue areas highlighting continental shelves, submarine ridges, and underwater mountains.

BIOSPHERE

Thousands of satellite images were combined to show a picture of biospheric productivity. In the oceans, red, yellow, and green indicate waters rich in phytoplankton. On land, green areas show high potential plant productivity; tan areas suffer from productivity limitations due to aridity and temperature.

THE

SAT

SOUTH POLAR REGION

ARCTIC OCEAN

Franz Josef Land
North Land

SIBERIA

Ural Mountains

EUROPE

Aral Sea
Black Sea

Lake Baikal

ASIA

Kamchatka Peninsula

GOBI

NORTH

PACIFIC

OCEAN

TROPIC OF CANCER

ARABIAN PENINSULA

INDIA

ARABIAN SEA

BAY OF BENGAL

PHILIPPINE SEA

SOUTH CHINA

AFRICA

Congo Basin

Madagascar

INDONESIA

MICRONESIA

MELANESIA

EQUATOR

Kalahari Desert

INDIAN

OCEAN

AUSTRALIA

SOUTH

PACIFIC

TROPIC OF CAPRICORN

Cape of Good Hope

SOUTHWEST INDIAN RIDGE

SOUTHEAST INDIAN RIDGE

KERGUELEN PLATEAU

TASMAN SEA

NEW ZEALAND

North Island

South Island

Wilkes Land

ANTARCTICA

SOUTH POLAR REGION

ANTARCTIC CIRCLE

Weddell Sea

Queen Maud Land

Antarctic Peninsula

Alexander I.

Bellingshausen Sea

ANTARCTICA

WEST ANTARCTICA

Marie Byrd Land

Transantarctic Mountains

South Pole

EAST ANTARCTICA

Ross Ice Shelf

Ross Sea

Wilkes Land

South Magnetic Pole

ANTARCTIC CIRCLE

THE NEED FOR SATELLITES

The Global Satellite Mosaic, along with the biosphere image (lower left) and the temperature image (lower right) provides an integrated view of our world. The very high elevations of the Himalaya and Tibet show up as a cold area (blue, temperature image)and as a plant-poor area (tan, biosphere image). Temperature, plant life, and landscape are interrelated. The need to understand the forces shaping environmental change has led to a space race among various countries. In 1997 alone some 85 rockets launched more than 140 satellites–mostly from China, Europe, Japan, Russia, and the United States. Some satellites provide vital communication links propelling economic development; other satellites supply data on patterns and trends associated with agricultural productivity, pollution monitoring, weather forecasting, and many other environmental concerns.

WINKEL TRIPEL PROJECTION, CENTRAL MERIDIAN 0°
SCALE 1:38,931,000
1 CENTIMETER = 389 KILOMETERS 1 INCH = 614 MILES AT THE EQUATOR

KILOMETERS

STATUTE MILES

WORLD

MAP

SURFACE TEMPERATURE

Reddish colors vividly show average high temperatures on the two largest continents, Africa and Asia, from the Sahara to Central Asia. Latitude, mountains, and oceans influence land temperatures.

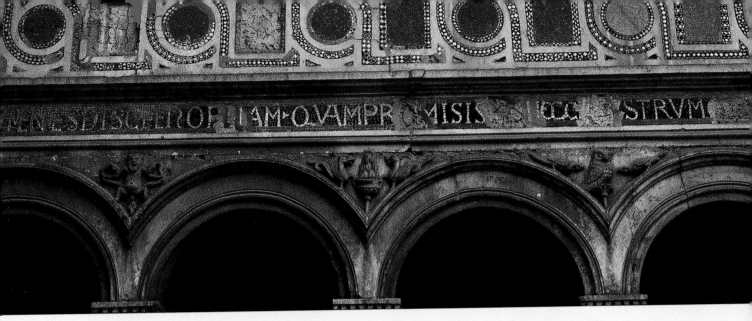

VOLUME C/FIFTEENTH EDITION

JUDITH G. COFFIN

ROBERT C. STACEY

BASED ON *WESTERN CIVILIZATIONS*

BY EDWARD McNALL BURNS

ROBERT E. LERNER

STANDISH MEACHAM

W · W · NORTON & COMPANY · NEW YORK · LONDON

WESTERN
CIVILIZATIONS

THEIR HISTORY
& THEIR CULTURE

W. W. Norton & Company has been independent since its founding in 1923, when William Warder Norton and Mary D. Herter Norton first published lectures delivered at the People's Institute, the adult education division of New York City's Cooper Union. The Nortons soon expanded their program beyond the Institute, publishing books by celebrated academics from America and abroad. By mid-century, the two major pillars of Norton's publishing program—trade books and college texts— were firmly established. In the 1950s, the Norton family transferred control of the company to its employees, and today—with a staff of four hundred and a comparable number of trade, college, and professional titles published each year—W. W. Norton & Company stands as the largest and oldest publishing house owned wholly by its employees.

Composition: TSI Graphics
Manufacturing by R. R. Donnelley
Book design by Antonina Krass
Director of Manufacturing/College: Roy Tedoff
Editor: Karl Bakeman
Associate Director, Electronic Media: Steven S. Hoge
Copy Editor: Barbara Gerr
Production Editor: Chris Granville
Editorial Assistants: Sarah England, Sarah Mann

Library of Congress Cataloging-in-Publication Data

Coffin, Judith G., 1952–
    Western civilizations: their history & their culture / Judith G. Coffin, Robert C. Stacey.—15th ed.
        p. cm.
    "Based on Western Civilizations by Robert E. Lerner, Standish Meacham,
Edward McNall Burns."
    Includes bibliographical references and index.
    ISBN 0-393-92699-0
    1. Civilization, Western—Textbooks. 2. Europe—Civilization—Textbooks. I. Stacey,
Robert C. II. Lerner, Robert E. Western civilizations, their history and their culture. III Title.

CB245.C65 2005
909'.09821—dc22   2004058148

W. W. Norton & Company, Inc., 500 Fifth Avenue, New York, NY 10110
www.wwnorton.com

W. W. Norton & Company Ltd., Castle House, 75/76 Wells Street, London W1T 3QT
1 2 3 4 5 6 7 8 9 0

To our families—Robin, Will, and Anna Stacey, and Willy, Zoe, and Aaron Forbath—for their patience and support. They reminded us that books such as this are worth the work, and also that there are other things in life.

To Robert Lerner, Standish Meacham, Edward McNall Burns, and Marie Burns, our predecessors who successfully guided *Western Civilizations* for thirteen editions, spanning six decades.

About the Book

Used by over 1,000,000 students *Western Civilizations* is renowned for its balanced presentation, clear prose, and exceptional treatment of cultural history. Originally published in 1942, the book began as an outgrowth of Edward McNall Burns's western civilizations course at Rutgers University. Robert Lerner (Northwestern University) and Standish Meacham (University of Texas at Austin) took over authorship in the ninth edition and extended the book's traditional strengths to include the new social history. Beginning with the fourteenth edition, Judith Coffin (University of Texas at Austin) and Robert Stacey (University of Washington) debuted as the third generation of authors to lead this book. While Coffin and Stacey maintain the balanced presentation of *Western Civilizations*, they have enlarged the conception of "Western Civilization" to take in the diversity of the European world.

About the Authors

Judith G. Coffin received her Ph.D. in modern French history from Yale University. She has taught at Harvard University and the University of California, Riverside, and is currently associate professor of history at the University of Texas at Austin, where she won a 1999 University of Texas President's Associates' Award for Teaching Excellence. Her research interests focus on the social and cultural history of gender, mass culture, slavery, race relations, and colonialism. She is the author of *The Politics of Women's Work: The Paris Garment Trades, 1750-1915.*

Robert C. Stacey is Dean of Social Sciences and Professor of History and Jewish Studies at the University of Washington in Seattle. A long-time teacher of western civilization and medieval European history, he has received Distinguished Teaching Awards from both the University of Washington and Yale University, where he taught from 1984 to 1988. The author or coauthor of four books, he is a Fellow of the Royal Historical Society and has held awards from the American Council of Learned Societies and from the Guggenheim Foundation. His current research deals with the history of Jews in medieval England.

Robert E. Lerner is professor of medieval history at Northwestern University, where he has served as director of the Humanities Program. He has won awards from the National Endowment for Humanities, the American Council of Learned Studies, the Guggenheim Foundation, and the Rockefeller Foundation. His books include *The Feast of Saint Abraham: Medieval Millenarians and the Jews; The Age of Adversity: The Fourteenth Century; The Heresy of Free Spirit in the Middle Ages;* and *The Powers of Prophecy.*

Standish Meacham is professor emeritus at the University of Texas at Austin. He has received grants from the Guggenheim Foundation, the American Council of Learned Studies, and the American Philosophical Society. His books include *Regaining Paradise: Englishness and the Early Garden City Movement; Henry Thornton of Clapman, 1760-1815; Lord Bishop: The Life of Samuel Wilberforce; A Life Apart: The English Working Class, 1890-1914;* and *Toynbee Hall and Social Reform, 1880-1914.*

CONTENTS

CHAPTER 20   FROM RESTORATION TO REVOLUTION,
1815–1848   704

DIGITAL HISTORY: Nationalism and Music

CHAPTER 21   WHAT IS A NATION? TERRITORIES, STATES,
AND CITIZENS, 1848–1871   742

PART VII   THE WEST AT THE
WORLD'S CENTER

CHAPTER 22   IMPERIALISM AND COLONIALISM
(1870–1914)   780

DIGITAL HISTORY: The Olympics Past and Present

DIGITAL HISTORY: Cold War

PART VIII   THE WEST AND THE WORLD

CHAPTER 27   THE COLD WAR WORLD: GLOBAL POLITICS, ECONOMIC RECOVERY, AND CULTURAL CHANGE   974

CHAPTER 28   RED FLAGS AND VELVET REVOLUTIONS: THE END OF THE COLD WAR, 1960–1990   1010

DIGITAL HISTORY: War and Technology

CHAPTER 29   A WORLD WITHOUT WALLS: GLOBALIZATION AND THE WEST   1044

MAPS

CHRONOLOGIES

Documents

PREFACE

Since the 1920s, the western civilization survey course has held a central place in the curricula of American universities and high schools. Yet the concept of "western civilization" remains both elusive and controversial. It seems appropriate, therefore, that we begin by defining our terms. How do we, as authors, conceive of our subject?

During much of the twentieth century, "western" civilization meant "the civilization of western Europe," to which the earlier history of the Ancient Near East was somewhat arbitrarily attached. Western civilization was therefore presented as beginning at Sumer, developing in Egypt, and then flowering in Greece. From Greece it passed to Rome, which transmitted it to France, Germany, England, Italy, and Spain, whose emigrating colonists then transferred it to the Americas after 1492. Rather like a train passing through stations, western civilization was thus conceived as picking up "cargo" at each of its stops, but always retaining the same engine and the same baggage cars.

This vision of western civilization was not only selective, it was often tied to a series of contentious assumptions. It cast the worldwide dominance of the European imperial powers between roughly 1800 and 1950 as the culmination of several thousand years of historical development, which it was the obligation of historians to explain. It also tended to presume that European global dominance in the nineteenth and twentieth centuries reflected and demonstrated the superiority of western European civilization over the African, Asian, and Native American civilizations the Europeans conquered during the heyday of their imperial expansion.

Historians today are keenly aware of how much such an account leaves out. It slights the use of force and fraud in European expansion. It ignores the sophistication, dynamism, and humanity of the many cultures it sidelines. By neglecting the crucial importance of Byzantium and Islam, it gives a misleadingly narrow account even of the development of European civilization. And it also misleads us about the western civilizations created in North and South America after 1492, which were creole, or hybrid, cultures, not simply European cultures transplanted to other shores. This is not to argue that a study of western civilization must give way to a study of world civilization. It is merely to insist that understanding the historical development of the West requires us to place this subject in a much wider geographical and cultural context; and that, shorn of its triumphalism, the history of western civilization becomes vastly more interesting.

In this textbook, we will argue that the West cannot be understood as a single, continuous historical culture. Rather, there have been a number of western civilizations, whose fundamental characteristics have changed markedly over time. We mean, therefore, for our title, *Western Civilizations,* to be taken seriously. We will treat "western" as a geographical designator referring to the major civilizations that developed in and around the Mediterranean Sea between 3500 B.C.E. ("Before the Common Era," equivalent to the Christian dating system B.C., "Before Christ") and 500 C.E. ("Common Era," equivalent to the Christian dating system A.D., "Anno Domini," "the Year of the Lord"). We will also treat as "western" the civilizations that emerged out of the Mediterranean world in the centuries after 500 C.E., as the Greco-Roman world of antiquity divided into Islamic, Byzantine, and Latin Christian realms. The interdependence and mutual influences of these three western civilizations upon each other will be a recurring theme of this book.

Western Civilizations rests on the efforts and learning of three generations of historians. Edward McNall Burns, Robert Lerner, and Standish Meacham constructed a textbook that combined a vigorous narrative style with wide-ranging attention to the diverse ways in which ordinary people have organized their lives in response to changing environments, visions, and goals. In continuing their work, we have tried to retain these traditional strengths by remaining attentive to narrative, by aiming for clarity and accessibility without compromising on accuracy or ignoring complexity, and by presenting "high" and "popular" politics and culture as part of a single, shared world of historical experience.

We have also made some significant changes to the book, reflecting the changing historical interests of teachers, students, and scholars. In keeping with our broadened understanding of western civilizations, we devote much more attention to the world outside western Europe than once was customary. We have continued to integrate new scholarly work in social and cultural history and the history of gender into our narrative, but we have also substantially increased the attention we pay to economic, religious, and military history. In this new edition, we also pay particular attention to the varying ways in which these different western civilizations sought to govern themselves and the territories they conquered. "Empire" has been a consistent theme

in the history of the West for more than four thousand years. In revising this book for its Fifteenth Edition, we have tried to do justice to its importance.

As we did for the Fourteenth Edition, we have substantially revised or completely rewritten most of the chapters in this volume, including many that were first composed only four years ago. New maps and new art have been added to every chapter, and the prose throughout the book has been tightened, resulting in a book that is more concise than its predecessor despite its expanded coverage of empire, religion, and gender. Users of the Fourteenth Edition will note particularly dramatic changes in Parts I, IV, and VI, in which chapters have been combined or reordered for greater clarity and concision, and in Part VIII, in which all the chapters have been completely rewritten. But in every chapter they will find arguments that have been modified and material that has been updated to reflect the most recent scholarship.

Responding to the requests of teachers, we have reorganized and rewritten Part I, "The Ancient Near East," to make it easier for students and their instructors to follow the development first of Mesopotamian civilization and then of ancient Egypt. We have also shortened Part I by combining three chapters into two and reducing some of the narrative detail. We have retained, however, our distinctive emphasis on the cultural interactions and historical dynamism of these early civilizations and added to our coverage of several subjects, including the Egyptian Middle Kingdom and the origins of the alphabet.

In Part II, the prose of Chapters 3 and 4 ("The Greek Experiment," "The Expansion of Greece") has been sharpened, the coverage updated, and the map program expanded and improved. Chapter 5, "Roman Civilization," has been reorganized and rewritten to link the social and economic changes of the late Republic more directly to the political struggles of the period. The discussion of Augustus has been rewritten and expanded to better explain the ideology of Augustan rule. More attention is also paid to Roman women, and to the economic difficulties of the third century C.E. In Chapter 6, "Christianity and the Transformation of the Roman World," readers will find an entirely new discussion of early Christianity and a much improved discussion of monasticism.

In Part III, Chapter 7 contains a revised discussion of Muslim philosophy, science, medicine, and literature and a fuller explanation of the importance of papermaking to Muslim cultural and intellectual life. We have also tried to bring greater clarity to the issue of

Iconoclasm in Byzantine religion. In Chapter 8, the account of English and French royal politics has been shortened and the entire chapter streamlined. In Chapter 9, readers will find a clearer account of the growth of schools and their relationship to the twelfth-century renaissance. Both chapters have also been thoroughly revised for style.

Part IV, "From Medieval to Modern," now begins with Chapter 10, "The Later Middle Ages," and ends with Chapter 14, "Religious Wars and State Building." The most important changes here are in Chapter 13, "Reformations of Religion," which has been rewritten (although not reconceived) from beginning to end, and in Chapter 14, where readers will find, among much else, a new account of the events that led to the English Civil War.

Part V opens with a new Chapter 15, "Absolutism and Empire, 1660–1789." This chapter brings the economic, cultural and political developments of this period together into a single narrative, instead of dividing them between two separate chapters as we did in the Fourteenth Edition. Part V then continues with two chapters, both newly composed for the Fourteenth Edition, on the Scientific Revolution and the Enlightenment. Both chapters are concerned with the context in which new ideas were forged and with how those ideas came to matter for a range of people, from philosophers, rulers, and bureaucrats to explorers, artists, and artisans. Here and throughout the Fifteenth Edition, we have continued to expand the treatment of gender. This has meant adding more material concerning women but also, more important, showing the ways in which family, sexuality, models of femininity, and the rights and duties of men and women became central to politics and culture at different historical moments.

In Part VI, two chapters from the Fourteenth Edition have been merged into a single new Chapter 19 on industrial society, focused on the relationship between social, economic, and cultural change—or on industry as a way of life. This new chapter is more explicit about different models of industrialization, about the global relationships that nineteenth-century industry fostered and thrived on, and about the environmental repercussions of industrialization. Chapters 20 and 21, on nineteenth-century politics, have been reorganized and shortened to make the tumultuous changes of the period easier to follow. Chapter 20 now goes from the conservative reaction against the French Revolution of 1789 to the renewed outbreak of revolution in 1848. We have clarified the discussion of nineteenth-century political ideologies and moved it into this chapter. We

have also revised the cultural history and added a new section on Romanticism as a way of seeing and understanding the wider world. Chapter 21 begins with the revolutions of 1848 in central and eastern Europe and then treats the issues those revolutions raised, nation and state building, as they played out elsewhere.

In Part VII, we have revised the introduction to imperialism and sharpened the focus of Chapter 23. Much more major revisions have been made in Part VIII, which has been reorganized and almost entirely rewritten. Chapter 27 analyzes the collapse of Europe's empires as an integral part of the postwar restructuring of Europe and of the emergence of a Cold War world. This chapter now includes material on a subject that has fascinated historians recently: how any culture recovers from a catastrophe on the order of World War II. Chapter 28 traces developments from the 1960s, including the worldwide upheaval of 1968, to the collapse of the USSR, which is now treated in more depth. Chapter 29 concludes the volume with a discussion of how historians look at globalization at the beginning of the twenty-first century.

INNOVATIVE PEDAGOGICAL PROGRAM

Western Civilizations, Fifteenth Edition, is designed for maximum readability. The crisp, clear, and concise narrative is also accompanied by a highly useful pedagogical program to help students study while engaging them in the subject matter. Highlights of this innovative program include:

- **NEW End-of-Chapter Key Terms.** In response to requests from professors, each chapter includes a list of ten to fifteen key terms to help students focus on the key ideas, events, or people in the chapter.

- **NEW Digital History Features.** Twelve Digital History Feature essays distributed throughout the text direct students to the Western Civilizations Digital History Center (www.wwnorton.com/wciv), where they can explore collections of primary sources on topics that include:
  The Primary Element—Water (Chapter 1)
  Women and Mystery Cults (Chapter 4)
  Grapes and Civilization (Chapter 6)
  The Market (Chapter 8)
  After the Black Death (Chapter 10)
  Spices (Chapter 12)
  Astrology, Astronomy, and Galileo (Chapter 15)
  Revolutionary Paris (Chapter 18)
  Nationalism and Music (Chapter 20)

Olympics (Chapter 23)
Cold War (Chapter 26)
Military Strategy and New Technology (Chapter 28)

- **In-Text Documents.** To add depth to the more focused narrative of *Western Civilizations*, each chapter contains an average of four primary sources, two of which are paired to convey a sense of historical complexity and diversity.

- **Map Program with Enhanced Captions.** Over 130 beautiful maps appear throughout the text, including twenty-five new maps, each accompanied by an enhanced caption designed to engage the reader analytically while conveying the key role that geography plays in the development of history and the societies of the world.

- **In-Chapter Chronologies.** Several brief chronologies built around particular events, topics, or periods appear in each chapter and are designed to provide road maps through the narrative detail.

- **Focus Question System.** To ensure that students remain alert to key concepts and questions on every page of the text, focus questions guide their reading in three ways: (1) a focus question box appears at the beginning of each chapter to preview the chapter's contents; (2) relevant questions reappear at the start of the section in which they are discussed; and (3) running heads on the righthand pages keep these questions in view throughout the chapter.

- **Pull Quotes.** Lifted directly from the narrative, pull quotes appear throughout each chapter to highlight key thoughts and keen insights while keeping students focused on larger concepts and ideas.

RESOURCES FOR STUDENTS

NEW Western Civilizations Digital History Center
www.wwnorton.com/wciv
by Steven Kreis, Wake Technical College
This online resource for students—designed specifically for use with *Western Civilizations*—provides access to online review and research materials. Its contents include:

Review Materials, consisting of chapter objectives and outlines, interactive chapter chronologies, focus questions and answers, interactive map exercises, and flash cards.

Online Primary Sources
Multimedia elements for each chapter are categorized by type—documents, images, maps, audio, and video.

Digital History Features
These twelve online explorations deal with topics that arc over several chapters in *Western Civilizations*. Each exploration is integrated with the text through a Digital History Feature essay that summarizes the topic and poses several critical thinking questions.

Media Analysis Worksheets
Each media element in the Digital History Features is accompanied by a Media Analysis Worksheet, which guides students through a three-part approach to the resources:
Observation: prompts students to articulate what they see, hear, or read
Expression: prompts students to write about or "voice" their observations
Connection: prompts students to place their responses within a historical context

NEW Study Guide
by Margaret Minor and Paul Wilson, both of Nicholls State University
The Study Guide gives students a comprehensive means for review and self-assessment. Each chapter contains a chapter outline, identifications, multiple-choice questions, matching, and true/false questions, chronologies, and short-answer and essay questions.

Resources for Instructors

NEW Instructor's Manual
by Steven Kreis, Wake Technical College
This valuable resource follows the chapter organization of the text and provides a wide array of teaching tools, including extensive lecture outlines, lecture launchers, key lecture topics, various classroom/recitation activities, and lists of suggested films and readings. New to this edition are suggestions for integrating electronic media into the classroom.

NEW Test-Item File
By Michael Halvorson, Pacific Lutheran University, and Michael Prahl, University of Northern Iowa
Available in both print and electronic formats, this test bank contains over one thousand multiple-choice ques-

tions, approximately thirty to forty per chapter, ranging from factual to conceptual. In addition, there are twelve basic identifications and four to six essay/short-answer questions per chapter.

Norton Media Library
These PowerPoint slides are optimized for lecture use and contain audio and visual files as well as many of the images and maps from the text.

Map Transparencies

ACKNOWLEDGMENTS

The drafts of the manuscript have benefited from careful reading by and suggestions from a group of professors to whom we are greatly indebted. Our sincere thanks to:

- Michael Bailey, St. Louis University
- Cindy Blackburn, Trident Technical College
- Jonathan Bone, William Paterson University
- Stephen A. Bourque, California State University, Northridge
- James Brophy, University of Delaware
- Pierre Cagniart, Texas State University—San Marcos
- Kevin K. Carroll, Arizona State University
- Mary Kay Carter, University of Michigan, Dearborn
- Christine Caldwell, St. Louis University
- Susan Carrafiello, Wright State University
- Katherine Crawford, Vanderbilt University
- Dora Dumont, State University of New York College at Oneonta
- Chiarella Esposito, University of Mississippi
- Mari Firkatian, University of Hartford
- Gerritdina (Ineke) Justitz, North Dakota State University
- Corbett Gottfried, Portland Community College
- Sylvia Gray, Portland Community College
- Michael Halvorson, Pacific Lutheran University
- Carla Hay, Marquette University
- Steven Kreis, Wake Technical College
- Michael Kulikowski, University of Tennessee, Knoxville
- Eileen Lyon, SUNY Fredonia
- Michael Meyer, California State University, Northridge
- John Montano, University of Delaware
- Fred Murphy, Western Kentucky University
- Heather O'Grady-Evans, Elmira College
- Michael Prahl, University of Northern Iowa
- George Robb, William Paterson University
- Shawn Ross, William Paterson University
- Geraldine Ryder, Ocean County College
- George Lawrence Simpson, High Point University
- Carol Taylor, SUNY Albany
- Stephen Wessley, York College
- Clayton Whisnant, Wofford College
- Linda York, Wallace Community College
- Margarita Youngo, Pima Community College
- Ina Zweiniger-Bargielowska, University of Illinois, Chicago

We want to thank Steve Forman and Jon Durbin at W. W. Norton & Company for their faith in this project; Karl Bakeman for his intelligent editing, attentiveness, and exceptional good cheer; and Sarah England, Chris Granville, and Sarah Mann for their help with all aspects of the production process

Robert Stacey is principally responsible for Chapters 1–15. He owes special thanks to Jason Hawke of Northern Illinois University for his extraordinary help in drafting Chapters 1–5. He would also like to acknowledge the assistance of a large number of friends and colleagues around the country who have taken the time to answer queries and offer suggestions: Jon Crump, Gerald Eck, Sandra Joshel, Mary O'Neil, Ben Schmidt, Julie Stein, Joel Walker, and Dan Waugh of the University of Washington; Michael Halvorson, University of Puget Sound; Michelle Ferry, University of California, Santa Barbara; and Byron Nakamura, Southern Connecticut State University. He owes special thanks to Robert Stiefel, University of New Hampshire, whose criticisms of the Fourteenth Edition's treatment of monasticism have greatly improved the new account offered here.

Judith Coffin is principally responsible for the revisions to Chapter 16–29. Many colleagues have supplied expertise and references, but she is especially grateful to Caroline Castiglione, David Crew, Paul Hagenloh, Standish Meacham, John Merriman, Gail Minault, Joan Neuberger, Paula Sanders, Daniel Sherman, James Sidbury, Robert Stephens, Michael Stoff, and Charters Wynn. Special thanks to Tony Hopkins for consulting on imperialism, to James Brophy for his consistently excellent advice on many matters, and to Geoffrey Clayton, who drafted Chapters 16 and 29 as well as significant portions of 24, 26, and 28. Patrick Timmons, Marion Barber, April Smith, and, especially, Cori Crider were terrific research assistants. Her greatest debt for this edition is to Justin Glasson, whose writing, editing, and intellectual energy have made this project a pleasure.

WESTERN
CIVILIZATIONS

PART VI
THE FRENCH AND INDUSTRIAL REVOLUTIONS AND THEIR CONSEQUENCES

FEW EVENTS more profoundly altered the shape of Western culture than the French and Industrial revolutions. The major developments of the nineteenth and early twentieth centuries—the decline of landed aristocracies and the rise of new social groups, the emergence of dramatically new forms of politics, changes in political and social thought, economic expansion, and Europe's expanding hegemony in the world—all had their roots in these two revolutions.

The French and Industrial revolutions took place at about the same time and affected many of the same people, though in different ways and to varying degrees. Together they brought about the collapse of absolutism, mercantilism, and what was left of feudalism. Together they produced the theory and practice of economic individualism and political liberalism. And together, the wrenching changes they wrought polarized Europe for several generations. What historians call the "age of revolution" lasted from the 1770s through at least half the nineteenth century.

Each revolution, of course, produced results peculiarly its own. The French Revolution helped make such terms as *citizen, nation,* and *liberty* central to the political vocabulary of modern times. It encouraged the growth of nationalism—in both liberal and authoritarian forms. The Industrial Revolution changed the economic and cultural landscape of Europe, with ramifications for the private worlds of men and women as well as the economic organization of the world. Despite their unique contributions, the two revolutions must be studied together, for the effects of each magnified the importance of the other.

	POLITICS	SOCIETY AND CULTURE	ECONOMY	INTERNATIONAL RELATIONS
1750		Johann Wolfgang von Goethe (1749–1852)	British export production increases 80 percent (1750–1770)	
	Reign of Catherine the Great of Russia (1762–1796)	William Blake (1757–1827)	British Parliament increases enclosures (1750–1860)	
	American Revolution (1774–1782)	William Wordsworth (1770–1850)	Spinning jenny, water frame, and spinning mule invented (1764–1799)	Poland partitioned by Russia, Austria, and Prussia (1772, 1793, 1795)
		Goethe's *Faust* (1790)	James Watt patents improved steam engine (1769)	
			Industrial Revolution (1780–1880)	
	Louis XVI calls Assembly of Notables (1788)			
	The French Revolution breaks out (1789)	Jeremy Bentham's *Introduction to the Principles of Morals and Legislation* (1789)		
	Great Fear in the French countryside (1789)			
	Declaration of the Rights of Man and of the Citizen (1789)			
	French National Assembly abolishes feudal rights and privileges (1789)			
1790	Slave revolt in St. Domingue (1791)	Edmund Burke's *Reflections on the Revolution in France* (1790)		Slave rebellion in St. Domingue sparks British and Spanish invasion (1791)
	Louis XVI of France overthrown and French Republic declared (1792)	Thomas Paine's *Rights of Man* (1791)		France declares war on Austria and Prussia (1792)
	Reign of Terror (1793–1794)	French Convention abolishes slavery and primogeniture (1793–1794)	Eli Whitney invents cotton gin (1793)	England enters war against France (1793)
	Maximilien Robespierre executed (1794)			Revolutionary France occupies Low Countries, Rhineland, and parts of Spain and Italy (1794–1796)
		Heinrich Heine, German poet (1797–1856)		
		Wordsworth's and Coleridge's *Lyrical Ballads* (1798)		
		Thomas Malthus's *Essay on the Principle of Population* (1798)		
		Eugène Delacroix, French painter (1799–1837)		
	Napoleon Bonaparte is declared temporary consul (1799)	Honoré de Balzac, French novelist (1799–1850)		
1800	President Thomas Jefferson (1800–1808)	Emergence of Romanticism (early 1800s)	Women make up 50 percent of British textile work force (c. 1800)	Peace of Amiens temporarily halts war between Britain and France (1801)
	Bonaparte's Concordat with the pope (1801)	Continental population doubles (1800–1850)		Napoleon unsuccessfully tries to restore slavery in St. Domingue (1801–1803)
	Bonaparte elected Consul for Life by plebiscite (1802)			Louisiana Purchase (1803)
	Bonaparte crowns himself Emperor Napoleon I (1804)	Napoleonic Code (1804)		Independent state of Haiti (formerly St. Domingue) (1804)
		George Sand, novelist (1804–1876)		Nelson's victory at Trafalgar breaks French naval power (1805)
			Napoleon's Continental System imposed (1806)	Napoleon defeats Austria and Russia at battle of Austerlitz (1805)
			Serfdom abolished in Prussia (1807)	
1808	Prussian reform era begins (1808)	Johann Gottlieb Fichte's *Addresses to the German Nation* (1808)		Napoleon invades Spain (1808)

POLITICS	SOCIETY AND CULTURE	ECONOMY	INTERNATIONAL RELATIONS	
			Napoleon marries Mary Louise of the Habsburgs (1809)	1809
	Grimm's Fairy Tales by the Brothers Grimm (1813)		Napoleon's Russian campaign (1812)	
Bourbon monarchy restored in France (1815)			Napoleon exiled to Elba (1814)	
			Congress of Vienna (1814–1815)	
			Napoleon defeated at Waterloo (1815)	
			German Confederation created by Congress of Vienna (1815)	
	Gustav Courbet, French painter (1819–1877)	Prussian Zollverein (customs union) founded (1818)	Quintuple Alliance formed (1818)	
			Greek war of independence (1821–1827)	
Decembrist Revolt in Russia (1825)			Monroe Doctrine (1823)	
Revolution in France, Belgium (1830)		First railway to carry passengers (1830)	Serbia emerges from within Ottoman empire (1828)	
Mazzini founds Young Italy society (1831)				
Electoral Reform Act in England (1832)				
Poor Laws Reform in England (1834)	Alexis de Tocqueville's *Democracy in America* (1835–1840)			
Reign of Queen Victoria (1837–1901)	*The Economist* is founded (1838)			
British Chartist movement (1838–1848)	Emergence of Realism in art and literature (1840s)	Rail transport spreads across Continent (1840s)		
	Great Famine in Ireland (1845–1849)	Zollverein expands to include nearly all German states (1840s)		
		Poor harvests contribute to economic crisis across Europe (1845)	Treaty of Guadalupe Hidalgo ends war between United States and Mexico (1848)	
Repression of revolutionary movements in central and eastern Europe (1848–1850)	Seneca Falls Convention (1848)	Great Irish Famine (1845–1849)		
		California gold rush (1849)	United States buys western territory, including California, for $15 million (1848)	
	Florence Nightingale's medical reforms (1850s)	Serfdom abolished in southern and eastern Europe (1850)		1850
Louis Napoleon Bonaparte overthrows Second Republic (1851)	Great Exhibit of the Works of Industry in All Nations, London (1851)	Great Exhibition of the Works of Industry in All Nations, London (1851)		
		Britain exports half of world's iron (1852)		
		Cotton accounts for 40 percent of domestic exports from Britain (1852)	Crimean War (1854–1856)	
	Charles Darwin's *On the Origin of Species* (1859)		Sardinia takes Lombardy, Papal States, and various duchies (1859)	
	John Stuart Mill's *On Liberty* (1859)	Agricultural laborers still largest work force in Britain (1860)		
Reign of Kaiser Wilhelm I (1861–1888)		Britain and France sign free-trade agreement (1860)		
Civil War in the United States (1861–1865)		Emancipation of serfs in Russia (1861)	Victor Emmanuel II claims title of king of Italy (1861–1878)	
Otto von Bismarck appointed prime minister of Germany (1862)	Victor Hugo's *Les Misérables* (1862)			
	Fyodor Dostoyevsky's *Crime and Punishment* (1866)	Slavery abolished in United States (1865)	Seven Week's War; Prussia takes Schleswig-Holstein (1866)	
Reform Bill of 1867 in England (1867)			Canada gains independence (1867)	
	Mill's *Subjection of Women* (1869)	Railroad connects Mississippi valley with Pacific coast (1869)		
			Franco-Prussian War (1870–1871)	1870
			Italians take Rome from Napoleon III's protection (1870)	
			German empire proclaimed (1871)	

Chapter EIGHTEEN

À MARAT.

DAVID.

THE FRENCH REVOLUTION

I N 1789, ONE EUROPEAN out of every five lived in France. Many Europeans considered France the center of European culture. It followed that a revolution in France would immediately command the attention of Europe and assume international significance. Yet the French Revolution attracted and disturbed men and women for much more important reasons. Both its philosophical ideals and its political realities mirrored attitudes, concerns, and conflicts that had occupied the minds of educated Europeans for several decades. When the revolutionaries pronounced in favor of liberty, they spoke not only with the voice of the eighteenth-century *philosophes*, but with that of the English aristocracy in 1688 and the North American revolutionaries of 1776.

They also raised issues that resonated across Europe. Absolutism was increasingly the bane of a wide spectrum of thoughtful opinion. Aristocrats across Europe and the colonies resented monarchical inroads on their ancient freedoms. Members of the middle class, many of whom were very successful, chafed under a system of official privilege that they increasingly considered outmoded. Peasants fiercely resented what seemed to them the never-ceasing demands of central government on their limited resources. Nor were resentments focused exclusively on absolutist monarchs. Tensions existed as well between country and city dwellers, between rich and poor, overprivileged and underprivileged, slave and free. The French Revolution marked part of a crisis that shook all of late eighteenth-century Europe and its colonies, bringing revolutionary movements to the British Empire, to Belgium and the Netherlands, and to South America. The age of revolution restructured the nations of the West.

The opening of the age of revolution came in the North American colonies. The American Revolution of 1776 was one of the last in a series of conflicts over colonial control of the New World, conflicts that had wracked England and France throughout the eighteenth century. It also became one of the first crises of the old regime at home. "The New World was where the fears and aspirations . . . were first dramatized, where extralegal associations of common citizens defied acts of a sovereign power, where abstract ideals of political philosophy were substantiated in the actions of ordinary men," as one historian recently said. Among

FOCUS QUESTIONS

- What were the causes of the French Revolution?

- How did popular uprisings shape the first stage of the French Revolution?

 • Why did the French Revolution become more radical?

- Why did the Directory fail?

- How did Napoleon centralize his authority?

- What led to Napoleon's downfall?

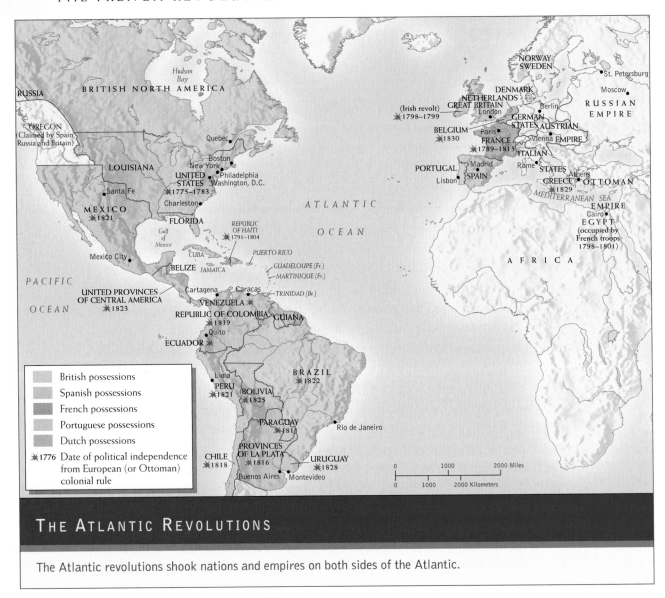

THE ATLANTIC REVOLUTIONS

The Atlantic revolutions shook nations and empires on both sides of the Atlantic.

"enlightened" Europeans, the success with which citizens of the new nation had thrown off British rule and formed a republic based on Enlightenment principles was the source of tremendous optimism. Change would come. Reform was possible. The costs would be modest.

If the American Revolution first dramatized Europeans' "fears and aspirations," the events in France deepened them. The French Revolution proved a more radical project, though it did not necessarily begin that way. It became immeasurably more costly—protracted, complex, and violent. It aroused much greater hopes and consequently, in many cases, bitter disillusionment. It raised issues that would not be settled for half a century.

THE FRENCH REVOLUTION: AN OVERVIEW

In Charles Dickens's *Tale of Two Cities* (1859), the source of many popular images of revolution, the French upheaval blurs into a frightening picture of bloodthirsty crowds watching a guillotine. The picture is memorable but misleading. The "French Revolution" is a shorthand for a complex series of events between 1789 and 1799. (Napoleon ruled from 1799 to 1814–1815.) To simplify, those events can be divided into three stages. In the first stage, running from 1788 to 1792, the struggle was constitutional and relatively peaceful.

An increasingly bold elite articulated its grievances against the king. Like the American revolutionaries, elites refused taxation without representation, attacked "despotism," or arbitrary authority, and offered an Enlightenment-inspired program to rejuvenate the nation. Reforms, many of them breathtakingly wide ranging, were instituted—some accepted or even offered by the king, and others passed over his protests. The peaceful, constitutional phase did not last. Unlike the American Revolution, the French Revolution did not stabilize around one constitution or one set of political leaders, for many reasons. Reforms met with resistance, dividing the country. The threat of change in France created international tensions. In 1792, these tensions exploded into war and the monarchy fell, to be replaced with a republic. The second stage of the Revolution, which lasted from 1792 to 1794, was one of crisis and consolidation. A ruthlessly centralized government mobilized all the country's resources to fight the foreign enemy as well as counterrevolutionaries at home, to destroy traitors and the vestiges of the Old Regime. The Terror, as this policy was called, did save the republic, but it exhausted itself in factions and recriminations. In the third phase, from 1794 to 1799, the government, still at war with Europe, drifted into corruption and almost inevitably into military rule under Napoleon. Napoleon continued the war until his final defeat in 1815.

THE COMING OF THE REVOLUTION

What were the causes of the French Revolution?

What were the long-term causes of the revolution in France? Historians long ago argued that the causes and outcomes should be understood in terms of class conflict. According to this interpretation, a rising bourgeoisie, or middle class, inspired by the political and economic ideology of the Enlightenment and by its own self-interest, overthrew what was left of the aristocratic order. This interpretation drew on the writings of the nineteenth-century philosopher Karl Marx and on much twentieth-century sociology.

Historians have substantially modified this bold thesis. Certainly, to understand the origins of the French

CHRONOLOGY		
PERIODS OF THE FRENCH REVOLUTION ERA, 1789–1815		
1) The First French Revolution		July 1789–August 1792
2) The Second French Revolution		August 1792–July 1794
3) The Directory		1794–1799
4) The Napoleonic Era		1799–1815

Revolution, we must first analyze late-eighteenth-century French society. Yet that society was not racked by conflict between a "bourgeois" class and the aristocracy. Instead, it was increasingly dominated by a new elite or social group that brought together aristocrats, officeholders, professionals, and, to a lesser degree, merchants and businessmen. To understand the Revolution, we need to understand this new social group and its conflicts with the government of Louis XVI.

French society was divided into three Estates. (An individual's "estate" marked his standing, or status, and it determined legal rights, taxes, and so on.) The First Estate comprised all the clergy; the Second Estate, the nobility. The Third Estate, by far the largest, included everyone else, from wealthy lawyers and businessmen to urban laborers and poor peasants. Within the political and social elite of the country, a small but powerful group, these legal distinctions often seemed artificial. To begin with, in the upper reaches of society, the social boundaries between nobles and wealthy commoners were ill defined. Noble title was accessible to those who could afford to buy an ennobling office. For example, close to fifty thousand new nobles were created between 1700 and 1789. The order depended for its vigor on a constant infusion of talent and economic power from the wealthy social groups of the Third Estate.

The case of the family of the revolutionary figure Honoré Gabriel Riqueti, the comte de Mirabeau, illustrates the changes. Mirabeau's sixteenth-century ancestors had been merchants. In 1570, however, one of them had purchased the seigneury of Mirabeau. In the following century another bought himself the title of marquis. Mirabeau, a lawyer, also held a commission in the cavalry that his grandfather once commanded.

Aristocrats spoke of a distinction between the nobility of the "sword" and of the "robe," the former supposedly of a more ancient and distinguished lineage derived from military service, the latter aristocrats because they had purchased administrative or judicial office (hence the robe). As the example of the Mirabeau family shows, even that distinction could be illusory.

Wealth did not take predictable forms. Most noble wealth was "proprietary," that is, tied to land, urban properties, purchased offices, and the like. Yet noble families did not disdain trade or commerce, as historians long thought. In fact, noblemen financed most industry, and they also invested heavily in banking and such enterprises as ship owning, the slave trade, mining, and metallurgy. Moreover, the very wealthy members of the Third Estate also preferred to invest in secure, proprietary holdings. Thus throughout the century, much "bourgeois" wealth was transformed into "noble" wealth, and a significant number of rich "bourgeois" became noblemen. This economically important bourgeois group did not see itself as a separate class. Its members recognized themselves as different from and often opposed to the common people, who worked with their hands. But they identified with the values of a nobility to which they frequently aspired.

There were, nonetheless, important social tensions. Less prosperous lawyers—and there were an increasing number of them—were jealous of the privileged position of a favored few in their profession. Over the

course of the century the price of offices rose, making it more difficult to buy one's way into the nobility, and creating tensions between middling members of the Third Estate and the very rich in trade and commerce who, by and large, were the only group able to afford to climb the social ladder. Not surprisingly, the more financially modest nobles resented the success of rich, upstart commoners whose income allowed them the luxury of life in the grand style that they could not have themselves. In sum, several fault lines ran through the elite and the middle classes. Despite these fissures, however, these social groups could join in attacking with mounting vehemence a government and an economy that were not serving their interests.

The new elite aired its frustrations in the widening circles of public debate (see Chapter 17). Although ideas did not "cause" the Revolution, they played a critical role in articulating the discontents felt by the elite and middle orders. The political theories of Locke, Voltaire, and Montesquieu could appeal to both discontented nobles and members of the middle class. Voltaire was popular because of his attacks on noble privileges; Locke and Montesquieu gained widespread followings because of their defense of private property and limited sovereignty. Montesquieu's ideas were especially congenial to the noble lawyers and officeholders who dominated France's powerful law courts, the *parlements*. They read his doctrine of checks and balances as a defense of parlements as the govern-

Prerevolutionary Propaganda, 1788–1789. These prints illustrate the popular view that the Third Estate (commoners) were carrying the burden of national taxation on its shoulders while doing the productive work of the nation.

mental bodies that would provide a check to the despotism of the king's government. When conflicts arose, noble leaders presented themselves as defenders of a national political community threatened by the king and his ministers.

The campaign for change was also fueled by proponents of economic reform. The "physiocrats," as they were called in France, urged the government to simplify the tax system and free the economy from mercantilist regulations. They urged the government to lift its controls on the price of grain, for example, which had been imposed to keep the cost of bread low but, they argued, had interfered with the natural workings of the market.

Whether or not the public accepted the physiocrats' prescriptions, it agreed with their diagnosis: the French economy was seriously ailing. A general price rise during much of the eighteenth century, which permitted the French economy to expand by providing capital for investment, created hardship for the peasantry and for urban tradesmen and laborers. Their plight deteriorated further at the end of the 1780s,

Evidence indicates that between 1787 and 1789 the unemployment rate in many parts of urban France was as high as 50 percent.

when poor harvests sent bread prices sharply higher. In 1788 families found themselves spending more than 50 percent of their income on bread, which made up the bulk of their diet. The following year the figure rose to as much as 80 percent. Poor harvests reduced demand for manufactured goods, and contracting markets in turn created unemployment. Many peasants left the countryside for the cities, hoping to find work there, only to discover that urban unemployment was far worse than that in rural areas. Evidence indicates that between 1787 and 1789 the unemployment rate in many parts of urban France was as high as 50 percent.

Peasants on the land were caught in a web of obligations to landlords, church, and state: a tithe, or levy on farm produce owed to the church; fees for the use of a landlord's mill or wine press; fees to the landlord as well when land changed hands. In addition, peasants paid a disproportionate share of both direct and indirect taxes—the most onerous of which was the salt tax—levied by the government. (For some time the production of salt had been a state monopoly; every individual was required to buy at least seven pounds a year from the government works. The result was a commodity whose cost was often as much as fifty or sixty times its actual value.) Further grievances stemmed from the requirement to maintain public roads (the corvée) and

from the hunting privileges that nobles for centuries had regarded as the distinctive badge of their order.

An inefficient tax system further weakened the country's financial position. Not only was taxation tied to differing social standings, it varied as well from region to region—some areas, for example, were subject to a much higher rate than others. Special circumstances and exemptions made the task of collectors all the more difficult. The financial system, already burdened by debts incurred under Louis XIV, all but broke down completely under the increased expenses brought on by French participation in the American Revolution. The cost of servicing the national debt of approximately 4 billion livres in the 1780s consumed 50 percent of the nation's budget.

Problems with the economy reflected weaknesses in France's administrative structure, ultimately the responsibility of the country's absolutist monarch, Louis XVI (1774–1792). Anxious to serve his people in "enlightened" ways, Louis wished to improve the lot of the poor, to abolish torture, and to shift the burden of taxation onto the richer classes. Yet he lacked the ability to put these reforms into effect. His well-intentioned attempts at reform ultimately undermined his own authority. He appointed such reformers as Anne-Robert-Jacques Turgot, a philosopher, physiocrat, and former provincial intendant, and Jacques Necker, a Swiss Protestant banker, as finance ministers, only to arouse opposition among traditionalist factions within the court. He allowed his wife, the young but strong-willed Marie Antoinette—daughter

CHRONOLOGY

ORIGINS OF THE FRENCH REVOLUTION, 1788–1789

Failure of fiscal reform	1787–1788
Louis XVI summons the Estates General	May 1788
Bread riots across France	Spring 1789
Estates General convenes in Paris	May 1789
Third Estate declares itself the National Assembly	May 1789
Oath of the Tennis Court	June 1789
Fall of the Bastille	July 14, 1789

Louis XVI. Louis inherited both absolutism and challenges to it.

of Austria's Maria Theresa—a free hand to dispense patronage among her friends. The result was constant intrigue and frequently reshuffled administrative alliances at Versailles.

Wrangling between the central government and the provincial parlements also slowed reform. As we have noted, the parlements had reasserted their independence during the early years of the reign of Louis XV. Throughout the century they had grown increasingly insistent on what they began to call their "constitutional" rights, or privileges. When Louis XVI pressed for new taxes to be paid by the nobility as well as the rest of the community after the expensive Seven Years' War, the parlements successfully defended the nobility's right to exemption from major national taxes. In the mid-1770s this episode was reenacted when Turgot, Louis XVI's principal financial minister, proposed reducing the debt by curtailing court expenses,

replacing the corvée with a small tax on landowners, and abolishing certain guild restrictions in order to stimulate manufacturing. The Paris parlement steadfastly opposed such innovations, claiming that Turgot was trampling on ancient prerogatives and privileges—and he was.

In the end, however, the plan failed because the king withdrew his support of Turgot. Although the parlements were jealous of their prerogatives, they could not indefinitely inhibit the reforms of a determined monarch. Louis XVI, however, was not determined. By 1788, a weak monarch, together with a chaotic financial situation and severe social tensions, brought absolutist France to the edge of political disaster.

THE DESTRUCTION OF THE OLD REGIME

How did popular uprisings shape the first stage of the French Revolution?

The fiscal crisis precipitated the Revolution. In 1787 and 1788 the king's principal ministers, Charles de Calonne and Loménie de Brienne, attempted to institute a series of reforms to stave off bankruptcy. To meet the mounting deficit, they proposed new taxes, notably a stamp duty and a direct tax on the annual produce of the land.

Hoping to persuade the nobility to agree to these reforms, the king summoned an Assembly of Notables from among the aristocracy. This group used the financial emergency to attempt major constitutional reforms. Most important, they insisted that any new tax scheme must have the approval of the Estates General, the representative body of the three estates of the realm, and that the king had no legal authority to arrest and imprison arbitrarily. In this, they echoed the English aristocrats of 1688 and the American revolutionaries of 1775.

Faced with economic hardship and financial chaos, Louis XVI summoned the Estates General (which had not met since 1614) to meet in 1789. His action appeared to many as the only solution to France's deepening problems. Long-term grievances and short-term hardships had produced bread riots across the country in the spring of 1789. Looting in Brittany, Flanders, Provence, and elsewhere was accompanied by demands that the king take measures to make bread affordable.

WHAT IS THE THIRD ESTATE?

The Abbé Emmanuel-Joseph Sieyès (1748–1836) was, by virtue of his office, a member of the First Estate of the Estates General. Nevertheless, his political savvy led him to be elected as a representative of the Third Estate from the district of Chartres. Sieyès was a formidable politician as well as a writer. His career during the Revolution, which he ended by assisting Napoleon to the imperial throne, began with one of the most important radical pamphlets of 1789. In What Is the Third Estate?, *Sieyès posed fundamental questions about the rights of the Estate, which represented the great majority of the population, and helped provoke its secession from the Estates General.*

The plan of this book is fairly simple. We must ask ourselves three questions.

1. What is the Third Estate? *Everything.*
2. What has it been until now in the political order? *Nothing.*
3. What does it want to be? *Something.*

It suffices to have made the point that the so-called usefulness of a privileged order to the public service is a fallacy; that without help from this order, all the arduous tasks in the service are performed by the Third Estate; that without this order the higher posts could be infinitely better filled; that they ought to be the natural prize and reward of recognized ability and service; and that if the privileged have succeeded in usurping all well-paid and honorific posts, this is both a hateful iniquity towards the generality of citizens and an act of treason to the commonwealth.

Who is bold enough to maintain that the Third Estate does not contain within itself everything needful to constitute a complete nation? It is like a strong and robust man with one arm still in chains. If the privileged order were removed, the nation would not be something less but something more. What then is the Third Estate? All; but an "all" that is fettered and oppressed. What would it be without the privileged order? It would be all; but free and flourishing. Nothing will go well without the Third Estate; everything would go considerably better without the two others.

Emmanuel-Joseph Sieyès. *What is the Third Estate?* Translated by M. Blondel, edited by S. E. Finer (London: Phaidon Press, 1964), pp. 53–63.

Fear that the forces of law and order were collapsing and that the common people might take matters into their own hands spurred the delegates to the Estates General. Each of the three orders elected its own deputies—the Third Estate indirectly through local assemblies. These assemblies were charged as well with the responsibility of drawing up lists of grievances (*cahiers des doléances*) further heightening expectations for fundamental reform.

The delegates of the Third Estate, though elected by assemblies chosen in turn by artisans and peasants, represented the outlook of the elite. Only 13 percent were men of business. About 25 percent were lawyers; 43 percent were government officeholders of some sort.

By tradition, each estate met and voted as a body. In the past, this had generally meant that the First Estate (the clergy) had combined with the Second (the nobility) to defeat the Third. Now the Third Estate made it clear it would not tolerate such an arrangement. The Third's interests were articulated most memorably by the Abbé Emmanuel Sieyès, a radical member of the clergy. "What Is the Third Estate?" asked Sieyès, in his famous pamphlet of January 1789. Everything, he answered, and pointed to eighteenth-century social changes to bolster his point. In early 1789, Sieyès' views were still unusually radical. But the leaders of the Third Estate agreed that the three orders should sit together and vote as individuals. More important, they insisted that the Third Estate should have twice as many members as the First and Second.

The king first opposed "doubling the Third," and then changed his position. His unwillingness to take a strong stand on voting procedures cost him support he might otherwise have obtained from the Third Estate.

Shortly after the Estates General opened at Versailles in May 1789, the Third Estate, angered by the king's attitude, took the revolutionary step of leaving the body and declaring itself the National Assembly. Locked out of the Estates General meeting hall on June 20, the Third Estate and a handful of sympathetic nobles and clergymen moved to a nearby indoor tennis court.

Here, under the leadership of the volatile, maverick aristocrat Mirabeau and the radical clergyman Sieyès, they bound themselves by a solemn oath not to separate until they had drafted a constitution for France. This Oath of the Tennis Court, sworn on June 20, 1789, can be seen as the beginning of the French Revolution. By claiming the authority to remake the government in the name of the people, the National Assembly was not merely protesting against the rule of Louis XVI but asserting its right to act as the highest sovereign power in the nation. On June 27 the king virtually conceded this right by ordering all the delegates to join the National Assembly.

The Tennis Court Oath, by Jacques Louis David (1748–1825). In June, 1789, in the hall where royalty played a game known as *jeu de paume* (similar to tennis) leaders of the Revolution swore to draft a constitution. In the center of this painting, standing on the table, is Jean Bailly, president of the National Assembly. Seated at the table below him is Abbé Sieyès. Mirabeau stands in the right foreground with a hat in his left hand.

HOW DID POPULAR UPRISINGS SHAPE THE FIRST STAGE OF THE FRENCH REVOLUTION?

THE DESTRUCTION OF THE OLD REGIME   639

FIRST STAGES OF THE FRENCH REVOLUTION

The first stage of the French Revolution extended from June 1789 to August 1792. In the main, this stage was moderate, its actions dominated by the leadership of liberal nobles and men of the Third Estate. Yet three events in the summer and fall of 1789 furnished evidence that the Revolution was to penetrate to the very heart of French society.

POPULAR REVOLTS

From the beginning of the political crisis, public attention was high. It was roused not merely by interest in political reform, but also by the economic crisis that, as we have seen, brought the price of bread to astronomical heights. Many believed that the aristocracy and the king were conspiring to punish the Third Estate by encouraging scarcity and high prices. Rumors circulated in Paris during the latter days of June 1789 that the king was about to stage a reactionary coup d'état. The electors of Paris (those who had voted for the Third Estate—workshop masters, artisans, shopkeepers) feared not only the king but also the Parisian poor, who had been parading through the streets and threatening violence. The common people would soon be referred to as *sans-culottes*. The term, which translates to "without breeches," was an antiaristocratic badge of pride: a man of the people wore full-length trousers rather than aristocratic breeches, stockings, and gold-buckled shoes. Led by the electors, the people formed a provisional municipal government and organized a militia of volunteers to maintain order. Determined to obtain arms, they made their way on July 14 to the Bastille, an ancient fortress where guns and ammunition were stored. Built in the Middle Ages, the Bastille had served as a prison for many years but was no longer much used. Nevertheless, it symbolized hated royal authority. When crowds demanded arms from its governor, he at first procrastinated and then, fearing a frontal assault, opened fire, killing ninety-eight of the attackers. The crowd took revenge, capturing the fortress (which held only seven prisoners—five common criminals and two persons confined for mental incapacity) and decapitating the governor. Similar groups assumed control in other cities across France. The fall of the Bastille was the first instance of the people's role in revolutionary change.

The second popular revolt occurred in the countryside. Peasants, too, anticipated and feared a monarchical and aristocratic counterrevolution. Rumors flew that

Women of Paris Leaving for Versailles, October 1789. A crowd of women, accompanied by Lafayette and the National Guard, marched to Versailles to confront the king about shortages and rising prices in Paris.

the king's armies were on their way, that Austrians, Prussians, or "brigands" were invading. Frightened and uncertain, peasants and villagers organized militias; others attacked and burned manor houses, sometimes to look for grain, but usually to find and destroy records of manorial dues. This "Great Fear," as historians have labeled it, compounded the confusion abroad in rural areas. The news, when it reached Paris, convinced deputies at Versailles that the administration had simply collapsed.

The third instance of popular uprising, the "October Days" of 1789, was brought on by economic crisis. This time Parisian women from the market district, angered by the soaring price of bread and fired by rumors of the king's continuing unwillingness to cooperate with the Assembly, marched to Versailles on October 5 and demanded to be heard. Not satisfied with its reception by the Assembly, the crowd broke through the gates to the palace, calling for the king to return to Paris from Versailles. On the afternoon of the following day the king yielded. The National Guard, sympathetic to the agitators, led the crowd back to Paris, the procession headed by a soldier holding aloft a loaf of bread on his bayonet.

Each of these popular uprisings shaped the political events unfolding at Versailles. The storming of the Bastille persuaded the king and nobles to agree to the creation of the National Assembly. The "Great Fear" compelled the most sweeping changes of the entire revolutionary period. In an effort to quell rural disorder, on the night of August 4 the Assembly took a giant step toward abolishing all forms of privilege. It eliminated the church tithe, the labor requirement known as the corvée, the nobility's hunting privileges, and a wide variety of tax exemptions and monopolies. In effect, these reforms obliterated the remnants of feudalism. One week later, the Assembly abolished the sale of offices, thereby sweeping away one of the fundamental institutions of the Old Regime. The king's return to Paris during the October Days undercut his ability to resist further changes.

THE NATIONAL ASSEMBLY AND THE LIBERAL REVOLUTION

The Assembly issued its charter of liberties, the Declaration of the Rights of Man and of the Citizen, in Sep-

tember 1789. It declared property to be a natural right, along with liberty, security, and "resistance to oppression." It declared freedom of speech, religious toleration, and liberty of the press inviolable. All citizens were to be treated equally before the law. No one was to be imprisoned or otherwise punished except in accordance with due process of law. Sovereignty was affirmed to reside in the people, and officers of the government were made subject to deposition if they abused the powers conferred on them. These were not new ideas; they represented the outcome of Enlightenment discussions and revolutionary debates and deliberations. The Declaration became the preamble to the new constitution, which the Assembly finished in 1791.

Whom did the Declaration mean by "man and the citizen"? The revolutionaries distinguished between "passive" citizens, guaranteed rights under law, and "active" citizens, who paid a certain amount in taxes, and could thus vote and hold office. About half the adult males in France qualified as "active" citizens. Even their power was curtailed, because they could only vote for "electors," men whose property ownership qualified them to hold office. Later in the revolution, the more radical republic abolished the distinction between active and passive, and the conservative regimes reinstated it. Which men could be trusted to participate in politics and on what terms was a hotly contested issue.

> The Assembly issued its charter of liberties, the Declaration of the Rights of Man and of the Citizen, in September 1789. It declared property to be a natural right, along with liberty, security, and "resistance to oppression." It declared freedom of speech, religious toleration, and liberty of the press inviolable.

So, to a certain extent, were the rights of religious minorities. The revolution gave full civil rights to Protestants, though in areas long divided by religious conflict those rights were challenged by Catholics. The revolution did, hesitantly, give civil rights to Jews, a measure that sparked protest in areas of eastern France. Religious toleration, a central theme of the Enlightenment, meant ending persecution; it did not mean that the regime was prepared to accommodate religious difference. The Assembly abolished serfdom and banned slavery in continental France. It remained silent on colonial slavery, and although delegations pressed the assembly on political rights for free people of color, the assembly exempted the colonies from the constitution's provisions. Events in the Caribbean, as we will see, later forced the issue.

The rights and roles of women became the focus of sharp debate, though most of the discussion centered on

DECLARATION OF THE RIGHTS OF MAN AND OF THE CITIZEN

One of the first important pronouncements of the National Assembly after the Tennis Court Oath was the Declaration of the Rights of Man and of the Citizen. The authors drew inspiration from the American Declaration of Independence, but the language is even more heavily influenced by the ideals of French Enlightenment philosophers, particularly Rousseau. Following are the Declaration's preamble and some of its most important principles.

The representatives of the French people, constituted as the National Assembly, considering that ignorance, disregard, or contempt for the rights of man are the sole causes of public misfortunes and the corruption of governments, have resolved to set forth, in a solemn declaration, the natural, inalienable, and sacred rights of man, so that the constant presence of this declaration may ceaselessly remind all members of the social body of their rights and duties; so that the acts of legislative power and those of the executive power may be more respected . . . and so that the demands of the citizens, grounded henceforth on simple and incontestable principles, may always be directed to the maintenance of the constitution and to the welfare of all. . . .

Article 1. Men are born and remain free and equal in rights. Social distinctions can be based only on public utility.

Article 2. The aim of every political association is the preservation of the natural and imprescriptible rights of man. These rights are liberty, property, security, and resistance to oppression.

Article 3. The source of all sovereignty resides essentially in the nation. No body, no individual can exercise authority that does not explicitly proceed from it.

Article 4. Liberty consists in being able to do anything that does not injure another; thus the only limits upon each man's exercise of his natural laws are those that guarantee enjoyment of these same rights to the other members of society.

Article 5. The law has the right to forbid only actions harmful to society. No action may be prevented that is not forbidden by law, and no one may be constrained to do what the law does not order.

Article 6. The law is the expression of the general will. All citizens have the right to participate personally, or through representatives, in its formation. It must be the same for all, whether it protects or punishes. All citizens, being equal in its eyes, are equally admissable to all public dignities, positions, and employments, according to their ability, and on the basis of no other distinction than that of their virtues and talents. . . .

Article 16. A society in which the guarantee of rights is not secured, or the separation of powers is not clearly established, has no constitution.

Declaration of the Rights of Man and of the Citizen, as cited in K. M. Baker, ed. *The Old Regime and the French Revolution* (Chicago: University of Chicago Press, 1987), pp. 238–239.

OLYMPE DE GOUGES, DECLARATION OF THE RIGHTS OF WOMAN AND OF THE CITIZEN

Opposition to the Declaration of the Rights of Man and of the Citizen *did not come from conservatives alone. Some radicals did not think the Declaration went nearly far enough. In this pamphlet from 1791 Olympe de Gouges, a literate butcher's daughter and political radical, chastised the Declaration's authors for their arrogance in presuming to speak for the rights and best interests of a large part of the Third Estate—its women. Note her satirical attack on the revolutionaries' fascination with "natural laws," a legacy of Enlightenment thought.*

Man, are you capable of being just? It is a woman who asks you this question; at least you will not deny her this right. Tell me! Who has given you the sovereign authority to oppress my sex? Your strength? Your talents? Observe the creator in his wisdom; regard nature in all her grandeur, with which you seem to want to compare yourself; and give me, if you dare, an example of this tyrannical empire. Go back to the animals, consult the elements, study the plants, then glance over the modifications of organized matter, and cede to the evidence when I offer you the means. Seek, search, and distinguish, if you can, the sexes in the administration of nature. Everywhere you will find them mingled, everywhere they cooperate in harmony with this immortal masterpiece.

Only man has fashioned himself a principle out of this exception. Bizarre, blind, bloated by science and degenerate, in this century of enlightenment and wisdom, he, in grossest ignorance, wishes to exercise the command of a despot over a sex that has received every intellectual faculty; he claims to rejoice in the Revolution and claims his rights to equality, at the very least.

"The Declaration of the Rights of Woman and of the Citizen," as cited in Susan Bell and Karen Offen, eds. *Women, the Family and Freedom: The Debate in Documents,* Vol. 1, *1750–1880* (Stanford: Stanford University Press, 1983), pp. 104–106.

the future of working women's guilds, or trade organizations, marriage and divorce, poor relief, and education. The Englishwoman Mary Wollstonecraft's milestone book *A Vindication of the Rights of Woman* (see Chapter 17) was penned during the revolutionary debate over national education. Should girls be educated? To what end? Wollstonecraft, as we have seen, argued strongly that it entailed nothing less than overthrowing prevailing ideas about female character, and forging a new concept of independent and equal womanhood. Even Wollstonecraft, however, only hinted at political representation, aware that such an idea would only "excite laughter." The marquis de Condorcet wrote a pamphlet in 1790 arguing for women's political rights.

Women's political rights found a colorful proponent in Marie Gouze, also known as Olympe de Gouges, the self-educated daughter of a butcher who had become an intellectual and playwright. Like many "ordinary" people who found in the explosion of revolutionary activity the opportunity to address the public by writing speeches, pamphlets, or newspapers, Gouges composed her own manifesto, the Declaration of the Rights of

HOW DID POPULAR UPRISINGS SHAPE THE FIRST STAGE OF THE FRENCH REVOLUTION?

THE DESTRUCTION OF THE OLD REGIME   643

Pays d'états
Main internal customs barriers
Seat of a parlement or other sovereign court

GOVERNMENT AND REGIONAL JURISDICTIONS IN FRANCE BEFORE 1789

Parlements were law courts. Pays d'etat had traditions of independence and their own Estates, which represented different social groups. How might such a system have challenged the monarchy? Why would the revolutionaries have wanted to change it?

Woman and the Citizen (1791). Beginning with the proposition that "social distinctions can only be based on the common utility," she declared that women had the same rights as men, including resistance to author-

ity, participation in government, and naming the fathers of illegitimate children—a revealing glimpse of issues of economic distress, shame, and isolation as experienced by women of the era. Women participated in the

Areas of insurrection

THE REVOLUTIONARY DEPARTMENTS OF FRANCE

Compare this map with the one on page 643. In what ways is this a more "rational" system of territorial administration? How would such a reorganization affect the power of the Church, the nobility, and older governing institutions? What might have been its effects on everyday life? Why did the insurrections occur in the regions indicated
on the map as opposed to others?

everyday activities of the revolution, joining clubs,
demonstrations, and debates; women artisans' organizations had a well-established role in municipal life;
market women were familiar public figures, often central to the circulation of news and spontaneous popular
demonstrations. The regime celebrated the support of
women "citizens," and female figures were allegories for
liberty. Those conceptions, however, were increasingly

tied to an image of women as supportive mothers, educators, and tenders of the private sphere, not to be involved in public.

In this early period of the revolution, the most divisive issue to confront the Assembly involved religion. In November 1789, the National Assembly resolved to confiscate the lands of the church and to use them as collateral for the issue of assignats, interest-bearing notes that eventually circulated as paper money. The Assembly hoped—vainly, as it turned out—that this device would resolve the country's inflationary crisis. In July of the following year it enacted the Civil Constitution of the Clergy, which provided that all bishops and priests should be subject to the authority of the state. Their salaries were to be paid out of the public treasury, and they were required to swear allegiance to the new state, making it clear they served France rather than Rome. The Assembly's aim was to make the Catholic Church of France a truly national and civil institution.

Reforming the church polarized large sections of France. The church's privileged position during the Old Regime, including its vast monastic land holdings, had earned it the resentment of many. On the other hand, the practice of centuries had made the parish church an institution of great local importance. The local priest not only baptized, married, and buried people, he helped with any written documents. The church provided poor relief and other services. In many areas peasants relied on and respected their priests. The dramatic changes embodied in the Civil Constitution of the Clergy thus encountered considerable resistance in some parts of rural France. When the pope threatened to excommunicate priests who signed the Civil Constitution, the stakes rose, driving many local people in the deeply Catholic areas of western France into counterrevolution.

The National Assembly made a series of economic and governmental changes with lasting effects. To raise money, it sold off church lands, although few of the genuinely needy could afford to buy them. To encourage the growth of economic enterprise, it abolished guilds. To rid the country of local aristocratic power, it reorganized local governments. France was divided into eighty-three equal departments. These measures aimed to defend individual liberty and freedom from ancient privilege. Their principal beneficiaries were, for the most part, members of the elite, people on their way up under the previous regime who were able to take advantage of the opportunities, such as buying land or being elected to office, that the new one offered.

A NEW STAGE: POPULAR REVOLUTION

Why did the French Revolution become more radical?

In the summer of 1792, the Revolution entered a second stage. The moderate leaders were toppled and replaced by much more radical "republicans" claiming to rule on behalf of the common people. Why this abrupt and drastic change? Was the Revolution "blown off course"? These are among the most difficult questions about the French Revolution. Answers need to take account of three factors: changes in popular politics, a crisis of leadership, and international polarization.

First, the revolution produced a remarkable politicization of the common people, especially in cities. Newspapers filled with political and social commentary multiplied, freed from restrictions on printing. From 1789 forward, a wide variety of political clubs became part of daily political life. Some were formal, almost like political parties, gathering members of the elite to debate issues facing the country and influence decisions in the assembly. Other clubs opened their doors to those excluded from formal politics, and they read aloud from newspapers and discussed the options facing the country, from the provisions of the constitution to the trustworthiness of the king and his

CHRONOLOGY

THE FIRST FRENCH REVOLUTION, 1789–1792

Fall of the Bastille	July 14, 1789
The "Great Fear"	Summer of 1789
Declaration of the Rights of Man and of the Citizen	August 1789
The "October Days"	1789
National Assembly enacts the Civil Constitution of the Clergy	July 1790
Royal family tries to escape Paris	June 1791
National Assembly declares war on Austria and Prussia	April 1792

ministers. This political awareness was heightened by the crisis of nearly constant shortages and fluctuating prices. Prices particularly exasperated those among the working people of Paris who had demanded changes in 1789 and had eagerly awaited change since then. Urban demonstrations, often led by women, demanded cheaper bread, while political leaders in clubs and newspapers called for the government to control rising inflation. Their leaders also articulated the frustrations of a mass of men and women who felt cheated by the constitution.

A second major reason for the change of course was a lack of effective national leadership. Louis XVI remained a weak, vacillating monarch. He was compelled to support measures personally distasteful to him, in particular the Civil Constitution of the Clergy. He was thus sympathetic to the plottings of the queen, who was in contrast with her brother Leopold II of Austria. Urged on by Marie Antoinette, Louis agreed to attempt an escape from France in June 1791, hoping to rally foreign support for counterrevolution. The members of the royal family managed to slip past their palace guards in Paris, but they were apprehended near the border at Varennes and brought back to the capital. Though the Constitution of 1791 declared France a monarchy, after Varennes, Louis was little more than a prisoner of the Assembly.

The third major reason for the dramatic turn of affairs was war. From the outset of the Revolution, men and women across Europe had been compelled, by the very intensity of events in France, to take sides in the conflict. In the years immediately after 1789, the Revolution in France won the enthusiastic support of a wide range of thinkers. The British poet William Wordsworth, who later became disillusioned, recalled his initial mood: "Bliss was it in that dawn to be alive. . . ." His sentiments were echoed across the Continent by poets and philosophers, including the German Johann Gottfried von Herder, who declared the Revolution the most important historical moment since the Reformation. Political societies in Britain proclaimed their allegiance to the principles of the new revolution, often quite incorrectly seeing it as nothing more than a French version of the events of 1688. In the Low Countries, a "patriot" group organized strikes and plotted a revolution of its own against dominant merchant oligarchies. Political revolutionaries in western Germany and Italy welcomed the possibility of invasion by the French as a means of achieving radical change within their own countries.

THE COUNTERREVOLUTION

Others opposed the course of the Revolution from the start. Exiled nobles, who had fled France for sympathetic royal courts in Germany and elsewhere, did all they could to stir up counterrevolutionary sentiment. In Britain the conservative cause was strengthened by the publication in 1790 of Edmund Burke's *Reflections on the Revolution in France.* A Whig politician who had sympathized with the American revolutionaries, Burke nevertheless attacked the Revolution in France as a monstrous crime against the social order. The French failure to pay proper respect to tradition and custom had destroyed the fabric of French civilization, woven by centuries of national history.

Burke's famous pamphlet, in which he painted a romantic and highly inaccurate picture of the French king and queen, helped arouse sympathy for the counterrevolutionary cause. That sympathy did not turn to active opposition until France became a threat to international stability and the individual ambitions of the great powers. It was that threat which led to war in 1792, and which kept the Continent in arms for a generation.

The first European states to express public concern about events in revolutionary France were Austria and Prussia. In August 1791, they declared that restoring order and the rights of the monarch of France was a matter of "common interest to all sovereigns of Europe." The leaders of the French government pronounced the declaration an affront to national sovereignty, hoping that enthusiasm for a war would unite the French people and strengthen the revolution. Monarchists both within and outside France played into their hands with plots and pronouncements against the government. On April 20, 1792, the Assembly declared war against Austria and Prussia.

Almost all of the various political factions in France welcomed the war. The Assembly's leaders expected an aggressive policy to shore up the people's loyalty and bring freedom to the rest of Europe. Counterrevolutionaries hoped the intervention of Austria and Prussia would begin to undo all that had happened since 1789. Radicals, suspicious of aristocratic leaders and the king, believed that war would expose all "traitors" who harbored misgivings about the Revolution

> Though the Constitution of 1791 declared France a monarchy, after Varennes, Louis was little more than a prisoner of the Assembly.

DEBATING THE FRENCH REVOLUTION: EDMUND BURKE AND THOMAS PAINE

The best-known debate on the French Revolution set the Irish-born conservative Edmund Burke against the British radical Thomas Paine. Burke opposed the French Revolution from the beginning. His Reflections on the Revolution in France *was published early, in 1790, when the French king was still securely on the throne. Burke disagreed with the premises of the Revolution. Rights, he argued, were not abstract and "natural," but the results of specific historical traditions. Remodeling the French government without reference to the past and failing to pay proper respect to tradition and custom had, in his eyes, destroyed the fabric of French civilization.*

Thomas Paine was one of many to respond to Burke. The Rights of Man *(1791–1792) defended the Revolution and, more generally, conceptions of human rights. In the polarized atmosphere of the revolutionary wars, simply possessing Paine's pamphlet was cause for imprisonment in Britain.*

EDMUND BURKE

You will observe, that from the Magna Charta to the Declaration of Right, it has been the uniform policy of our constitution to claim and assert our liberties, as an entailed inheritance derived to us from our forefathers. . . . We have an inheritable crown; an inheritable peerage; and a house of commons and a people inheriting privileges, franchises, and liberties, from a long line of ancestors. . . .

You had all these advantages in your ancient states, but you chose to act as if you had never been moulded into civil society, and had every thing to begin anew. You began ill, because you began by despising every thing that belonged to you. . . . If the last generations of your country appeared without much luster in your eyes, you might have passed them by, and derived your claims from a more early race of ancestors. . . . Respecting your forefathers, you would have been taught to respect yourselves. You would not have chosen to consider the French as a people of yesterday, as a nation of low-born servile wretches until the emancipating year of 1789. . . . [Y]ou would not have been content to be represented as a gang of Maroon slaves, suddenly broke loose from the house of bondage, and therefore to be pardoned for your abuse of liberty to which you were not accustomed and ill fitted. . . .

. . . The fresh ruins of France, which shock our feelings wherever we can turn our eyes, are not the devastation of civil war; they are the sad but instructive monuments of rash and ignorant councel in time of profound peace. They are the display of inconsiderate and presumptuous, because unresisted and irresistible authority. . . .

Nothing is more certain, than that of our manners, our civilization, and all the good things which are connected with manners, and with civilization, have, in this European world of ours, depended upon two principles; and were indeed the result of both combined; I mean the spirit of a gentleman, and the spirit of religion. The nobility and the clergy, the one by profession, the other by patronage, kept learning in existance, even in the midst of arms and confusions. . . . Learning paid back what it received to nobility and priesthood. . . . Happy if they had all continued to know their indissoluble union, and their proper place. Happy if learning, not debauched by ambition, had been satisfied to continue the instructor, and not aspired to be the master! Along with its natural protectors and guardians, learning will be cast into the mire, and trodden down under the hoofs of a swinish multitude.

Edmund Burke. *Reflections on the Revolution in France* (1790) (New York: Anchor Books, 1973), pp. 45, 48, 49, 52, 92.

THOMAS PAINE

Mr. Burke, with his usual outrage, abuses the *Declaration of the Rights of Man*. . . . Does Mr. Burke mean to deny that man has any rights? If he does, then he must mean that there are no such things as rights any where, and that he has none himself; for who is there in the world but man? But if Mr. Burke means to admit that man has rights, the question will then be, what are those rights, and how came man by them originally?

The error of those who reason by precedents drawn from antiquity, respecting the rights of man, is that they do not go far enough into antiquity. They stop in some of the intermediate stages of an hundred or a thousand years, and produce what was then a rule for the present day. This is no authority at all. . . .

To possess ourselves of a clear idea of what government is, or ought to be, we must trace its origin. In doing this, we shall easily discover that governments must have arisen either *out* of the people, or *over* the people. Mr. Burke has made no distinction. . . .

What were formerly called revolutions, were little more than a change of persons, or an alteration of local circumstances. They rose and fell like things of course, and had nothing in their existance or their fate that could influence beyond the spot that produced them. But what we now see in the world, from the revolutions of America and France, is a renovation of the natural order of things, a system of principles as universal as truth and the existence of man, and combining moral with political happiness and national prosperity.

Thomas Paine. *The Rights of Man* (New York: Anchor Books, 1973), pp. 302, 308, 383.

---

and flush out those who sympathized with the king and the European counterrevolutionaries. As the radicals expected, the French forces met serious reverses. By August 1792 the allied armies of Austria and Prussia had crossed the frontier and were threatening to capture Paris. Many, including soldiers, believed that the military disasters were evidence of the king's treason. On August 10, Parisian crowds, organized by their radical leadership, attacked the royal palace. The king was imprisoned and a second and far more radical revolution began.

THE JACOBINS

From this point, the country's leadership passed into the hands of the more egalitarian leaders of the Third Estate. These new leaders were known as Jacobins, the name of the political club to which they belonged. Although their headquarters were in Paris, their membership extended throughout France. Their members included large numbers of professionals, government officeholders, and lawyers, but they proclaimed themselves spokesmen for the people and the nation. An increasing number of artisans joined Jacobin clubs as the movement grew, and other, more democratic clubs expanded as well.

A National Convention, elected by free white men, became the effective governing body of the country for the next three years. It was elected in September 1792, at a time when disturbances across France reached a new height. The so-called September Massacres occurred when revolutionary Paris crowds, hearing a rumor that political prisoners were plotting to escape from their prisons, responded by hauling them before hastily convened tribunals and sentencing them to swift execution. More than one thousand supposed enemies of the Revolution were killed in less than a week. Similar riots engulfed Lyons, Orléans, and other French cities.

The newly elected Convention was far more radical than its predecessor, the Assembly, and its leadership was determined to end the monarchy. On September 21, the Convention declared France a republic. In December it placed the king on trial, and in January he was condemned to death by a narrow margin. The heir to the grand tradition of French absolutism met his end bravely as "Citizen Louis Capet," beheaded by the guillotine, the frightful mechanical headsman that had become the symbol of revolutionary fervor.

Meanwhile, the Convention turned its attention to further domestic reforms. Among its most significant accomplishments over the next three years were the abolition of slavery in French colonies (see below) and the repeal of primogeniture, so that property would not be inherited exclusively by the oldest son but would be divided in substantially equal portions among all immediate heirs. The Convention also confiscated the property of enemies of the Revolution for the benefit of the government and the lower classes.

The Execution of Louis XVI. A revolutionary displays the king's head moments after it is severed by the guillotine in January 1793.

Some large estates were broken up and offered for sale to poorer citizens on relatively easy terms. It abruptly canceled the policy of compensating nobles for their lost privileges. To curb rising prices, the government set maximum prices for grain and other necessities. In an astonishing effort to root out Christianity from everyday life, the Convention adopted a new calendar. The calendar year began with the birth of the republic (September 22, 1792), and divided months in such a way as to eliminate the Catholic Sunday.

Much of this program, particularly price ceilings and requisitioning, was the consequence of desperate political necessity and pressure from the urban sans-culottes. In the three years after 1790, prices had risen staggeringly: wheat by 27 percent, beef by 136 percent, potatoes by 700 percent. While the government imposed its maximums in Paris, small armies of urban sans-culottes attacked those they considered hoarders and profiteers. Left to its own economic inclinations, the Jacobin leadership would have pursued policies in line with liberal, reformist thinking that had challenged absolutist cen-

tralization and control. Yet the dire circumstances of Continental warfare and domestic turmoil forced the leaders to acquiesce to the sans-culottes' demands.

The Convention also accomplished an astonishingly successful reorganization of its armies. By February 1793, Britain, Holland, Spain, and Austria were in the field against the French. Britain's entrance into the war was dictated by both strategic and economic reasons. The British feared French penetration into the Low Countries directly across the Channel; they were also concerned that French expansion might pose a serious threat to Britain's own growing economic hegemony around the globe. The allied coalition, though united only in its desire to contain this fearsome revolutionary phenomenon, was nevertheless a formidable force. To counter it, the French organized an army that was able to win engagement after engagement during these years. In August 1793, the revolutionary government mustered all men capable of bearing arms. Fourteen hastily drafted armies were flung into battle under the leadership of young and inexperienced officers. What they lacked in training and discipline they made up for in organization, mobility, flexibility, courage, and morale. (In the navy, however, where skill was of paramount importance, the revolutionary French never succeeded in matching the performance of the British.) In 1793–1794, the French armies preserved their homeland. In 1794–1795, they occupied the Low Countries, the Rhineland, and parts of Spain, Switzerland, and Savoy. In 1796, they invaded and occupied key parts of Italy and broke the coalition that had arrayed itself against them.

THE REIGN OF TERROR

These achievements exacted a heavy price. To ensure their accomplishment, the rulers of France resorted to a bloody authoritarianism that has come to be known as the Terror. Although the Convention succeeded in 1793 in drafting a new democratic constitution based on male suffrage, it deferred its introduction because of wartime emergency. Instead, the Convention prolonged its own life year after year, and increasingly delegated its responsibilities to a group of twelve leaders, or the Committee of Public Safety.

Foremost among the political leadership were Jean Paul Marat, Georges Jacques Danton, and Maximilien Robespierre, the latter two members of the Committee of Public Safety. Jean Paul Marat was educated as a physician, and by 1789 had already earned enough distinction in that profession to be awarded an honorary degree by St. Andrews University in Scotland. Marat opposed nearly all of his moderate colleagues' assumptions, including their admiration for Great Britain, which Marat considered corrupt and despotic. Soon made a victim of persecution and forced to take refuge in unsanitary sewers and dungeons, he persevered as the editor of the popular news sheet, *The Friend of the People.* Exposure to infection left him with a chronic skin disease, from which he could find relief only through frequent bathing. In the summer of 1793, at the height of the crisis of the revolution, he was stabbed in his bath by Charlotte Corday, a young royalist, and became a revolutionary martyr.

Georges Jacques Danton, like Marat, was a popular political leader, well known in the more plebian clubs of Paris. Elected a member of the Committee of Public Safety in 1793, he had much to do with organizing the Terror. As time went on, however, he wearied of

The Death of Marat. This painting by the French artist David immortalized Marat. The note in the slain leader's hand is from Charlotte Corday, his assassin.

> Marat opposed nearly all of his moderate colleagues' assumptions, including their admiration for Great Britain, which Marat considered corrupt and despotic.

ruthlessness and displayed a tendency to compromise that gave his opponents in the Convention their opportunity. In April 1794 Danton was sent to the guillotine. On mounting the scaffold he is reported to have said, "Show my head to the people; they do not see the like every day."

The most famous and perhaps the greatest of the radical leaders was Maximilien Robespierre. Born of a family reputed to be of Irish descent, Robespierre was trained for the law and speedily achieved modest success as a lawyer. His eloquence, and his consistent, or ruthless, insistence that leaders respect the "will of the people" eventually won him a following in the Jacobin Club. Later he became president of the National Convention and a member of the Committee of Public Safety. Though he had little to do with starting the Terror, he was nevertheless responsible for enlarging its number of executions as high as twenty-five to thirty thousand in France as a whole, fewer than twenty thousand of whom were condemned by the courts. In addition, approximately five hundred thousand were incarcerated between March 1793 and August 1794. Few victims of the Terror were aristocrats. Many more were peasants or laborers accused of hoarding, treason, or counterrevolutionary activity. Anyone who appeared to threaten the republic, no matter what his or her

Maximilien Robespierre. Robespierre presented himself as the "Incorruptible," the one willing to repudiate all private interests and follow the general will.

scope. He came to justify ruthlessness as necessary to revolutionary progress.

The two years of the Terror brought stern dictatorship in France. Pressed by foreign enemies from without, the Committee faced opposition from both the political right and left at home. In June 1793, responding to the need for absolute political control, leaders of the "Mountain," a party of radicals allied with Parisian artisans, purged moderates from the Convention. Rebellions broke out in the provincial cities of Lyons, Bordeaux, and Marseilles, ruthlessly repressed by the Committee and its local representatives. The government also faced counterrevolution in the west. The peasantry there resented the government's assault on its religious institutions. The government's attempts to conscript troops into the revolutionary armies fanned long-smoldering resentments into open rebellion. By the summer, the peasant forces in the west posed a serious threat to the Convention. Determined to stabilize France, whatever the cost, the Committee dispatched commissioners into the countryside to suppress the enemies of the state.

During the period of the Terror, from September 1793 to July 1794, the most reliable estimates place the

FRANCE AND ITS SISTER REPUBLICS

The French revolutionaries, fighting against the conservative monarchs of Europe, conquered and annexed large sections of Italy, the Austrian Netherlands, and Switzerland. Napoleon did not begin these wars, though he continued and greatly expanded them.

social or economic position, was at risk. When some time later the Abbé Sieyès was asked what he had done to distinguish himself during the Terror, he responded dryly, "I lived."

THE LEGACY OF THE SECOND FRENCH REVOLUTION

Several points need to be made concerning this "second" French Revolution. First, for a time revolutionary enthusiasm affected the everyday life of French men, women, and children in a remarkably direct way. The city-based sans-culottes imposed their style of dress on their fellow citizens. Workers' trousers replaced the breeches that had been a sartorial badge of the middle classes and the nobility. A red cap, said to symbolize freedom from slavery, became popular headgear, wigs vanished. Men and women addressed each other as "citizen" or "citizeness." Public life was marked by ceremonies designed to dramatize the break with the Old Regime. In the early stages of the revolution, these festivals galvanized and expressed popular enthusiasm for new ways of living and thinking. Under the Committee of Public Safety, they became didactic and hollow.

Second, the radical revolution of 1792–1793 dramatically reversed the trend toward decentralization. The Assembly replaced local officials, some of them still royalist in sympathy, with "deputies on mission," whose task was to conscript troops and generate patriotic fervor. When these deputies appeared too eager to act independently, they were in turn replaced by "national agents," with instructions to report directly to the Committee. In another effort to stabilize authority, the Assembly closed down all the women's political clubs, decreeing them a political and social danger.

Third, the Revolution eroded the strength of those traditional institutions—church, guild, parish—that had for centuries given people a common bond. In their place now stood patriotic organizations and a culture that insisted on loyalty to one national cause. Those institutions started with the election campaigns, meetings, and pamphlet wars of 1788 and the interest they heightened. They included the political clubs and local assemblies, which at the height of the revolution (1792–1793) met every day of the week, and offered an apprenticeship in politics. In addition to the national army (*fédérés*), they included the people's armies, which were vigilante groups of sans-culottes sent from the town into the countryside to requisition food and materials.

Patriotic Women's Club. The members of this patriotic club wear "constitutional bonnets" to show their support for the Revolution and the reforms of the Convention.

Those who sided with the Revolution were not the only ones mobilized. Counterrevolutionary movements were also "popular" movements, enlisting peasants and artisans who believed their local areas were being invaded, and who fought for their local priest, or against the summons from the revolutionaries' conscription boards. The Revolution divided France. But it also forged new bonds. The sense that the rest of Europe, carrying what the verses of the *Marseillaise*, the most famous anthem of the Revolution, called the "blood-stained flag of tyranny," would crush the new nation and its citizens unquestionably strengthened French national identity.

CHRONOLOGY

THE SECOND FRENCH REVOLUTION, 1792–1794

First Republic established	Summer 1792
National Convention elected	September 1792
Execution of the king	January 1793
War between Britain, Holland, Spain, and France	February 1793
"Reign of Terror"	September 1793–July 1794
Purge of the Jacobins	July 27, 1794
Execution of Robespierre	July 28, 1794

FROM THE TERROR TO BONAPARTE: THE DIRECTORY

Why did the Directory fail?

The Committee of Public Safety, though able to save France, could not save itself. Inflation became catastrophic. The long string of military victories convinced growing numbers that the Committee's demands for continuing self-sacrifice, as well as its insistence on the necessity of the Terror, were no longer justified. By July 1794, the Committee was virtually without allies. On July 27 (9 Thermidor, according to the new calendar), Robespierre was shouted down by his enemies while attempting to speak on the floor of the Convention. The following day, along with twenty-one other conspirators, he met his death by guillotine as an enemy of the state.

The end of the Terror did not immediately bring "moderation." Jacobins were driven into hiding and hunted by vigilante groups of royalists. The repeal of the Maximum, or price controls, combined with the worst winter in a century, caused widespread misery. Other measures which had constituted the Terror were gradually repealed. In 1795 the National Convention adopted a new and more conservative constitution. It granted suffrage to all adult male citizens who could read and write. Yet it set up indirect elections: citizens voted for electors, who in turn chose the legislative body. Wealthy citizens thus held authority. Eager to avoid personal dictatorship, it vested executive authority in a board of five men known as the Directory, chosen by the legislative body. The new constitution included not only a bill of rights but also a declaration of the duties of the citizen.

Although the Directory lasted longer than its revolutionary predecessor, it could not stabilize the government. Its members faced discontent on both the radical left and the conservative right. On the left, the Directory successfully quashed various radical movements to abolish private property and parliamentary-style government, including the movement led by the radical "Gracchus Babeuf," most of whose followers were executed or deported. Dispatching threats from the right proved more challenging. Elections in March 1797—the first free elections held in France as a republic—returned a large number of constitutional monarchists to the councils of government. Leading politicians, among them some who had voted to execute Louis XVI, took alarm. With the support of the army, the Directory annulled most of the election results. Two years later, after more uprisings and purges, and with the country still plagued by severe inflation, the Directors grew desperate. This time they called the brilliant young general Napoleon Bonaparte to their assistance.

Bonaparte's first military victory in 1793, the recapture of Toulon from royalist and British forces, had earned him promotion from captain to brigadier general at the age of twenty-four. Though arrested as a Terrorist after Robespierre's fall, he subsequently won the Directory's gratitude. In October 1795, he had delivered what he called a "whiff of grapeshot" that saved the Convention from attack by opponents of the new constitution. He had registered a remarkable series of victories in Italy, forcing Austria to withdrawal (temporarily) from the war. Most recently, he had attempted to defeat Britain by staging an attack on British forces in Egypt and the Near East. That campaign had gone well on land, but when the French fleet was defeated by Admiral Horatio Nelson (Abukir Bay, 1798), Bonaparte found himself trapped by the British. A year of further fighting had not brought him nearer to decisive victory.

It was at this point that the call came from the Directory. Bonaparte slipped away from Egypt and appeared in Paris, already having agreed to participate in a coup d'état with the leading Director, that former revolutionary champion of the Third Estate, the Abbé Sieyès. On November 9, 1799 (18 Brumaire), Bonaparte was declared a "temporary consul." He was the answer to the prayers of the Directory: a strong, popular leader who was not a king. Sieyès declared that Bonaparte would provide "Confidence from below, authority from above." With those words Sieyès pronounced the end of the revolutionary period.

> On November 9, 1799 (18 Brumaire), Bonaparte was declared a "temporary consul." He was the answer to the prayers of the Directory: a strong, popular leader who was not a king.

THE HAITIAN REVOLUTION

Throughout all of these events, the French colonies across the Atlantic were reshaping the revolution and its legacy. The Caribbean islands of Guadeloupe, them. Their refusal sparked a mulatto rebellion in St. Domingue. The colonial authorities repressed the movement quickly and brutally, capturing Vincent Ogé, a member of the mulatto delegation to Paris and one of the leaders of the rebellion, and publicly executing him and his allies by breaking on the wheel and decapitation. Radical deputies, in Paris, including Robespierre, expressed outrage but could do little to change the Assembly's policy.

In August 1791 the largest slave rebellion in history broke out in St. Domingue. How much that rebellion owed to revolutionary propaganda is unclear; like many rebellions during the period, it had its own roots and followed its own logic. The British and the Spanish invaded St. Domingue, confident they could crush the rebellion and take the island. In the spring of 1792, the French government, on the verge of collapse and war with Europe, scrambled to win allies in St. Domingue by making free men of color citizens. Soon after the revolution of August 1792, the new French Republic dispatched commissioners to St. Domingue with troops and instructions to hold the island. The volatile combination of Spanish and British troops, and rebellious St. Domingue planters and slaves, proved more than the Republican forces could handle on their own. In this context, the local French commissioners capitulated to a successful slave revolution, and in 1793 promised freedom to slaves who would join the French. A year later, the Assembly in Paris extended to all the colonies what had already been accomplished in St. Domingue.

The new situation brought new leaders to the fore, chief among them a former slave, Toussaint Bréda, later Toussaint L'Ouverture, meaning "the one who opened the way." Over the course of the next five years, Toussaint and his soldiers, now allied with the French army, emerged victorious over the French planters, the British (in 1798), and the Spanish (in 1801). Toussaint also broke the power of his rival generals in both the mulatto and former slave armies, becoming the statesman of the revolution. In 1801, Toussaint set up a constitution, swearing allegiance to France but denying France any right to interfere in St. Domingue affairs. The constitution abolished slavery, reorganized the military, and established Christianity as the state religion (this entailed a rejection of vodoun, a blend of Christian and various West and Central African traditions) and made Toussaint governor for life. It was an extraordinary moment in the revolutionary period: the formation of an authoritarian society but also an utterly unexpected symbol of the universal potential of revolutionary ideas.

Toussaint L'Ouverture. A portrait of L'Ouverture, leader of what would become the Haitian revolution, as a general.

Martinique, and St. Domingue occupied a central role in the French economy because of the sugar trade. Their planter elites had powerful influence in Paris. The French National Assembly (like its American counterpart) declined to discuss the matter of slavery in the colonies, unwilling to encroach on the property rights of slave owners and fearful of losing the lucrative sugar islands to their British or Spanish rivals should discontented slave owners talk of independence from France. More difficult, from the point of view of the French men in the Assembly, was the question of rights for free men of color, a group that included a significant number of wealthy owners of property (and slaves).

St. Domingue had about forty thousand whites of different social classes, thirty thousand free people of color, and five hundred thousand slaves, most of them recently enslaved in West Africa. In 1790, free people of color from St. Domingue sent a delegation to Paris, asking to be seated by the Assembly, underscoring that they were men of property and, in many cases, of European ancestry. The Assembly refused to seat

Toussaint's accomplishments, however, put him on a collision course with the other French general he admired and whose career was remarkably like his own: Napoleon Bonaparte. St. Domingue stood at the center of Bonaparte's ambitions for the New World, and in January 1802, he dispatched twenty thousand troops to bring the island under control. Toussaint, captured when he arrived for discussions with the French, was shipped under heavy guard to a prison in the mountains of eastern France where he died in 1803. Fighting continued in St. Domingue, however, with fires now fueled by Bonaparte's determination to restore slavery. The war turned into a nightmare for the French. Yellow fever killed thousands of French troops, including one of Napoleon's best generals. Armies on both sides committed atrocities. By December 1803, the French army had collapsed. In January 1804, Jean-Jacques Dessalines, a general in the army of former slaves, declared the independent state of Haiti.

> The Haitian revolution remained, in significant ways, an anomaly. It was the only successful slave revolution in history, and by far the most radical of the revolutions that occurred in this age.

The Haitian revolution remained, in significant ways, an anomaly. It was the only successful slave revolution in history, and by far the most radical of the revolutions that occurred in this age. It suggested that the emancipatory ideas of the revolution and Enlightenment might apply to non-Europeans and enslaved peoples—a suggestion that residents of Europe attempted to ignore but one that struck home with planter elites in North and South America. Combined with later rebellions in the British colonies, it contributed to the British decision to end slavery in 1838. And it cast a long shadow over nineteenth-century slave societies from the southern United States to Brazil.

NAPOLEON AND IMPERIAL FRANCE

How did Napoleon centralize his authority?

Few figures in Western history have compelled the attention of the world as Napoleon Bonaparte did during the fifteen years of his rule in France. Few men lived on with such persistence as myth, not just in their own countries, but across the West. For the great majority of ordinary Europeans, memories of the French Revolution were dominated by those of the Napoleonic wars, which devastated Europe, convulsed its politics, and traumatized its peoples for a generation. What had begun as political revolution and popular revolt ended in war and efforts to create a new kind of European empire. To many observers, that transformation seemed embodied in the career of one man. From the onset of war in 1792, France's revolutionaries had turned to the armies of France for defense and survival. It seemed all too natural that the future of the Revolution should be bound up with the successes of its greatest general, Napoleon Bonaparte.

Bonaparte's relationship to the Revolution, however, was not simple. His regime consolidated some of the revolution's political and social changes but sharply repudiated others. He presented himself as the son of the revolution, but he also borrowed freely from very different regimes, fashioning himself as the heir to Charlemagne, or to the Roman empire. His regime remade revolutionary politics and the French state, transformed the nature of European warfare, and left a legacy of conflict and legends of French glory that lingered in the dreams, or nightmares, of Europe's statesmen and citizens for more than a century.

CONSOLIDATING AUTHORITY: 1799–1804

Napoleon's early career reinforced the claim that the Revolution rewarded the efforts of able men. The son of a provincial Corsican nobleman, he attended the Ecole Militaire in Paris. In pre-Revolutionary France, he would have been unable to rise beyond the rank of major, which required buying a regimental command. The Revolution, however, had abolished the purchase of military office, and Bonaparte quickly became a general. Here, then, was a man who had risen from obscurity because of his own gifts, which he lent happily to the service of France's revolution. His character seemed suited to the age as well, at least to his early admirers, who noted his wide range of talents and intellectual interests. He pursued serious interests in history, law, and mathematics. His particular strengths as a leader lay in his ability to create financial, legal, or military plans and then to master their every detail; in his capacity for inspiring others, even those initially opposed to him; and in his belief that he was the destined savior of France. That last conviction eventually led to Napoleon's undoing.

In the first five years of his reign, Bonaparte quickly consolidated personal power. When he overthrew the government in 1799, he assumed the title of First Consul and governed in the name of the Republic. A new constitution established universal white male suffrage and set up two legislative bodies. Elections, however, were indirect, and the power of the legislative bodies sharply curbed. "The government?" said one observer. "There is Bonaparte." Bonaparte instituted what has since become a common authoritarian device, the plebiscite, which put a question directly to popular vote. This allows the head of state to bypass politicians or legislative bodies who might disagree with him—as well as permitting local officials to tamper with ballot boxes. In 1802, flush with victory abroad, he asked the legislature to proclaim him consul for life. When the Senate refused to do so, Bonaparte's Council of State stepped in, offered him the title, and had it ratified by plebiscite. Throughout, his regime retained the appearance of consulting with the people, but its most important feature was the centralization of authority.

That authority came from reorganizing the state. Bonaparte's regime confirmed the abolition of privilege, thereby promising "careers open to talent." Through centralization of the administrative departments, he established what no recent French regime had yet achieved: an orderly and generally fair system of taxation. More efficient tax collection and fiscal management also helped him halt the inflationary spiral that had crippled the revolutionary governments, although Bonaparte's regime relied heavily on resources from areas he had conquered to fund his military ventures. As we have seen, the revolutionaries began the work of reorganizing the administration, abolishing the ancient fiefdoms with their separate governments, and setting up a uniform system of departments. Bonaparte continued that work, but with an accent on centralization. He replaced elected officials and local self-government with centrally appointed "prefects" and "subprefects" whose administrative duties were defined in Paris, where local government policy was made as well. Napoleon's state was a point midway between absolutism and the modern state.

LAW, EDUCATION, AND A NEW ELITE

Napoleon's most significant accomplishment, and one exported to the areas he conquered, was the completion of the legal reforms begun during the revolutionary period and the promulgation of a new legal code in 1804. The Napoleonic Code reflected two principles that had threaded their way through all the constitutional changes since 1789: uniformity and individualism. The code cleared through the thicket of different legal traditions, creating one uniform law. It confirmed the abolition of feudal privileges of all kinds: not only noble and clerical privileges but the special rights of craft guilds, municipalities, and so on. It set the conditions for exercising property rights: the drafting of contracts, leases, and stock companies. The code's provisions on the family, which Napoleon developed personally, insisted on the importance of paternal authority and the subordination of women and children. In 1793, during the most radical period of the revolution, men and women had been declared "equal in marriage"; now Napoleon's code affirmed the "natural supremacy" of the husband. Married women could not sell property, run a business, or have a profession without their husbands' permission. Fathers had the sole right to control their children's financial affairs, consent to their marriages, and (under the ancient right to correction) to imprison them for up to six months without showing cause. Divorce remained legal, but under unequal conditions; a man could sue for divorce on the grounds of adultery, but a woman could only do so if her husband moved his "concubine" into the family's house. Most important to the common people, the code prohibited paternity suits for illegitimate children. The new criminal code consolidated some of the gains of the revolution, treating citizens as equals before the law and outlawing arbitrary arrest and imprisonment. Yet it, too, reintroduced harsher measures that the revolutionaries had abolished, such as branding and cutting off the hands of parricides. The Napoleonic code was more egalitarian than law under the Old Regime, but no less concerned with authority.

> The Napoleonic Code reflected two principles that had threaded their way through all the constitutional changes since 1789: uniformity and individualism.

Bonaparte also rationalized the educational system. He ordered the establishment of *lycées* (high schools) in every major town to train civil servants and army officers and a school in Paris to train teachers. To supplement these changes, Napoleon brought the military and technical schools under state control and founded a national university to supervise the entire system. Like almost all his reforms, this one reinforced reforms introduced during the Revolution, and it intended to abolish privilege and create "careers open to talent." Napoleon also embraced the burgeoning social and physical sciences of the Enlightenment. He sponsored the Academie Française and retained several of the revolutionaries' more practical attempts to rationalize society and commerce, such as the metric system.

Who benefited from these changes? Like Bonaparte's other new institutions, the new schools helped confirm the power of a new elite. The new elite included businessmen, bankers, and merchants, but was still composed primarily of powerful landowners. What was more, at least half of the fellowships to the high schools went to the sons of military officers and high civil servants. Finally, like most of Bonaparte's reforms, changes in education aimed to strengthen the power of the state: "My object in establishing a teaching corps is to have a means of directing political and moral opinion," Napoleon said bluntly.

Bonaparte's early measures were ambitious. To win support for them, he made allies without regard for their past political affiliations. He admitted back into the country exiles of all political stripes. His two fellow consuls were a regicide of the Terror and a bureaucrat of the Old Regime. His minister of police had been an extreme radical republican; his minister of foreign affairs was the aristocrat and opportunist Charles Talleyrand. The most remarkable act of political reconciliation came in 1801, with Bonaparte's concordat with the pope, an agreement that put an end to more than a decade of hostility between the French state and the Catholic Church. Although it shocked anticlerical revolutionaries, Napoleon, ever the pragmatist, believed that reconciliation would create domestic harmony and international solidarity. The agreement gave the pope the right to depose French bishops and to discipline the French clergy. In return, the Vatican agreed to forgo any claims to church lands expropriated by the Revolution. That property would remain in the hands of its new middle-class rural and urban proprietors. The concordat did not revoke the principle of religious freedom established by the Revolution, but it did win Napoleon the support of conservatives who had feared for France's future as a godless state.

Such political balancing acts increased Bonparte's general popularity. Combined with early military successes (peace with Austria in 1801 and with Britain in 1802), they muffled any opposition to his personal ambitions. He had married Josephine de Beauharnais, a Creole from Martinique and an influential mistress of the Revolutionary period. Josephine had given the Corsican soldier-politician legitimacy and access among the revolutionary elite early in his career. Neither Bonaparte nor his ambitious wife were content to be first among equals, however, and in December of 1804, he finally cast aside any traces of republicanism. In a ceremony that evoked the splendor of medieval kingship

Coronation of Napoleon and Josephine. Napoleon crowned himself, but Jaques Louis David diplomatically painted the moment when he bestowed a crown on his wife, Josephine.

and Bourbon absolutism, he crowned himself Emperor Napoleon I in the Cathedral of Notre Dame in Paris. Napoleon did much to create the modern state, but he did not hesitate to proclaim his links to the past.

IN EUROPE AS IN FRANCE: NAPOLEON'S WARS OF EXPANSION

The nations of Europe had looked on—some in admiration, others in horror, all in astonishment—at the phenomenon that was Napoleon. A coalition of European powers led by Austria, Prussia, and Britain had fought France from 1792 until 1795, in hopes of maintaining European stability. This first coalition collapsed in disarray, defeated by the French armies and by financial exhaustion. The coalition was revived in 1798, at Britain's behest, but in the end it fared no better than the first effort. Despite Napoleon's debacle in Egypt, French victories in Europe split the alliance.

Russia and Austria withdrew from the fray in 1801, and even the intransigent British were forced to make peace the following year.

Out of these victories Napoleon created his new empire and affiliated states. These included a series of small republics carved from Austria's empire and the old German kingdoms. These were presented as France's revolutionary gift of independence to patriots elsewhere in Europe, but in practice they were a military buffer and a system of client states for a new French empire. A loose federation of German states, known as the Confederation of the Rhine, seemed to glorify France's role in "liberating" Europe, but also brought the French Revolution's practical consequences—a powerful, centralizing state and an end to old systems of privilege—to Europe's doorstep. In the case of Britain, these successes stretched beyond Europe as the British were forced to return territories recently captured in colonial warfare, although they retained the important islands of Trinidad and Ceylon.

Napoleon's reign accelerated developments already underway in the territories of central Europe. The French introduced a system of administration based on the notion of careers open to talent, equality before the law, and the abolition of ancient customs and privileges. The Napoleonic program of reform applied to the empire principles that had already transformed France. It eliminated manorial and church courts. It joined previously separate provinces into an enormous bureaucratic network that reached directly back to Paris. It codified laws and modernized tax systems, and freed individuals to work at whatever trade they chose. These new freedoms of law, property, and profession, however, did not extend to politics. All governmental direction emanated from Paris, and therefore from Napoleon.

The effect of these changes on the men and women who experienced them was profound. In those small principalities previously ruled by princes—the patchwork states of Germany, for example, or the repressive kingdom of Naples—reforms that provided for more efficient, less corrupt administration, a workable tax structure, and an end to customary privilege were welcomed by most of the local population. Yet the Napoleonic presence proved a mixed blessing. Vassal states contributed heavily to the maintenance of the emperor's military power. The French levied taxes, drafted men, and required states to support occupying armies. In Italy, the policy was called "liberty and requisitions," and the Italians, Germans, and Dutch paid an especially high price for reforms. From the point of view of the common people, the local lord and priest had been replaced by the French tax collector and army recruiting board.

This arrogance slowly but irretrievably cost Napoleon the support of revolutionaries, former Enlightenment thinkers, and liberals across the Continent. The German composer Ludwig van Beethoven originally planned to dedicate his Third Symphony, the *Eroica*, to Napoleon. Like so many European idealists, Beethoven at first hoped that Bonaparte would bring liberty to the whole continent. But Napoleon's empire building and his self-coronation in 1804 forced a swift and bitter change of judgment. Beethoven revoked the dedication to Bonaparte, declaring, "Now he, too, will trample on all the rights of man and indulge only his ambition."

THE RETURN TO WAR AND NAPOLEON'S DEFEAT: 1806–1815

What led to Napoleon's downfall?

Napoleon's boldest attempt at consolidation, a policy banning British goods from the Continent, was a dangerous failure. Britain had bitterly opposed each of France's revolutionary regimes since the death of Louis XVI; now it tried to rally Europe against Napoleon with promises of generous financial loans and trade. The Continental System, established in 1806, sought to starve Britain's trade and force its surrender. The system failed for several reasons. Throughout the war Britain retained control of the seas. The British naval blockade of the Continent, begun in 1807, effectively countered Napoleon's system. While the French empire strained to transport goods and raw materials overland to avoid the British blockade, the British successfully developed a lively trade with South America. A second reason for the failure of the system was its internal tariffs. Europe divided into economic camps, at odds with each other as they tried to subsist on what the Continent alone could produce and manufacture. Finally, the system hurt the Continent more than Britain. Stagnant trade in Europe's ports and unemployment in its manufacturing centers eroded public faith in Napoleon's dream of a working European empire.

The Continental System was Napoleon's first serious mistake. A second cause of his decline was his unmasterable ambition. Napoleon's goal was to remake Europe as a new Roman empire, ruled from Paris. The symbols of his empire—reflected in painting, architecture, and the

Napoleon on the Battlefield of Eylau. Amidst bitter cold and snow, Napoleon engaged with the Russian army in February of 1807. Although technically a victory for the French, it was only barely that, with the French losing at least 10,000 men, and the Russians twice as many. This painting, characteristic of Bonaparte propaganda, emphasizes not the losses but the Emperor's saint-like clemency—even enemy soldiers reach up toward him.

design of furniture and clothing—were deliberately Roman in origin. This was not a novelty; the early revolutionaries, Jacobins in particular, harked back to the Roman republic as their model for political virtue, drawing on its imagery in art and political rhetoric. But the triumphal columns and arches Napoleon had erected to commemorate his victories recalled the ostentatious monuments of the Roman emperors. He made his brothers and sisters the monarchs of his newly created kingdoms, which Napoleon controlled from Paris while their mother reportedly sat at court, anxiously wringing her hands and repeating to herself, "If only it lasts!" In 1809 he divorced the empress Josephine and ensured himself a successor of royal blood by marrying Marie Louise, daughter of Francis I of the powerful and respectable house of Habsburg. Even Napoleon's admirers began to wonder if his empire would reflect simply a larger, more efficient, and ultimately more dangerous absolutism than the monarchies of the eighteenth century.

War had broken out again in 1805, with the Russians, Prussians, Austrians, and Swedes joining the British in an attempt to contain France. Their efforts were to no avail. Napoleon's military superiority led to defeats, in turn, of all three Continental allies. Napoleon was a master of well-timed, well-directed shock attacks on the battlefield. He led an army that had transformed European warfare: first raised as a revolutionary militia, it was now a trained, conscript army of native Frenchmen, loyal, well supplied by a nation whose economy was committed to serving the war effort, and led by generals promoted largely on the basis of talent. This new kind of army, directed with Napoleon's lethal flair, inflicted crushing defeats on his enemies. The battle of Austerlitz, in December 1805, was a mighty triumph for the French against the combined forces of Austria and Russia and became a symbol of the emperor's apparent invincibility. His subsequent victory against the Russians at Friedland in 1807 only added to his reputation.

TWO LETTERS FROM NAPOLEON

Napoleon placed his brothers on the thrones of different vassal states in conquered territories throughout Europe. The first excerpt below is from a letter to his brother Eugène, head of one of the new Italian states, in which Napoleon explains how Italy's lucrative silk trade was to be diverted in order to damage English commercial interests and bolster the French empire. It provides a revealing glimpse of Napoleon's vision of a united Europe, with the other countries' futures tied to France's.

On March 1, 1815, Napoleon landed in the south of France, having escaped from his exile on the island of Elba. The restored Bourbon king abdicated, and Napoleon ruled for one hundred more days, until his defeat at the battle of Waterloo in June. The second selection below is excerpted from a proclamation, addressed to the sovereigns of Europe, explaining the emperor's return. It is an excellent illustration of Napoleon's self-image, his rhetoric, and his belief that he represented the force of history itself.

LETTER TO PRINCE EUGÈNE, 23 AUGUST 1810

I have received your letter of August 14. All the raw silk from the Kingdom of Italy goes to England, for there are no silk factories in Germany. It is therefore quite natural that I should wish to divert it from this route to the advantage of my French manufacturers: otherwise my silk factories, one of the chief supports of French commerce, would suffer substantial losses. I cannot agree with your observations. My principle is *France first*. You must never lose sight of the fact that, if English commerce is supreme on the high seas, it is due to her sea power: it is therefore to be expected that, as France is the strongest land power, she should claim commercial supremacy on the continent: it is indeed our only hope. And isn't it better for Italy to come to the help of France, in such an important matter as this, than to be covered with Customs Houses? For it would be short-sighted not to recognise that Italy owes her independence to France; that it was won by French blood and French victories; that it must not be misused; and that nothing could be more unreasonable than to start calculating what commercial advantages France gets out of it.

Piedmont and Parma produce silk too; and there also I have prohibited its export to any country except France. It is no use for Italy to make plans that leave French prosperity out of account; she must face the fact that the interests of the two countries hang together. Above all, she must be careful not to give France any reason for annexing her; for if it paid France to do this, who could stop her? So make this your motto too—*France first*.

CIRCULAR LETTER TO THE SOVEREIGNS OF EUROPE, 4 APRIL 1815

Monsieur, My Brother,

You will have learnt, during the course of last month, of my landing again in France, of my entry into Paris, and of the departure of the Bourbon family. Your Majesty must by now be aware of the real nature of these events. They are the work of an irresistible power, of the unanimous will of a great nation conscious of its duties and of its rights. A dynasty forcibly reimposed upon the French people was no longer suitable for it: the Bourbons refused to associate themselves with the natural feelings or the national customs; and France was forced to abandon them. The popular voice called for a liberator. The expectation which had decided me to make the supreme sacrifice was in vain. I returned; and from the place where my foot first touched the shore I was carried by the affection of my subjects into the bosom of my capital.

My first and heartfelt anxiety is to repay so much affection by the maintenance of an honourable peace. The re-establishment of the Imperial throne was necessary for the happiness of Frenchmen: my dearest hope is that it may also secure repose for the whole of Europe. Each national flag in turn has had its gleam of glory: often enough, by some turn of fortune, great victories have been followed by great defeats. . . . I have provided the world in the past with a programme of great contests; it will please me better in future to acknowledge no rivalry but that of the advocates of peace, and no combat but a crusade for the felicity of mankind. It is France's pleasure to make a frank avowal of this noble ideal. Jealous of her independence, she will always base her policy upon an unqualified respect for the independence of other peoples. . . .

Monsieur my Brother,
Your good Brother,
Napoléon.

K. M. Baker, ed. *The Old Regime and the French Revolution* (Chicago: University of Chicago Press, 1987), pp. 419–20, 426–27.

Over time, the bitter tonic of defeat began to have an effect on Napoleon's enemies, who changed their own approach to waging war in response to his devastating victories. After the Prussian army was humiliated at Jena in 1806 and forced out of the war, a whole generation of younger Prussian officers reformed their military and their state by demanding rigorous practical training for commanders and a genuinely national army made up of patriotic Prussian citizens rather than well-drilled mercenaries.

The myth of Napoleon's invincibility worked against him as well, as he took ever greater risks with France's military and national fortunes. Russian numbers and Austrian artillery inflicted horrendous losses on the French at Wagram in 1809, although these difficulties were forgotten in the glow of victory. Napoleon's allies and supporters shrugged off the British admiral Horatio Nelson's victory at Trafalgar in 1805 as no more than a temporary check to the emperor's ambitions. But Trafalgar broke French naval power in the Mediterranean and helped lead to a rift with Spain, which had been France's equal partner in the battle and suffered equally in the defeat. In the Americas, too, Napoleon was forced to cut growing losses, giving up on St. Domingue in the face of disaster and selling France's territories along the Mississippi to the United States for badly needed cash.

A crucial moment in Napoleon's undoing came with his invasion of Spain in 1808. The invasion aimed, eventually, toward the conquest of Portugal, which had remained a stalwart ally of the British. Napoleon overthrew the Spanish king, installed his own brother on the throne, and then imposed a series of reforms similar to those he had instituted elsewhere in Europe. But he reckoned without two factors that led to the ultimate failure of his Spanish mission: the presence of British forces under Sir Arthur Wellesley (later the duke of Wellington), and the determined resistance of the Spanish people. They particularly detested Napoleon's interference in the affairs of the church. The peninsular wars, as the Spanish conflicts were called, were long and bitter. The smaller British force learned how to concentrate a devastating volume of gunfire on the French pinpoint attacks on the open battlefield, and laid siege to French garrison towns. The Spanish quickly began to wear down French numbers, supplies, and morale through what was called "guerrilla" warfare. Terrible atrocities were committed by both sides; the French military's torture and execution of Spanish guerrillas and civilians was immortalized by the Spanish artist Francisco Goya (1746–1828) with sickening accuracy in his prints and paintings. Though at one point Napoleon himself took charge of his army, he could not achieve anything more than temporary victory. The Spanish campaign was the first indication that Napoleon could be beaten, and it encouraged resistance elsewhere.

The second, and most dramatic stage in Napoleon's downfall began with the disruption of his alliance with Russia. As an agricultural country, Russia had suffered a severe economic crisis when it was no longer able to trade its surplus grain for British manufactures. The consequence was that Tsar Alexander I began to wink at trade with Britain and to ignore or evade the protests from Paris. By 1811 Napoleon decided that he could endure this flouting of their agreement no longer.

Accordingly, he collected an army of six hundred thousand and set out for Russia in the spring of 1812. Only a third of the soldiers in this "Grande Armée" were French: nearly as many were Polish or German, joined by soldiers and adventurers from the rest of France's client states. It was the grandest of Napoleon's imperial expeditions, an army raised from across Europe and sent to punish the autocratic tsar. It ended in disaster. The Russians refused to make a stand, drawing the French farther and farther into the heart of their country. Just before Napoleon reached the ancient Russian capital of Moscow, the Russian army drew the French forces into a bloody, seemingly pointless battle in the narrow streets of a town called Borodino, where both sides suffered terrible losses of men and supplies, harder on the French who were now so far from home. After the battle, the Russians permitted Napoleon to occupy Moscow. But on the night of his entry, Russian partisans put the city to the torch, leaving little but the blackened walls of the Kremlin palaces to shelter the invading troops.

Hoping that the tsar would eventually surrender, Napoleon lingered amid the ruins for more than a month. On October 19 he finally ordered the homeward march. The delay was a fatal blunder. Long before he had reached the border, the terrible Russian winter was on his troops. Frozen streams, mountainous drifts

of snow, and bottomless mud slowed the retreat almost to a halt. To add to the miseries of frostbite, disease, and starvation, mounted Cossacks rode out of the blizzard to harry the exhausted army. Each morning the miserable remnant that pushed on left behind circles of corpses around the campfires of the night before. On December 13 a few thousand broken soldiers crossed the frontier into Germany—a fragment of the once proud Grande Armée. Nearly three hundred thousand of its soldiers and untold thousands of Russians lost their lives in Napoleon's Russian adventure.

Following the retreat from Russia, the anti-Napoleonic forces took renewed hope. United by a belief that they might finally succeed in defeating the emperor, Prussia, Russia, Austria, Sweden, and Britain renewed their attack. Citizens of many German states in particular saw this as a war of liberation, and indeed most of the fighting took place in Germany. The climax of the campaign occurred in October 1813 when, at what was thereafter known as the Battle of the Nations, fought near Leipzig, the allies dealt the French a resounding defeat. Meanwhile, allied armies won significant victories in the Low Countries and Spain. By the beginning of 1814, they had crossed the Rhine into France. Left with an inexperienced army of raw youths, Napoleon retreated to Paris, urging the French people to further resistance despite constant setbacks at the hands of the

Execution of the Rebels on 3 May 1808, by Francisco Goya. This painting of the execution of Spanish rebels by Napoleon's army as it marched through Spain is one of the most memorable depictions of a nation's martyrdom.

NAPOLEON'S EMPIRE AT ITS HEIGHT

EUROPE IN 1812
- French territory
- French dependencies
- Allied with Napoleon
- Independent states

NAPOLEON'S INVASION OF RUSSIA, 1812
- → Advance
- ◄-- Retreat
- ✳ Battle sites

What did Napoleon want from the rest of Europe? Where was he successful; where did he fail, and why? Where did his rule leave the most lasting impact? Could he have maintained his empire?

larger invading armies. On March 31, Tsar Alexander I of Russia and King Frederick William III of Prussia made their triumphant entry into Paris. Napoleon was forced to abdicate unconditionally and was sent into exile on the island of Elba, off the Italian coast.

Napoleon was back on French soil in less than a year. In the interim the allies had restored the Bourbon dynasty to the throne, in the person of Louis XVIII, brother of Louis XVI. Despite his administrative abilities, Louis could not fill the void left by Napoleon's abdication. It was no surprise that, when the former emperor staged his escape from Elba, his fellow countrymen once more rallied to his side. By the time Napoleon reached Paris, he had generated enough

support to cause Louis to flee the country. The allies, meeting in Vienna to conclude peace treaties with the French, were stunned by the news of Napoleon's return. They dispatched a hastily organized army to meet the emperor's typically bold offensive push into the Low Countries. At the battle of Waterloo, fought over three bloody days from June 15 to 18, 1815, Napoleon was stopped by the forces of his two most persistent enemies, Britain and Prussia, and suffered his final defeat. This time the allies took no chances and shipped their prisoner off to the bleak island of St. Helena in the South Atlantic. The once-mighty emperor, now the exile Bonaparte, lived out a dreary existence writing self-serving memoirs until his death in 1821.

C H R O N O L O G Y

REIGN OF NAPOLEON, 1799–1815

Napoleon becomes First Consul	1799
Concordat with the pope	1801
Napoleon becomes consul for life	1802
Napoleon abolishes the republic and crowns himself emperor	1804
Napoleonic Code	1804
The Continental System	1806
Napoleon invades Spain	1808
Invasion of Russia	1812
Abdication of Napoleon	1814
Return and final exile of Napoleon	1815

CONCLUSION

The tumultuous events in France formed part of a broad pattern of late-eighteenth-century democratic upheaval. The French Revolution was the most violent, protracted, and contentious of the revolutions of the era, but the dynamics of revolution were much the same everywhere. One of the most important developments of the French Revolution was the emergence of a popular movement, which included political clubs representing people previously excluded from politics, newspapers read by and to the common people, and political leaders who spoke for the sans-culottes. In the French Revolution as in other revolutions, the popular movement challenged the early and moderate revolutionary leadership, pressing for more radical and democratic measures. And as in other revolutions, the popular movement in France was defeated, and authority was reestablished by a quasi-military figure. Likewise, the revolutionary ideas of liberty, equality, and fraternity were not specifically French; their roots lay in the social structures of the eighteenth century and in the culture of the Enlighten-

ment. Yet French armies brought them, literally, to the doorsteps of many Europeans.

What was the larger impact of the Revolution and the Napoleonic era? Its legacy is partly summed up in three key concepts: liberty, equality, and nation. Liberty meant individual rights and responsibilities, and more specifically freedom from arbitrary authority. By equality, as we have seen, the revolutionaries meant the abolition of legal distinctions of rank among European men. Though their concept of equality was limited, it became a powerful mobilizing force in the nineteenth century. The most important legacy of the revolution may have been the new term *nation*. Nationhood was a political concept. A "nation" was formed of citizens, not a king's subjects. A nation was ruled by law and treated citizens as equal before the law. Sovereignty did not lie in dynasties or historic fiefdoms, but in the nation of citizens. Loyalty and affinity to this new kind of nation was bred in the hearts of the French people when their citizen armies repelled attacks against their newly won freedoms. By the Napoleonic period, this new political body of freely associated citizens was most powerfully embodied in a centralized state, its army, its greatest general turned Emperor of the French, and a kind of citizenship defined by individual commitment to the needs of "the nation" at war.

The revolutionary concept of nationhood spread throughout Europe in response to French aggression. The French did not hesitate to champion their revolutionary principles abroad. France's enemies responded with a growing sense of their own commonality. In the German and Italian principalities the domination of an alien emperor and his unwelcome agents helped forge opposition and a national identity of their own.

When the revolutionary period closed, the three concepts of liberty, equality, and nationality were no longer merely ideas. They had taken shape in new communities and institutions. They had created new alliances between countries. They also polarized Europe and much of the world, giving rise to debates, grievances, and conflict that would shape the nineteenth century.

KEY TERMS

Louis XVI	Olympe de Gouges	Napoleon Bonaparte
Third Estate	Jacobins	lycées
Declaration of the Rights of Man and of the Citizen	Committee of Public Safety	
	St. Domingue	

SELECTED READINGS

Applewhite, Harriet B., and Darline G. Levy, eds. *Women and Politics in the Age of the Democratic Revolution.* Ann Arbor, 1990. Essays cover women's activities in France, Britain, the Netherlands, and the United States.

Bergeron, Louis. *France under Napoleon.* Princeton, 1981. Concentrates on the social history of the Napoleonic period.

Best, Geoffrey. *War and Society in Revolutionary Europe, 1770–1870.* Leicester, 1982.

Blackburn, Robin. *The Overthrow of Colonial Slavery.* London and New York, 1988.

Blum, Carol. *Rousseau and the Republic of Virtue: The Language of Politics in the French Revolution.* Ithaca, N.Y., 1986. Excellent on how Rousseau was read by the revolutionaries.

Bruun, Geoffrey. *Europe and the French Imperium, 1799–1814.* Westport, Conn., 1983. Describes the impact of Napoleon on Europe.

Cobb, Richard. *The People's Armies.* New Haven, 1987. Brilliant and detailed analysis of the sans-culottes.

Cobban, Alfred. *The Social Interpretation of the French Revolution.* Cambridge, 1964. A penetrating critique of the radical interpretation of the Revolution, more important for its questions than for its conclusions.

Doyle, William. *Oxford History of the French Revolution.* New York, 1989.

———. *Origins of the French Revolution.* 2d ed. New York, 1988. A revisionist historian surveys recent research on the political and social origins of the Revolution and identifies a new consensus.

Forrest, Alan. *The French Revolution and the Poor.* New York, 1981. An account that argues the poor fared little better under revolutionary governments than under the Old Regime.

Furet, Francois. *Revolutionary France, 1770–1880.* Translated by Antonia Nerill. Cambridge, Mass., 1992.

Geyl, Pieter. *Napoleon: For and Against.* Rev. ed. New Haven, 1964. The ways in which Napoleon was interpreted by French historians and political figures.

Hesse, Carla. *Publishing and Cultural Politics in Revolutionary Paris 1789–1810.* Berkeley, 1991.

Hunt, Lynn. *Politics, Culture, and Class in the French Revolution.* Berkeley, 1984. An analysis of the interaction between political events and sociocultural phenomena out of which grew a new culture of democracy and republicanism.

———. *The French Revolution and Human Rights.* Boston, 1996.

Landes, Joan B. *Women and the Public Sphere in the Age of the French Revolution.* Ithaca, N.Y., 1988. Discusses the revolutionaries' exclusionary policy toward women.

Lefebvre, Georges. *The Coming of the French Revolution.* Princeton, 1947. An excellent study of the causes and early events of the Revolution.

———. *The French Revolution.* 2 vols. New York, 1962–1964. An impressive synthesis by the greatest modern scholar of the Revolution.

———. *The Great Fear of 1789.* New York, 1973. The best account of the rural disturbances.

Lewis, G., and C. Lucas. *Beyond the Terror: Essays in French Regional and Social History, 1794–1815.* New York, 1983.

O'Brien, Connor Cruise. *The Great Melody: A Thematic Biography of Edmund Burke.* Chicago, 1992.

Palmer, R. R. *The Age of the Democratic Revolution: A Political History of Europe and America, 1760–1800.* 2 vols. Princeton, 1964. Impressive for its scope; places the French Revolution in the larger context of a worldwide revolutionary movement.

———. *Twelve Who Ruled: The Year of the Terror in the French Revolution.* Princeton, 1958. Excellent biographical studies of the members of the Committee of Public Safety.

Rudé, George. *The Crowd in the French Revolution.* Westport, Conn., 1986. An important monograph that analyzes the composition of the crowds that participated in the great uprisings of the Revolution.

Schama, Simon. *Citizens: A Chronicle of the French Revolution.* New York, 1989. Particularly good on art and politics.

Soboul, Albert. *The Sans-Culottes: The Popular Movement and Revolutionary Government, 1793–1794.* Garden City, N.Y., 1972. A classic study of the pressures on the Convention in the year of the Terror.

Sutherland, D. M. G. *France, 1789–1815: Revolution and Counterrevolution.* Oxford, 1986. An important synthesis of work on the revolution, especially in social history.

Thompson, J. M. *Robespierre and the French Revolution.* London, 1953. An excellent short biography.

Tilly, Charles. *The Vendée: A Sociological Analysis of the Counter-Revolution of 1793.* Cambridge, Mass., 1964. An important economic and social analysis of the factors that led to the reaction in the Vendée.

Tocqueville, Alexis de. *The Old Regime and the French Revolution.* Garden City, N.Y., 1955. Originally written in 1856, this remains a classic analysis of the causes of the French Revolution.

Trouillot, Michel Rolph. *Silencing the Past.* Boston, 1995.

Woloch, Isser. *The New Regime: Transformations of the French Civic Order, 1789–1820.* New York, 1994. The fate of revolutionary civic reform.

Woolf, Stuart. *Napoleon's Integration of Europe.* New York, 1991.

REVOLUTIONARY PARIS

Frenchmen, it is for you to give to the world the example which Paris has given to France; prepare yourselves by order and by confidence in your destiny for the firm institutions which you are about to be called upon to establish.

— *Proclamation of the Provisional Government,* Paris, February 24, 1848

THE FRENCH REVOLUTION of 1789 has long stood as a watershed in the history of modern Europe. Although the revolution began with the rather moderate aim of creating a constitution, it developed into a struggle between the forces of republicanism and the *ancien regime*. The city of Paris played a formative role in the revolutionary spirit of late-eighteenth-century France. However, Paris was again visited by revolutions in 1830, 1848, 1871, and 1968. How is it possible that one European city should serve as the heart of so much revolutionary activity?

Although each revolution was precipitated by different forces, there is little doubt that the intellectuals, professionals, artisans, commoners, and students of Paris were the engines of social, political, and economic change. In each instance, there were specific grievances that needed to be addressed by the government. In 1789, near financial collapse led Louis XVI to convoke the Estates General. Ten years later, the *ancien regime* had been destroyed. In 1830, the Bourbons were overthrown and replaced by the more liberal regime of Louis-Philippe. 1848 was a revolutionary year throughout Europe. The euphoria that brought Louis-Philippe to the throne was short-lived, and those students and workers who had fought on the barricades in 1830 remained unrepresented. On March 18, 1871, the revolutionary workers of Paris barricaded the streets and established the Commune. The French government fled to Versailles and declared war on Paris. Almost a century later, in May 1968, students at the Sorbonne fought against the "system," and the people of Paris sided with the students. In the end, 12 million workers went on strike and more than 120 factories were occupied.

The images and documents in the *Revolutionary Paris* Digital History Feature at www.wwnorton.com/wciv highlight the similarities between the French Revolution of 1789 and the subsequent revolutions up to the student protests of 1968. As you explore the *Revolutionary Paris* feature, consider the following:

• In what ways did the "language" of revolution change between 1789 and 1968?

• What social, political, economic, and intellectual forces made Paris such a focus of revolutionary activity?

• Is there any continuity between these various revolutions, or were they all the result of specific historical circumstances?

• How did the student revolt at the Sorbonne in 1968 serve as a rallying point for the workers of Paris?

CHAPTER NINETEEN

CHAPTER CONTENTS

THE INDUSTRIAL REVOLUTION AND NINETEENTH-CENTURY SOCIETY

T HE FRENCH REVOLUTION TRANSFORMED the political and diplomatic landscape of Europe suddenly and dramatically. The transformation of industry came more gradually. By the 1830s or 1840s, however, writers and social thinkers were increasingly aware of unexpected and extraordinary changes in their economic world. They spoke of an "industrial revolution," one that seemed to parallel the ongoing revolution in politics. The term has stayed with us. The Industrial Revolution spanned the hundred years after 1780. It represented the first breakthrough from an agricultural, artisanal, and overwhelmingly rural economy to one characterized by larger-scale manufacturing, more capital-intensive enterprises, and urbanization. It involved new sources of energy and power, faster transportation, mechanization, higher productivity, and new ways of organizing human labor. It triggered social changes with revolutionary consequences for the West and its relationship with the world.

Of all the changes, perhaps the most revolutionary came at the very root of human endeavor: new forms of energy. Over the space of two or three generations, a society and an economy that had drawn on water, wind, and wood for most of its energy needs came to depend on steam engines and coal. In 1800, the world produced 10 million tons of coal. In 1900, it produced 1 billion: one hundred times more. The Industrial Revolution brought the beginning of the "fossil fuel age." It shattered the constraints of previous times, it opened an era of unprecedented economic growth, and it began to alter irrevocably the balance of humanity and the environment. Within a few more generations, by the end of the nineteenth century, the new energy regime would include oil and electricity—but historians refer to that period as the second Industrial Revolution.

Machines gripped contemporaries' imaginations, dazzling some observers and disquieting others. The novelist Charles Dickens, for instance, compared the piston of the steam engine working "monotonously up and down" to "the head of an elephant in a state of melancholy madness." Mechanization made possible enormous gains in productivity in some sectors; in so doing it shifted the basis of the economy, in some

FOCUS QUESTIONS

• Why did the Industrial Revolution first take hold in Britain?

• What specific changes did the Industrial Revolution bring?

 • How was the Industrial Revolution different on the Continent?

• What were the consequences of industrialization?

• Who were the new middle classes?

cases creating entirely new livelihoods and industrial regions while rendering others obsolete. Yet to focus on mechanization can be misleading. Especially at the outset, mechanization was limited to a few sectors of the economy and did not always lead to a dramatic break with techniques used in the past. Above all, technology did not dispense with human toil. Historians emphasize that the Industrial Revolution intensified human labor—carrying water or iron rails, digging trenches, harvesting cotton, sewing by hand, or pounding hides—much more often than it eased it.

One historian suggests we speak of an "industrious revolution." The "revolution" did not lie in machines themselves. Instead, it lay in the mushrooming growth of new economic system based on mobilizing capital and labor on a much larger scale. Its sweeping effects redistributed wealth, influence, and power. It created new social classes and produced new social tensions.

> The "revolution" did not lie in machines themselves. Instead, it lay in the mushrooming growth of new economic system based on mobilizing capital and labor on a much larger scale.

It also prompted deep-seated cultural shifts. The English cultural critic Raymond Williams has pointed out that in the eighteenth century, "industry" referred to a human quality: a hard-working woman was "industrious;" an ambitious clerk showed "industry." By the middle of the nineteenth century, "industry" had come to mean an economic system, one that followed its own inner logic and worked on its own—seemingly independent of humans. This is our modern understanding of the term, and it was born during the early nineteenth century. As the Industrial Revolution altered the foundations of the economy, it also changed the very assumptions with which people approached economics and the ways in which they regarded the role of human beings in the economy. These new assumptions could foster a sense of power—but also anxieties about powerlessness.

Living as we do in the early twenty-first century, an age of economic and technological transformations, we may identify with the 1840s' sense of extraordinary, far-reaching, and little-understood change. We feel the economic and social world shifting but are unable to grasp the effects, and the changes are simultaneously exhilarating and unsettling. The cascading effects of new technologies, new forms of communication, and new economic imperatives make it difficult to differentiate results from causes. Are new technologies the driving force of change, or are they the effects of other structural transformations? What sectors of the economy and which kinds of employment will expand and which become obsolete? Will dizzying rises in productivity benefit workers? Will all social groups share in economic growth? These questions and others that haunt us today arose during the first Industrial Revolution. Only in retrospect can we piece together the answers.

The dramatic changes of the late eighteenth and early nineteenth centuries built on developments in earlier times. Overseas commercial exploration and development had opened new territories to European trade. The continents of India, Africa, and North and South America had been woven into the pattern of European economic expansion. Expanding networks of trade and finance created new markets for goods and sources for raw materials; and they made it easier to mobilize capital for investment. All these developments paved the way for industrialization. The seventeenth and eighteenth centuries had seen significant "proto-industrialization," or the spread of manufacturing in rural areas in specific regions (see Chapter 15). Especially in England, as we will see, it had also brought changes in agriculture and property holding with far-reaching ramifications. Population growth, which began in the eighteenth century, was also a key factor. Last, more elusive social and cultural developments, such as more secure property rights or new forms of social mobility, played an essential role in the revolution that created the modern industrial world.

The "industrial revolution" itself began in northern England and western Scotland during the late eighteenth century and from there moved slowly and unevenly across continental Europe. Various factors (supplies of labor, resources, or capital) and important developments (technological innovations, the emergence of new economic institutions, government subsides, or legal changes) came together in different ways at different moments. For that reason, industrialization did not follow any single path across the various regions of Europe. Nor did it sweep aside older forms of production. New machines coexisted with intensive, old-fashioned hand labor. Manufacturing regions developed alongside vast areas of seemingly unchanged subsistence agriculture within the same nation. We begin with early industrialization in Great Britain and then turn to the more diverse changes that came later elsewhere.

WHY DID THE INDUSTRIAL REVOLUTION FIRST TAKE HOLD IN BRITAIN?

THE INDUSTRIAL REVOLUTION IN BRITAIN, 1760–1850   671

THE INDUSTRIAL REVOLUTION IN BRITAIN, 1760–1850

Why did the Industrial Revolution first take hold in Britain?

Great Britain in the eighteenth century had a fortunate combination of natural, economic, and cultural resources. It was a small and secure island nation with a robust empire and control over crucial lanes across the oceans. It had ample supplies of coal, rivers, and a well-developed network of canals—all of which proved important at different stages of early industrialization.

Industrialization's roots lay in agriculture. By the middle of the eighteenth century, agriculture in Britain was more thoroughly commercialized than it was elsewhere. British agriculture had been transformed by a combination of new techniques, new crops, and changes in patterns of property holding, especially the "enclosure" of fields and pastures, which turned small holdings, and in many cases commonly held lands, into large fenced tracts that were privately owned and individually managed by commercial landlords. The British Parliament encouraged enclosure with a series of bills in the second half of the eighteenth century. Commercialized agriculture was more productive, and yielded more food for a growing and increasingly urban population. The concentration of property in fewer hands drove small farmers off the land, sending them to look for work in other sectors of the economy. Last, commercialized agriculture produced higher profits and more wealth for a class of landed investors, wealth that would be invested in industry.

A key precondition for industrialization was Britain's growing supply of available capital, in the forms of private wealth and well-developed banking and credit institutions. London had become the leading center for international trade, and the city was a headquarters for the transfer of raw material, capital, and manufactured products throughout the world. Portugal alone channeled as much as fifty thousand pounds in Brazilian gold per week into London. Nor was banking limited to London; it was well established in the provinces as well. British merchants and financiers had accumulated substantial and well-organized resources and they had established relatively secure banking. This made capital more readily available to underwrite new economic enterprises, and eased the transfer of money and goods—importing, for instance, silks from points east or Egyptian and North American cottons.

Social and cultural conditions also encouraged investment in enterprises. In Britain far more than on the Continent, the pursuit of wealth was perceived to be a worthy goal. Since the Renaissance the nobility of Europe had cultivated the notion of "gentlemanly" conduct, in part to hold the line against those moving up from below. British aristocrats, whose ancient privileges were meager when compared with those of Continental nobles, respected commoners with a talent for making money and did not hesitate to invest themselves. Their scramble to enclose their lands reflected a keen interest in commercialization and investment. Outside the aristocracy, an even lower barrier separated merchants from the rural gentry. Indeed, many of the entrepreneurs of the early Industrial Revolution came from the small gentry or independent (yeoman) farmer class. Eighteenth-century Britain was not by any means free of social snobbery: lords looked down on bankers and bankers looked down on craft workers. But a lord's disdain might well be tempered by the fact that his own grandfather had worked in the counting house.

Growing domestic and international markets made eighteenth-century Britain prosperous. The British were voracious consumers. The court elite followed and bought up yearly fashions, and so did most of Britain's landed and professional society. "Nature may be satisfied with little," one London entrepreneur declared. "But it is the wants of fashion and the desire of novelties that causes trade." The country's small size and the fact that it was an island encouraged the development of a well-integrated domestic market. Unlike Continental Europe, Britain did not have a system of internal tolls and tariffs, so goods could be moved freely to wherever they might fetch the best price. A constantly improving transportation system boosted that freedom of movement. So did a favorable political climate. Some members of Parliament were

> Unlike Continental Europe, Britain did not have a system of internal tolls and tariffs, so goods could be moved freely to wherever they might fetch the best price. A constantly improving transportation system boosted that freedom of movement. So did a favorable political climate.

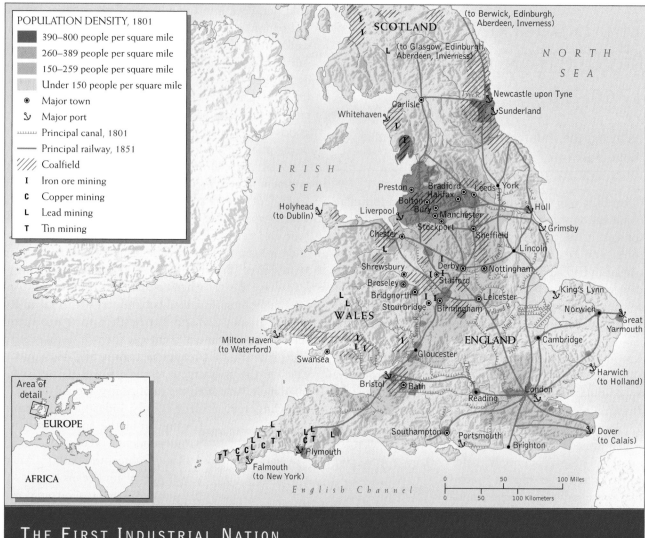

POPULATION DENSITY, 1801
- 390–800 people per square mile
- 260–389 people per square mile
- 150–259 people per square mile
- Under 150 people per square mile
- ⊙ Major town
- ⚓ Major port
- ⠿⠿⠿ Principal canal, 1801
- —— Principal railway, 1851
- ⫽⫽⫽ Coalfield
- I   Iron ore mining
- C   Copper mining
- L   Lead mining
- T   Tin mining

Area of detail
EUROPE
AFRICA

THE FIRST INDUSTRIAL NATION

The Industrial Revolution first took hold in Great Britain. How did its size and status as an island effect industrialization? Why did Great Britain build its first railroad between Durham and Darlington? Why did the railroad system expand more quickly in Great Britain than on the continent?

businessmen themselves; others were investors, and both groups were eager to encourage by legislation the construction of canals, the establishment of banks, and the enclosure of common lands. In the late eighteenth century Parliament passed acts to finance turnpike building at the rate of forty roads per year, to construct canals, and to open up harbors and navigable streams.

Foreign markets promised even greater returns than domestic ones, though with greater risks. British foreign policy responded to its commercial needs. At the end of every major eighteenth-century war, Britain wrested overseas territories from its enemies. At the same time, Britain was penetrating hitherto unexploited territories, such as India and South America, in search of further potential markets and resources. In 1759, over one third of all British exports went to the colonies; by 1784, if we include the former colonies in North America, that figure had increased to one half. Production for export production rose by 80 percent between 1750 and 1770; production for domestic consumption gained just 7 percent over the same period. The British possessed a merchant marine capable of

WHY DID THE INDUSTRIAL REVOLUTION FIRST TAKE HOLD IN BRITAIN?

THE INDUSTRIAL REVOLUTION IN BRITAIN, 1760–1850   673

transporting goods around the world, and a navy practiced in the art of protecting its commercial fleets. By the 1780s, Britain's markets, together with its fleet and its established position at the center of world commerce, gave its entrepreneurs unrivaled opportunities for trade and profit. These factors enabled Britain to experience the first great changes that would become an "industrial revolution."

INNOVATION IN THE TEXTILE INDUSTRIES

The Industrial Revolution began with dramatic technological leaps in a few well-placed industries, the first of which was cotton textiles. The industry was already long established. Tariffs prohibiting imports of East Indian cottons, which Parliament had imposed to protect British woolen goods, had spurred the manufacture of British cotton. British textile manufacturers imported raw materials from India and the American South, and borrowed patterns from Indian spinners and weavers. What, then, were the "revolutionary" breakthroughs?

In 1733, John Kay's invention of the flying shuttle speeded the process of weaving. The task of spinning thread, however, had not kept up. A series of comparatively simple mechanical devices eliminated this spinning-to-weaving bottleneck. The most important device was the spinning jenny, invented by James Hargreaves, a carpenter and hand-loom weaver, in 1764 (patented 1770). The spinning jenny, named after the inventor's wife, was a compound spinning wheel, capable of producing sixteen threads at once—though the threads were not strong enough to be used for the longitudinal fibers, or warp, of cotton cloth. The invention of the water frame by Richard Arkwright, a barber, in 1769, made it possible to produce both warp and woof (latitudinal fibers) in great quantity. In 1799 Samuel Compton invented the spinning mule, which combined the features of both the jenny and the frame. All of these important technological changes were accomplished by the end of the eighteenth century.

The water frame and the spinning mule had enormous advantages over the spinning wheel. A jenny could spin from six to twenty-four times more yarn than a hand spinner. By the end of the eighteenth century, a mule could produce two to three hundred times more. Just as important, the new machines made better-quality—stronger and finer—thread. These machines revolutionized production across the textile

Cotton Mill in Lancashire, 1834. Women and girls prepare the cotton by carding, drawing, and roving the fibers.

THE FACTORY SYSTEM, SCIENCE, AND MORALITY: TWO VIEWS

Reactions to the Industrial Revolution and the factory system it produced ranged from celebration to horror. Dr. Andrew Ure, a Scottish professor of chemistry, was fascinated with these nineteenth-century applications of Enlightenment science. He believed that the new machinery and its products would create a new society of wealth, abundance, and, ultimately, stability through the useful regimentation of production.

Friedrich Engels (1820–1895) was one of the many socialists to criticize Dr. Ure as shortsighted and complacent in his outlook. Engels was himself part of a factory-owning family and so was able to examine the new industrial cities at close range. He provides a classic nineteenth-century analysis of industrialization. The Condition of the Working Class in England *is compellingly written, angry, and revealing about middle-class concerns of the time, including female labor.*

DR. ANDREW URE

This island [Britain] is preeminent among civilized nations for the prodigious development of its factory wealth, and has been therefore long viewed with a jealous admiration by foreign powers. This very pre-eminence, however, has been contemplated in a very different light by many influential members of our own community, and has even been denounced by them as the certain origin of innumerable evils to the people, and of revolutionary convulsions to the state. . . .

The blessings which physico-mechanical science has bestowed on society, and the means it has still in store for ameliorating the lot of mankind, has been too little dwelt upon; while, on the other hand, it has been accused of lending itself to the rich capitalists as an instrument for harassing the poor, and of exacting from the operative an accelerated rate of work. It has been said, for example, that the steam-engine now drives the power-looms with such velocity as to urge on their attendant weavers at the same rapid pace; but that the hand-weaver, not being subjected to this restless agent, can throw his shuttle and move his treddles at his convenience. There is, however, this difference in the two cases, that in the factory, every member of the loom is so adjusted, that the driving force leaves the attendant nearly nothing at all to do, certainly no muscular fatigue to sustain, while it produces for him good, unfailing wages, besides a healthy workshop *gratis*: whereas the non-factory weaver, having everything to execute by muscular exertion, finds the labour irksome, makes in consequence innumerable short pauses, separately of little account, but great when added together; earns therefore proportionally low wages, while he loses his health by poor diet and the dampness of his hovel.

Andrew Ure. *The Philosophy of Manufacturers: or, An Exposition of the Scientific, Moral and Commercial Economy of the Factory System of Great Britain*, 1835, as cited in J. T. Ward, *The Factory System*, v. 1. (New York: Barnes and Noble, 1970), pp. 140–41.

FRIEDRICH ENGELS

Histories of the modern development of the cotton industry, such as those of Ure, Baines, and others, tell on every page of technical innovations. . . . In a well-ordered society such improvements would indeed be welcome, but social war rages unchecked and the benefits derived from these improvements are ruthlessly monopolized by a few persons. . . . Every improvement in machinery leads to unemployment, and the greater the technical improvement the greater the unemployment. Every improvement in machinery affects a number of workers in the same way as a commercial crisis and leads to want, distress, and crime. . . .

Let us examine a little more closely the process whereby machine- continually supesedes hand-labour. When spinning or weaving machinery is installed practically all that is left to be done by the hand is the piecing together of broken threads, and the machine does the rest. This task calls for nimble fingers rather than muscular strength. The labour of grown men is not merely unnecessary but actually unsuitable. . . . The greater the degree to which physical labour is displaced by the introduction of machines worked by water- or steam-power, the fewer grown men need be employed. In any case women and children will work for lower wages than men and, as has already been observed, they are more skillful at piecing than grown men. Consequently it is women and children who are employed to do this work. . . . When women work in factories, the most important result is the dissolution of family ties. If a woman works for twelve or thirteen hours a day in a factory and her husband is employed either in the same establishment or in some other works, what is the fate of the children? They lack parental care and control. . . . It is not difficult to imagine that they are left to run wild.

Friedrich Engels, *The Condition of the Working Class in England in 1844*, trans. and eds. W. O. Henderson and W. H. Chaloner (New York: Macmillan, 1958), pp. 150–51, 158, 160.

industry. Last, the cotton gin, invented by the American Eli Whitney in 1793, mechanized the process of separating cotton seeds from the fiber, thereby speeding up the production of cotton and reducing its price. The supply of cotton fibers could now expand to keep pace with rising demand from cotton cloth manufacturers. This cotton gin had many effects, including, paradoxically, changing the economics of slavery in the United States. The cotton-producing slave plantations in the American south became significantly more profitable, their labor now enmeshed in the very brisk and lucrative trade with merchant exporters of raw cotton and manufacturers who produced cotton textiles in the northern United States and England.

The first textile machines were inexpensive enough to be used by spinners in their own cottages. But as machines grew in size and complexity, they were housed instead in workshops or mills located near water that could be used to power the machines. Eventually, the further development of steam-driven equipment allowed manufacturers to build mills wherever they could be used. Frequently those mills went up in towns and cities in the north of England, away from the older commercial and seafaring centers, but where local politicians were interested in textile manufacturing and the money and growth it brought in its wake. From 1780 on, British cotton textiles flooded the world market. Numbers testify to the revolutionary changes in the expanding industry. Between 1760 and 1800, British exports of cotton goods from £250,000 worth a year to £5 million. In 1760, Britain imported 2.5 million pounds of raw cotton; in 1787, 22 million pounds; in 1837, 366 million pounds. By 1815, the export of cotton textiles amounted to 40 percent of the value of all domestic goods exported from Great Britain. Although the price of manufactured cotton goods fell dramatically, the market expanded so rapidly that profits continued to increase.

Behind these statistics lay a revolution in clothing. Cotton in the form of muslins and calicos was fine enough to appeal to wealthy consumers. Cotton was also light and washable. For the first time, ordinary people could have sheets, table linens, curtains, and underwear. (Wool was too scratchy.) As one writer commented in 1846, the revolution in textiles had ushered in a "brilliant transformation" in dress. "Every woman used to wear a blue or black dress that she kept ten years without washing it for fear that it would fall to pieces. Today her husband can cover her in flower-printed cotton for the price of a day's wages."

Child Labor in the Mines. This engraving of a young worker pulling a coal cart up through the narrow shaft of a mine accompanied a British Parliamentary report on child labor.

The explosive growth of textiles also prompted a debate about the benefits and "tyranny" of the new industries. The British Romantic poet William Blake famously wrote in biblical terms of the textile mills' blight on the English countryside.

> And did the Countenance Divine
> Shine forth upon our clouded hills?
> And was Jerusalem builded here
> Among these dark Satanic mills?

By the 1830s, the British House of Commons was holding hearings on employment and working conditions in factories, recording testimony about working days that stretched from 3:00 A.M. to 10:00 P.M., the employment of very small children, and workers who lost hair and fingers in the mills' machinery. Women and children counted for roughly two thirds of the labor force in textiles. The principle of regulating any labor (and emphatically that of adult men), however, was controversial. Only gradually did a series of "factory acts" prohibit hiring children under nine and limit the labor of persons under eighteen to ten hours a day.

COAL AND IRON

Meanwhile, decisive changes were transforming the production of iron. As in the textile industry, many important technological changes came during the eighteenth century. A series of innovations (coke smelting, rolling, and puddling) enabled the British to substitute coal, which they had in abundance, for wood, which was scarce and inefficient, to heat molten metal and make iron. The new "pig iron" was higher quality and could be used in building an enormous variety of iron products: machines, engines, railway tracks, agricultural implements, and hardware. Those iron products became, literally, the infrastructure of industrialization. Britain found itself able to export both coal and iron to rapidly expanding markets around the industrializing regions of the world. Between 1814 and 1852, exports of British iron doubled, rising to over 1 million tons of iron, over half of the world's total production.

CHRONOLOGY

THE INDUSTRIAL REVOLUTION IN GREAT BRITAIN, 1733–1825

Invention of the fly shuttle	1733
Invention of the spinning jenny	1764
Invention of the water frame	1769
Invention of the steam engine	1769
Invention of the spinning mule	1779
Invention of the cotton gin	1793
First railroad built	1825

WHY DID THE INDUSTRIAL REVOLUTION FIRST TAKE HOLD IN BRITAIN?

THE INDUSTRIAL REVOLUTION IN BRITAIN, 1760–1850   677

Rising demand for coal required mining deeper veins. In 1711, Thomas Newcomen had devised a cumbersome but remarkably effective steam engine for pumping water from mines. Though it was immensely valuable to the coal industry, its usefulness in other industries was limited by the amount of fuel it consumed. In 1763, James Watt, who made scientific instruments at the University of Glasgow, was asked to repair a model of the Newcomen engine. While tinkering with the machine, he hit on a way to improve it: adding a separate chamber to condense the steam eliminated the need to cool the cylinder. Watt patented his first engine incorporating this device in 1769. Watt's genius as an inventor far surpassed his ability as a businessman. He admitted that he would "rather face a loaded cannon than settle a disputed account or make a bargain." As a consequence, he fell into debt in attempting to place his machines on the market. He was rescued by Matthew Boulton, a wealthy hardware manufacturer from Birmingham. The two men formed a partnership, with Boulton providing the capital. By 1800 the firm had sold 289 engines for use in factories and mines. Watt and Boulton made their fortune from their invention's efficiency; the price for Watt's engines was a regular percentage of the increased profits from each mine that operated one.

Steam power was still energy consuming and expensive and so only slowly replaced traditional water power. A series of improvements over the course of the nineteenth century made steam engines vastly more powerful than they had been in Watt's day. Even in its early form, however, the steam engine decisively transformed the nineteenth-century world with one application: the steam-driven locomotive. Railroads revolutionized industry, markets, public and private financing, and ordinary people's conceptions of space and time.

THE COMING OF RAILWAYS

Transportation had improved during the years before 1830, but moving heavy materials, particularly coal, remained a problem. It is significant that the first modern railway, built in England in 1825, ran from the Durham coal field of Stockton to Darlington, near the coast. Coal had traditionally been hauled short dis-

tances via tramways, or tracks along which horses pulled coal carts. The Stockton-to-Darlington railway was a logical extension of a tramway, designed to answer the transportation needs produced by constantly expanding industrialization. The man primarily responsible for the design of the first steam railway was George Stephenson, a self-educated engineer who had not learned to read until he was seventeen. The locomotives on the Stockton-Darlington line traveled at fifteen miles per hour, the fastest rate at which machines had yet moved goods overland. Soon they would move people as well, transforming transportation in the process.

Building railways became a massive enterprise and a risky but potentially profitable opportunity for investment. No sooner did the first combined passenger and goods service open in 1830, operating between Liverpool and Manchester, England, than plans were formulated and money pledged to extend rail systems throughout Europe, the Americas, and beyond. In 1830, there were no more than a few dozen miles of railway in the world. By 1840, there were over 4,500 miles; by 1850, over 23,000. British engineers, industrialists, and investors were quick to realize the global opportunities available in constructing railways overseas; a large part of Britain's industrial success in the later nineteenth century came through building other nations' infrastructures. The English contractor Thomas Brassey, for instance, built railways in Italy, Canada, Argentina, India, and Australia.

Throughout the world, a veritable army of construction workers built the railways. In Britain, they were called "navvies," derived from "navigator," a term first used for the construction workers on Britain's eighteenth-century canals. Navvies were a rough lot, living with a few women in temporary encampments as they migrated across the countryside. Often they were immigrant workers and faced local hostility. A sign posted by local residents outside a mine in Scotland in 1845 warned the Irish navvies to get "off the ground and out of the country" in a week, or else be driven out "by the strength of our armes and a good pick shaft." Later in the century railway building projects in Africa and the Americas were lined with camps of immigrant Indian and Chinese laborers, who also

British engineers, industrialists, and investors were quick to realize the global opportunities available in constructing railways overseas; a large part of Britain's industrial success in the later nineteenth century came through building other nations' infrastructures.

Navvies and Steam Excavation Machine. Despite help from new construction technology, much of the work on mid-eighteenth century railways was manual labor done by navvies, many of whom were immigrant workers.

became targets of nativist (a term that means opposed to foreigners) anger.

The magnitude of the navvies' accomplishment was extraordinary. In Britain and in much of the rest of the world, mid-nineteenth-century railways were constructed almost entirely without the aid of machinery. An assistant engineer on the London-to-Birmingham line, calculated that the labor involved was the equivalent of lifting 25 billion cubic feet of earth and stone one foot high. He compared this feat with building the Great Pyramid, a task he estimated had involved the hoisting of some 16 billion tons. The building of the pyramid, however, had required over two hundred thousand men and had taken twenty years. The construction of the London-to-Birmingham railway was accomplished by twenty thousand men in less than five years. If we translated this into individual terms, a navvy was expected to move an average of twenty tons of earth per day. Railways were produced by toil as much as by technology, by human labor as much as by engineering; they illustrate why some historians prefer to use the term "industrious revolution."

Steam engines, textile machines, new ways of making iron, and railways—all these were interconnected. Changes in one area endorsed changes in another. Pumps run by steam engines made it possible to mine deeper veins of coal; steam-powered railways made it possible to transport coal. Mechanization fueled the production of iron for machines and the mining of coal to run steam engines. The railway boom multiplied the demand for iron products: rails, locomotives, carriages, signals, switches, and the iron to make all of these. Building railroads called for engineering expertise: scaling mountains, designing bridges and tunnels. Railway construction, which required capital investment beyond the capacity of any single individual, forged new kinds of public and private financing. The scale of production expanded and the tempo of economic activity quickened, spurring the search for more coal, the production of more iron, the mobilization of more capital, and the recruitment of more labor. Steam and speed were becoming the foundation of the economy and of a new way of life.

THE INDUSTRIAL REVOLUTION ON THE CONTINENT

How was the Industrial Revolution different on the Continent?

Continental Europe, with its different natural, economic, and political resources, followed a different path. Eighteenth-century France, Belgium, and Germany did have manufacturing districts in regions with raw materials, access to markets, and long-standing traditions of craft and skill. Yet for a variety of reasons, changes along the lines seen in Britain did not occur until the 1830s. Britain's transportation system was highly developed; those of France and Germany were not. France was far larger than England: its rivers more difficult to navigate; its seaports, cities, and coal deposits farther apart. Much of Central Europe was divided into small principalities, each with its own set of tolls and tariffs, which complicated the transportation of raw materials or manufactured goods over any considerable distance. The Continent had fewer raw materials, coal in particular, than Britain. The abundance and cheapness of wood discouraged exploration that might have resulted in new discoveries of coal. It also meant that high-energy-consuming, coal-run steam engines were less economical on the Continent. Capital, too, was less readily available. Early British industrialization was underwritten by private wealth; this was less feasible elsewhere. And different patterns of landholding formed obstacles to the commercialization of agriculture. In the east, serfdom was a powerful disincentive to labor-saving innovations. In the west, especially in France, the large number of small peasants, or farmers, stayed put on the land.

The wars of the French Revolution and Napoleon did hasten legal changes and the consolidation of state power, but they disrupted economies. During the eighteenth century, the population had grown and mechanization had begun in a few key industries. The ensuing political upheaval, the financial strains of warfare, and the thundering hooves of armies, however, did virtually nothing to help economic development. Napoleon's Continental System and British destruction of French merchant shipping hurt commerce badly. The ban on British-shipped cotton stalled the growth of cotton textiles for decades, though the armies' greater demand for woolen cloth kept that sector of textiles humming. Iron processing increased to satisfy the military's rising needs, but techniques for making iron remained largely unchanged. Probably the revolutionary change most beneficial to industrial advance in Europe was the removal of previous restraints on the movement of capital and labor—for example, the abolition of craft guilds and the reduction of tariff barriers across the Continent.

After 1815, a number of factors combined to change the economic climate. In those regions with a well-established commercial and industrial base—the northeast of France, Belgium, and swaths of territory across the Rhineland, Saxony, Silesa, and northern Bohemia (see map on p. 681)—population growth further boosted economic development. Rising population did not by itself produce industrialization, however: in Ireland, where other necessary factors were absent, more people meant less food.

Transportation improved. The Austrian empire added over 30,000 miles of roads between 1830 and 1847; Belgium almost doubled its road network in the same period; France built not only new roads but 2,000 miles of canals. These improvements, combined with the construction of railroads in the 1830s and 1840s, opened up new markets and encouraged new methods of manufacturing. It is nonetheless the case that in many of the Continent's manufacturing regions, industrialists could long continue to tap large pools of skilled but inexpensive labor. Thus older methods of putting out industry and handwork persisted alongside new-model factories.

In what other ways was the Continental model of industrialization different? Governments played a considerably more direct role in industrialization. France and Prussia, for instance, granted considerable subsidies to private companies that built railroads. After 1849, the Prussian state took on the task itself, as did Belgium and, later, Russia—an undertaking that required importing material and expertise but that often yielded significant profits. In Prussia, the state also

> It is nonetheless the case that in many of the Continent's manufacturing regions, industrialists could long continue to tap large pools of skilled but inexpensive labor. Thus older methods of putting out industry and handwork persisted alongside new-model factories.

operated a large proportion of that country's mines. Governments on the Continent provided incentives for and laws favorable to industrialization. Limited-liability laws, to take the most important example, allowed investors to own shares in a corporation or company without becoming liable for the company's debts—and it enabled enterprises to recruit many small investors to put together the capital for massive investments in railroads, other forms of industry, and commerce.

Mobilizing capital for industry was one of the challenges of the century. In Great Britain, overseas trade had created well-organized financial markets; on the Continent, capital was dispersed and in short supply. New joint-stock investment banks, unlike private banks, could sell bonds to and take deposits from individuals and smaller companies. They could offer start-up capital in the form of long-term, low-interest commercial loans to aspiring entrepreneurs. The Belgian Société Générale dated from the 1830s, the Austrian Creditanstalt and the French Crédit Mobilier from the 1850s. The Crédit Mobilier, for instance, founded in 1852 by the wealthy and well-connected Périere brothers, assembled enough capital to finance insurance companies, the Parisian bus system, six municipal gas companies, transatlantic shipping, enterprises in other European countries, and, with the patronage of the state, the massive railroad-building spree of the 1850s. The Périeres' success earned them reputations as upstart speculators, and the Crédit Mo-bilier collapsed in scandal, but the revolution in banking was well underway.

Finally, Continental Europeans actively promoted invention and technological development. They were willing for the state to establish educational systems whose aim, among others, was to produce a well-trained elite capable of assisting in the development of industrial technology. In sum, what Britain had produced almost by chance, the Europeans began to reproduce by design.

INDUSTRIALIZATION AFTER 1850

Until 1850 Britain remained the preeminent industrial power. Individual British factories were small by the standards set later in the century, let alone those of modern times. Still, their output was tremendous and their ability to sell to home and foreign markets was unrivaled. Between 1850 and 1870, however, France, Germany, Belgium, and the United States emerged as challengers to the power and place of British manufacturers. The British iron industry remained the largest in the world (in 1870 Britain still produced half the world's pig iron), but it grew more slowly than did its counterparts in France or Germany. Most of continental Europe's gains came as a result of continuing changes in those areas we recognize as important for sustained industrial growth: transport, commerce, and government policy. The spread of railways encouraged the free movement of goods. International monetary unions were established, and restrictions removed on international waterways such as the Danube. Free trade went hand in hand with removing guild barriers to entering trades and ending restrictions on practicing business. Guild control over artisanal production was abolished in Austria in 1859 and in most of Germany by the mid-1860s. Laws against usury, most of which had ceased to be enforced, were officially abandoned in Britain, Holland, Belgium, and in many parts of Germany. Governmental regulation of mining was surrendered by the Prussian state in the 1850s, freeing entrepreneurs to develop resources as they saw fit. Investment banks continued to form, encouraged by an increase in the money supply and an easing of credit after the California gold fields opened in 1849.

Silk Weavers of Lyons, 1850. The first significant working-class uprisings in nineteenth-century France occurred in Lyons in 1831 and 1834. Note the domestic character of the working conditions.

Moscow

RUSSIAN EMPIRE

St. Petersburg

Uppsala
Stockholm

SWEDEN

NORWAY

DENMARK
Copenhagen

NORTH SEA

ATLANTIC OCEAN

BALTIC SEA

Warsaw

Lodz

Posen

SILESIA

Berlin

Breslau

Cracow

Lemberg

GERMAN EMPIRE

Hamburg

Bremen

Dresden

Leipzig

Kassel

Zwickau

Chemnitz

Prague

Pilsen

AUSTRIAN EMPIRE

Vienna

Budapest

BLACK SEA

OTTOMAN EMPIRE

Essen
RUHR
Cologne

Eisenach

Frankfurt

Nuremberg

Munich

Steyr

NETHERLANDS

Amsterdam

Brussels

BELGIUM

Liège

Lille

Le Havre

Amiens

Paris

Orléans

Tours

Nantes

Karlsruhe
SAAR
Strasbourg
Mulhouse

Stuttgart

Basel

Zurich
SWITZ.

Turin

Milan

ITALY

Florence

Livorno

Rome

Naples

MEDITERRANEAN SEA

FRANCE

Limoges

Lyons

Avignon

Marseilles

Barcelona

UNITED KINGDOM

Glasgow

Darlington

Leeds

Sheffield

Liverpool

Manchester

Birmingham

Cardiff

London

Dublin

Gijon
Oviedo
Santander
Bilbao

Madrid

Granada
Seville
Jerez

Lisbon

PERCENT OF POPULATION LIVING IN CITIES OF 100,000 OR MORE

- 5 percent or less
- 6 to 10 percent
- 20 percent or more

— Railroads in 1850
□ Centers of industry
• Iron ore deposits
• Coal and lignite deposits

300 Miles
0   100   200   300

300 Kilometers
0   100   200   300

Area of detail

EUROPE

AFRICA

THE INDUSTRIAL REVOLUTION

Why were the effects of the Industrial Revolution more rapidly apparent in Great Britain and in north central Europe? How did the presence of an extensive railroad system help to accelerate industrialization? What effects did the Industrial Revolution have on urban population densities?

The first phase of the "industrial revolution," one economic historian reminds us, was confined to a narrow set of industries, and can be summed up rather simply: "cheaper and better clothes (mainly made of cotton), cheaper and better metals (pig iron, wrought iron, and steel) and faster travel (mainly by rail)." The second half of the century brought changes farther afield, and in areas where the Great Britain's early advantages were no longer decisive. Transatlantic cable (starting in 1865) and the telephone (invented in? 1876) laid the ground for a revolution in communications. New chemical processes, dyestuffs, and pharmaceuticals emerged. So did new sources of energy: electricity, in which the United States and Germany led both invention and commercial development; and oil, which was being refined in the 1850s and widely used by 1900. Among the early exploiters of Russian oil discoveries were the Swedish Nobel brothers and the French Rothschilds. The developments that eventually converged to make the automobile came primarily from Germany and France. The internal combustion engine, important because it was small, efficient, and could be used in a very wide variety of situations, was developed by Carl Benz and Gottlieb Daimler in the 1880s. The removable pneumatic tire was patented in 1891 by Edouard Michelin, a painter who had joined with his engineer brother in running the family's small agricultural-equipment business. These developments are discussed fully in Chapter 23, but their pioneers' familiar names illustrate how industry and invention had diversified over the course of the century.

In eastern Europe, the nineteenth century brought different patterns of economic development. Spurred by the ever-growing demand for food and grain, large sections of eastern Europe developed into concentrated, commercialized agriculture regions which played the specific role of exporting food to the West. Many of those large agricultural enterprises were based on serfdom and remained so, in the face of increasing pressure for reform, until 1850. Peasant protest and liberal demands for reform only gradually chipped away at the nobility's determination to hold onto its privilege and system of labor. Serfdom was abolished in most parts of eastern and southern Europe by 1850, and in Poland and Russia in the 1860s.

Although industry continued to take a back seat to agriculture, eastern Europe had several important manufacturing regions. By the 1880s, the number of men and women employed in the cotton industry in the Austrian province of Bohemia exceeded that in the German state of Saxony. In the Czech region, textile industries, developed in the eighteenth century, continued to thrive. By the 1830s, there were machine-powered Czech cotton mills and iron works. In Russia, a factory industry producing coarse textiles—mostly linens—had grown up around Moscow. At mid-century, Russia was purchasing 24 percent of the total British machinery exports to mechanize its own mills. Many who labored in Russian industry actually remained serfs until the 1860s—about 40 percent of them employed in mines. Of the over eight hundred thousand Russians engaged in manufacturing by 1860, however, most were employed in small workshops of about forty persons.

By 1870, then, the core industrial nations of Europe included Great Britain, France, Germany, Italy, the Netherlands, and Switzerland. Austria stood at the margins. Russia, Spain, Bulgaria, Greece, Hungary, Romania, and Serbia formed the industrial periphery—and some regions of these nations seemed virtually untouched by the advance of industry. What was more, even in Great Britain, the most fully industrialized nation, agricultural laborers still constituted the single largest occupational category in 1860 (although they formed only 9 percent of the overall population). In Belgium, the Netherlands, Switzerland, Germany, France, Scandinavia, and Ireland, 25 to 50 percent of the population still worked on the land. In Russia, the number was 80 percent. "Industrial," moreover, did not mean automation or machine production, which long remained confined to a few sectors of the economy. As machines were introduced in some sectors to do specific tasks, they usually intensified the tempo of handwork in other sectors. Thus even in the industrialized regions, much work was still accomplished in tiny workshops—or at home.

> As machines were introduced in some sectors to do specific tasks, they usually intensified the tempo of handwork in other sectors. Thus even in the industrialized regions, much work was still accomplished in tiny workshops—or at home.

INDUSTRY AND EMPIRE

From an international perspective, nineteenth-century Europe was the most industrial region of the world. Europeans, particularly the British, jealously guarded their international advantages. They preferred to do so through financial leverage. Britain, France, and other European nations gained control of the national debts of China, the Ottoman empire, Egypt, Brazil, Argentina, and other non-European powers. They also supplied large loans to other states, which bound those nations to their European investors. If the debtor nations expressed discontent, as Egypt did in the 1830s when it attempted to establish its own cotton textile industry, they confronted financial pressure and shows of force. Coercion, however, was not always necessary or even one sided. Social change in other empires—China, Persia, and the Mughal empire of India, for example—made those empires newly vulnerable and created new opportunities for the European powers and their local partners. Ambitious local elites often reached agreements with Western governments or groups such as the British East India Company. These trade agreements transformed regional economies on terms that sent the greatest profits to Europe after a substantial gratuity to the Europeans' local partners. Where agreements could not be made, force prevailed, and Europe took territory and trade by conquest.

Industrialization tightened global links between Europe and the rest of the world, creating new networks of trade and interdependence. To a certain extent, the world economy divided between the producers of manufactured goods—Europe itself—and suppliers of the necessary raw materials and buyers of finished

goods—everyone else. Cotton growers in the southern United States, sugar growers in the Caribbean, and wheat growers in Ukraine accepted their arrangements with the industrialized West and typically profited by them. If there were disputes, however, those suppliers often found that Europe could look elsewhere for the same goods or dictate the terms of trade down the business end of a bank ledger or a cannon barrel.

In 1811 Britain imported 3 percent of the wheat it consumed. By 1891, that portion had risen to 79 percent. Why? In an increasingly urban society, fewer people lived off the land. The commercialization of agriculture, which began early in Britain, had taken even firmer hold elsewhere, turning new regions—Australia, Argentina, and North America (Canada and the United States)—into centers of grain and wheat production. New forms of transportation, finance, and communication made it easier to shuttle commodities and capital through international networks. Those simple percentages, in other words, dramatize the new interdependence of the nineteenth century; they illustrate as well as any statistics can how ordinary Britons' lives—like their counterparts' in other nations—were embedded in an increasingly global economy.

British Clipper Ships in Calcutta Harbor, 1860. Calcutta, a long-established city on the eastern coast of India, was one of the hubs of the British empire—a center for trade in cotton, jute, opium, and tea. The dazzling new clipper ships, first built in the 1830s and 1840s, were very fast and were central to the global economy of the nineteenth century.

THE SOCIAL CONSEQUENCES OF INDUSTRIALIZATION

❧ What were the consequences of industrialization?

We have mentioned population growth as one factor in industrial development, but it deserves treatment on its own terms. By any measure, the nineteenth century constituted a turning point in European demographic history. In 1800 the population of Europe as a whole was estimated roughly at 205 million. By 1850, it had risen to 274 million; by 1900, 414 million; on the eve of World War I it was 480 million. (Over the same span of time, world population went from about 900 million to 1.6 billion.) Britain, with its comparatively high standard of living, saw its population rise from 16 million to 27 million. Increases, however, came in the largely rural regions as well. In Russia, the population rose from 39 to 60 million during the same period.

POPULATION

How do historians explain this population explosion? Some speculate that the cyclical potency of microbes made certain fatal diseases less virulent. From 1796 on, Edward Jenner's technique of vaccinating for smallpox gradually gained acceptance and made the disease less fatal. Improved sanitation helped to curb cholera, though not until much later in the nineteenth century. Governments were better able and more determined to monitor and improve the lives of their people. Less expensive foods of high nutritional value—most notably the potato—and the ability to transport foodstuffs cheaply by railroad meant that many European populations were better nourished and so less susceptible to debilitating illness. But real changes in mortality and life expectancy only came late in the nineteenth or the beginning of the twentieth century. In 1880, the average male life expectancy in the city of Berlin was no more than 30 years, and in rural districts nearby it was 43. Historians now attribute the population growth of the nineteenth century to rising fertility rather than to falling mortal-

ity. Men and women married earlier, which raised fertility (the number of births per woman) and family size. Peasants tended to set up households at a younger age. The spread of rural manufacturing allowed couples in the countryside to marry and set up households—even before they inherited any land. Not only did the age of marriage fall, but more people married. And population growth has its own dynamic, increasing the number of young and fertile people, thus raising significantly the ratio of births to total population.

LIFE ON THE LAND: THE PEASANTRY

Even as the West grew more industrial, the majority of people continued to live on the land. Conditions in the countryside were harsh. Peasants—as farmers of humble origin were called in Europe—still did most of their sowing and harvesting by hand. Millions of tiny farms produced, at most, a bare subsistence living, and families wove, spun, made knives, and sold butter to make ends meet. The average daily diet for an entire family in a "good" year might amount to no more than two or three pounds of bread—a total of about 3,000 calories daily. By many measures, living conditions for rural inhabitants of many areas in Europe grew worse in the first half of the nineteenth century, a fact of considerable political importance in the 1840s. Rising population put more pressure on the land. Small holdings and indebtedness were chronic problems in regions where peasants scraped by on their own lands. The uncertainties of the market compounded the unpredictability of the weather and the harvest. Over the course of the century some 37 million people—most of them peasants—left Europe, eloquent testimony to the bleakness of rural life. They settled where land was plentiful and inexpensive: the vast majority in the United States and others in places from South America, northern Africa, New Zealand, and Australia to Siberia. In many cases, governments encouraged emigration to ease overcrowding.

The most tragic combination of famine, poverty, and population in the nineteenth century came to Ireland in the Great Famine of 1845–1849. Potatoes, which had come to Europe from the New World, fundamentally transformed the diets of European peasants, providing much more nutrition for less money than corn and grain. They also grew more densely, an enormous advantage for peasants scraping a living

> By many measures, living conditions for rural inhabitants of many areas in Europe grew worse in the first half of the nineteenth century, a fact of considerable political importance in the 1840s.

THOMAS MALTHUS ON POPULATION AND POVERTY

Thomas Malthus's enormously influential Essay on the Principle of Population *(1798) marked a shift away from Enlightenment optimism about the "perfectibility of society" and a break with a long tradition of considering a large population to be a sign of economic strength. The English cleric (1766–1834) argued that hopes for prosperity ran up against a simple and grim law of nature: population grew more rapidly than food supply. Famine, disease, poverty, infant malnutrition: Malthus considered all of these inevitable, indeed "positive," checks on population. Governments could do nothing to alleviate poverty, he argued; instead the poor had to exercise "moral restraint," postpone marriage, and have fewer children. Note how Malthus's conception of nature differs from that of Enlightenment thinkers and how his influence registers in the documents on the Irish famine.*

I say, that the power of population is indefinitely greater than the power in the earth to produce subsistence for man.

Population, when unchecked, increases in a geometrical ratio. Subsistence increases only in an arithmetical ratio. A slight acquaintance with numbers will shew the immensity of the first power in comparison of the second.

By that law of our nature which makes food necessary to the life of man, the effects of these two unequal powers must be kept equal.

This implies a strong and constantly operating check on population from the difficulty of subsistence. This difficulty must fall somewhere and must necessarily be severely felt by a large portion of mankind.

Through the animal and vegetable kingdoms, nature has scattered the seeds of life abroad with the most profuse and liberal hand. She has been comparatively sparing in the room and the nourishment necessary to rear them. The germs of existence contained in this spot of earth, with ample food, and ample room to expand in, would fill millions of worlds in the course of a few thousand years. Necessity, that imperious all pervading law of nature, restrains them within the prescribed bounds. The race of plants and the race of animals shrink under this great restrictive law. And the race of man cannot, by any efforts of reason, escape from it. Among plants and animals its effects are waste of seed, sickness, and premature death. Among mankind, misery and vice. The former, misery, is an absolutely necessary consequence of it. Vice is a highly probable consequence, and we therefore see it abundantly prevail, but it ought not, perhaps, to be called an absolutely necessary consequence. The ordeal of virtue is to resist all temptation to evil.

This natural inequality of the two powers of population and of production in the earth, and that great law of our nature which must constantly keep their effects equal, form the great difficulty that to me appears insurmountable in the way to the perfectibility of society. All other arguments are of slight and subordinate consideration in comparison of this. I see no way by which man can escape from the weight of this law which pervades all animated nature. No fancied equality, no agrarian regulations in their utmost extent, could remove the pressure of it even for a single century. And it appears, therefore, to be decisive against the possible existence of a society, all the members of which should live in ease, happiness, and comparative leisure; and feel no anxiety about providing the means of subsistence for themselves and families.

Consequently, if the premises are just, the argument is conclusive against the perfectibility of the mass of mankind.

Thomas Malthus, *An Essay on the Principle of Population*, edited by Philip Appleman, Norton Critical Edition, 2nd edition, 2004, pp. 19–20.

Potato Fields. A scene from the Irish countryside in the late eighteenth century showing potatoes densely planted on a hillside.

from small plots of land. Nowhere did they become more important than in Ireland, where the climate and soil made growing grain difficult, and both overpopulation and poverty were rising. When a fungus hit the potato crop, first in 1845 and again, fatally, in 1846 and 1847, no alternate foods were at hand. At least one million Irish died of starvation, of dysentery from spoiled foods, or of fever, which spread through villages and the overcrowded poorhouses. Before the famine, tens of thousands of Irish were already crossing the Atlantic to North America; they accounted for one third of all voluntary migration to the New World. In the ten years after 1845, 1.5 people million left Ireland for good. The potato blight also struck in Germany, Scotland, and the Netherlands, but with less catastrophic results. Europe had known deadly famines for centuries. The tragic Irish famine came late, however, at a time when many thought that starvation was receding into the past, and it illustrated just how vulnerable the nineteenth-century countryside remained to bad harvests and shortages.

Changes in the land depended partly on particular governments. States that were more sympathetic to commercialized agriculture passed legislation making it simpler to transfer and reorganize land, encouraging the elimination of small farms and the creation of

> When a fungus hit the potato crop, first in 1845 and again, fatally, in 1846 and 1847, no alternate foods were at hand. At least one million Irish died of starvation, of dysentery from spoiled foods, or of fever, which spread through villages and the overcrowded poorhouses.

larger, more efficient units of production. In Britain, over half the total area of the country, excluding waste land, was composed of estates of a thousand acres or more. In Spain, the fortunes of large-scale commercial agriculture fluctuated with changes in the political regime: in 1820, the liberal regime passed legislation encouraging the free transfer of land; when absolutism was restored in 1823 the law was repealed. In Russia land was worked in vast blocks; some of the largest landowners possessed over half a million acres. Until the emancipation of the serfs in the 1860s, landowners claimed the labor of dependent peasant populations for as much as several days per week. But the system of serfdom gave neither landowners nor serfs much incentive to improve farming or land-management techniques.

European serfdom, which bound hundreds of thousands of men, women, and children to particular estates for generations, made it difficult to buy and sell land freely, and created an obstacle to the commercialization and consolidation of agriculture. Yet the opposite was also the case. In France, peasant landholders who had benefited from the the French Revolution's sale of lands and laws on inheritance stayed in the countryside, continuing to work their small farms. Although French peasants were poor, they could sustain themselves on

THE IRISH FAMINE:
INTERPRETATIONS AND RESPONSES

When the potato blight appeared for the second year in a row in 1846, famine came to Ireland. The first letter excerpted below is from Father Theopold Mathew, a local priest, to Charles Edward Trevelyan, the English official in charge of Irish relief. While Father Mathew attributes the potato blight to "divine providence," he also worries that businessmen opposed to government intervention in a free market will let the Irish starve.

The second and third excerpts are from letters that Trevelyan wrote to other British officials concerned with the crisis. Trevelyan makes clear that while he does not want the government to bear responsibility for starving its people, he believes that the famine will work to correct "social evils" in Ireland, by which he means everything from families having too many children to farmers failing to plant the right crops. In the nineteenth century, reactions to food crises were reshaped by the rise of new economic doctrines, changing social assumptions, and the shifting relationship between religion and government. These letters provide a good example of those changes and how they affected government officials.

Rev. Theobald Mathew to Trevelyan

Cork, 7 August 1846.

Divine providence, in its inscrutable ways, has again poured out upon us the viol [sic] of its wrath. A blot more destructive than the simoom of the desert has passed over the land, and the hopes of the poor potato-cultivators are totally blighted, and the food of a whole nation has perished. On the 27th of last month I passed from Cork to Dublin, and this doomed plant bloomed in all the luxuriance of an abundant harvest. Returning on the 3rd instant, I beheld, with sorrow, one wide waste of putrefying vegetation. In many places the wretched people were seated on the fences of their decaying gardens, wringing their hands and wailing bitterly the destruction that had left them foodless.

It is not to harrow your benevolent feelings, dear Mr. Trevelyan, I tell this tale of woe. No, but to excite your sympathy in behalf of our miserable peasantry. It is rumoured that the capitalists in the corn and flour trade are endeavoring to induce government not to protect the people from famine, but to leave them at their mercy. I consider this a cruel and unjustifiable interference.

Trevelyan to Routh

Treasury, 3 February 1846.

That indirect permanent advantages will accrue to Ireland from the scarcity and the measures taken for its relief, I entertain no doubt; but if we were to pursue these incidental objects to the neglect of any of the precautions immediately required to save the people from actual starvation, our responsibility would be fearful indeed. Besides, the greatest improvement of all which could take place in Ireland would be to teach the people to depend upon themselves for developing the resources of their country, instead of having recourse to the assistance of the government on every occasion. Much has been done of late years to put this important matter on its proper footing; but if a firm stand is not made against the prevailing disposition to take advantage of this crisis to break down all barriers, the true permanent interest of the country will, I am convinced, suffer in a manner which will be irreparable in our time.

TREVELYAN TO LORD MONTEAGLE

To the Right Hon. Lord Monteagle.

My Dear Lord,

I need not remind your lordship that the ability even of the most powerful government is extremely limited in dealing with a social evil of this description. It forms no part of the functions of government to provide supplies of food or to increase the productive powers of the land. In the great institution of the business of society, it falls to the share of government to protect the merchant and the agriculturist in the free exercise of their respective employments; but not itself to carry on those employments; and the condition of a community depends upon the result of the efforts which each member of it makes in his private and individual capacity. . . .

I must give expression to my feelings by saying that I think I see a bright light shining in the distance through the dark cloud which at present hangs over Ireland. A remedy has been already applied to that portion of the maladies of Ireland which was traceable to political causes, and the morbid habits which still to a certain extent survive are gradually giving way to a more healthy action. The deep and inveterate root of social evil remains, and I hope I am not guilty of irreverence in thinking that, this being altogether beyond the power of man, the cure has been applied by the direct stroke of an all-wise providence in a manner as unexpected and unthought of as it is likely to be effectual. God grant that we may rightly perform our part and not turn into a curse what was intended for a blessing. The ministers of religion and especially the pastors of the Roman Catholic Church, who possess the largest share of influence over the people of Ireland, have well performed their part; and although few indications appear from any proceedings which have yet come before the public that the landed proprietors have even taken the first step of preparing for the conversion of the land now laid down to potatoes to grain cultivation, I do not despair of seeing this class in society still taking the lead which their position requires of them, and preventing the social revolution from being so extensive as it otherwise must become.

Believe me, my dear lord, yours very sincerely,

C. E. Trevelyan. Treasury, 9 October 1846.

Noel Kissane. *The Irish Famine: A Documentary History* (Dublin: National Library of Ireland, 1995), pp. 17, 47, 50–51.

---

the land. This had important consequences. France suffered less agricultural distress, even in the 1840s, than did other European countries; migration from country to city was slower than in the other nations; far fewer peasants left France for other countries.

Industrialization came to the countryside in other forms. Improved communication networks not only afforded rural populations a keener sense of events and opportunities elsewhere, but also made it possible for governments to intrude into the lives of these men and women to a degree previously impossible. Central bureaucracies now found it easier to collect taxes from the peasantry and to conscript sons of peasant families into armies. Some rural cottage industries faced direct competition from factory-produced goods, which meant less work or lower piece rates and falling incomes for families, especially during winter months. In other sectors of the economy, industry spread out into the countryside, making whole regions producers of shoes, shirts, ribbons, cutlery, and so on in small shops and workers' homes. Changes in the market could usher in prosperity, or they could bring entire regions to the verge of starvation.

Vulnerability often led to political violence. Rural rebellions were common in the early nineteenth century. In southern England in the late 1820s, small farmers and day laborers joined forces to burn barns and haystacks protesting the introduction of threshing machines, a symbol of the new agricultural capitalism. They masked and otherwise disguised themselves, riding out at night under the banner of their mythical leader, "Captain Swing." Their raids were preceded by anonymous threats such as the one received by a large-scale farmer in the county of Kent: "Pull down your threshing machine or else [expect] fire without delay. We are five thousand men [a highly inflated figure] and will not be stopped." In the southwest of France, peasants, at night and in disguise, attacked local authorities who had barred them from collecting wood in the forests. Since forest wood was in demand for new furnaces, the peasants' traditional gleaning rights had come to an end. Similar rural disturbances

Agricultural Disturbances. Violence erupted in southern England in 1830 in protest against the introduction of threshing machines.

broke out across Europe in the 1830s and 1840s: insurrections against landlords, against "tithes," or taxes to the church, against laws curtailing customary rights, against unresponsive governments. In Russia, serf uprisings were a reaction to continued bad harvests and exploitation.

Many onlookers considered the nineteenth-century cities dangerous seedbeds of sedition. Yet conditions in the countryside and frequent flareups of rural protest remained the greatest source of trouble for governments, and rural politics exploded, as we will see, in the 1840s. Peasants were land poor, deep in debt, and precariously dependent on markets. More important, however, a government's inability to contend with rural misery made it look autocratic, indifferent, or inept—all political failings.

THE URBAN LANDSCAPE

The growth of cities was one of the most important facts in nineteenth-century social history, and one with significant cultural reverberations. Over the course of the nineteenth century, as we have seen, the overall population of Europe doubled. The percentage of that population living in cities tripled—that is, urban populations rose sixfold. Like industrialization, urbanization generally moved from the northwest of Europe to the southeast, but it also followed very specific demands for resources, labor, and transportation. In mining and manufacturing areas, or along newly built railway lines, it sometimes seemed that cities (like Manchester, Birmingham, or Essen) sprang up from nowhere. Industrialization swelled the size of port cities such as Danzig (modern Gdansk), Le Havre, and Rotterdam. Most striking to contemporaries was the very rapid expansion of Europe's old cities. Sometimes the rates of growth were dizzying. Between 1750 and 1850, London (Europe's largest city) grew from 676,000 to 2.3 million. The population of Paris went from 560,000 to 1.3 million, adding 120,000 new residents between 1841 and 1846 alone! Berlin, which like Paris became the hub of a rapidly expanding railway system, nearly tripled in size during the first half of the century alone. Such rapid expansion was almost necessarily unplanned, and the combination of unregulated growth and the pressure of numbers brought in its wake new social problems.

Almost all nineteenth-century cities were overcrowded and unhealthy, their largely medieval infrastructures strained by the burden of new population and the demands of industry. Construction lagged far behind population growth, especially in the working-class districts of the city. In many of the larger cities, old and new, working men and women who had left families behind in the country lived in temporary lodging houses. The poorest workers dwelt in wretched basement or attic rooms, often without any light or drainage. A local committee appointed to investigate conditions in the British manufacturing town of Huddersfield—by no means the worst of that country's urban centers—reported that there were large areas without paving, sewers, or drains, "where garbage and filth of every description are left on the surface to ferment and rot; where pools of stagnant water are almost constant; where dwellings adjoining are thus necessarily caused to be of an inferior and even filthy description; thus where disease is engendered, and the health of the whole town perilled."

Governments gradually adopted measures in an attempt to cure the worst of these ills, if only to prevent

Nineteenth-Century Working-Class Housing. As cities grew, medieval neighborhoods with tiny narrow streets were cleared to make way for new, improved buildings such as the ones in this photograph.

luted water of "Coketown," the fictional city in *Hard Times* is deservedly well known:

> It was a town of red brick, or of brick that would have been red if the smoke and ashes had allowed it. . . . It was a town of machines and tall chimneys, out of which interminable serpents of smoke trailed themselves forever and ever, and never got uncoiled. It had a black canal in it, and a river that ran purple with ill-smelling dye, and vast piles of building full of windows where there was a rattling and a trembling all day long . . .

Wood-fired manufacturing and heating for home had long spewed smoke across the skies, but the new concentration of industrial activity and the transition to coal made the air measurably worse. In London especially, where even homes switched to coal early, smoke from factories, railroads, and domestic chimneys hung heavily over the city, and the last third of the century brought the most intense pollution in its history. Over all of England, air pollution took an enormous toll in health, contributing to the bronchitis and tuberculosis that accounted for 25 percent of British deaths. The coal-rich and industrial regions of North America (especially Pittsburgh) and Central Europe were other concentrations of pollution; the Ruhr in particular by the end of the century had the most polluted air in Europe.

Toxic water—produced by industrial pollution and human waste—posed the second critical environmenal hazard in urban areas. London and Paris led the way in building municipal sewage systems, though those emptied into the Thames and the Seine. Cholera, typhus, and tuberculosis were natural predators in areas without adequate sewage facilities or fresh water. The Rhine river, which flowed through central Europe's industrial heartland and intersected with the Ruhr, was thick with detritus from coal mining, iron-processing, and the chemical industry. Spurred by several epidemics of cholera, in the late nineteenth century the major cities began to purify their water supplies, but conditions in the air, rivers, and land continued to worsen until at least the mid-twentieth century.

the spread of catastrophic epidemics. Legislation was designed to rid cities of their worst slums by tearing them down, and to improve sanitary conditions by supplying both water and drainage. Yet by 1850, these projects had only just begun. Paris, perhaps better supplied with water than any other European city, had enough for no more than two baths per person per year; in London, human waste remained uncollected in two hundred fifty thousand domestic cesspools; in Manchester, fewer than a third of the dwellings were equipped with toilets of any sort.

INDUSTRY AND ENVIRONMENT IN THE NINETEENTH CENTURY

The Industrial Revolution began many of the environmental changes of the modern period. Nowhere were those changes more visible than in the burgeoning cities. Dickens' description of the choking air and pol-

SEX IN THE CITY

Prostitution flourished in nineteenth-century cities; in fact it offers a microsom of the nineteenth-century urban economy. At mid-century the number of prostitutes in Vienna was estimated to be fifteen thousand; in Paris, where prostitution was a licensed trade, fifty

View of London with Saint Paul's Cathedral in the Distance by William Henry Crome. Despite the smog-filled skies and intense pollution, many entrepreneurs and politicians celebrated the new prosperity of the Industrial Revolution. As W. P. Rend, a Chicago businessman, wrote in 1892, "Smoke is the incense burning on the altars of industry. It is beautiful to me. It shows that men are changing the merely potential forces of nature into articles of comfort for humanity."

thousand; in London, eighty thousand. London newspaper reports of the 1850s catalogued the elaborate hierarchies of the vast underworld of prostitutes and their customers. Those included entrepreneurs with names like Swindling Sal who ran lodging houses; the pimps and "fancy men" who managed the trade of prostitutes on the street; and the relatively few "prima donnas" or courtesans who enjoyed the protection of rich, upper-middle-class lovers, who entertained lavishly and whose wealth allowed them to move on the fringes of more respectable high society. The heroines of Alexandre Dumas's novel *La Dame aux Camélias* and of Giuseppe Verdi's opera *La Traviata* ("the lost one") were modeled on these women. Yet the vast majority of prostitutes were not courtesans but rather women (and some men) who worked long and dangerous hours in port districts of cities, or at lodging houses in the overwhelmingly male working-class neighborhoods. Most prostitutes were young women who had just arrived in the city or working women trying to manage during a period of unemployment.

Many observers considered prostitution but one of the dangers and corruptions of urban life. The overcrowded poor neighborhoods of cities with their accompanying problems captured the attention of those watching changes taking place. Political leaders, social scientists, and public health officials across all of Europe issued thousands of reports—many of them several volumes—on criminality, water supply, sewers, prostitution, tuberculosis and cholera, alcoholism, wet nursing, wages, and unemployment. Against the backdrop of the French revolution of 1789 and subsequent revolutions in the nineteenth century (as we will see in the following chapters), the new cities and their poor inhabitants seemed to pose dangers that were not just social but political. Surveys and studies like these—or early social science—provided direct inspiration for novelists such as Honoré de Balzac, Charles Dickens, and Victor Hugo. In his novel *Les Misérables* (1862) Hugo even used the sewers of Paris as a central metaphor for the general condition of urban existence. Both Hugo and Dickens wrote sympathetically of the poor, of juvenile delinquency, and of child labor; revolution was never far from their minds. The French writer Honoré de Balzac had little sympathy for the poor, but he shared his fellow writers' views on the corruption of modern life. His *Human Comedy* (1829–1855) was a series of 95 novels and stories including *Eugenie Grandet, Old Goriot, Lost Illusions,* and *A Harlot High and Low.* Balzac was biting in his observations about ruthless and self-promoting young men and about the cold calculations behind romantic liaisons. And he was but one of many writers to use prostitution as a metaphor for what he considered the deplorable materialism and desperation of his time.

> The middle class was not one homogeneous unit, in terms of occupation or income. Movement within middle-class ranks was often possible in the course of one or two generations.

THE MIDDLE CLASSES

Who were the new middle classes?

Balzac's many novels aimed to be a sweeping portrait of middle-class society in the early to mid-nineteenth century. They are peopled with characters from all walks of life—journalists, courtesans, small-town mayors, mill owners, shopkeepers, and students. Balzac's main argument throughout is clear: he believed the political changes of the French revolution and the social changes of industrialization had done no more than replace an older aristocracy (for which Balzac was nostalgic) with a new and materialistic middle class (which he disdained). Older hierarchies expressed as rank, status, and privilege, he believed, had given way to gradations based on wealth, or social class. Not surprisingly, Balzac (although he was deeply conservative) was Karl Marx's favorite novelist. Balzac's point was echoed by many others: by Dickens, whose middle-class characters are often heartless, rigid, and obtuse; by the French artist Honoré Daumier, whose famous caricatures of

early nineteenth-century lawyers are veritable portraits of power and arrogance; and by the British novelist William Makepeace Thackeray in his similarly panoramic *Vanity Fair* (1847–1848). One of Thackeray's characters observes caustically that "Ours is a ready-money society. We live among bankers and city bigwigs . . . and every man, as he talks to you, is jingling his guineas in his pocket." Works of literature need to be approached cautiously, for their characters express their authors' points of view. Still literature and art offer offers us an extraordinary source of social historical detail and insight. And we can safely say that the rising visibility of the middle classes, and their new political and social power—lamented by some writers but hailed by others—was a central fact of nineteenth-century society.

Who were the middle classes? (Another common term for this social group, the *bourgeoisie*, originally meant city (*bourg*) dweller.) The middle class was not one homogeneous unit, in terms of occupation or income. Movement within middle-class ranks was often possible in the course of one or two generations. Very few, however, moved from the working class into the middle class. Most middle-class success stories began in the middle class itself, with the children of relatively well-off farmers, skilled artisans, or professionals. Upward mobility was almost impossible without education, and education was a rare, though not unattainable, luxury for working-class children. Careers open to talents, that goal achieved by the French Revolution, frequently meant opening jobs to middle-class young men who could pass exams. The examination system was an important path upward within government bureaucracies.

The journey from middle class to aristocratic, landed society was equally difficult. In Britain, mobility of this sort was easier to achieve than on the Continent. Sons from wealthy upper-middle-class families, if they were sent to elite schools and universities, and if they left the commercial or industrial world for a career in politics, might actually move up. William Gladstone, son of a Liverpool merchant, attended the exclusive educational preserves of Eton (a private boarding school) and Oxford University, married into the aristocratic Grenville family, and became prime minister of England. Yet Gladstone was an exception to the rule, even in Britain, and most upward mobility was much less spectacular.

Nevertheless, the European middle class helped sustain itself with the belief that it was possible to get ahead by means of intelligence, pluck, and serious devotion to work. The Englishman Samuel Smiles, in his extraordinarily successful how-to-succeed book *Self-Help* (1859), preached a gospel dear to the middle class. "The spirit of self-help is the root of all genuine growth in the individual," Smiles wrote. "Exhibited in the lives of many, it constitutes the true source of national vigor and strength." As Smiles also suggested, those who suceeded were obliged to follow middle-class notions of respectability. The middle-classes' claim to political power and cultural influence rested on arguments that they constituted a new and deserving social elite, superior to the common people yet sharply different from the older aristocracy, and the rightful custodians of the nation's future. Thus middle-class "respectability," like a code, stood for many values. It meant financial independence, providing responsibly for one's family, avoiding gambling and debt. It suggested merit and character as opposed to aristocratic privilege, and hard work as opposed to living off noble estates. "Respectable" middle-class gentlemen might be wealthy, but they should live modestly and soberly, avoiding conspicuous consumption, lavish dress, womanizing and other forms of "dandyish" behavior associated with the aristocracy. We need to emphasize that these were aspirations and codes, not social realities. They nonetheless remained key to the middle-class sense of self and understanding of the world.

PRIVATE LIFE AND MIDDLE-CLASS IDENTITY

Family and home played a central role in forming middle-class identity. Few themes were more common in nineteenth-century fiction than men and women pursuing mobility and status by or through marriage. Families served intensely practical purposes: sons, nephews, and cousins were expected to assume responsibility in family firms when it came their turn, wives managed accounts, and parents-in-law provided business connections, credit, inheritance, and so on. The family's role in middle-class thought, however, did not arise only from these practical considerations; family was part of a larger world view. A well-governed household offered a counterpoint to the business and confusion of the world, and families offered continuity and tradition in a time of rapid change.

GENDER AND THE CULT OF DOMESTICITY

There was no single type of "middle-class" family or home. Yet many people held powerful convictions about how a respectable home should be run, and about the rituals, hierarchies, and distinctions that should prevail therein. According to advice manuals, poetry, and middle-class journals, wives and mothers were supposed to occupy a "separate sphere" of life, in which they lived in subordination to their spouses. "Man for the field and woman for the hearth; man for the sword and for the needle she. . . . All else confusion," wrote the British poet Alfred Lord Tennyson in 1847. These prescriptions were directly applied to young people. Boys were educated in secondary schools; girls at home. This nineteenth-century conception of "separate spheres" needs to be understood in relation to much longer-standing traditions of paternal authority which were codified in law. Throughout Europe, laws subjected women to their husbands' authority. The Napoleonic Code, a model for other countries after 1815, classified women,

A Lawyer, by Honoré Daumier. Lawyers with their theatrical poses, dramatic robes, and displays of power were among Daumier's favorite subjects, and he drew countless caricatures of the courtroom.

children, and the mentally ill together as legally incompetent. In Britain, a woman transferred all her property rights to her husband on marriage. Although unmarried women did enjoy a degree of legal independence in France and Austria, laws generally assigned them to the "protection" of their fathers. Gender relations in the nineteenth century rested on this foundation of legal inequality. Yet the idea or doctrine of "separate spheres" was meant to underscore that men's and women's spheres complemented each other. Thus, for instance middle-class writings were full of references to spiritual equality between men and women, and middle-class people wrote, proudly, of marriages in which the wife was a "companion" and "helpmate."

It is helpful to recall that members of the middle class articulated their values in opposition to aristocratic customs on the one hand and the lives of the common people on the other. They argued, for instance, that middle-class marriages did not aim to found aristocratic dynasties and were not arranged to accumulate power and privilege; instead they were to be based on mutual respect and division of responsibilities. A "respectable" middle-class woman should be free from the unrelenting toil that was the lot of a woman of the people. Called in Victorian Britain the "angel in the house," the middle-class woman was responsible for the moral education of her children. It was

Called in Victorian Britain the "angel in the house," the middle-class woman was responsible for the moral education of her children.

understood that being a good wife and mother was a demanding task, requiring an elevated character. This belief, sometimes called the "cult of domesticity," was central to middle-class Victorian thinking about women. Home life, and by extension the woman's role in that life, were infused with new meaning. As one young woman put it after reading a popular book on female education, "What an important sphere a woman fills! How thoroughly she ought to be qualified for it—I think hers the more honourable employment than a man's." In sum, the early nineteenth century brought a general reassessment of femininity. The roots of this reassessment lay in early nineteenth-century religion and efforts to moralize society, largely to guard against the disorders of the French and Industrial Revolutions.

As a housewife, a middle-class woman had the task of keeping the household functioning smoothly and harmoniously. She maintained the accounts and directed the activities of the servants. Having at least one servant was a mark of middle-class status, and in wealthier families governesses and nannies cared for children, idealized views of motherhood notwithstanding. The middle classes, however, included many gradations of wealth, from a well-housed banker with a governess and five servants to a village preacher with one. Moreover, the work of running and maintaining a home was enormous. Linens and clothes had to be made and mended. Only the wealthy had the luxury of running water, and others had to carry and heat water for cooking, laundry, and cleaning. Heating with coal and lighting with kerosene involved hours of cleaning, and so on. If the "angel in the house" was a cultural ideal, it was partly because she had real economic value.

Outside the home, women had very few respectable options for earning a living. Unmarried women might act as companions or governesses—the British novelist Charlotte Brontë's heroine Jane Eyre did so and led a generally miserable life until "rescued" by marriage to her difficult employer. But nineteenth-century convictions about women's moral nature, combined as they were with middle-class aspirations to political leadership, encouraged middle-class wives to undertake voluntary charitable work or to campaign for social reform. In Britain and the United States, women played an important role in the struggle to abolish the slave trade and slavery in the British empire. Many of these movements also drew on the energies of religious, especially Protestant, organizations, committed to the eradication of social evils and moral improvement. Throughout Europe, a wide range of movements to improve conditions for the poor in schools and hospitals, for temperance, against prostitution, or for legislation on factory hours were often run by women. Florence Nightingale, who went to the Crimean Peninsula in Russia to nurse British soldiers fighting there in the 1850s, remains the most famous of those women, whose determination to right social wrongs compelled them to defy conventional notions of woman's "proper" sphere. Equally famous—or infamous, at the time—was the French female novelist George Sand (1804–1876), whose real name was Amandine Aurore Dupin Dudevant. Sand dressed like a man and smoked cigars, and her novels often told the tales of independent women thwarted by convention and unhappy marriage.

Queen Victoria, who came to the British throne in 1837, labored to make her solemn public image reflect contemporary feminine virtues of moral probity and dutiful domesticity. Her court was eminently proper, a marked contrast to that of her uncle George IV, whose cavalier ways had set the style for high life a generation before. Though possessing a bad temper, Victoria trained herself to curb it in deference to her ministers and her public-spirited, ultrarespectable husband, Prince Albert of Saxe-Coburg. She was a successful queen because she embodied the traits important to the middle class, whose triumph she seemed to epitomize and whose habits of mind we have come to call Victorian. Nineteenth-century ideas about gender had an impact on masculinity as well femininity. Soon after the revolutionary and Napoleonic period, men began to dress in sober, practical clothing—and to see as "effeminate" or "dandyish" the wigs, ruffled collars, and tight breeches that had earlier been the pride of aristocratic masculinity.

"PASSIONLESSNESS": GENDER AND SEXUALITY

"Victorian" ideas about sexuality are among the most remarked-on features of nineteenth-century culture. They have become virtually synonymous with anxiety, prudishness, and ignorance. An English mother counseling her daughter about her wedding night is said to have told her to "lie back and think of the Empire." Etiquette apparently required that piano legs be covered. Many of these anxieties and prohibitions, however, have been caricatured. More recently historians have tried to disentangle the teachings or prescriptions of etiquette books and marriage manuals from the actual beliefs of men and women. Equally important, they have sought to understand each on its own terms. Beliefs about sexuality followed from convictions, described above, concerning "separate spheres." Indeed, one of the defining aspects of nineteenth-century ideas about men and women is the extent to which they rested on scientific arguments about nature. Codes of morality and methods of science combined to reinforce the certainty that specific characteristics were inherent to each sex. Men and women had different social roles, and those differences were rooted in their bodies. The French social thinker Auguste Comte provides a good example: "Biological philosophy teaches us that, through the whole animal scale, and while the specific type is preserved, radical differences, physical and moral, distinguish the sexes." Comte also spelled out the implications of biological difference: "[T]he equality of the sexes, of which so much is said, is incompatible with all social existence. . . . The economy of the human family could never be inverted without an entire change in our cerebral organism." Women were unsuited for higher education because their brains were smaller, or because their bodies were fragile. "Fifteen or 20 days of 28 (we may say nearly always) a woman is not only an invalid, but a wounded one. She ceaselessly suffers from love's eternal wound," wrote the well-known French author Jules Michelet about menstruation.

Finally, scientists and doctors considered women's alleged moral superiority to be literally embodied in an absence of sexual feeling, or "passionlessness."

Queen Victoria with Her Granddaughters. The queen's image was carefully tailored to reflect middle-class morals and the ideal of the dutiful Victorian mother.

MARRIAGE, SEXUALITY, AND THE FACTS OF LIFE

In the nineteenth century sexuality became the subject of much anxious debate, largely because it raised other issues: the roles of men and women, morality, and social respectability. Doctors threw themselves into the discussion, offering their expert opinions on the health (including the sexual lives) of the population. Yet doctors did not dictate people's private lives. Nineteenth-century men and women responded to what they experienced as the facts of life more than to expert advice. The first document provides an example of medical knowledge and opinion. The second offers a glimpse of the daily realities of family life.

A FRENCH DOCTOR DENOUNCES CONTRACEPTION

One of the most powerful instincts nature has placed in the heart of man is that which has for its object the perpetuation of the human race. But this instinct, this inclination, so active, which attracts one sex towards the other, is liable to be perverted, to deviate from the path nature has laid out. From this arises a number of fatal aberrations which exercise a deplorable influence upon the individual, upon the family and upon society. . . .

We hear constantly that marriages are less fruitful, that the increase of population does not follow its former ratio. I believe that this is mainly attributable to genesiac frauds. It might naturally be supposed that these odious calculations of egotism, these shameful refinements of debauchery, are met with almost entirely in large cities, and among the luxurious classes, and that small towns and country places yet preserve that simplicity of manners attributed to primitive society, when the *pater familias* was proud of exhibiting his numerous offspring. Such, however, is not the case, and I shall show that those who have an unlimited confidence in the patriarchal habits of our country people are deeply in error. At the present time frauds are practiced by all classes. . . .

The laboring classes are generally satisfied with the practice of Onan [withdrawal]. . . . They are seldom familiar with the sheath invented by Dr. Condom, and bearing his name.

Among the wealthy, on the other hand, the use of this preservative is generally known. It favors frauds by rendering them easier; but it does not afford complete security. . . .

Case X.—This couple belongs to two respectable families of vintners. They are both pale, emaciated, downcast, sickly. . . .

They have been married for ten years; they first had two children, one immediately after the other, but in order to avoid an increase of family, they have had recourse to conjugal frauds. Being both very amorous, they have found this practice very convenient to satisfy their inclinations. They have employed it to such an extent, that up to a few months ago, when their health began to fail, the husband had intercourse with his wife habitually two and three times in twenty-four hours.

The following is the condition of the woman: She complains of continual pains in the lower part of the abdomen and kidneys. These pains disturb the functions of the stomach and render her nervous. . . . By the touch we find a very intense heat, great sensibility to pressure, and all the signs of a chronic metritis. The patient attributes positively her present state to the too frequent approaches of her husband.

The husband does not attempt to exculpate himself, as he also is in a state of extreme suffering. It is not in the genital organs, however, that we find his disorder, but in the whole general nervous system; his history will find its place in the part of this work relative to general disturbances. . . .

DEATH IN CHILDBIRTH

Mrs. Ann B. Pettigrew was taken in Labour after returning from a walk in the garden, at 7 o'clock in the evening of June 30, 1830. At 40 minutes after 11 o'clock, she was delivered of a daughter. A short time after, I was informed that the Placenta was not removed, and, at 10 minutes after 12 was asked into the room. I advanced to my dear wife, and kissing her, asked her how she was, to which she replied, I feel very badly. I went out of the room, and sent for Dr. Warren.

I then returned, and inquired if there was much hemorrhage, and was answered that there was. I then asked the midwife (Mrs. Brickhouse) if she ever used manual exertion to remove the placenta. She said she had more than fifty times. I then, fearing the consequences of hemorrhage, observed, Do, my dear sweet wife, permit Mrs. Brickhouse to remove it: To which she assented. . . . After the second unsuccessful attempt, I desired the midwife to desist. In these two efforts, my dear Nancy suffered exceedingly and frequently exclaimed: "O Mrs Brickhouse you will kill me," and to me, "O I shall die, send for the Doctor." To which I replied, "I have sent."

After this, my feelings were so agonizing that I had to retire from the room and lay down, or fall. Shortly after which, the midwife came to me and, falling upon her knees, prayed most fervently to God and to me to forgive her for saying that she could do what she could not. . . .

The placenta did not come away, and the hemorrhage continued with unabated violence until five o'clock in the morning, when the dear woman breathed her last 20 minutes before the Doctor arrived.

So agonizing a scene as that from one o'clock, I have no words to describe. O My God, My God! have mercy on me. I am undone forever. . . .

Cited in Erna Olafson Hellerstein, Leslie Parker Hume, and Karen M. Offen, eds. *Victorian Women: A Documentary Account of Women's Lives in Nineteenth-Century England, France, and the United States* (Stanford: Stanford University Press, 1981), pp. 193–94, 219–20.

Scientists and doctors considered male sexual desire natural, if not admirable—an unruly force that had to be channeled. Many governments legalized and regulated prostitution—which included the compulsory examination of women for venereal disease—precisely because it provided an outlet for male sexual desire. Doctors disagreed about female sexuality, but the British doctor William Acton stood among those who asserted that women functioned differently:

> I have taken pains to obtain and compare abundant evidence on this subject, and the result of my inquiries I may briefly epitomize as follows:—I should say that the majority of women (happily for society) are not very much troubled with sexual feeling of any kind. What men are habitually, women are only exceptionally.

Like other nineteenth-century men and women, Acton also believed that more open expressions of sexuality were disreputable and, also, that working-class women were less "feminine."

Convictions like these reveal a great deal about Victorian science and medicine, but they did not necessarily dictate people's intimate lives. As far as sexuality was concerned, the absence of any reliable contraception mattered more in people's experiences and feelings than sociologists' or doctors' opinions. Abstinence and withdrawal were the only common techniques for preventing pregnancy. Their effectiveness was limited, since until the 1880s doctors continued to believe that a woman was most fertile during and around her menstrual period. Midwives and prostitutes knew of other forms of contraception and abortifacients (all of them dangerous and most ineffective), and surely some middle-class women did as well, but such information was not respectable middle-class fare. Concretely, then, sexual intercourse was directly related to the very real dangers of frequent pregnancies. In England, one in one hundred childbirths ended in the death of the mother; at a time when a woman might become pregnant eight or nine times in her life, this was a sobering prospect. Those dangers varied with social class, but even among wealthy and better-cared-for women, they took a real toll. Not surprisingly, middle-class women's diaries and letters are full of their anticipations of childbirth, both joyful and anxious. Queen Victoria, who bore nine children, declared that childbirth was the "shadow side" of marriage—and she was a pioneer in using anesthesia!

MIDDLE-CLASS LIFE IN PUBLIC

The public life of middle-class families literally re-shaped the nineteenth-century landscape. Houses and their furnishings were powerful symbols of material security. Solidly built, heavily decorated, they proclaimed the financial worth and social respectability of those who dwelt within. In provincial cities they were often freestanding "villas." In London, Paris, Berlin, or Vienna, they might be in rows of five- or six-story townhouses, or large apartments. Whatever particular shape they took, they were built to last a long time. The rooms were certain to be crowded with furniture, art objects, carpets, and wall hangings. The size of the rooms, the elegance of the furniture, the number of servants—all depended, of course, on the extent of one's income. A bank clerk did not live as elegantly as a bank director. Yet they shared many standards and aspirations, and those common values helped bind them to the same class, despite the differences in their material way of life.

As cities grew, they became increasingly segregated. Middle-class people lived far from the unpleasant sights and smells of industrialization. Their residential areas, usually built to the west of the cities, out of the path of the prevailing breeze and therefore of industrial pollution, were havens from congestion. The public buildings in the center, many constructed during the nineteenth century, were celebrated as signs of development and prosperity. The middle classes increasingly managed their cities' affairs, although members of the aristocracy retained considerable power, especially in Central Europe. And it was these new middle-class civic leaders who provided new industrial cities with many of their architectural landmarks: city halls, stock exchanges, museums, opera houses, outdoor concert halls, and department stores. One historian has called these buildings the new cathedrals of the industrial age; projects intended to express the community's values and represent public culture, they were monuments to social change.

The suburbs changed as well. The advent of the railways made outings to concerts, parks, and bathing spots popular. They made it possible for families of relatively moderate means to take one- or two-week-long trips to the mountains or to the seashore. New resorts opened, offering racetracks, mineral springs baths, and cabanas on the beach. Mass tourism would not come until the twentieth century. But the now familiar Impressionist paintings of the 1870s and 1880s testify to something that was dramatically new in the nineteenth century: a new range of middle-class leisures.

WORKING-CLASS LIFE

Like the middle class, the working class was divided into various subgroups and categories, determined in this case by skill, wages, gender, and workplace. Workers' experiences varied, depending on where they worked, where they lived, and, above all, how much they earned. A skilled textile worker lived a life far different from that of a ditch digger, the former able to afford the food, shelter, and clothing necessary for a decent existence, the latter barely able to scrape by.

Some movement from the ranks of the unskilled to the skilled was possible, if children were provided, or

Apartment Living in Paris. This print shows that on the Continent rich and poor often lived in the same buildings, the rich on the lower floors, the poor at the top. This sort of residential mixing was unknown in Britain.

provided themselves, with at least a rudimentary education. Yet education was considered by many parents a luxury, especially since children could be put to work at an early age to supplement a family's meager earnings. Downward mobility from skilled to unskilled was also possible, as technological change—the introduction of the power loom, for example—drove highly paid workers into the ranks of the unskilled and destitute.

Working-class housing was unhealthy and unregulated. In older cities single-family dwellings were broken up into apartments, often of no more than one room per family. In new manufacturing centers, rows of tiny houses, located close by smoking factories, were built back to back, thereby eliminating any cross-ventilation or space for gardens. Crowding was commonplace. A newspaper account from the 1840s noted that in Leeds, a textile center in northern Britain, an "ordinary" worker's house contained no more than 150 square feet, and that in most cases those houses were "crammed almost to suffocation with human beings both day and night."

Household routines, demanding in the middle classes, were grinding for the poor. The family remained a survival network, in which everyone played a crucial role. In addition to working for wages, wives were expected to house, feed, and clothe the family on the very little money different members of the family earned. A "good wife" was able to make ends meet even in bad times. Working women's daily lives involved constant rounds of carrying and boiling water, cleaning, cooking, and doing laundry—in one- and two-room crowded, unventilated, poorly lit apartments. Families could not rely on their own gardens to help supply them with food. City markets catered to their needs for cheap goods, but these were regularly stale, nearly rotten, or dangerously adulterated. Formaldehyde was added to milk to prevent spoilage. Pounded rice was mixed into sugar. Fine brown earth was introduced into cocoa.

WORKING WOMEN IN THE INDUSTRIAL LANDSCAPE

Few figures raised more public anxiety and outcry in the nineteenth century than the working woman. Contemporaries worried out loud about the "promiscuous mixing of the sexes" in crowded and humid workshops.

Nineteenth-century writers, starting in England and France, chronicled what they considered to be the economic and moral horrors of female labor: unattended children running in the streets, small children caught in accidents at the mills or the mines, pregnant women hauling coal, or women laboring alongside men in shops.

Women's work was not new. Industrialization made it more visible. Women and children formed nearly half the labor force in some of the most "modern" industries, such as textiles. Women workers were paid less and were considered less likely to make trouble; manufacturers sought to recruit women mill hands from neighboring villages, paying good wages by comparison with other jobs open to women; in some cases they asked poor-law officials to find "needy and suitable families" for the mills. Most began to work at the age of ten or eleven old; and once they had children they either put their children out to wet nurses, brought them to the mills, or continued to earn wages doing piecework (paid by the piece rather than by the hour) at home. One of the common causes of labor protest during the period was the introduction of women workers to do jobs considered the "property" of men.

Still, most women did not work in factories and the gender division of labor remained remarkably unchanged. Most women labored at home or in small workshops—"sweatshops," as they came to be called—for notoriously low wages, paid not by the hour but by the piece for each shirt stitched or each matchbox glued. And by far the greatest number of unmarried working-class women worked, less visibly, in domestic service, a job that brought low wages and, to judge by a great many women's testimony, coercive sexual relationships with male employers or their sons. Domestic service, however, provided room and board. In a time when a single woman simply could not survive on her own wages, a young woman who had just arrived in the city had few choices: marriage, which was unlikely to happen right away; renting a room in a boardinghouse, many of which were often centers of prostitution; domestic service; or living with someone. How women balanced the demands for money and the time for household work varied with the number and age of their children. Mothers were actually more likely to work when their children were very small, for there

> Most women labored at home or in small workshops—"sweatshops," as they came to be called—for notoriously low wages, paid not by the hour but by the piece for each shirt stitched or each matchbox glued.

were more mouths to feed and the children were not yet old enough to earn wages.

Poverty, the absence of privacy, and the particular vulnerabilities of working-class women made working-class sexuality very different from its middle-class counterpart. Illegitimacy rose dramatically between 1750 and 1850. In Frankfurt, Germany, for example, where the illegitimacy rate had been a mere 2 percent in the early 1700s, it reached 25 percent in 1850. In Bordeaux, France, in 1840, one third of the recorded births were illegitimate. Reasons for this increase are difficult to establish. Greater mobility and urbanization meant weaker family ties, more opportunities for young men and women, and more vulnerabilities. Premarital sex was an accepted practice in preindustrial villages, but because of the social controls that dominated village life, it was almost always followed by marriage. These controls were weaker in the far more anonymous setting of a factory town or commercial city. The economic uncertainties of the early industrial age meant that a young workingman's promise of marriage based

on his expectation of a job might frequently be difficult to fulfill. Economic vulnerability drove many single women into temporary relationships that produced children and a continuing cycle of poverty and abandonment. Historians have shown, however, that in the city as in the countryside, many of these temporary relationships became enduring ones: the parents of illegitimate children would marry later. Again, nineteenth-century writers dramatized what they considered the disreputable sexuality of the "dangerous classes" in the cities. Some of them attributed illegitimacy, prostitution, and so on, to the moral weakness of working-class people, others to the systematic changes wrought by industrialization. Both sides, however, overstated the collapse of the family and the destruction of traditional morality. Working-class families transmitted expectations about gender roles and sexual behavior: girls should expect to work, daughters were responsible for caring for their younger siblings as well as for earning wages, sexuality was a fact of life, midwives could help desperate pregnant girls, marriage was an avenue to re-

CAPITAL AND LABOUR.

"Capital and Labour." In its earliest years, the British magazine *Punch,* though primarily a humorous weekly, manifested a strong social conscience. This 1843 cartoon shows the capitalists are seen reveling in the rewards of their investments while the workers shiver in cold and hunger.

spectability, and so on. The gulf that separated these expectations and codes from those of middle-class women was one of the most important factors in the development of nineteenth-century class identity.

A LIFE APART: "CLASS" CONSCIOUSNESS

The new demands of factory life also created common experiences and difficulties. The factory system, emphasizing as it did standard rather than individual work patterns, denied skilled laborers the pride in craft they had previously enjoyed. Many workers found themselves stripped of the protections of guilds and formal apprenticeships that had bound their predecessors to a particular trade or place, and that were outlawed or sharply curtailed by legislation in France, Germany, and Britain in the first half of the nineteenth century. Factory hours were long; before 1850 workdays were usually twelve to fourteen hours long. Textile mills remained unventilated, so that minute particles of material lodged in workers' lungs. Machines were unfenced and posed a particular danger to child workers, often hired, because of their supposed agility, to clean under and around the moving parts. Surveys by British physicians in the 1840s catalogued the toll that long factory hours and harsh working conditions were taking, particularly on young workers, such as spinal curvature and other bone malformations that resulted from standing hour after hour in unnatural positions at machines. And what was true of factories was true as well of mines, in which over fifty thousand children and young people were employed in Britain in 1841. Children were used to haul coal to underground tramways or shafts. The youngest were set to work—often for as long as twelve hours at a stretch—operating doors that regulated the ventilation in the mines. When they fell asleep during long shifts they jeopardized the safety of the entire work force.

Factories also imposed new routines and disciplines. Artisans in earlier times worked very long hours for very little pay. But at least to some degree, they could set their own hours and structure their own activities, moving from their home workshops to their small garden plots and back again as they wished. In a factory, all "hands" learned the discipline of the whistle. To function efficiently, a factory demanded that all employees begin and end work at the same time. Most workers could not tell time; fewer possessed clocks. None was accustomed to the relentless pace of the machine. In order to increase production, the factory system encouraged the breaking down of the manufacturing process into specialized steps, each with its own assigned time, an innovation that upset workers accustomed to completing a task at their own pace. Workers began to see machinery itself as the tyrant that had changed their lives and bound them to a kind of industrial slavery. A radical working-class song written in Britain in the 1840s expressed the feeling: "There is a king and a ruthless king; / Not a king of the poet's dream; / But a tyrant fell, white slaves know well, / And that ruthless king is steam."

Yet the defining feature of working-class life was vulnerability—to unemployment, sickness, accidents in dangerous jobs, family problems, and spikes in the prices of food. Seasonal unemployment, high in almost all trades, made it impossible to collect regular wages. Markets for manufactured goods were small and unstable, producing cyclical economic depressions; when those came, thousands of workers found themselves laid off with no system of unemployment insurance to sustain them. The early decades of industrialization were also marked by several severe agricultural depressions and economic crises. During the crisis years of the 1840s, half the working population of Britain's industrial cities was unemployed. In Paris, eighty-five thousand went on relief in 1840. Families survived by working several small jobs, pawning their possessions, and getting credit from local wineshops and grocery stores. The chronic insecurity of working-class life helped fuel the creation of workers' self-help societies, fraternal associations, and early socialist organizations. It also meant that economic crises, could have explosive consequences (see Chapter 20).

By mid-century, various experiences were beginning to make working people conscious of themselves as different from and in opposition to the middle classes. Changes in the workplace—whether the introduction of machines and factory labor, speedups, subcontracting to cheap labor, or the loss of guild protections— were part of the picture. The social segregation of the rapidly expanding nineteenth-century cities also contributed to the sense that working people lived a life apart. Class differences seemed embedded in a very wide array of everyday experiences and beliefs: work, "private" life, expectations for children, the roles of men and women, and definitions of respectability. Industrialization did not simply create a class society. Yet over the course of the nineteenth century, all of these different experiences gave concrete, specific meaning to the word "class."

CONCLUSION

Between 1800 and 1900, the population of Europe doubled. Over that same period, Europe's gross national product more than doubled. Yet even startling statistics on growth only begin to suggest how profoundly Europe's economics, politics, and culture were transformed. The Industrial Revolution was one of the turning points in the history of the world. It did not happen overnight and it did not happen evenly. In 1900 agriculture was still the largest single sector of employment. Villages and farms in vast stretches of Europe could seem virtually untouched by industry. Landowners still exercised enormous political and social clout, even when they had to share power with new elites. Yet the changes were by any measure extraordinary; they reached across the globe and into the private lives of ordinary people. Family structures changed. Industry changed the European landscape and, even more fundamentally, humanity's relationship to the environment. As we will see in later chapters, the revolutionary transformations in communication,

transportation, and economics had among their many effects the expansion of national states and bureaucracies. Europe's economic surge forward also decisively altered the global balance of power, tilting the scales toward an increasingly industrialized West. Economic development became a new yardstick of value, technology a measure of progress. Increasingly, the "West" came to be associated with—or even defined as—those nations with advanced industrial economies.

Industrialization created new forms of wealth alongside new kinds of poverty. It also fostered an acute awareness of the disparity between social groups. In the eighteenth century, that disparity would have been described in terms of birth, rank, or privilege. In the nineteenth century, it was increasingly seen in terms of class. Champions and critics of the new order alike spoke of a "class society," and new class identities were another key feature of the period. They were embodied in the growing and overcrowded working-class districts of the new cities, in the daily experiences of work, in new conceptions of "respectability," and in middle-class homes. Those new identities would be sharpened in the political events to which we now turn.

KEY TERMS

enclosure

spinning jenny

James Watt

"navvies"

Irish Potato Famine

Charles Dickens

Human Comedy

"cult of domesticity"

Queen Victoria

sweatshops

SELECTED READINGS

Berg, Maxine. *The Age of Manufactures: Industry, Innovation, and Work in Britain, 1700–1820.* Oxford, 1985. Good on new scholarship and on women.

Bridenthal, Renate, Claudia Koonz, and Susan Stuard, eds. *Becoming Visible: Women in European History*, 2d ed. Boston, 1987. Excellent, wide-ranging introduction.

Briggs, Asa. *Victorian Cities.* New York, 1963. A survey of British cities, stressing middle-class attitudes toward the new urban environment.

Cameron, R. E. *France and the Industrial Development of Europe.* Princeton, 1968. Valuable material on the Industrial Revolution outside Britain.

Chevalier, Louis. *Laboring Classes and Dangerous Classes during the First Half of the Nineteenth Century.* New York, 1973. An im-

portant, though controversial, account of crime, class, and middle-class perceptions of life in Paris.

Cipolla, Carlo M., ed. *The Industrial Revolution, 1700–1914.* New York, 1976. A collection of essays that emphasizes the wide range of industrializing experiences in Europe.

Cott, Nancy. *The Bonds of Womanhood: "Woman's Sphere" in New England, 1780–1935.* New Haven and London, 1977. One of the most influential studies of the paradoxes of domesticity.

Davidoff, Leonore, and Catherine Hall. *Family Fortunes: Men and Women of the English Middle Class, 1780–1850.* Chicago, 1985. A brilliant and detailed study of the lives and ambitions of several English families.

Ferguson, Niall. "The European Economy, 1815–1914." In *The Nineteenth Century*, edited by T.C.W. Blanning. Oxford and New York, 2000. See, by the same author, *The Cash Nexus: Money and Power in the Modern World, 1700–2000* (New York,

2001) for a very stimulating and fresh overview of the period.

Gay, Peter. *The Bourgeois Experience: Victoria to Freud*. New York, 1984. A multivolume, path-breaking study of middle-class life in all its dimensions. See also Gay's synthesis of some of those arguments in *Schnitzler's Century: The Making of Middle-Class Culture, 1815–1914*. New York and London, 2002.

Hellerstein, Erna, Leslie Hume, and Karen Offen, eds. *Victorian Women: A Documentary Account*. Stanford, 1981. Good collection of documents, with excellent introductory essays.

Hobsbawm, Eric J. *The Age of Capital, 1848–1875*. London, 1975. Among the best introductions.

———. *The Age of Revolution, 1789–1848*. London, 1962.

Hobsbawm, Eric, and George Rudé. *Captain Swing: A Social History of the Great English Agricultural Uprising of 1830*. New York, 1975. Analyzes rural protest and politics.

Kemp, Tom. *Industrialization in Nineteenth-Century Europe*. London, 1985.

Kindelberger, Charles. *A Financial History of Western Europe*. London, 1984.

Landes, David S. *The Unbound Prometheus: Technological Change and Industrial Development in Western Europe from 1750 to the Present*. London, 1969. Excellent and thorough on technological change and its social and economic context.

Langer, William L. *Political and Social Upheaval, 1832–1852*. New York, 1969. Comprehensive and detailed survey.

McNeill, J.R. *Something New Under the Sun: An Environmental History of the Twentieth-Century World*. New York and London, 2000.

Mokyr, Joel. *The Lever of Riches: Technological Creativity and Economic Progress*. New York, 1992.

O'Gráda, Cormac. *The Great Irish Famine*. Cambridge, 1989. A fascinating and recent assessment of scholarship on the famine.

———. *Black '47 and Beyond: The Great Irish Famine*. Princeton, 1999.

Rendall, Jane. *The Origins of Modern Feminism: Women in Britain, France and the United States, 1780–1860*. New York, 1984. Helpful overview.

Rose, Sonya O. *Limited Livelihoods: Gender and Class in Nineteenth-Century England*. Berkeley, 1992.

Sabean, David Warren. *Property, Production, and Family Neckarhausen, 1700–1870*. New York, 1990. Brilliant and very detailed study of gender roles and family.

Sabel, Charles, and Jonathan Zeitlin. "Historical Alternatives to Mass Production." *Past and Present* 108 (August 1985): 133–76.

Schivelbusch, Wolfgang. *The Railway Journey*. Berkeley, 1986.

Thompson, E. P. *The Making of the English Working Class*. London, 1963. Shows how the French and Industrial Revolutions fostered the growth of working-class consciousness. A brilliant and important work.

Tilly, Louise, and Joan Scott. *Women, Work and the Family*. New York, 1978. Now the classic study.

Valenze, Deborah. *The First Industrial Woman*. New York, 1995. Excellent and readable on industrialization and economic change in general.

Williams, Raymond. *Keywords: A Vocabulary of Culture and Society*. New York, 1976

Zeldin, Theodore. *France, 1848–1945*, 2 vols. Oxford, 1973–1977.

CHAPTER TWENTY

CHAPTER CONTENTS

FROM RESTORATION TO REVOLUTION, 1815–1848

WHEN NAPOLEON LEFT THE FIELD OF BATTLE at Waterloo on June 18, 1815, headed back to his Elysée palace and, eventually, to lonely exile on the rocky shore of St. Helena in the South Atlantic, his victorious opponents hoped the age of revolution had ended. The Austrian foreign minister Klemens von Metternich, perhaps the most influential conservative diplomat of the early nineteenth century, called revolution a "sickness," "plague," and "cancer," and with his allies set out to inoculate Europe against any further outbreaks. As Metternich and others saw it, revolution produced war. Peace, therefore, rested on avoiding political turmoil and keeping a firm grip on domestic affairs in all the countries of Europe.

Within Metternich's lifetime, however, waves of revolution would again sweep across Europe—in the 1820s, 1830s, and again in 1848. Conservative efforts to restore the old order only succeeded in part. Why? To begin with, the developments of the eighteenth century proved impossible to reverse. The expansion of an informed reading public, a development that went back to the Enlightenment, continued. The word *citizen* (and the political rights that it implied) was controversial in the tumultuous aftermath of the French Revolution, but it was difficult to banish the term from the West's vocabulary. More people thought about and participated in politics. New political ideologies, new political groups and allegiances made the early nineteenth century very different from the world that conservatives sought to retrieve. Second, industrialization and the far-reaching changes we surveyed in the last chapter eroded the foundations of the conservative order. Steam presses transformed printing; railroads changed the speed at which newspapers traveled. Cities became centers of political activity. Above all, social changes created new antagonisms and conflicts.

This is not to say that the revolutionaries carried the day. Many of the revolutions failed or were repressed. And although the old order was not restored, conservatism, renovated and adapted, gained a new foothold. This period offers a fascinating case study in sudden changes, vaulting hopes, partial successes, unintended consequences, and political adaptation—for revolutionaries and conservatives alike.

FOCUS QUESTIONS

• What principles guided the Congress of Vienna?

• What were the new political ideologies of the nineteenth century?

• What were the key themes of Romanticism?

• How did the events of 1830 bring the restoration to an end?

In culture as well as in politics, imagination and a sense of possibility were among the defining characteristics of the first half of the century. Romanticism broke with what many artists considered the cold Classicism and formality of eighteenth-century art. The Enlightenment had championed reason; the Romantics prized subjectivity, feeling, and spontaneity. Their revolt against eighteenth-century conventions had ramifications far beyond literature and painting. The Romantics had no single political creed: some were fervent revolutionaries and others fervent traditionalists who looked to the past, to religion or history for inspiration. Their sensibility, however, infused politics and culture. And to look ahead, their collective search for new means of expression sent nineteenth-century art off in a new direction.

BACK TO THE FUTURE: RESTORING ORDER, 1815–1830

What principles guided the Congress of Vienna?

In 1814 the victorious European powers met at the Congress of Vienna. The peace settlement aimed high, seeking to satisfy the great powers' territorial ambitions and guarantee international tranquillity. The Congress became a long affair and produced two peace treaties: one in 1814 and another in 1815, after Napoleon's startling escape from exile and his final defeat at Waterloo. Thus conservatives had months to celebrate the defeat of the upstart revolutionary emperor, holding expensive banquets with elaborate aristocratic etiquette, where dignitaries and relieved members of European royalty and the nobility jockeyed for positions at table.

THE CONGRESS OF VIENNA AND THE RESTORATION

The central cast at the Congress were the major powers, with Tsar Alexander I (1801–1825) and the Austrian diplomat Klemens von Metternich (1773–1859) in dominant roles. The French prince Charles Maurice de Talleyrand (1754–1838) had a surprisingly strong supporting role, considering he represented the de-

feated nation. In the wake of Napoleon's fall Russia had emerged as the most powerful Continental state. The Russian tsar Alexander, raised in the court of Catherine the Great, had taken in both Enlightenment doctrines from his French tutor and notions of absolutist authority from his autocratic father, Tsar Paul. In 1801 he succeeded his murdered father and during the Napoleonic wars he presented himself as the "liberator" of Europe. Many feared that he would substitute an all-powerful Russia for an all-powerful France. Talleyrand, the French representative to the Congress, had been a bishop and a revolutionary, had survived the Terror by going into exile in the United States, and had returned to serve as Napoleon's foreign minister before turning on the emperor and becoming foreign minister to the restored Louis XVIII. That he was present at Vienna testified to his diplomatic skill—or opportunism.

Klemens von Metternich, the architect of the peace, grew up the son of an Austrian diplomat in the unstable patchwork of the small German states. As a student at the University of Strasbourg the young Metternich witnessed popular violence connected with the French Revolution and to this he attributed his lifelong hatred of political change. He had tried to upset the 1807 alliance between Napoleon and Tsar Alexander in the interest of Austria and had played some part in arranging the marriage of Napoleon to the Austrian archduchess Marie Louise. Metternich once said he admired spiders, "always busy arranging their houses with the greatest of neatness in the world." At the Congress of Vienna, he attempted at every turn to arrange international affairs with equal neatness to suit his own diplomatic designs. His central concerns, nearly obsessions, were checking Russian expansionism and preventing political and social change. He feared that Tsar Alexander might provoke revolution in order to establish Russian supremacy in Europe. For this reason he favored treating the defeated French with moderation. Indeed, at one point he was ready to restore Napoleon as emperor of the French—under the protection and supervision of the Habsburg monarchy. Metternich was an archconservative who readily resorted to harsh repressive tactics, including secret police and spying. Yet the peace he crafted was enormously significant and helped to prevent a major European war until 1914.

The Congress sought to restore order and "legitimate" authority. It recognized Louis XVIII as the legitimate sovereign of France and confirmed the restoration of Bourbon rulers in Spain and the two Sicilies. The other monarchs of Europe had no interest in undermining the French restoration: Louis XVIII was their bulwark against revolution. But after Napoleon's Hundred Days in 1815, when the French people seemed to welcome him back from exile, the allies became sterner; France was compelled to pay an indemnity of 700 million francs and support an allied army of occupation for five years. Its boundaries were to remain essentially the same as in 1789, more restricted than the "greater France" of the revolutionary years, but the boundaries were not so punitive as they might have been.

The peace built strong barriers against any renewed French expansions. Here the guiding principle was the balance of power, according to which no country should be powerful enough to destabilize international relations. The Dutch Republic, conquered by the French in 1795, was restored as the kingdom of the

THE CONGRESS OF VIENNA

Note how the borders of European nations were established after the final defeat of Napoleon. How had Napoleon's conquests irrevocably changed the political geography of Europe. Did the delegates at Vienna build on some of Napoleon's ideas for organizing his own empire? Was the settlement reached at Vienna a success? What were the major social and political concerns of the diplomats, and how did they try to address them?

Netherlands. Its territory now expanded into Belgium, formerly the Austrian Netherlands. This now substantial power would discourage any future French expansion. For the same reason, the allies ceded the German left bank of the Rhine to Prussia. Austria expanded its empire in northern Italy, regaining the territories lost to Napoleon.

The peace of 1815 had especially important consequences for Germany and Poland. Napoleon had reorganized the German states into the Confederation of the Rhine. At Vienna the great powers reduced the number of German states and principalities from over 300 to 39 and linked them with Prussia into a loose German Confederation under the honorary presidency of Austria. This Confederation would later become the basis for German unification, but such was not the intent of the peacemakers. To check possible Russian aggression, the other European nations supported the German Confederation and maintaining the independent kingdoms of Bavaria, Wurttemburg, and Saxony. Poland, which had been partitioned out of existence by Russia, Austria, and Prussia in the 1790s, became a bone of contention and an object of the great powers' territorial ambitions. In the end, the parties compromised. They created a nominally independent kingdom of Poland but gave control over it to Tsar Alexander. Sections of Poland also went to Prussia and Austria. Prussia took a part of Saxony. Like the other victorious powers, Britain demanded compensation for long years at war and received territories that had been under French dominion in South Africa and South America, as well as the island of Ceylon. Britain's military successes in the Napoleonic wars helped secure her growing commercial empire (see Chapter 19).

The Congress of Vienna also called for a "Concert of Europe" to secure the peace and create permanent stability. Britain, Austria, Prussia, and Russia formed the Quadruple Alliance (renamed the Quintuple Alliance when France was admitted in 1818). Its members pledged to meet regularly and to cooperate in the suppression of any disturbances—either attempts to overthrow legitimate governments or to change international boundaries. Tsar Alexander I persuaded the allies to join him in the declaration of a "Holy Alliance" dedicated to establishing justice, Christian charity, and peace. Yet this second alliance only made Europe's leaders suspicious of

Alexander's intentions. Many of the aristocratic statesmen gathered at Vienna were steeped in the values of the Enlightenment and wary of crusading. Many might have shared the British foreign minister's belief that the Holy Alliance was "a piece of sublime mysticism and nonsense." In any event, they attempted to forge a different conception of authority, centered on "legitimacy." What made a ruler "legitimate" and reinforced his power was not divine right but international treaties, support, and a series of guarantees.

> King Leopold of the Belgians, placed on his throne by the allies, observed that war now threatened to become "a conflict of principles"—a conflict sparked by revolutionary ideas, and setting "peoples" against emperors.

King Leopold of the Belgians, placed on his throne by the allies, observed that war now threatened to become "a conflict of principles"—a conflict sparked by revolutionary ideas, and setting "peoples" against emperors. "From what I know of Europe," he continued, "such a conflict would change her form and overthrow her whole structure." Metternich and many of his fellow diplomats at Vienna dedicated the rest of their lives to seeing that such a conflict would never take place.

REVOLT AGAINST RESTORATION

From the beginning, the restoration met opposition. Much of the early resistance was clandestine, centered in secret organizations driven underground by repressive tactics. In Metternich's own backyard, for instance, the Italian Carbonari (a group that took its name from the charcoal with which members blackened their faces) vowed to oppose the government in Vienna and its conservative allies, whose power extended down into the Italian peninsula. The Carbonari's influence spread through southern Europe and France during the 1820s. Members of the organization identified one another through obscure rituals and met in hiding. Their political views were murky. Some Carbonari called for constitutions, political representation, and other liberal reforms. Others sang the praises of Bonaparte. The former emperor, indeed, became more popular in exile—where he became a mythologized alternative to the restored Bourbons—than he had been during his war-torn reign. Veterans of the Napoleonic armies helped create what came to be called the Napoleonic legend, and military officers were prominent among the ranks of the Carbonari.

In Spain, and in Naples and Piedmont on the Italian peninsula, opposition to the restoration turned to revolt. In both cases, restored monarchs who had pledged to respect constitutional reforms abandoned their promises, attempting to squelch elections and reinstate privileges. Alarmed at the threat to Austrian power on the Italian peninsula but determined to have international support, Metternich summoned Austrian, Prussian, and Russian representatives to a meeting. They issued the Troppau memorandum (1820), declaring that they would aid each other in suppressing revolution. France and Britain declined to sign. Although they agreed that any revolution threatened international stability, they did not want their hands tied by treaties. Metternich felt he had diplomatic permission to suppress the uprisings in Italy, forcing the rebels into prison or exile. The French took on the Spanish revolution. They sent two hundred thousand troops to the Iberian Peninsula in 1823. This force crushed the Spanish revolutionaries and restored the beleaguered King Ferdinand's authority. Ferdinand tortured and publicly executed hundreds of rebels.

Secret meeting of the Carbonari. Not all resistance took the form of open protest. An Italian organization named for the charcoal that obscured the faces of its members, the Carbonari were an underground expression of opposition to the restoration.

REVOLUTION IN LATIN AMERICA

Ferdinand's empire in Latin America, however, would not be restored. Napoleon's earlier conquest of Spain (1807) had shaken the foundations of colonial rule. Elites in the Spanish colonies had long chafed under imperial control, resenting taxes, restrictive trade policies, and privileges granted to *peninsulares* (persons born in Spain). With the king under house arrest, guarded by French troops, they saw an opportunity for self-government—an opportunity that made them unlikely to accept the restoration of Ferdinand's authority after the French had been driven out. From 1810 on, independence movements gathered momentum, beginning in Río de la Plata (now Argentina), which declared its independence in 1816. The general of the Río de la Plata forces, José de San Martín (1778–1850), led an extraordinary march across the Andes to confront royalist forces and liberate Chile and Peru. The other key military and political figure of the South American revolutions, Simón Bolívar (1783–1830), led a series of uprisings from Venezuela across to Bolivia, eventually joining forces with San Martín. The two men had very different visions of postrevolutionary government. San Martín was a monarchist. Bolívar, however, was a republican, willing to mobilize free people of color, slaves, and Indians to fight against Spanish rule, and aiming to forge a large pan-American republic on the continent along the lines of the United States or Napoleonic France. Neither leader realized his ambitions. Political revolt unleashed conflict and in many cases violent civil war. On the one hand were elites who aimed only to free themselves from Spain and, on the other, more radical groups that wanted land reform, an end to slavery, or the dismantling of social and racial hierarchies. In the end, the radical movements were repressed, and the newly independent nations were dominated by an alliance of conservative landowners and military officers.

Metternich and his conservative allies would have preferred to prevent the Latin American revolutions. But they ran up against two forces: the newly ambitious United States and Britain. In 1823 the American president James Monroe issued the Monroe Doctrine, warning Europe's great powers that he would regard any effort to intervene in the affairs of the New World as an unfriendly act. The new U.S. doctrine would have remained a dead letter, however, without British support. Britain was ready to recognize the independence of the South American republics to gain new trading partners and used its navy to keep Spain from

MEXICO
(1821)

Gulf of Mexico

CUBA
(Spanish)

Mexico
City •

ATLANTIC

OCEAN

SANTO
DOMINGO
(1821)

BRITISH
HONDURAS

HAITI
(1804)

PUERTO
RICO
(Spanish)

*CARIBBEAN
SEA*

UNITED PROVINCES
OF CENTRAL AMERICA
(1823)

• Caracas

VENEZUELA
(1830)

GUIANA (British)
SURINAME (Dutch)
GUIANA (French)

•Bogotá

COLOMBIA
(1819)

ECUADOR
(1822)   Quito •

PACIFIC

OCEAN

PERU
(1824)

• Lima

BRAZIL
(1822)

BOLIVIA
(1825)

PARAGUAY
(1811)

São Paulo
•

• Rio de Janeiro

Asunción
•

CHILE
(1818)

ARGENTINA
(1816)

URUGUAY (1828)

Santiago
•

Buenos Aires
•

Montevideo
•

ATLANTIC

OCEAN

| 0 | 500 | 1000 Miles |
| 0 | 500 | 1000 Kilometers |

New Nations of Latin America

After Haiti became the Western Hemisphere's second independent nation, many areas of Central and South America also broke away from colonial rule. Whereas the North American colonists had revolted against a vibrant and powerful empire, many of the Latin American revolutionaries took advantage of the disorder created by the Napoleonic wars. How had Napoleon's grab for the Spanish and Portuguese crowns facilitated the independence movement in South America?

intervening. By the middle of the 1820s, then, the once enormous Spanish empire in the New World had vanished. Portugal's colonial foothold in Latin America also ended when Brazil declared independence in 1822. These revolutions which brought sweeping changes to the entire continent, arguably marked the end of an age that had opened in 1492. They also dramatized the global significance of the French revolution of 1789, which reached well beyond the core states of Europe and remade states across a significant portion of the world.

RUSSIA: THE DECEMBRISTS

Revolt also broke out in Russia, the heart of the conservative alliance. In 1825, Tsar Alexander died, and uncertainty about his heir sparked an uprising among a group of army officers. Many of the Decembrists, as they were called, came from noble families and were members of elite regiments. Many of them had served in the tsarist armies that drove Napoleon back to France and had been posted there during the years while the peace was being settled. Young and idealistic, they took seriously Tsar Alexander's claim that Russia was the "liberator" of Europe. If Russia was to assume that kind of "moral greatness," though, it needed to reform. Serfdom contradicted the promise of liberation, and so did the autocratic tsar's monopoly on political power. Not only were Russian peasants enslaved, they argued, but Russian nobles were "slaves to the tsar."

The Decembrists had no single political program. They ranged from constitutional monarchists to Jacobin republicans. The rebels hoped to persuade Alexander's liberal-minded brother, Constantine, to assume the throne and guarantee a constitution. The attempt failed. Constantine was unwilling to usurp power from the rightful heir, a third brother, Nicholas. The officers themselves failed to attract support from the rank-and-file peasant soldiers and without such support were doomed to fail. This does not mean that repression was easy. The new tsar, Nicholas I (1825–1855), ruthlessly interrogated hundreds of mutinous soldiers, sentencing many to hard labor and exile. The five leaders, sentenced to death, were more troublesome. Young members of the elite, they were the "cream of the cream," and attractive candidates for martyrdom. The tsar ordered them hanged at dawn inside the walls of the Peter and Paul Fortress in St. Petersburg and buried in secret graves, so that neither their funerals nor their gravesites could provide occasions for unrest.

Nicholas went on to rule in the manner of his predecessor. Among his most autocratic acts was the creation of the Third Section, a political police force, to prevent further domestic disorder. Like the secret police of so many conservative powers, it was overstretched and undermanned, but its very existence contributed to a culture of fear and suspicion. Nicholas became perhaps Europe's most uncompromising conservative. Still, Russia showed signs of change. Bureaucracy became more centralized and more efficient, and less dependent on the nobility for political support and everyday operation. The government systematically codified laws in 1832. Rising demand for Russian grain encouraged large landowners to reorganize their estates for more effective production and the state to build railways to transport grain to western markets. Other opponents of the regime, like Alexander Herzen, who admired the Decembrists, would carry on the Decembrists' unresolved political legacy.

SOUTHEASTERN EUROPE: GREECE AND SERBIA

The conservative European powers were more open to rebellion when it was directed against rival empires. Such was the case in Greece and Serbia, both provinces in the Balkan region of the sprawling and once powerful Ottoman empire, where local movements began to demand autonomy and to ask the Europeans to sponsor their struggles. The first Greek uprising of 1821 was led by Alexander Ypsilantis, a former officer in the Russian army who enjoyed close relations with Tsar Alexander. Alexander refused to intervene. A second rising, however, drew not only support from the British government, but also hundreds of volunteers from Europe.

Of all the revolts of the early nineteenth century, none captured more attention and sympathy than the Greek war for independence (1821–1827). Why was this conflict significant? The answer has little to do with realities in the Balkans; it lies instead in conceptions of European identity. Christians in European cast the rebellion as a part of an ongoing struggle between Christianity and Islam. From a secular point of view, the Greeks' battle could be interpreted as both a crusade for liberty and a struggle to preserve the ancient classical heritage of the land. Increasingly Europeans spoke of Greece as the birthplace of the West. "We are all Greeks," wrote Percy Shelley, the Romantic poet. "Our laws, our literature, our religion, our arts have

The Massacre at Chios, by Eugène Delacroix (1798–1863). Delacroix was a Romantic painter of dramatic and emotional scenes. Here he put his brush to work for the cause of liberty, eulogizing the more than twenty thousand Greeks slain by the Turks during the Greek war of independence in 1822. The painting illustrates the fusion of Romanticism and nationalism so characteristic of the period.

their roots in Greece. But for Greece . . . we might still have been savages and idolators." George Gordon, Lord Byron (1788–1824), another Romantic poet, fought in Greece. The French Romantic painter Eugène Delacroix memorialized the Greek struggle in his *Massacre at Chios* (1824). "Philhellenic" (devoted to classical Greece) committees in cities across Europe raised money and sent volunteers; men and women in Paris wore blue and white ribbons to show they had given to the Greek cause. Celebrating the Greeks went hand in hand with demonizing the Turks and reviving the theme of "Turkish despotism," which had figured prominently in the Enlightenment. A British official remarked, "Almost the whole extent of European Turkey presents a dreadful picture of anarchy, rebellion, and barbarism." Europeans of different political persuasions sought to identify themselves with a Greek heritage which they contrasted with images of "eastern" or "Islamic" tyranny. Europeans, in short, saw the struggle through their own lens.

On the ground in Greece, both sides were ruthless. On several occasions Greek forces besieged Turkish towns and killed the inhabitants. In March of 1822, Greeks invaded and proclaimed the independence of the island of Chios, then inhabited by Turks and Greeks who remained loyal to the Ottomans. When Ottoman troops arrived to retake the island, the Greek invaders killed their Turkish prisoners and fled. The Turks took their revenge by slaughtering thousands of Greeks and selling forty thousand more into slavery. Delacroix's *Massacre at Chios,* characteristically, depicted only Turkish brutality.

Ultimately, Greek independence depended on great power politics. In 1827, British, French, and, now, Russian troops went in against the Turks. (Tsar Alexander's successor, Nicholas, favored intervention.) Two London Protocols, in 1829 and 1830, established Greek independence from the Ottoman empire, although one year later the allies put the son of the king of Bavaria on the Greek throne.

The struggle between the European powers and the Ottomans similarly helped to create the independent nation of Serbia in 1828. With Russian encouragement and aid Serbia became semi-independent: an Orthodox Christian principality (with significant minority populations) under Ottoman rule. Serbia went on to press for more territory, claiming territories held by another power in the region, the Austrian empire, a struggle that would escalate at the end of the nineteenth century.

In sum, when the leaders of independence movements could take advantage of conflict between the great powers, or when those movements fell in line with Europe's ongoing struggle against the Ottoman empire, as in Greece and Serbia, they were more likely to succeed. Both of those new nations, however, were

CHRONOLOGY

CONCERT OF EUROPE, 1815–1830

Congress of Vienna	1814–1815
Quintuple Alliance	1818
France restores King Ferdinand in Spain	1823
South American revolutions	1810–1825
Decembrist revolt in Russia	1825
Greek war of independence	1821–1827
Serbian independence	1828

WHAT WERE THE NEW POLITICAL IDEOLOGIES OF THE NINETEENTH CENTURY?

TAKING SIDES: NEW IDEOLOGIES IN POLITICS   713

small and fragile. Only eight hundred thousand Greeks actually lived in the new Greek state. Serbia's existence was protected by the great powers until 1856. Moreover, neither of the new nations broke their close links with the Ottomans. Greek and Serbian overseas merchants, bankers, and administrators were still well ensconced in the Ottoman empire. The region, then, remained one of the borderlands of the West, a multiethnic and multireligious meeting point between Europe and the Ottoman empire, a region whose peoples alternated between tolerant coexistence and bitter conflict.

TAKING SIDES: NEW IDEOLOGIES IN POLITICS

What were the new political ideologies of the nineteenth century?

These rebellions made it clear that issues raised by the French Revolution were very much alive. Early nineteenth-century politics did not have parties as we know them today. But more clearly defined groups and competing doctrines, or ideologies, took shape during this time. An ideology may be defined as a coherent system of thought regarding the social and politcal order, one that consciously competes with other views of how the world is or should be. The major political ideologies of modern times—conservatism, liberalism, socialism, and nationalism—were first articulated in this period. Their roots lay in earlier times, but ongoing political battles brought them to the fore. So did the Industrial Revolution (see Chapter 19) and the social changes that accompanied it, which proved a tremendous spur to political and social thought. Would the advance of industry yield progress or misery? What were the "rights of man," and who would enjoy them? Did equality necessarily go hand in hand with liberty? This exceptionally fertile period cast up several different responses. A brief survey of the political horizon will show how these alternatives were taking shape, and dramatize how the ground had shifted since the eighteenth century.

> Conservatives believed that change had to be slow, incremental, and managed in order to strengthen the structures of authority. Conserving the past and cultivating tradition would ensure an orderly future.

PRINCIPLES OF CONSERVATISM

At the Congress of Vienna and in the Restoration generally, the most important guiding concept was "legitimacy." Legitimacy had broad appeal as a general antirevolutionary policy. It might be best understood as a code word for a new political order. Conservatives aimed to make legitimate—and thus to solidify—both the monarchy's authority and a hierarchical social order. The most thoughtful conservatives of the period did not believe that the old order would survive completely intact or that time could be reversed, especially after the events of the 1820s made it clear the restoration would be challenged. They did believe, however, that the monarchy guaranteed political stability, that the nobility were the rightful leaders of the nation, and that both needed to play active and effective roles in public life. They insisted that, as a matter of strategy, the nobility and the crown shared a common interest, despite their disagreements in the past. Conservatives believed that change had to be slow, incremental, and managed in order to strengthen the structures of authority. Conserving the past and cultivating tradition would ensure an orderly future.

Edmund Burke's writings became a point of reference for nineteenth-century conservatives. His *Reflections on the Revolution in France* was more influential in this new context than it had been during the 1790s, when it was first published. Burke did not oppose all change; he had argued, for instance, that the British should let the North American colonies go. But he opposed talk of natural rights, which he considered dangerous abstractions. He believed enthusiasm for constitutions to be misguided and the Enlightenment's emphasis on what he called the "conquering power of reason" to be dangerous. Instead, Burke counseled deference to experience, tradition, and history. Other conservatives such as the French writers Joseph de Maistre (1753–1821) and Louis-Gabriel-Ambroise Bonald (1754–1840) penned carefully elaborated defenses of absolute monarchy and its main pillar of support, the Catholic Church. De Maistre, for instance, blamed the Enlightenment's critique of the Catholic Church for the French revolution, and he assailed Enlightenment individualism for ignoring the bonds and collective institutions (the church, for instance, or family) that he believed held society together. As

Magdalen Chapel in London, 1809. A revival of religion in the early nineteenth century was one expression of the conservative reaction to revolution. Conservatives considered the Church one of the pillars of social and political order.

conservatives saw it, monarchy, aristocracy, and the church were the mainstays of the social and political order. Those institutions needed to stand together in face of the challenges of the new century.

Conservatism was not simply the province of intellectuals. A more broadly based revival of religion in the early nineteenth century also expressed a popular reaction against revolution and an emphasis on order, discipline, and tradition. What was more, conservative thinkers also exercised influence well beyond their immediate circle. Their emphasis on history, on the untidy and unpredictable ways in which history unfolded, and their awareness of the past became increasingly central to social thought and artistic visions of the first half of the century.

LIBERALISM

Liberalism's core was a commitment to individual liberties, or rights. Liberals believed that the most important function of government was to protect liberties, and that doing so would benefit all, promoting justice, knowledge, progress, and prosperity. Liberalism had three components. First, liberalism called for equality before the law, which meant ending traditional privileges and the restrictive power of rank and hereditary authority. Second, liberalism held that government needed to be based on political rights and the consent of the governed. Third, in economics, liberalism meant a belief in the benefits of unfettered economic activity, or economic individualism.

The roots of legal and political liberalism lay in the late seventeenth century, in the work of John Locke, who had defended the English Parliament's rebellion against absolutism, and the "inalienable" rights of the British people (see Chapter 15). Liberalism had been developed by the Enlightenment writers of the eighteenth century and, especially, the founding texts of the American and French revolutions (the Declaration of Independence and the Declaration of the Rights of Man). Freedom from arbitrary authority, imprisonment, or censorship; freedom of the press, the right to assemble and deliberate: these principles were the starting points for nineteenth-century liberalism. Liberals believed in individual rights, that those rights were inalienable, and that they should be guaranteed in written constitutions. (Conservatives, as we saw above, considered constitutions abstract and dangerous.) Most liberals called for constitutional as opposed to hereditary monarchy; all agreed that a monarch who abused power could legitimately be overthrown.

Liberals advocated direct representation in government—at least for those who had the property and public standing to be trusted with the responsibilities of power. Liberalism by no means required democracy. To the contrary, who should have the right to vote was a hotly debated issue. Nineteenth-century liberals, with fresh memories of the French Revolution of 1789, were torn between their belief in rights and their fears of political turmoil. They considered property and education essential prerequisites for participation in politics. Wealthy liberals opposed extending the vote to the common people. To demand universal male suffrage was radical indeed, and to speak of enfranchising women or people of color even more so. As far as slavery was concerned, nineteenth-century liberalism inherited the contradictions of the Enlightenment. Belief

WHAT WERE THE NEW POLITICAL IDEOLOGIES OF THE NINETEENTH CENTURY?

TAKING SIDES: NEW IDEOLOGIES IN POLITICS   715

in individual liberty collided with vested economic interests, determination to preserve order and property, and increasingly "scientific" theories of racial inequality (see Chapter 19).

Economic liberalism was newer. Its founding text was Adam Smith's *Wealth of Nations* (1776), which attacked mercantilism (the government practice of regulating manufacturing and trade in order to raise revenues) in the name of free markets. Smith's argument that the economy should be based on a "system of natural liberty" was reinforced by a second generation of economists and popularized in journals such as the *Economist*, founded in 1838. The economists (or political economists, as they were called) sought to identify basic economic laws: the law of supply and demand, the balance of trade, the law of diminishing returns, and so on. They argued that economic policy had to begin by

Adam Smith pointing to his book *The Wealth of Nations* (1776). Smith was an Enlightenment thinker whose work was popularized in the nineteenth century, and he helped to establish "political economy," or economics.

recognizing these laws. David Ricardo (1772–1823) of Britain, for example, set out laws of wages and of rents, trying to determine the long-run outcomes of fluctuations in each. The political economists believed that economic activity should be unregulated. Labor should be contracted freely, unhampered by guilds or unions. Property should be unencumbered by feudal restrictions. Goods should circulate freely, which meant, concretely, an end to government-granted monopolies and traditional practices of regulating markets, especially in valuable commodities such as grain, flour, or corn. At the time of the Irish famine, for instance, their writings played a role in hardening opposition to government intervention or relief (see Chapter 19). The functions of the state should be kept to a minimum. Government's role was to preserve order and protect property, but not to interfere with the natural play of economic forces, a doctrine known as *laissez-faire*, which translates, roughly, as "leave things to go on their own." This strict opposition to government intervention makes nineteenth-century liberalism significantly different from liberalism as we know it today.

Liberty and freedom meant different things in different countries. In lands occupied by other powers, liberal parties demanded freedom from foreign rule. The colonies of Latin America demanded "liberty" from Spain, and similar struggles set Greece and Serbia against the Ottoman empire, northern Italy against the Austrians, Poland against Russian rule, and so on. In central and southeastern Europe, liberty meant eliminating feudal privilege and allowing at least the educated elite access to political power, more rights for local parliaments, and creating representative national political institutions. Some cited the British system of government as a model; others the French declaration of the rights of man. Most shied away from the radicalism of the French Revolution. The issue was constitutional, representative government. In such countries as Russia, Prussia, and France under the restored Bourbon monarchy, liberty meant political freedoms, such as the right to vote, assemble, and print political opinions without censorship.

In Great Britain, where political freedoms were relatively well established, liberals focused on expanding the franchise, on laissez-faire economics and free trade, and on reforms aiming to create limited and efficient government. In this respect, one of the most influential British liberals was Jeremy Bentham (1748–1832). Bentham's major work, *The Principles of Morals and Legislation* (1789), illustrates how nineteenth-century liberalism continued the Enlightenment legacy and also transformed it. Unlike, for instance, Smith, Bentham did not believe that human interests were naturally harmonious or that a stable social order could emerge naturally from a body of self-interested individuals. Instead he proposed that society adopt the organizing principle of utilitarianism. Social institutions and laws (an electoral system, for instance, or a tariff) should be measured according to their social usefulness—according to whether or not they produced the "greatest happiness of the greatest number." If a law passed this test, it could remain on the books; if it failed, it should be jettisoned. Utilitarians acknowledged the importance of the individual. Each individual best understood his or her own interests, and was therefore best left free, whenever possible, to pursue those interests as he or she saw fit. Only when an individual's interests conflicted with the interests—the happiness—of the greatest number was individual freedom to be curtailed. The intensely practical spirit of utilitarianism enhanced its influence as a creed for reform.

RADICALISM, REPUBLICANISM, AND EARLY SOCIALISM

The liberals were flanked on their left by two radical groups: republicans and socialists. Whereas liberals advocated a constitutional monarchy (in the name of stability and keeping power in hands of men of property), republicans, as their name implies, pressed further, demanding a government by the people, an expanded franchise, and democratic participation in politics. Where liberals called for individualism and laissez-faire, socialists put the accent on equality. To put it in the terms that were used at the time, socialists raised the "social question." How could growing social inequality and the miseries of working people be remedied? The "social question," they insisted, was an urgent political matter. Socialists offered varied responses to this question and different ways of redistributing economic and social power. These solutions ranged from cooperation and new ways of organizing everyday life to collective ownership of the means of production; some were speculative, others intensely practical.

Socialism was a nineteenth-century system of thought and a response in large measure to the visible problems ushered in by industrialization: the intensification of labor, the poverty of working-class neighborhoods in

> To put it in the terms that were used at the time, socialists raised the "social question." How could growing social inequality and the miseries of working people be remedied?

industrial cities, and the widespread perception that a hierarchy based on rank and privilege had been abolished only to be replaced by one based on social class. For the socialists, the problems of industrial society were not incidental; they arose from the core principles of competition, individualism, and private property. The socialists did not oppose industry and economic development. On the contrary, what they took from the Enlightenment was a commitment to reason and human progress. They believed society could be both industrial and humane.

These radical thinkers were often explicitly utopian. Robert Owen, a wealthy industrialist turned reformer, bought a large cotton factory at New Lanark in Scotland and proceeded to organize the mill and the surrounding town according to the principles of cooperation rather than those of profitability. New Lanark organized good housing and sanitation, good working conditions, child care, free schooling, and a system of social security for the factory's workers. Owen advocated a general reorganization of society on the basis of cooperation and mutual respect and he tried to persuade other manufacturers of the rightness of his cause. The Frenchman Charles Fourier, too, tried to organize utopian communities based on the abolition of the wage system, the division of work according to people's natural inclinations, the complete equality of the sexes, and collectively organized child care and household labor. The charismatic socialist Flora Tristan (1803–1844) toured France speaking to workers about the principles of cooperation and the equality of men and women. Numerous men and women followed like-minded leaders into experimental communities. That so many took utopian visions seriously is a measure of people's unhappiness with early industrialization, and of their conviction that society could be organized along radically different lines.

Other socialists proposed simpler, practical reforms. Louis Blanc, a French politician and journalist, campaigned for universal male suffrage with an eye to giving working-class men control of the state. Instead of protecting private property and the manufacturing class, the transformed state would become "banker of the poor," extending credit to those who needed it, and establishing "associations of production," a series of workshops governed by laborers which would guarantee jobs and security for all. Such workshops were established, fleetingly, during the French revolution of

WHAT WERE THE NEW POLITICAL IDEOLOGIES OF THE NINETEENTH CENTURY?

TAKING SIDES: NEW IDEOLOGIES IN POLITICS   717

Quadrille Dancing at Lanark. Robert Owen's model community. Owen's Scottish experiment with cooperative production and community building, including schooling for infants, was only one of many utopian ventures in early nineteenth-century Europe and North America.

1848. So were clubs promoting women's rights. Pierre-Joseph Proudhon (1809–1865) also proposed establishing producers' cooperatives that would sell goods at a price workers could afford, working-class credit unions, and so on. Proudhon's "What is Property?"—to which the famous answer was "property is theft"—became one of the most widely read socialist pamphlets, familiar to artisans, laborers, and middle-class intellectuals, including Karl Marx. As we will see, a period of economic depression and widespread immiseration in the 1840s brought the socialists many more working-class followers.

KARL MARX'S SOCIALISM

The father of modern socialism, Karl Marx (1818–1883), was barely known in the early nineteenth century. His reputation rose later, after 1848, when a wave of revolutions and violent confrontation seemed to confirm his distinctive theory of history and make earlier socialists' emphasis on cooperation, setting up experimental communities, and peaceful reorganization of industrial society seem naive.

Marx grew up in Trier, in the western section of Germany, in a region and a family keenly interested in the political debates and movements of the revolutionary era. His family was Jewish, but his father had converted to Protestantism in order to be able to work as a lawyer. Marx studied law briefly at the University of Berlin before turning instead to philosophy and particularly the ideas of Georg Wilhelm Friedrich Hegel. With the so-called Young Hegelians, a group of rebellious students who chafed under the narrow thinking of a deeply conservative Prussian university system, Marx appropriated Hegel's concepts for his radical politics. His radicalism (and atheism, for he repudiated all his family's religious affiliations) made it impossible for him to get a post in the university. He became a journalist, writing now famous articles on, for instance, peasants "stealing" wood from forests that used to be common land. From 1842 to 1843 he edited the *Rhineland Gazette (Rheinische Zeitung)*. The paper's criticism of legal privilege and political repression put it on a collision course with the Prussian government, which closed it down and sent Marx into exile—first in Paris, then Brussels, and eventually London.

While in Paris Marx studied early socialist theory, economics, and the history of the French Revolution. He also began a lifelong intellectual and political partnership with Friedrich Engels (1820–1895). Engels was the son of a textile manufacturer from the German Rhineland and had been sent to learn business with a merchant firm in Manchester, one of the heartlands of England's industrial revolution (see Chapter 19). Rather than follow in his father's footsteps, however, Engels took up his pen to denounce the miserable working and living conditions in Manchester and what he saw as the systematic inequalities of capitalism (*The Condition of the Working Classes in England*, 1844). Marx and Engels joined a small international group of radical artisans called the League of the Just, in 1847 renamed the Communist League. The league asked Marx to draft a statement of its principles, published in 1848 as the *Communist Manifesto*.

The *Communist Manifesto* laid out Marx's theory of history in short form. World history had passed through three major stages, each characterized by conflict between social groups: master and slave in ancient slavery, lord and serf in feudalism, and bourgeois and proletariat in capitalism. According to Marx's theory, the stage of feudal or aristocratic property relations had ended in 1789, when the French Revolution overthrew the old order, ushering in bourgeois political power and industrial capitalism. In the *Communist Manifesto*, Marx and Engels admired the revolutionary accomplishments of capitalism, saying that the bourgeoisie had "created more impressive and more colossal productive forces than had all preceding generations together." But, they argued, the revolutionary character of capitalism would also undermine the bourgeois economic order. As capital became more concentrated in the hand of the few, a growing army of wage workers would become increasingly aware of its economic and political disenfranchisement; struggle between these classes was central to industrial capitalism itself. Eventually, the *Communist Manifesto* predicted, recurring economic crises, caused by capitalism's unending need for new markets and the cyclical instability of overproduction, would bring capitalism to collapse. Workers would seize the state, reorganize the means of production, abolish private property, and eventually create a communist society.

What was distinctive about Marx's version of socialism? It took up the disparity between public proclamations of progress and workers' daily experiences in a systematic, scholarly manner. Marx was an inexhaustible reader and thinker, with a extraordinarily broad range. He took insights where he found them: in British economics, French history, and German philosophy. He wove other's ideas that labor was the source of value and that property was expropriation into a new theory of history that was also a thoroughgoing critique of nineteenth-century liberalism.

From Hegel, Marx imported the view of history as a dynamic process, with an inner logic, moving toward human freedom. (This is a good example of the larger influence of conservative historical thinking.) In Hegel's view, the historical process did not unfold in any simple and predictable way. Instead history proceeded "dialectically" or through conflict. Hegel saw the conflict as one between ideas: a "thesis" produced an "anti-thesis" and the clash between the two created a distinctive and new "synthesis." Marx applied Hegel's notions to the specifics of history. He did not begin with ideas, as

Karl Marx (1818–1883). The young Marx created a theory of history and philosophy of Socialism that combined European thought and politics in the 1840s. The *Communist Manifesto* published on the eve of the revolutions of 1848, became much more influential in their aftermath.

WHAT WERE THE NEW POLITICAL IDEOLOGIES OF THE NINETEENTH CENTURY?

TAKING SIDES: NEW IDEOLOGIES IN POLITICS   719

Hegel had, but rather with the material (social and economic) forces that he believed drove history. Hence the term dialectical materialism, which is used to describe Marxist thought.

Marx synthesized international cross-currents of European thought and politics in the 1840s. His concerns with the relationship between economic and politics were characteristic of his time. Like other radicals, he addressed the gap between liberal demands for freedom and liberal silence on social equality. He was only one of many socialists, however, and before the revolutions of 1848 one of the least well known. Those revolutions erupted the same year the *Communist Manifesto* was published, but well before it had any effect. Only in the second half of the century would Marxism become the leading socialist doctrine.

CITIZENSHIP AND COMMUNITY: NATIONALISM

Of all the political ideologies of the early nineteenth century, nationalism is most difficult to grasp. Its premises are elusive. What, exactly, counted as a nation? Who demanded a nation, and what did their demand mean? In the early nineteenth century, nationalism was usually aligned with liberalism. As the century progressed, however, it became increasingly clear that nationalism could be molded to fit any doctrine.

The meaning of nation has changed over time. The term comes from the Latin verb *nasci*, "to be born," and suggests "common birth." In sixteenth-century England, the "nation" designated the aristocracy, or those who shared noble birthright. The French nobility also referred to itself as the "nation." Those earlier and unfamiliar usages are important. They highlight the most significant development of the late eighteenth and early nineteenth centuries: the French Revolution redefined "nation" to mean the people, or the sovereign people. The revolutionaries of 1789 boldly claimed that the nation, and no longer the king, was the sovereign power. "Vive la nation," or "long live the nation"—a phrase found everywhere, from government decrees to revolutionary festivals, engravings, and memorabilia—celebrated a new political community, not a territory or an ethnicity. Philosophically, the French revolutionaries and the others who developed their views took from Jean-Jacques

Rousseau the argument that a regenerated nation, based on the equality of its members (on the limits of that equality, see Chapter 18), was not only more just, but more powerful. On a more concrete level, the revolutionaries built a national state, army, and legal system whose jurisdiction trumped the older regional powers of the nobility, a national system of law, and a national army. In the aftermath of the French Revolution of 1789, the "nation" became what one historian calls "the collective image of modern citizenry."

In the early nineteenth century, then, "nation" symbolized legal equality, constitutional government, and unity, or an end to feudal privileges and divisions. Conservatives disliked the term. National unity and the creation of national political institutions threatened to erode the local power of aristocratic elites. New nations rested on constitutions, which, as we have seen, conservatives considered dangerous, rights-bearing abstractions. Nationalism became an important rallying cry for liberals across Europe in the early nineteenth century precisely because it was associated with political transformation. It celebrated the achievements and political "awakening" of the common people.

Nationalism also went hand in hand with liberal demands for economic modernity. Economists, such as the influential German economist Friedrich List (1789–1846), sought to develop national economies and national infrastructures: larger, stronger, better integrated, and more effective systems of banking, trade, transportation, production, and distribution. List linked ending the territorial fragmentation of the German states and the development of manufacturing to "culture, prosperity, and liberty."

> Nationalism became an important rallying cry for liberals across Europe in the early nineteenth century precisely because it was associated with political transformation. It celebrated the achievements and political "awakening" of the common people.

Nationalism, however, could easily undermine other liberal values. When liberals insisted on the value and importance of individual liberties, those committed to building nations replied that their vital task might require the sacrifice of some measure of each citizen's freedom. The Napoleonic army, a particularly powerful symbol of nationhood, appealed to conservative proponents of military strength and authority as well as to liberals who wanted an army of citizens.

Nineteenth-century nationalists wrote as if as if national feeling were natural, inscribed in the movement of history. They waxed poetic about the sudden awakening of feelings slumbering within the collective consciousness of a "German," an "Italian," a "French,"

EUROPEAN LANGUAGE GROUPS, c. 1850

Examine the distribution of language groups throughout Europe. What is the relationship between language and nationalism? How did states encourage the development of a national identity? Why would the divisions between language groups have created problems for the European empires?

or a "British" people. This is misleading. National identity (like religious, gender, or ethnic identities) developed and changed historically. It rested on specific nineteenth-century political and economic developments, or rising literacy, on the creation of national institutions such as schools or the military, and on the new importance of national rituals, from voting to holidays and village festivals. Nineteenth-century governments sought to develop national feeling, to link their peoples more closely to their states.

State-supported educational systems taught a "national" language, fighting the centrifugal forces of traditional dialects. Italian became the official language of the Italian nation, despite the fact that only 2.5 percent of the population spoke it. In other words, even a minority could define a "national" culture. Textbooks and self-consciously nationalist theater, poetry, and painting helped to elaborate and sometimes "invent" a national heritage.

Political leaders associated the nation with specific causes. But ordinary activities, such as reading a daily newspaper in the morning, helped people to imagine and identify with their fellow citizen. As one influential historian puts it, "[A]ll communities larger than primordial villages of face-to-face contact (and perhaps even these) are imagined." The nation is imagined as "limited," "sovereign", and "finally, it is imagined as a community, because regardless of the actual inequality and exploitation that may prevail in each, the nation is always conceived as a deep, horizontal comradeship." The different meanings of "nationhood," the various political beliefs it evoked, and the powerful emotions it tapped made nationalism exceptionally unpredictable.

These were the principal political ideologies of the early nineteenth century. They were rooted in the eighteenth-century but brought to the forefront by the political turmoil of early nineteenth century. Some were continuations of the French revolutionary trio: liberty (from arbitrary authority), equality (or the end of legal privilege), and fraternity (the creation of new communities of citizens). Others, like conservatism, were reactions against the French revolution. All could be reinterpreted. All became increasingly common points of reference as the century unfolded.

CULTURAL REVOLT: ROMANTICISM

What were the key themes of Romanticism?

Romanticism, the most significant cultural movement of the early nineteenth century, also took form in the polarized aftermath of Enlightenment and revolution. An exceptionally diverse intellectual movement, it touched all the arts and permeated politics as well. Put most simply, it marked a reaction against the Classicism of the eighteenth century and against many of the values of the Enlightenment. Eighteenth-century Classical art had aspired to reason, discipline, and harmony. Romanticism, in contrast, stressed emotion, freedom, and imagination. Romantic artists prized the individual, individuality, and subjective experience; many were personally rebellious and sought out intense experiences. In contrast to Enlightenment thinkers, they considered intuition, emotion, and feelings better guides to truth—and to human happiness—than reason and logic.

BRITISH ROMANTIC POETRY

Romanticism developed earliest in England and Germany, where it arose as part of a reaction against the Enlightenment and French classicism; it came later to France. Like any intellectual or artistic movement, Romanticism did not completely break with its predecessors. Indeed, the early Romantics developed themes first raised by dissenting figures of the Enlightenment, especially Jean-Jacques Rousseau (see Chapter 17). Rousseau's key themes—nature, simplicity, and feeling—ran through the very influential *Lyrical Ballads* (1798) of William Wordsworth (1770–1850) and Samuel Taylor Coleridge (1772–1834). Wordsworth considered emotions, or soul, the core of humanity; for him, poetry was "the spontaneous overflow of powerful feelings." Like Rousseau, Wordsworth also emphasized the ties of compassion and feeling that bind all of humankind, regardless of social class. "We have all of us one human heart," he wrote; "men who do not wear fine clothes can feel deeply." Like Rousseau, Wordsworth considered nature to be humanity's most trustworthy teacher, and he considered the experience of nature the source of true feeling. Poetic insights could be inspired by landscapes and the memories those evoked—in Wordsworth's case the wild hills and tumbledown cottages of England's Lake District. At the head of his poem "The Ruined Cottage," Wordsworth quoted from the Scottish romantic poet Robert Burns:

> Give me a spark of Nature's fire,
> 'Tis the best learning I desire…
> My muse, though homely in attire,
> May touch the heart.

The Lake Poets, as Wordsworth and Coleridge were sometimes called, offered one key theme of nineteenth-century Romanticism: a view of nature that rejected the abstract mechanism of eighteenth-century thought. Nature was not a system whose operations were to be observed with a critical eye. Instead, humanity was immersed in nature; the human soul needed to be opened to nature's sublime (literally, inspiring wonder and awe) power.

Like Wordsworth, the poet William Blake (1757–1827) championed the individual imagination and poetic vision, and saw both as transcending the narrow limits of the material world. Blake was a fierce and brilliant critic of industrial society and its daily corruptions, of the factories (which he called the "dark satanic mills") that blighted the English landscape, and of the values of a market culture in which everything was for sale. For Blake, imagination did not just lead to poetry. Imagination could awaken human sensibilities and sustain belief in different values, breaking humanity's "mind-forged manacles," or constraints of the contemporary world. In this, Blake's poetry paralleled early socialist efforts to imagine a better world. And like many Romantics, Blake looked back to a past in which he thought society had been more organic, united, and humane.

Lord Byron. One of the great English romantic poets, Byron's liberal politics also helped make him a romantic hero. He went to Greece to fight in the independence movement against the Ottoman Turks, but ended up dying there of tuberculosis.

English Romanticism reached its height with the next generation of English romantic poets—George Gordon, Lord Byron (1788–1824), Percy Bysshe Shelley (1792–1822), and John Keats (1795–1821). Some of these poets' lives and loves appealed as much as their writing, for their adventures seemed to personify their poetic themes. Lord Byron, for instance, took the Romantic emphasis on creativity, imagination, and spontaneity to new levels. Poetry, he wrote, was the "lava of the imagination, whose eruption prevents an earthquake." Byron was also an aristocrat, well known as rich, handsome, and defiant of nineteenth-century English conventions. His countless love affairs helped create the association between Romanticism and rebellion against conformity and inhibition. Those affairs were hardly carefree. Byron entered into an ill-starred marriage with an unhappy woman, whom he treated cruelly and drove away after a year. The powerful images in his poetry offer glimpses of his excruciating inner turmoil. Byron also rebelled against political convention; his Romanticism was inseparable from liberal politics. He assailed British political leaders as corrupt, narrow minded, and repressive, defended working-class movements in the name of liberty, and sailed off to fight in the Greek movement for independence from the Ottoman Turks. When he died in Greece (of tuberculosis, not in battle) he seemed to epitomize the liberal Romantic hero. Byron's close friend Percy Shelley continued to take Romantic poetry and politics to new heights. The subject of Shelley's *Prometheus Unbound* (1820) virtually defines romantic heroism and its cult of individual audacity. Prometheus, defying Zeus, had stolen fire for humanity and as punishment found himself chained to a rock while an eagle tore out his heart.

WOMEN WRITERS, GENDER, AND ROMANTICISM

Perhaps the best-known work of Romantic fiction, however, is Mary Godwin Shelley's *Frankenstein* (1818). Mary was the daughter of two radical literary "celebrities": the philosopher William Godwin and the feminist Mary Wollstonecraft (see Chapter 17), who died as her daughter was born. Mary Godwin met Shelley at sixteen, had three children by him before they married, and published *Frankenstein* when she was twenty. The novel captures especially well the Romantic critique of Enlightenment reason and early nineteenth-century ambivalence about science. Shelley herself was fasci-

Mary Shelley's *Frankenstein*. Perhaps the best-known work of Romantic fiction, *Frankenstein* joined the Romantic critique of Enlightenment reason with early nineteenth-century ambivalence about science to create a striking horror story. Mary Shelley (pictured at right at 19, around the time she published *Frankenstein*) was the daughter of the philosopher William Godwin and the feminist Mary Wollstonecraft, and married the poet Percy Shelley.

nated with scientific developments of her times—from electricity to mesmerism—and with their dangers as well as their promise. The story turns around a madly ambitious and eccentric Swiss scientist determined to find the secret of human life. Along the way he prowls through charnel houses where the dead were kept before burial, studying corpses, the parts of the body, and stages of decomposition. Shelley said she was often asked how a young girl "came to think of, and to dilate upon, so very hideous an idea." Dr. Frankenstein finally does produce life, in the form of a freakish monster. Though the monster is artificially made, he has human feelings, and when he finds himself spurned by his horrified creator, he becomes consumed by loneliness, longing, and murderous self-hatred, wreaking havoc on all. Shelley cast the novel in characteristically Romantic fashion, as a twisted creation myth, a story of individual genius gone wrong, and a study of agonizingly powerful feeling. For all these reasons, the novel became a point of reference in Western culture. Dr. Frankenstein,

forced to acknowledge that he "had been the author of unalterable evils," became one of its most memorable characterizations of the limits of reason and the impossibility of controlling nature.

First, then, Romanticism stressed the limits of reason and the power of emotion. Second, it insisted on the uniqueness and subjectivity of individual experience. The mind was not a "blank tablet" on which one's senses imprinted knowledge, which was John Locke's image, and central to most Enlightenment philosophy. Instead Romantics regarded the mind as a source of imagination and creativity. The Romantics' belief in individuality and creativity led in several directions. It became a cult of artistic genius—of the "inexplicably and uniquely creative individual" who was able to see things that others could not. It led artists—and ordinary people—to seek out experiences that would elicit intense emotions and spark leaps of imagination and creativity, experiences that could range from traveling to "exotic" lands to using opium. The Romantic style encouraged the daring to defy conventionality, as did Lord Byron, the Shelleys, or the French women writers Germaine de Staël and George Sand (Amandine Aurore Lucile Dupin, 1804–1876). George Sand, like Lord Byron, cultivated a persona. In her case this meant earning a living as a woman writer, taking lovers as she liked, and wearing men's clothing—all in rebellion against middle-class moral codes.

Women played an important role in Romantic letters, and Romanticism stimulated new thinking about gender and artistic creativity. In the eighteenth and nineteenth centuries it was common to assert that men were rational and women emotional, or intuitive. Romanticism, though, valued the emotional and intuitive as creative. Madame de Staël (1766–1817), who emigrated from France to Germany during the revolutionary period, played a key part in popularizing German romanticism in France in her *De l'Allemagne* ("Germany," 1810) and wrote many books of history. The language of Romanticism helped Madame de Staël describe

herself as a "genius." Claiming the role of artist-genius became a way for some women to subvert social norms. Romanticism also suggested that men could be emotional, and that men and women shared a common human nature. Last, and perhaps most important to literate middle-class people, by emphasizing the search for individuality, and valuing emotion and the soul as well as sensuality, the romantics forged new ways of writing—and indeed thinking—about love. Some historians have called Romanticism a "cultural style," and as such it reached well beyond small circles of artists, into the everyday writing and thoughts of men and women.

ROMANTIC PAINTING

Painters of the early nineteenth century carried the Romantic interest in subjectivity and imagination onto their canvases. In Great Britain, romantic painting was best represented by John Constable (1776–1837) and

Stormy Sea on a Shore, by J.M.W. Turner. By using energetic brush strokes and other techniques that made his paintings border on the abstract, Turner pushed Romantic painting toward experiments with imagination and subjectivity.

J. M. W. Turner (1775–1851). Both British painters tried to develop more emotional and poetic approaches to nature. "It is the soul that sees," wrote Constable, echoing Wordsworth. Constable pored over Isaac Newton's prisms, studying the properties of light, but with an eye to capturing the "poetry" of a rainbow. His landscapes emphasized the artist's individual technique and way of seeing. Turner's intensely subjective, personal, and imaginative paintings were even more unconventional. Turner experimented with brush strokes and color to produce some of the most remarkable paintings of his time. Critics assailed the paintings, saying they were too abstract, incomprehensible. "I did not paint it to be understood," Turner retorted on one occasion. Turner's concerns were those of his contemporaries: imagination, the creativity of the artist, and

the force of nature. Yet his technique took Romantic painting to a new level.

In France the leading Romantic painters were Théodore Géricault (1791–1824) and Eugène Delacroix (1799–1863). Delacroix's paintings look very different from Turner's. But Delacroix's ideas about subjectivity and the creative process, which he set out in detailed diaries, shared much with Turner's. The poet Charles Baudelaire, who represents the last stages of French Romanticism, credited Delacroix with showing him new ways to see: "The whole visible universe is but a storehouse of images and signs. . . . All the faculties of the human soul must be subordinated to the imagination." Romanticism opened new ways visualizing the world and pointed the way toward experiments, later in the century, that launched modernism.

Weymouth Bay, by John Constable. "It is the soul that sees," wrote Constable. Like other romantic artists, Constable explored new forms of feeling and perception.

ROMANTIC POLITICS: LIBERTY, HISTORY, AND NATION

Romanticism had many dimensions, and Romantic artists championed contradictory causes. "Romanticism, so often ill-defined, is only . . . liberalism in literature. Liberty in Art, liberty in Society, behold the double banner that rallies the intelligence." So wrote Victor Hugo (1802–1885) whose poetry, plays, and immensely influential historical novels focused sympathetically on the experience of the common people. *Nôtre Dame de Paris* (1831) and *Les Misérables* (1862) are the most famous. Delacroix's *Liberty Leading the People* represented revolutionary Romanticism (see page 731). So did the poetry of Shelley and Byron.

Yet Romantics could be ardently conservative. The French conservative François Chateaubriand's *Genius of Christianity* (1802) argued that the religious experiences of the national past were woven into the present, and could not be unraveled without destroying the fabric of culture. In characteristically Romantic terms, Chateaubriand put the accent on religious emotion, feeling, and subjectivity. Artistic and literary interest in religion had much wider resonance, and the period witnessed a broad and popular religious revival. It also renewed interest in medieval literature, art, and architecture. Romanticism cut across political lines, providing imagery for both conservatives and liberals.

Early nineteeth-century nationalism was suffused with Romantic imagery. The Romantic emphasis on individuality was easily transmuted into an insistence on the uniqueness of cultures. Among the most influential nationalist thinkers was the German Johann von Herder, a Protestant pastor and theologian and author of *Ideas for a Philosophy of Human History*. For Herder, civilization did not arise from a learned, cultivated, and international elite—here, as elsewhere, Romantic thinkers took their distance from the Enlightenment *philosophes*. Instead, Herder argued, civilization sprang from the culture of the common people, in German the *Volk*. Each culture had to express its own unique historical character, or *Volksgeist*, the spirit (genius) of the people. Whereas some Romantics prized individual genius, Herder extolled the particular genius of a people and insisted that each nation must be true to its own particular heritage, in Germany's case its culture and language.

The Romantics' keen interest in historical development and destiny also sealed their place in the nationalist tradition. The brothers Grimm, editors of the famous collection of fairy tales (1812–1815), traveled across Germany to study native dialects and collected folktales that were published as part of a national heritage. The poet Friedrich Schiller retold the drama of the Swiss hero William Tell (1804) to make it a rallying cry for German national consciousness, though ironically, the Italian composer Gioacchino Rossini turned Schiller's poem into an opera that promoted Italian nationalism. In Britain, Sir Walter Scott retold in many of his novels the popular history of Scotland; Wordsworth's *Lyrical Ballads* sought to evoke the simplicity and virtue of the English people. The Pole Adam Mickiewicz wrote the national epic *Pan Tadeusz* ("Lord Thaddeus") as a vision of a recently lost way of life.

ORIENTALISM

The same cultural currents—a passion for grand theories of cultures, their distinctive characteristics, and their historical development—also created a wave of interest in the "Orient." Napoleon had invaded Egypt in 1798, seeking military advantage against the British, but also and perhaps more important in the long run, knowledge, cultural splendor, and imperial glory. "This Europe of ours is a molehill," Napoleon wrote in his characteristic style. "Only in the East, where 600 million human beings live, is it possible to found great empires and realize great revolutions." The dozens of scholars who accompanied Napoleon's Army of the Orient established the Egyptian Institute, charged with systematically collecting facts about Egyptian natural history, culture, and industry. Other discoveries during the same period opened a new world of knowledge. Among the many artifacts the French took from Egypt was the soon to be famous Rosetta Stone, a block with what scholars discovered to be versions of the same text in three different languages and scripts: hieroglyphic writing (pictorial script), demotic (a version of early alphabetic script), and Greek, which, since it was familiar, enabled scholars to begin deciphering the first two. Egyptian obelisks, with their now readable hieroglyphic inscriptions, yielded more clues about ancient Egypt. The twenty-three-volume, lavishly illustrated *Description of Egypt*, published in French between 1809 and 1828, became an intellectual

> The twenty-three-volume, lavishly illustrated *Description of Egypt*, published in French between 1809 and 1828, became an intellectual event in Europe, heightening the soaring interest in Eastern languages and history. "We are now all orientalists," wrote Victor Hugo in 1829.

Women of Algiers, by Eugène Delacroix. This is one of many paintings done during Delacroix's trips through North Africa and a good example of the Romantics' "Orientalism."

eager to explore new regions but also quick to classify the East as the land of bold color, sensuality, mystery, and irrationality. Delacroix's and, later, Renoir's paintings of women in Algeria are good examples of this viewpoint. The religious revival of the period had similar effects; scholars and artists looking for the roots of Christianity hoped to find them in what they thought of as the "unchanged habits of the East." Fascination with medieval history and religion also fired up images of medieval crusades—important subjects for such Romantics as Scott and Chateaubriand. The "Oriental renaissance" supplied a rich imagery for nineteenth-century Western painting, literature, and scholarship. It also helped create what would become well-established habits of mind. Europeans built up oversimplified images of the differences between "the West" and "the Orient."

GOETHE AND BEETHOVEN

Many artists of the turn of the century are hard to classify. Johann Wolfgang von Goethe (1749–1832) had an enormous influence on the Romantic movement and on German writers trying to cast off the French style and develop their own language and voice. His early novel *The Sorrows of Young Werther* (1774), a story of a young man's yearnings and restless love, captivated readers all over Europe. Yet Goethe backed away from what he came to consider the excessiveness of Romanticism: its cult of feeling over restraint and order, which Goethe considered self-indulgent and "morbid." In 1790 Goethe published the first part of his masterpiece, *Faust,* a drama in verse, which he finished one year before he died in 1832. The play retold the German legend of the man who sold his soul to the devil in return for eternal youth and universal knowledge. It was more classical in its tone than other works of the Romantic era, though it still reflected a Romantic concern with spiritual freedom and humanity's daring.

The composer Ludwig van Beethoven (1770–1827) considered himself a Classicist and was steeped in the principles of the eighteenth century. The glorification of nature and Romantic individuality ring clearly through his work, and his insistence that instrumental music (without vocal accompaniment) could become more poetic and expressive of emotion made him the key figure for later Romantic composers. "Music is a

event in Europe, heightening the soaring interest in Eastern languages and history. "We are now all orientalists," wrote Victor Hugo in 1829. Great-power rivalries in Egypt, the British incursions into India, the Greek civil war, the French invasion of Algeria in 1830: all these developments raised Europeans' interests in the region and were the political accompaniment to the "Oriental renaissance."

Nineteenth-century Europeans cast the "Orient" in a specific political and cultural role. In the words of one scholar, "[T]he Orient has helped to define Europe (or the West) as its contrasting image, idea, personality, experience." We saw above that during the 1820s Greek rebellion against the Ottoman Turks, Europeans sought to identify themselves with a Greek heritage and against what they insisted was "Oriental" or "Islamic" cruelty and despotism. Rebelling against the rules of eighteenth-century Classicism, social conventions, and Enlightenment rationalism, European artists and intellectuals were not only fascinated with ethnography and

The writer Johann Wolfgang von Goethe (1749–1832) and the composer Ludwig van Beethoven (1770–1827), both important figures in the transition from eighteenth to nineteenth-century art.

more sublime revelation than all wisdom and all philosophy," he wrote, "[and] it is the wine that inspires and leads to fresh creations." His musical achievements did indeed raise the standing of music as an art form and placed it at the center of the Romantic movement. Beethoven's life and politics also became part of his legacy. Like many of his contemporaries he was caught up in a burst of enthusiasm for the French Revolution of 1789. Disillusionment set in when Napoleon, whom he had admired as a revolutionary and for whom he had originally named the *Eroica* Symphony, crowned himself emperor and repudiated his principles, and Beethoven's disappointment continued through the Napoleonic wars. At the same time, by the age of thirty-two, Beethoven knew that he was losing his hearing. He hoped the problem could be cured, but it slowly put an end to his career as a virtuoso pianist, and by 1819 he was completely deaf. As his condition worsened and his disenchantment deepened, he withdrew into composing, his solitude a powerful symbol of alienation and extraordinary creativity.

Beethoven and Goethe were transitional figures between the eighteenth and nineteenth centuries. They also illustrate the elusiveness of a simple definition of Romanticism. The Romantic movement was composed of many different currents that sometimes cut across each other: a critique of eighteenth-century Classicism, a quasi-mystical view of nature, a return to history, a cult of individual heroism, defiance, and creativity, and a search for a new way of seeing. At Romanticism's core lay an insistence that the arts needed to find a new way of expressing emotion and feeling, a search that sent nineteenth-century art in a new direction.

REFORM AND REVOLUTION

How did the events of 1830 bring the Restoration to an end?

In the 1820s, the conservative restoration faced scattered opposition. The most decisive blow against it came in 1830 in France. There, the Congress of Vienna had returned a Bourbon monarch to the throne. Louis XVIII was the oldest of the former king's surviving brothers. Louis claimed absolute power, but in the name of reconciliation he granted a "charter," and conceded some important rights: legal equality, careers open to talent, and a two-chamber parliamentary government. Voting rights excluded most citizens from government. This narrowly based rule, combined with the sting of military defeat, nostalgia for a glorious Napoleonic past and, for some, memories of the revolution, undermined the Restoration in France.

THE 1830 REVOLUTION IN FRANCE

In 1824, Louis was succeeded by his far less conciliatory brother Charles X (1824–1830), who was determined to reverse the legacies of the revolutionary and Napoleonic eras. At Charles' direction the French assembly voted to compensate members of the nobility whose land had been confiscated and sold during the revolution. Doing so appeased the ultra-royalists, as the extreme right wing was called, but it antagonized property holders who had benefited from the revolution. Charles's regime also restored the Catholic Church to its traditional place in French classrooms. These policies provoked widespread discontent, several votes of no confidence in the monarch, and a series of elections that brought liberal opponents of the regime to the French Chamber of Deputies. The rising tide of liberal public opinion was also swollen by economic hard times. In Paris and the provinces, worried police reports flagged the extent of unemployment, hunger, and anger. Confronted with alarming evidence of the regime's unpopularity, Charles and his ministers called new elections, and when those went against them, the king tried, essentially, to overthrow the parliamentary regime. The so-called July Ordinances of 1830 (1) dissolved the newly elected chamber before it had even met; (2) imposed strict censorship on the press; (3) further restricted suffrage so as to exclude almost completely anyone outside the nobility; and (4) called for new elections.

In return for these measures, Charles got revolution. Parisians—especially workers, artisans, students, and writers—took to the streets. Three days of intense street battles followed in which the revolutionaries, fighting behind hastily constructed barricades, defied the army and the police, neither of which was willing to fire into the crowds. Aware that his support had evaporated, Charles abdicated. Many of the revolutionaries on the barricades wanted a republic. But other leaders of the movement wanted to avoid the domestic and international turmoil of the revolution of 1789. They ushered in the duke of Orléans as King Louis Philippe (1830–1848), promoting him as a constitutional monarch accountable to the people: king of the French, not king of France. The new regime, called the July Monarchy, doubled the number of eligible voters. Yet voting was still a privilege, not a right, and was still based on steep requirements of property ownership. The major beneficiaries of the revolution were the propertied classes. Still, the revolution of 1830 brought the common people back into politics, reviving the memories of the revolution of 1789, and it spurred movements elsewhere.

For opponents of the restoration across Europe, 1830 assumed enormous importance. It suggested that history was moving in a new direction and that the political landscape had changed, opening up new possibilities.

BELGIUM AND POLAND IN 1830

In 1815, the Congress of Vienna had agreed to join Belgium (then called the Austrian Netherlands) to Holland, forming one large state as a buffer against France. The union had never been popular in Belgium, and news of the July revolution in France catalyzed Belgian opposition. The city of Brussels rebelled; the Dutch king sent in troops; faced with barricades and intense street fighting, the troops withdrew. The great powers, preoccupied with other matters and unwilling to allow one of the group intervene, agreed to guarantee Belgian neutrality—a provision that remained in force in 1914.

Revolt also spread to Poland, where it faced the far more formidable forces of the Russian empire. Poland was not an independent state; by the provisions of the Congress of Vienna it was under Russian governance. It did, however, have its own parliament (or *diet*), a relatively broad electorate, a constitution, and guarantees of basic liberties of speech and the press—guarantees that were increasingly ignored by the Russian-imposed head of state, the tsar's brother Constantine. In Poland as in Belgium, news of the French revolution of 1830 tipped the country into revolt. The revolutionaries— an initially well-organized coalition of Polish aristocrats defending their autonomy and students, military officers, and middle-class people demanding political reforms—drove Constantine out. Within less than a year, however, Russian forces retook Warsaw. The fiercely conservative tsar Nicholas crushed the Polish revolt with the same heavy hand that he had just used on the Decembrists at home and put Poland under military rule.

REFORM IN GREAT BRITAIN

Why was there no revolution in England? One answer is that there almost was. After an era of political conservatism that paralleled that on the Continent, British politics took a different direction, and Britain became one of the most liberal nations in Europe.

POPULAR UNREST IN PARIS, 1828

Throughout Europe the police regularly reported on the mood of the common people. This police report, filed in Paris in 1828, captured the rising anger of citizens in the capital. Poor grain harvests in the years before had helped to drive up prices. In the working-class districts of Paris, the economic crisis fueled criticism of the regime. The document also reflects the anxieties of the police, who were not persuaded they could enforce order.

A handwritten placard has been put up at the corner of the rue Saint-Nicolas in the quartier des Quinze-Vingts: "Long live Napoleon! War to the death against Charles X and the priests who are starving us to death!" Several workers cheered, saying that "they would make an end of it, if die they must, since there was no work for them. . . ." Similar leaflets have been distributed in the rue de Charenton and the rue de Charonne in the faubourg Saint-Marceau and the faubourg Saint-Martin. . . . People are saying in the wine shops and workshops that the people must assemble and march on the Tuileries to demand work and bread and that they do not fear the soldiery, since many of them have been won over. This exasperation on the part of the workers has been noted ever since the recent rise in prices, and professional agitators (there are plenty of them in the faubourgs) are trying to exploit it to incite the workers to indulge in excesses. Circumstances are favorable. A great many workers have been suffering for a long time and the price of bread is driving them to utter despair. . . . I have begged the Prefect of Police to get some digging and similar work started from which they can earn at least a pittance.

From Louis Chevalier, *Laboring Classes and Dangerous Classes in Paris during the First Half of the Nineteenth Century* (Princeton: Princeton University Press, 1973), p. 266.

The end of the Napoleonic wars brought with it a major agricultural depression in Britain, and the combination of low wages, unemployment, and bad harvests provoked regular social unrest. In the new industrial towns of the north, where economic conditions were especially bad, radical members of the middle class joined with workers to demand increased representation in Parliament. In 1819 a crowd of sixty thousand gathered to demonstrate for political reform in St. Peter's Field in Manchester. The militia and some soldiers on horseback charged the crowd, killing eleven and injuring four hundred, including 113 women. British radicals condemned what they called "Peterloo," a domestic Waterloo where the nation's army had turned against its own citizens. Parliament quickly passed the Six Acts (1819), which outlawed "seditious and blasphemous" literature, increased the stamp tax on newspapers, allowed the searching of houses for arms, and restricted the rights of public meeting.

Prodded by pressure from below, British political leaders reversed their opposition to reform. Ironically, reforms began under the conservative Tory party. British foreign policy became less conservative, and Catholics and dissenting Protestants (non-Anglicans, such as Baptists, Congregationalists, and Methodists) were allowed to participate in public political life. Tories, however, refused to reform political representation in the House of Commons. For centuries Parliament had represented the interests of the major propertied class. About two thirds of the members of the House of Commons were either directly nominated by or indirectly owed their election to the patronage of the richest titled landowners in the country. Many of the parliamentary electoral districts, or boroughs, which returned members to the House of Commons, were controlled by landowners who used their power to return candidates sympathetic to their interests. These were the "rotten" or "pocket" boroughs, so called because they were said to be in the pockets of those men who controlled them. Defenders of the system argued that Parliament looked after the interests of the

nation at large, which they perceived to coincide with the interests of landed property.

Liberals in the opposing Whig party, the new industrial middle class, and radical artisans argued passionately for reform. Liberals in particular were not proponents of democracy; they wanted to enfranchise only "responsible" citizens. Yet they made common cause with well-organized middle- and working-class radicals to intensify the push for reform. A Birmingham banker named Thomas Attwood, for instance, organized a Political Union of the Lower and Middle Classes of the People. By July 1830, similar organizations had arisen in several provincial cities, some willing to

Among the best-known images of the revolutions of 1830 is "Liberty Leading the People" by Eugene Delacroix, the same artist who had mourned the extinction of liberty in his painting of the "Massacre of Chios" in Greece (see page 712). The allegorical female figure of liberty leads representatives of the united people: a middle-class man (identified by his top hat), a worker, and a boy of the streets wielding a pistol. Neither middle class people nor children fought on the barricades, and the image of revolutionary unity was romanticized. But optimistic images of what the French called the "Three Glorious Days" of July 1830 were widespread.

engage in bloody clashes with army units and police. Middle-class shopkeepers announced they would withhold taxes and, if necessary, form a national guard. Also plagued by an outbreak of cholera, the country appeared to be on the verge of serious general disorder, if not outright revolution. Lord Grey, head of the Whig party, seized the opportunity to press through reform.

The Reform Bill of 1832 eliminated the "rotten boroughs" from Parliament. It reallocated 143 parliamentary seats, most of them from the rural south, to the industrial north. It expanded the franchise, but with property qualifications only one in six men could vote. Produced by nearly revolutionary conditions, the bill ended as a relatively modest measure. It reduced but did not destroy the political strength of landed aristocratic interests. It admitted British liberals, including some of the industrial middle classes, into a junior partnership with the landed elite that had ruled Britain for centuries and was to rule it for at least one more generation.

What changes did the new regime bring? The most striking example of middle class power came with the repeal of the Corn Laws in 1846. The Corn Laws (the British term for wheat is corn) protected British landlords and grain farmers from foreign competition. Although those laws had been modified in the 1820s, they continued to keep the price of bread artificially high. More important, the industrial middle classes increasingly viewed them as special protections for the aristocracy. The campaign to accomplish repeal was superbly orchestrated and relentless, combining the support of those who believed, in principle, in reform and free trade and those who had a direct economic stake in a new system. The Anti–Corn Law League, which drew surprisingly broad support, held large meetings throughout the north of England and lobbied members of Parliament. In the end the league achieved a crucial victory, persuading Prime Minister Sir Robert Peel that repealing the Corn Laws was both inevitable and necessary for Britain's economic health and global power. The free trade policy inaugurated in 1846 endured until the 1920s.

BRITISH RADICALISM AND THE CHARTIST MOVEMENT

Disappointment with the narrow gains of the 1832 reform focused attention on farther-reaching political change, in the form of what was called the "People's Charter." This document, circulated across the country by committees of Chartists, as they were known, and

CHRONOLOGY

REFORM IN GREAT BRITAIN, 1832–1867

Electoral Reform Bill	1832
Slavery abolished in British West Indies	1838
Chartist Movement	1840s
Corn Laws repealed	1846
Great Reform Bill	1867
Woman Suffrage movement grows	1860s

signed by millions, contained six demands: universal white male suffrage, institution of the secret ballot, abolition of property qualifications for membership in the House of Commons, annual parliamentary elections, payment of salaries to members of the House of Commons, and equal electoral districts.

As economic conditions deteriorated in the 1840s, Chartism spread. The movement also tapped into local traditions of worker self-help and organization. Chartists disagreed about tactics and goals. Should immigrant Irish Catholics in England be included in the movement, or excluded as dangerous competitors for scarce jobs? Should the franchise be extended only to workingmen, representing their families as respectable, "interested" members of society, or to women as well? Three examples will illustrate the range of Chartist positions. The Chartist William Lovett, a cabinetmaker, was as fervent a believer in self-improvement as any member of the middle class. He advocated a union of educated workers to acquire their fair share of the nation's increasing industrial bounty. The Chartist Feargus O'Connor, a member of a minor Anglo-Irish landholding family but a political radical, appealed to the more impoverished and desperate class of workers. He attacked industrialization and the resettlement of the poor on agricultural allotments. Another Chartist, Bronterre O'Brien, openly admired Robespierre and shocked crowds by attacking "the big-bellied, little-brained, numbskull aristocracy." Chartism comprised many smaller movements with different emphases, but its goal was political democracy as a means to social justice.

Democracy was a very radical demand in the 1840s. Not surprisingly, Chartists faced fierce opposition. They persisted. Committees presented massive petitions for the Charter to Parliament in 1839 and 1842; on both occasions they were summarily rejected. In the north of England, political demands took shape

WOMEN IN THE ANTI–CORN LAW LEAGUE, 1842

The campaign to repeal the Corn Laws enlisted many middle-class women in its ranks. For many such women, the anti–Corn Law campaign led to other causes, such as woman suffrage. The following article, hostile to the reform campaign, deplores women's participation in the endeavor. The author raises characteristically Victorian objections to women's participation in politics. The article also offers a glimpse of the reformers' arguments and tactics.

We find that the council of the Manchester Anti-Corn-Law Association had invited the inhabitants to 'an *anti-Corn-law tea-party*, to be held on the 20th of May, 1841—gentlemen's tickets, 2s.; ladies 1s. 6d.' . . . [L]adies were advertised as *stewardesses* of this assembly. So now the names of about 300 Ladies were pompously advertised as the *Patroness* and *Committee* of the *National Bazaar.* We exceedingly wonder and regret that the members of the Association . . . and still more that anybody else, should have chosen to exhibit their wives and daughters in the character of political agitators; and we most regret that so many ladies—modest, excellent, and amiable persons we have no doubt in their domestic circles—should have been persuaded to allow their names to be *placarded* on such occasions—for be it remembered, this Bazaar and these *Tea-parties* did not even pretend to be for any *charitable* object, but entirely for the purposes of *political agitation.* . . .

We have before us a letter from Mrs. Secretary Woolley to one body of workmen. . . . She 'appeals to them to stand forth and denounce as *unholy*, unjust, and cruel all restrictions on the food of the people'. She acquaints them that 'the ladies are resolved to perform *their* arduous part in the attempt to *destroy a monopoly* which, for *selfishness* and its *deadly* effects, has no parallel in the history of the world'. 'We therefore', she adds, 'ask you for contributions. . . .' Now surely . . . not only should the *poorer classes* have been exempt from such unreasonable solicitations, but whatever subscriptions might be obtainable from the wealthier orders should have been applied, not to *political agitation* throughout England, but to charitable relief at home.

J. Croker, "Anti–Corn Law Legislation," *Quarterly Review*, December, 1842, as cited in Patricia Hollis, ed. *Women in Public: The Women's Movement 1850–1900* (London: G. Allen & Unwin, 1979), p. 287.

against a backdrop of strikes, trade-union demonstrations, and attacks on factories and manufacturers who imposed low wages and long hours, or who harassed unionists. The combination of political and social radicalism did not sway the government; conservatives saw anarchy, and liberals repudiated any interest in revolution. The movement peaked in April of 1848. Partly inspired by revolution in continental Europe, Chartist leaders planned a major demonstration and show of force in London. A procession of twenty-five thousand workers assembled, and carried to Parliament a petition containing 6 million signatures demanding the six points. Confronted once again with the specter of open class conflict, special constables and contingents of the regular army were marshaled under the now aged duke of Wellington, hero of the battle of Waterloo, to resist

The Great Chartist Rally of April 10, 1848. 1848 brought revolution to continental Europe and militant protest to England. This photo shows the April rally in support of the Chartists' six points, which included expanding the franchise, abolishing property qualifications for representatives, and instituting a secret ballot.

this threat to order. In the end, only a small delegation of leaders presented the petition to Parliament. Rain, poor management, and unwillingness on the part of many to do battle with the well-armed constabulary put an end to the Chartists' campaign. A relieved liberal observer, Harriet Martineau, observed, "From that day it was a settled matter that England was safe from revolution."

THE HUNGRY FORTIES

The economic and political conditions that sowed unrest in England produced revolution on the Continent. Poor harvests began in the early 1840s. In 1845–1846, the crisis became acute. For two years in a row, the grain harvest failed completely. The potato blight struck, bringing starvation to Ireland (see page 732) and hunger to Germany, another potato-growing region. By 1846–1847, food prices had, on average, doubled. Bread riots broke out across Europe. City and village dwellers attacked carts carrying grain, either refusing to let merchants take it to other markets or simply taking the grain and selling it at what they considered a fair price. Compounding the problem was

a cyclical industrial slowdown across Europe, which threw thousands of workers into unemployment. Starving peasants and unemployed laborers swamped public-relief organizations. The years 1846 and 1847 were "probably the worst of the entire century in terms of want and human suffering," and the decade has earned the name of "the Hungry Forties."

Hunger itself does not cause revolution. It does, however, test governments' abilities and their legitimacy. When the inadequate public relief systems in France foundered, when troops moved to repress potato riots in Berlin, or when regimes armed middle-class citizens to protect themselves against the poor, governments looked both authoritarian and inept. Under those circumstances, states lost the confidence of their supporters, starting a wave of revolution that swept across Europe, breaking first in France.

THE FRENCH REVOLUTION OF 1848

The French monarchy installed after the July revolution of 1830 seemed to differ little from its predecessor. The new king, Louis Philippe, gathered around him representatives of the banking and industrial elite.

The regime often gave the impression of complacency. When confronted with demands to enfranchise more of the middle class, the prime minister quipped that everyone was free to rise into the ranks of the wealthy. "Enrich yourselves," he counseled. Construction projects and the expansion of the railway system presented ample opportunities for graft. The regime disappointed the high hopes that it had inspired. Republican societies proliferated, especially in such cities as Paris and Lyons, where worker and artisans associations had long political traditions. In 1834, the government declared radical political organizations illegal. Rebellions broke out in Lyons and Paris, bringing two days of repression, death, and arrests. The government's authoritarian image and refusal to expand the franchise drove even moderates into opposition. By 1847, the opposition had organized a campaign for electoral reform throughout France. Since political meetings were outlawed, the opposition organized political "banquets," where opponents of the regime drank toasts to reform—though not to outright revolution. Defying the king's threats, the opposition called a final, giant banquet for February 22, 1848. When the government banned the meeting, revolution broke out. In a surprisingly short time, Louis Philippe abdicated the throne.

> Defying the king's threats, the opposition called a final, giant banquet for February 22, 1848. When the government banned the meeting, revolution broke out.

The provisional government of the new republic was a remarkable group, consisting of a combination of liberals, republicans and, for the first time, socialists. It set about making a new constitution, with elections based on universal male suffrage. Yet tensions between middle-class republicans and socialists, which had momentarily dissolved in opposition to Louis Philippe, now reemerged. Among working men and women, the most widely supported demand was the "right to work," which meant the ability to earn a living wage, to be able to support oneself. The provisional government cautiously supported this demand, creating what were called National Workshops, a program of public works in and around Paris. Initial plans called for the employment of no more than ten or twelve thousand persons. But with unemployment running as high as 65 percent in the construction trades and 51 percent in textiles and clothing, workers streamed in, as many as sixty-six thousand by April, and one hundred twenty thousand by June 1848.

Popular politics flourished. The provisional government lifted restrictions on freedom of speech and political activity. One hundred seventy new journals and more than two hundred clubs formed within weeks. Delegations claiming to represent the oppressed of all European countries—Chartists, Hungarians, Poles—moved freely about the city, attracting attention, if not devoted followings. Women's clubs and newspapers appeared, with names like *The Voice of Women* or *The Opinion of Women* and demands ranging from real, universal suffrage to living wages. This revival of popular politics, though, convinced rising numbers of middle-class onlookers that stern measures were needed. Elections reinforced the concern for order. Universal male suffrage by no means guaranteed radical victory, and rural voters, worried about revolutionary Paris, elected moderate republicans and monarchists.

By late spring 1848, a majority of the French assembly believed that the workshop system had become a financial drain and, worse, a serious threat to social order. At the end of May, the government closed the workshops to new enrollment, excluded anyone who had resided

The Revolution of 1848 in France. A contemporary engraving celebrating the triumph of the people. Note the themes borrowed from Delacroix's painting of 1830 (see p. 731).

The Barricade, by Ernest Meissonier (1815–1891).
A very different view of 1848, one that foreshadows the
defeat of revolutionary hopes.

in Paris for less than six months, and sent all members between the ages of eighteen and twenty-five to the army. On June 21, the government simply ended the program, repudiating any responsibility for the social question. The reaction brought some of the bloodiest conflict of the period. Laborers, journeymen, the unemployed, traditional manual laborers, socialists, and some republican leaders once more built barricades across Paris. For four days, June 23–26, they defended themselves in an ultimately hopeless military battle against armed forces recruited, in part, from willing provincials eager enough to assist in the repression of the urban working class. The repression itself was ferocious, shocking many observers. About three thousand were killed and twelve thousand more arrested, the majority of whom were deported to Algerian labor camps.

In the aftermath of the "June Days," the French government moved quickly to bring order to the country.

Assembly members hoped a strong leader bring dissidents to heel. Four candidates ran for president of the republic: Alphonse de Lamartine, the moderate republican; General Louis Eugène Cavaignac, who had commanded the troops in June; Alexandre August Ledru-Rollin, a socialist; and Louis Napoleon Bonaparte, nephew of the former emperor, who polled more than twice as many votes as the other three candidates combined.

"All facts and personages of great importance in world history occur twice . . . the first time as tragedy, the second as farce." This was how Karl Marx (no admirer of Napoleon I) summarized the relationship of Louis Napoleon to his uncle. The upstart, rumored by other detractors to be illegitimate, had spent most of his life in exile. His name gave him a wide and suitably vague appeal. Conservatives believed he would protect property and order. Some people on the left had heard of his book *The Extinction of Pauperism* or of his correspondence with important socialists. "Napoleon" evoked glory and greatness. Whatever his origins, as one historian puts it, "he was very precisely the son of the Napoleonic myth." His role as an "an all purpose personage" helped secure his electoral victory. As one old peasant expressed it, "How could I help voting for this gentleman—I whose nose was frozen at Moscow?"

Not surprisingly, Louis Napoleon used his position to consolidate his power. He enlisted the support of the Catholics by restoring the Church's role in education and by sending an expedition to Rome in 1849 to rescue the pope from revolutionaries. (The Italian revolutions are discussed in the next chapter.) The regime hastened to demobilize radicals across the country, banning meetings, workers' associations, and so on. In 1851 he invited the people to grant him the power to draw up a new constitution. A plebiscite shortly thereafter authorized his actions. After one year Louis Napoleon Bonaparte ordered another plebiscite and, with the approval of over 95 percent of the voters, established the Second Empire and assumed the title of Napoleon III (1852–1870), emperor of the French.

Why was the French Revolution of 1848 significant? First, its dynamics would be repeated elsewhere. The middle classes played a pivotal political role. Louis Philippe's regime had been proudly "bourgeois" but ended up alienating many of its supporters. Denied a direct political voice, key groups of the middle class swung to the opposition, allying themselves with radicals who never would have toppled the regime alone. Yet demands for reform soon ran up against fears of

TWO VIEWS OF THE JUNE DAYS, FRANCE, 1848

These two passages make for an interesting comparison. The socialist Karl Marx reported on the events of 1848 in France as a journalist for a German newspaper. For Marx, the bloodshed of the June days shattered the "fraternal illusions" of February 1848, when the king had been overthrown and the provisional government established. That bloodshed also symbolized a new stage in history: one of acute class conflict.

The French liberal politician Alexis de Tocqueville also wrote about his impressions of the revolution. (Tocqueville's account, however, is retrospective, for he wrote his memoirs well after 1848.) For Marx, a socialist observer, the June Days represented a turning point: "the working class was knocking on the gates of history." For Tocqueville, a member of the government, the actions of the crowd sparked fear and conservative reaction. Unlike Marx, Tocqueville was not sympathetic to the revolutionaries of June. Yet he, too, underscored the historical significance of the events.

KARL MARX'S JOURNALISM

The last official remnant of the February Revolution, the Executive Commission, has melted away, like an apparition, before the seriousness of events. The fireworks of Lamartine [French Romantic poet and member of the provisional government] have turned into the war rockets of Cavaignac [French general, in charge of putting down the workers' insurrection]. *Fraternité*, the fraternity of antagonistic classes of which one exploits the other, this *fraternité*, proclaimed in February, on every prison, on every barracks—its true, unadulterated, its prosaic expression is civil war, civil war in its most fearful form, the war of labor and capital. This fraternity flamed in front of all the windows of Paris on the evening of June 25, when the Paris of the bourgeoisie was illuminated, whilst the Paris of the proletariat [Marxist term for the working people] burnt, bled, moaned. . . . The February Revolution was the beautiful revolution, the revolution of universal sympathy, because the antagonisms, which had flared up in it against the monarchy, slumbered peacefully side by side, still undeveloped, because the social struggle which formed its background had won only a joyous existence, an existence of phrases, of words. The June revolution is the ugly revolution, the repulsive revolution, because things have taken the place of phrases, because the republic uncovered the head of the monster itself, by striking off the crown that shielded and concealed it.— Order! was the battle cry of Guizot . . . Order! shouts Cavaignac, the brutal echo of the French National Assembly and of the republican bourgeoisie. Order! thundered his grape-shot, as it ripped up the body of the proletariat. None of the numerous revolutions of the French bourgeoisie since 1789 was an attack on order; for they allowed the rule of the class, they allowed the slavery of the workers, they allowed the bourgeois order to endure, however often the political form of this rule and of this slavery changed. June has attacked this order. Woe to June!"

Neue Rheinische Zeitung (New Rhineland Gazette), June 29, 1848; from Karl Marx, *The Class Struggles in France* (New York: International Publishers, 1964), pp. 57–58.

Alexis de Tocqueville Remembers the June Days

Now at last I have come to that insurrection in June which was the greatest and the strangest that had ever taken place in our history, or perhaps in that of any other nation: the greatest because for four days more than a hundred thousand men took part in it, and there were five generals killed; the strangest, because the insurgents were fighting without a battle cry, leaders, or flag, and yet they showed wonderful powers of coordination and a military expertise that astonished the most experienced officers.

Another point that distinguished it from all other events of the same type during the last sixty years was that its object was not to change the form of government, but to alter the organization of society. In truth it was not a political struggle (in the sense in which we have used the word "political" up to now), but a class struggle, a sort of "Servile War." . . . One should not see it only as a brutal and a blind, but as a powerful effort of the workers to escape from the necessities of their condition, which had been depicted to them as an illegitimate depression, and by the sword to open up a road towards that imaginary well-being that had been shown to them in the distance as a right. It was this mixture of greedy desires and false theories that engendered the insurrection and made it so formidable. These poor people had been assured that the goods of the wealthy were in some way the result of a theft committed against themselves. They had been assured that inequalities of fortune were as much opposed to morality and the interests of society as to nature. This obscure and mistaken conception of right, combined with brute force, imparted to it an energy, tenacity and strength it would never have had on its own.

From Alexis de Tocqueville, *Recollections: The French Revolution of 1848.* Edited by J. P. Mayer and A. P. Kerr, translated by George Lawrence. (New Brunswick,N.J.: Transaction Books, 1987), pp. 436–437.

disorder and desire for a strong state. This familiar dynamic led to the collapse of the republic and to the rule of Louis Napoleon Bonaparte. Second, many contemporaries saw the June Days as simply naked class struggle. The violence of the June Days shattered many of the liberal aspirations of the earlier period. The romantic image of revolutionary unity captured in Delacroix's *Liberty Leading the People* now seemed naïve. In the aftermath of 1848, the interests and politics of middle- and working-class people were more sharply differentiated and more directly at odds. Socialism would come into its own as an independent political force.

Conclusion

The French revolution of 1789 had polarized Europe; in its aftermath new political identities formed and new political ideologies were spelled out. The Congress of Vienna, or peace settlement of 1815, had aimed to establish a new international system and to inoculate Europe against revolution. It succeeded in the first aim, but only partially in the second. The combination of new politics with industrialization and rapid social change undermined the conservative order. From the 1820s through the 1840s, a combination of social grievances and political disappointments created powerful movements for change, first in Latin America and the Balkans, then in western Europe and Great Britain.

The French revolution of 1848 (the second since the defeat of Napoleon) became the opening act of a much larger drama. In Southern and Central Europe, as we will see in the next chapter, the issues were framed differently. Still, the dynamics of revolution in France foreshadowed the turn of events in other lands: exhilarating revolutionary successes were followed by the unraveling of revolutionary alliances and the emergence of new forms of conservative government. Throughout the West, the mid-century crisis of 1848 became a turning point. In its aftermath, the kinds of broad revolutionary alliances that had produced revolution were vanquished by class politics, and utopian socialism gave way to Marxism. In culture as in politics Romanticism faded, its expansive sense of possibility replaced by the more biting viewpoint of realism. Economies and states changed. Conservatism, liberalism, and socialism adapted to new political conditions. How this happened, and the explosive role of nationalism in the process, are the subjects of the next chapter.

KEY TERMS

Congress of Vienna
Simón Bolívar
Nicholas I
Greek Civil War
conservatism

liberalism
The Wealth of Nations
socialism
The Communist Manifesto
nationalism

Romanticism
Chartist Movement
French Revolution of 1848

SELECTED READINGS

Agulhon, Maurice. *The Republican Experiment, 1848–1852.* New York, 1983. A full treatment of the revolution in France.

Anderson, Benedict. *Imagined Communities: Reflections on the Origin and Spread of Nationalism.* London, 1983. The most influential recent study of the subject, highly recommended for further reading.

Briggs, Asa. *The Age of Improvement, 1783–1867.* New York, 1979. A survey of England from 1780 to 1870, particularly strong on Victorian attitudes.

Colley, Linda. *Britons: Forging the Nation, 1707–1837.* New Haven, 1992. An important analysis of Britain's emerging national consciousness in the eighteenth and early nineteenth centuries.

Furet, François. *Revolutionary France, 1770–1880.* New York, 1970. An excellent and fresh overview by one of the preeminent historians of the revolution of 1789.

Gilbert, Sandra M., and Susan Gubar. *The Madwoman in the Attic: The Woman Writer and the Nineteenth-Century Literary Imagination.* New Haven and London, 1970. A study of the history of women writers and on examination of women writers as historians of their time.

Hobsbawm, Eric. *The Age of Revolution: Europe 1789 to 1848.* New York, 1970. A classic, and still very useful, account of the period.

Kramer, Lloyd. *Nationalism: Political Cultures in Europe and America, 1775-1865.* London, 1998. Excellent recent overview.

Langer, William. *Political and Social Upheaval, 1832–1851.* New York, 1969. Long the standard, and still the most comprehensive survey.

Laven, David and Lucy Riall. *Napoleon's Legacy: Problems of Government in Restoration Europe.* London, 2002. A new collection of essays.

Levinger, Matthew. *Enlightened Nationalism: The Transformation of Prussian Political Culture 1806–1848.* New York, 2000. A new and nuanced study of Prussian conservatism, with implications for the rest of Europe.

Macfie, A. L. *Orientalism.* London, 2002. Introductory but very clear.

Merriman, John M., ed. *1830 in France.* New York, 1975. Emphasizes the nature of revolution and examines events outside Paris.

Pinkney, David. *The French Revolution of 1830.* Princeton, N.J., 1972. A reinterpretation, now the best history of the revolution.

Porter, Roy, and Mikulas Teich, eds. *Romanticism in National Context.* Cambridge, 1988.

Raeff, Marc. *The Decembrist Movement.* New York, 1966. A study of the Russian uprising with documents.

Sahlins, Peter. *Forest Rites: The War of the Demoiselles in Nineteenth-Century France.* Cambridge, Mass., 1994. A fascinating study of relations among peasant communities, the forests, and the state.

Said, Edward W. *Orientalism.* New York, 1979. A brilliant and biting study of the imaginative hold of the "Orient" on European intellectuals.

Saville, John. *1848: The British State and the Chartist Movement.* New York, 1987. A detailed account of the movement's limited successes and ultimate failure.

Schroeder, Paul. *The Transformation of European Politics, 1763–1848.* Oxford and New York, 1994. For those interested in international relations and diplomacy; massively researched and a fresh look at the period. Especially good on the Congress of Vienna.

Sewell, William H. *Work and Revolution in France: The Language of Labor from the Old Regime to 1848.* Cambridge, 1980. A very influential study of French radicalism and its larger implications.

Smith, Bonnie. *The Gender of History: Men, Women, and Historical Practice.* Cambridge, Mass., 1998. On Romanticism and the historical imagination.

Wordsworth, Jonathan, Michael C. Jaye, and Robert Woof. *William Wordsworth and the Age of English Romanticism.* New Brunswick, 1987. Wide ranging and beautifully illustrated, a good picture of the age.

DIGITAL HISTORY

NATIONALISM AND MUSIC

I think our reputation as a musical nation is fairly old and well-known, and to preserve this, to infuse new spirit into it and to enhance it more and more is the task of every artist who is at the same time inspired by true patriotism. As for me, I am merely making the beginning.
—Smetana, Bedřich, and František Bartoš. Bedřich Smetana, Letters and Reminiscences. Prague: Artia, 1955. p. 70

Toward the end of the eighteenth century, a vast cultural movement began to sweep across Europe. The movement, known as Romanticism, called into question many of the principles of the eighteenth-century Enlightenment—human reason, the uniformity of human nature, and the life of the mind. The Romantics were a mixed bag of philosophers, historians, painters, poets, and musicians who believed that the excessive rationality of the eighteenth-century *philosophe* had actually done more harm than good. Because they emphasized the diversity of humanity, and the importance of spontaneity, creativity, emotion, and passion, the Romantics appeared to be an antidote or corrective to many aspects of European cultural and intellectual life.

Within the Romantic movement, a group of composers were inspired by new ideas about national identity and the revolutions occurring throughout Europe. They merged the political ideology of nationalism, its celebration of the nation in all its simplicity and history, with Romantic music to create a new movement called Musical Nationalism. In Eastern Europe and Russia, composers began to tap into folk heroes, tales, songs, and dances in order to establish a new identity, a nationalist one. Musical nationalism in Germany, Hungary, Czechoslovakia, Russia, and elsewhere helped create a new soul of the nation, one that celebrated the people and their traditions. In operas and symphonic poems, the nineteenth-century musical nationalists exposed the distant and exotic for all to see. In this way, the ideals of the Enlightenment were challenged at the same time that many nations began to develop distinct cultural identities.

The primary sources in the Nationalism and Music Digital History Feature at www.wwnorton.com/wciv reveal how composers expressed the new national fervor felt by millions of people throughout Central, Southern, and Eastern Europe. While reading some of the writings of the musical nationalists and listening to their music, think about the following questions:

• Why did musical nationalism appear in the nineteenth century and not earlier? What forces were largely responsible for its development?

• Why did musical nationalism appear in Eastern Europe and Russia first?

• Is there American nationalist music?

• Do you think that musical nationalism helped create new national identities?

CHAPTER TWENTY-ONE

WHAT IS A NATION? TERRITORIES, STATES, AND CITIZENS, 1848–1871

Eighteen forty-eight was a tumultuous year. From Berlin to Budapest to Rome, insurgents rushed to hastily built barricades, forcing kings and princes to beat an equally hasty—though only temporary—retreat. Across the Atlantic, the treaty of Guadalupe Hidalgo ended the war between Mexico and the United States with a massive territorial transaction: for a sum of $15 million, the United States acquired half a million square miles of western territory, including California. The exchange nearly completed the United States' continental expansion, but it also ushered in conflicts that led to the American Civil War. In July of 1848, the Seneca Falls Convention marked the emergence of an organized movement for woman suffrage in the United States, which was paralleled in Europe. The New York *Herald* detected a disturbing connection among the year's events and commented nervously that "To whatever part of the world the attention is directed, the political and social fabric is crumbling. . . . [T]he work of revolution is no longer confined to the Old World, nor to the masculine gender." It was in 1848, too, that miners struck gold in California, launching an event with transatlantic resonance, the gold rush. When news of California gold reached Paris in the fall of 1848 after a summer of bitter social conflict, Karl Marx acidly remarked that "golden dreams were to supplant the socialist dreams of the Paris workers."

The social and political upheavals of 1848 marked the high point of the "age of revolution" and their failure signaled the end of that age. Yet the mid-century crisis was an equally important turning point in the history of nationalism and nation building. Nationalism, as defined in the last chapter, is the sense of belonging to a community that shares historical, geographic, cultural, or political traditions. As historians point out, this sense is both powerful and diffuse and so could be—and was—cultivated by intellectuals, revolutionaries, and governments for different purposes. Nationalism could serve liberal or conservative politics and goals. During the first part of the nineteenth century, nationalism was usually linked to liberal goals; by the end of the century it had been given a conservative meaning; 1848 was an important moment in this larger sea change.

FOCUS QUESTIONS

- What different forms did nationalism take and why?
- Why did the efforts to unify Italy and Germany succeed during the 1860s?

- What were the similarities between slavery and serfdom?
- How did journalists' depictions of the Crimean War reflect cultural trends?

Nation building refers to the process of creating new states and reconstructing older ones, a process in which the nineteenth century marked a crucial stage. Territorial changes, such as the treaty of Guadalupe Hidalgo, which dramatically transformed the boundaries of the United States, were significant. But so were political reforms and new state structures that changed how governments worked and how they related to their citizens. The American Civil War, and the unification of Italy and of Germany involved wrenching political change as well as territory, and all three had far-reaching ramifications for the international order. France, Britain, Russia, and Austria were also rebuilt during this period—their bureaucracies overhauled and their electorates expanded, relations between ethnic groups reorganized, Russian serfdom, like American slavery, abolished. Changing relations between states and those they governed lay at the heart of nation building. And these changes were hastened by reactions against the revolutionary upheavals of 1848.

NATIONALISM AND REVOLUTION IN 1848

What different forms did nationalism take and why?

In central and eastern Europe, the spring of 1848 brought a dizzying sequence of revolution and repression. The roots of revolution lay in social antagonisms, economic crisis, and political grievances. But these conflicts were also shaped decisively by nationalism. To be sure, reformers and revolutionaries had liberal goals: representative government, an end to privilege, economic development, and so on. But they also sought some form of national unity. Indeed, reformers in Germany, Italy, Poland, and the Austrian empire believed that their liberal goals might only be realized in a vigorous, "modern" nation-state. The fate of the 1848 revolutions in these regions demonstrated nationalism's power to mobilize opponents of the regime, but also its potential to splinter revolutionary alliances and to override other allegiances and values entirely.

WHO MAKES A NATION? GERMANY IN 1848

In 1815, there was no "Germany." The Congress of Vienna had created a "German Confederation," a loose organization of thirty-eight states, including Austria and Prussia but not their non-German territories in sections of Poland and Hungary. The Confederation was intended to provide only common defense. It had no real executive power. As a practical matter, Prussia was, with Austria, the great power in the area, and would play a central role in German politics.

In 1806, Prussia had been defeated by the French under Napoleon. Many Prussians considered the defeat an indictment of the country's inertia since the reign of Frederick the Great (1740–1786). Aiming to revive "patriotism and a national honor and independence," they instituted a series of aggressive reforms, imposed from above. Prussian reformers reconstituted the army, following the Napoleonic example. Officers were recruited and promoted on the basis of merit rather than birth, although the large majority continued to come from the Junker (aristocratic) class. Other reforms modernized training at the royal cadet school in Berlin and encouraged the middle class to take a more active role in the civil service. In 1807, serfdom and the estate system were abolished. A year later, in a conscious attempt to increase middle-class Germans' sense of themselves as citizens, cities and towns were allowed to elect their councilmen and handle their own finances. (Justice and security continued to be administered by the central government in Berlin.) The Prussian reformers expanded facilities for both primary and secondary education and founded the University of Berlin, which numbered among its faculty several ardent nationalists.

Prussia aimed to establish itself as the leading German state and a counter to Austrian power in the region. Prussian's most significant victory in this respect came with the Zollverein, or customs union, in 1834, which established free trade among the German states and a uniform tariff against the rest of the world—an openly protectionist policy advocated by the economist Friedrich List. By the 1840s, the union included almost all of the German states except German Austria and offered manufacturers a market of almost 34 million people. The spread of the railways after 1835 accelerated exchange within this expanded internal market.

During the 1840s, in both Prussia and the smaller German states, political clubs of students and other radicals joined with middle-class groups of lawyers, doctors, and businessmen to press new demands for representative government and reform. Newspapers multiplied, defying censorship. Liberal reformers resented both Prussian domination of the German Confederation and the conservatism of the Habsburgs who ruled the Austrian empire. They attacked the combination of autocracy and bureaucratic authority that stifled political life in Prussia and Austria. German nationhood, they reasoned, would break Austrian or Prussian domination and end the sectional fragmentation that made reform so difficult.

When Frederick William IV (1840–1861) succeeded to the Prussian throne in 1840, hopes ran high. The new kaiser did gesture toward liberalizing reforms. Faced when economic troubles hit the 1840s, however, the regime reverted to authoritarianism. Frederick William sent the army to crush a revolt among the textile weavers of Silesia, who were protesting British imports, and, more generally, riled by unemployment, falling wages, and hunger. The brutality of the regime's response shocked many. The kaiser also opposed constitutionalism, and any representative participation in issues of legislation and budgets.

As in France, liberals and radicals in Prussia and the German states continued their reform campaigns. And when revolution came to France in the spring of 1848, unrest spread across the Rhine. In the smaller German states, kings and princes yielded surprisingly quickly to revolutionary movements. The governments promised freedom of the press, elections, expanded suffrage, jury trials, and other liberal reforms. In Prussia, Frederick William IV, shaken by unrest in the countryside and stunned by a showdown in Berlin between the army and revolutionaries in which two hundred and fifty were killed, finally capitulated.

GERMAN CONFEDERATION, 1815

Compare this map with the one on page 761. What helped to bring the various states of the German Confederation together? What was their relationship with German-speaking Prussia? What factors prevented a more formally unified German state at this time?

THE FRANKFURT ASSEMBLY AND GERMAN NATIONHOOD

The second and most idealistic stage of the revolution began with the election of delegates to an all-German assembly in Frankfurt, where representatives from Prussia, Austria, and the small German states met to discuss the unification of a single German nation. Most of the delegates came from the professional classes—lawyers, professors, administrators—and most were moderate liberals. Many had assumed that the Frankfurt Assembly would draft a constitution for a liberal, unified Germany, much as an assembly of Frenchmen had done for their country in 1789. The comparison was severely. In 1789 a French nation-state and a centralized sovereign power already existed, to be reformed and redirected by the assembled Frenchmen. By contrast, the Frankfurt Assembly had no resources, no sovereign power to take, no single legal code. It did not even have a suitable meeting place: for eleven months the delegates worked in a single public room in an old church with terrible acoustics—no place to debate and decide on legislation. Although the Assembly benefited from the energy, idealism, and devotion of the delegates, it faced enormous obstacles, and at times it teetered on the brink of chaos.

> The Prussian Monarch wanted both the crown and a larger German state, but on his own terms. After a brief protest, summarily suppressed by the military, the delegates went home, disillusioned by their experience and convinced that their liberal and nationalist goals were incompatible.

On the Assembly floor, questions of nationality proved contentious and destructive. Which Germans would be in the new state? A majority of the Assembly's delegates argued that Germans were all those who, by language, culture, or geography, felt themselves bound to the enterprise of unification. They believed the German nation should include as many Germans as possible—a position encouraged by the spectacle of disintegration in the Habsburg empire. This was the "Great German" position. It was countered by a minority who called for a "Small Germany," one that left out all lands of the Habsburg empire, including German Austria. Great Germans had a majority, but were stymied by other nationalities unwilling to be included in their fold. The Czechs in Bohemia, for instance, wanted no part of Great Germany. After a long and difficult debate, and when the Austrian emperor withdrew his support, the Assembly retreated to the "Small German" solution and in April of 1849 offered the crown of the new German nation to Frederick William IV.

Frederick William refused the offer. The Assembly's proposed constitution, he argued, was too liberal, and to owe his crown to a parliament would be demeaning; he called it the "crown from the gutter." The Prussian Monarch wanted both the crown and a larger German state, but on his own terms. After a brief protest, summarily suppressed by the military, the delegates went home, disillusioned by their experience and convinced that their liberal and nationalist goals were incompatible. Some fled repression by emigrating to the United States. Others convinced themselves to sacrifice their liberal views for the seemingly realistic goal of nationhood. In Prussia itself, the army dispatched what remained of the revolutionary forces.

Beyond the walls of the church in Frankfurt, popular revolution took its own course. Peasants ransacked tax offices and burned castles; workers smashed machines. In towns and cities, a groundswell of political activity produced citizen militias, new daily newspapers, pamphleteering, and political clubs. For the first time, many of these clubs admitted women, although they denied

Procession of the German Assembly to Its Opening Session at Saint Paul's Church, Frankfurt, May 1848.

FREDERICK WILLIAM IV REFUSES THE "THRONE FROM THE GUTTER"

In March 1849, after months of deliberation and constitution making, the Frankfurt Assembly offered the throne of its proposed German state to the Prussian monarch Frederick William IV, who quickly turned it down. He had already reflected on the matter. In an earlier (December, 1848) letter to one of his advisors, the diplomat Christian von Bunsen, he had set out his reasoning as follows.

I want the princes' approval of neither *this* election nor *this* crown. Do you understand the words emphasized here? For you I want to shed light on this as briefly and brightly as possible. First, *this* crown is no crown. The crown which a Hohenzoller [the Prussian royal house] could accept, *if* circumstances *permitted*, is not one *made* by an assembly sprung from a revolutionary seed in the genre of the crown of cobble stones of Louis Philippe—even if this assembly was established with the sanction of princes . . . but one which bears the stamp of God, one which makes [the individual] on whom it [the crown] is placed, after his anointment, a "divine right" monarch—just as it has elevated more than 34 princes to Kings of the Germans by divine right and just as it bonds the last of these to his predecessors. The crown worn by Ottonians, Staufens [earlier German royal houses], Habsburgs can of course also be worn by a Hohenzoller; it honors him overwhelmingly with the luster of a thousand years. But *this* one, to which you regrettably refer, overwhelmingly dishonors [its bearer] with its smell of the gunpowder of the 1848 revolution—the silliest, dumbest, worst, though—thank God!—not the most evil of this century. Such an imaginary headband, baked out of dirt and the letters of the alphabet, is supposed to be welcome to a legitimate divine right king: to put it more precisely, to the King of Prussia who is blessed with a crown which may not be the oldest but, of all those which have never been stolen, is the most noble? . . . I will tell you outright: if the thousand-year-old crown of the German nation . . . should be bestowed again, it will be *I* and my equals who will bestow it. And woe to those who assume [powers] to which they have no title.

Ralph Menning, *The Art of the Possible: Documents on Great Power Diplomacy, 1814–1914* (New York: McGraw-Hill, 1996), p. 82.

them the right to speak. In Berlin and other German cities newly founded women's clubs sought to participate in an expanded political world. Such popular unrest made moderate reformers uneasy, however; full male suffrage alone was a deeply disturbing prospect. Peasant and worker protests had forced the king to make concessions in the early spring of 1848. Now moderate reformers found popular movements threatening.

National unification increasingly appealed to moderates as a way to maintain order. "In order to realize our ideas of freedom and equality, we want above all a strong and powerful government," claimed one candidate during the election campaigns for the Frankfurt Assembly. Popular sovereignty, he continued, "strengthened by the authority of a hereditary monarchy, will be able to repress with an iron hand any disorder and any violation of

CHRONOLOGY

NATION BUILDING IN GERMANY, 1800–1850

Napoleon defeats Prussia	1806
Edict abolishing serfdom	1807
Municipal Ordinance of 1808	
Creation of the Zollverein	1834
Liberal protests	1820s–1840s
Revolution of 1848	
Frankfurt Assembly meets	1848
Frederick Willam grants Prussian constitution	1850

the law." In this context, nationhood stood for a new constitution and political community, but also for a sternly enforced rule of law.

PEOPLES AGAINST EMPIRE: THE HABSBURG LANDS

In the sprawling Austrian empire, nationalism played a different, centrifugal role. The empire included a wide array of ethnic and language groups: Germans, Czechs, Magyars, Poles, Slovaks, Serbs, and Italians, to name only the most prominent. In some areas of the empire, these groups lived in relative separation and isolation. Elsewhere they co-existed, though not always harmoniously. The Habsburgs found it increasingly difficult to hold their empire together as these groups' varying national demands escalated after 1815.

In the Polish territories of the empire, nationalist sentiment was strongest among aristocrats, who were especially conscious of their historic role as leaders of the Polish nation. Here, the Habsburg empire successfully set Polish serfs against Polish lords, ensuring that social grievances dampened ethnic nationalism. In the Hungarian region, national claims were likewise advanced by the relatively small Magyar aristocracy. Yet they resonated broadly under the gifted and influential leadership of Lajos (Louis) Kossuth. A member of the lower nobility, Kossuth was by turns a lawyer, publicist, newspaper editor, and political leader. To protest the closed-door policy of the empire's barely representative Diet (Parliament) Kossuth published transcripts of parliamentary debates and distributed them to a broader public. He campaigned for independence and a separate Hungarian parliament, but he also (and

more influentially) wanted to bring politics to the people. Kossuth staged political "banquets" like those in France, where local and national personalities made speeches in the form of toasts, and interested citizens could eat, drink, and participate in politics. The Hungarian political leader combined aristocratic style with rabble-rousing politics: a delicate balancing act but one that, when it worked, catapulted him to the center of Habsburg politics. He was as well known in the Habsburg capital of Vienna as he was in Pressburg and Budapest.

The other major nationalist movement that plagued the Habsburg empire was pan-Slavism. Slavs included Russians, Poles, Ukrainians, Czechs, Slovaks, Slovenes, Croats, Serbs, Macedonians, and Bulgarians. Before 1848 pan-Slavism was primarily a cultural movement united by a general pro-Slavic sentiment. It was internally divided, however, by the competing claims of different Slavic languages and traditions. Pan-Slavism inspired the works of the Czech historian and political leader, František Palacký, author of the *History of the Bohemian People*, and the Slovak Jan Kollár, whose book *Salvy Dcera* ("Slava's Daughter") mourned the loss of identity among Slavs in the Germanic world. The movement also influenced the Polish romantic poet Adam Mickiewicz, who sought to rekindle Polish nationhood against foreign oppression.

Tsar Nicholas of Russia sought to use pan-Slavism to his advantage, making arguments about "Slavic" uniqueness part of his "autocracy, orthodoxy, nationality" ideology after 1825. Yet the tsar's Russian-sponsored pan-Slavism alienated Western-oriented Slavs who resented Russian rule, providing a good example of the tangled web of alliances and antagonisms that nationalist sentiments created. Pan-Slavism was a volatile and unpredictable political force in the regions of Eastern Europe where Austrian and Russia vied for power and influence.

1848 IN AUSTRIA AND HUNGARY: SPRINGTIME OF PEOPLES AND THE AUTUMN OF EMPIRE

Eighteen forty-eight brought the empire's combustive combination of political, social, and ethnic tensions to the point of explosion. The Habsburgs faced multiple challenges to their authority. The opening salvo came from the Hungarians. Emboldened by uprisings in France and Germany, Kossuth stepped up his reform campaigns, pillorying the "Metternich system" of Habsburg autocracy and control, de-

Romance
- French
- Italian
- Romanian
- Walloon

Germanic
- Dutch
- German
- Flemish
- Danish
- Swedish

Slavonic
- Ukrainian
- Polish
- Serbian
- Croatian
- Slovak
- Czech
- Slovenian
- Great Russian

Baltic
- Lithuanian
- Latvian

Finno-Ugrian
- Magyar
- Estonian

Mixed use of languages

LANGUAGES OF THE AUSTRIAN EMPIRE

This map shows the distribution of languages across the German Confederation and the Austrian Empire. Note the pattern of linguistic groups in comparison to the political boundaries. Did this disparity encourage or discourage nationalism in central and southeastern Europe? How did the emergence of identities based on language help redraw the map of Europe?

Committee of Citizens took shape, as did a middle-class militia, or National Guard, determined at once to maintain order and to press demands for reform. The Habsburg regime tried to shut the movement down by closing the university, but that only unleashed more popular anger. The regime found itself forced to retreat almost entirely. Metternich, whose political system had weathered so many storms, fled to Britain in disguise—a good indication of the political turmoil—leaving the emperor Ferdinand I in Vienna. The government conceded to radical demands for male suffrage and a single house of representatives. It agreed to withdraw troops from Vienna, and to put forced labor and serfdom on a path to abolition. The government also yielded to Czech demands in Bohemia, granting that kingdom its own constitution. To the south, Italian liberals and nationalists attacked the empire's territories in Naples and Venice. In Milan, the forces of King Charles Albert of Piedmont routed the Austrians, raising hopes of victory. As what would be called "the springtime of peoples" unfolded, Habsburg control of its various provinces seemed to be coming apart.

manding representative institutions throughout the empire and autonomy for the Hungarian "Magyar" nation. The Hungarian Diet prepared to draft its own constitution. In Vienna, the seat of Habsburg power, a popular movement of students and artisans demanding political and social reforms built barricades and attacked the imperial palace. A Central

Yet the explosion of national sentiment that shook the empire later allowed it to recoup its fortunes. The paradox of nationalism in central Europe was that no cultural or ethnic majority could declare independence in a given region without prompting rebellion from other minority groups that inhabited the same area. In Bohemia, for instance, Czechs and Germans who lived side by side had worked together to pass reforms scuttling feudalism. Within a month, however, nationalism began to fracture their alliance. German Bohemians set off to attend the all-important Frankfurt Assembly (see above), but the Czech majority refused to send representatives and indeed countered by convening a confederation of Slavs in Prague. What did the delegates at the Slav confederation want? Some were hostile to what the Russian anarchist Mikhail Bakunin called the "monstrous Austrian empire." But the majority of delegates preferred to be ruled by the Habsburgs (though with some autonomy) than to be dominated by either the Germans or the Russians.

This bundle of animosities allowed the Austrians to divide and conquer. In May 1848, during the Slav Congress, a student- and worker-led insurrection broke out in Prague. On the orders of the newly installed liberal government, Austrian troops entered the city to restore order, sent the Slav congress packing, and reasserted control in Bohemia. For economic as well as political reasons, the new government was determined to keep the empire intact. The regime also sent troops to regain control in the Italian provinces of Lombardy and Venetia, and quarrels among the Italians helped the Austrians succeed.

Nationalism and counternationalism in Hungary set the stage for the final act of the drama. The Hungarian parliament had passed a series of laws including new provisions for the union of Hungary and Austria. In the heat of 1848 Ferdinand I had little choice but to accept them. To prevent a peasant insurrection, the Hungarian parliament also abolished serfdom and ended noble privilege. It also established freedom of the press and of religion, and changed the suffrage requirements, enfranchising small property holders. Many of these measures (called the March laws) were hailed by Hungarian peasants, Jewish communities, and liberals. But other provisions, particularly the extension of Magyar control, provoked opposition from the Croats, Serbs, and Romanians within Hungary. The Austrian government took advantage of these divisions. It appointed the anti-Magyar Josip Jelacic as governor of the breakaway province of Croatia. Encouraged by the Austrians, Jelacic first broke off links with Hungary and then launched an attack. In response, Kossuth rallied the Hungarian forces and turned the tide in their favor. On April 14, 1848, Kossuth upped the ante, severing all ties between Hungary and Austria. The new Austrian emperor, Franz Josef, now played his last card: he asked for military support from Nicholas I of Russia. The Habsburgs were unable to win their "holy struggle against anarchy," but the Russian army of over three

Hungarian revolutionary Lajos Kossuth, 1851. A leader of the Hungarian nationalist movement who combined aristocratic style with rabble-rousing politics, Kossuth almost succeeded in an attempt to separate Hungary from Austria in 1849.

hundred thousand found it an easier task. By mid-August 1849, the Hungarian revolt was crushed.

In the city of Vienna itself, the revolutionary movement had lost ground. When economic crisis and unemployment helped spark a second popular uprising, the emperor's forces, with Russian support, descended on the capital. On October 31, the liberal government capitulated. The regime reestablished censorship, disbanded the National Guard and student organizations, and put twenty-five revolutionary leaders to death in front of a firing squad. Kossuth went into hiding in Turkey, and lived the rest of his life in exile.

1848 AND THE EARLY STAGES OF ITALIAN UNIFICATION

The Italian penninsula had not been united since the Roman empire. At the beginning of the nineteenth century it was a patchwork of small states. Austria occupied the northernmost states of Lombardy and Venetia, which were also the most urban and industrial. Habsburg dependents also ruled Tuscany, Parma, and Modena, extending Austria's influence over the north of the penninsula. The independent Italian states included the southern kingdom of the Two Sicilies, governed by members of the Bourbon family; the Papal States, ruled by Pope Gregory XVI (1831–1846); and most important, Piedmont-Sardinia, ruled by the reform-minded monarch Charles Albert (1831–1849) of the House of Savoy. Charles Albert had no particular commitment to creating an Italian national state, but by virtue of Piedmont-Sardinia's economic power, geographical location, and long tradition of opposition to the Habsburgs, Charles Albert's state played a central role in nationalist and anti-Austrian politics.

The leading Italian nationalist in this period—one whose republican politics Charles Albert disliked— was Giuseppe Mazzini (1805–1872) from the city of Genoa, in Piedmont. Mazzini began his political career as a member of the Carbonari (see Chapter 20), a underground society pledged to resisting Austrian control of the region and establishing constitutional rule. In 1831 Mazzini founded his own society, Young Italy, which was anti-Austrian and in favor of constitutional reforms but also dedicated to Italian unification. Charismatic and persuasive, Mazzini was one of the best-known nationalists of his time. He spoke in characteristically Romantic tones of the awakening of the Italian people and of the common people's mission to bring republicanism to the world. Under his leadership Young Italy clubs multiplied. Yet the organization's favored tactics, plotting mutinies and armed rebellions, proved ineffective. In 1834, Mazzini launched an invasion of the kingdom of Sardinia. Without sufficient support, it fizzled, driving Mazzini into exile in England.

Mazzini's republican vision of a united Italy clashed with the goals of his potential allies. Many liberals shared his commitment to creating a single Italian state, but not his enthusiasm for the people and popular movements. They hoped instead for a merger of existing governments into a some form of constitutional monarchy or, in a few cases, for a government under the pope. Mazzini's insistence on a democratic republic, committed to social and political transformation, struck pragmatic liberals as utopian, and well-to-do members of the middle classes as dangerous.

The turmoil that swept across Europe in 1848 raised hopes for political and social change and put Italian unification on the agenda. Popular revolts forced the

> Charismatic and persuasive, Mazzini was one of the best-known nationalists of his time. He spoke in characteristically Romantic tones of the awakening of the Italian people and of the common people's mission to bring republicanism to the world.

conservative, independent kingdoms on the peninsula to grant civil liberties and parliamentary government. In the north, the provinces of Venetia and Lombardy rebelled against the Austrian occupation. Charles Albert of Piedmont-Sardinia provided them with military support and took up the banner of Italian nationalism, although many charged that he was primarily interested in expanding his own power. In Rome, a popular uprising challenged the power of the pope and established a republic, with Mazzini as its head. These movements were neither coordinated nor ultimately successful. Within a year, the Austrians had regained the upper hand in the north. French forces under Louis Napoleon intervened in the Papal States, and although they met fierce resistance from the Roman republicans joined by Giuseppe Garibaldi (see below), they nonetheless restored the pope's power. Like most of the radical movements of 1848, these uprisings failed. Still, they raised the hopes of nationalists who spoke of a *risorgimento*, or Italian resurgence, that would restore the nation to the position of leadership it had held in Roman times and during the Renaissance.

Giuseppe Mazzini.

BUILDING THE NATION-STATE

Why did the efforts to unify Italy and Germany succeed during the 1860s?

In the wake of the revolutions of 1848, new nation-states were built—often, ironically, by former critics of nationalism. Since the French Revolution of 1789, conservative politicians had associated "nationhood" with liberalism: constitutions, reforms, new political communities. Nationalism evoked memories of popular movements clashing with authoritarian governments. During the second half of the century, however, the political ground shifted dramatically. States and governments took the national initiative. Alarmed by revolutionary ferment, they promoted economic development, pressed social and political reforms, and sought to shore up their base of support. Rather than allow popular nationalist movements to emerge from below, statesmen consolidated their governments' powers and built nations from above.

FRANCE UNDER NAPOLEON III

Napoleon III, like his uncle, believed in personal rule and the development of a centralized state. His constitution, modeled on that of the first French empire, gave control of finance, the army, and foreign affairs exclusively to the emperor. The assembly, elected by universal male suffrage, held virtually no power and could only approve legislation drafted at the emperor's direction by a Council of State. Through bureaucratic expansion, the regime aimed to put the countryside under the political and administrative thumb of the modern state, undermining traditional elites and cultivating a new relationship with the people. "The confidence of our rough peasants can be won by an energetic authority," as one of the regime's representatives put it.

Napoleon III and his government also took steps to develop the economy, harboring a near utopian faith in the ability of industrial expansion to bring prosperity, political support, and national glory. An advisor to the emperor expressed it this way: "I see in industry, machinery and credit the indispensable auxiliaries of humanity's moral and material progress." The government thus encouraged a variety of progressive economic de-

velopments, including credit and other new forms of financing. It passed new limited-liability laws to spur growth and signed a free-trade treaty with Britain in 1860. The government also supported the founding of the Crédit Mobilier, an investment banking institution that sold shares publicly and financed such enterprises as railroads, insurance and gas companies, the coal and construction industries, and the building of the Suez Canal (see Chapter 22). In a different vein, Napoleon III also reluctantly permitted the existence of trade unions and the legalization of strikes. By appealing to both workers and the middle class, he sought to symbolize his country's reemergence as a leading world power.

Perhaps the best illustration of the Second Empire's policies was the transformation of the nation's capital. In Paris, as in other nineteenth-century cities, the medieval infrastructure was buckling under the weight of industrial development. Cholera epidemics had killed twenty thousand in 1832 and nineteen thousand in 1849. In 1850, only one house in five had running water. Economic and public-health incentives to rebuild were multiplied by political concerns, for such "unhealthy conditions" bred not only disease but also crime—and revolution. The massive rebuilding, financed by the Crédit Mobilier among other investment institutions, razed much of the medieval center of the city and erected thirty-four thousand new buildings, including elegant new hotels with the first elevators. The construction installed new water pipes and sewer lines (a popular attraction at the 1867 International Exposition), laid out 200 kilometers of new streets, and rationalized the traffic flow (perhaps unsuccessfully) around the Arc de Triomphe. Wide new boulevards, many named for Napoleon I's most famous generals, radiated outward from the Arc. This wholesale renovation did not benefit everyone. Although the regime built model worker residences, demolitions and rising rents drove working people out of the city center into the increasingly segregated suburbs. Baron Haussmann, who presided over the project, considered the city a monument to "cleanliness and order"; but others called him an "artist of demolition." For centuries monarchs had taken on massive building projects, but this was different, an unprecedented and conscious state effort to change what contemporaries conceived of as the "mechanics" or "system" of modern urban life.

With a similar intent on grandeur, Napoleon III pursued an aggressive foreign policy. First came mixed results against Russia in the Crimea, then success against the Austrians in Italy, then an adventurous expedition to Mexico, where his attempt to help establish another

WHY DID THE EFFORTS TO UNIFY ITALY AND GERMANY SUCCEED DURING THE 1860S?

BUILDING THE NATION-STATE   753

Paris rebuilt. Much of the medieval infrastructure of Paris was razed by Baron Haussman and replaced with new streets and buildings. This photograph shows the new design for the area surrounding the Arc de Triomphe in an "etoile" (star) pattern, with the wide boulevards named after Napoleon I's famous generals.

empire met with costly failure. Finally and most disastrously, the emperor was drawn into a war with Prussia that brought the collapse of his regime in 1870.

VICTORIAN BRITAIN AND THE SECOND REFORM BILL (1867)

Less roiled by the revolutionary wave of 1848, Great Britain was more willing and able to chart a course of significant social and political reform, continuing a process that had begun in 1832 with the First Reform Bill. The government faced mounting demands to extend the franchise beyond the middle classes. Industrial expansion sustained a growing stratum of highly

skilled and relatively well-paid workers (almost exclusively male). These workers, concentrated for the most part within the building, engineering, and textile industries, turned away from the tradition of militant radicalism that had characterized the "Hungry Forties." Instead they favored collective self-help through cooperative societies or trade unions, whose major role was to accumulate funds for insurance against old age and unemployment. They saw education as a tool for advancement, and patronized the mechanics' institutes and similar institutions founded by them or on their behalf. These prosperous workers created real pressure for electoral reform.

Some argued for the vote in the name of democracy. Others borrowed arguments from earlier middle-class campaigns for electoral reform: they were responsible workers, respectable and upstanding members of society, with strong religious convictions and patriotic feelings. Unquestionably loyal to the state, they deserved the vote and direct representation just as much as the middle class. These workers were joined in their campaign by many middle-class Dissenting reformers in the Liberal party, whose religious beliefs (as dissenters from the Church of England) linked them to the workers' campaigns for reform. Dissenters had long been discriminated against. They were denied posts in the civil service and the military that liberals felt should be open to talent, and for centuries had been excluded from the nation's premier universities, Oxford and Cambridge, unless they renounced their faith and subscribed to the articles of the Anglican church. Moreover, they resented paying taxes to support the Church of England, which was largely staffed by sons of the gentry and run in the interests of landed society. The fact that the community of "dissent" crossed class lines was vital to Liberal party politics and the campaign for reforming the vote.

Working-class leaders and middle-class dissidents joined in a countrywide campaign for a new reform bill and a House of Commons responsive to their interests. They were backed by some shrewd Conservatives, such as Benjamin Disraeli (1804–1881), who argued that political life would be improved, not disrupted, by including the "aristocrats of labor." In actuality, Disraeli was betting that the newly enfranchised demographic would vote Conservative, and in 1867, he steered through Parliament a bill that reached farther than anything proposed by his political opponents. The 1867 Reform Bill doubled the franchise by extending the vote to any men who paid poor rates or rent of ten pounds or more a year in urban areas (this meant, in general, skilled workers), and to rural tenants paying rent of twelve pounds or more. As in 1832, the bill redistributed seats, with large northern cities gaining representation at the

expense of the rural south. The "responsible" working class had been deemed worthy to participate in the affairs of state.

The reform bill was silent on women; but an important minority insisted that liberalism should include women's enfranchisement. These advocates mobilized a woman suffrage movement, building on women's remarkable participation in earlier reform campaigns, especially the Anti–Corn Law League and the movement to abolish slavery. Their cause found a passionate supporter in John Stuart Mill, perhaps the century's most brilliant, committed, and influential defender of personal liberty. Mill's father had worked closely with the Utilitarian philosopher Jeremy Bentham, and the young Mill had been a convinced Utilitarian himself (see Chapter 20). He went on, however, to develop much more expansive notions of human freedom. In 1859, Mill wrote *On Liberty*, which many consider the classic defense of individual freedom in the face of the state and the "tyranny of the majority." During the same period he coauthored—with his lover and eventual wife, Harriet Taylor—essays on women's political rights, the law of marriage, and divorce. At the time, Taylor was trapped in an unhappy marriage and divorce

MILL'S LOGIC, OR FRANCHISE FOR FEMALES
" Pray clear the way, there, for these—ah—persons."

John Stuart Mill and Suffragettes. Cartoon published in 1860, by which time Mill had established a reputation as a liberal political philosopher and supporter of woman suffrage. The famous political thinker Mill argued that women's enfranchisement was essential to personal liberty and to social progress.

WHY DID THE EFFORTS TO UNIFY ITALY AND GERMANY SUCCEED DURING THE 1860S?

BUILDING THE NATION-STATE   755

required an act of Parliament. Taylor's relationship with Mill thus added a measure of personal scandal to their political views, which contemporaries considered scandalous enough. His *The Subjection of Women* (1869), published after Harriet died, argued what few could even contemplate: that women had to be considered individuals on the same plane as men, and that women's freedom was a measure of social progress. *Subjection* was an international success, and with *On Liberty* became one of the defining texts of Western liberalism. Mill's arguments, however, did not carry the day. Only militant suffrage movements and the crisis of World War I brought women the vote.

The decade or so following the passage of the Reform Bill of 1867 marked the high point of British liberalism. By opening the doors of political participation, liberalism had accomplished a peaceful restructuring of political institutions and social life. It did so under considerable pressure from below, however, and in Britain as elsewhere, liberal leaders made it clear that these doors were unquestionably not open to everyone. Their opposition to woman suffrage is interesting for what it reveals about their views on male and female "nature" and their insistence that female individuality was incompatible with family stability. Yet it also speaks to their conception of the vote: casting a ballot was a specific privilege granted to specific social groups in return for their contributions to and interests in society. Men of property might champion the rule of law and representative government, but they balked at the prospect of a truly democratic politics and did not shy from heavy-handed, law-and-order politics. The expansion of the franchise had created new constituencies with new ambitions, however, and paved the way for of socialist and labor politics in the last quarter of the century. These tensions within liberalism made it possible for liberals to work within a variety of different political regimes, but they also forecast conflicts in the future.

ITALIAN UNIFICATION: CAVOUR AND GARIBALDI

The failed efforts to unify Italy in 1848 left behind two different visions of Italian statehood. The first was most closely associated with Mazzini who, as we have seen, believed in a republican Italy, built by the people.

Mazzini's cause was taken up by the colorful figure Giuseppe Garibaldi. No political theorist, Garibaldi was a guerilla fighter who had been exiled twice: first in Latin America, where he fought along with independence movements, and again in the United States. Like Mazzini, Garibaldi was committed to achieving national unification through a popular movement.

A decidedly different route to unification—a constitutional monarchy—was favored by more moderate nationalists, who sought economic and political reforms but intended to steer clear of democracy and the forces it might unleash. Rather than arousing popular movements, these moderates pinned their hopes on the kingdom of Piedmont-Sardinia, whose king, Charles Albert, had taken up the anti-Austrian cause in 1848. Though Charles Albert had been defeated and died in exile, his son Victor Emmanuel II (1849–1861) brought a man into his government who would

> No political theorist, Garibaldi was a guerilla fighter who had been exiled twice: first in Latin America, where he fought along with independence movements, and again in the United States.

Giuseppe Garibaldi.

embody the conservative vision of nationhood: the shrewd Sardinian nobleman Count Camillo Benso di Cavour (1810–1861). "In Italy a democratic movement has almost no chance of success," Cavour declared. He instead pursued ambitious but pragmatic reforms guided by the state. First as minister of commerce and agriculture and then as prime minister, he promoted economic expansion, encouraged the construction of a modern transportation infrastructure, reformed the currency, and sought to raise Piedmont-Sardinia's profile in international relations. Garibaldi and Cavour thus represented two different routes to Italian unification: Garibaldi stood for unification from below, Cavour for unification guided from above.

Cavour's plan depended on diplomacy. Since Piedmont-Sardinia did not have the military capacity to counter the Austrians in northern Italy, Cavour skillfully cultivated an alliance with one of Austria's traditional rivals: Napoleonic France. In 1858 Cavour held a secret meeting with Napoleon III, who agreed to cooperate in driving the Austrians from Italy if Piedmont would cede Savoy and Nice to France. A war with Austria was duly provoked in 1859, and for a time all went well for the Franco-Italian allies. After the conquest of Lombardy, however, Napoleon III suddenly withdrew, concerned that he might either lose the battle or antagonize French Catholics, who were alienated by Cavour's hostility to the pope. Deserted by the French, Piedmont could not expel the Austrians from Venetia. Yet the campaign made extensive gains. Piedmont-Sardinia annexed Lombardy. The duchies of Tuscany, Parma, and Modena agreed by plebiscite to join the new state. By the end of this process in 1860, Piedmont-Sardinia had grown to more than twice its original size and was far the most powerful state in Italy.

As Cavour consolidated the northern and central states, events in the southern states seemed to put those areas up for grabs as well. The unpopular Bourbon king of the Two Sicilies, Francis II (1859–1860), faced a fast-spreading peasant revolt that rekindled the hopes of earlier insurrections of the 1820s and 1840s. That revolt, in turn, got a much needed boost from Garibaldi, who landed in Sicily in May of 1860. "The Thousand," as Garibaldi's volunteer fighters called themselves, embodied the widespread support for Italian unification: they came from the north as well as the south, and counted among them members of the middle class, as well as workers and artisans. Garibaldi's troops took Sicily in the name of Victor Emmanuel (though

> "In Italy a democratic movement has almost no chance of success," Cavour declared. He instead pursued ambitious but pragmatic reforms guided by the state.

Garibaldi insisted that Sicily keep its autonomy), and then continued on to the mainland. By November 1860, Garibaldi's forces, alongside local insurgents, had taken Naples and toppled the kingdom of Francis II. Emboldened by success, Garibaldi looked to Rome, where French troops guarded the pope.

Garibaldi's rising popularity put him on a collision course with Cavour. "Now what will happen? It is impossible to forsee," the prime minister wrote a friend as he contemplated developments in the south. Cavour worried that Garibaldi's forces would bring French or Austrian intervention, with unknown consequences. He feared Garibaldi's "irresistible" prestige. Above all Cavour preferred that Italian unification happen quickly, under Piedmont-Sardinia's stewardship, without domestic turmoil or messy, unpredictable negotiations with other Italian states. "As long as he [Garibaldi] is faithful to his flag, one has to march along with him," Cavor wrote. "This does not alter the fact that it would be eminently desirable for the revolution . . . to be accomplished without him." Determined to recoup the initiative, Cavour dispatched Victor Emmanuel and his army to Rome. Flush with success, the king ordered Garibaldi to cede him military authority, and Garibaldi obeyed. Most of the peninsula was united under a single rule, and Victor Emmanuel assumed the title of king of Italy (1861–1878). Cavour's vision of Italian nationhood had won the day.

The final steps of Italy's territorial nation building came indirectly. Venetia remained in the hands of the Austrians until 1866, when Austria was defeated by Prussia and forced to relinquish their last Italian stronghold. Rome had resisted conquest largely because of the military protection that Napoleon III accorded the pope. But in 1870 the outbreak of the

CHRONOLOGY

UNIFICATION OF ITALY, 1848–1870

Revolutions of 1848	
Italian war with Austria	1859
Conquest of the kingdom of Two Sicilies	1860
Austria cedes Venetia	1866
Occupation of Rome	1870
Law of Papal Guaranties enacted	1870

WHY DID THE EFFORTS TO UNIFY ITALY AND GERMANY SUCCEED DURING THE 1860S?

BUILDING THE NATION-STATE 757

The Kingdom of Sardinia at the time of the Congress of Vienna, 1815

Territories acquired, 1859–1860

Territories acquired, 1861–1870

THE UNIFICATION OF ITALY

Why did the Austrian von Metternich call Italy nothing but a "geographic expression" at mid-century? Why did Cavour see French support and sympathy as crucial to the cause of unification? Why did leadership of the unification movement fall to Piedmont? Why did the Papal States oppose the unification of Italy? Why did Cavour and his southern rival Garibaldi both consider popular support crucial, whereas Bismarck achieved German unification through military and diplomatic means?

Franco-Prussian War compelled Napoleon to withdraw his troops. That September, Italian soldiers occupied Rome, and in July 1871, Rome became capital of the united Italian kingdom.

What of the pope's authority? The Italian parliament passed a Law of Papal Guaranties to define and limit the pope's status—an act promptly defied by the reigning pontiff, Pius IX, who refused to have anything to

BUILDING THE ITALIAN NATION: THREE VIEWS

MAZZINI AND ROMANTIC NATIONALISM

The charismatic revolutionary Giuseppe Mazzini left more than fifty volumes of memoirs and writings. In this excerpt, he sets out his vision of the "regeneration" of the Italian nation and the three Romes: ancient Rome, the Rome of the popes, and (in the future) the Rome of the people, which would emancipate the peoples of Europe. Mazzini's conception of Italian nationalism was Romantic in its interpretation of Italy's distinctive history and destiny, and revolutionary in its emphasis on the Italian people rather than on statesmen.

I saw regenerate Italy becoming at one bound the missionary of a religion of progress and fraternity. . . .

The worship of Rome was a part of my being. The great Unity, the One Life of the world, had twice been elaborated within her walls. Other peoples—their brief mission fulfilled—disappeared for ever. To none save to her had it been given twice to guide and direct the world. . . . There, upon the vestiges of an epoch of civilization anterior to the Grecian, which had had its seat in Italy . . . the Rome of the Republic, concluded by the Caesars, had arisen to consign the former world to oblivion, and borne her eagles over the known world, carrying with them the idea of right, the source of liberty.

In later days . . . she had again arisen, greater than before, and at once constituted herself, through her Popes—the accepted center of a new Unity. . . .

Why should not a new Rome, the Rome of the Italian people . . . arise to create a third and still vaster Unity; to link together and harmonize earth and heaven, right [law] and duty; and utter, not to individuals but to peoples, the great word Association—to make known to free men and equal their mission here below?

Giuseppe Mazzini, *The Life and Writings of Joseph Mazzini.* (London: Smith, Elder & Co., 1964) as cited in Denis Mack Smith, *The Making of Italy, 1796–1870* (New York: Harper & Row, 1968), pp. 48–49.

THE POLITICAL CREED OF THE NATIONAL SOCIETY, FEBRUARY, 1858

The National Society was formed in 1857 to support Italian unification. By the 1860s, the society had over five thousand members. It was especially strong in Piedmont, where it was formed, and central Italy. Giuseppe la Farina was a tenacious organizer; he drafted the society's political creed and had it printed and sold throughout Italy. The society's practical nationalism differed from Mazzini's Romantic vision.

Italian independence should be the aim of every man of spirit and intelligence. Neither our educational system in Italy, nor our commerce and industry, can ever be flourishing or properly modernized while Austria

keeps one foot on our neck. . . . What good is it to be born in the most fertile and beautiful country in the world, to lie midway between East and West with magnificent ports in both the Adriatic and Mediterranean, to be descended from the Genoese, the Pisans, the men of Amalfi, Sicily and Venice? What use is it to have invented the compass, to have discovered the New World and been the progenitor of two civilizations? . . .

To obtain political liberty we must expel the Austrians who keep us enslaved. To win freedom of conscience we must expel the Austrians who keep us slaves of the Pope. To create a national literature we must chase away the Austrians who keep us uneducated. . . .

Italy must become not only independent but politically united. Political unity alone can reconcile various interests and laws, can mobilize credit and put out collective energies to speeding up communications. Only thus will we find sufficient capital for large-scale indus-try. Only thus will we create new markets, suppress internal obstacles to the free flow of commerce, and find the strength and reputation needed for traffic in distant lands. . . .

Everything points irresistibly to political unification. Science, industry, commerce, and the arts all need it. No great enterprise is possible any longer if we do not first put together the skill, knowledge, capital and labor of the whole of our great nation. The spirit of the age is moving toward concentration, and woe betide any nation that holds back!

A. Franchi, ed. *Scritti politici di Giuseppe La Farina*, Vol. 2. (Milan, 1870), pp. 83–98, as cited in Denis Mack Smith, *The Making of Italy, 1796–1870* (New York: Harper & Row, 1968), pp. 224–225.

COUNT CAVOUR AS A LEADER

The unification of Italy owed as much to Cavour's hard-nosed diplomacy as it did to middle-class movements for unification. In 1862, one of Cavour's contemporaries offered the following assessment of the count and how he had found "an opening in the complicated fabric of European politics."

Count Cavour undeniably ranks as third among European statesmen after Lord Palmerston [British prime minister 1885–1858, 1859–1865] and the Emperor Napoleon. . . . Count Cavour's strength does not lie in his principles; for he has none that are altogether inflexible. But he has a clear, precise aim, one whose greatness would—ten years ago—have made any other man reel: that of creating a unified and independent Italy. Men, means, circumstances were and still are matters of indifference to him. He walks straight ahead, always firm, often alone, sacrificing his friends, his sympathies, sometimes his heart, and often his conscience. Nothing is too difficult for him. . . .

Count Cavour . . . always has the talent to assess a situation and the possibilities of exploiting it. And it is this wonderful faculty that has contributed to form the Italy of today. As minister of a fourth-rate power, he could not create situations like Napoleon III, nor has he possessed the support of a great nation like Palmerston.

Count Cavour had to seek out an opening in the complicated fabric of European politics; he had to wriggle his way in, conceal himself, lay a mine, and cause an explosion. And it was by these means that he defeated Austria and won the help of France and England. Where other statesmen would have drawn back, Cavour plunged in headlong—as soon as he had sounded the precipice and calculated the possible profit and loss. The Crimean expeditionary force . . . the cession of Nice, the invasion of the Papal States last autumn [i.e., in 1860], were all the outcome of his vigorous stamina of mind.

There in brief you have the man of foreign affairs. He is strong; he is a match for the situation, for the politicians of his time or indeed of any time.

F. Petruccelli della Gattina, *I moribundi del Palazzo Carignano* (Milan, 1862), pp. 58–65, as cited in Denis Mack Smith, *The Making of Italy, 1796–1870* (New York: Harper & Row, 1968), pp. 181–182.

do with a disrespectful secular government. His successors continued to close themselves off in the Vatican until 1929, when a series of agreements between the Italian government and Pius XI settled the dispute.

In 1871, Italy was a state, but nation building was hardly over. A minority of the "Italian" population spoke Italian; the rest used local and regional dialects so diverse that schoolteachers sent from Rome to Sicily were mistaken for foreigners. As one politician remarked, "We have made Italy; now we must make Italians." The task did not prove easy. The gap between an increasingly industrialized north and a poor and rural south remained wide. Cavour and those who succeeded him as prime minister had to contend with those economic and social inequalities, with rising tensions between landlords and agricultural workers in rural regions, and with lingering resentments of the centralized, northern-oriented state. Banditry in the territory of the former kingdom of the Two Sicilies compelled the central administration to dispatch troops to quell serious uprisings, killing more people than in the war of unification. Regional differences and social tensions, then, made building the Italian nation an ongoing process.

THE UNIFICATION OF GERMANY: REALPOLITIK

In 1853, the former revolutionary August Ludwig von Rochau wrote a short book with a long title: *The Principles of* Realpolitik *Applied to the Conditions of Germany.* Rochau banished the idealism and revolutionary fervor of his youth. "The question of who ought to rule . . . belongs in the realm of philosophical speculation," he wrote. "Practical politics has to do with the simple fact that it is power alone than can rule." In Rochau's view, power would not accrue to those with a "just" cause—those who supported constitutions and Enlightenment conceptions of rights. Instead power came indirectly, through diverse forms such as the expansion of the economy and social institutions. In several important ways, Rochau's views captured the changing outlook of broad sections of the German middle classes. "Realpolitik" became the watchword of the 1850s and 1860s and was most closely associated with the deeply conservative and pragmatic Otto von Bismarck, whose skillful diplomacy and power politics played such an important role in German unification. Yet the German nation was not built by one statesman's efforts. It was the product of the growth of national feeling, recalculations of middle-class interests, diplomacy, war, and struggles between the regime and its opponents.

Despite its decisive defeat in 1848, German liberalism had revived within a decade, in the face of considerable odds. The staunchly antirevolutionary King Frederick William had granted a Prussian constitution that established a bicameral (two-house) parliament, with the lower lower house elected by universal male suffrage. A series of edicts, however, modified the electoral system to reinforce hierarchies of wealth and power. The new provisions divided voters into three classes based on the amount of taxes they paid, and their votes were apportioned accordingly. (This new system was considered an improvement over the traditional practice of representation by estates, which had been dismantled in France in 1789.) Thus, the relatively few wealthy voters who together paid one third of the country's taxes elected one third of the legislators, meaning a large landowner or industrialist exercised nearly a hundred times the voting power of a common workingman. In 1858 William I, who had led troops against the revolutionaries of 1848 in his youth, became prince regent of Prussia. (William became king in 1861 and ruled until 1888.) Although a notoriously conservative state, Prussia was not a monolith. A decade of industrial growth had expanded the size and confidence of the middle class. By the late 1850s, Prussia had an active liberal intelligensia, a thoughtful and engaged press, and a liberal civil service dedicated to political and economic modernization. These changes helped to forge a liberal political movement that won a majority in elections to the lower house and could confidently confront the king.

The particular bone of contention (though hardly the only issue) between liberals and the king was military spending. William wanted to expand the standing army, reduce the role of reserve forces (a more middle-class group), and, above all, ensure that military matters were not subject to parliamentary control. Opponents in Parliament suspected the king of making the military his own private force, or a state within a state. Between 1859 and 1862 relations deteriorated, and when liberals' protests went unanswered, they refused to approve the regular budget. Faced with a crisis, in 1862 William named Otto von Bismarck minister-president of Prussia. (A prime minister answers to Parliament; Bismarck did not.) This crucial moment in Prussian domestic politics became a decisive turning point in the history of German nationhood.

Born into the Junker class of conservative, land-owning aristocrats, Bismarck not only supported the monarchy during the revolutionary period of 1848–1849, he had fiercely opposed the liberal movement. He was not a nationalist. He was before all else a Prussian. He did not institute domestic reforms because he favored the "rights"

WHY DID THE EFFORTS TO UNIFY ITALY AND GERMANY SUCCEED DURING THE 1860S?

BUILDING THE NATION-STATE   761

TOWARD THE UNIFICATION OF GERMANY

This map outlines the stages leading to the unification of the German state. How did the German state of Prussia expand at the expense of Poland and the Austrian empire? How did the nineteenth-century wars with France strengthen the emergent Prussian state? Examine closely the fragmented states of the region. What challenges did Bismarck face in building a unified Germany? What cultural and historical factors could he use to his advantage?

of a particular group, but because he thought that these policies would unify and strengthen Prussia. When he maneuvered to bring other German states under Prussian domination, he did so not in pursuit of a grand German design, but because he believed that union in some form

was inevitable and that Prussia had to seize the initiative. Bismarck happily acknowledged that he admired power and that he considered himself destined for greatness. At one point he had considered a career in the military, a common choice for someone with aristocratic origins, and he later regretted that he was compelled to serve his country from behind a desk rather than at the front. Whatever his post, he intended to command and to turn opportunities to his advantage. "I want to play the tune the way it sounds good to me or not at all," he declared. He had a reputation for cynicism, arrogance, and uninhibited frankness in expressing his views. Yet the Latin phrase he fondly quoted distills his more careful assessment of politics, and of the relationship between even masterful individuals and history: "Man cannot create or control the tide of time, he can only move in the same direction and try to direct it."

In Prussia, Bismarck defied parliamentary opposition. When the liberal majority refused to levy taxes, he dissolved Parliament and collected them anyway, claiming that the constitution, whatever its purposes, had not been designed to subvert the state. His most decisive actions, however, were in foreign policy. Once opposed to nationalism, Bismarck skillfully played the national card to preempt his liberal opponents at home and to make German nation building an accomplishment—and an extension—of Prussian authority.

The other "German" power was Austria, which wielded considerable influence within the German Confederation and especially over the largely Catholic regions in the south. Bismarck saw a stark contrast between Austrian and Prussian interests, believed that the Confederation had outlived its usefulness, and skillfully exploited Austria's economic disadvantages and the Habsburgs' internal ethnic struggles. He inflamed a long-smoldering dispute with Denmark over Schleswig and Holstein, two provinces peopled by Germans and Danes and claimed by both the German Confederation and Denmark. Liberal-nationalist feeling about the provinces ran high in the German Confederation, and a German liberal noble who claimed to be the rightful heir to Schleswig-Holstein became a minor public hero. In 1864, the Danish king attempted to annex the provinces, prompting a German nationalist outcry. Bismarck cast the conflict as a Prussian matter, and persuaded Austria to join Prussia in a war against Denmark. The war was short, and it forced the Danish ruler to cede the two provinces to Austria and Prussia. As Bismarck hoped, the victorious alliance promptly fell apart. In 1866 casting Prussia as the defender of larger German interests, he declared war on Austria. The conflict, known as the Seven Weeks' War, ended in Prussian victory. Austria gave up all claims to Schleswig and Holstein, surrendered Venetia to the Italians, and agreed to dissolve the German Confederation. In its place Bismarck created the North German Confederation, a union of all the German states north of the Main River.

Bismarck Sweeping Away the Stubborn Germans.
Bismarck helped provoke the Franco-Prussian War of 1870–71 by cultivating the perception that France was a threat to Germany. This caricature reads "Here is Bismarck, still with his big broom, who scolds and picks up all of the recalcitrant Germans. Let's go! Go or die! Faster than that! Or the French will eat your sauerkraut!"

Bismarck "played power politics with an eye to public opinion." Both wars had strong public support, and Prussian victories weakened liberal opposition to the king and his president-minister. In the aftermath of the Austrian defeat, Prussian liberals gave up their battle over budgets, the military, and constitutional provisions. Bismarck also neutralized his opponents by other means. He admired Napoleon III's use of plebiscites to strengthen his regime, and like the French emperor sought support among the masses. He understood that Germans did not necessarily support business elites, the bureaucracies of their own small states, or the Austrian Habsburgs. The constitution of the North German Confederation gave the appearance of a more liberal political body, with a bicameral legislature, freedom of the press, and universal male suffrage in the lower house. Its structure, however, gave Prussia and the con-

WHY DID THE EFFORTS TO UNIFY ITALY AND GERMANY SUCCEED DURING THE 1860S?

BUILDING THE NATION-STATE 763

servative emperor a decisive advantage in the North German Confederation—and in the soon to be expanded empire (see Chapter 20).

The final step in the completion of German unity was the Franco-Prussian War of 1870–1871. Bismarck hoped that a conflict with France would arouse German nationalism in Bavaria, Württemberg, and other southern states still outside the Confederation and overcome their historic wariness of Prussia. A diplomatic tempest concerning the right of the Hohenzollerns (Prussia's ruling family) to occupy the Spanish throne created an opportunity to foment a Franco-German misunderstanding. King William agreed to meet with the French ambassador at the resort spa of Ems in Prussia to discuss the Spanish succession. William initially acquiesced in French demands, but when the French blundered by asking for "perpetual exclusion" of the Hohenzollern family from the Spanish throne, Bismarck seized his opportunity. He edited a telegraph from the kaiser and released portions of it to the press so as to make it appear that King William had rebuffed the ambassador. Once the redacted report reached France, the nation reacted with a call for war. Prussia echoed the call, and Bismarck published evidence that he claimed proved French designs on the Rhineland.

As soon as war was declared, the south German states rallied to Prussia's side. The conflict was quickly over. No European powers came to France's aid. Austria, the most likely candidate, remained weakened by its recent war with Prussia. The Hungarian Magyars welcomed a strengthened Prussia, for the weaker Austria was as a "German" power, the stronger would be the Magyar claims to power sharing in the empire. In the battlefield, France could not match Prussia's professionally trained and superbly equipped forces. The war began in July and ended in September with the defeat of the French and the capture of Napoleon III at Sedan in France. Insurrectionary forces in Paris continued to hold out against the Germans through the winter of 1870–1871, but the French imperial government collapsed.

On January 18, 1871, in the Hall of Mirrors at Versailles, symbol of the powerful past of French absolutism, the German empire was proclaimed. All the German states that had not already been absorbed into the Prussian fold, except Austria, declared their allegiance to William I, henceforth emperor or kaiser. Four months later, at Frankfurt, a treaty between the French and Germans ceded the border region of Alsace to the new German empire, and forced the French to pay an indemnity of 5 billion francs. Prussia accounted for 60 percent of the new state's territory and population. The Prussian kaiser, prime minister, army, and most of the bureaucracy remained intact, now reconfigured as the German nation-state. This was not the new nation for which Prussian liberals had hoped. It marked a "revolution from above" rather than from below. Still, the more optimistic believed that the German empire would evolve in a different political direction, that they could eventually "extend freedom through unity."

> On January 18, 1871, in the Hall of Mirrors at Versailles, symbol of the powerful past of French absolutism, the German empire was proclaimed.

THE STATE AND NATIONALITY: CENTRIFUGAL FORCES IN THE AUSTRIAN EMPIRE

Germany emerged from the 1860s a stronger, unified nation. The Austrian empire faced a very different situation, with different resources, and emerged a weakened, precariously balanced, multiethnic Dual Monarchy, also called Austria-Hungary.

As we have seen, ethnic nationalism was a powerful force in the Habsburg monarchy in 1848. Yet the Habsburg state, with a combination of military repression and tactics that divided its enemies, had proved more powerful. It abolished serfdom but made few other concessions to its opponents. The Hungarians, who had nearly won independence in the spring of 1848, were essentially reconquered. The Imperial Council, which developed into a House of Lords, nominally accommodated representatives of the nationalities. Other developments were also intended to strengthen the Habsburg state. Administrative reforms

CHRONOLOGY	
UNIFICATION OF GERMANY, 1854–1871	
Crimean War	1854–1856
Bismarck becomes prime minister	1862
Danish War	1864
Seven Weeks' War	1866
Franco-Prussian War	1870–1871

created a new and more uniform legal system, rationalized taxation, and imposed a single-language policy that favored German. The issue of managing ethnic relations, however, only grew more difficult. Through the 1850s and 1860s the subject nationalities, as they were often called, bitterly protested the powerlessness of their local Diets (or parliaments), military repression, cultural disenfranchisement, and electoral districts that reduced their representation. The Czechs in Bohemia, for instance, grew increasingly alienated by policies that favored the German minority of the province and increasingly insistent on their Slavic identity—a movement welcomed by Russia, willing enough to become the sponsor of a broad pan-Slavism. The Hungarians, or Magyars, the most powerful of the subject nationalities, sought to reclaim the autonomy they had glimpsed in 1848.

In this context, Austria's damaging defeats at the hands of Piedmont-Sardinia in 1859 and Prussia in 1866 became especially significant. The 1866 war in particular forced the emperor Francis Joseph to renegotiate the very structure of the empire. In order to stave off a revolution by the Hungarians, Francis Joseph agreed to a new federal structure in the form of the Dual Monarchy. Austria-Hungary had a common system of taxation, a common army, and made foreign and military policy together. Francis Joseph was emperor of Austria and king of Hungary. But internal and constitutional affairs were separated. The Ausgleich, or Settlement, allowed the Hungarians to establish their own constitution, their own legislature, and their own capital, combining the cities of Buda and Pest.

What of the other nationalities? The official policy of the Dual Monarchy stated that they were not to be discriminated against, and that they could use their own languages. Official policy was only loosely enforced. More important, elevating the Hungarians and conferring on them alone the benefits of political nationhood could only exacerbate relations with other groups. On the Austrian side of the Dual Monarchy, minority nationalities such as the Poles, Czechs, and Slovenes resented their second-class status. On the Hungarian side, the regime embarked on a project of Magyarization, attempting to make the state, the civil service, and the schools more thoroughly Hungarian—an effort that did not sit well with Serbs and Croats.

It was impossible, then, to speak of national unification in the Habsburg lands. The Austrian emperor remained deeply opposed to nationalism, considering it, rightly, a centrifugal force that would destroy his king-

dom. Unlike the governments of France, England, Italy, or Germany, the Habsburgs did not seek to build a nation state based on a common cultural identity. It tried instead to build a state and administrative structure strong enough to keep the pieces from spinning off, playing different minorities off against each other, and conceding autonomy only when essential. As the nineteenth century unfolded, subject nationalities would appeal to other powers—Serbia, Russia, the Ottomans—and this balancing act would become more difficult.

NATION AND STATE BUILDING IN RUSSIA, THE UNITED STATES, AND CANADA

What were the similarities between slavery and serfdom?

The challenges of nationalism and nation building also occupied Russia, the United States, and Canada. In all three countries, nation building entailed territorial and economic expansion, the incorporation of new peoples, and, in Russia and the United States, contending with the enormous problems of slavery and serfdom.

TERRITORY, THE STATE, AND SERFDOM: RUSSIA

Serfdom in Russia, which had been legally formalized in 1649, had begun to draw significant protest from the intelligentsia under the reign of Catherine the Great (1762–1796). After 1789, and especially after 1848, the abolition of serfdom elsewhere in Europe made the issue more urgent. Abolishing serfdom became part of the larger project of building Russia as a modern nation. How that should happen was the subject of much debate. Two schools of thought emerged. The "Slavophiles," or Romantic nationalists, sought to preserve Russia's distinctive features. They idealized traditional Russian culture and the peasant commune, rejecting Western secularism, urban commercialism, and bourgeois culture. In contrast, the "westernizers"

The Emancipation of the Serfs. This engraving depicts officials delivering the formal decree liberating serfs. A massive reform granting legal rights to millions of people, emancipation was undermined by the payments serfs owed to their former owners.

wished to see Russia adopt European developments in science, technology, and education, which they believed to be the foundation for Western liberalism and the protection of individual rights. Both groups agreed that serfdom must be abolished. The Russian nobility, however tenaciously opposed emancipation. Tangled debates about how lords would be compensated for the loss of "their" serfs, and how emancipated serfs would survive without full-scale land redistribution, also checked progress on the issue. The Crimean War (see below) broke the impasse. In its aftermath, Alexander II (1855–1881) forced the issue. Worried that the persistence of serfdom had sapped Russian strength and contributed to its defeat in the war, and persuaded that serfdom would only continue to prompt violent conflict, he ended serfdom by decree in 1861.

The emancipation decree of 1861 was a reform of massive scope, but paradoxically, it produced limited change. It granted legal rights to some 22 million serfs and authorized their title to a portion of the land they had worked. It also required the state to compensate landowners for the properties they relinquished. Large-scale landowners vastly inflated their compensation claims, however, and managed to retain much of the most profitable acreage for themselves. As a result, the land granted to peasants was often of poor quality and insufficient to sustain themselves and their families. Moreover, the newly liberated serfs had to pay in installments for their land, which was not in fact granted to them individually, but rather to a village commune that collected their payments. As a result, the pattern of rural life in Russia did not change drastically. The system of payment kept peasants in the villages—not as free-standing farmers, but as agricultural laborers for their former masters.

While the Russian state undertook reforms, it also expanded its territory. After mid-century, the Russians pressed east and south. They invaded and conquered several independent Islamic kingdoms along the former "Silk Road" and expanded into Siberia in search of

THE ABOLITION OF SERFDOM IN RUSSIA

Tsar Alexander II's Decree Emancipating the Serfs, 1861

The abolition of serfdom was central to Tsar Alexander II's program of modernization and reform after the Crimean War. Emancipated serfs were now allowed to own their land, ending centuries of peasant bondage. The decree, however, emphasized the tsar's benevolence and the nobility's generosity—not peasant rights. The government did not want emancipation to bring revolution to the countryside; it sought to reinforce the state's authority, the landowners' power, and the peasants' obligations. After spelling out the detailed provisions for emancipation, the decree added:

And We place Our hope in the good sense of Our people.

When word of the Government's plan to abolish the law of bondage [serfdom] reached peasants unprepared for it, there arose a partial misunderstanding. Some [peasants] thought about freedom and forgot about obligations. But the general good sense [of the people] was not disturbed in the conviction that anyone freely enjoying the goods of society correspondingly owes it to the common good to fulfill certain obligations, [a conviction held] both by natural reason and by Christian law, according to which "every soul must be subject to the governing authorities." . . .

Rights legally acquired by the landlords cannot be taken from them without a decent return or [their] voluntary concession; and that it would be contrary to all justice to make use of the lords' land without bearing the corresponding obligation.

And now We hopefully expect that the bonded people, as a new future opens before them, will understand and accept with gratitude the important sacrifice made by the Well-born Nobility for the improvement of their lives.

James Cracraft, ed., *Major Problems in the History of Imperial Russia* (Lexington, Mass.: D. C. Heath, 1994), pp. 340–344.

EMANCIPATION: THE VIEW FROM BELOW

Emancipation did not solve problems in the Russian countryside. On the contrary, it unleashed a torrent of protest, including complaints from peasants that nobles were undermining attempts to reform. These petitions detail the struggles that came in the wake of emancipation in two villages.

PETITION FROM PEASANTS IN PODOSINOVKA
(VORONEZH PROVINCE) TO ALEXANDER II, MAY 1863

The most merciful manifesto of Your Imperial Majesty from 19 February 1861, with the published rules, put a limit to the enslavement of the people in blessed Russia. But some former serfowners—who desire not to im-

prove the peasants' life, but to oppress and ruin them—apportion land contrary to the laws, choose the best land from all the fields for themselves, and give the poor peasants . . . the worst and least usable lands.

To this group of squires must be counted our own, Anna Mikhailovna Raevskaia. . . . Of our fields and resources, she chose the best places from amidst our strips, and, like a cooking ring in a hearth, carved off 300 dessiatines [measures of land] for herself. . . . But our community refused to accept so ruinous an allotment and requested that we be given an allotment in accordance with the local Statute. . . . The peace arbitrator . . . and the police chief . . . slandered us before the governor, alleging that we were rioting and that it is impossible for them to enter our village.

The provincial governor believed this lie and sent 1,200 soldiers of the penal command to our village. . . . Without any cause, our village priest Father Peter—rather than give an uplifting pastoral exhortation to stop the spilling of innocent blood—joined these reptiles, with the unanimous incitement of the authorities. . . . They summoned nine township heads and their aides from other townships. . . . In their presence, the provincial governor—without making any investigation and without interrogating a single person—ordered that the birch rods be brought and that the punishment commence, which was carried out with cruelty and mercilessness. They punished up to 200 men and women; 80 people were at four levels (with 500, 400, 300 and 200 blows); some received lesser punishment . . . and when the inhuman punishment of these innocent people had ended, the provincial governor said: "If you find the land unsuitable, I do not forbid you to file petitions wherever you please," and then left. . . .

We dare to implore you, Orthodox emperor and our merciful father, not to reject the petition of a community with 600 souls, including wives and children. Order with your tsarist word that our community be allotted land . . . as the law dictates without selecting the best sections of fields and meadows, but in straight lines. . . . [Order that] the meadows and haylands along the river Elan be left to our community without any restriction; these will enable us to feed our cattle and smaller livestock, which are necessary for our existence.

Gregory L. Freeze, ed., *From Supplication to Revolution: A Documentary Social History of Imperial Russia* (New York: Oxford University Press, 1988), pp. 170–173.

PETITION FROM PEASANTS IN BALASHOV DISTRICT TO GRAND DUKE CONSTANTIN NIKOLAEVICH, JANUARY 25, 1862

Your Imperial Excellency! Most gracious sire! Grand Duke Konstantin Nikolaevich! . . .

After being informed of the Imperial manifesto on the emancipation of peasants from serfdom on 1861 . . . we received this [news] with jubilation. . . . But from this moment, our squire ordered that the land be cut off from the entire township. But this is absolutely intolerable for us: it not only denies us profit, but threatens us with a catastrophic future. He began to hold repeated meetings and [tried to] force us to sign that we agreed to accept the above land allotment. But, upon seeing so unexpected a change, and bearing in mind the gracious manifesto, we refused. . . . After assembling the entire township, they tried to force us into making illegal signatures accepting the land cut-offs. But when they saw that this did not succeed, they had a company of soldiers sent in. . . . Then [Colonel] Globbe came from their midst, threatened us with exile to Siberia, and ordered the soldiers to strip the peasants and to punish seven people by flogging in the most inhuman manner. They still have not regained consciousness.

Gregory L. Freeze, ed., *From Supplication to Revolution: A Documentary Social History of Imperial Russia* (New York: Oxford University Press, 1988), pp. 170–173.

natural resources. Russian diplomacy wrung various commercial concessions from the Chinese that led to the founding of the Siberian city of Vladivostok in 1860. Racial, ethnic, and religious differences made governing a daunting task. In most cases, the Russian state did not try to assimilate the populations of the new territories: an acceptance of ethnic particularity was a pragmatic response to the difficulties of governing such a heterogeneous population. When the state did make sporadic efforts to impose Russian culture, the results were disastrous. Whether power was wielded by the nineteenth-century tsars or, later, by the Soviet Union, powerful centrifugal forces pulled against genuine unification. Expansion helped Russia create a vast empire that was geographically of one piece, but by no means one nation.

TERRITORY, THE NATION-STATE, AND SLAVERY: THE UNITED STATES

The American Revolution had bequeathed to the United States a loose union of slave and free states, tied together in part by a commitment to territorial expansion. The so-called Jeffersonian Revolution combined democratic aspirations with a drive to expand the nation's boundaries. Leaders of the movement, under the Democratic-Republican president Thomas Jefferson (1801–1809), campaigned to add a Bill of Rights to the Constitution and were almost exclusively responsible for its success. Though they supported, in principle, the separation of powers, they believed in the supremacy of the people's representatives and viewed with alarm attempts of the executive and judicial branches to increase their power. They supported a political system based on an aristocracy of "virtue and talent," in which respect for personal liberty would be the guiding principle. They opposed the establishment of a national religion and special privilege, whether of birth or of wealth. Yet the Jeffersonian vision of the republic rested on the independence of yeomen farmers, and the independence and prosperity of those farmers depended on the availability of new lands. This made territorial expansion, as exemplified by the Louisiana Purchase in 1803, central to Jeffersonian America. Expansion brought complications. While

AMERICAN EXPANSION IN THE EARLY NINETEENTH CENTURY

A crucial turning point in American westward expansion came in 1803, when the Louisiana Purchase transferred a vast expanse of land from Napoleon I's France to the United States. Napoleon had failed to reconquer Saint-Domingue and restore slavery there, and he urgently needed to regroup his forces for war in Europe. Both factors persuaded him to give up visions of a North American empire. How did the withdrawal of a major colonial power reshape American attitudes about the western frontier? What further issues did the Louisiana Purchase raise?

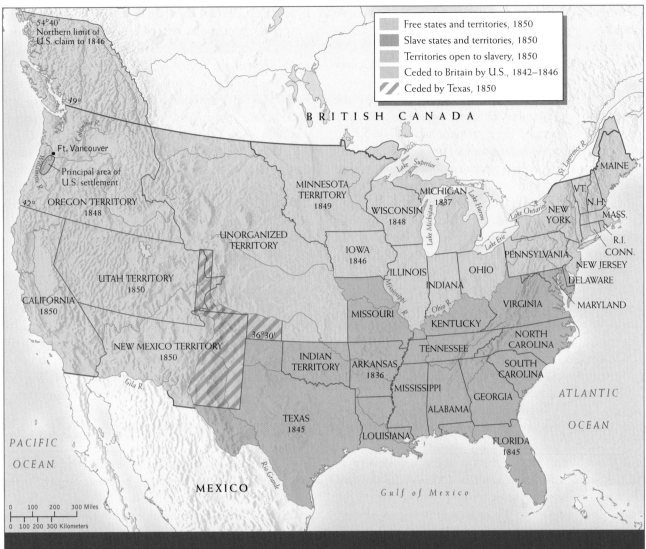

	Free states and territories, 1850
	Slave states and territories, 1850
	Territories open to slavery, 1850
	Ceded to Britain by U.S., 1842–1846
	Ceded by Texas, 1850

AMERICAN EXPANSION IN THE LATE NINETEENTH CENTURY

Note the stages by which American settlement progressed across the North American continent, and the organization of newly acquired territory by the American government. How was American expansion different from European colonialism? How was it similar? What considerations informed the compromises made by the American government in establishing less ambitious northern borders? Why were the Utah and New Mexico territories opened to slavery even though the West and Southwest had previously been considered free? What role did California statehood play in such considerations?

it did provide land for many yeomen farmers in the North and South, it also added millions of acres of prime cotton land, thus extending the empire of slavery. The purchase of the port of New Orleans made lands in the South well worth developing, but led the American republic forcibly to remove Native Americans from the Old South west of the Mississippi River. This process of expansion and expropriation stretched

from Jefferson's administration through the age of Jackson, or the 1840s.

Under Andrew Jackson (1829–1837), the Democrats (as some of the Democratic-Republicans were now called) transformed the circumscribed liberalism of the Jeffersonians. They campaigned to extend the suffrage to all white males; they argued that all office-holders should be elected rather than appointed; and they sought the frequent rotation of men in positions of political power—a doctrine that permitted politicians to use patronage to build national political parties. Moreover, the Jacksonian vision of democracy and nationhood carried over into a crusade to incorporate more territories into the republic. It was the United States' "Manifest Destiny," wrote a New York editor, "to overspread the continent allotted by Providence for the free development of our yearly multiplying millions." That "overspreading" brought Oregon and Washington into the Union through a compromise with the British, and brought Arizona, Texas, New Mexico, Utah, Nevada, and California through war with Mexico—all of which led to the wholesale expropriation of Native American lands. In the North, these changes heightened belief in "democratic rule" and "free-labor"; in the South they fueled a sense of isolation and deepened white southerners' commitments to an economy and society based on plantation slavery. Ultimately, the changes pushed southern political leaders toward secession.

Territorial expansion made it impossible for the United States government to avoid the question of slavery. The Haitian revolution had begun the long and uneven process of dismantling slavery. Great Britain ended the transatlantic slave trade in 1807, as did the United States; Britain abolished slavery in 1838. Spanish America abolished slavery in the first decades of the nineteenth century; France during the revolution of 1848. In the face of growing antislavery sentiment, southern planters, like Russian serf owners, continued to insist that without the slave system they would go bankrupt. Like the Russian nobility, they responded to abolitionists with arguments based on theories of inherited inferiority and warnings of the chaos they believed abolition would bring. As the country expanded west, North and South engaged in a protracted tug of war about whether new states were to be "free" or "slave." The failure of a series of elaborate compromises led to the outbreak of the Civil War in 1861.

The protracted and costly struggle—a first experience of the horrors of modern war—decisively transformed the nation. First, it abolished slavery. Second, it established the preeminence of the national government over states' rights. The Fourteenth Amendment to the Constitution stated specifically that all Americans were citizens of the United States, and not of an individual state or territory. In declaring that no citizen was to be deprived of life, liberty, or property without due process of law, it established that "due process" was to be defined by the national, not the state or territorial, government. Third, in the aftermath of the Civil War, the United States' economy expanded with stunning rapidity. In 1865, there were thirty-five thousand miles of railroad track in the United States; by 1900, there were almost two hundred thousand. Industrial and agricultural production rose, putting the United States in a position to compete with Great Britain. As we will see later on, American industrialists, bankers, and retailers introduced innovations in assembly-line manufacturing, corporate organization, and advertising that startled their European counterparts and gave the United States new power in world politics. These developments were all part of the process of nation building. They did not overcome deep racial, regional, or class divides. Though the war brought the South back into the Union, the rise of northern capitalism magnified the "backwardness" of the South as an underdeveloped agricultural region whose wealth was extracted by northern industrialists. The railroad corporations, which pieced together the national infrastructure, became the classic foe of labor and agrarian reformers. In these ways, the Civil War laid the foundations for the modern American nation-state.

TERRITORIAL EXPANSION: CANADA

The expansion of the United States also had an important effect on its neighbor to the north. In 1763, the Treaty of Paris had passed the territories of New France to Britain. Throughout the nineteenth century, relations were strained between the French-speaking, largely Roman Catholic inhabitants of what came to be called Québec and the more recently arrived, largely Protestant British settlers. However fragile, unity among European settlers was forged, as in the United States, by westward expansion, which dispossessed native populations and forced their resettlement in separate territories. The drive westward, which made available vast wheat lands and timber resources in the Canadian prairies and forests, fueled demands for greater autonomy. The fear of falling prey to the United States' expansionist drive, however, made English-speaking Canadians less eager to break completely with British rule. In 1867, an Act of Parliament gave Canada independence, but the country remained a "dominion" within the British Commonwealth. With dominion status in place, the Canadian government, like its American counterpart, pursued a policy of economic expansion and settlement. It annexed territories, offered attractive homestead grants to lure European immigrants, policed settler-Indian relations, and built vast

HOW DID JOURNALISTS' DEPICTIONS OF THE CRIMEAN WAR REFLECT CULTURAL TRENDS?

EASTERN QUESTIONS AND INTERNATIONAL RELATIONS   771

railroads. The government encouraged economic developments that connected Canadian cities, forging networks independent of the United States. Canada's new railways linked the vast wheatfields in the west with seaports that would ship that wheat to Canada's major overseas buyer, Great Britain. In culture, commerce, and matters of national defense, ties between independent Canada and the "mother country" remained strong.

EASTERN QUESTIONS AND INTERNATIONAL RELATIONS

How did journalists' depictions of the Crimean War reflect cultural trends?

During the nineteenth century, questions of national identity and international power were inextricable from contests over territory. War and diplomacy drew and redrew boundaries as European nations groped toward a tenable balance of power. The rise of new powers, principally the German empire, posed one set of challenges to Continental order. The waning power of older regimes proved equally destabilizing. The Crimean War, which lasted from 1854 to 1856, was a particularly gruesome attempt to cope with the most serious such collapse. As the Ottoman empire lost its grip on its provinces in southeastern Europe, the "Eastern Question" of who would benefit from Ottoman weakness drew Europe into war. At stake were not only raw territorial gains, but also strategic interests, alliances, and the balance of power in Europe. And though the war occurred before the unification of the German and Italian states, it structured the system of Great Power politics that guided Europe until (and indeed toward) the First World War.

THE CRIMEAN WAR, 1854–1856

The root causes of the war lay in the "Eastern Question." The crisis that provoked it, however, involved religion, namely French and Russian claims to protect religious minorities and the Holy Places of Jerusalem within the Muslim Ottoman Empire. In 1853 a three way quarrel between France (on behalf of Roman Catholics), Russia (representing Eastern Orthodox Christians) and Turkey devolved into a Russian confrontation with the Turkish sultan. Confident that Turkey would be unable to resist, concerned that other powers might take advantage of Turkish weakness, and persuaded (mistakenly) that they had British support, the Russians moved troops into the Ottoman governed territories of Moldavia and Walachia. (These territories lie north and west of the point where the Danube river meets the Black Sea.) In October, 1853, also persuaded they would be supported by the British, Turkey declared war on Russia. The war became a disaster for the Turks, who lost their fleet at the battle of Sinope in November. But Russia's success alarmed the British and the French, who considered Russian expansion a threat to their interests in the Balkans, the eastern Mediterranean, and, for the British, the route to India. Determined to check that expansion, France and Britain each declared war on Russia in March, 1854. In September, they landed on the Russian peninsula of Crimea, headed for the Russian naval base at Sevastopol, to which they laid siege. France, Britain, and the Ottomans were joined in 1855 by the small but ambitious Italian state of Piedmont-Sardinia, all fighting against the Russians. This was the closest Europe had come to a general war since 1815.

The war was relatively short, but its conduct was devastating. Conditions on the Crimean Peninsula were dire, and the disastrous mismanagement of supplies and hygiene by the British and French led to epidemics among the troops. At least as many soldiers died from typhus or cholera as in combat. The fighting was bitter, marked by such notoriously inept strategies as the British "charge of the Light Brigade," in which a British cavalry unit was slaughtered by massed Russian artillery. Vast battles pitted tens of thousands of British and French troops against Russian formations, combat that was often settled with bayonets. Despite the disciplined toughness of the British and French troops, and despite their nations' dominance of the seas around Crimea, the Russians denied them a clear victory. Sevastopol, under siege for nearly a year, did not fall until September, 1855. The bitter, unsatisfying conflict was ended by treaty in 1856.

For the French and Sardinians, the bravery of their soldiers bolstered positive national sentiments at home; for the British and Russians, however, the poorly managed war provoked waves of intense criticism. As far as international relations were concerned, the peace settlement was a severe setback for Russia, whose influence in the Balkans was drastically curbed. The provinces of Moldavia and Walachia were united as Romania and became an independent nation. And Austria's refusal to come to the aid of Russia cost it the support of that powerful erstwhile ally. The Crimean War embarrassed

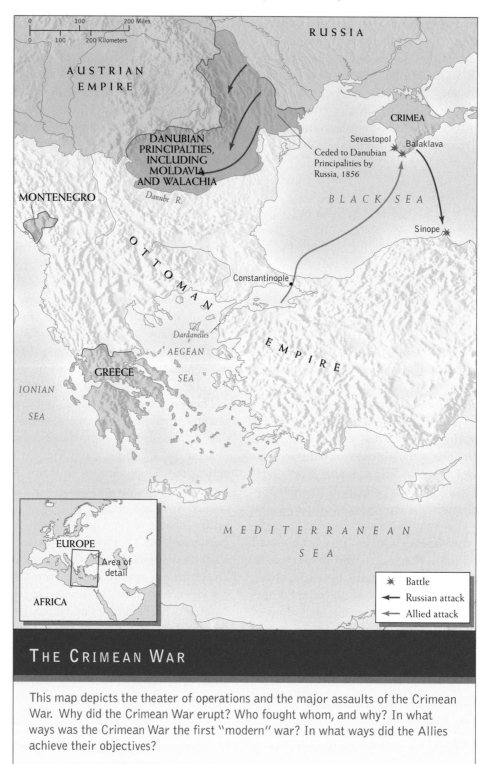

THE CRIMEAN WAR

This map depicts the theater of operations and the major assaults of the Crimean War. Why did the Crimean War erupt? Who fought whom, and why? In what ways was the Crimean War the first "modern" war? In what ways did the Allies achieve their objectives?

France and left Russia and Austria considerably weaker, opening an advantage for Bismarck in the 1860s, as we saw above.

The Crimean War was important in other ways as well. Though fought largely with the same methods and mentalities employed in the Napoleonic Wars forty years earlier, the war brought a handful of innovations that forecast the direction of modern warfare. It saw the first significant use rifled muskets, underwater mines, and trench warfare, as well as the first tactical use of railroads and telegraphs. In addition, the war was covered by the first modern war correspondents and photo-

HOW DID JOURNALISTS' DEPICTIONS OF THE CRIMEAN WAR REFLECT CULTURAL TRENDS?

EASTERN QUESTIONS AND INTERNATIONAL RELATIONS   773

journalists, making it the most "public" war to date. Reports from the theater of war were sent "live" by telegraph to Britain and France with objective and sobering detail; the (London) *Times* reporter William Howard Russell, for instance, heaped criticism on the government for the deplorable conditions its soldiers endured. The care and supply of the troops became national scandals in the popular press, prompting dramatic changes in the military's administrative and logistical systems, and making heroes of individual doctors and nurses such as Florence Nightingale. The British government and commercial publishers both sent photographers to document the war's progress, and perhaps also to counter charges that troops were undersupplied and malnourished. Roger Fenton, the most prominent and prolific of these war photographers, employed the new medium to capture the grim realities of camp life, though technological limitations and political considerations kept him from photographing the more gruesome carnage of the battlefield. Nonetheless, Fenton's photographs lacked the elegant distortions of paintings and engravings and thus introduced a new level of realism and immediacy to the public's conception of war.

REALISM: "DEMOCRACY IN ART"

The journalistic reporting from the Crimean War was in part remarkable because it avoided the heroic and jingoistic language to which nineteenth-century readers were accustomed. In this way, it reflected a dominant cultural trend of the mid-nineteenth century: the rise of the artistic movement known as realism. In both painting and literature, realism signaled a strict rejection of artistic "conventions" and ready-made formulas in favor of what artists saw as more honest, objective, and authentic representations of the world. Whereas Romanticism had sought higher truths, with an emphasis on emotion and imagination, realism trained its gaze on empirical reality. As the French painter Gustave Courbet (1819–1877) claimed, "[T]he art of painting can only consist of the representation of objects which are visible and tangible for the artist."

Realism's focus on the material world owed much to the ideals of nineteenth-century science, which seemed to cut through traditional moral and philosophical concerns in pursuit of empirical facts. The French novelist Émile Zola (1840–1902), who along with Honoré de

The Stone Breakers by Gustave Courbet, 1849. Courbet was a French Realist painter who depicted everyday men and women in an honest and unromantic manner. Considered one of his most imortant works, this painting of two ordinary peasants building a road was destroyed in Dresden during World War II.

Balzac and Gustave Flaubert was among the most prominent realist writers, aimed for an exact, scientific presentation of society. He read Darwin's theories of evolution and often grimly cast his characters as victims of heredity and social circumstance. Like many realists, Zola was also motivated by a powerful sympathy for common people and a desire for social justice. His novels confronted the many social problems of working-class industrial life—alcoholism, poverty, hunger, strikes—as did the famous works of Charles Dickens, which included vivid descriptions of urban squalor, tempered by a humanitarian spirit. Realist painters also shared this sympathy for the common man (and woman) and they shocked refined sensibilities by making beggars, miners, laundry women, railroad workers, prostitutes, and peasants the subjects of their work.

Inherent in the realists' sympathies for the poor and dispossessed was a sharp critique of contemporary society. Paralleling demands for the democratization of politics and society, artists and writers called for "democracy in art," the phrase Courbet used to describe Realism. Born in the wake of the 1848 upheavals, realism was often considered a direct manifestation of the revolutionary spirit, and indeed many of its proponents were self-conscious political radicals. Critics scornfully noted that "the vile multitude, chased out of politics, [was] reappearing in painting." Yet realism was also marked by the disillusionment that characterized the postrevolutionary era of conservative reaction. The movement's politics were ambivalent. What united the realists was a belief that the lower classes had a right to literary and artistic representation, and that this required a meticulous observation of characters and their environment.

In Russia, writers felt similarly compelled to take on social and political issues such as poverty, crime, and gender roles, but they joined those topics to larger philosophical themes, creating a distinctive hybrid of realism and Romanticism. Ivan Turgenev, who spent much of his life in France, was the first Russian novelist to become well known to western Europe. His brooding novel *Fathers and Sons* (1861), which condemned the existing social order, inspired a group of young Russian intellectuals who sought to reform society by abandoning their parents' emphasis on status, wealth, and leisure, turning instead to serve "the people." Feodor Dostoevsky (1821–1811), whose novels mirrored his harrowing personal life, explored the psychology of anguished minds with broad sympathy and morbid intensity. The third outstanding novelist of the late nineteenth century, Leo Tolstoy, examined Russian society in such epic novels as *War and Peace* (1862–1869) which focused on the fate of individuals caught up in powerful movements of history.

CONCLUSION

The twenty years between 1850 and 1870 were a time of intense nation building in the Western world. The unification of Germany and Italy changed the map of Europe, with important consequences for the balance of power. The emergence of the United States as a major power also had international ramifications. For old as well as new nation-states, economic development and political transformation—often on a very large scale—were important means of increasing and securing the state's power. Yet demands for more representative government, the abolition of privilege, and land reform had to be reckoned with, as did the systems of slavery and serfdom. Trailing the banner of nationhood was an explosive set of questions about how to balance the power and interests of minorities and majorities, of the wealthy and poor, of the powerful and the dispossessed. In short, nation building forced a transformation of relations between states and their citizens.

Yet these transformations were anything but predictable. Nationalism showed itself to be a volatile, erratic, and malleable force during the mid-nineteenth century. It provided much of the fuel for revolutionary movements in 1848, but it also helped to tear their movements apart, undermining liberal gains. Those who had linked their democratic goals to the rise of new nation-states were sorely disappointed. In the aftermath of the defeated revolutions, most nation building took a conservative tack. Nationalism came to serve the needs of statesmen and bureaucrats who did not seek an "awakening of peoples," and who had serious reservations about popular sovereignty. For them, nations simply represented modern, organized, and stronger states. The upshot of this fit of nation building was a period of remarkable stability on the Continent, which ushered in an era of unprecedented capitalist and imperial expansion. The antagonisms unleashed by German unification and the crumbling of the Ottoman empire would reemerge, however, in the Great Power politics that precipitated the First World War.

KEY TERMS

Frankfurt Assembly

pan-Slavism

Giuseppe Mazzini

John Stuart Mill

Giuseppe Garibaldi

Camillo Benso di Cavour

Realpolitik

Otto von Bismarck

Crimean War

realism

SELECTED READINGS

Beales, Derek. *The Risorgimento and the Unification of Italy.* New York, 1971. Objective, concise survey of Italian unification.

Blackbourn, David. *The Long Nineteenth Century: A History of Germany, 1780–1918.* New York, 1998.

Blackburn, Robin. *The Overthrow of Colonial Slavery.* London, 1988. Brilliant and detailed overview of the social history of slavery and antislavery movements.

Brophy, James M. *Capitalism, Politics, and Railroads in Prussia, 1830–1870.* Columbus, 1998. Important, clear, and helpful.

Coppa, Frank. *The Origins of the Italian Wars of Independence.* London, 1992.

Craig, Gordon. *Germany, 1866–1945.* New York, 1978. An excellent and thorough synthesis.

Deak, Istvan. *The Lawful Revolution: Louis Kossuth and the Hungarians, 1848–1849.* New York, 1979.

Eyck, Erich. *Bismarck and the German Empire.* 3d ed. London, 1968. The best one-volume study of Bismarck.

Hamerow, Theodore S. *The Social Foundations of German Unification, 1858–1871.* 2 vols. Princeton, N.J., 1969–1972. Concentrates on economic factors that determined the solution to the unification question. An impressive synthesis.

———. *The Birth of a New Europe: State and Society in the Nineteenth Century.* Chapel Hill, N.C., 1983. A discussion of political and social change, and their relationship to industrialization and the increase in state power.

Higonnet, Patrice. *Paris: Capital of the World.* London, England, 2002. Brilliant and imaginative study of Paris as "capital of the nineteenth century."

Hobsbawm, Eric J. *Nations and Nationalism since 1870: Programme, Myth, Reality.* 2d ed. Cambridge, 1992. A clear, concise analysis of the historical and cultural manifestations of nationalism.

Howard, Michael. *The Franco-Prussian War.* New York, 1981. The war's effect on society.

Hutchinson, John, and Anthony Smith, eds. *Nationalism.* New York, 1994. A recent collection of articles, not particularly historical, but with the merit of discussing non-European nationalisms.

Johnson, Susan. *Roaring Camp.* New York, 2000. A fascinating story of one mining camp in California, and a microhistory of the larger forces changing the West and the world.

Kolchin, Peter. *Unfree Labor: American Slavery and Russian Serfdom.* Cambridge, Mass., 1987. Pioneering comparative study.

Mack Smith, Denis. *Cavour and Garibaldi.* New York, 1968.

———. *The Making of Italy, 1796–1870.* New York, 1968. A narrative with documents.

Nochlin, Linda. *Realism.* New York, 1971.

Pflanze, Otto. *Bismarck and the Development of Germany.* 2d ed. 3 vols. Princeton, N.J., 1990. Extremely detailed analysis of Bismarck's aims and policies.

Pinkney, David. *Napoleon III and the Rebuilding of Paris.* Princeton, N.J., 1972. An interesting account of the creation of modern Paris during the Second Empire.

Robertson, Priscilla. *Revolutions of 1848: A Social History.* Princeton, N.J., 1952. Old-fashioned narrative, but very readable.

Sammons, Jeffrey L. *Heinrich Heine: A Modern Biography.* Princeton, N.J., 1979. An excellent historical biography, as well as a study of culture and politics.

Sheehan, James J. *German Liberalism in the Nineteenth Century.* Chicago, 1978. Fresh and important synthesis.

Sperber, Jonathan. *Rhineland Radicals: The Democratic Movement and the Revolution of 1848–1849.* Princeton, N.J., 1993. A detailed study of Germany, by the author of the most recent overview of the revolutions of 1848.

———. *The European Revolutions, 1848–1851.* New York, 1994. Now the best single volume on the period, with new bibliography.

Stearns, Peter N. *1848: The Revolutionary Tide in Europe.* New York, 1974. Stresses the social background of the revolutions.

Zeldin, Theodore. *The Political System of Napoleon III.* Compact and readable, by one of the major scholars of the period.

PART VII
THE WEST AT THE WORLD'S CENTER

THE YEARS BETWEEN 1870 and 1945 have been called the "European era." Three developments run through this period. The first is the rapid and dramatic expansion of European empires. The industrial development of western Europe and the United States gave those nations unprecedented power in the world arena. The West's trade, its wars, and its methods of wielding political power were global. That newfound, worldwide power produced both confidence and crisis. Although the economic might of the Western nations enabled them to dominate the less-developed quarters of the globe, it also created new and dangerous competition among them. The old system of the "balance of power," designed to preserve peace by ensuring that no one country could dominate others, was strained to the breaking point by rivalries that grew swiftly and stretched around the world. The second development, slower and more uneven, was the emergence of "mass" politics and culture: the expansion of suffrage and of liberal and parliamentary democracy, new techniques for mobilizing (or manipulating) citizens, and modern cultural forms ranging from mass-market newspapers and advertising to radio and movies. The third theme to consider involves the wrenching transformations brought by war. Twice during the period, in 1914 and 1939, international and domestic pressures exploded. Twice during the period, war proved shockingly different from what citizens, soldiers, or political leaders expected. And twice during the period, in 1918 and 1945, Europeans awoke to a world they barely recognized. The two world wars had far reaching consequences, among them the fracturing of the European empires and the transformation of Europe's place in the world.

POLITICS	SOCIETY AND CULTURE	ECONOMY	INTERNATIONAL RELATIONS
		Britain monopolizes opium trade in China (1830s)	British expand foothold in India (1797–1818)
			Opium Wars (1839–1842)
		Production of steel alloys revolution-ized (1850–1870s)	Treaty of Nanjing (1842)
	Karl Marx and Friedrich Engels publish *Communist Manifesto* (1848)		
Reign of Alexander II (1855–1881)	Gustave Flaubert's *Madame Bovary* (1856)		
Sepoy Rebellion in India (1857–1858)	Darwin's *On the Origin of Species* (1859)		
1860 American Civil War (1861–1864)	Leo Tolstoy's *War and Peace* (1862–1869)		
Emancipation of serfs in Russia (1861)	Fyodor Dostoyevsky's *Crime and Punishment* (1866)		
Otto von Bismarck unifies Germany (1862–1871)			
Reform Bill of 1867 in England (1867)			
Pope Pius IX's pronouncement of papal infallibility (1869)		Limited liability laws change invest-ment strategies (1870)	Franco-Prussian War (1870–1871)
Bismarck's Kulturkampf (1871–1878)	First Impressionist salon with Claude Monet and others (1874)	Birth of vertical and horizontal monopolies (1870)	European scramble for Africa (1870–1900)
Paris Commune repressed (1871)			Britain gains control of Suez Canal (1875)
Third French Republic (1875)		Electricity demand rises (1880s)	Congress of Berlin redraws Balkan states (1878)
1880 The progressive movement in the United States (1880–1914)		Rockefeller's Standard Oil Company controls over 90 percent of U.S. oil (1880s)	British occupation of Egypt begins (1882)
Alexander III and the Counter Reforms (1881–1894)		Russia launches industrialization program (1880–1890s)	France moves into Vietnam, Laos, and Cambodia (1883–1893)
Bismarck's health and social legislation (1883–1884)	Friedrich Nietzsche's *Thus Spoke Zarathustra* (1883)	Sherman Anti-Trust Act in the United States (1890)	Berlin West Africa Conference (1884–85)
Reform Bill expands male suffrage in Britain (1884)	Émile Zola's *Germinal* (1885)		
Kaiser Wilhelm II ascends throne (1888)	Completion of the Eiffel Tower (1889)		
	Anti-Semitic League founded in Paris (1889)		
	Vincent Van Gogh's *The Starry Night* (1889)	Birth of the department store (1890s)	Sino-Japanese War (1894–1905)
Bismarck resigns (1890)			Italian forces defeated by Ethiopians (1896)
			Fashoda Crisis (1898)
			Boer War (1898–1901)
The Dreyfus Affair (1894–1899)			Spanish-American War (1898)
			United States annexes Puerto Rico and makes Cuba a Protectorate (1898)
1900 Boxer Rebellion in China (1900)	Sigmund Freud publishes *The Interpreta-tion of Dreams* (1899)	Discovery of oil fields in Russia, Bor-neo, Persia, and Texas (1900)	London Pan-African Conference (1900)
Sinn Fein party forms in Ireland (1900)			
French laws separate church and state (1901–1905)			
Labour party established in Britain (1901)			
Vladimir Lenin's "What Is to Be Done?" (1902)			
Russian Marxists split into Bolsheviks and Mensheviks (1903)			United States occupies Panama (1903)
British House of Lords loses veto power (1911)			First and Second Balkan Wars (1912–1913)
			First World War (1914–1918)
			Battle of the Marne (1914)
	Albert Einstein proposes theory of relativity (1915)		*Lusitania* sunk by German U-boat (1915)
			Battles of Verdun and the Somme (1916)
Russian Revolution in February and October (1917)		Bread riots and strikes against wartime shortages in Britain (1917)	United States enters World War I (1917)

POLITICS	SOCIETY AND CULTURE	ECONOMY	INTERNATIONAL RELATIONS	
		Vladimir Lenin's *Imperialism: The Highest Stage of Capitalism* (1917)	Treaty of Brest-Litovsk (1918)	1917
Russian Civil War (1918–1920)				
Britain extends vote to men and women over age thirty (1918)				
German (Weimar) Republic declared (1918)				
Nineteenth Amendment gives American women vote (1919)	Dadaist and Surrealist artistic movements flourish (1920–1940)	Hyperinflation in Weimar Republic (1920–1924)	Treaty of Versailles (1919–1920)	
Separate parliaments for north and south Ireland (1920)	Marie Stopes opens birth control clinic in London (1921)	Beginning of New Economic Policy in U.S.S.R. (1921)		
Mussolini's fascists march on Rome (1922)	T. S. Eliot's *The Waste Land* (1922)			
	Hitler writes *Mein Kampf* in prison (1924)			
Joseph Stalin's Revolution from Above (1927–1928)		Joseph Stalin's First Five-Year Plan for modernization of Russian economy (1928–1932)	Kellogg-Briand Pact (1928)	
		American stock market crash (1929)		
		Great Depression (1929–1933)		
Hitler appointed chancellor of Germany, proclaims the Third Reich (1933)	James Chadwick discovers the neutron (1932)	Britain abandons gold standard (1931)	Japan invades Manchuria (1931)	1930
Concentration camp for political prisoners opens at Dachau (1933)	German laws exclude Jews from public office (1933)	United States abandons gold standard (1933)		
Popular Front government formed by Leon Blum (1936)	Leni Riefenstahl's *Triumph of the Will* (1934)	One third of American workers unemployed (1933)		
Spanish Civil War (1936–1939)		President Franklin Roosevelt announces the New Deal (1933)	Italy conquers Ethiopia (1935–1936)	
Great Terror of Stalin (1937–1938)			Germany and Italy form Axis (1935)	
Nazis begin deporting Jews in occupied territories to ghettos (1939)	Otto Hahn and Fritz Strassman split the atom (1939)		Germany annexes Austria (1938)	
			Hitler invades Czechoslovakia (1939)	
			Soviet Union signs nonaggression pact with Germany (1939)	
			Soviets and Germans invade Poland (1939)	
			Britain and France declare war on Germany (1939)	
Winston Churchill becomes prime minister of England (1940)	Charlie Chaplin's *The Great Dictator* (1940)	Winston Churchill brokers Lend-Lease program with Franklin Roosevelt (1940)	France surrenders to Germany (1940)	1940
			Battle of Britain (1940–1941)	
			Germany invades the Soviet Union (1941)	
			Japan strikes Pearl Harbor; United States enters World War II (1941)	
			Japan invades Philippines (1941)	
	Enrico Fermi stages first controlled nuclear chain reaction (1942)		American island-hopping campaigns in the Pacific (1942)	
			Rommel and the Afrika Korps defeated in Tunisia (1942)	
			Warsaw ghetto uprising (1943)	
			D-Day: Allies land at Normandy (1944)	
			Germany surrenders (1945)	1945
			United States detonates nuclear bombs over Hiroshima and Nagasaki in August (1945)	
			Conferences at Potsdam and Yalta (1945)	
			Nuremberg trials (1945)	
			United Nations founded (1945)	

Chapter Twenty-Two

Chapter Contents

IMPERIALISM AND COLONIALISM, 1870–1914

IN 1869, THE SUEZ CANAL opened with a grandiose celebration. The imperial yacht *Eagle*, Empress Eugénie of France on board, entered the canal on November 17, followed by sixty-eight steamships carrying the rest of the party—the emperor of Austria, the crown prince of Prussia, the grand duke of Russia, and scores of other dignitaries. Flowery speeches flowed freely, as did the Champagne. The ceremony cost a staggering £1.3 million. Even so, the size of the celebration paled in comparison to the canal itself. The largest project of its kind, and a masterful feat of engineering, the canal sliced through one hundred miles of Egyptian desert to link the Mediterranean and Red seas, which cut the trip from London to Bombay in half. As a fast, cheap, and efficient route to the East, the canal had instant strategic importance. Moreover, the canal dramatically showcased—and to many Europeans, justified—the abilities of Western power and technology to transform the globe.

The building of the canal was the result of half a century of France and Britain's increasingly pervasive commercial, financial, and political involvement in Egypt. French troops under Napoleon led the way, but Britain's bankers soon followed. European financial interests developed a close relationship with those who governed Egypt as a semi-independent state inside the Ottoman empire. By 1875 the canal itself had come under the control of Britain, which had purchased 44 percent of the shares in the canal from the khedive (viceroy) of Egypt when he was threatened with bankruptcy. By the late 1870s, these economic and political relationships had produced debt and instability in Egypt, and consternation among European investors who wanted returns on their loans. In a bid to produce both an independent state and an Egyptian nation—not so different from the European model—free of foreign "interference," a group of Egyptian army officers (led by 'Urabi Pasha) took control of Egypt's government in 1882.

After much debate, the British government decided to intervene. They did not believe Suez to be at risk, but they were determined to protect their investments by controlling the budget and enforcing a debt settlement. The Royal Navy shelled

FOCUS QUESTIONS

• What were the causes of the "new imperialism"?

• How was the Indian empire reorganized after the Mutiny of 1857?

• How did Western countries "open" China?

• What was the "civilizing mission"?

• What events set off the "scramble for Africa"?

• How did empire affect European identity?

• Why was the Boer War unique?

Egyptian forts along the canal into rubble. A special task force of troops led by Britain's most successful colonial general, "Garnet" Wolseley, landed along the shore of the canal near 'Urabi Pasha's central base. Wolseley planned his attack down to the last detail—the order of maneuvers looked very much like a railway timetable—and overwhelmed the Egyptian lines just before dawn, at bayonet point. This striking success rallied immediate popular support at home, but the political consequences ran much deeper and lasted for more than seventy years. Britain took over effective control of the province of Egypt. Lord Evelyn Baring (immediately nicknamed "Over" Baring by British anticolonialists) assumed the role of "proconsul" in a power-sharing

EUROPE IN 1871

How did European borders change as the nation-states consolidated their power? Did these boundaries lead to further social and cultural integration between the diverse people within the new nation-states? Outside of Europe, where did the European states expand their political and economic control? Why were North Africa and the Middle East attractive to the Europeans?

relationship with Egyptian authorities—a relationship in which all the real power rested with Britain. Britain put conditions on the repayment of loans owed by the former Egyptian government, and regulated the trade in Egyptian cotton that helped supply Britain's textile mills. Most important, intervention secured the route to India and the markets of the East.

The convergence of technology, money, and politics involved in the Suez Canal epitomizes the interplay of economics and empire in late-nineteenth-century Europe. The years 1870 to 1914 brought both rapid industrialization throughout the West and the stunningly rapid expansion of Western power abroad. The "new imperialism" of the late nineteenth century was distinguished by its scope, intensity, and long-range consequences. It transformed cultures, economies, and states. Projects such as the Suez Canal changed—literally— the landscape and map of the world. They not only brought together newly made money and fresh desires for power, they also represented an ideology: the belief in technology and in Western superiority. Physically and imaginatively, the opening of the Suez Canal undermined notions of an "Orient" divided from the West. In the minds of imperialists, the elimination of geographic barriers had opened the entire world, its lands and peoples, to the administrative power of the West.

The new imperialism, however, was not a one-way street, nor did it allow the West simply to conquer vast territories and dictate its terms to the rest of the world. The new political and economic relationships between colonies and dependent states on the one hand and the "metropole" (the colonizing power) on the other ran both ways, bringing changes to the both parties. Fierce competition among nations upset the balance of power. The new imperialism was an expression of European strength, but it was also profoundly destabilizing.

IMPERIALISM

What were the causes of the "new imperialism"?

"Imperialism" is the process of extending one state's control over another—a process that takes many forms. Historians begin by distinguishing between formal and informal imperialism. "Formal imperialism," or colonialism, was sometimes exercised by direct rule: the colonizing nations annexed territories outright and established new governments to subjugate and administer other states and peoples. Sometimes colonialism worked through indirect rule: the conquering Europeans reached agreements with indigenous leaders and governed them. There was no single technique of colonial management; as we will see, resistance forced colonial powers to shift strategies frequently. "Informal imperialism" refers to a more subtle and less visible exercise of power, in which the stronger state allowed the weaker state to maintain its independence while reducing its sovereignty. Informal imperialism took the form of carving out zones of European sovereignty and privilege, such as treaty ports, within other states. It could mean using European economic, political, and cultural power to get advantageous treaties or terms of trade. Informal imperialism was not only common, it played an even more fundamental role in shaping global power relations.

Both formal and informal imperialism expanded dramatically in the nineteenth century. The "scramble for Africa" was the most sudden and startling case of formal imperialism: from 1875 to 1902 Europeans seized up to 90 percent of the continent. The overall picture is no less remarkable: between 1870 and 1900, a small group of Western states (France, Britain, Germany, the Netherlands, Russia, and the United States) colonized about one quarter of the world's land surface. In addition to these activities, Western states extended informal empire in sections of China and Turkey, across South and East Asia, and into Central and South America. So striking was this expansion of European power and sovereignty that by the late nineteenth century contemporaries were speaking of the "new imperialism."

Imperialism was not new. It is more helpful to think of nineteenth-century developments as a new stage of European empire building. The "second European empires" took hold after the first empires, especially those in the New World, had by and large collapsed. The British empire in North America was shattered in 1776 by the American Revolution. French imperial ambitions across the Atlantic were toppled along with Napoleon. Spanish and Portuguese domination of Central and South America ended with the Latin American revolutions of the early nineteenth century. In what ways were the second, nineteenth-century European empires different?

The nineteenth-century empires developed against the backdrop of developments we have considered in the preceding chapters: industrialization, liberal revolutions, and the rise of nation-states. These developments changed Europe, and they changed European imperialism. First, industrialization created new economic needs for raw materials. Second, industrialization, liberalism, and science forged a new view of the world, history, and the future. A distinguishing feature of nineteenth-century imperialism lay in Europeans' conviction that economic development and technological advances would inevitably bring progress to the rest of the world. Third, especially in the case of Britain and France, the nineteenth-century imperial powers were also in principle democratic nations, where government authority rested on consent and on the equality of most citizens. This made conquest and subjugation more difficult to justify and raised increasingly thorny questions about the status of colonized peoples. Nineteenth-century imperialists sought to distance themselves from earlier histories of conquest. They

spoke not of winning souls for the church or subjects for the king, but rather of building railroads and harbors, encouraging social reform, and fulfilling Europe's secular mission to bring civilization to the world.

The "new" aspects of nineteenth-century imperialism, however, resulted equally from changes and events outside Europe. Resistance, rebellion, and recognition of colonial failures obliged Europeans to develop new strategies of rule. The Haitian revolution of 1804, echoed by slave rebellions in the early nineteenth century, compelled the British and French, slowly, to end the slave trade and slavery in their colonies in the 1830s and 1840s, although new systems of forced labor cropped up to take their places. The example of the American Revolution encouraged the British to grant self-government to white settler states in Canada

The Inauguration of the Suez Canal. This allegory illustrates the union of the Mediterranean and Red Seas attended by Ismail Pasha, the Khedive of Egypt, Abdul Aziz, Sultan of the Ottoman empire, Ferdinand de Lesseps, President of the Suez Canal Company, Empress Eugenie of France, and several mermaids. It also represents the nineteenth-century vision of imperialism as a bearer of global progress, promoting technological advance and breaking down barriers between the "Orient" and the West.

(1867), Australia (1901), and New Zealand (1912). In India, as we will see, the British responded to rebellion by taking the area away from the East India Company and putting it under control of the crown, by requiring civil servants to undergo more training, and by much more careful policing of indigenous peoples. Almost everywhere, nineteenth-century empires established carefully codified racial hierarchies to organize relationships between Europeans and different indigenous groups. (Apartheid in South Africa is but one example.) In general, nineteenth-century imperialism involved less independent "entrepreneurial" activity by merchants and traders (such as the East India Company) and more "settlement and discipline." This meant that empire became a vast project, involving legions of administrators, schoolteachers, and engineers. Nineteenth-century imperialism, then, arose from new motives. It produced new forms of government and management in the colonies. Last, it created new kinds of interactions between Europeans and indigenous peoples.

THE NEW IMPERIALISM AND ITS CAUSES

All historical events have many causes. The causes of a development with the scope, intensity, and long-range importance of the "new imperialism" inevitably provoke heated controversy. The most influential and long-standing interpretation points to the economic dynamics of imperialism. As early as 1902, the British writer J. A. Hobson charged that what he named the "scramble for Africa" had been driven by the interests of a small group of wealthy financiers. British taxpayers subsidized armies of conquest and occupation, and journalists whipped up the public's "spectatorial lust of jingoism," but Hobson believed that the core interests behind imperialism were those of international capitalists. At a time when fierce economic competition was producing protectionism and monopolies, he argued, and when western Europe did not provide the markets that industry needed, investors sought out secure investment opportunities overseas, in colonies. Hobson saw investors and international bankers as the central players: "large savings are made which cannot find any profitable investment in this country; they must find employment elsewhere." Yet investors were not alone. Their interests matched those of manufacturers involved in colonial trade, the military, and the armaments industry. Hobson was a reformer and social critic. His point was that international finance and business had distorted conceptions of England's real national interests. He hoped that genuine democracy would be an antidote to the country's imperial tendencies.

Hobson's analysis, still widely read, inspired the most influential Marxist critique of imperialism, which came from the Russian socialist and revolutionary leader Vladimir Ilich Lenin (see Chapter 21). Like Hobson, Lenin underscored the economics of imperialism. Unlike Hobson, he considered imperialism to be an integral part of late-nineteenth-century capitalism. Competition and the monopolies that it produced had lowered domestic profits. Capitalists, Lenin argued, could only enlarge their markets at home by raising workers' wages, which would have the effect of further reducing profits. Thus the "internal contradictions" of capitalism produced imperialism, compelling capitalists to invest and to search for new markets overseas. If this were the case, it followed that Hobson's hopes for democratic reform were misplaced; only overthrowing capitalism itself could check imperialist expansion, conflict, and violence. Lenin published his book (*Imperialism: The Highest Stage of Capitalism*, 1917) at the height of World War I, a war many considered imperialist. The timing gave real urgency to his argument that revolution alone could topple capitalism, imperialism, and the forces that had brought the world to the brink of disaster.

Historians now would agree that economic pressures were one, though only one, important cause of imperialism. In the case of Great Britain, roughly half its total of £4 billion in foreign investments was at work within its empire. As Hobson, Lenin, and their contemporaries correctly noted, late-nineteenth-century London was rapidly becoming the banker of the world. In all western European countries, demand for raw materials made colonies seem a necessary investment and helped persuade governments that imperialism was a worthwhile policy. Rubber, tin, and minerals from the colonies supplied European industries, and foods, coffee, sugar, tea, wool, and grain supplied European consumers. Yet the economic explanation has limits. Colonial markets were generally too

> British taxpayers subsidized armies of conquest and occupation, and journalists whipped up the public's "spectatorial lust of jingoism," but Hobson believed that the core interests behind imperialism were those of international capitalists.

poor to meet the needs of European manufacturers. Africa, the continent over which Europeans frantically "scrambled," was the poorest and least profitable to investors. Regarding overseas investment, before 1914 only a very small portion of German capital was invested in German colonies. Only one fifth of French capital was so invested; indeed, the French had more capital invested in Russia, hoping to stabilize that ally against the Germans, than in all their colonial possessions. Yet some of these calculations are clear only in retrospect. Many nineteenth-century Europeans expected the colonies to produce profits. French newspapers, for instance, reported that the Congo was "rich, vigorous, and fertile virgin territory," with "fabulous quantities" of gold, copper, ivory, and rubber. Such hopes certainly contributed to expansionism, even if the profits of empire did not match Europeans' expectations.

A second interpretation of imperialism emphasizes strategic and nationalist motives more than economic interests. International rivalries reinforced the belief that vital national interests were at stake, and made European powers more determined to control both the governments and economies of less-developed nations and territories. French politicians supported imperialism as a means of restoring national prestige and honor, lost in the humiliating defeat by the Prussians in 1870–1871. The British, on the other hand, looked with alarm at the accelerating pace of industrialization in Germany and France and feared losing their existing and potential world markets. The Germans, recently unified in a modern nation, viewed overseas empire as a "national" birthright possession and as a way of entering the "club" of Great Powers.

This second, noneconomic, interpretation stresses the new links between imperialism and nineteenth-century state and nation building. That nations should be empires was not always self-evident. Otto von Bismarck, the architect of German unification, long considered colonialism overseas a distraction from far more serious issues on the continent of Europe. By the last decades of the century, however, Germany had joined France and England in what seemed an urgent race for territories. Advocates of colonialism—from businessmen and explorers to writers (such as Rudyard Kipling) and political theorists—spelled out why empire was important to a new nation. Colonies did more than demonstrate military power; they showed the vigor of a nation's economy, the strength of its convictions, the will of its citizenry, the force of its laws, and the power of its culture. A strong national community could assimilate others, bring progress to new lands and new peoples.

One German proponent of expansion called colonialism the "national continuation of the German desire for unity." Lobby groups such as the German Colonial Society, the French Colonial Party, and the Royal Colonial Institute argued for empire in similar terms, as did newspapers, which also recognized the attractions of sensational stories of overseas conquest. Presented in this way, as part of nation building, imperialism seemed to rise above particular interests or mundane cost-benefit analysis. Culture, law, religion, and industry were vital national products, and their value rose as they were exported and defended abroad.

Third, imperialism had important cultural dimensions. A French diplomat once described the British imperial adventurer Cecil Rhodes as "a force cast in an idea"; the same might be said of imperialism itself. Imperialism as an idea excited such explorers as the Scottish missionary David Livingston, who believed that the British conquest of Africa would put an end to the East African slave trade, and "introduce the Negro family into the body of corporate nations." Rudyard Kipling, the British poet and novelist, wrote of the "white man's burden" (see p. 807), a notorious phrase that referred to the European mission to "civilize" what Kipling and others considered the "barbaric" and "heathen" quarters of the globe. Taking arms against the slave trade, famine, disorder, and illiteracy seemed to many Europeans not only a reason to invade Africa and Asia, but also a duty and proof of a somehow superior civilization. These convictions did not cause imperialism, but they illustrate how central empire building became to the West's self-image.

In short, it is difficult to disentangle the economic, political, and strategic "causes" of imperialism. It is more important to understand how the motives over-

CHRONOLOGY

MAJOR IMPERIAL CONFLICTS, 1857–1905

First Opium War, China	1839–1842
Great Mutiny, India	1857–1858
Siege of Khartoum, Sudan	1884–1885
Italian invasion of Ethiopa	1896
Crisis of Fashoda, Sudan	1898
Spanish-American War	1898
Boer War, South Africa	1899–1902
Boxer Rebellion, China	1900
Russo-Japanese War	1904–1905

HOW WAS THE INDIAN EMPIRE REORGANIZED AFTER THE MUTINY OF 1857?

IMPERIALISM IN SOUTH ASIA   787

lapped. Strategic interests often persuaded policy makers that economic issues were at stake. Different constituencies—the military, international financiers, missionaries, colonial lobby groups at home—held different and often clashing visions of the purpose and benefits of imperialism. "Imperial policy" was less a matter of long-range planning than of a series of quick responses, often improvised, to particular situations. International rivalries led policy makers to redefine their ambitions. So did individual explorers, entrepreneurs, or groups of settlers who established claims to hitherto unknown territories that home governments then felt compelled to recognize and defend. Finally, Europeans were not the only players on the stage. Their goals and practices were shaped by social changes in the countries in which they became involved, by the independent interests of local peoples, and by resistance, which, as often as not, they found themselves unable to understand and powerless to stop.

Is there any reason to call nineteenth-century imperialism "new"? Economic integration, or developing lines of investment and trade to the advantage of the Europeans, was not new. The "informal" and subterranean exercise of European power at work in Latin America, China, and the Ottoman empire was a much more long-term process. This kind of power expanded more or less continuously through the modern period. But nineteenth-century imperialism did have new aspects, or specific features stamped on it by developments within Europe and by indigenous resistance to Europeans.

IMPERIALISM IN SOUTH ASIA

How was the Indian empire reorganized after the Mutiny of 1857?

India was the center of the British empire, the jewel of the British crown. It was also an inheritance from eighteenth-century empire building, secured well before the period of the "new imperialism." The conquest of most of the subcontinent began in the 1750s and quickened during the age of revolution. Conquering India helped compensate for "losing" North America.

General Cornwallis, defeated at Yorktown, went on to a brilliant career in India. By the mid-nineteenth century, India had become the focal point of Britain's newly expanded global power, which reached from southern Africa across South Asia and to Australia. Keeping this region involved changing tactics and forms of rule.

Until the mid-nineteenth century, British territories in the subcontinent were under the control of the British East India Company. The company had its own military, divided into European and (far larger) Indian divisions. The company held the right to collect taxes on land from Indian peasants. Until the early nineteenth century, the company had legal monopolies over trade in all goods, including indigo, textiles, salt, minerals, and, most lucrative of all, opium. The British government had granted trade monopolies in its northern American colonies. Unlike North America, however, India never became a settler state. In the 1830s Europeans were a tiny minority, numbering forty-five thousand in an Indian population of 150 million. The company's government was military and repressive. Soldiers collected taxes; civil servants wore military uniforms; British troops brashly commandeered peasants' oxen and carts for their own purposes. Typically, though, the company could not enforce its rule uniformly. It governed some areas directly, others through making alliances with local leaders, and others still by simply controlling goods and money. Indirect rule, here as in other empires, meant finding indigenous collaborators and maintaining their good will. Thus the British cultivated groups that had provided administrators in earlier regimes, the Rajputs and Bhumihars of North India, whom they considered especially effective soldiers, and merchants of big cities such as Calcutta. They offered economic privileges, state offices, or military posts to either groups or entire nations that agreed to ally with the British against others.

British policy shifted between two poles: one group wanted to "westernize" India, another believed it safer, and more practical, to defer to local culture. Christian missionaries, whose numbers rose as occupation expanded, were determined to replace "blind superstition" with the "genial influence of Christian light and truth." Indignant at such practices as child marriage and sati (in which a widow immolated herself on her husband's funeral pyre), they sought support in England for a wide-ranging assault on Hindu culture. Secular reformers, many of them liberal, considered

> By the mid-nineteenth century, India had become the focal point of Britain's newly expanded global power, which reached from southern Africa across South Asia and to Australia. Keeping this region involved changing tactics and forms of rule.

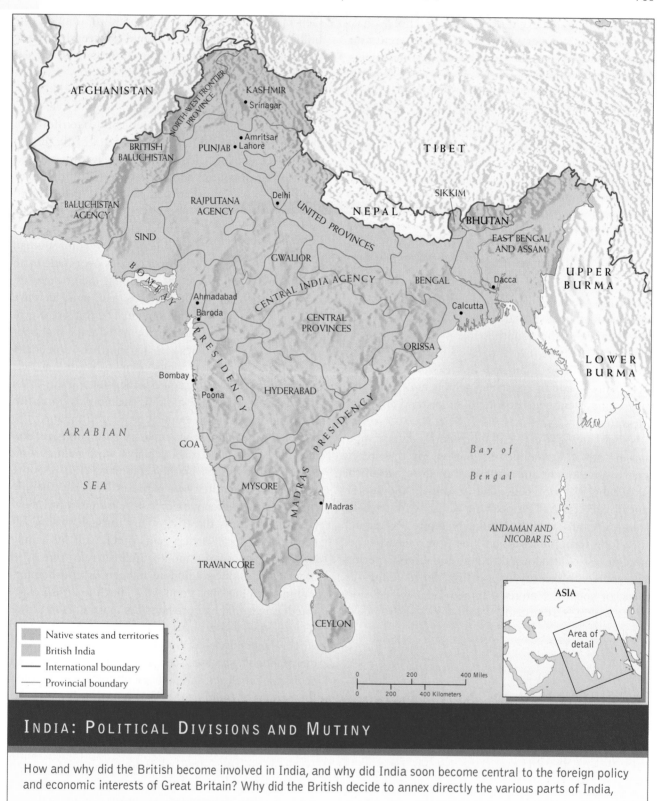

INDIA: POLITICAL DIVISIONS AND MUTINY

How and why did the British become involved in India, and why did India soon become central to the foreign policy and economic interests of Great Britain? Why did the British decide to annex directly the various parts of India,

"Hindoos" and "Mahommedans" susceptible to forms of despotism—in both the family and in the state. They turned their reforming zeal to legal and political change. But other company and British administrators warned their countrymen not to meddle with Indian institutions and practices. "Englishmen are as great

HOW WAS THE INDIAN EMPIRE REORGANIZED AFTER THE MUTINY OF 1857?

IMPERIALISM IN SOUTH ASIA   789

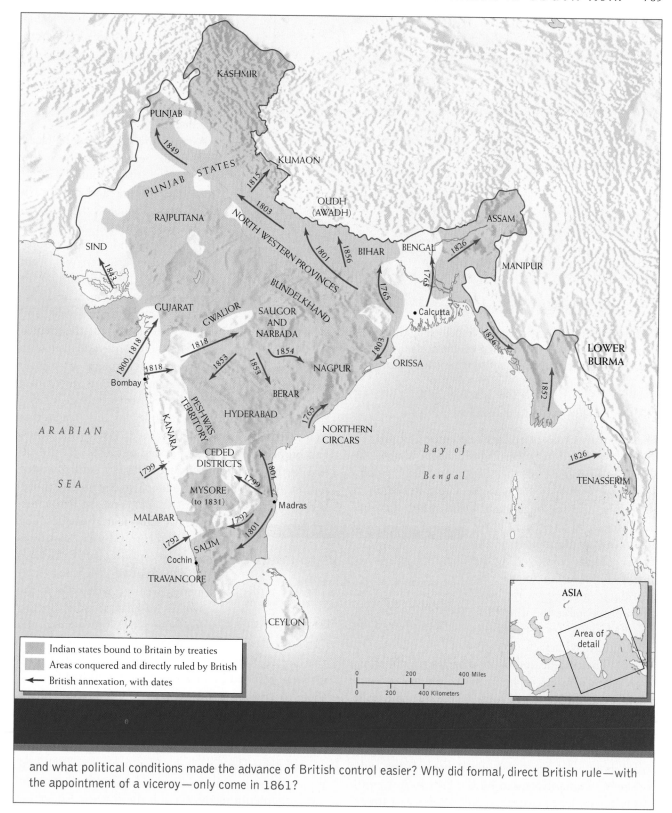

and what political conditions made the advance of British control easier? Why did formal, direct British rule—with the appointment of a viceroy—only come in 1861?

fanatics in politics as Mahommedans in religion. They suppose that no country can be saved without English institutions," said one British administrator. Indirect rule, they argued, would only work with the cooperation of local powers. Conflicts such as these meant that the British never agreed on any single cultural policy.

British executing leaders of Indian Rebellion of 1857. The British were determined to make an example of the rebel Indian soldiers of the Great Mutiny. This engraving shows executions in which the condemned were blown apart by cannons.

FROM MUTINY TO REBELLION

The company's rule often met resistance and protest. In 1857–1858, it was particularly badly shaken by what the British called the "Sepoy [soldiers'] Rebellion," now known in India as the Great Rebellion of 1857. The uprising began near Delhi, when the military disciplined a regiment of sepoys (the traditional term for Indian soldiers employed by the British) for refusing to use rifle cartridges greased with pork fat—unacceptable to either Hindus or Muslims. Yet as the British prime minister Disraeli later observed, "The decline and fall of empires are not affairs of greased cartridges." The causes of the mutiny were much deeper and involved social, economic, and political grievances. Indian peasants attacked law courts and burned tax rolls, protesting debt and corruption. In areas such as Oudh, which had recently been annexed, rebels defended their traditional leaders, who had been summarily ousted by the British. Army officers from privileged castes resented arbitrary treatment at the hands of the British; they were first promoted as loyal allies and then forced to serve without what they considered titles and honors. The mutiny spread through large areas of northwest India. European troops, which counted for fewer than one fifth of those

in arms, found themselves losing control. Religious leaders, both Hindu and Muslim, seized the occasion to denounce Christian missionaries sent in by the British and their assault on local traditions and practices.

At first the British were faced with a desperate situation, with areas under British control cut off from one another and pro-British cities under siege. Loyal Indian troops were brought south from the frontiers, and British troops, fresh from the Crimean War, were shipped directly from Britain to suppress the rebellion. The fighting lasted more than a year, and the British matched the rebels' early massacres and vandalism with a systematic campaign of repression. Whole rebel units were either killed rather than being allowed to surrender, or else tried on the spot and executed. Towns and villages that supported the rebels were burned, just as the rebels had burned European homes and outposts. Yet the defeat of the rebellion caught the British public's imagination. After the bloody, inconclusive mess of Crimea, the terrifying threat to British India and the heroic rescue of European hostages and British territory by British troops were electrifying news. Pictures of the Scottish highland regiments (wearing wool kilts in the sweltering heat of India) liberating besieged white women and children went up in homes across the United Kingdom. At a political level, British leaders were stunned by how close the revolt had brought them to disaster and were determined never to repeat the same mistakes.

> At a political level, British leaders were stunned by how close the revolt had brought them to disaster and were determined never to repeat the same mistakes.

After "the mutiny," the British were compelled to reorganize their Indian empire, developing new strategies of rule. The East India Company was abolished, replaced by the British crown. The British raj (or rule) was governed directly, though the British also sought out collaborators and cooperative interest groups. Princely India was left to the indigenous princes, who were subject to British advisors. The British also reorganized the military, and tried to change relations among soldiers. Indigenous troops were separated

LORD CURZON ON THE IMPORTANCE OF INDIA AND INDIANS TO THE BRITISH EMPIRE

Lord George Nathaniel Curzon (1859–1925) served as viceroy of India from 1898 to 1905, and foreign secretary from 1919 to 1924. He made his reputation in India, and as a prominent Tory politician he became among the most vocal proponents of the new imperialism. In this speech Curzon spells out the benefits of empire and underscores British dependence on India.

If you want to save your Colony of Natal from being over-run by a formidable enemy, you ask India for help, and she gives it; if you want to rescue the white men's legations from massacres at Peking, and the need is urgent, you request the Government of India to despatch an expedition, and they despatch it; if you are fighting the Mad Mullah in Somaliland, you soon discover that Indian troops and an Indian general are best qualified for the task, and you ask the Government of India to send them; if you desire to defend any of your extreme out-posts or coaling stations of the Empire, Aden, Mauritius, Singapore, Hong-Kong, even Tien-tsin or Shan-hai-kwan, it is to the Indian Army that you turn; if you want to build a railway to Uganda or in the Soudan, you apply for Indian labour. When the late Mr. Rhodes was engaged in developing your recent acquisition of Rhodesia, he came to me for assistance. It is with Indian coolie labor that you exploit the plantations equally of Demerara and Natal; with Indian trained officers that you irrigate and dam the Nile; with Indian forest officers that you tap the resources of Central Africa and Siam; with Indian surveyors that you explore all the hidden places of the earth. . . . [Moreover,] India is a country where there will be much larger openings for the investment of capital in the future than has hitherto been the case, and where a great work of industrial and commercial exploitation lies before us.

William Roger Louis, editor in chief, *The Oxford History of the British Empire*, vol. 3, *The Nineteenth Century*, edited by Andrew Porter (Oxford: Oxford University Press, 1999), p. 403.

from each other, in order to avoid the kind of "fraternization" that proved subversive. As one British officer put it, "If one regiment mutinies I should like to have the next so alien that it would fire into it." Even more than before, the British sought to rule through the Indian upper classes rather than in opposition to them. Queen Victoria, now empress of India, set out the principles of indirect rule: "We shall respect the rights, dignity and honour of native princes as our own, and we desire that they, as well as our own subjects, should enjoy that prosperity and that social advancement which can only be secured by internal peace and good government." Civil-service reform opened up new positions to members of the Indian upper classes. The British had to reconsider their relationship to Indian cultures. Missionary activity was subdued, and the British channeled their reforming impulses into the more secular projects of economic development,

British Imperialism. This cartoon, "The Execution of 'John Company,'" appeared in *Punch* magazine in 1857. It celebrates the end of the British East India Company's corrupt rule. Note the reference to executions such as the ones on page 790.

Kipling urged the British and the Americans to "take up the white man's burden" (see p. 807), Curzon pleaded with his countrymen to see how central India was to the greatness of Britain.

What did India provide to Great Britain? By the eve of World War I, India was Britain's largest export market. One tenth of all the British empire's trade passed through India's port cities of Madras, Bombay, and Calcutta. India mattered enormously to Britain's balance of payments; surpluses earned there compensated for deficits with Europe and the United States. Equally important to Great Britain were the human resources of India. Indian laborers worked on tea plantations in Assam, near Burma, and they built railways and dams in southern Africa and Egypt. British rule cast an enormous diaspora of Indian workers throughout the empire. Over a million indentured Indian servants left their country in the second half of the century. India also provided the British empire with highly trained engineers, land surveyors, clerks, bureaucrats, school-teachers, and merchants. The nationalist leader Mohandas Gandhi, for instance, first came into the public eye as a young lawyer in Pretoria, South Africa, where he worked for an Indian law firm. The British deployed Indian troops across the empire. (They would later call up roughly 1.2 million troops in World War I.) For all these reasons, men such as Curzon found it impossible to imagine their empire, or even their nation, without India.

How did the British raj shape Indian society? The British practice of indirect rule sought to create an Indian elite that would serve British interests, a group "who may be the interpreters between us and the millions whom we govern—a class of persons Indian in colour and blood, but English in tastes, in opinion, in morals, and in intellect," as one British writer put it. Eventually, this practice created a large social group of British-educated Indian civil servants and businessmen, well trained for government and skeptical about British claims that they brought progress to the subcontinent. This group provided the leadership for the nationalist movement that challenged British rule in India. At the same time, this group became increasingly distant from the rest of the nation. The overwhelming majority of Indians remained desperately poor peasants, many of them unable to pay taxes and thus in debt to British landlords, all struggling to subsist on diminishing plots of land, villagers working in the textile trade beaten down by imports of cheap manufactured goods from England, all residents of what would become the most populous nation in the world.

railways, roads, irrigation, and so on. Still, consensus on effective colonial strategies was elusive. Some administrators counseled more reform and change; others sought to give the princes more support; the British tried both, in fits and starts, until the end of British rule in 1947.

In India, the most prominent representative of the "new imperialism" was Lord Curzon, a prominent conservative and the viceroy of India from 1898 to 1905. Curzon deepened British commitments to the region. Concerned about the British position in the world, he warned of the need to fortify India's borders against Russia. He urged continued economic investment. Curzon worried out loud that the British would be worn down by resistance to the raj, and that confronted with their apparent inability to transform Indian culture, they would become cynical, get "lethargic and think only of home." In the same way that Rudyard

IMPERIALISM IN CHINA

How did Western countries "open" China?

In China, too, European imperialism escalated early, well before the period of the "new imperialism." Yet there it took a different form. Europeans did not conquer and annex whole regions. Instead, they forced favorable trade agreements at gunpoint, set up treaty ports where Europeans lived and worked under their own jurisdiction, and established outposts of European missionary activity—all with such dispatch that the Chinese spoke of their country as being "carved up like a melon."

Since the seventeenth century European trade with China—in coveted luxuries such as silk, porcelain, art objects, and tea—had run up against resistance from the Chinese government, which was determined to keep foreign traders, and foreign influence in general, at bay. By the early nineteenth century, however, Britain's global ambitions and rising power were setting the stage for a confrontation. Freed from the task of fighting Napoleon, the British set their sights on improving the terms of the China trade, demanding the rights to come into open harbors and to have special trading privileges. The other source of constant friction involved the harsh treatment of British subjects by Chinese law courts—including the summary execution of several Britons convicted of crimes. And by the 1830s, these diplomatic conflicts had been heightened by the opium trade.

THE OPIUM TRADE

Opium provided a direct link among Britain, British India, and China. Since the sixteenth century, the drug had been produced in India and carried by Dutch, and later, British traders. In fact, opium (derived from the poppy plant) was one of the very few commodities that Europeans could sell in China, and for this reason it became crucial to the balance of East-West trade. When the British conquered northeast India, they also annexed one of the richest opium-growing areas and became deeply involved in the trade—so much so that historians do not shy from calling East India Company rule a "narco-military empire." British agencies designated specific poppy-growing regions and gave cash advances to Indian peasants who would cultivate the crop. Producing opium was a labor-intensive process: peasant cultivators collected sap from the poppy seeds, others cleaned the sap and formed it into opium balls, which were dried before being weighed and shipped out. In the opium-producing areas northwest of Calcutta, "factories" employed as many as one thousand Indian workers forming and curing the opium, as well as young boys whose job it was to turn the opium balls every four days.

From India, the East India Company sold the opium to "country traders"—small fleets of British, Dutch, and Chinese shippers who carried the drug to southeast Asia and China. Silver paid for the opium came back to the East India Company, which used it, in turn, to buy Chinese goods for the European market. The trade, therefore, was not only profitable, it was key to a triangular European-Indian-Chinese economic relationship. Production and export rose dramatically in the early nineteenth century. By the 1830s, when the

An Opium Factory in Patna, India, c. 1851. Balls of opium dry in a huge warehouse before being shipped to Calcutta for export to China and elsewhere.

British-Chinese confrontation was taking shape, opium provided British India with more revenues than any other source except taxes on land.

People all over the world consumed opium, for medicinal reasons as well as for pleasure. The Chinese market was especially lucrative. Eighteenth-century China had witnessed a craze for tobacco smoking that taught users how to smoke opium. A large, wealthy Chinese elite of merchants and government officials provided much of the market, but opium smoking also became popular among soldiers, students, and Chinese laborers. In the nineteenth century opium imports followed Chinese labor all over the world—to southeast Asia and San Francisco. In an effort to control the problem, the Chinese government banned opium imports, prohibited domestic production, criminalized smoking, and in the 1830s began a

The Opium Trade, 1880s. A European merchant examines opium.

full-scale campaign to purge the drug from China. That campaign set the Chinese emperor on a collision course with British opium traders. In one confrontation the Chinese drug commissioner Lin confiscated 3 million pounds of raw opium from the British and washed it out to sea. In another the Chinese authorities blockaded British ships in port, and local citizens demonstrated angrily in front of British residences.

THE OPIUM WARS

In 1839, these simmering conflicts broke into what was called the first "Opium War." Drugs were not the core of the matter. They highlighted larger issues of sovereignty and economic status: the Europeans' "rights" to trade with whomever they pleased, bypassing Chinese monopolies; to set up zones of European residence in defiance of Chinese sovereignty; and to proselytize and open schools. War flared up several times over the course of the century. After the first war of 1839–1842, in which British steam vessels and guns overpowered the Chinese fleet, the Treaty of Nanking (1842) compelled the Chinese to give the British

> In the nineteenth century opium imports followed Chinese labor all over the world— to southeast Asia and San Francisco.

trading privileges, the right to reside in five cities, and the port of Hong Kong "in perpetuity." After a second war, the British secured yet more treaty ports and privileges, including the right to send in missionaries. In the aftermath of those agreements between the Chinese and British, other countries demanded similar rights and economic opportunities. By the end of the nineteenth century, during the period of the new imperialism, the French, Germans, and Russians had claimed mining rights and permission to build railroads, to begin manufacturing with cheap Chinese labor, and to arm and police European communities in Chinese cities. In Shanghai, for instance, seventeen thousand foreigners lived with their own courts, schools, churches, and utilities. The United States, not wanting to be shouldered aside, demanded its own "open door policy." Japan was an equally active imperialist power in the Pacific, and the Sino-Japanese war of 1894–1895 was a decisive moment in the history of the region. The Japanese victory forced China to concede trading privileges, the independence of Korea, and the Liaotung Peninsula in Manchuria. It opened a scramble for spheres of influ-

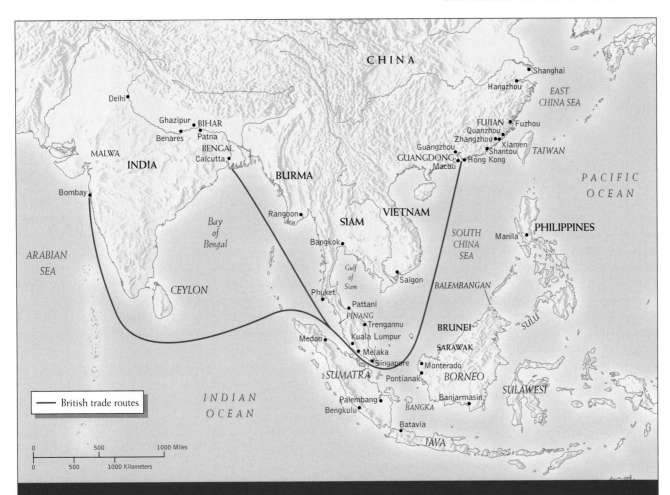

BRITISH OPIUM TRADE ROUTES

This map depicts the major trade routes used by the British in the shipment of opium in Asia. How did opium come to play such an important role? How did the intensification of the opium trade affect the British position in this part of the world? What social and political problems did it create?

ence and for mining and railway concessions. The demand for reparations forced the Chinese government to levy greater taxes. All these measures heightened resentment and destabilized the regime.

Surrendering privileges to Europeans and the Japanese seriously undermined the authority of the Chinese Qing (Ching) emperor at home, and only heightened popular hostility to foreign intruders. Authority at the imperial center had been eroding for more than a century by 1900, hastened by the Opium Wars and by the vast Taiping Rebellion (1852–1864), an enormous, bitter, and deadly conflict in which radical Christian rebels in south-central China challenged the authority of the emperors themselves. On the defensive against the rebels, the dynasty hired

foreign generals, including the British commander Charles Gordon to lead its forces. The war devastated China's agricultural heartland, and the death toll, never confirmed, may have reached 20 million. This ruinous disorder, and the increasing inability of the emperor to keep order and collect the taxes necessary to stabilize trade and repay foreign loans, led European countries to take more and more direct control of their side of "the China trade."

THE BOXER REBELLION

From a Western perspective, the most important of the nineteenth-century rebellions against the corruptions of foreign rule was the Boxer Rebellion of 1900.

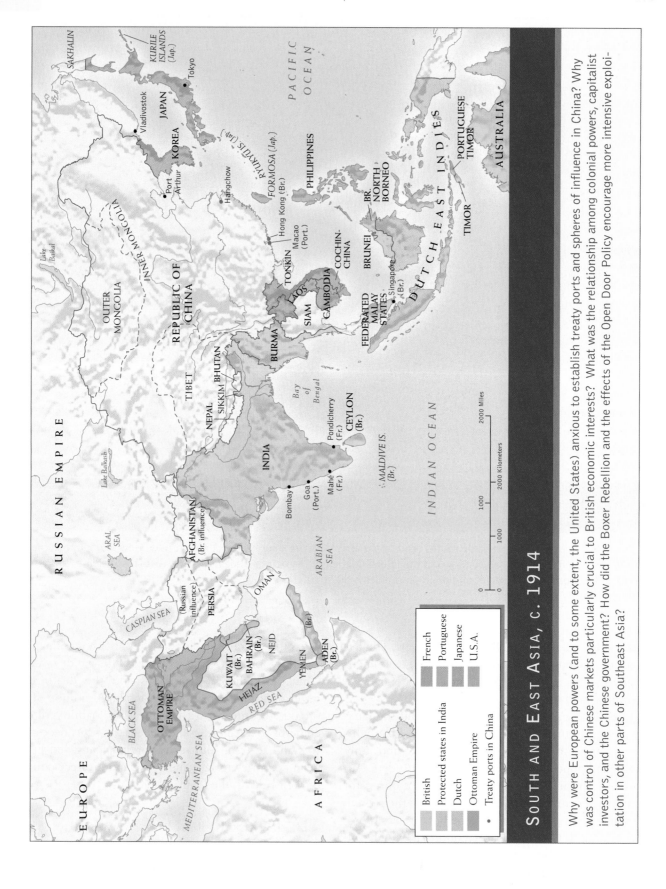

SOUTH AND EAST ASIA, C. 1914

Legend:
- British
- Protected states in India
- Dutch
- Ottoman Empire
- Treaty ports in China
- French
- Portuguese
- Japanese
- U.S.A.

Why were European powers (and to some extent, the United States) anxious to establish treaty ports and spheres of influence in China? Why was control of Chinese markets particularly crucial to British economic interests? What was the relationship among colonial powers, capitalist investors, and the Chinese government? How did the Boxer Rebellion and the effects of the Open Door Policy encourage more intensive exploitation in other parts of Southeast Asia?

The Boxers were a secret society of young men trained in Chinese martial arts and believed to have spiritual powers. Antiforeign and antimissionary, they provided the spark for a loosely organized but widespread uprising in northern China. Bands of Boxers attacked foreign engineers, tore up railway lines, and in the spring of 1900 marched on Beijing. They laid siege to the foreign legations in the city, home to several thousand Western diplomats and merchants and their families. The legations' small garrison defended their walled compound with little more than rifles, bayonets, and improvised artillery, but they withstood the siege for fifty-five days until a large relief column arrived. The rebellion, particularly the siege at Beijing, mobilized a global response. Europe's Great Powers, rivals everywhere else in the world, drew together in response to this crisis in order to tear China apart. An expedition numbering twenty thousand troops—combining the forces of Britain, France, the United States, Germany, Italy, Japan, and Russia—ferociously repressed the Boxer movement. The outside powers then demanded indemnities, new trading concessions, and reassurances from the Chinese government.

The maneuvering, spying, and support of friendly puppet governments by Russia and Britain became known as the "Great Game," and foreshadowed Western countries' jockeying for the region's oil resources in the twentieth century.

The Boxer Rebellion was one of several anti-imperialist movements at the end of the nineteenth century. The rebellion testified to the vulnerability of Europeans' imperial power. It dramatized the resources Europeans would have to devote to maintaining their far-flung influence. In the process of repression, the Europeans became committed to propping up corrupt and fragile governments in order to protect their agreements and interests, and they were drawn into putting down popular uprisings against local inequalities and foreign rule.

In China the age of the "new imperialism" capped a century of conflict and expansion. By 1900, virtually all of Asia had been divided up among the European powers. Japan, an active imperial power in its own right, alone had maintained its independence. British rule extended from India across Burma, Malaya, Australia, and New Zealand. The Dutch, Britain's long-standing trade rivals, secured Indonesia. During the 1880s, the French moved into Indochina. Imperial rivalries (among Britain, France, and Russia, China and Japan, Russia and Japan) caused the struggle for influence and economic advantage in Asia; that struggle, in turn exacerbated nationalist feeling. Imperial expansion, the expression of European power, was showing its destabilizing effects.

RUSSIAN IMPERIALISM

Russia was a persistently imperialist power throughout the nineteenth century. Its rulers championed a policy of annexation—by conquest, treaty, or both—of lands bordering on the existing Russian state. Beginning in 1801, with the acquisition of Georgia following a war with Persia, the tsars continued to pursue their expansionist dream. Bessarabia and Turkestan (taken from the Turks) and Armenia (from the Persians) vastly increased the empire's size. This southward colonization brought the Russians close to war with the British twice: first in 1881, when Russian troops occupied territories in the transCaspian region, and again in 1884–1887, when the tsar's forces advanced to the frontier of Afghanistan. In both cases the British feared incursions into areas they deemed within their sphere of influence in the Middle East. They were concerned, as well, about a possible threat to India. The maneuvering, spying, and support of friendly puppet governments by Russia and Britain became known as the "Great Game," and foreshadowed Western countries' jockeying for the region's oil resources in the twentieth century.

Russian expansion also moved east. In 1875, the Japanese traded the southern half of Sakhalin Island for the previously Russian Kurile Islands. The tsars' eastward advance was finally halted in 1904. Russian expansion in Mongolia and Manchuria came up against Japanese expansion, and the two powers went to war. Russia's huge imperial army more than met its match in a savage, bloody conflict. Russia's navy was sent halfway round the world to reinforce the beleaguered Russian troops, but was ambushed and sunk by the better-trained and equipped Japanese fleet. This national humiliation (see Chapter 23) helped provoke a revolt in Russia and led to an American-brokered peace treaty in 1905. The defeat shook the already unsteady regime of the tsar, and proved that European nations were not the only ones who could play the imperial game successfully.

THE FRENCH EMPIRE AND THE CIVILIZING MISSION

What was the "civilizing mission"?

Like British expansion into India, French colonialism in Northern Africa began before the so-called new imperialism of the late nineteenth century. By the 1830s, the French had created a general government of their possessions in Algeria, the most important of which were cities along the Mediterranean coast. From the outset the Algerian conquest was different from most other colonial ventures: Algeria became a settler state, one of the few apart from South Africa. Some of the early settlers were utopian socialists, out to create ideal communities; some were workers the French government deported after the revolution of 1848 to be "resettled" safely as farmers; some were winegrowers whose vines at home had been destroyed by an insect infestation. The settlers were by no means all French; they included Italian, Spanish, and Maltese merchants and shopkeepers of modest means, laborers, and peasants. By the 1870s, in several of the coastal cities, this new creole community outnumbered indigenous Algerians, and within it, other Europeans outnumbered the French. With the French military's help, the settlers appropriated land, and French business concerns took cork forests and established mining in copper, lead, and iron. Economic activity was for European benefit. The first railroads, for instance, did not even carry passengers; they took iron ore to the coast for export to France, where it would be smelted and sold.

The settlers and the French government did not necessarily pursue common goals. In the 1870s, the new and still fragile Third Republic (founded after Napoleon III was defeated in 1870; see Chapter 21), in an effort to ensure the settlers' loyalty, made the colony a department of France. This gave the French settlers the full rights of republican citizenship. It also gave them the power to pass laws in Algeria that consolidated their privileges and community (naturalizing all Europeans, for instance) and further disenfranchised indigenous populations, who had no voting rights at all. French politicians in Paris occasionally objected to the settlers' contemptuous treatment of indigenous peoples, arguing that it subverted the project of "lifting up" the natives. The French settlers in Algeria had little interest in such a project; although they paid lip service to republican ideals, they wanted the advantages of "Frenchness" for themselves. Colonial administrators and social scientists differentiated the "good" mountain-dwelling Berbers, who could be brought into French society, from the "bad" Arabs, whose religion made them supposedly inassimilable. In Algeria, then, colonialism was at the very least a three-way relationship, and illustrates the dynamics that made colonialism in general a contradictory enterprise.

Before the 1870s, colonial activities aroused relatively little interest among the French at home. But after the humiliating defeat in the Franco-Prussian war (1870–1871) and the establishment of the Third Republic, colonial lobby groups and, gradually, the government, became increasingly adamant about the benefits of colonialism. These benefits were not simply economic. Taking on the "civilizing mission" would reinforce

Surrender of the Berber People to the French. In Algeria French colonialism created a settler state; by the 1870s, in order to secure European settlers' loyalty, the colony was made a department of France.

the purpose of the French republic and the prestige of the French people. It was France's duty "to contribute to this work of civilization." Jules Ferry, a republican political leader, successfully argued for expanding the French presence in Indochina, saying, "We must believe that if Providence deigned to confer upon us a mission by making us masters of the earth, this mission consists not of attempting an impossible fusion of the races but of simply spreading or awakening among the other races the superior notions of which we are the guardians." Those "superior notions" included a commitment to economic and technological progress and to liberation from slavery, political oppression, poverty, and disease. In what Ferry ironically considered an attack on the racism of his contemporaries, he argued that "the superior races have a right vis-à-vis the inferior races . . . they have a right to civilize them."

Under Ferry, the French acquired Tunisia (1881), northern and central Vietnam (Tonkin and Annam; 1883), and Laos and Cambodia (1893). They also carried this "civilizing mission" into their colonies in West Africa. European and Atlantic trade with the west coast of Africa, in slaves, gold, and ivory, had been well established for centuries. In the late nineteenth century, trade gave way to formal administration. The year 1895 saw the establishment of a Federation of French West Africa, a loosely organized administration to govern an area nine times the size of France, including Guinea, Senegal, and the Ivory Coast. Even with reforms and centralization in 1902, French control remained uneven. Despite military campaigns of pacification, resistance remained, and the French dealt gingerly with tribal leaders, at some times deferring to their authority and at others trying to break their power. They established French courts and law only in cities, leaving Islamic or tribal courts to run other areas. The federation aimed to rationalize the economic exploitation of the area, and to replace "booty capitalism" with a more careful management and development of resources. The French called this "enhancing the value" of the region, which was part of the civilizing mission of the modern republic. The federation embarked on an ambitious program of public works. Engineers rebuilt the huge harbor at Dakar, the most important on the coast, to accommodate rising exports.

With some utopian zeal they redesigned older cities, tried to improve sanitation and health, improved water systems, and so on. The French republic was justifiably proud of the Pasteur Institute for bacteriological research, which opened in France in 1888; overseas institutes became part of the colonial enterprise. One plan called for a large-scale West African railroad network to lace through the region. A public-school program built free schools in villages not controlled by missionaries. Education, though, was not compulsory and was usually for boys.

Such programs plainly served French interests. "Officially this process is called civilizing, and after all, the term is apt, since the undertaking serves to increase the degree of prosperity of our civilization," remarked one Frenchman who opposed the colonial enterprise. None of these measures aimed to give indigenous peoples political rights. As one historian puts it, "the French Government General was in the business not of making citizens, but of civilizing its subjects." More telling, however, the French project was not often successful. The French government did not have the resources to carry out its plans, which proved much more expensive and complicated than anyone imagined. Transportation costs ran very high. Labor posed the largest problems. Here as elsewhere, Europeans faced massive resistance from the African peasants, whom they wanted to do everything from building railroads to working mines and carrying rubber. The Europeans resorted to forced labor, signing agreements

Slaves in Chains, 1896. In Africa, native labor was exploited by Europeans and by other natives, as here.

with local tribal leaders to deliver workers, and they turned a blind eye to the continuing use of slave labor in the interior. For all of these reasons, the colonial project did not produce the profits some expected. In important respects, however, the French investment in colonialism was cultural. Railroads, schools, and projects such as the Dakar harbor were, like the Eiffel Tower (1889), symbols of the French nation's modernity, power, and world leadership.

THE "SCRAMBLE FOR AFRICA" AND THE CONGO

What events set off the "scramble for Africa"?

French expansion into West Africa was but one instance of Europe's voracity on the African continent. The scope and speed with which the major European powers conquered and colonized, asserting formal control was astonishing. The effects were profound. In 1875, 11 percent of the continent was in European hands. By 1902, the figure was 90 percent. European powers mastered logical problems of transport and communication; they learned how to keep diseases at bay. They also had new weapons. The Maxim gun, adopted by the British army in 1889 and first used by British colonial troops, pelted out as many as five hundred rounds a minute; it turned encounters with indigenous forces into bloodbaths and made armed resistance virtually impossible.

THE CONGO FREE STATE

In the 1870s, the British had formed new imperial relationships along the costs of south and east Africa, and in the north and west. A new phase of European involvement struck right at the heart of the continent. Until the latter part of the nineteenth century this territory had been out of bounds for Europeans. The rapids downstream on such strategic rivers as the Congo and the Zambezi made it difficult to move inland, and tropical diseases against which Europeans had little or no resistance were lethal to most explorers. But during the 1870s, a new drive into central Africa produced results. The target was the fertile valleys around the river Congo, and the European colonizers were a privately financed group of Belgians paid

by their king, Leopold II (1865–1909). They followed in the footsteps of Henry Morton Stanley, an American newspaperman and explorer who later became a British subject and a knight of the realm. Stanley hacked his way through thick canopy jungle and territory where no European had previously set foot. His "scientific" journeys inspired the creation of a society of researchers and students of African culture in Brussels, in reality a front organization for the commercial company set up by Leopold. The ambitiously named International Association for the Exploration and Civilization of the Congo was set up in 1876, and set about signing treaties with local elites that opened the whole Congo River basin to commercial exploitation. The vast resources of palm oil and natural rubber, and the promise of minerals (including diamonds) were now within Europeans' reach.

The strongest resistance that Leopold's company faced came from other colonial powers, particularly Portugal, which objected to this new drive for occupation. In 1884, a conference was called in Berlin to settle the matter of control over the Congo River basin. It was chaired by the master of European power politics, Otto von Bismarck, and attended by all the leading colonial nations, as well as the United States. The conference established ground rules for a new phase of European economic and political expansion. Europe's two great overseas empires, Britain and France, and the strongest emerging power inside Europe, Germany, joined forces and settled the Congo issue. Their dictates seemed to be perfectly in line with nineteenth-century liberalism. The Congo valleys would be open to free trade and commerce; a slave trade still run by some of the Islamic kingdoms in the region would be suppressed in favor of free labor; and a Congo Free State would be set up, denying the region to the formal control of any single European country.

In reality the "Congo Free State" was run by Leopold's private company, and the region was opened up to unrestricted exploitation by a series of large European corporations. The older slave trade was suppressed, but the European companies took the "free" African labor guaranteed in Berlin and placed workers in equally bad conditions. Huge tracts of land, larger than whole European countries, became diamond mines or plantations for the extraction of palm oil, rubber, or cocoa. African workers labored in appalling conditions, with no real medicine or sanitation, too little food, and according to production schedules that made European factory labor look mild by comparison. Hundreds of thousands of African workers died from disease and overwork. Because European managers did not respect the different cycle of seasons in central Africa, whole crop years were lost, leading to famines. Laborers working in the heat of the dry season often carried individual loads on their backs that would have been handled by heavy machinery in a European factory. Thousands of Africans were pressed into work harvesting goods Europe wanted. They did so for little or no pay, under the threat of beatings and ritual mutilation for dozens of petty offenses against the plantation companies, who made the laws of the "Free State." Eventually the scandal of the Congo became too great to go on unquestioned. A whole generation of authors and journalists, most famously Joseph Conrad in his *Heart of Darkness*, publicized the arbitrary brutality and the vast scale of suffering. In 1908, Belgium was forced to take direct control of the Congo, turning it into a Belgian colony. A few restrictions at least were imposed on the activities of the great plantation companies that had brought a vast new store of raw materials to European industry by using slavery in all but name.

THE PARTITION OF AFRICA

The occupation of Congo, and its promise of great material wealth, pressured other colonial powers into expanding their holdings. By the 1880s, the "scramble for Africa" was well underway, hastened by stories of rubber forests or diamond mines in other parts of central and southern Africa. The guarantees made at the 1884 Berlin conference allowed the Europeans to take further steps. The French and Portugese increased their holdings. Italy moved into territories along the Red Sea, beside British-held land and the independent kingdom of Ethiopia.

Germany came relatively late to empire overseas. Bismarck was reluctant to engage in an enterprise that he believed would yield few economic or political advantages. Yet he did not want either Britain or France to dominate Africa, and Germany seized colonies in strategic locations. The German colonies in Cameroon and most of modern Tanzania separated the territories of older, more established powers. Though the Germans were not the most enthusiastic colonialists, they were still fascinated by the imperial adventure, and jealous of their territories. When the

CHRONOLOGY	
THE "SCRAMBLE FOR AFRICA," 1870–1908	
European drive into Central Africa	1870s
French acquire Tunisia	1881
Berlin Congress	1884
Germany colonizes Cameroon and Tanzania	1884
Federation of French West Africa	1895
Congo becomes a Belgian colony	1908

Herero people of German Southwest Africa (now Namibia) rebelled in the early 1900s, the Germans responded with a vicious campaign of village burning and ethnic killing that nearly annihilated the Herero.

Great Britain and France had their own ambitions. The French aimed to move west to east across the continent, an important reason for the French expedition to Fashoda (in the Sudan) in 1898 (see below). Britain's part in the "scramble" took place largely in southern and eastern Africa, and was encapsulated in the dreams and career of one man: the diamond tycoon, colonial politician, and imperial visionary Cecil Rhodes. Rhodes, who made a fortune from the South African diamond mines in the 1870s and 1880s and founded the diamond-mining company DeBeers, became prime minister of Britain's Cape Colony in 1890. (He left part of this fortune for the creation of the Rhodes scholarships to educate future leaders of the empire at Oxford.) In an uneasy alliance with the Boer settlers in their independent republics and with varying levels of support from London, Rhodes pursued two great personal and imperial goals. The personal goal was to build a southern African empire that was founded on diamonds. "Rhodesia" would fly the Union Jack out of pride but send its profits into Rhodes' own companies. Through bribery, double dealing, careful coalition politics with the British and Boer settlers, warfare, and outright theft, Rhodes helped carve out territories occupying the modern nations of Zambia, Zimbabwe, Malawi, and Botswana—most of the savannah of southern Africa. Rhodes had a broader imperial vision, one that he shared with the new British colonial secretary in the late 1890s, Joseph Chamberlain. The first part of

> Eventually the scandal of the Congo became too great to go on unquestioned. A whole generation of authors and journalists, most famously Joseph Conrad in his Heart of Darkness, publicized the arbitrary brutality and the vast scale of suffering.

ATLANTIC
OCEAN

Algiers (Fr.)
Ceuta (Sp.) Melilla (Sp.)
ALGIERS   TUNIS
MOROCCO   MEDITERRANEAN SEA

TRIPOLI   EGYPT
British occupied
(nominally Turkish
suzerainty)
RIO DE ORO

RED SEA

SENEGAL   MAHDIST
STATE   ERITREA
GAMBIA   OBOCK (Fr.)
TUKOLOR
EMPIRE   DAHOMEY   Lake Chad
BORNU   ABYSSINIAN
PORT.   SAMORI'S   SOKOTO   EMPIRE
GUINEA   STATE   CALIPHATE   (ETHIOPIA)
SIERRA   ASHANTI   BRITISH
LEONE   LIBERIA   ROYAL NIGER   SOMALILAND
COY. SPHERE
IVORY COAST
GOLD COAST   Porto   CAMEROON   BUNYORO
TOGO   Novo
LAGOS   (Fr.)   BUGANDA KINGDOM
OIL RIVERS   Lake Victoria
FERNANDO PO (Sp.)   FRENCH   CONGO   Witu (Ger.)
SÃO THOMÉ (Port.)   CONGO   FREE   BRITISH EAST AFRICA SPHERE
RIO MUNI (Sp.)   STATE
SULTANATE OF
ZANZIBAR
ATLANTIC   Lake
Tanganyika   GERMAN EAST AFRICA
OCEAN   KATANGA   COY. SPHERE
ANGOLA   Lake
TEKE   Nyasa

MOZAMBIQUE   MADAGASCAR

MATABELE   INDIAN
SOUTH-   LAND
WEST   HERERO   OCEAN
AFRICA
WALVIS BAY (Br.)   NAMA
TRANSVAAL
REPUBLIC
BECHUANALAND   SWAZILAND
PROTECTORATE   ZULULAND
BRITISH   NATAL
BECHUANALAND   CAPE   BASUTOLAND
COLONY
ORANGE FREE STATE

Legend:
- Indigenous power
- Turkish suzerainty
- Portuguese
- British
- King Leopold's State
- German
- Boer
- French
- Italian
- Spanish

0   500   1000 Miles
0   500   1000 Kilometers

AFRICA, c. 1886

Before World War I, who were the "winners" and "losers" in the scramble for Africa? Although the French claim
was the largest, why were the British imperial gains more impressive? Given their late arrival as a unified nation
and colonial power, how did Germany fare in the race for colonial possessions? Why did Italy, despite an advan-

AFRICA, c. 1914

tageous geographical relationship to Africa, fare so poorly in carving out an African empire? What does the ultimate result of the prewar scramble for Africa suggest to us about the ways in which European powers regarded each other, and why they felt maintaining economic and material resources was so important?

ATROCITIES IN THE CONGO

George Washington Williams (1849–1891), an African American pastor, journalist, and historian, was among a hand-ful of international observers who went to the Congo in the 1890s to explore and report back on conditions. He wrote sev-eral reports: one for the United States government, another that he presented at an international antislavery conference, several newspaper columns, and an open letter to King Léopold, from which the following is excerpted.

Good and Great Friend,

I have the honour to submit for your Majesty's consideration some reflections respecting the Independent State of Congo, based upon a careful study and inspection of the country and character of the personal Government you have established upon the African Continent. . . .

I was led to regard your enterprise as the rising of the Star of Hope for the Dark Conti-nent, so long the habitation of cruelties. . . . When I arrived in the Congo, I naturally sought for the results of the brilliant programme:—*"fostering care," "benevolent enterprise,"* an *"honest and practical effort"* to increase the knowledge of the natives *"and secure their welfare."* . . .

I was doomed to bitter disappointment. Instead of the natives of the Congo "adopting the fostering care" of your Majesty's Government, they everywhere com-plain that their land has been taken from them by force; that the Government is cruel and arbitrary, and declare that they neither love nor respect the Govern-ment and its flag. Your Majesty's Government has se-questered their land, burned their towns, stolen their property, enslaved their women and children, and committed other crimes too numerous to mention in detail. It is natural that they everywhere shrink from *"the fostering care"* your Majesty's Government so eagerly proffers them.

There has been, to my absolute knowledge, no *"hon-est and practical effort made to increase their knowledge and secure their welfare."* Your Majesty's Government has never spent one franc for educational purposes, nor instituted any practical sys-tem of industrialism. Indeed the most un-practical measures have been adopted *against* the natives in nearly every respect; and in the capital of your Majesty's Govern-ment at Boma there is not a native employed. The labour system is radically unpractical. . . .

[R]ecruits are transported under circumstances more cruel than cattle in European countries. They eat their rice twice a day by the use of their fingers; they often thirst for water when the season is dry; they are exposed to the heat and rain, and sleep upon the damp and filthy decks of the vessels often so closely crowded as to lie in human ordure. And, of course, many die. . . .

All the crimes perpetrated in the Congo have been done in *your* name, and *you* must answer at the bar if Public Sentiment for the misgovernment of a people, whose lives and fortunes were entrusted to you by the august Conference of Berlin, 1884–1885. . . .

George Washington Williams, "An Open Letter to His Serene Majesty Leopold II, King of the Belgians, and Sovereign of the Independent State of Congo, July 1890" in John Hope Franklin, *George Washington Williams: A Biography* (Chicago: University of Chicago Press, 1985), pp. 243–254.

Left: **"The Rhodes Colossus."** This cartoon, which appeared in *Punch* magazine, satirized the ambitions of Cecil Rhodes, the driving force behind British imperialism in South Africa. Right: **"Now We Shant Be Long to Cairo."** So read the banner across Engine No. 1 taking the first train from Umtali to Salisbury, Rhodesia. In Cecil Rhodes's vision, Capetown-to-Cairo railway symbolized British domination of the African continent.

that vision was a British presence along the whole of eastern Africa, symbolized by the goal of a "Cape-to-Cairo" railway. The second was that the empire should make Britain self-sufficient, with British industry able to run on the goods and raw materials shipped in from its colonies, then exporting many finished products back to those lands. Once the territories of "Zambeziland" and "Rhodesia" were taken, Rhodes found himself turning against the European settlers in the region, a conflict that led to outright war in 1899 (see below).

This battle over strategic advantage, diamonds, and European pride was symbolic of the "scramble." As each European power sought its "place in the sun," in the famous phrase of the German kaiser William II, they brought more and more of Africa under direct colonial control. It created a whole new scale of plunder as companies were designed and managed to strip the continent of its resources, and African peoples faced a combination of direct European control and "indirect rule" which allowed local elites friendly to European interests literally to lord over those who resisted. The partition of Africa was the most striking instance of the new imperialism, with international and domestic repercussions.

IMPERIAL CULTURE

How did empire affect European identity?

The relationship between the metropole and the colonies was not carried on at a distance; imperialism was thoroughly anchored in late nineteenth-century Western culture. Images of empire were everywhere in the metropole. They were not just in the propagandist literature distributed by the proponents of colonial expansion, but on tins of tea and boxes of cocoa, as background themes in posters advertising everything from dance halls to sewing machines. Museums and world's fairs displayed the products of empire and introduced spectators to "exotic peoples" who were now benefiting from European "education." Music halls rang to the sound of imperialist songs. Empire was almost always present in novels of the period, sometimes appearing as a faraway setting for fantasy, adventure, or stories of self-discovery. Sometimes imperial themes and peoples were presented as a subtly menacing presence at home. Even in the tales of Sherlock Holmes, which were set in London and not overtly imperialist, the furnishings of empire provided instantly recognizable signs of opulence and decadence. In *The Sign of Four*, Holmes visits a gentleman in a lavish apartment: "Two great tigerskins thrown athwart [the carpet] increased the suggestion of Eastern luxury, as did a huge hookah which stood upon a mat in the corner." In "The Man with the Twisted Lip," Watson wanders into one of the supposed opium dens in the East End of London, and is waited on by a "sallow Malay attendant." The "dens" themselves were largely an invention; police records of the time show very few locations in London that supplied the drug. As a realm of fantasy, overseas empires and "exotic" cultures became part of the century's sexual culture. Photos and postcards of North African harems or "unveiled" Arab women were common in European pornography, as were colonial memoirs that chronicled the sexual adventures of their authors.

Empire, however, was not simply background; it played an important part in establishing European identity. In the case of France, the "civilizing mission" demonstrated to French citizens the grandeur of their nation. Building railroads and "bringing progress to other lands" illustrated the vigor of the French republic. Many British writers spoke in similar tones. One called the British empire "the greatest secular agency for good known to the world." Another, using more religious language, argued, "The British race may safely be called a missionary race. The command to go and teach all nations is one that the British people have, whether rightly or wrongly, regarded as specially laid upon themselves." The sense of high moral purpose was not restricted to male writers or authority figures. In England, the United States, Germany, and France, the speeches and projects of women's reform movements were full of references to empire and the civilizing mission. Britain's woman suffrage movement, for instance, was fiercely critical of the British government but often equally nationalist and imperialist. Asking that women be brought into British politics seemed to involve calling on them to take on imperial, as well as civic, responsibilities. British women reformers wrote about the oppression of Indian women by child marriage and sati, and saw themselves shouldering the "white woman's burden" of reform. The French suffragist Hubertine Auclert wrote a book entitled *Arab Women in Algeria* (1900), which angrily indicted both French colonial administrators for their indifference to the

> Empire, however, was not simply background; it played an important part in establishing European identity.

condition of women in their domains and the French republic for shrugging off the claims of women at home. Her arguments stung precisely because they rested on the assumption that European culture should be enlightened. Arab women were "victims of Muslim debauchery," wrote Auclert, and polygamy led to "intellectual degeneracy." The image of women languishing in the colonies not only dramatized the need for reform, it enabled European women in their home countries to see themselves as bearers of progress. The liberal writer and political theorist John Stuart Mill (see Chapter 20) regularly used the colonial world as a foil. When he wanted to drive home a point about freedom of speech or religion, he pointed to India as a counter example, trading in stereotypes about Hindu or Muslim "obscurantism," and appealing to British convictions that theirs was the superior civilization. This contrast between colonial backwardness or moral degeneration and European civility and stability shaped Western culture and political debate.

Imperial culture also gave new prominence to theories of race. In the 1850s, Count Arthur de Gobineau (1816–1882) had written a massive tome on *The Inequality of the Races*, but the book sparked little interest until the period of the new imperialism, when it was translated into English and widely discussed. For Gobineau, race offered the "master key" to understanding problems in the modern world. He argued, "The racial question overshadows all other problems of history . . . the inequality of the races from whose fusion a people is formed is enough to explain the whole course of its destiny." Some of Gobineau's ideas followed from earlier Enlightenment projects that compared and examined different cultures and governments. Unlike his Enlightenment predecessors, however, Gobineau did not believe that environment had any effect on politics, culture, or morals. Race was all. He argued that a people degenerated when it no longer had "the same blood in its veins, continual adulteration having gradually affected the quality of that blood." Enlightenment thinkers often argued that slavery made its victims unable to understand liberty. Gobineau, by contrast, asserted that slavery proved its victims' racial inferiority.

Houston Stewart Chamberlain (1855–1927), the son of a British admiral, tried to improve Gobineau's theories and make them more "scientific." That meant tying racial theories to the new scientific writing about evolution, Charles Darwin's natural science, and

RUDYARD KIPLING AND HIS CRITICS

Rudyard Kipling (1865–1936) remains one of the most famous propagandists of empire. His novels, short stories, and poetry about the British imperial experience in India were defining texts for the cause in which he believed. Kipling's poem, "The White Man's Burden," reprinted below, was published in 1899 during the Spanish-American War and the struggle for the Philippines. The poem called on the United States to shoulder the burden of empire. It became an instant classic and, as the response on the follwing page shows, it soon became part of the turn-of-the-century debate about imperialism.

Take up the White Man's burden—
    Send forth the best ye breed—
Go, bind your sons to exile
    To serve your captives' need;
To wait, in heavy harness,
    On fluttered folk and wild—
Your new-caught sullen peoples,
    Half devil and half child.

Take up the White Man's burden—
    In patience to abide,
To veil the threat of terror
    And check the show of pride;
By open speech and simple,
    An hundred times made plain,
To seek another's profit
    And work another's gain.

Take up the White Man's burden—
    The savage wars of peace—
Fill full the mouth of Famine,
    And bid the sickness cease;
And when your goal is nearest
    (The end for others sought)
Watch sloth and heathen folly
    Bring all your hope to nought.

Take up the White Man's burden—
    No iron rule of kings,
But toil of serf and sweeper—
    The tale of common things.
The ports ye shall not enter,
    The roads ye shall not tread,

Go, make them with your living
    And mark them with your dead.

Take up the White Man's burden,
    And reap his old reward—
The blame of those ye better
    The hate of those ye guard—
The cry of hosts ye humour
    (Ah, slowly!) toward the light:—
"Why brought ye us from bondage,
    Our loved Egyptian night?"

Take up the White Man's burden—
    Ye dare not stoop to less—
Nor call too loud on Freedom
    To cloak your weariness.
By all ye will or whisper,
    By all ye leave or do,
The silent sullen peoples
    Shall weigh your God and you.

Take up the White Man's burden!
    Have done with childish days—
The lightly-proffered laurel,
    The easy ungrudged praise:
Comes now, to search your manhood
    Through all the thankless years,
Cold, edged with dear-bought wisdom,
    The judgment of your peers.

Rudyard Kipling, "The White Man's Burden," *McClure's Magazine* 12 (Feb. 1899).

To the Editor of *The Nation*:

Sir: The cable informs us that "Kipling's stirring verses, the 'Call to America,' have created a . . . profound impression" on your side. What that impression may be, we can only conjecture. There is something almost sickening in this "imperial" talk of assuming and bearing burdens for the good of others. They are never assumed or held where they are not found to be of material advantage or ministering to honor or glory. Wherever empire (I speak of the United Kingdom) is extended, and the climate suits the white man, the aborigines are, for the benefit of the white man, cleared off or held in degradation for his benefit. . . .

Taking India as a test, no one moves a foot in her government that is not well paid and pensioned at her cost. No appointments are more eagerly contended for than those in the Indian service. A young man is made for life when he secures one. The tone of that service is by no means one "bound to exile," "to serve . . . captives' need," "to wait in heavy harness," or in any degree as expressed in Mr. Kipling's highfalutin lines. It is entirely the contrary: "You are requested not to beat the servants" is a not uncommon notice in Indian hotels. . . . So anxious are we, where good pay is concerned, to save Indians the heavy burden of enjoying them, that, while our sons can study and pass at home for Indian appointments, her sons must study and pass in England; and even in India itself whites are afforded chances closed to natives. . . .

There never was a fostered trade and revenue in more disastrous consequences to humanity than the opium trade and revenue. There never was a more grinding and debilitating tax than that on salt. . . .

Alfred Webb, "Mr. Kipling's Call to America," *The Nation* 68 (Feb. 23, 1899).

Herbert Spencer's views about the evolution of societies. (On Darwin and Spencer, see Chapter 23.) Like other European thinkers concerned with race, Chamberlain used the concept of evolutionary change to show that races changed over time. Chamberlain's books proved extremely popular, selling tens of thousands of copies in England and Germany. Francis Galton (1822–1911), a British scientist who studied evolution, similarly explored how hereditary traits were communicated from generation to generation. In 1883, Galton first used the term "eugenics" to refer to the science of improving the "racial qualities" of humanity through selective breeding of "superior types." Karl Pearson (1857–1936), who did pioneering work in the use of statistics, turned his systematic analysis to studies of intelligence and "genius," sharing Galton's worries that only new policies of racial management would check Europe's impending decline. These theories did not, by themselves, produce an imperialist mindset, and they were closely linked with other developments in European culture, particularly renewed antagonism about social class and a fresh wave of European anti-Semitism (see Chapter 23). Yet the increasingly scientific racism of late-nineteenth-century Europe made it easier for many to reconcile the rhetoric of progress, individual freedom, and the "civilizing mission" with contempt for other peoples. It also provided a rationale for imperial conquest and a justification for the bloodshed that imperialism brought, for instance, in Africa.

Still, Europeans disagreed on these issues. Politicians and writers who championed imperialism, or offered racial justifications for it, met with opposition. Such thinkers as Hobson and Lenin condemned the entire imperial enterprise as an act of greed and antidemocratic arrogance. Writers such as Joseph Conrad, who shared many of their contemporaries' racism, nevertheless believed that imperialism signaled deeply rooted pathologies in European culture. In short, one result of imperialism was serious debate on its effects and causes. Many of the anti-imperialists were men and women from the colonies themselves, who brought their case to the metropole. The British Committee of the Indian National Congress, for instance, gathered together many members of London's Indian community determined to educate British public opinion about the exploitation of Indian peoples and resources. This work involved speaking tours, demonstrations, and meetings with potentially sympathetic British radicals and socialists.

Perhaps the most defiant of all anti-imperialist actions was the London Pan-African conference of

1900, staged at the height of the "scramble for Africa" and during the Boer War (see below). The conference grew out of an international tradition of African American, British, and American antislavery movements, and out of groups like the African Association (founded in 1897), which brought the rhetoric used earlier to abolish slavery to bear on the tactics of European imperialism. They protested forced labor in the mining compounds of South Africa as akin to slavery, and asked in very moderate tones for some autonomy and representation for native African peoples. The Pan-African Conference of 1900 was small, but it drew delegates from the Caribbean, West Africa, and North America, including the thirty-two-year-old Harvard Ph.D. and leading African American intellectual W. E. B. Dubois (1868–1963). The conference issued a proclamation "To the Nations of the World," with a famous introduction written by DuBois. "The Problem of the twen-

tieth century is the problem of the color line. . . . In the metropolis of the modern world, in this the closing year of the nineteenth century," the proclamation read, "there has been assembled a congress of men and women of African blood, to deliberate solemnly the present situation and outlook of the darker races of mankind." The British government ignored the conference completely. Yet Pan-Africanism, like Indian nationalism, grew by sudden (and, for imperialists, disturbing) leaps after World War I.

In recent years historians have become increasingly interested in colonial cultures, or the results of the imperial encounter across the world. Cities such as Bombay, Calcutta, and Shanghai boomed in the period, more than tripling in size. Hong Kong and other "treaty ports", run as outposts of European commerce and culture, were transformed as Europeans built banks, shipping enterprises, schools, and military

Imperialism gave new prominence to dramatically different theories of race. British scientist Francis Galton (left) originated the term "eugenics" and helped to develop the scientific racism that justified imperial conquest. African American intellectual W.E.B. Dubois (right) attended the Pan-African conference of 1900, and was one of those whose anti-imperialism sprung from his work with the antislavery movement.

academies, and engaged in missionary activities. The variety of national experiences makes generalization very difficult, but we can underscore a few points. First, colonialism created new, hybrid cultures. Both European and indigenous institutions and practices, especially religion, were transformed by their contact with each other. Second, although Europeans often considered the areas they annexed "laboratories" for creating well-disciplined and orderly societies, the social changes Europeans brought in their wake confounded such plans. In both western and southern Africa, European demands for labor brought men out of their villages, leaving their families behind, and crowded them by the thousands into the shantytowns bordering sprawling new cities. Enterprising locals set up all manner of illegal businesses catering to transitory male workers, disconcerting European authorities in the process. Hopes that European rule would create a well-disciplined labor force and well-patrolled cities were quickly dashed.

Third, authorities on both side of the colonial encounter worried enormously about preserving national traditions and identity in the face of an inevitably hybrid and constantly changing colonial culture. Especially in China and India, debates about whether education should be "westernized" or continue on traditional lines set off fierce debates. Chinese elites, already divided over such customs as foot binding and concubinage (the legal practice of maintaining formal sexual partners for men outside their marriage), found their dilemmas heightened as imperialism became a more powerful force. Uncertain whether such practices should be repudiated or defended, they wrestled with great anguish over the ways in which their own culture had been changed by the corruption of colonialism. Proponents of reform and change in China or India had to sort through their stance toward "modern" Western culture, the culture of the colonizers, and "traditional" popular culture. For their part, British, French, and Dutch colonial authorities fretted that too much familiarity between colonized and colonizer would weaken European traditions and undermine European power. In Phnom Penh, Cambodia (then part of French Indochina), where French citizens lived in neighborhoods separated from the rest of the city by a moat, colonial authorities nonetheless required "dressing appropriately and keeping a distance from the

> Proponents of reform and change in China or India had to sort through their stance toward "modern" Western culture, the culture of the colonizers, and "traditional" popular culture.

natives." Scandalized by what he considered the absence of decorum among the French in the city, a French journalist asserted that a French woman should never be seen in the public market. "The Asians cannot understand such a fall." European women were to uphold European standards and prestige.

Not surprisingly, sexual relations provoked the most anxiety and also the most contradictory responses. "In this hot climate, passions run higher" wrote a French administrator in Algeria. "The French soldiers seek out Arab women due to their strangeness and newness." "It was common practice for unmarried Englishmen resident in China to keep a Chinese girl, and I did as others did," reported a British man stationed in Shanghai. But when he followed convention and married an English woman, he sent his Chinese mistress and their three children to England to avoid any awkwardness. European administrators fitfully tried to prohibit liaisons between European men and indigenous women, labeling such affairs as "corrupting" and "nearly always disastrous." They grew increasingly hostile to the children of such unions. But such prohibitions only drove relations underground, increasing the gap between the public façade of colonial rule and the private reality of colonial lives. In this and other spheres, colonial culture forced a series of compromises about "acceptability," and created changing, sometimes subtle, ethnic hierarchies. And such local and personal dramas were no less complex than the Great Powers' clashes over territories.

CRISES OF EMPIRE AT THE TURN OF THE TWENTIETH CENTURY

Why was the Boer War unique?

The turn of the twentieth century brought a series of crises to the Western empires. Those crises did not end European rule. They did, however, create sharp tensions between Western nations. The crises also drove imperial nations to expand their economic and military commitments in territories overseas. They shook Western confidence. In all of these ways, they became central to Western culture in the years before World War I.

FASHODA

The first crisis, in the fall of 1898, pitted Britain against France at Fashoda, in the Egyptian Sudan. Britain's establishment of a "protectorate" in Egypt after the 1880s Suez Canal confrontation had several important effects. It changed British strategy in east Africa, encouraging Rhodes's "Cape to Cairo" ideas. It also opened up the archaeological and cultural treasures of Egypt's past to British adventurers and academics, keen students—and self-aggrandizing editors—of history. It seemed that the most ancient civilization was now linked to the most successful modern one, and British explorers could trace the "source of the Nile" by traveling up waters that were governed under a British flag.

Explorers were not the only Britons to venture farther up the Nile. In the name of protecting the new, pro-British ruler, Britain intervened in an Islamic uprising in the Sudan. An Anglo-Egyptian force was sent to the Sudanese capital, Khartoum, led by the most flamboyant—and perhaps least sensible—of Britain's colonial generals, Charles "Chinese" Gordon, well known for his role in suppressing the Taiping Rebellion. The Sudanese rebels, led by Mahdi (a religious leader who claimed to be the successor to the prophet Muhammad), besieged Gordon. British forces were ill prepared to move south on the Nile in strength; Gordon ended up dying a "hero's death" as the rebels stormed Khartoum. Avenging Gordon occupied officials in Egypt and the British popular imagination for more than a decade. In 1898, a second large-scale rebellion provided the opportunity. An Anglo-Egyptian army commanded by a methodical and ambitious engineer, General Horatio Kitchener, sailed south up the Nile and attacked Khartoum. Using modern rifles, artillery, and machine guns, they massacred the Mahdi's army at the town of Omdurman and retook Khartoum. Gordon's body was disinterred and reburied with pomp and circumstance as the British public celebrated a famous and easy victory.

That victory brought complications, however. France, which held territories in central Africa next door to the Sudan, saw the British presence along the eastern side of Africa as a prelude to Britain's dominance of the whole continent. A French expedition was sent to the Sudanese town of Fashoda to challenge British claims to the southernmost part of the territory. The French faced off with troops from Kitchener's army. For a few weeks in September 1898 the situation teetered on the brink of war. The matter was resolved, however, when Britain not only called France's bluff but also provided guarantees against further expansion by cementing borders for the new "Anglo-Egyptian Sudan," an even greater extension of the political control that had begun with the Suez Canal.

ETHIOPIA

Traditional methods of imperial rule and notions of European military and moral superiority faced other challenges at the turn of the century. The Boxer Rebellion in China was one of a number of indigenous revolts against Western imperial methods and its consequences. The Russo-Japanese war was a dangerously large conflict between two imperial powers that challenged notions of inherent European superiority over all the peoples of the world.

Other complications for European powers arose as well. During the 1880s and 1890s Italy had been developing a small empire of its own along the shores of the Red Sea. Italy annexed Eritrea and parts of Somalia, and shortly after the death of Gordon at Khartoum defeated an invasion of its new colonies by the Mahdi's forces. These first colonial successes encouraged Italian politicians, still trying to build a modern industrial nation, to mount a much more ambitious imperial project. In 1896, an expedition was sent to conquer Ethiopia. Ethiopia was a mountainous, inland empire, the last major independent African kingdom. Its emperor, Menelik II, was a savvy politician and shrewd military commander. His subjects were largely Christian, and the empire's trade had allowed Menelik to invest in the latest European artillery to guard his vast holdings. The expedition, which consisted of a few thousand professional Italian soldiers and many more Somali conscripts, marched into the mountain passes of Ethiopia. Menelik let them come, knowing that by keeping to the roads the Italian commanders would have to divide their forces. Menelik's own huge army moved over the mountains themselves, and as the

> Britain's establishment of a "protectorate" in Egypt after the 1880s Suez Canal confrontation had several important effects. It changed British strategy in east Africa, encouraging Rhodes's "Cape to Cairo" ideas.

Emperor Menelik II. Ethiopia was the last major independent African kingdom, its prosperity a counter to the European opinion of African cultures. Menelik soundly defeated the Italian attempt to conquer his kingdom in 1896.

Company in the early 1800s, and who had a long and troubled relationship with their imperial neighbor, Great Britain. Over the course of the nineteenth century the Afrikaners trekked inland from the Cape, setting up two independent republics away from the influence of Britain: the Transvaal and the Orange Free State. In the mid 1880s, gold reserves were discovered in the Transvaal. The British diamond magnate and imperialist Cecil Rhodes had actually tried to provoke war between Britain and the Boers in hopes of adding the Afrikaners' prosperous diamond mines and pastureland to his own territory of "Rhodesia." In 1899, as the result of a series of disputes, Britain did go to war with the Afrikaners. Despite the recent British victory in the Sudan, the British army was woefully unprepared for the war: supplies, communications, and medicine for

disorganized Italian command tried to regroup near the town of Adowa in March 1896, the Ethiopian army set on the separate columns and destroyed them completely, killing six thousand. Adowa was a national humiliation for Italy, and an important symbol for African political radicals and reformers during the early twentieth century. Menelik's prosperous kingdom seemed a puzzling and perhaps dangerous exception to European judgments about African cultures generally.

SOUTH AFRICA: THE BOER WAR

Elsewhere in Africa vaulting ambitions led to an even more troubling kind of conflict: Europeans fighting European settlers. The Afrikaners, also called Boers (an appropriation of the Dutch word for "farmer"), were settlers from the Netherlands and Switzerland who had arrived in South Africa with the Dutch East India

LA GUERRE AU TRANSVAAL
Les camps de reconcentration

An English Concentration Camp during the Boer War. In an attempt to block support to guerrilla fighters, the English restricted Afrikaner civilians to camps where appalling conditions led to the death of nearly 20,000 people over 2 years. This illustration appeared in *Le Petit Journal* in 1901.

Boer Commandos under Louis Botha. Botha became the first prime minister of the Union of South Africa following the Boer War.

the army in South Africa were a shambles. These initial problems were followed by several humiliating defeats as British columns were shot to pieces by Afrikaner forces who knew the terrain. British garrisons at the towns of Ladysmith and Mafeking were besieged. Angered and embarrassed by these early failures the British government, particularly the colonial secretary Joseph Chamberlain, refused any compromise. The new British commander, Sir Robert Roberts, used superior British resources and the railroads built to service the diamond mines to his advantage. British forces steamrolled the Boers, relieved the besieged British garrisons, and took the Afrikaner capital at Pretoria. There were celebrations in London, and hopes that the war was now over.

The Afrikaners, however, were determined never to surrender. Supplied by other European nations, particularly Germany and the Netherlands, the Afrikaners took to the wilderness in "commandos" (small raiding parties) and fought a guerrilla war that dragged on for another three years. British losses due to the commandos and disease led British generals to take most of the comprehensive and brutal steps to which later Western armies would frequently resort in the face of guerrilla warfare. Armored blockhouses were set up to guard strategic locations, shooting at anything that moved. Special cavalry units—often using Irish or Australian horsemen fighting for the "mother country," Britain— were sent in to fight the guerrillas on their own terms, each side committing its share of atrocities. Black Africans, despised by both sides, suffered the effects of famine and disease as the war destroyed valuable farm-

land. The British also instituted "concentration camps"—the first use of the term—where Afrikaner civilians were rounded up and forced to live in appalling conditions so that they would be unable to lend aid to the guerrillas. Nearly twenty thousand civilians died due to disease and poor sanitation over the course of two years. These measures provoked an international backlash. European and American newspapers lambasted the British as imperial bullies. The concentration camps bred opposition in Britain itself where protesters, labeled "pro-Boers" by the conservative press, campaigned against these violations of white Europeans' rights while saying very little about the fate of native Africans in the conflict. In the end, the Afrikaners acquiesced. Afrikaner politicians signed their old republics over to a new, British "Union of South Africa" that gave them a share of political power. The settlement created an uneasy alliance between English settlers and Afrikaners; politicians for both parties preserved their high standards of living by relying on cheap African labor and, eventually, a system of racial segregation known as apartheid.

U.S. IMPERIALISM

Another imperial power began to emerge in the 1890s: the United States. During the late nineteenth century, American governments and private interests that supported imperial expansion played a double game. The United States acted as the champion of the underdeveloped countries in the Western Hemisphere when they were threatened from Europe. Yet America was willing, whenever it suited, to prey on its neighbors either "informally" or formally. This ultimately brought conflict with another, fragile Western empire. Spain's feeble hold on its Caribbean and Pacific colonies was plagued by rebellion in the 1880s and 1890s. The American popular press talked up the cause of the rebels, and when an American battleship accidentally exploded in port at Havana, Cuba, American imperialists and the press clamored for a war of revenge. The administration of President William McKinley was extremely wary of going to war, but McKinley also understood political necessity. The United States stepped in to protect its investments, to guarantee the maritime security of trade routes in the Americas and the Pacific, and to demonstrate the power of the newly built-up American navy. It declared war on Spain in 1898 on trumped-up grounds and swiftly won. In Spain, the Spanish-American War provoked an entire generation of writers, politicians, and intellectuals to national soul searching. This led to the end of the Spanish monarchy in 1912 and the germination of political tensions that eventually exploded in the Spanish Civil War of the 1930s.

In the same year that the United States won its "splendid little war" against Spain, it also annexed Puerto Rico, established a "protectorate" over Cuba, and fought a short but brutal war against Philippine rebels who liked American colonialism no better than the Spanish kind. In the Americas, the United States continued its interventions. When the Colombian province of Panama threatened to rebel in 1903, the Americans quickly backed the rebels, recognized Panama as a republic, and then proceeded to grant it protection while Americans built the Panama Canal on land leased from the new government. The Panama Canal (which opened officially in 1914), like Britain's canal at Suez, cemented American dominance of the seas in the Americas and the eastern Pacific. Interventions in Hawaii and later Santo Domingo were further proof that the United States was no less an imperial power than the nations of Europe.

CONCLUSION

In the last quarter of the nineteenth century, the long-standing relationship between European nations and the rest of the world entered a new stage. That stage was distinguished by the stunningly rapid extension of formal European control and by new patterns of discipline and settlement. It was driven by the rising economic needs of the industrial West, by territorial conflict, and by nationalism, which by the late nineteenth century linked nationhood to empire. Among its immediate results was the creation of a "self-consciously imperial" culture in the West. At the same time, however, it plainly created unease in Europe, and contributed powerfully to the sense of crisis that swept through the late-nineteenth-century West.

For all its force, this European expansion was never unchallenged. Imperialism provoked resistance and required constantly changing strategies of rule. During World War I, mobilizing the resources of empire would become crucial to victory. In the aftermath, reimposing the conditions of the late nineteenth century would become nearly impossible. And over the longer term, the political structures, economic developments, and patterns of race relations established in this period would be contested throughout the twentieth century.

KEY TERMS

New imperialism   Leopold II   Boer War
Indian Rebellion of 1857   Arthur de Gobineau   Spanish-American War
Opium Wars   Eugenics
Boxer Rebellion   Pan-African Conference

SELECTED READINGS

Adas, Michael. *Machines as the Measure of Man: Science, Technology, and Ideologies of Western Dominance.* Ithaca and London, 1989.

Bayly, C. A. *Indian Society and the Making of the British Empire.* Cambridge, 1988. A good introduction, and one that bridges eighteenth- and nineteenth-century imperialisms.

Burton, Antoinette. *Burdens of History: British Feminists, Indian Women, and Imperial Culture, 1865-1915.* Chapel Hill, 1994.

Cain, P. J., and A. G. Hopkins. *British Imperialism, 1688-2000.* London, 2002. A new edition of one of the most influential studies. Excellent overview and exceptionally good on economics.

Clancy Smith, Julia, and Frances Gouda. *Domesticating the Empire: Race, Gender, and Family life in French and Dutch Colonialism.* Charlottesville and London, 1998. A particularly good collection of essays that both breaks new historical ground and is accessible to nonspecialists. Essays cover daily life and private life in new colonial cultures.

Conklin, Alice. *A Mission to Civilize: The Republican idea of Empire in France and West Africa, 1895–1930.* Stanford, 1997.

Cooper, Frederick, and Ann Laura Stoler. *Tensions of Empire: Colonial Cultures in a Bourgeois World.* Berkeley, 1997. New approaches, combining anthropology and history, with an excellent bibliography.

Headrick, Daniel R. *The Tools of Empire: Technology and European Imperialism in the Nineteenth Century.* Oxford, 1981. A study of the relationship between technological innovation and imperialism.

Hobsbawm, Eric. *The Age of Empire, 1875–1914.* New York, 1987. Surveys the European scene at a time of apparent stability and real decline.

Lorcin, Patricia. *Imperial Identities: Stereotyping, Prejudice and Race in Colonial Algeria.* New York, 1999.

Louis, William Roger. *The Oxford History of the British Empire.* 5 vols. Oxford, 1998. Excellent and wide-ranging collection of the latest research.

Metcalf, Thomas. *Ideologies of the Raj.* Cambridge, 1995.

Pakenham, Thomas. *The Scramble for Africa, 1876–1912.* London, 1991. A well-written narrative of the European scramble for Africa in the late nineteenth century.

Prochaska, David. *Making Algeria French: Colonialism in Bône, 1870–1920.* Cambridge, 1990.

Robinson, Ronald, and J. Gallagher. *Africa and the Victorians: The Official Mind of Imperialism.* London, 1961.

Said, Edward. *Culture and Imperialism.* New York, 1993.

Sangari, Kumkum, and Sudesh Vaid. *Recasting Women: Essays in Colonial History.* New Delhi, 1989.

Schneer, Jonathan. *London 1900: The Imperial Metropolis.* New Haven, 1999. Excellent recent study of the empire—and opposition to empire—in the metropole.

Spence, Jonathan. *The Search for Modern China.* New York, 1990.

Chapter Twenty-Three

Modern Industry and Mass Politics, 1870–1914

"We are on the extreme promontory of ages!" decreed the Italian poet and literary editor F. T. Marinetti in 1909. In a bombastic manifesto—a self-described "inflammatory declaration" printed on the front page of a Paris newspaper—Marinetti introduced Europe to an aggressive art movement called futurism. Revolting against what he considered the tired and impotent conservatism of Italian culture, Marinetti called for a radical renewal of civilization through "courage, audacity, and revolt." Enamored with the raw power of modern machinery, with the dynamic bustle of urban life, he trumpeted "a new form of beauty, the beauty of speed." Most notably, Marinetti celebrated the heroic violence of warfare and disparaged the moral and cultural traditions that formed the bedrock of nineteenth-century liberalism.

At the time Marinetti issued his manifesto, five years before the First World War, people across Europe indeed felt themselves to be living in a radically new world. In the years since 1870, a series of explosive developments had unfolded across Europe. A second industrial revolution spurred enormous growth in the scope and scale of industry. Mass consumption became a fact of life, as did mass politics. New blocs of voters brought new demands to the political arena, and national governments struggled to maintain order and legitimacy. Socialists mobilized growing numbers of industrial workers, while suffragists demanded the franchise for women. In the arts and sciences, new theories challenged age-old notions of nature, society, truth, and beauty. These changes, however, did not simply ride roughshod over nineteenth-century traditions. Few Europeans embraced the modern era with the unflinching abandon of the futurists. As we will see, the great dynamism and signifacnce of this period arose from the ambivalent, uneven way that groups, individuals, and governments responded to the challenge of a changing world.

FOCUS QUESTIONS

- What developments sparked the second industrial revolution?

- Why did working-class movements grow so dramatically during this period?

- What rights did women claim, and why were they so controversial?

- How did nation-states respond to the rise of mass politics?

- What impact did new scientific theories have on culture?

New Technologies and Global Transformations

What developments sparked the second industrial revolution?

In the last third of the nineteenth century, new technologies transformed the face of manufacturing in Europe, leading to new levels of economic growth and complex realignments among industry, labor, and national governments. Like Europe's first industrial revolution, which began in the late eighteenth century and centered on coal, steam, and iron, this "second" industrial revolution relied on innovation in three key areas: steel, electricity, and chemicals.

Harder, stronger, and more malleable than iron, steel had long been prized as a construction material. But until the mid-nineteenth century, producing steel cheaply and in large quantities was impossible. That changed between the 1850s and 1870s, as three different processes for refining and mass-producing alloy steel revolutionized the metallurgical industry—one by the Englishman Henry Bessemer, the others in tandem between the German Siemen brothers and the French engineer Pierre Martin. Although iron did not disappear overnight, it was soon eclipsed by soaring steel production. Britain's shipbuilders made a quick and profitable switch to steel construction, and thus kept their lead in the industry. Germany and America, however, dominated the rest of the steel industry. By 1901 Germany was producing almost half again as much steel as Britain, allowing Germany to build a massive national and industrial infrastructure.

Annual Output of Steel (in millions of metric tons)

Year	Britain	Germany	France	Russia
1875–1879	0.90	—	0.26	0.08
1880–1884	1.82	0.99	0.46	0.25
1885–1889	2.86	1.65	0.54	0.23
1890–1894	3.19	2.89	0.77	0.54
1895–1899	4.33	5.08	1.26	1.32
1900–1904	5.04	7.71	1.70	2.35
1905–1909	6.09	11.30	2.65	2.63
1910–1913	6.93	16.24	4.09	4.20

Source: Carlo Cipolla, *The Fontana Economic History of Europe*, vol. 3(2) (London: Collins/Fontana Books, 1976), p. 775.

Like steel, electricity had been discovered earlier, and its advantages were similarly well known. Easily transmitted over long distances to be converted into heat, light, and other types of energy, electricity was finally made available for commercial and domestic use by another set of nineteenth-century innovations. In 1800, the Italian Alessandro Volta invented the chemical battery. In 1831, the English scientist Michael Faraday discovered electromagnetic induction, which led to the first electromagnetic generator in 1866. By the 1880s, engineers and technicians had developed alternators and transformers capable of producing high-voltage alternating current. By century's end, large power stations, which often utilized cheap water power, could send electric current over vast distances. In 1879 Thomas Edison and his associates invented the incandescent-filament lamp and changed electricity into light. The demand for electricity skyrocketed, and soon entire metropolitan areas were electrified. As a leading sector in the new economy, electrification powered subways, tramways, and, eventually, long-distance railroads; it made possible new techniques in the chemical and metallurgical industries; and gradually, it dramatically altered living habits in ordinary households.

The chemical industry was a third sector of important new technologies. The efficient production of alkali and sulfuric acid transformed the manufacture of such consumer goods as paper, soaps, textiles, and fertilizer. Britain and particularly Germany became leaders in the field. The British led the way in the production of hand soap and household cleaners. Heightened concerns for household hygiene and new techniques in mass marketing enabled the British entrepreneur Harold Lever to market his soaps and cleansers around the world. German production, on the other hand, focused on industrial use, such as developing synthetic dyes and methods for refining petroleum, and came to control roughly 90 percent of the world's chemical market.

Other innovations contributed to the second industrial revolution. For instance, the growing demand for efficient power spurred the invention of the liquid-fuel internal combustion engine. Already, improved steam turbines had engines running at record speeds, but internal combustion engines offered two major advantages: they were more efficient and did not require stoking, as did steam engines. By 1914 most navies had converted from coal to oil, as had domestic steamship companies. The new engines' dependence on crude petroleum and distilled gasoline at first threatened

A German electrical engineering works illustrates the scale of production during the second industrial revolution.

their general application, but the discovery of oil fields in Russia, Borneo, Persia, and Texas around 1900 allayed fears. Protecting these oil reserves thus became a vital state prerogative. The adoption of oil-powered machinery had another important consequence: industrialists who had previously depended on nearby rivers or coal mines for power were free to take their enterprises to regions bereft of natural resources. The potential for worldwide industrialization was in place. Of course, the internal combustible engine would bring even more radical changes to twentieth-century transportation in the future, but the automobile and the airplane were both still in their infancies before 1914.

CHANGES IN SCOPE AND SCALE

These technological changes were part of a much larger process—impressive increases in the scope and scale of industry. Technologies were both causes and consequences of the Western race toward a bigger, faster, cheaper, and more efficient world. At the end of the nineteenth century, size mattered. The rise of

heavy industry and mass marketing had factories and cities growing hand in hand, while advances in media and mobility advanced the creation of national mass cultures. For the first time, ordinary people followed the news on national and global levels. They watched as European powers divided the globe, enlarging their empires with prodigious feats of engineering mastery; railroads, dams, canals, and harbors grew to monumental proportions. Such projects embodied the ideals of modern European industry. They also generated enormous income for builders, investors, bankers, entrepreneurs, and, of course, makers of steel and concrete. Canals in central Europe, railroads in the Andes, and telegraph cables spanning the ocean floors: these "tentacles of empire," as one historian dubs them, stretched across the globe.

Yet industrialization also brought profound, if less spectacular, changes in Europe. The population grew constantly, particularly in central and eastern Europe. Russia's population increased by nearly a quarter and Germany's by half in the space of a generation. Britain's population, too, grew by nearly one third between

THE INDUSTRIAL REGIONS OF EUROPE

Note the distribution of mineral resources, rail lines and industrial activity marked on this map. What nations enjoyed advantages in the development of industry and why? What resources were have been most important for industrial growth in the nineteenth century?

Map labels

RUSSIA
Moscow
St. Petersburg
FINLAND
SWEDEN
Stockholm
NORWAY
BALTIC SEA
Warsaw
NORTH SEA
DENMARK
Berlin
GREAT BRITAIN
IRELAND
London
NETHERLANDS
BELGIUM
GERMANY
Breslau
Nuremberg
Paris
FRANCE
Limoges
St. Etienne
Toulouse
ATLANTIC OCEAN
SWITZ.
Vienna
AUSTRIA-HUNGARY
Laibach
Marseilles
ITALY
Rome
Naples
Salerno
MONTE-NEGRO
ALBANIA
SERBIA
Belgrade
BULGARIA
ROMANIA
GREECE
Constantinople
TURKEY
BLACK SEA
MEDITERRANEAN SEA
Barcelona
SPAIN
Madrid
PORTUGAL
Lisbon

Legend

Railroad Development
Lines completed by 1848
Area of main railroad completed by 1870
Lines after 1870

Steel
Engineering
Chemicals
Electrical industry
Oil production

Mining
Low-grade coal
High-grade coal
Iron ore
Petroleum

Industrial Concentration
• Cities
Areas

Scale

300 Miles
300 Kilometers
200
100
0

Inset

Area of detail
EUROPE
AFRICA

Population Growth in Major States between 1871 and 1911
(population in millions)

	c. 1871	c. 1911	% increase
German Empire	41.1	64.9	57.8
France	36.1	39.6	9.7
Austria-Hungary*	35.8	49.5	38.3
Great Britain	31.8	45.4	42.8
Italy	26.8	34.7	29.5
Spain	16.0	19.2	20.0

*Not including Bosnia-Herzegovina.
Source: Colin Dyer, *Population and Society in Twentieth Century France* (New York: Holmes and Meier, 1978), p. 5.

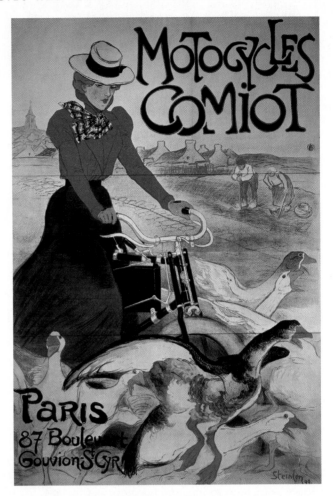

Poster for *Motocycles Comiot,* 1899. The rise in consumer consumption created a new emphasis on advertising, leading to lavish portrayals of merchandise aimed at the middle class.

1881 and 1911. Thanks to improvements in both crop yields and shipping, food shortages declined, which rendered entire populations less susceptible to illness and high infant mortality. Advances in medicine, nutrition, and personal hygiene diminished the prevalence of dangerous diseases such as cholera and typhus, and improved conditions in housing and public sanitation transformed the urban environment.

Changes in scope and scale not only transformed production, they also altered consumption. Indeed it was in this period that consumption began to shift, slowly, to the center of economic activity and theory. The era in which economists would worry about consumer confidence and experts could systematically track the public's buying habits did not begin until the middle of the twentieth century, but developments pointed toward that horizon. Department stores offering both practical and luxury goods to the middle class were one mark of the times—of urbanization, economic expansion, and the new importance attached to merchandising. Advertising took off as well. The lavishly illustrated posters of the late nineteenth century advertising concert halls, soaps, bicycles, and sewing machines were only one sign of underlying economic changes. Even more significant, by the 1880s new stores sought to attract working-class people by introducing the all-important innovation of credit payment. In earlier times, working-class families pawned watches, mattresses, or furniture to borrow money—now they began to buy on credit, a change that would eventually have seismic effects on both households and national economies.

These new, late nineteenth-century patterns of consumption, however, were largely urban. In the countryside peasants continued to save money under mattresses; pass down a few pieces of furniture for generations; make, launder, and mend their own clothes and linens; and offer a kilo of sugar as a generous household gift. Only slowly did retailers whittle away at these traditional habits. Mass consumption remained difficult to imagine in what was still a deeply stratified society.

THE RISE OF THE CORPORATION

Economic growth and the demands of mass consumption spurred reorganization, consolidation, and regulation of capitalist institutions. Although capitalist enterprises had been financed by individual investors through the joint-stock principle at least since the sixteenth century, it was during the late nineteenth century that the modern corporation came into its

THE DANGERS OF CONSUMER CULTURE

By 1880 the Bon Marché in Paris, the world's first department store, was turning over the astronomical sum of 80 million francs annually and came to embody the new rhythm and tempo of mass consumer culture. The vast scale of selling sparked debate about the decline of the family store, the recreation of browsing and window shopping, and, above all, the "moral disaster" of women's limitless desire for goods. In writing the novel The Ladies' Paradise *(1883), Émile Zola noted he wanted to "write the poem of modern activity." The passage below captures the fascination for Denise, a clerk in her uncle's fabric shop, of the fictitious department store the Ladies' Paradise.*

But what fascinated Denise was the Ladies' Paradise on the other side of the street, for she could see the shop-windows through the open door. The sky was still overcast, but the mildness brought by rain was warming the air in spite of the season; and in the clear light, dusted with sunshine, the great shop was coming to life, and business was in full swing.

Denise felt that she was watching a machine working at high pressure; its dynamism seemed to reach to the display windows themselves. They were no longer the cold windows she had seen in the morning; now they seemed to be warm and vibrating with the activity within. A crowd was looking at them, groups of women were crushing each other in front of them, a real mob, made brutal by covetousness. And these passions in the street were giving life to the materials: the laces shivered, then drooped again, concealing the depths of the shop with an excit-ing air of mystery; even the lengths of cloth, thick and square, were breathing, exuding a tempting odour, while the overcoats were throwing back their shoulders still more on the dummies, which were acquiring souls, and the huge velvet coat was billowing out, supple and warm, as if on shoulders of flesh and blood, with heaving breast and quivering hips. But the furnace-like heat with which the shop was ablaze came above all from the selling, from the bustle at the counters, which could be felt behind the walls. There was the continuous roar of the machine at work, of customers crowding into the departments, dazzled by the merchan-dise, then propelled towards the cash-desk. And it was all regulated and organized with the remorseless-ness of a machine: the vast horde of women were as if caught in the wheels of an inevitable force. . . .

Émile Zola, *The Ladies' Paradise*, translated by Brian Nelson (New York: Oxford University Press, 1995), pp. 15–16.

own. To mobilize the enormous funds needed for large-scale enterprises, entrepreneurs needed to offer better guarantees on investors' money. To provide such protection, most European countries enacted or improved their limited- liability laws, which ensured that stockholders could lose only the value of their shares in the event of bankruptcy. Insured in this way, many thousands of middle-class men and women now considered corporate investment a promising ven-ture. After 1870, stock markets ceased to be primarily a clearinghouse for state paper and railroad bonds, and instead attracted new commercial and industrial ventures.

Limited liability was one part of a larger trend of incorporation. Whereas most firms had been small or middle sized, companies now incorporated to attain the necessary size for survival. In doing so, they tended to shift control from company founders and local directors to distant bankers and financiers. Because financial institutions represented the interests of investors whose primary concern was the bottom line, bankers' control over industrial growth encouraged an ethos of impersonal finance capital.

Equally important, the second industrial revolution created a strong demand for technical expertise, which undercut traditional forms of family management. University degrees in engineering and chemistry became more valuable than on-the-job apprenticeships. The emergence of a white-collar class (middle-level salaried managers who were neither owners nor laborers) marked a significant change in work life and for society's evolving class structure.

The drive toward larger business enterprises was spurred by a desire for increased profits. It was also encouraged by a belief that consolidation protected society against the hazards of boom-and-bust economic fluctuations and against the wasteful inefficiencies of unbridled, "ruinous" competition. Some industries combined vertically, attempting to control every step of production from the acquisition of raw materials to the distribution of finished products. Andrew Carnegie's steel company in Pittsburgh controlled costs by owning the iron and coal mines necessary for steel production as well as acquiring its own fleet of steamships and railways to transport ore to the mills. A second form of corporate self-protection was horizontal alignment. Organizing into cartels, companies in the same industry would band together to fix prices and control competition, if not eliminate it outright. Coal, oil, and steel companies were especially suited to the organization of cartels, since only a few major players could front the huge expense of building, equipping, and running mines, refineries, and foundries. In 1894, for example, German entrepreneurs organized the Rhenish-Westphalian Coal Syndicate, which captured 98 percent of Germany's coal market by using ruthless tactics against small competitors, who could join the syndicate or face ruin. Through

similar tactics, both legal and illegal, John D. Rockefeller's Standard Oil company came to control the refined petroleum market in the United States, producing over 90 percent of the country's oil by the 1880s. The monopoly was sustained through the Standard Oil Trust, a legal innovation that enabled Rockefeller to control and manage assets of allied companies through the government. Cartels were particularly strong in Germany and America but less so in Britain, where dedication to free-trade policies made price fixing difficult, and in France, where family firms and laborers both opposed cartels, and where there was also less heavy industry.

Though governments sometimes tried to stem the burgeoning power of cartels (in the United States, for instance, where the "trust-buster" president Theodore Roosevelt put teeth into earlier antitrust laws) the dominant trend of this period was increased cooperation between governments and industry. Contrary to the laissez-faire mentality of early capitalism, corporations developed close relationships with the states in the West—most noticeably in colonial industrial projects, such as the construction of railroads, harbors, and seafaring steamships. These efforts were so costly, or so unprofitable, that private enterprise would not have undertaken them alone. But because they served larger political and strategic interests, governments funded them willingly.

> Coal, oil, and steel companies were especially suited to the organization of cartels, since only a few major players could front the huge expense of building, equipping, and running mines, refineries, and foundries.

Such interdependence was underscored by the appearance of businessmen and financiers as officers of state. The German banker Bernhard Dernburg was the German secretary of state for colonies. Joseph Chamberlain, the British manufacturer and mayoral boss of industrial Birmingham, also served as the colonial secretary. And in France, Charles Jonnart, president of the Suez Canal Company and the Saint-Étienne steel works, was later governor general of Algeria. Tied to imperial interests, the rise of modern corporations had an impact around the globe.

INTERNATIONAL ECONOMICS

From the 1870s on, the rapid spread of industrialization heightened competition among nations. The search for markets, goods, and influence fueled much of the imperial expansion and, consequently, often put countries at odds with each other. Trade barriers arose again to protect home markets. All nations except Britain raised tariffs, arguing that the needs of the nation-state trumped laissez-faire doctrine. Yet changes in international economics fueled the continuing growth of an interlocking, worldwide system of manufacturing, trade, and finance. For example, the near universal adoption of the gold standard in currency exchange greatly facilitated world trade. Pegging the value of currencies, particularly Britain's powerful pound sterling, against the value of gold meant that currencies could be readily exchanged. The common standard also allowed nations to use a third country to mediate trade and exchange to mitigate trade imbalances—a common problem for the industrializing West. Almost all European countries, dependent on vast supplies of raw materials to sustain their rate of industrial production, imported more than they exported. To avoid the mounting deficits that would otherwise have resulted from this practice, they relied on "invisible" exports: shipping, insurance, and banking services. The extent of Britain's exports in these areas was far greater than that of any other country. London was the money market of the world, to which would-be borrowers looked for assistance before turning elsewhere. By 1914, Britain had $20 billion invested overseas, compared with $8.7 billion for France and $6 billion for Germany. Britain also used its invisible trade to secure relationships with food-producing nations, becoming the major overseas buyer for the wheat of the United States and Canada, the beef of Argentina, and the mutton of Australia. These goods, shipped cheaply aboard refrigerated vessels, kept down food prices for working-class families and eased the demand for increased wages.

During this period the relationship between European manufacturing nations and the overseas sources of their materials was transformed, as detailed in the last chapter. Those changes, in turn, reshaped economies and cultures on both sides of the exchange with different degrees of expectations and benefits. This international push toward mass manufacturing and commodity production necessarily involved changes in deep-seated patterns in consumption as well as in production. It altered the landscape and habits of India as well as those of Britain. It brought new rhythms of life to women working in clothing factories in Germany, to porters carrying supplies to build railways in Senegal, to workers dredging the harbor of Dakar.

LABOR POLITICS, MASS MOVEMENTS

Why did working-class movements grow so dramatically during this period?

The rapid capitalist expansion of the late nineteenth century brought a parallel growth in the size, cohesion, and activism of Europe's working classes. The men and women who worked as wage laborers resented corporate power—a shared antagonism fostered not only by the exploitation and inequalities they experienced on the job, but also by the creation of distinctive working-class communities in Europe's expanding cities. Corporations had devised new methods of protecting and promoting their interests, and workers did the same. Labor unions, which were traditionally limited to skilled male workers in small-scale enterprises, evolved during the late nineteenth century into mass, centralized, nationwide organizations. This "new unionism" stressed organization across entire industries, and for the first time, brought unskilled workers into the ranks. The new unions' broad scope gave labor increased power to negotiate wages and job conditions. More important, though, the creation of national unions provided a framework for a new type of political movement: the socialist mass party.

The emergence of socialist parties across Europe after 1870 resulted in part from changes in national political structures. By the 1860s, the advance of parliamentary constitutionalism had opened the political process to new participants, including proponents of socialism. Now part of the legislative process, socialists in parliament led efforts to expand the franchise in the 1860s and 1870s. Their successful efforts created new constituencies of working-class men. At the same time, labor's traditional struggles with management were recast on a national scale, as governments aligned with business interests and countered working-class agitation with antilabor and antisocialist laws. To leaders of the radical left, the organization of national mass political movements seemed the only effective way to contest capitalist political authority. Thus, during this period, socialist movements abandoned their earlier

> Now part of the legislative process, socialists in parliament led efforts to expand the franchise in the 1860s and 1870s. Their successful efforts created new constituencies of working-class men.

WHY DID WORKING-CLASS MOVEMENTS GROW SO DRAMATICALLY DURING THIS PERIOD?

LABOR POLITICS, MASS MOVEMENTS   825

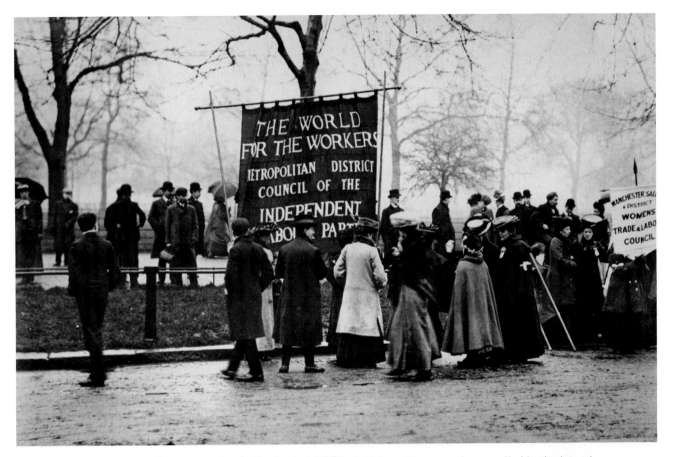

Independent Labor Party Demonstration in England, c. 1893. Activism among workers swelled in the late nineteenth century. Increasingly powerful labor unions had a profound impact on politics.

traditions of insurrectionary radicalism (exemplified by the romantic image of barricaded streets) in favor of legal, public competition within Europe's parliamentary systems.

This shift to popular mass politics, and the accompanying success of labor movements, owed as much to an upsurge in activism by intellectuals as it did to the efforts of workers and unions. Chief among these intellectuals was Karl Marx, whose early career was discussed in Chapter 20. Since the 1840s Marx and his collaborator Fredrick Engels had been intellectuals and activists, writing pamphlets and participating in the organization of fledgling socialist movements. Then, in 1867, Marx published the first of three volumes of *Capital*, a work he believed was his greatest contribution to the struggle for human emancipation. It provided historical materialism with a theoretical foundation, and it also attacked capitalism on the battlefield of economics. In the spirit of nineteenth-century science, Marx claimed to offer a systematic analysis of how capitalism forced workers to exchange their labor for subsistence

wages while enabling owners of the means of production to amass both wealth and power. Splicing together the scholarly study of economics with calls for revolutionary politics, the book became the preeminent socialist critique of capitalism.

For a variety of reasons, Marxism's explosive synthesis of thought and action appealed to workers and intellectuals across the West. First, Marxism made some of the most radical, insistent arguments for democracy and political inclusion of the period. Throughout Europe, though particularly in the western nations, Marxist socialism provided a crucial foundation for building a democratic mass politics. Few other groups pushed so strongly to secure civil liberties, expand conceptions of citizenship, or build a welfare state. As a theoretical matter, Marxism also made powerful claims for gender equality, though in practice woman suffrage took a backseat to class politics. Marxist utopianism was a crucial element, too, for its powerful promise of a better and attainable future for laborers rallied large numbers of workers to the cause.

Socialist Party Pamphlet, c. 1895. Socialism emerged as a powerful political force throughout Europe in the late nineteenth century although in different forms depending on the region. This German pamphlet quotes from the Communist Manifesto of 1848, calling for workers of the world to unite.

Not all working-class movements, however, were Marxist. Even as Marxist thought was taken up in various political and labor organizations, differences between the philosophies, objectives, and methods of varying left-wing groups remained strong. Such differences were amplified across industries, occupation, regions, and nations; there was no homogenous workers' movement. The most divisive issues, however, were the role of violence and whether socialists should cooperate with liberal, or "bourgeois" governments—and if so, to what end. Some "gradualists," particularly in Britain, were willing to work with liberals for piecemeal reform, while more radical socialists sought parliamentary power as a way to hasten the overthrow of capitalism. Anarchists and syndicalists rejected parliamentary politics altogether. This first pivotal debate over this issue occurred at the International Working Men's Association, or First International, which was founded in 1864 to promote coordinated labor activity throughout Europe. Marx and his supporters argued fiercely in favor of political mass movements; anarchists such as Mikhail Bakunin rejected centralized organizations of all kinds (whether nation-states or socialist parties) and called instead for terror and violence. Though this protracted argument prevented the International from drawing a clear map of political action, its goals remained at the fore for subsequent socialist organizations.

THE SPREAD OF SOCIALIST PARTIES— AND ALTERNATIVES

After the First International folded in 1876, organized labor politics developed rapidly, and in varying directions. Most prominently, Marxist socialism spread through a number of socialist and social democratic parties founded between 1875 and 1905 in Germany, Belgium, France, Austria, and Russia. These parties were disciplined, politicized workers' organizations aimed at seizing control of the state for revolutionary change: the model among them was the SPD, the German Social Democratic party. Formed in 1875, the SPD first aimed for political change within Germany's parliamentary political system, but after an era of oppressive antisocialist laws, it adopted an explicitly Marxist platform—preparing a politically conscious proletariat for the imminent collapse of capitalism. By the outbreak of the First World War, the Social Democrats were the largest, best organized workers' party in the world. Several key factors made Germany particularly receptive to social democracy: rapid and extensive industrialization, a large urban working class, a new parliamentary constitution, a national government hostile to organized labor, and no tradition of liberal reform.

The importance of this last factor is most evident when we consider the case of Britain, which was the world's first—and most—industrialized country, yet which had a much smaller, and more moderate, socialist presence than other European nations. Through the end of the nineteenth century, much of the progressive socialist agenda was advanced by radical Liberals in Britain, which forestalled the growth of an independent socialist party. Even when a separate Labour party was formed in 1901, it remained distinctively moderate, committed to incremental reform of the capitalist system rather than its overthrow. Its efforts focused on

WHY DID WORKING-CLASS MOVEMENTS GROW SO DRAMATICALLY DURING THIS PERIOD?

LABOR POLITICS, MASS MOVEMENTS   827

Anarchism and Syndicalism. Anarchists, with their reliance on violence, stood at the radical end of the socialist spectrum. Anarchists committed several high-profile political assassinations such as the assassination of French president Marie Francois Carnot in 1894 (left). Syndicalists, also on the radical side of the socialist spectrum, favored massive movements of direct action, such as the general strike depicted in this poster (right).

pragmatic reforms such as public housing, welfare benefits, and improved wages. For the range of political activists who belonged to the Labour party, and for Britain's many trade unions as well, Parliament remained a legitimate vehicle for effecting social change, limiting the appeal of revolutionary Marxism.

If parliamentary reform provided one popular alternative to the Marxist program, the doctrine of anarchism provided another. As suggested above, proponents of anarchism vied with Marxists over the direction socialism would take in Europe. Opposed to centrally organized economies and politics, and to the very existence of state authority, anarchists advocated individual sovereignty and small-scale, localized democracy. They shared an underlying set of values with the Marxists, but differed radically on how to advance them. Renouncing parties, unions, or any form of modern mass organization, anarchists fell back on the tradition of conspiratorial vanguard violence, which Marx had so forcefully opposed. Consequently, one of anarchism's defining characteristics was its reliance on terrorism, or what the Italian anarchists called "propaganda by the deed." Though not all adopted such methods, anarchists infamously assassinated Tsar Alexander II in 1881, and five other heads of

state in the following years. Influential anarchists such as Peter Kropotkin and Mikhail Bakunin believed that "exemplary terror" could spark popular revolt. Revealing the vulnerability of powerful political leaders, they thought, would create chaos and embolden the people. Though anarchism (perhaps inherently) made no substantial gains as a movement, it kept alive a radical, violent alternative to Marxism's emphasis on parliamentary politics.

Another type of socialist movement, known as syndicalism, gained popularity around the turn of the century, particularly among agricultural laborers in France, Italy, and Spain. Following socialist principles, syndicalism demanded that workers share ownership and control of the means of production, and that the capitalist state be overthrown and replaced by workers' syndicates, or trade associations. Although often elided with anarchism (as in the term *anarcho-syndicalism*), syndicalism was a distinct doctrine that did not call for terror, but rather for mass forms of direct action, including strikes and sabotage. The most widely read theorist of syndicalism, the French intellectual Georges Sorel, argued that a general strike of all industrial workers would do more to bring down the state than would electoral politics. When Sorel later moved to the extreme right, however, more popular and practical leaders emerged in France, where they joined with other French union leaders in 1895 to create a General Confederation of Labor. Committed to working outside the legally constituted framework of French politics, the confederation and other syndicalist organizations helped to spur radicalism among socialists—especially after the attempted revolution in Russia in 1905—but did not build a lasting presence in European politics.

THE LIMITS OF SUCCESS

By the turn of the century, popular socialist movements had made impressive gains all across Europe: in 1895, seven socialist parties had captured between a quarter and a third of the votes in their countries. But just as socialists gained a permanent foothold in national politics, they were also straining under limitations and internal conflicts that had hindered their parties from the outset. Working-class movements, in fact, had never gained anywhere near full worker support. Although some workers remained loyal to older liberal traditions or to religious parties, many others were excluded from socialist politics by its narrow definition of who constituted the working class—that is, only male industrial workers. In terms of elections at least, socialist parties were running up against a wall that they themselves had constructed.

At the same time, the enduring conflict between revolutionaries and reformers, between casting votes and throwing stones, erupted with renewed intensity after 1900. On one side, committed socialists began to question Marx's core assumptions about the inevitability of workers' impoverishment and the collapse of the bourgeois order. A German group of so-called revisionists, led by Eduard Bernstein, challenged Marxist doctrine and called for a shift to moderate reform. Though Bernstein's faction failed to win a majority of votes at either domestic or international congresses, his pragmatism appealed to socialists and workers across the Continent. At the other end of the spectrum, however, were advocates of increased radicalism and direct action. Inspired by the unexpected (and unsuccessful) revolutionary uprising in Russia in 1905, German Marxists such as Rosa Luxembourg called for mass strikes, hoping to seize the moment and ignite a widespread proletarian revolution.

Conflicts over strategy peaked just before the First World War, as moderates, reformists, and orthodox Marxists debated about how to respond to the threat of international conflict. Yet these divisions did not diminish the strength and appeal of turn-of-the-century socialism. Indeed, on the eve of the war, governments discreetly consulted with labor leaders about rank-and-file workers' willingness to enlist and fight. Having built impressive organizational and political strength since the 1870s, working-class parties now affected the ability of nation-states to wage war. In short, they had come of age.

DEMANDING EQUALITY: SUFFRAGE AND THE WOMEN'S MOVEMENT

What rights did women claim, and why were they so controversial?

Since the 1860s, the combination of working-class activism and liberal constitutionalism had expanded male suffrage rights across Europe: by 1884, Germany, France, and Britain had enfranchised most men. But nowhere did women have the right to vote. Nineteenth-century political ideology relegated women to the status of second-class citizens, and even egalitarian-minded socialists seldom challenged this entrenched hierarchy. Excluded from the workings of parliamentary and mass party politics, women pressed their interests through independent organizations and through forms of direct action. The new women's movement won some crucial legal reforms during this period, and after the turn of the century, its militant campaign for suffrage fed the growing sense of political crisis, most notably in Britain.

Women's organizations, such as the General German Women's Association, pressed first for educational and legal reforms. In Britain, women's colleges were established at the same time that women won the right to control their own property. (Previously women surrendered their property, including wages, to their husbands.) Laws in 1884 and 1910 gave Frenchwomen the same right, and the ability to divorce their husbands. German women, too, won more favorable divorce laws by 1870, and in 1900 they were granted full legal rights. After these important changes in women's status, suffrage crystallized as the next logical goal. Indeed, votes became *the* symbol for women's ability to attain full personhood. As the suffragists saw it, enfranchisement

WHAT RIGHTS DID WOMEN CLAIM, AND WHY WERE THEY SO CONTROVERSIAL?

DEMANDING EQUALITY: SUFFRAGE AND THE WOMEN'S MOVEMENT   829

meant not merely political progress but economic, spiritual, and moral advancement as well. By the last third of the century, middle-class women throughout western Europe had founded clubs, published journals, organized petitions, sponsored assemblies, and initiated other public activities to press for the vote. The number of middle-class women's societies rapidly multiplied; some, such as the German League of Women's Voting Rights, established in 1902, were founded solely to advocate votes. To the left of middle-class movements were organizations of feminist socialists, women such as Clara Zetkin and Lily Braun who believed that only a socialist revolution would free women from economic as well as political exploitation.

> The new women's movement won some crucial legal reforms during this period, and after the turn of the century, its militant campaign for suffrage fed the growing sense of political crisis, most notably in Britain.

In Britain, woman suffrage campaigns exploded in violence. Millicent Fawcett, a distinguished middle-class woman with connections to the political establishment, brought together sixteen different organizations into the National Union of Women's Suffrage Societies (1897), committed to peaceful, constitutional reform. But the movement lacked the political or economic clout to sway a male legislature. They became increasingly exasperated by their inability to win over either the Liberal or Conservative party, each of which feared that female suffrage would benefit the other. For this reason Emmeline Pankhurst founded the Women's Social and Political Union in 1903, which adopted tactics of militancy and civil disobedience. WSPU women chained themselves to the visitors' gallery in the House of Commons, slashed paintings in museums, inscribed VOTES FOR WOMEN in acid on the greens of golf courses, disrupted political meetings, burned politicians' houses, and smashed department-store windows. The government countered violence with repression. When arrested women went on hunger strikes in prisons, wardens fed them by force—tying them down, holding their mouths open with wooden and metal clamps, and running tubes down their throats. In 1910 the suffragists' attempt to enter the House of Commons set off a six-hour riot with policemen and bystanders, shocking and outraging a nation unaccustomed to such kinds of violence from women. The intensity of suffragists' moral claims was dramatically embodied by the 1913 martyrdom of Emily Wilding Davison who, wearing a "Votes for Women" sash, threw herself in front of the king's horse on Derby Day and was trampled to death.

REDEFINING WOMANHOOD

The campaign for woman suffrage was perhaps the most visible and inflammatory aspect of a larger cultural shift, in which traditional Victorian gender roles were redefined. In the last third of the nineteenth century, economic, political, and social changes were undermining the view that men and women should occupy distinctly different spheres. Women became increasingly visible in the work force as growing numbers of them took up a greater variety of jobs. Some working-class women joined the new factories and workshops in an effort to stave off their families' poverty, in spite of some working-class men's insistence that stable families required women at home. In addition, the expansion of government and corporate bureaucracies, coupled with a scarcity of male labor in the face of industrial growth, brought middle-class women to the work force as social workers and clerks. The increase in hospital services and the advent of national compulsory education required more nurses and teachers. Again, a shortage of male workers and a need to fill so many new jobs as cheaply as possible made women

Militant Martyrdom for Woman Suffrage. Emily Davison throwing herself under the king's horse at the Derby in 1913.

Changes in white-collar work. Male clerical work underwent great change at the end of the nineteenth century to accommodate the cadres of women office workers.

women's new political participation had been laid earlier in the century. Reform movements of the early nineteenth century depended on women and raised women's standing in public. First with charity work in religious associations and later with hundreds of secular associations, women throughout Europe directed their energies toward poor relief, prison reform, Sunday school, temperance, ending slavery and prostitution, and expanding educational opportunities for women. Reform groups brought women together outside the home, encouraging them to speak their minds as free-thinking equals, and to pursue political goals—a right denied them as individual females. And while some women in reform groups supported political emancipation, many others were drawn into reform politics by appeals to the belief that they had a special moral mission: they saw their public activities as merely an extension of feminine domestic duties. Nonetheless, nineteenth-century reform movements had opened up the world beyond the home, particularly for the middle classes, and widened the scope of possibilities for later generations.

These changes in women's roles were paralleled by the emergence of a new social type, dubbed the "new woman." A "new" woman demanded education and a job; she refused to be escorted by chaperones when she went out; she rejected the restrictive corsets of mid-century fashion. In other words, she claimed the right to a physically and intellectually active life and refused to conform to the norms that defined nineteenth-century womanhood. The new woman was an image—in part the creation of artists and journalists, who filled newspapers, magazines, and advertising billboards with pictures of women riding bicycles in bloomers (voluminous trousers with a short skirt); smoking cigarettes; and enjoying the cafés, dance halls, tonic waters, soaps, and other emblems of consumption. Very few women actually fitted this image: among other things, most were too poor. Still, middle- and working-class women demanded more social freedom and redefined gender norms in the

a logical choice. Thus women, who had campaigned vigorously for access to education, began to see doors opening to them. Swiss universities and medical schools began to admit women in the 1860s. In the 1870s and 1880s, British women established their own colleges at Cambridge and Oxford. Parts of the professional world began to look dramatically different: in Prussia, for instance, 14,600 full-time women teachers were staffing schools by 1896. These changes in women's employment began to deflate the myth of female domesticity.

In addition, some women began to work in the political arena—an area previously termed off limits. This is not to say that female political activity was unprecedented; in important ways, the groundwork for process. For some onlookers, women's new-found independence amounted to shirking domestic responsibilities, and they attacked women who defied convention as ugly "half-men," unfit and unable to marry. For supporters, though, these "new women" symbolized a welcome era of social emancipation.

Opposition to these changes was intense, sometimes violent, and not exclusively male. Men scorned the women who threatened their elite preserves in universities, clubs, and public offices, but a wide array of female antisuffragists also denounced the movement. Conservatives such as Mrs. Humphrey Ward maintained that bringing women into the political arena would sap the virility of the English empire. Octavia Hill, a noted social worker, stated that women should refrain from politics and in so doing, "temper this wild struggle for place and power." Christian commentators criticized suffragists for bringing moral decay through selfish individualism. Still others believed feminism would dissolve the family, a theme that fed into a larger discussion on the decline of the West amid a growing sense of cultural crisis. Indeed, the struggle for women's rights provided a flashpoint for an array of European anxieties over labor, politics, gender, and biology—all of which suggested that an orderly political consensus, so ardently desired by middle-class society, was slipping into the realm of impossibility.

Organized anti-feminism. Male students demonstrate against opening some universities to women.

LIBERALISM AND ITS DISCONTENTS: NATIONAL POLITICS AT THE TURN OF THE CENTURY

How did nation-states respond to the rise of mass politics?

Having championed doctrines of individual rights throughout the nineteenth century, middle-class liberals found themselves on the defensive after 1870. Previously, political power had rested on a balance between middle-class interests and traditional elites. The landed aristocracy shared power with industrial magnates; monarchical rule coexisted with constitutional freedoms. But during the late nineteenth century, the rise of mass politics upset this balance. An expanding franchise and rising expectations brought newcomers to the political stage. As we have seen, trade unions, socialists, and feminists all challenged Europe's governing classes by demanding that political participation be open to all. Governments responded in turn, with a mix of conciliatory and repressive measures. As the twentieth century approached, political struggles became increasingly fierce, and by World War I, the foundation of liberal parliamentary politics was crumbling. For both the left and the right, for both insiders and outsiders, negotiating this unfamiliar terrain required the creation of new and distinctly modern forms of mass politics.

FRANCE: THE EMBATTLED REPUBLIC

The Franco-Prussian War of 1870, which completed the unification of the victorious Germany, was a bruising defeat for France. The government of the Second Empire folded. In its wake, the French proclaimed a republic whose legitimacy was contested from the start. Crafting a durable republican system proved difficult. The new constitution of the Third Republic, which was finally instituted in 1875, signaled a triumph of democratic and parliamentary principles. Establishing democracy, however, was a volatile process, and the Third Republic faced class conflicts scandals and the rise of new forms of right-wing politics that would would poison politics for decades to come.

No sooner had the government surrendered than it faced a crisis that pitted the nation's representatives against the radical city of Paris. During the war, the city had appointed its own municipal government, the Commune. Paris not only refused to surrender to the Germans, it proclaimed itself the true government of France. The city had been besieged by the Germans for four months; most people who could afford to flee had done so and the rest, hungry and radicalized, defied the French government sitting in Versailles and negotiating the terms of an armistice with the Germans. The armistice signed, the French government turned its attention to the city. After long and fruitless negotiations, in March 1871 the government sent troops to disarm the capital. Since the Commune's strongest support came from the workers of Paris, the conflict became a class war. For a week, the "communards" battled against the government's troops, building barricades to stop the invaders, taking and shooting hostages, and retreating very slowly into

The January 1, 1895 edition of *Le Petit Journal* depicts the military degradation of Alfred Dreyfus.

the northern working-class neighborhoods of the city. The French government's repression was brutal. At least twenty-five thousand Parisians were executed, killed in fighting, or consumed in the fires that raged through the city; thousands more were deported to the penal colony of New Caledonia in the South Pacific. The Paris Commune was a brief episode, but it cast a long shadow and reopened old political wounds. For Marx, who wrote about the Commune, and for other socialists, it illustrated the futility of an older insurrectionary tradition on the left and the need for more mass-based democratic politics.

THE DREYFUS AFFAIR AND ANTI-SEMITISM AS POLITICS

On the other side of the French political spectrum, new forms of radical right-wing politics emerged that would foreshadow developments elsewhere. As the age-old foundations of conservative politics, the Catholic church and the landed nobility, slipped, more radical right-wing politics took shape. Stung by the defeat of 1870 and critical of the republic and its premises, the new right was nationalist, anti-parliamentary, and anti-

liberal (in the sense of commitment to individual liberties). Maurice Barrès, for instance, elected deputy in 1889, declared that parliamentary government had sown "impotence and corruption" and was too weak to defend the nation. During the first half of the nineteenth century, nationalism had been associated with the left (see Chapter 20). Now it was more often invoked by the right, and linked to xenophobia (fear of foreigners) in general and anti-Semitism in particular.

Édouard Drumont's career provides a case in point. Drumont was an extraordinarily successful anti-Semitic journalist, who attributed all of late-nineteenth-century France's problems to the baneful influence of an international Jewish conspiracy and labeled all of the right wing's enemies "Jewish." Drumont merged three strands of anti-Semitism: (1) long-standing Christian anti-Semitism, which damned the Jewish people as Christ-killers; (2) economic anti-Semitism, which insisted that the wealthy banking family of Rothschild was representative of all Jews; and (3) late-nineteenth-century racial thinking, which opposed the Aryan (Indo-European) race to the (inferior) Semitic race. Drumont packed these themes into a powerful ideology of hatred. "Jews in the army" subverted the national interest; financial scandals came from "international conspiracies"; mass

ANTI-SEMITISM IN LATE-NINETEENTH-CENTURY FRANCE

Over the course of the nineteenth century, European (though not Russian) Jewish people slowly gained more legal and political rights: access to occupations from which they had been barred, the right to vote and hold political office, the right to marry non-Jews, and so on. France, the land of the revolution of 1789, appeared to many European Jews the beacon of liberty. But in the late nineteenth century, France also proved the birthplace of new forms of anti-Semitism. This excerpt from Édouard Drumont's best-selling Jewish France *(1885) illustrates some themes of that ideology: the effort to displace economic grievances, conservative hatred of the republic, parliamentary government, and the legacy of 1789, and conservative nationalism.*

The only one who has benefitted from the Revolution [of 1789] is the Jew. Everything comes from the Jew; everything returns to the Jew.

We have here a veritable conquest, an entire nation returned to serfdom by a minute but cohesive minority, just as the Saxons were forced into serfdom by William the Conqueror's 60,000 Normans.

The methods are different, the result is the same. One can recognize all the characteristics of a conquest: an entire population working for another population, which appropriates, through a vast system of financial exploitation, all of the profits of the other. Immense Jewish fortunes, castles, Jewish townhouses, are not the fruit of any actual labor, of any production: they are the booty taken from an enslaved race by a dominant race.

It is certain, for example, that the Rothchild family, whose French branch alone possesses a declared fortune of three billion [francs], did not have that money when it arrived in France; it has invented nothing, it has discovered no mine, it has tilled no ground. It has therefore appropriated these three billion francs from the French without giving them anything in exchange. . . .

Thanks to the Jews' cunning exploitation of the principles of '89, France was collapsing into dissolu-tion. Jews had monopolized all of the public wealth, had invaded everything, except the army. The representatives of the old [French] families, whether noble or bourgeois . . . gave themselves up to pleasure, and were corrupted by the Jewish prostitutes they had taken as mistresses or were ruined by the horse-sellers and money-lenders, also Jews, who aided the prostitutes. . . .

The fatherland, in the sense that we attach to that word, has no meaning for the Semite. The Jew . . . is characterized by an *inexorable universalism.*

I can see no reason for reproaching the Jews for thinking this way. What does the word "Fatherland" mean? Land of the fathers. One's feelings for the Fatherland are engraved in one's heart in the same way that a name carved in a tree is driven deeper into the bark with each passing year, so that the tree and the name eventually become one. You can't become a patriot through improvization; you are a patriot in your blood, in your marrow.

Can the Semite, a perpetual nomad, ever experience such enduring impressions? . . .

Édouard Drumont, *La France juive. Essai d'histoire contemporaine* (Paris: C. Marpon and E. Flammarion, 1885), excerpt translated by Cat Nilan, 1997.

culture, the women's movement, dance halls, and all the developments that were supposedly corrupting French culture simply demonstrated the strength of "cosmopolitan and international Jewish interests"; "wealthy Jewish bankers" or "greedy Jewish socialists and trade unionists" preyed on the peasants and small shopkeepers of France. Drumont pounded at these themes in his newspaper, *La Libre Parole* ("*Free Speech*") founded in 1892, through his Anti-Semitic League, and in his massive, five-hundred-page bestseller, *Jewish France* (1886), which sold one hundred thousand copies in the first two months.

This politicized anti-Semitism exploded with the Dreyfus Affair, a pivotal political moment in the life of the French Republic. In 1894 a group of monarchist officers in the French army accused Alfred Dreyfus, a Jewish captain on the French general staff, of selling military secrets to Germany. Tried by court-martial, Dreyfus was convicted, stripped of his rank, and deported for life to Devil's Island, a ghastly prison in the Atlantic Ocean. In 1896 Colonel Georges Picquart, a new head of the Intelligence Division, questioned the verdict and, after an initial probe, announced that the trial documents were forgeries.

When the War Department denied Dreyfus a new trial, the "case" became an "affair," polarizing the country. Republicans, socialists, liberals, and such figures as the writer Émile Zola backed Dreyfus. As the Dreyfusards, as they were called, saw it, they stood for progress and justice against reaction and prejudice, and the survival of the republic lay in the balance. Zola, for instance, blasted the French establishment in a provocative newspaper essay "J'accuse!" that accused the government, the courts, and the military of falsifying documents, covering up treason, and blatantly ignoring basic issues of justice. On the other side, the anti-Dreyfusards included other socialists, who considered the affair a distraction from more important economic issues, monarchists, militarists, and some clergy. One Catholic newspaper insisted that the question was not whether Dreyfus was guilty or innocent but whether Jews and unbelievers were not the "secret masters of France."

After six years of bitter controversy, an executive order in 1899 set Dreyfus free. In 1906, the Supreme Court cleared him of all guilt, reinstating him in the army as a major and inducting him into the Legion of Honor. Among the Affair's many consequences was the separation of church and state in France. Republicans were convinced that the church and the army were hostile to the republic. Laws passed between 1901 and 1905 prohibited religious orders in France not authorized by the state, forbade clerics to teach in schools, and, finally, dissolved the union of the Catholic church and the state.

The Third Republic emerged stronger in the first decade of the new century. At the same time, the radical right and anti-Semitism were plainly political forces across Europe. The mayor of Vienna in 1897 was elected on an anti-Semitic platform. The Russian secret police forged and published a book called *The Protocols of the Learned Elders of Zion* (1903 and 1905), which imagined a Jewish plot to dominate the world. The Russian state also helped frame Mendel Beiless, a Jewish clerk from Ukraine who was arrested in 1911, convicted of murder, and kept in prison two years before being cleared. Political anti-Semitism as theorized by Drumont and practiced by others across Europe, intimately linked to late-nineteenth-century nationalism, insistently cast social and political issues as racial ones.

ZIONISM

Among the many people to watch with alarm as the Dreyfus Affair unfolded was Theodor Herzl (1860–1904), a Hungarian-born journalist working in Paris. The rise of virulent anti-Semitism in the land of the French Revolution troubled Herzl deeply. He considered the Dreyfus Affair "only the dramatic expression of a much more fundamental malaise." Despite Jewish emancipation, or the granting of civil rights, Herzl came to believe Jewish people might never be assimilated into Western culture, and that staking the Jewish community's hopes on acceptance and tolerance was dangerous folly. Herzl endorsed a different strategy of Zionism, or building a separate Jewish homeland outside of Europe (though not necessarily in Palestine). A small movement of Jewish settlers, mainly refugees from Russia, had already begun to establish settlements outside of Europe. Herzl was not the first to voice these goals, but he was the most effective advocate of political Zionism. He argued that Zionism should be recognized as a modern nationalist movement, capable of negotiating with other states. In 1896 Herzl published *The State of the Jews* (1896); a year later he convened the first Zionist Congress in Switzerland. Throughout he

> Despite Jewish emancipation, or the granting of civil rights, Herzl came to believe Jewish people might never be assimilated into Western culture, and that staking the Jewish community's hopes on acceptance and tolerance was dangerous folly.

JEWISH MIGRATION IN THE LATE 19TH CENTURY

What drove Jewish people to flee from eastern Europe in the late nineteenth century? Why did certain cities have larger Jewish populations than others? Why did many Jewish people migrate to the United States or to Palestine?

was involved in high politics, meeting with British and Ottoman heads of state. Herzl's vision of a Jewish homeland had strong utopian elements, for he believed that building a new state had to be based on a new and transformed society, eliminating inequality and establishing rights. Although Herzl's writings met with much

skepticism, they received an enthusiastic reception in areas of Eastern Europe where anti-Semitism was especially violent. During the turmoil of World War I, specific wartime needs prompted the British to become involved in the issue, embroiling Zionism in international diplomacy (see Chapter 24).

GERMANY'S SEARCH FOR IMPERIAL UNITY

Through deft foreign policy, three short wars, and a groundswell of national sentiment, Otto von Bismarck united Germany under the banner of Prussian conservatism during the years 1864 to 1871. In constructing a federal political system, Bismarck sought to create the centralizing institutions of a modern nation-state while safeguarding the privileges of Germany's traditional elites, including a dominant role for Prussia. Bismarck's constitution assigned administrative, educational, and juridical roles to local state governments and established a bicameral parliament to oversee Germany's national interests. The appointed delegates of the upper house (the Bundesrat) served as a conservative counterbalance to the more democratic lower house (the Reichstag), which was elected through universal male suffrage. In the executive branch, power rested solely with Wilhelm I, the Prussian king and German kaiser (emperor), who wielded full control of foreign and military affairs. Unlike in France or Britain, Germany's cabinet ministers had no responsibility to the parliament but answered only to kaiser.

Under a government that was neither genuinely federal nor democratic, building a nation with a sense of common purpose was no easy task. The German government successfully created imperial agencies for banking, coinage, federal courts, and railroads, all of which fostered administrative and economic union. But the question of political unity remained. Many states

had, after all, sided with Austria in 1866, and had only acquiesced in German unity under the threat of French conquest. Three fault lines in Germany's political landscape especially threatened to crack the national framework: the divide between Catholics and Protestants; a growing Social Democratic party; and the potentially divisive economic interests of agriculture and industry.

Between 1866 and 1876, Bismarck governed principally with liberal factions interested in promoting free trade and economic growth. To strengthen ties with these liberal coalitions, Bismarck unleashed an anti-Catholic campaign in Prussia. In what is known as the *Kulturkampf*, or "cultural struggle," Bismarck appealed to long-standing sectarian tensions over such issues as secular public education and civil marriage, and to anxieties about Catholics' allegedly torn loyalty between the nation and the pope. With the support of a majority of Protestant liberals, he passed laws that imprisoned priests for political sermons, banned Jesuits from Prussia, and curbed the church's control over education and marriage. The campaign backfired, however, and public sympathy for the persecuted clergy helped the Catholic Center party to win fully one quarter of the seats in the Reichstag in 1874. Recognizing that he needed Catholic support for new economic legislation, Bismarck negotiated an alliance of convenience with the Catholic Center party in 1878.

An economic downturn had undercut support for free trade policies in the late 1870s, prompting Bismarck to fashion a new coalition that included agricultural and industrial interests, as well as socially conservative Catholics. This new alliance passed protectionist legislation (grain tariffs, duties on iron and steel) that riled both laissez-faire liberals and the German working class, which was represented by the Social Democratic party. Just as Bismarck had used anti-Catholic sentiments to solidify his previous alliance, he now turned against a new "enemy of the empire"—Social Democrats—and couched his protectionist and antisocial legislation in terms of defending a "Christian moral order." In 1878, after two separate attempts on the life of the emperor, Bismarck declared a national crisis to push through a series of antisocialist laws that forbade Social Democrats to as-

Contemporary Cartoon depicting Bismarck stuffing the antisocialist law of 1878 down the throat of the German parliament. The caption read: "Devour it, Bird, or die!"

semble or distribute their literature. Additional legislation further expelled socialists from major cities. In effect, these laws obliged the Social Democratic party (known as the SPD) to become a clandestine organization, fostering a subculture of workers who increasingly viewed socialism as the sole answer to their political needs.

Having made the stick to beat down organized-labor politics, Bismarck now offered a carrot to German workers with an array of social reforms. Workers were guaranteed sickness and accident insurance, rigorous factory inspection, limited working hours for women and children, a maximum workday for men, public employment agencies, and old-age pensions. By 1890, Germany had put together a raft of social legislation, with the exception of unemployment insurance, that became a prototype for the majority of Western nations in the decades to come. Yet significantly, the laws failed to achieve Bismarck's short-term political goal of winning workers' loyalty. In spite of all legal hindrances, votes for the Social Democratic party more than quadrupled between 1881 and 1890, the year that Bismarck resigned.

The embittered atmosphere created by Bismarck's domestic politics prompted the new kaiser, Wilhelm II, to move in a new direction; he dramatically suspended the antisocialist legislation in 1890, legalizing the SPD. By 1912, the Social Democrats polled a third of the votes cast and elected the largest single bloc to the Reichstag; yet the kaiser refused to allow any meaningful political participation beyond a tight-knit circle of elites. Meanwhile, commercial, industrial, and agriculture interests deadlocked over tariffs. German

> By 1912, the Social Democrats polled a third of the votes cast and elected the largest single bloc to the Reichstag; yet the kaiser refused to allow any meaningful political participation beyond a tight-knit circle of elites.

politics were fast approaching a stalemate, but any conclusion to this volatile standoff was preempted by the outbreak of World War I.

BRITAIN: FROM MODERATION TO MILITANCE

During the half century before 1914, the British prided themselves on what they believed to be an orderly and workable system of government. Following the passage of the Second Reform Bill in 1867, which extended suffrage to more than a third of the nation's adult males, the two major political parties, Liberal and Conservative, vied with each other to win the support of these growing voting blocs. Parliament responded to new voters' concerns with laws that recognized the legality of trade unions, commissioned the rebuilding of large urban areas, provided elementary education for all children, and permitted male religious dissenters to attend the elite universities of Oxford and Cambridge. In 1884, suffrage expanded to include more than three fourths of adult males.

Two central figures, the Conservative Benjamin Disraeli and the Liberal William Gladstone, dominated the new parliamentary politics. Disraeli, a converted Jew and best-selling novelist, was eminently pragmatic, while Gladstone, a devout Anglican and moral reformer, viewed politics as "morality writ large." Despite their opposing sensibilities and bitter parliamentary clashes, the two men led parties that, in retrospect, seem to share largely similar outlooks. Managed by cabinet ministers drawn from the upper middle class and the landed gentry, both Liberals and Conservatives offered moderate programs that appealed to the widening electorate. Cabinet ministers prepared legislation but acknowledged the ultimate authority of the House of Commons, which could remove a governing cabinet with a vote of no confidence. Steered by men whose similar education and outlooks promised middling solutions, the British political system was stable and "reasonable."

Even Britain's working-class movements were notably moderate until the turn of the century, when at last new trade unions and middle-class socialist societies combined to create an independent Labour party in 1901. Pressed from the left, the Liberal ministry that took office in 1906 passed sickness, accident, old-age,

CHRONOLOGY

GERMANY'S QUEST FOR POLITICAL UNITY, 1871–1890

Bismarck's Kulturkampf	1871–1878
Conciliation with the Vatican	1878
Bismarck's antisocialist legislation	1878–1884
Bismarck launches social legislation	1883–1890
Bismarck resigns	1890

and unemployment insurance acts, along with other concessions to trade unions. To pay for the new welfare programs—and for a larger navy to counter the German buildup—the chancellor of the exchequer (finance minister), David Lloyd George, proposed an explosively controversial budget in 1909 that included progressive income and inheritance taxes, designed to make the wealthy pay at higher rates. The bill provoked a rancorous showdown with the House of Lords, which was forced not only to pass the budget, but also to surrender permanently its power to veto legislation passed by the Commons. The acrimony of this debate pointed to an increasingly militant tenor in British politics, which to many seemed headed for chaos.

Indeed, after 1900, Britain's liberal parliamentary framework, which had so successfully channeled the rising demands of mass society since the 1860s, began to buckle, as an array of groups rejected legislative activity in favor of radical action. Industrial militants launched enormous labor protests, including nationwide strikes of coal and rail workers and citywide transportation strikes in London and Dublin. Woman suffragists adopted violent forms of direct action, discussed above. Meanwhile, in Ireland, radical nationalists began to favor armed revolution as the simplest solution to the parliamentary wrangling over the details of Irish home rule, or self-government.

Ireland had been put under the direct government of the British Parliament in 1800, and various political and military efforts to regain Irish sovereignty over the course of the nineteenth century had failed. By the 1880s, a modern nationalist party (the Irish Parliamentary party) had begun to make substantial political gains through the legislative process, but as with other reform-minded groups (such as women's suffrage), its agenda was increasingly eclipsed toward the turn of the century by more radical organizers. These proponents of "new nationalism" disdained the party's representatives as ineffectual and out of touch. New groups revived interest in Irish history and culture and provided organizational support to the radical movement, as did such militant political organizations as Sinn Féin and the Irish Republican Brotherhood. In 1913, as a Liberal plan to grant home rule was once again on the table (prompting panic in Ulster, the Protestant-majority counties of northern Ireland, which feared Catholic rule) Irish nationalists called a number of paramilitary groups into action. Already awash in domestic crises, Britain now seemed on the verge of a civil war—a prospect delayed only by the outbreak of the World War in Europe.

RUSSIA: THE ROAD TO REVOLUTION

The industrial and social changes that swept Europe proved especially unsettling in Russia. An autocratic political system was ill equipped to handle conflict and the pressures of modern society. Western industrialization challenged Russia's military might. Western political doctrines—liberalism, democracy, socialism—threatened its internal political stability. Like other nations, tsarist Russia negotiated these challenges with a combination of repression and reform.

In the 1880s and 1890s Russia launched a program of industrialization that made it the world's fifth largest economy by the early twentieth century. The state largely directed this industrial development, for despite the creation of a mobile work force after the emancipation of the serfs in 1861, no independent middle class capable of raising capital and stewarding industrial enterprises emerged. In fact, the Russian state financed more domestic industrial development than any other major European government during the nineteenth century.

Rapid industrialization heightened social tensions. The transition from country to city life was sudden and harsh. Men and women left agriculture for factory work, straining the fabric of village life and rural culture. In the industrial areas, workers lived in large barracks and were marched, military style, to and from the factories, where working conditions were among the worst in Europe. They coped by leaving their villages only temporarily and returning to their farms for planting or the harvest. Social change strained Russia's legal system, which did not recognize trade unions or employers' associations. Laws still distinguished among nobles, peasants, clergy, and town dwellers, categories

C H R O N O L O G Y

THE RUSSIAN ROAD TO REVOLUTION, 1861–1905

Emancipation of the serfs	1861
State-directed industrialization begins	1880s–1890s
Alexander II assassinated	1881
Alexander III launches counterreforms	1881–1894
Nicholas II continues "Russification" policies	1894–1905
Russo-Japanese War	1904–1905
The first Russian revolution: "Bloody Sunday" and October Manifesto	1905

Execution of the conspirators against Alexander II. Known as the liberator of the serfs, Tsar Alexander II grew increasingly restrictive and unpopular late in his reign, and was assassinated in 1881 by radicals. Six were ultimately hanged for the crime, although the execution of the woman at the center was delayed due to her pregnant state.

that did not correspond to an industrializing society. Outdated banking and financial laws failed to serve the needs of a modern economy.

Real legal reform, however, would threaten the regime's stability. Alexander II (1855–1881), the "Tsar Liberator" (emancipator of the serfs), had grown wary of change. Instead of loosening restrictions, he tightened them. The regime set up a system of provincial and county assemblies, or zemstvos, elected by all social classes (though dominated by the nobility) in 1864, only to curtail their rights and ability to discuss politics. It extended censorship to the press and schools as well. When the tsar was killed by a radical assassin in 1881, his successor, Alexander III (1881–1894), steered the country sharply to the right. Russia had nothing in common with western Europe, Alexander III claimed; his people had been nurtured on mystical piety for centuries and would be utterly lost without a strong autocratic system. This principle guided stern repression. The regime curtailed all powers of the zemstvos, increased the authority of the secret police, and subjected villages to the governmental authority of nobles appointed by the state.

Nicholas II (1894–1917) continued these "Counter Reforms." Like his father, he ardently advocated Russi-

fication, or government programs to extend the language, religion, and culture of Greater Russia over the empire's non-Russian subjects. Russification amounted to coercion, expropriation, and physical oppression: Finns lost their constitution, Poles studied their own literature in Russian translation, and Jews perished in pogroms. (*Pogrom* is a Russian term for violent attacks on civilians, which in the late nineteenth century were usually aimed at Jewish communities.) The Russian government did not organize pogroms, but it was openly anti-Semitic and made a point of looking the other way when villagers massacred Jews and destroyed their homes, businesses, and synagogues. Other groups whose repression by the state led to long-lasting undercurrents of anti-Russian nationalism included the Georgians, Armenians, and Azerbaijanis of the Caucasus Mountains.

The most important radical political group in late-nineteenth-century Russia was a large, loosely knit group of men and women who called themselves populists. Populists believed that Russia needed to modernize on its own terms, not the West's. They envisioned an egalitarian Russia based on the ancient institution of the village commune (*mir*). Advocates of populism sprang primarily from the middle class; many of its adherents were young students, and women made up about 15 percent—a significantly large proportion for the period. They formed secret bands, plotting the overthrow of tsarism through anarchy and insurrection. They dedicated their lives to "the people," attempting wherever possible to live among common laborers so as to understand and express the popular will. Populism's historical importance lies less in what it accomplished, which was little, than in what it promised for the future. It acted as a seedbed of organized agitation in Russia, which would in time produce revolution. Populists read Marx's *Capital* and revised his ideas to produce a doctrine suited to Russia. Populists' emphasis on peasant socialism influenced the Social Revolutionary party, formed in 1901, which also concentrated on increasing the political power of the peasant and building a socialist society based on the agrarian communalism of the *mir*.

The emergence of industrial capitalism and a new, desperately poor working class created Russian Marxism. Organized as the Social Democratic party, Russian Marxists concentrated their efforts on behalf of urban workers and saw themselves as part of the international working-class movement. They made little headway in a peasant-dominated Russia before the First World War, but they provided disaffected urban factory workers and intellectuals alike with a powerful ideology that stressed the necessity of overthrowing the tsarist regime and the inevitability of a better future. Autocracy would give way to capitalism and capitalism to an egalitarian, classless society. Russian Marxism blended radical, activist opposition with a rational, scientific approach to history, furnishing revolutionaries with a set of concepts with which to understand the upheavals of the young twentieth century.

In 1903 the leadership of the Social Democratic party split over an important disagreement on revolutionary strategy. One group, temporarily in the majority and quick to name itself the Bolsheviks ("majority group"), believed that the Russian situation called for a strongly centralized party of active revolutionaries. The Bolsheviks also insisted that the rapid industrialization of Russia meant that they did not have to follow Marx's model for the West. Instead of working for liberal capitalist reforms, Russian revolutionaries could skip a stage, and immediately begin to build a socialist state. The Mensheviks ("minority group") were more cautious or "gradualist," seeking slow changes and reluctant to depart from Marxist orthodoxy. When the Mensheviks regained control of the Social Democratic party, the Bolsheviks formed a splinter party under the leadership of the young, dedicated revolutionary Vladimir Ilyich Ulanov, who lived in political exile in western Europe between 1900 and 1917. He wrote under the pseudonym of Lenin from the Lena river in Siberia, where he was exiled.

Lenin's theoretical abilities and organizational energy commanded respect, enabling him to remain the leader of the Bolsheviks even while living abroad. From exile Lenin preached unrelenting class struggle, the need for a coordinated revolutionary socialist movement throughout Europe, and, most important, the belief that Russia was passing into an economic stage that made it ripe for revolution. It was the Bolsheviks' responsibility to organize a revolutionary party on behalf of workers, for without the party's discipline, workers could not effect change. Lenin's treatise *What Is to Be Done?* (1902) set out his vision of Russia's special destiny, and it denounced gradualists who had urged collaboration with moderate parties. Lenin considered revolution the only answer to Russia's problems, and he argued that organizing for revolution needed to be done, soon, by "vanguard" agents of the party acting in the name of the working class.

> From exile Lenin preached unrelenting class struggle, the need for a coordinated revolutionary socialist movement throughout Europe, and, most important, the belief that Russia was passing into an economic stage that made it ripe for revolution.

THE FIRST RUSSIAN REVOLUTION

The revolution that came in 1905, however, took all of these radical movements by surprise. Its unexpected occurrence resulted from Russia's resounding defeat in the Russo-Japanese War of 1904–1905. But the revolution had deeper roots. Rapid industrialization had transformed Russia unevenly; certain regions were heavily industrial, while others were less integrated into the market economy. The economic boom of the 1880s and 1890s turned to bust in the early 1900s, as demand for goods tapered off, prices plummeted, and the nascent working class suffered high levels of unemployment. At the same time, low grain prices resulted in a series of peasant uprisings, which, combined with students' energetic radical organizing, became overtly political.

As dispatches reported the defeats of the tsar's army and navy, the Russian people grasped the full extent of

LENIN'S VIEW OF A REVOLUTIONARY PARTY

At the turn of the century, Russian revolutionaries debated political strategy. How could Russian autocracy be defeated? Should they follow the programs of their counterparts in the West? Or did the Russian situation require different tactics? In What is To Be Done? *(1902) Lenin (Vladimir Ilyich Ulyanov, 1870–1924) argued that Russian socialists needed to revise the traditional Marxist view, according to which a large and politically conscious working class would make revolution. In Russia, Lenin argued, revolution required a small but dedicated group of revolutionaries to lead the working class. Lenin's vision was important, for it shaped the tactics and strategies of the Bolsheviks in 1917 and beyond.*

[T]he national tasks of Russian Social-Democracy are such as have never confronted any other socialist party in the world. We shall have occasion further on to deal with the political and organisational duties which the task of emancipating the whole people from the yoke of autocracy imposes upon us. At this point, we wish to state only that the *role of vanguard fighter can be fulfilled only by a party that is guided by the most advanced theory. . . .*

I assert: (1) that no revolutionary movement can endure without a stable organisation of leaders maintaining continuity; (2) that the broader the popular mass drawn spontaneously into the struggle, which forms the basis of the movement and participates in it, the more urgent the need for such an organisation, and the more solid this organisation must be (for it is much easier for all sorts of demagogues to side-track the more backward sections of the masses); (3) that such an organisation must consist chiefly of people professionally engaged in revolutionary activity; (4) that in an autocratic state, the more we *confine* the membership of such an organisation to people who are professionally engaged in revolutionary

activity and who have been professionally trained in the art of combating the political police, the more difficult will it be to unearth the organisation; and (5) the *greater* will be the number of people from the working class and from the other social classes who will be able to join the movement and perform active work in it. . . .

Social-Democracy leads the struggle of the working class, not only for better terms for the sale of labour-power, but for the abolition of the social system that compels the propertyless to sell themselves to the rich. Social-Democracy represents the working class, not in its relation to a given group of employers alone, but in its relation to all classes of modern society and to the state as an organised political force. Hence, it follows that not only must Social-Democrats not confine themselves exclusively to the economic struggle. . . . We must take up actively the political education of the working class and the development of its political consciousness.

Vladimir Lenin, "What is To Be Done?" from *Collected Works of V. I. Lenin,* vol. 5 (Moscow: Progress Publishers, 1964), pp. 369–70, 373, 375.

Bloody Sunday. Demonstrating workers who sought to bring their grievances to the attention of the tsar were met and gunned down by government troops, January 1905.

the regime's inefficiency. Hitherto apolitical middle-class subjects clamored for change, and radical workers organized strikes and held demonstrations in every important city. Trust in the benevolence of the tsar was severely shaken on January 22, 1905—"Bloody Sunday"—when a group of two hundred thousand workers and their families, led by a priest, Father Gapon, went to demonstrate their grievances at the tsar's winter palace in St. Petersburg. When guard troops killed 130 demonstrators and wounded several hundred, the government seemed not only ineffective, but arbitrary and brutal. Over the course of 1905 general protest grew. Merchants closed their stores, factory owners shut down their plants, lawyers refused to plead cases in court. The autocracy lost control of entire rural towns and regions as local authorities were ejected and often killed by enraged peasants. Forced to yield, Tsar Nicholas II issued the October Manifesto, pledging guarantees of individual liberties, a moderately liberal franchise for the election of a Duma, and genuine legislative veto powers for the Duma. Although the 1905 revolution brought the tsarist system perilously close to collapse, it failed to convince the tsar that fundamental political change was necessary. Between 1905 and 1907 Nicholas revoked most of the promises made in the October Manifesto. Above all, he deprived the Duma of its principal powers and decreed that it be elected indirectly on a class basis, which ensured a legislative body of obedient followers.

Nonetheless, the revolt of 1905 persuaded the tsar's more perceptive advisers that reform was urgent. The agrarian programs sponsored by the government's leading minister, Peter Stolypin, were especially significant. Between 1906 and 1911 the Stolypin reforms provided for the sale of 5 million acres of royal land to peasants, granted permission to peasants to withdraw from the *mir* and form independent farms, and canceled peasant property debts. Further decrees legalized labor unions, reduced the working day (to ten hours in most cases), and established sickness and accident insurance. Liberals could reasonably hope that Russia was on the way to becoming a progressive nation on the Western model, yet the tsar remained stubbornly autocratic. Russian agriculture remained suspended between an emerging capitalist system and the traditional peasant commune; Russian industry, though powerful enough to allow Russia to maintain its status as a world power, had hardly created a modern, industrial society capable of withstanding the enormous strains that Russia would face during the First World War.

NATIONALISM AND IMPERIAL POLITICS: THE BALKANS

In southeastern Europe rising nationalism continued to divide the disintegrating Ottoman empire. Before 1829 the entire Balkan peninsula, bounded by the Aegean, Black, and Adriatic seas, was controlled by the Turks. Over the course of the next eighty-five years, however, the Turkish empire ceded territories to rival European powers, especially Russia and Austria, as well as to nationalist revolts by the empire's Christian subjects. Once a formidable world power, the Ottoman empire was now dubbed the "sick man of Europe." In 1829, at the conclusion of a war between Russia and Turkey, Sultan Abdul Hamid II (1876–1909) acknowledged the independence of Greece and granted autonomy to both Serbia and the provinces that later became Romania. As the years passed, resentment against Ottoman rule spread through other Balkan territories. In 1875–1876 there were uprisings in Bosnia, Herzegovina, and Bulgaria, which the sultan suppressed with effective ferocity. Reports of atrocities against Christians gave Russia an excuse to renew its long-standing struggle for domi-

THE DISMEMBERMENT OF THE OTTOMAN EMPIRE

What helps to explain the slow decline of Ottoman power in relationship to Europe and the emerging global economy? How did the Europeans discovery of trade routes around Africa—and the acquisition of overseas empires adversely affect the Ottoman economy? How did the rising tide of nationalism in eastern Europe undermine Ottoman control there, and what did European governments do to encourage this trend? Why did Britain and France have an interest in placing certain portions of the Ottoman empire under "protectorates" following World War I?

nation of the Balkans. In this Russo-Turkish War (1877–1878) the armies of the tsar won a smashing victory. The Treaty of San Stefano, which terminated the conflict, forced the sultan to surrender nearly all of his territory in Europe, except for a remnant around Constantinople. But at this juncture the Great Powers intervened. Austria and Great Britain were especially opposed to granting Russia jurisdiction over so large a portion of the Near East. In 1878 a congress of the

Great Powers, meeting in Berlin, transferred Bessarabia to Russia, Thessaly to Greece, and Bosnia and Herzegovina to the control of Austria. Montenegro, Serbia, and Romania also became independent states, thus launching the modern era of Balkan nationalism. Seven years later the Bulgars, who had been granted some degree of autonomy by the Congress of Berlin, seized the province of Eastern Rumelia from Turkey. In 1908 they established the independent kingdom of Bulgaria. In

Legend:
- Bosnia and Herzegovina placed under Austrian control (not annexed)
- Serbia, Montenegro and Romania become independent (had been under Ottoman control)
- Bulgaria as amended by Congress of Berlin, 1878
- Ottoman Empire

EUROPE AFTER THE CONGRESS OF BERLIN, 1878

What events precipitated the Congress of Berlin? What issues did the delegates hope to resolve? How did the Congress strengthen the German position within Europe, and why? What national groups won sovereignty and independence, and at whose expense? How did the settlement complicate matters for supranational empires, such as Austria-Hungary?

1908 Austria annexed the provinces of Bosnia and Herzegovina, which it had administered since 1878, and in 1911–1912 Italy entered into war with Turkey. The power vacuum in the Orient significantly strained Europe's imperial balance of power.

A nationalist movement also emerged in Turkey itself. For some time informed Turks had grown increas-

ingly impatient with the sultan's weakness and his government's incompetence. Those who had been educated in European universities advocated national rejuvenation through the introduction of Western science and democratic reforms. Invoking a Western liberal variant of nationalism, these reformers called themselves "Young Turks" and in 1908 successfully forced the sultan to establish a constitutional government. The following year, in the face of a reactionary movement, they deposed Sultan Abdul Hamid II and placed on the throne his brother, Mohammed V (1909–1918). The real powers of government were now entrusted to a grand vizier and ministers responsible to an elected parliament. The new representative government did not, however, extend liberties to the empire's non-Turkish inhabitants. On the contrary, the Young Turks launched a vigorous effort to "Ottomanize" all their imperial subjects, trying to bring both Christian and Muslim communities under more centralized control and to spread Turkish culture. That effort, intended to compensate for the loss of territories in Europe, undercut the popularity of the new reformist regime.

THE SCIENCE AND SOUL OF THE MODERN AGE

What impact did new scientific theories have on culture?

The decades before the First World War brought a profound shift in society's relationship to both science and art. Ninteenth-century liberals had confidence in science. Not only did science deliver technological and material progress, it also confirmed liberals' faith in the power of human reason to uncover and command the laws of nature. Toward the end of the century, however, scientific developments defied these expectations. Evolutionary theory, psychology, and social science all introduced visions of humanity that were sharply at odds with conventional wisdom. At the same time, artists and intellectuals mounted their own revolt against nineteenth-century conventions. Morals, manners, institutions, traditions: all established values and assumptions were under question, as a generation of self-consciously avant-garde artists called for a radical break with the past. These upheavals in the world of ideas unsettled older conceptions of individuality, culture, and consciousness. The modern individual no longer seemed the free and rational agent of Enlightenment thought, but rather the product of irrational inner drives and uncontrollable external circumstances. As Georg Simmel, one of the founders of modern sociology, wrote in 1902: "The deepest problems of modern life derive from the claim of the individual to preseve the autonomy and individuality of his existence in the face of overwhelming social forces, of historical heritage, of external culture, and of the technique of life."

DARWIN'S REVOLUTIONARY THEORY

If Marx changed conceptions of society, Charles Darwin did him one better, perhaps, for his theory of organic evolution by natural selection transformed conceptions of nature itself. As both a scientific explanation and an imaginative metaphor for political and social change, Darwin's theory of evolution introduced an unsettling new picture of human biology, behavior, and society. As with Marxism, its core concepts were embraced by some and abhorred by others, and were interpreted and deployed in a variety of unexpected, often conflicting, ways that profoundly shaped the late nineteenth and early twentieth centuries.

Theories of evolution did not originate with Darwin but none had gained widespread scientific or popular currency. Geologists and other other scientists in the nineteenth century had challenged the biblical account of creation with evidence that the world was formed by natural processes over millions of years. The nature of those processes remained unknown, however, particularly the question of how different species arose. One important attempt at an answer was proposed in the early nineteenth century by the French biologist Jean Lamarck, who argued that behavioral changes could alter an animal's physical characteristics within a single generation, and that these new traits would be passed on to offspring. (In a famous example, Lamarck believed that giraffes' long necks resulted from generations of giraffes reaching for ever higher leaves.) Over time, Lamarck suggested, the inheritance of acquired characteristics produced new species of animals. Though widely attacked, Lamarck's hypothesis had its adherents, and absent an understanding of genetic inheritance, it persisted as a popular conception of evolution into the twentieth century.

A more convincing hypothesis of organic evolution appeared in 1859, however, with the publication of the *Origin of Species* by British naturalist Charles Darwin. The son of a small-town physician, Darwin had spent five years in the 1830s as an unpaid naturalist aboard the H.M.S. *Beagle*, a ship that had been chartered for scientific exploration on a trip around the world. The voyage gave Darwin an unparalleled opportunity to observe firsthand the manifold variations of animal

DARWIN AND HIS READERS

Charles Darwin's Origin of Species *(1859) and his theory of natural selection transformed Western knowledge of natural history. The impact of Darwin's work, however, extended well beyond scientific circles. It assumed a cultural importance that exceeded even Darwin's scholarly contribution. How Darwinism was popularized is a complex question, for writers and readers could mold Darwin's ideas to fit a variety of political and cultural purposes. The first excerpt below comes from the conclusion to* The Origin of Species *itself, and it sets out the different laws that Darwin thought governed the natural world. The second excerpt, on the next page, comes from the autobiography of Nicholas Osterroth (1875–1933), a clay miner from western Germany. Osterroth was ambitious and self-educated. The passage recounts his reaction to hearing about Darwin and conveys his enthusiasm for late-nineteenth-century science.*

The natural system is a genealogical arrangement, in which we have to discover the lines of descent by the most permanent characters, however slight their vital importance may be.

The framework of bones being the same in the hand of a man, wing of a bat, fin of the porpoise, and leg of the horse,—the same number of vertebrae forming the neck of the giraffe and of the elephant,—and innumerable other such facts, at once explain themselves on the theory of descent with slow and slight successive modifications. The similarity of pattern in the wing and leg of a bat, though used for such different purposes,—in the jaws and legs of a crab,—in the petals, stamens, and pistils of a flower, is likewise intelligible on the view of the gradual modification of parts or organs, which were alike in the early progenitor of each class. . . .

It is interesting to contemplate an entangled bank, clothed with many plants of many kinds, with birds singing on the bushes, with various insects flitting about, and with worms crawling through the damp earth, and to reflect that these elaborately constructed forms, so different from each other, and dependent on each other in so complex a manner, have all been produced by laws acting around us. These laws, taken in the largest sense, being Growth with Reproduction; Inheritance which is almost implied by reproduction; Variability from the indirect and direct action of the external conditions of life, and from use and disuse; a Ratio of Increase so high as to lead to a Struggle for Life, and as a consequence to Natural Selection, entailing Divergence of Character and the Extinction of less-improved forms. Thus, from the war of nature, from famine and death, the most exalted object which we are capable of conceiving, namely, the production of the higher animals, directly follows. There is grandeur in this view of life, with its several powers, having been originally breathed into a few forms or into one; and that, whilst this planet has gone cycling on according to the fixed law of gravity, from so simple a beginning endless forms most beautiful and most wonderful have been, and are being, evolved.

Charles Darwin, *The Origin of Species* (Harmondsworth: Penguin, 1968), pp. 450–51, 458–60.

The book was called *Moses or Darwin?* . . . Written in a very popular style, it compared the Mosaic story of creation with the natural evolutionary history, illuminated the contradictions of the biblical story, and gave a concise description of the evolution of organic and inorganic nature, interwoven with plenty of striking proofs.

What particularly impressed me was a fact that now became clear to me: that evolutionary natural history was monopolized by the institutions of higher learning; that Newton, Laplace, Kant, Darwin, and Haeckel brought enlightenment only to the students of the upper social classes; and that for the common people in the grammar school the old Moses with his six-day creation of the world still was the authoritative world view. For the upper classes there was evolution, for us creation; for them productive liberating knowledge, for us rigid faith; bread for those favored by fate, stones for those who hungered for truth!

Why do the people need science? Why do they need a so-called Weltanschauung [world view]? The people must keep Moses, must keep religion; religion is the poor man's philosophy. Where would we end up if every miner and every farmhand had the opportunity to stick his nose into astronomy, geology, biology, and anatomy? Does it serve any purpose for the divine world order of the possessing and privileged classes to tell the worker that the Ptolemaic heavens have long since collapsed; that out there in the universe there is an eternal process of creation and destruction; that in the universe at large, as on our tiny earth, everything is in the grip of eternal evolution; that this evolution takes place according to inalterable natural laws that defy even the omnipotence of the old Mosaic Jehovah; . . . Why tell the dumb people that Copernicus and his followers have overturned the old Mosaic creator, and that Darwin and modern science have dug the very ground out from under his feet of clay?

That would be suicide! Yes, the old religion is so convenient for the divine world order of the ruling class! As long as the worker hopes faithfully for the beyond, he won't think of plucking the blooming roses in this world. . . .

The possessing classes of all civilized nations need servants to make possible their godlike existence. So they cannot allow the servant to eat from the tree of knowledge.

Alfred Kelly, ed., *The German Worker: Working-Class Autobiographies from the Age of Industrialization* (Berkeley: University of California Press, 1987), pp. 185–86.

life. He contrasted island-dwelling species with related animals on nearby continents and compared the traits of living creatures with those of fossilized remains. From a familiarity with pigeon breeding (a popular Victorian hobby), Darwin knew that particular traits could be artificially selected by means of controlled mating. Was a similar process of "selection" at work in nature?

Darwin's revolutionary answer was *yes*. He theorized that variations within a population (such as longer beaks or protective coloring) made certain individual organisms better equipped for survival, increasing their chances of breeding and thus passing their advantageous traits to the next generation. To reach this conclusion, Darwin drew on the ideas of the economist and demographer Thomas Malthus, who earlier argued that in nature many more individuals are born than can survive, and that consequently, the weaker ones must perish in the struggle for food. In Darwin's explanation, this Malthusian competition led to adaptation and, if adaptation was successful, to survival. The environment, he argued, "selects" those variants among offspring that are best able to survive and reproduce while eliminating other, less "fit" biological traits.

Darwin used this theory of variation and natural selection to explain the origin of new species. He believed that individual plants and animals with favorable characteristics would transmit their inherited qualities to their descendants over generations, and that successive eliminations of the least fit would eventually produce a new species. Darwin applied his concept of evolution not only to plant and animal species but also to humans. In his view, the human race had evolved from an apelike ancestor, long since extinct, but probably a common precursor of the existing anthropoid apes and humans. Darwin introduced this unsettling idea in his second great work, *The Descent of Man* (1871). At least since Newton, science had inspired faith in human ability to understand and master the natural world; the Darwinian revolution seemed to put such faith in jeopardy.

DARWINIAN THEORY AND RELIGION

The implications of Darwin's writings went far beyond the domain of the evolutionary sciences. Most notably, they challenged the basis of deeply held religious beliefs, sparking a public discussion on the existence and knowability of God. Although popular critics denounced Darwin for contradicting literal interpretations of the Bible, those contradictions were not what made religious middle-class readers uncomfortable. The work of prominent theologians, such as David Friedrich Strauss, had already helped Christians adapt their faith to biblical inaccuracies and inconsistencies. They did not need to abandon either Christianity or faith simply because Darwin showed (or argued) that the world and its life forms had developed over millions of years rather than six days. What religious readers in the nineteenth century found difficult to accept was Darwin's challenge to their belief in a benevolent God and a morally guided universe. By Darwin's account, the world was governed not by order, harmony, and divine will, but by random chance and constant, undirected struggle. Moreover, the Darwinian world view seemed to redefine notions of good and bad only in terms of an ability to survive, thus robbing humanity of critical moral certainties. Darwin himself was able to reconcile his theory with a belief in God, but others latched on his work to fiercely attack Christian orthodoxy. One such figure was the philosopher Thomas Henry Huxley, who earned himself the nickname of "Darwin's bulldog" by inveighing against Christians who were appalled by the implications of Darwinian theory. Huxley called himself an agnostic (from the Greek *agnostos*, or "unknowable"), a person who believed that neither the existence nor the nature of God could be known, and asserted that "there is no evidence of the existence of such a being as the God of the theologians." Opposed to all forms of dogma, Huxley argued that the thinking person should simply follow reason "as far as it can take you," and recognize that the ultimate character of the universe lay beyond his or her grasp.

SOCIAL DARWINISM

The theory of natural selection also influenced the social sciences, which were just developing at the end of the nineteenth century. New disciplines such as sociology, psychology, anthropology, and economics aimed to apply scientific methods to the analysis of society, and introduced new ways of quantifying, measuring, and interpreting human experience. Under the authoritative banner of "science," these disciplines exerted a powerful influence on society, oftentimes to improve the health and well-being of European men and women. But, as we will see with the impact of "Social Darwinism," the social sciences could also provide justification for forms of economic, imperial, and racial dominance.

The so-called Social Darwinists, whose most famous proponent was the English philosopher Herbert Spencer (1820–1903), adapted Darwinian thought in a way that would have shocked Darwin himself, by applying his concept of individual competition and survival to relationships among classes, races, and nations. Spencer, who coined the phrase "survival of the fittest," used evolutionary theory to expound the virtues of free competition and attack state welfare programs. As a champion of individualism, Spencer condemned all

Herbert Spencer, c. 1885. The most famous philosopher of Social Darwinism, Spencer converted Charles Darwin's scientific principles into a doctrine that justified economic and racial imperialism in the name of individualism and "survival of the fittest."

forms of collectivism as primitive and counterproductive, relics of an earlier stage of social evolution. Government attempts to relieve economic and social hardships—or to place constraints on big business—were, in Spencer's view, hindrances to the vigorous advancement of civilization, which could only occur through individual adaptation and competition. Particularly in America, such claims earned Spencer high praise from some wealthy industrialists, who were no doubt glad to be counted among the "fittest."

Unlike the science of biological evolution, the popularized notion of Social Darwinism was easy to comprehend, and its concepts (centering on a struggle for survival) were soon integrated into the political vocabulary of the day. Proponents of laissez-faire capitalism and opponents of socialism used Darwinist rhetoric to justify marketplace competition and the "natural order" of rich and poor. Nationalists embraced Social Darwinism to rationalize imperialist expansion and warfare. Spencer's doctrine also became closely tied to theories of racial hierarchy and white superiority, which claimed that the white race had reached the height of evolutionary development and had thus earned the right to dominate and rule other races (see Chapter 25). Ironically, some progressive middle-class reformers relied on a similar set of racial assumptions: their campaigns to improve the health and welfare of society played to fears that Europe, though dominant, could possibly regress down the evolutionary ladder. Despite its unsettling potential, Darwinism was used to advance a range of political objectives and to shore up an array of ingrained prejudices.

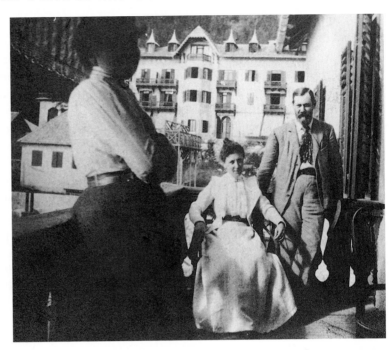

Sigmund Freud and his Family.

EARLY PSYCHOLOGY: PAVLOV AND FREUD

Although the new social scientists self-consciously relied on the use of rational, scientific principles, their findings often stressed the opposite: the irrational, even animalistic nature of human experience. Darwin had already called into question the notion that humanity was fundamentally superior to the rest of the animal kingdom, and similarly discomfitting conclusions came from the new field of psychology. Physiological experiments, which could establish connections between body and mind, promised an entirely new way to comprehend the mental makeup of humans. For instance, the work of the Russian physician Ivan Pavlov (1849–1936) explained a type of behavior called "classical conditioning," in which a random stimulus can be made to produce a (sometimes unintended) physical reflex reaction. Pavlov's famous experiment showed that if dogs were fed following the ringing of a bell, the animals would eventually salivate at the sound of the bell alone, exactly as if they smelled and saw food. Moreover, Pavlov insisted that such conditioning constituted a significant part of human behavior as well. Known as "behaviorism," this type of physiological psychology eschewed vague concepts such as mind and consciousness, concentrating instead on the reaction of muscles, nerves, glands, and visceral organs. Rather than being governed by reason, human activity was recast by behavorists as a bundle of physiological responses to stimuli in the environment.

Like behavorism, a second major school of psychology also suggested that human behavior was largely motivated by unconcious and irrational forces. Founded by the Austrian physician Sigmund Freud (1856–1939), the discipline of psychoanalysis posited a new, dynamic, and unsettling theory of the mind, in which a variety of unconscious drives and desires conflict with a rational and moral conscience. Developed over many years of treating patients with nervous ailments, Freud's model of the psyche contained three elements: (1) the id, or undisciplined desires for pleasure, sexual gratification, aggression, and so on; (2) the superego, or conscience, which registers the prohibitions of morality and culture; and (3) the ego, the arena in which the conflict between id and superego works itself out. Freud believed that most cases of mental disorder result from an irreconcilable tension between natural drives and cultural restraints, which leave innate impulses buried in the subconscious. Freud believed that by studying such disorders, as well as dreams and slips of the tongue, scientists could glimpse the submerged areas of consciousness, and thus formulate an objective understanding of seemingly "irrational" behavior. Indeed, Freud's seach for an all-encompassing theory of the mind was deeply grounded in the tenets of nineteenth-century science. By stressing the irrational, however, Freud's theories fed a growing anxiety about the value and limits of human reason. Likewise, they brought to fore a powerful critique of the constraints imposed by the moral and social codes of Western civilization.

NIETZSCHE'S ATTACK ON TRADITION

No one provided a more sweeping or more influential assault on Western values than the German philosopher Friedrich Nietzsche (1844–1900). With an exuberant embrace of emotion, instinct, and irrationality, Nietzsche skewered the moral certainties of the nineteenth century. Like Freud, Nietzsche had observed a middle-class culture dominated by illusions and self-deceptions, and he sought to unmask them. In a series of works that rejected rational argumentation in favor of an elliptical, suggestive prose style, Nietzsche presented his critque of Western culture. Essentially, he argued that bourgeois faith in such concepts as science, progress, democracy, and religion represented a futile, and thus reprehensible, search for security and truth. Nietzsche categorically denied the possibility of knowing "truth" or "reality," since all knowlege comes filtered through linguistic, scientific, or artistic systems of representation. He also famously ridiculed Judeo-Christian morality for instilling a repressive conformity that drained civilization of its vitality. Though Nietzsche's philosophy did not offer any concrete political or social objectives, it resounded with themes of personal liberation, especially from the stranglehold of history and tradition. Indeed, Nietzsche's ideal individual, or

Though Nietzsche's philosophy did not offer any concrete political or social objectives, it resounded with themes of personal liberation, especially from the stranglehold of history and tradition.

"superman," was one who abandoned the burdens of cultural conformity and created an independent set of values based on artistic vision and strength of character. Only through individual struggle against the chaotic universe did Nietzsche forecast salvation for Western civilization. His publications, including *Thus Spake Zarathustra* (1883), *Beyond Good and Evil* (1886), and *On the Genealogy of Morals* (1887), achieved widespread fame beginning in the 1890s, just when the strains of modernization were beginning to crack the foundations of European society.

RELIGION AND ITS CRITICS

Faced with these various scientific and philosophical challenges, the institutions responsible for the maintenance of traditional faith found themselves on the defensive. The Roman Catholic Church responded to the encroachments of secular society by appealing to its dogma and venerated traditions. In 1864 Pope Pius IX issued a Syllabus of Errors, condemning what he regarded as the principal religious and philosophical "errors" of the time. Among them were materialism, free thought, and "indifferentism," or the idea that one religion is as good as another. The pope also convoked the first church council since the Catholic Reformation, which in 1871 pronounced the dogma of papal infallibility. This meant that in his capacity "as pastor and doctor of all Christians," the pope was infallible in regard to all matters of faith and morals. Though generally accepted by pious Catholics, the claim of papal infallibility provoked a storm of protest and was denounced by the governments of several Catholic countries, including France, Spain, and Italy. The death of Pius IX in 1878 and the accession of Pope Leo XIII, however, brought a more accommodating climate to the church. The new pope acknowledged that there was "good" as well as "evil" in modern civilization. He added a scientific staff to the Vatican and opened archives and observatories, but made no further concessions to liberalism in the political sphere.

Protestants were also compelled to respond to a modernizing world. Since they were taught to understand God with the aid of little more than the Bible and a willing conscience, Protestants, unlike Catholics, had little in the way of doctrine to help them defend their faith. Some fundamentalists chose to ignore the implications of scientific and philosophical inquiry altogether, and continued to believe in the literal truth of the Bible. Others were willing to agree with the school of American philosophers known as pragmatists (principally Charles S. Peirce and William James), who taught that "truth" was whatever produced useful, practical results; by their logic, if belief in God provided mental peace or spiritual satisfaction, then the belief was true. Other Protestants sought solace from religious doubt in founding missions, laboring among the poor, and other good works. Many adherents to this "social gospel" were also "modernists," who accepted the ethical teachings of Christianity but discarded beliefs in miracles and original sin.

NEW READERS AND THE POPULAR PRESS

The effect of various scientific and philosophical challenges on the men and women who lived at the end of the nineteenth century cannot be measured precisely. Millions undoubtedly went about the business of life untroubled by the implications of evolutionary theory, content to believe as they had believed before. Certainly, for most members of the middle class, the challenge of socialism was understood as "real" in a way that the challenges of science and philosophy probably were not. Socialism threatened specific interests.

The theories of Darwin and Freud, though "in the air" and troubling, did not matter to the same degree. Men and women could postpone thoughts about their origins and ultimate destiny. Furthermore, as we have seen, many religious men and women could reconcile faith and religion with the new science. Yet the changes we have been discussing eventually had a profound impact. Darwin's theory was not too complicated to be popularized. If educated men and women had neither the time nor inclination to read the *Origin of Species*, they read magazines and newspapers that summarized (not always correctly) its implications. They encountered some of its central concepts in other places, from political speeches to novels and crime reports.

The diffusion of these new ideas was facilitated by rising literacy rates and by new forms of printed mass culture. Between 1750 and 1870, readership had expanded from the aristocracy to include middle-class circles and, thereafter, to an increasingly literate general population. In 1850 approximately half the population of Europe was illiterate. In subsequent decades, country after country introduced state-financed elementary and secondary education to provide opportunities for social advancement, to diffuse technical and scientific knowledge, and to inculcate civic and national pride. Britain instituted elementary education in 1870, Switzerland in 1874, Italy in 1877. France expanded its existing system between 1878 and 1881. After 1871

The New Power of the Press. With the spread of literacy, newspapers adapted to the needs and desires of the new mass audience. Here British railway passengers scramble for the latest edition.

Germany instituted a state system modeled on Prussia's. By 1900, approximately 85 percent of the population in Britain, France, Belgium, the Netherlands, Scandinavia, and Germany could read. The era of mass readership had arrived. Elsewhere, however, the percentages were far lower, ranging between 30 and 60 percent.

In those countries where literacy rates were highest, commercial publishers such as Alfred Harmsworth in Britain and William Randolph Hearst in the United States hastened to serve the new reading public. Middle-class readers had for some time been well supplied with newspapers catering to their interests and point of view. The *Times* of London had a readership of well over fifty thousand by 1850; the *Presse* and the *Siècle* in France, a circulation of seventy thousand. By 1900, however, other newspapers were appealing to the newly literate, and doing so by means of sensational journalism and spicy, easy-to-read serials. Advertisements drastically lowered the costs of the mass-market newspapers, enabling even workers to purchase one or two newspapers a day. The "yellow" journalism of the penny presses merged entertainment and sensationalism with the news, aiming to increase circulation and thus secure more lucrative advertising sales. Publishers and marketing men weren't the only ones eager to reach this emerging mass market, however. As the new century progressed, artists, activists, politicians—and above all, governments—would become increasingly preoccupied with communicating their messages to the masses.

THE FIRST MODERNS: INNOVATIONS IN ART

In the crucible of late-nineteenth-century Europe—bubbling with scientific, technological, and social transformations—artists across the Continent began critically and systematically to reexamine the nature of art in the modern world. New generations of painters, poets, writers, and composers began to question the moral and cultural values of liberal, middle-class society. Some did so with grave hesitation, others with heedless abandon. In a dizzying array of experiments,

innovations, ephemeral art movements, and bombastic manifestos, the pioneers of what would later be termed "modernism" developed the artistic forms and aesthetic values that came to dominate much of the twentieth century. Like all such terms, *modernism* is notoriously difficult to define: it encompassed a diverse and often contradictory set of theories and practices than spanned the entire range of cultural production—from painting, sculpture, literature, and architecture to theater, dance, and musical composition. Despite such diversity, however, modernist movements did share certain key characteristics: first, a self-conscious sense of rupture from history and tradition; second, a rejection of established values and assumptions; and third, a radical insistence on expressive and experimental freedom.

> Despite such diversity, however, modernist movements did share certain key characteristics: first, a self-conscious sense of rupture from history and tradition; second, a rejection of established values and assumptions; and third, a radical insistence on expressive and experimental freedom.

In addition to these trends, early modernism was distinguished by a new understanding of the relationship between art and society. Though some artists and writers did indeed turn inward, toward investigations of purely aesthetic questions, many others embraced the notion that art could effect profound social and spiritual change. The abstract painter Wassily Kandinsky (1866–1944), for instance, who was a devotee of occult mysticism (especially popular around the turn of the century), believed that visionary artists would carry society from "the soulless-material life of the nineteenth century" toward "the psychic-spiritual life of the twentieth century." Notions that contemporary society was materialistic and morally bankrupt figured prominently in modernist critiques of European culture. And while artists like Kandinsky pointed to salvation in a utopian future, others used their art to examine the present unflinchingly, probing the psychological and social pathologies of urban industrial society. In the political arena, modernist hostility toward conventional values sometimes translated into support for antiliberal movements at the political peripheries—radical anarchism on the left and proto-fascism on the right. This push toward the ideological edges mirrored the modernists' aesthetic tendencies. In the words of one scholar: "After the nineteenth century had established a remarkably safe, intimate center where the artist and the audience could dwell, the modernist age reached out to the freakish circumferences of art."

Black Lines by Wassily Kandinsky, 1913. Kandinsky broke from the traditional representational approach of 19th century painting with his abstractions, and was one of a generation of turn-of-the-century artists who reexamined and experimented with their art forms.

THE REVOLT ON CANVAS

Like most artistic movements, modernism defined itself in opposition to a set of earlier principles. For painters in particular, this meant a rejection both of mainstream academic art, which affirmed the chaste and moral outlook of museumgoers, and of the socially conscious realist tradition (discussed in Chapter 20), which strove for rigorous, even scientific exactitude in representing material reality. The rebellion of modern artists went even further, however, by discarding altogether the centuries-old tradition of representation, or what French painter Paul Gauguin (1848–1903) called the "shackles of verisimilitude." Since the Renaissance, Western art had sought to accurately depict three-dimensional visual reality; paintings were considered

to be "mirrors," or "windows" on the world. But during the late nineteenth century, artists turned their backs to the visual world, focusing instead on subjective, psychologically oriented, intensely emotional forms of self-expression. As the Norwegian painter Edvard Munch claimed: "Art is the opposite of nature. A work of art can come only from the interior of man."

Though challenges to the tradition of representational art occurred earlier in the nineteenth century, the first significant breaks emerged with the French impressionists, who came to prominence as young artists in the 1870s. Strictly speaking, the impressionists were realists. Steeped in scientific theories about sensory perception, they attempted to record natural phenomena objectively. Instead of painting objects themselves, they captured the transitory play of light on surfaces,

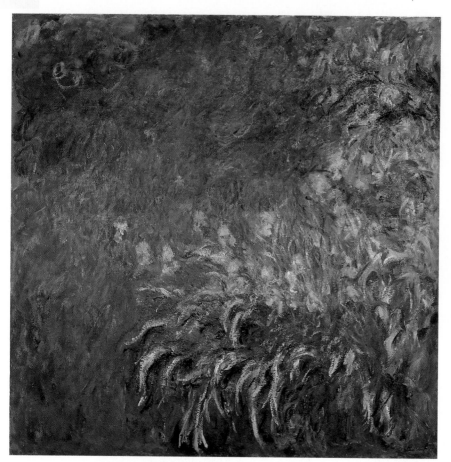

Iris Beside a Pond by Claude Monet (1840–1926). Monet called some of his paintings impressions, and the name soon came to designate a school.

man Paul Cézanne (1839–1906), whose efforts to "make of Impressionism something solid and durable" entailed a reduction of natural forms to their geometric equivalents, a rejection of traditional perspective, and (most important) an emphasis on the subjective arrangement of color and form. Perhaps more so than anyone, Cézanne shattered the window of representational art. Instead of a reflection of the world, painting became a vehicle for an artist's self-expression. The Dutchman Vincent van Gogh also explored art's expressive potential, with greater emotion and subjectivity. For Van Gogh, painting was a labor of faith, a way to channel his violent passions. For Paul Gauguin, who fled to the Pacific islands in 1891, art promised a utopian refuge from the corruption of Europe. Gauguin in particular was influenced by the symbolist movement around the turn of the century. The symbolists were a group of artists and writers who were deeply suspicious of material reality, and who sought transcendental truth though imagination, personal feelings, and psychological perceptions.

giving their works a sketchy, ephemeral quality that differed sharply from realist art. And though subsequent artists revolted against what they deemed the sterile objectivity of this scientific approach, the impressionist painters, most famously Claude Monet (1840–1926) and Pierre-Auguste Renoir (1841–1919), left two important legacies to the European avant-garde. First, by developing new techniques without reference to past styles, the impressionists paved the way for younger artists to experiment more freely. Second, because the official salons rejected their work, the impressionists organized their own independent exhibitions from 1874 to 1886. These shows effectively undermined the French Academy's centuries-old monopoly on artistic display and aesthetic standards, and they established a tradition of autonomous outsider exhibits, which figures prominently in the history of modernism.

In the wake of impressionism, a handful of innovative artists working at the end of the nineteenth century laid the groundwork for an explosion of creative experimentation after 1900. Chief among them was the French-

Especially in Germany, avant-garde artists expressed a wrenching disillusionment with modern society. Emil Nolde (1867–1956) railed against the "irresponsible voraciousness" with which European empires "annihilated peoples and races—and always under the hypocritical pretext of the best intentions." Emphasizing the parallel corruption of artistic culture, Nolde's contemporary James Ensor (1860–1949) later wrote that "All the rules, all the canons of art vomit death exactly like their bronze-mouthed brothers of the battlefield." Collectively referred to as expressionists, these painters turned to acid colors, violent figural distortions, and crude depictions of sexuality that shocked middle-class viewers. Inspired by the psychological dramas of his compatriot Henrik Ibsen, Edvard Munch (1863–1944) sought to express the interior consciousness of the human mind. The Austrian Egon Schiele (1890–1918) explored sexuality and the body with disturbingly raw, graphic imagery.

After the turn of the century, a diverse crop of avant-garde movements flowered across Europe. In bohemian Paris, the Frenchman Henri Matisse (1869–1954) and Pablo Picasso (1881–1973), a Catalan Spaniard, pursued their groundbreaking aesthetic experiments in relative quiet. Clamoring for attention, on the other hand, were groups of artists who reveled in the energetic dynamism of modern life. The cubists in Paris, vorticists in Britain, and futurists in Italy all embraced a hard, angular aesthetic of the machine age. While other modernists sought an antidote to fin-de-siècle malaise by looking "backward" to so-called primitive cultures, these new movements embraced the future in all its uncertainty—often with the kind of aggressive, hypermasculine language that later emerged as a hallmark of fascism. In the futurist Manifesto, for instance, F. T. Marinetti pro-

claimed: "We will glorify war—the only true hygiene of the world—militarism, patriotism, the destructive gesture of anarchist, the beautiful Ideas which kill." In Russia and Holland, meanwhile, a few intensely idealistic painters made perhaps the most revolutionary aesthetic leap of early modernism, into totally abstract, or "object-less" painting.

The breadth and diversity of modern art defy simple categories and explanations. The profound changes that swept the visual arts were paralleled across the cultural spectrum (developments discussed in Chapter 28). And though they remained the province of a small group of artists and intellectuals before 1914, these radical revisions of artistic values entered the cultural mainstream soon after the First World War.

Mont Sainte-Victoire by Paul Cézanne (1839–1906). Cézanne's reduction of the exterior world to forms and planes of color provided an important bridge between impressionism and cubism.

CHRONOLOGY

THE CHALLENGE OF SCIENCE AND PHILOSOPHY

Darwin, *Origin of Species*	1859
Tolstoy, *War and Peace*	1862–1869
Pius IX issues Syllabus of Errors	1864
Dostoyevsky, *Crime and Punishment*	1866
Darwin, *The Descent of Man*	1871
Pius IX's pronouncement of papal infallibility	1871
Ibsen, *A Doll's House*	1879
Zola, *Germinal*	1885
Nietzsche, *Beyond Good and Evil*	1886
Nietzsche, *On the Genealogy of Morals*	1887
Van Gogh, *The Starry Night*	1889

CONCLUSION

Many Europeans who had grown up in the period from 1870 to 1914, but lived through the hardship of the First World War, looked back on the prewar period as a golden age of European civilization. In one sense this retrospective view is apt. After all, the Continental powers had successfully avoided major wars, enabling a second phase of industrialization to provide better living standards for the growing populations of mass society. An overall spirit of confidence and purpose pervaded Europe's perceived mission to exercise political, economic, and cultural dominion in the far reaches of the world. Yet European politics and culture also registered the presence of powerful—and destabilizing—forces of change. Industrial expansion, relative abundance, and rising literacy produced a political climate of rising expectations. As the age of mass politics arrived, democrats, socialists, and feminists clamored for access to political life, threatening violence, strikes, and revolution. Marxist socialism especially changed radical politics, redefining the terms of debate for the next century. Western science, literature, and the arts explored new perspectives on the individual, undermining some of the cherished beliefs of nineteenth-century liberals. The competition and violence central to Darwin's theory of evolution, the subconscious urges that Freud found in human behavior, and the rebellion against representation in the arts all pointed in new and baffling directions. These experiments, hypotheses, and nagging questions accompanied Europe into the Great War of 1914. They would help to shape Europeans' responses to the enormity of mass death and destruction that devastated the continent. After the war, the political changes and cultural unease of the period from 1870 to 1914 would reemerge in the form of mass movements and artistic developments that would define the twentieth century.

KEY TERMS

second industrial revolution	Dreyfus Affair	Charles Darwin
Capital	Irish home rule	Sigmund Freud
anarchism	"Bloody Sunday"	Friedrich Nietzsche
woman suffrage	"Young Turks"	modernism

SELECTED READINGS

Berlanstein, Lenard. *The Working People of Paris, 1871–1914.* Baltimore, 1984. A social history of the workplace and its impact on working men and women.

Berlin, Isaiah. *Karl Marx: His Life and Environment.* 4th ed. New York, 1996. An excellent short account.

Blackbourn, David. *The Long Nineteenth Century: A History of Germany, 1780–1918.* New York, 1998. The best current survey of German society and politics.

Bredin, Jean-Denis. *The Affair: The Case of Alfred Dreyfus.* New York, 1986. Detailed, up to date, and readable.

Burns, Michael. *Dreyfus: A Family Affair.* New York, 1992. Follows the story Dreyfus through the next generations.

Chipp, Herschel B. *Theories of Modern Art: A Source Book by Artists and Critics.* Berkeley, 1968.

Clark, T. J. *The Painting of Modern Life: Paris in the Art of Manet and His Followers.* New York, 1985. Argues for seeing impressionism as a critique of French society.

Eley, Geoff. *Forging Democracy.* Oxford, 2002. Wide-ranging and multinational account of European radicalism from 1848 to the present.

Gay, Peter. *The Bourgeois Experience: Victoria to Freud,* 5 vols. New York, 1984–2000. Imaginative and brilliant study of private life and middle class culture.

———. *Freud: A Life of Our Time.* New York, 1988. Beautifully written and lucid about difficult concepts; now the best biography.

Herbert, Robert L. *Impressionism: Art, Leisure, and Parisian Society.* New Haven, 1988. An accessible and important study of the impressionists and the world they painted.

Hughes, H. Stuart. *Consciousness and Society.* New York, 1958. A classic study on late-nineteenth-century European thought.

Jelavich, Peter. *Munich and Theatrical Modernism: Politics, Playwriting, and Performance, 1890–1914.* Cambridge, Mass., 1985.

Jones, Gareth Stedman. *Outcast London.* Oxford, 1971. Studies the breakdown in class relationships during the second half of the nineteenth century.

Joyce, Patrick. *Visions of the People: Industrial England and the Question of Class, 1848–1914.* New York, 1991. A social history of the workplace.

Kelly, Alfred. *The German Worker: Autobiographies from the Age of Industrialization.* Berkeley, 1987. Excerpts from workers' autobiographies provide fresh perspective on labor history.

Kern, Stephen. *The Culture of Time and Space.* Cambridge, Mass., 1983. A cultural history of the late nineteenth century.

Landes, David. *The Unbound Prometheus: Technological Change and Industrial Development in Western Europe from 1750 to the Present.* New York, 1969. Includes a first-rate analysis of the second industrial revolution.

Lidtke, Vernon. *The Alternative Culture: Socialist Labor in Imperial Germany.* New York, 1985. A probing study of working-class culture.

Marrus, Michael Robert. *The Politics of Assimilation: A Study of the French Jewish Community at the Time of the Dreyfus Affair.* Oxford, 1971.

Micale, Mark S. *Approaching Hysteria: Disease and Its Interpretations.* Princeton, N.J., 1995. Important study of the history of psychiatry before Freud.

Rupp, Leila J. *Worlds of Women: The Making of an International Women's Movement.* Princeton, N.J., 1997.

Silverman, Deborah L. *Art Nouveau in Fin-de-Siècle France: Politics, Psychology, and Style.* Berkeley, 1989. A study of the relationship between psychological and artistic change.

Smith, Bonnie. *Changing Lives: Women in European History since 1700.* New York, 1988. A useful overview of European women's history.

Tickner, Lisa. *The Spectacle of Women: Imagery of the Suffrage Campaign, 1907–14.* Chicago, 1988. A very engaging study of British suffragism.

Verner, Andrew. *The Crisis of Russian Autocracy: Nicholas II and the 1905 Revolution.* Princeton, N.J., 1990. A detailed study of this important event.

Vital, David. *A People Apart: A Political History of the Jews in Europe, 1789-1939.* Oxford and New York, 1999. Comprehensive and extremely helpful.

Weber, Eugen. *Peasants into Frenchmen: The Modernization of Rural France, 1870–1914.* Stanford, 1976. A study of how France's peasantry was assimilated into the Third Republic.

Wynn, Charters. *Workers, Strikes, and Pogroms: The Donbass-Dnepr Bend in Late Imperial Russia, 1870–1905.* Princeton, N.J., 1992. Excellent on Russian industrialization and Russian workers' politics.

DIGITAL HISTORY

THE OLYMPICS PAST AND PRESENT

The goal of Olympism is to place everywhere sport at the service of the harmonious development of man, with a view to encouraging the establishment of a peaceful society concerned with the preservation of human dignity. To this effect, the Olympic Movement engages, alone or in cooperation with other organizations and within the limits of its means, in actions to promote peace.
—The Olympic Charter (July 4, 2003)

The first recorded Olympic Games took place in the Valley of Olympia in 776 B.C.E. and were held at four-year intervals ("Olympiads") until 394 C.E., when they were abolished by the Roman emperor Theodosius I. Begun as a religious festival, the first Olympics contained only one event, the foot race, but over time boxing, wrestling, the javelin throw, and chariot racing were added. Winners received a simple olive tree branch, which the Greeks believed would bring the victor the vitality of the sacred tree. The winning athlete gave thanks to Zeus, and his city-state was considered to be in favor with the gods.

In 1894, Pierre de Coubertin created the institutional structure of Olympism, and the modern Olympic Games were born. Hoping to revive the flagging French educational system, Coubertin saw sport as a vehicle for social and moral change. In 1896, the International Olympic Committee (IOC) oversaw the first modern Olympics at Athens—245 athletes (all men) from fourteen nations competed in the ancient Panathenaic stadium before huge crowds.

The modern Olympic movement is now more than a century old. Technology has changed the training and execution of all sport, and digital records are made of every event. Media coverage can make or break a young star's career. Commercial endorsements are numerous, and the lines between amateur and professional athletes are more blurred than ever. Meanwhile, cities around the globe vie for the honor of hosting the Olympic Games.

There is, however, one constant—athletic competition—with which the modern Olympic movement continues to inspire all who participate in and view its games.

The images and documents in the "The Olympics Past and Present" Digital History Feature at www.wwnorton.com/wciv, reveal how the significance of international athletic competition has changed from the ancient world until the present. As you explore this feature, consider the following:

• What role did athletic competition play in the ancient Greek world?

• How have the lines between professional and amateur been blurred by modern sport?

• To what extent are the modern Olympic Games driven by economics and politics?

• Do you think the goals of modern Olympism as stated by the IOC are still valid?

CHAPTER
TWENTY-FOUR

CHAPTER CONTENTS

THE FIRST
WORLD WAR

I N SEVERAL CRUCIAL RESPECTS, the twentieth century began in August 1914, with the outbreak of the First World War—a four-year conflict that spurred the collapse of nineteenth-century ideals and institutions. Soldiers marched into battle with the confidence and ambition bred by imperial successes. The leading nations of Europe were at the height of their power. Europe was the center of the world economy and commanded far-flung empires. Many Europeans entered the war with faith in modernity, and in its ability to deliver not only prosperity but all the advantages of "civilization," especially peace and progress.

Despite those expectations, many people harbored fears about the future. The war justified that quiet dread. The "Great War" introduced the ugly face of industrial warfare and the grim capacities of the modern world. It caught Europeans unprepared not only militarily, but economically and politically. In a catastrophic combination of old mentalities and new technologies, the war left 9 million dead soldiers in its wake. Yet soldiers were not the only casualties. World War I was waged against entire nations and had profound economic and political ramifications for the people of Europe. Four years of fighting destroyed many of the institutions and assumptions of the previous century, from monarchies and empires to European economic hegemony. The war strained relations between classes and generations. It disillusioned many, even citizens of the victorious nations. As the British writer Virginia Woolf put it, "It was a shock—to see the faces of our rulers in the light of shell-fire." The war eroded the foundations of nineteenth-century economies and unleashed social upheaval. It banished older forms of authoritarianism and ushered in new ones that bore the distinctive mark of the twentieth century. Finally, the war proved nearly impossible to settle; antagonisms bred in battle only intensified in the war's aftermath, and would eventually lead to the Second World War. Postwar Europe faced more problems than peace could manage.

• What were the causes of World War I?

• Why did the Schlieffen Plan fail?

• Why did the war become a stalemate?

• Why did the Allies persist with an offensive strategy?

 • What was the role of empire in World War I?

• How did the war change women's lives?

• How did the Bolsheviks seize power?

• How did the Allies win the war?

THE JULY CRISIS

What were the causes of World War I?

In 1914 Europe had built a seemingly stable peace. Through the complex negotiations of Great Power geopolitics, Europe had settled into two systems of alliance: the Triple Entente (later the Allied Powers) of Britain, France, and Russia rivaled the Triple Alliance (later the Central Powers) of Germany, Austria-Hungary, and Italy. Within this balance of power, the nations of Europe challenged one another for economic, military, and imperial advantage. The scramble for colonies abroad accompanied a fierce arms race at home, where military leaders assumed that superior technology and larger armies would result in a quick victory in a European war. Indeed, in the prevailing atmosphere of international suspicion, such a war seemed likely to many of Europe's political and military elites. Yet none of the diplomats, spies, military planners, or cabinet ministers of Europe—nor any of their critics—predicted the war they eventually got. Nor did many expect that the Balkan crisis of July 1914 would touch off that conflict, engulfing all of Europe in just over a month's time.

The Great Powers had long been involved in the affairs of southeast Europe. The Balkans lay between two venerable but unsteady empires, the Austro-Hungarian and the Ottoman. The region was also home to newly formed states under the sway of ambitious nationalist movements, pan-Slavic ethnic crusaders, and local power brokers. Balkan politics were a traditional focus for Russian intervention in European affairs, and also for German and British diplomacy. Despite these entanglements, the Great Powers tried to avoid direct intervention, seeking instead to bring the new Balkan states into the web of alliances. In 1912 the independent states of Serbia, Greece, Bulgaria, and Montenegro launched the First Balkan War against the Ottomans; in 1913, the Second Balkan War was fought over the spoils of the first. Through reasonable diplomacy, the Great Powers steered clear of entanglement, and these wars remained localized. But if diplomacy failed, as it ultimately did in the summer of 1914, the Great Powers' system of alliances would actually hasten the outbreak of a wider war.

The link between Balkan conflict and continental war would be the Austro-Hungarian empire, which was struggling to survive amid increasing nationalist ambitions. The "dual monarchy," as it was called after reforms in 1876, had frustrated many ethnic groups excluded from the arrangement. Czechs and Slovenes protested their second-class status in the German half of the empire; Poles, Croats, and ethnic Romanians chafed at Hungarian rule. The province of Bosnia was particularly volatile, home to several Slavic ethnic groups and formerly part of the Ottoman empire. In 1878, the Austrians had occupied and then annexed Bosnia, drawing hatred and resistance from most of Bosnia's ethnic groups. Bosnian Serbs, in particular, had hoped to secede and join the independent kingdom of Serbia. But now the Austrians blocked their plans. So with the support of Serbia, the Bosnian Serbs began an underground war against the empire to achieve their goals. Bosnia would be the crucible of European conflict.

On June 28, 1914, Franz Ferdinand (1889–1914), archduke of Austria and heir to the Austro-Hungarian Empire, paraded through Sarajevo, the capital of Bosnia. As a hotbed of Serb resistance, Sarajevo was an admittedly dangerous place for the head of the hated empire to parade in

Franz Ferdinand and His Wife, Sophie. The Austrian archduke and archduchess, in Sarajevo on June 28, 1914, approaching their car before they were assassinated.

EUROPEAN ALLIANCES ON THE EVE OF WORLD WAR I

Study the pattern of alliances shown in this map. How had the alliance system emerged to protect the varied interests and the integrity of the balance of power in Europe? Why were Germany and the Austro-Hungarian empire allied? Why would the Ottoman empire join such an alliance? Why would the Russian empire gravitate toward Great Britain and France? Did colonial rivalries inform this pattern at all? How did such a system of alliances contribute to global conflict?

public. The archduke had escaped an assassination attempt earlier in the day, with a bomb barely missing his automobile; but when his car made a wrong turn and stopped to back up, a nineteen-year-old Bosnian student named Gavrilo Princip shot Ferdinand and his wife at point-blank range. Princip was a member of the Young Bosnian Society, a national liberation group with close links to Serbia. He saw his violent act as a part of a struggle for his people's independence—we see it as the start of World War I.

Shocked by Ferdinand's death, the Austrians saw the assassination as a direct attack by the Serbian government. Eager for retribution, Austria issued an ultimatum to Serbia three weeks later, demanding that the Serbian government denounce the aims and activities of the Bosnian Serbs, prohibit further propaganda and subversion, and allow Austro-Hungarian officials to prosecute and punish Serbian officials who the Austrians believed were involved in the assassination. The demands were deliberately unreasonable. Austria wanted war, a punitive

THE BALKANS, 1878 AND 1914

How did the decline of the Ottoman empire affect the Balkans? Why did the European empires get involved in the affairs of southeast Europe? What were the most important changes in the region between 1878 and 1914? Why was Bosnia-Herzegovina particularly volatile?

campaign to restore order in Bosnia and crush Serbia. The Serbs recognized the provocation and mobilized their army three hours before sending a reply, which agreed to all but the most important Austrian demands. Austria responded with its own mobilization and declared war three days later, on July 28, 1914.

For a brief moment, it seemed possible to avoid a wider war. At first diplomats and politicians hoped to write the confrontation off as another crisis in the Balkans. Austria's steady escalation, coupled with Russia's traditional ties to Serbia, ultimately made that impossible. (Many historians also fault Germany here, for failing to coax allied Austria back from the brink.) For Austria, the conflict was a matter of prestige and power politics—a chance to reassert the fraying empire's authority. For Russia, too, the emerging conflict was an opportunity to regain some of the tsar's authority by standing up for the rights of "brother Slavs." Initially,

WHAT WERE THE CAUSES OF WORLD WAR I?

Russia planned to respond to Austria's threat with a partial mobilization, but when the orders came down on July 30, Russia mobilized fully—its troops were readied to fight both Austria and Germany.

The crisis spread, and the Germans were prepared. Sitting in the most precarious geographic position, Germany had the most detailed plans for fighting a war of necessity. Its military planners were among those who considered war inevitable, and an opportunity to settle the nation's future in continental Europe. As Russia began to mobilize, Kaiser William II (1888–1918) sent an ultimatum to St. Petersburg demanding that Russian mobilization cease within twelve hours; the Russians refused. Meanwhile, the German ministers demanded to know France's intentions. Premier René Viviani (1914–1915) replied that France would act "in accordance with her interests"—which meant an immediate mobilization against Germany. Finally facing the dual threat it had long anticipated, Germany mobilized on August 1 and declared war on Russia—two days later, on France. The next day, the German army invaded Belgium on its way to take Paris.

The invasion of neutral Belgium provided a convenient rallying cry for the British generals and diplomats who wanted Britain to join the nascent continental conflict. Despite Britain's secret pacts with France and despite its public guarantee of Belgium's neutrality, British entry into the Great War was not a foregone conclusion. The Liberal government opposed entry and acquiesced primarily for fear of being turned out of office. Indeed, one historian has recently suggested (rather controversially) that Germany's war aims and imperial ambitions did not pose a substanital threat to Britain's empire, and that the United Kingdom's best interest was to remain neutral in 1914. Proponents of war, however, could resort to an irrefutable tenet of British foreign policy: that to maintain the balance of power, no single nation should be allowed to dominate the Continent. Thus, on August 4, Britain entered the war against Germany.

Other nations were quickly drawn into the struggle. On August 7 the Montenegrins joined the Serbs in fighting Austria. Two weeks later the Japanese declared war on Germany, mainly to attack German possessions in the Far East. On August 1 Turkey allied with Germany, and in October began the bombardment of Russian ports on the Black Sea. Italy had been allied with Germany and Austria before the war, but at the outbreak of hostilities, the Italians cited a strict interpretation of their obligations and declared neutrality. They insisted that since Germany had invaded neutral Belgium, they owed Germany no protection.

The diplomatic maneuvers during the five weeks that followed the assassination at Sarajevo have been characterized as "a tragedy of miscalculation." Diplomats' hands were tied, however, by the strategic thinking and rigid timetables set by military leaders. Speed was of prime importance to generals. To them, once war seemed certain, time spent on diplomacy was time lost on the battlefield. A number of other factors also contributed to the outbreak of war when it came. For instance, while Austria negotiated about its ultimatum for three weeks, during the delay both Russia and Germany felt obliged to make shows of strength. Reasoned debate about the problem never occurred. During the crisis government officials had little contact with each other, and even less with the diplomats and ambassadors of other countries. Several heads of state, including the kaiser and the president of France, along with many of their ministers, spent most of July on vacation; they returned to find their generals holding orders for mobilization, waiting for signature. Austria's mismanagement of the crisis and Russia's inability to find a way to intervene without mobilizing its army contributed greatly to the spiraling confrontation. It is clear, however, that powerful German officials were arguing that war was inevitable. They insisted that Germany should fight before Russia recovered from its 1905 loss to Japan, and before the French army could benefit from its new three-year conscription law, which would put more men in uniform. The same sense of urgency characterized the strategies of all combatant countries. The lure of a bold, successful strike against one's enemies, and the fear that too much was at stake to risk losing the advantage, created a rolling tide of military mobilization that carried Europe into battle.

CHRONOLOGY

WORLD WAR I BEGINS

Assassination of Archduke Franz Ferdinand of Austria	June 28, 1914
Austria and Russia mobilize for war	July 28, 1914
Germany declares war on Russia and France	August 1–3, 1914
Britain enters war against Germany	August 4, 1914

TOWARD WORLD WAR I: DIPLOMACY IN THE SUMMER OF 1914

The assassination of Franz Ferdinand in Sarajevo on June 28, 1914 set off an increasingly desperate round of diplomatic negotiations. As the following exchanges show, diplomats and political leaders on both sides swung from trying to provoke war to attempting to avert or, at least, contain it.

EMPEROR FRANZ JOSEPH OF AUSTRIA-HUNGARY TO KAISER WILLIAM II OF GERMANY, JULY 5, 1914

A week after his nephew, the heir to the throne, was shot, Franz Joseph set out his interpretation of the long-standing conflict with Serbia and its larger implications.

The plot against my poor nephew was the direct result of an agitation carried on by the Russian and Serb Pan-Slavs, an agitation whose sole object is the weakening of the Triple Alliance and the destruction of my realm.

So far, all investigations have shown that the Sarajevo murder was not perpetrated by one individual, but grew out of a well-organized conspiracy, the threads of which can be traced to Belgrade. Even though it will probably be impossible to prove the complicity of the Serb government, there can be no doubt that its policy, aiming as it does at the unification of all Southern Slavs under the Serb banner,

encourages such crimes, and that the continuation of such conditions constitutes a permanent threat to my dynasty and my lands. . . .

This will only be possible if Serbia, which is at present the pivot of Pan-Slav policies, is put out of action as a factor of political power in the Balkans.

You too are [surely] convinced after the recent frightful occurrence in Bosnia that it is no longer possible to contemplate a reconciliation of the antagonism between us and Serbia and that the [efforts] of all European monarchs to pursue policies that preserve the peace will be threatened if the nest of criminal activity in Belgrade remains unpunished.

AUSTRO-HUNGARIAN DISAGREEMENTS OVER STRATEGY

The following comes from an account of a meeting of the Council of Ministers of the Austro-Hungarian empire on July 7, 1914. The ministers disagreed sharply about diplomatic strategies and about how crucial decisions should be made.

[Count Leopold Berchtold, foreign minister of Austria-Hungary] . . . both Emperor Wilhelm and [chancellor] Bethmann Hollweg had assured us emphatically of Germany's unconditional support in the event of military complications with Serbia. . . . It was clear to him

that a military conflict with Serbia might bring about war with Russia. . . .

[Count Istvan Tisza, prime minister of Hungary] . . . We should decide what our demands on Serbia will be [but] should only present an ultimatum if Serbia rejected them. These demands must be hard but not so that they cannot be complied with. If Serbia accepted them, we could register a noteworthy diplomatic success and our prestige in the Balkans would be enhanced. If Serbia rejected our demands, then he too would favor military action. But he would already now go on record that we could aim at the down-sizing but not the complete annihilation of Serbia because, first, this would provoke Russia to fight to the death and, second, he—as Hungarian premier—could never consent to the monarchy's annexation of a part of Serbia. Whether or not we ought to go to war with Serbia was not a matter for Germany to decide. . . .

[Count Berchtold] remarked that the history of the past years showed that diplomatic successes against Serbia might enhance the prestige of the monarchy temporarily, but that in reality the tension in our relations with Serbia had only increased.

[Count Karl Stürgkh, prime minister of Austria] . . . agreed with the Royal Hungarian Prime Minister that we and not the German government had to determine whether a war was necessary or not . . . [but] Count Tisza should take into account that in pursuing a hesitant and weak policy, we run the risk of not being so sure of Germany's unconditional support. . . .

[Leo von Bilinsky, Austro-Hungarian finance minister] . . . The Serb understands only force; a diplomatic success would make no impression at all in Bosnia and would be harmful rather than beneficial. . . .

AUSTRO-HUNGARY'S ULTIMATUM TO SERBIA

The British foreign secretary Sir Edward Grey, for one, was shocked by Austria's demands, especially its insistence that Austrian officials would participate in Serbian judicial proceedings. The Serbian government's response was more conciliatory than most diplomats expected, but diplomatic efforts to avert war still failed. The Austrians' ultimatum to Serbia included the following demands:

The Royal Serb Government will publish the following declaration on the first page of its official *journal* of 26/13 July:

"The Royal Serb Government condemns the propaganda directed against Austria-Hungary, and regrets sincerely the horrible consequences of these criminal ambitions.

"The Royal Serb Government regrets that Serb officers and officials have taken part in the propaganda above-mentioned and thereby imperiled friendly and neighbourly relations.

"The Royal Government . . . considers it a duty to warn officers, officials and indeed all the inhabitants of the kingdom [of Serbia], that it will in future use great severity against such persons who may be guilty of similar doings.

The Royal Serb Government will moreover pledge itself to the following:

1. to suppress every publication likely to inspire hatred and contempt against the Monarchy;

2. to begin immediately dissolving the society called *Narodna Odbrana**; to seize all its means of propaganda and to act in the same way against all the societies and associations in Serbia, which are busy with the propaganda against Austria-Hungary.

3. to eliminate without delay from public instruction everything that serves or might serve the propaganda against Austria-Hungary, both where teachers or books are concerned;

4. to remove from military service and from the administration all officers and officials who are guilty of having taken part in the propaganda against Austria-Hungary, whose names and proof of whose guilt the I. and R. Government [Imperial and Royal, that is, the Austro-Hungarian empire] will communicate to the Royal Government;

5. to consent to the cooperation of I. and R. officials in Serbia in suppressing the subversive movement directed against the territorial integrity of the Monarchy;

6. to open a judicial inquest [*enquête judiciaire*] against all those who took part in the plot of 28 June, if they are to be found on Serbian territory; the I. and R. Government will delegate officials who will take an active part in these and associated inquiries;

The I. and R. Government expects the answer of the Royal government to reach it not later than Saturday, the 25th, at six in the afternoon. . . .

*Narodna Odbrana, or National Defense, was pro-Serbian and anti-Austrian, but nonviolent. The Society of the Black Hand, to which Franz Ferdinand's assassin belonged, considered Narodna Odbrana too moderate.

Ralph Menning, *The Art of the Possible: Documents on Great Power Diplomacy, 1814–1914* (New York: McGraw Hill, 1996), pp. 400, 402–403, and 414–415 (source for all three document excerpts).

THE MARNE AND ITS CONSEQUENCES

Why did the Schlieffen Plan fail?

Declarations of war were met with a mix of public fanfare and private concern. Though saber-rattling romantics envisioned a war of national glory and spiritual renewal, plenty of Europeans recognized that a continental war put decades of progress and prosperity at risk. Bankers and financiers, who might have hoped to profit from increased wartime production or from captured colonial markets, were among those most opposed to the war. They correctly predicted that a major war would create financial chaos. Many young men, however, enlisted with excitement. On the continent, volunteer soldiers added to the strength of conscript armies, while in Britain (where conscription wasn't introduced until 1916) over seven hundred thousand men joined the army in the first eight weeks alone. Like many a war enthusiast, these men expected the war to be over by Christmas.

If less idealistic, the expectations of the politicians and generals in charge were also soon to be disproved. Military planners foresaw a short, limited, and decisive war—a tool to be used where diplomacy failed. They thought that a modern economy simply could not function amid a sustained war effort, and that modern weaponry made protracted war impossible. They placed their bets on size and speed: bigger armies, more powerful weapons, and faster offensives would win the war. But for all of their planning, they were unable to respond to the uncertainty and confusion of the battlefield. In the Great War, one historian has noted, military success was achieved "through improvisation, not planning."

The Germans based their offensive on the plans of Count Alfred von Schlieffen. The Schlieffen Plan was designed to suit Germany's efficient, well-equipped, but outnumbered army. It called for attacking France first to secure a quick victory that would neutralize the Western Front, and free the German

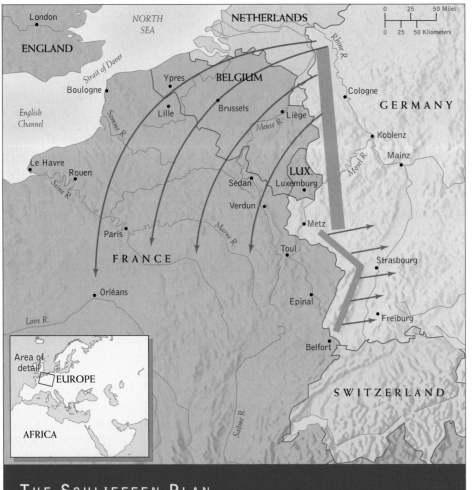

THE SCHLIEFFEN PLAN

This map details the plan developed by the Prussian general and strategist Alfred von Schlieffen in the 1890s. Schlieffen outlined the plan as part of what he believed was inevitable conflict with Russia. Why did Schlieffen seek to send German military resources to France in the event of a war with Russia? Why would he wish to defeat France first? What does the willingness of the German high command to commit to the violation of neutral territory (in this case Belgium) suggest about the breakdown of the diplomatic system carved out over the previous two generations?

army to fight Russia in the east. With France expecting an attack through Alsace-Lorraine, the Germans would instead invade through Belgium and sweep down through northwestern France to fight a decisive battle near Paris. For over a month, the German army advanced swiftly. Yet the plan overestimated the army's physical and logistical capabilities. The speed of the operation—advancing twenty to twenty-five miles a day—was simply too much for soldiers and supply lines to keep up with. They were also slowed by the resistance of the poorly armed but determined Belgian army and by the intervention of Britain's small but highly professional field army, whose trained marksmen caused terrible losses among the advancing Germans.

There were also changes of plan. First, fearing the Russians would move faster than expected, German commanders altered Schlieffen's plan by dispatching some troops to the east instead of committing them all to the assault on France. Second, they chose to attack Paris from the northeast instead of circling to the southwest.

Nevertheless, German plans seemed to be working during August. French attacks into Alsace-Lorraine were a chaotic failure, and casualties mounted as the French lines retreated toward Paris. Yet German successes began to erode. The Belgian and British defense collapsed the German front into a single major thrust toward Paris. The French commander, Jules Joffre, who was immensely calm under pressure and almost callously indifferent to casualties, reorganized his armies and slowly drew the Germans into a trap. In September, with the Germans just thirty miles outside of the capital, Britain and France launched a successful counteroffensive at the battle of the Marne. The German line retreated to the Aisne river, and the Schlieffen Plan was dead. After the Marne unable to advance, the armies tried to outflank one another to the north, creating a race to the sea that neither side won. After four months of swift charges across open ground, Germany set up a fortified, defensive position that the Allies could not break. Along an immovable front, stretching over four hundred miles from the northern border of Switzerland to the English Channel, the Great Powers dug fortifications for a protracted battle. By Christmas, trench warfare was born, and the war had just begun.

The Marne proved to be the most strategically important battle of the entire war. This single battle upended Europe's expectations of war

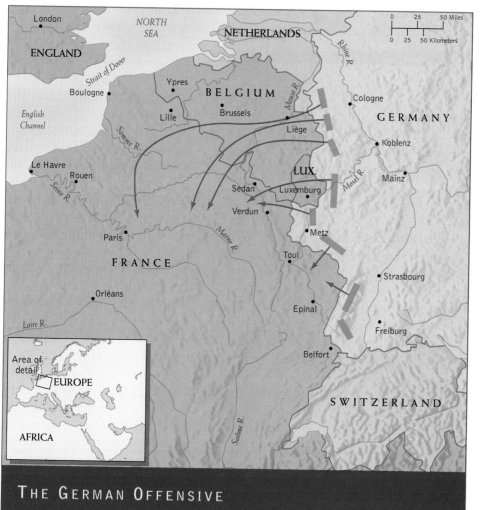

THE GERMAN OFFENSIVE

In what ways was the Schlieffen Plan a success? How did the French help to frustrate the Schlieffen Plan despite leaving Paris dangerously vulnerable? Note how close the German advance came to Paris. How did the German command staff's decision not to commit the entire German military to the defeat of France undermine the success of the Schlieffen Plan?

and dashed hopes of a quick finish. The war of movement had stopped dead in its tracks, where it would remain for four years. The war would prove long, costly, and deadly. Politicians and generals began a continual search for ways to break the stalemate and to bring the war out of trenches, seeking new allies, new theaters, and new weapons. But they also remained committed to offensive tactics on the Western Front. Whether through ignorance, stubbornness, callousness, or desperation, military leaders continued to order their men to go "over the top."

Part of the success of the Marne resulted from an unexpectedly strong Russian assault in eastern Prussia, which pulled some German units away from the war in the west. But Russia's initial gains were obliterated at the battle of Tannenberg, August 26–30. Plagued with an array of problems, the Russian army was tired and half-starved; the Germans devastated it, taking one hundred thousand prisoners and virtually destroying the Russian Second Army. The Russian general killed himself on the battlefield. Two weeks later, the Germans won another decisive victory at the battle of the Masurian Lakes, forcing the Russians to retreat from German territory. Despite this, Russian forces were able to defeat Austrian attacks to their south, inflicting terrible losses and thereby forcing the Germans to commit more troops to face the poorly armed but enormous Russian army. Through 1915 and 1916, the Eastern Front remained bloody and indecisive, with neither side able to capitalize on its gains.

> Politicians and generals began a continual search for ways to break the stalemate and to bring the war out of trenches, seeking new allies, new theaters, and new weapons. But they also remained committed to offensive tactics on the Western Front.

STALEMATE, 1915

Why did the war become a stalemate?

In the search for new points of attack, both the Allies and the Central Powers added new partners. The Ottoman empire (Turkey) joined Germany and Austria at the end of 1914. In May 1915, Italy joined the Allies, persuaded by the popular support of its citizens and by the lure of land and money. The Treaty of London of April 1915 promised Italy financial reparations, parts of Austrian territory, and pieces of Germany's African colonies when (and if) the Allies won the war. Bulgaria also hoped to gain territory in the Balkans and joined the war on the side of the Central Powers a few months later. The entry of these new belligerents expanded the geography of the war and introduced the possibility of breaking the stalemate in the west by waging offensives on other fronts.

GALLIPOLI AND NAVAL WARFARE

Turkey's involvement, in particular, altered the dynamics of the war, for it threatened Russia's supply lines and endangered Britain's control of the Suez Canal. To defeat Turkey quickly—and in hopes of bypassing the western stalemate—the British First Lord of the Admiralty, Winston Churchill (1911–1915), argued for a naval offensive in the Dardanelles, the narrow strait separating Europe and Asia Minor. Under particularly incompetent leadership, however, the Royal Navy lacked adequate planning, supply lines, and maps to mount a successful campaign. Thus, the Allied attack began with a series of ineffective naval bombardments and mine sweeps, resulting in the loss or damage of six Allied ships. The Allies then attempted a land invasion of the Gallipoli peninsula, beginning on April 25, 1915. The combined force of French, British, Australian, and New Zealand troops made little headway, however. The Turks defended the narrow coast from positions high on fortified cliffs, and the shores were covered with nearly impenetrable barbed wire. During the disastrous landing, a British officer recalled, "the sea behind was absolutely crimson, and you could hear the groans through the rattle of musketry." The battle became entrenched on the beaches at Gallipoli, and the casualties mounted for seven months before the Allied commanders admitted defeat and ordered a withdrawal in December. The Gallipoli campaign—the first large-scale amphibious attack in history—was a major defeat for the Allies. It brought death into London's neighborhoods and the cities of Britain's industrial north. Casualties were particularly devastating in the "white dominions"—practically every town and hamlet in Australia, New Zealand, and Canada lost young men, sometimes all the sons of a single family. The campaign cost the Allies two hundred thousand soldiers and did little to

Lusitania, drawing by Claus Bergen, 1915. The sinking of the passenger liner *Lusitania* by a German submarine provoked outrage from the Allied countries, as well as the United States.

shift the war's focus away from the deadlocked Western Front. In fact, the failure of "going around" simply reinforced the logic of fighting in the trenches.

By 1915 both sides realized that fighting this prolonged and costly "modern" war would require countries to mobilize all of their resources. As one captain put it in a letter home, "It is absolutely certainly a war of 'attrition,' as somebody said here the other day, and we have got to stick it out longer than the other side and go on producing men, money, and material until they cry quits, and that's about it, as far as I can see."

The Allies started to wage war on the economic front. Germany was vulnerable, dependent as it was on imports for at least one third of its food supply. The Allies' naval blockade against all of central Europe aimed to slowly drain their opponents of food and raw materials. Germany responded with a submarine blockade, threatening to attack any vessel in the seas around Great Britain. On May 7, 1915, the German submarine *U-20*, without warning, torpedoed the passenger liner *Lusitania,* which was secretly carrying war supplies. The attack killed 1,198 people, including 128 Americans.

The attack provoked the animosity of the United States, and Germany was forced to promise that it would no longer fire without warning. (This promise proved only temporary: in 1917 Germany would again declare unrestricted submarine warfare, drawing America into the war.) Although the German blockade against Britain destroyed more tonnage, the blockade against Germany was more devastating in the long run, as the continued war effort placed increasing demands on the national economy.

TRENCH WARFARE

While the war escalated economically and politically, life in the trenches remained largely the same: a cramped and miserable existence of daily routines and continual killing. "When all is said and done," an English officer later wrote, "the war was mainly a matter of holes and ditches." Indeed, some twenty-five thousand miles of trenches snaked along the Western Front, normally in three lines on each side of "No Man's Land." The front line was the attack trench, lying anywhere from fifty yards to a mile away from the enemy. Behind the front was the second line, a support trench; and behind that, a third trench for reserves. But despite the similar layouts, the two sides' trenches were remarkably different. The Germans saw their position as permanent, and they built elaborate bunkers—fully enclosed rooms with electric light, running water, and overstuffed furniture. Some even had kitchens, wallpaper, curtains, and doorbells. These comforts contrasted sharply with the ramshackle constructions of the French and British, who refused to abandon their offensive strategy, and so saw little value in fortifying a defensive position. "The result," one soldier realized, was "that we lived a mean and impoverished sort of existence in lousy scratch holes."

The British trenches were wet, cold, and filthy. Rain turned the dusty corridors into squalid mud pits and flooded the floors up to waist level. Soldiers lived with lice and large black rats, which fed on the dead soldiers and horses that cast their stench over everything. Cadavers could go unburied for months, and were often just embedded in the trench walls. It was little wonder that soldiers were rotated out of the front lines frequently—after only three to seven days—to be relieved from what one soldier called "this present, ever-present, eternally present misery, this stinking world of sticky, trickling earth ceilinged by a strip of threatening sky." Indeed, the threat of enemy fire was constant: seven thousand British men were killed or wounded daily. This "wastage," as it was called, was part of the routine, along with the inspections, rotations, and mundane duties of life on the Western Front. Despite this danger, the trenches were a relatively reliable means of protection, especially compared to the casualty rates of going on the offensive.

As the war progressed, new weapons added to the frightening dimensions of daily warfare. Besides artillery, machine guns, and barbed wire, the instruments of war now included exploding bullets, liquid fire, and poison gas. Gas, in particular, brought visible change to the battlefront. First used effectively by the Germans in April 1915 at the second battle of Ypres, poison gas was not only physically devastating—especially in its later forms—but also psychologically disturbing. The deadly cloud frequently hung over the trenches, although the quick appearance of gas masks limited its effectiveness. Like other new weapons, poison gas solidified the lines and took more lives, but could not end the stalemate. The war dragged through its second year, bloody and stagnant. Soldiers grew accustomed to the stalemate, while their leaders plotted ways to end it.

SLAUGHTER IN THE TRENCHES: THE GREAT BATTLES, 1916–1917

Why did the Allies persist with an offensive strategy?

The bloodiest battles of all—those that epitomize the First World War—occurred in 1916–1917. Massive campaigns in the war of attrition, these assaults produced hundreds of thousands of casualties and only minor territorial gains. These battles encapsulated the military tragedy of the war: a strategy of soldiers in cloth uniforms marching against machine guns. The result, of course, was carnage. The common response to these staggering losses was to replace the generals in charge. But though commanders changed, commands did not. Military planners continued to believe that their original strategies were the right ones, and that their plans had simply been frustrated by bad luck and German determination. The "cult of the offensive" insisted that a breakthrough was possible with enough troops and enough weapons.

But the manpower needed could not be moved efficiently or protected adequately. Railroad networks made it possible to bring large numbers of troops to the front, but mobility ended there. Heavy mud, labyrinthine trenches, and tangles of barbed wire made movement arduous, if not impossible. More important, the new technologies of killing made movement deadly. Unprotected soldiers armed with rifles, grenades, and bayonets were simply no match for machine guns and deep trenches. Another major problem of military strategy—and another explanation for the continued slaughter—was the lack of effective communication between the front lines and general headquarters. If something went wrong at the front (which happened frequently) it was impossible for the leaders to know in time to make meaningful corrections. As the great battles of the Great War illustrate, firepower had outpaced mobility, and the Allied generals simply did not know how to respond.

VERDUN

The first of these major battles was the German attack on the French stronghold of Verdun, near France's east-

Verdun, 1916. French soldiers look out from their trenches during a round of shelling. A dead body lies at the right.

ern border, in February 1916. Verdun had little strategic importance, but it quickly became a symbol of France's strength and was defended at all costs. Germany's goal was not necessarily to take the city, but rather to break French morale—France's "remarkable devotion"—at a moment of critical weakness. As the German general Erich von Falkenhayn (1914–1916) said, the offensive would "compel the French to throw in every man they have. If they do so the forces of France will bleed to death." One million shells were fired on the first day of battle, inaugurating a ten-month struggle of back-and-forth fighting offensives and counteroffensives of intense ferocity at enormous cost and zero gain. Led by General Henri Pétain (1914–1918), the French pounded the Germans with artillery and received heavy bombardment in return. The Germans relied on large teams of horses, seven thousand of which were killed in a single day, to drag their guns through the muddy, cratered terrain. The French moved supplies and troops into Verdun continually: twelve thousand delivery trucks were employed for service, as were 259 of 330 regiments of the French army (including the future president Charles de Gaulle, who was captured during a raid on a German fort). Neither side could gain a real

> By the end of June, over four hundred thousand French and German soldiers were dead. "Verdun," writes one historian, "had become a place of terror and death that could not yield victory."

advantage—one small village on the front changed hands thirteen times in one month alone—but both sides incurred devastating losses of life. By the end of June, over four hundred thousand French and German soldiers were dead. "Verdun," writes one historian, "had become a place of terror and death that could not yield victory." In the end, however, the advantage fell to the French. They simply survived, and bled the Germans as badly as they suffered themselves.

THE SOMME

Meanwhile, the British opened their own offensive against Germany farther west, beginning the battle of the Somme on June 24, 1916. The Allied attack began with a fierce five-day bombardment, blasting the German lines with a massive amount of artillery. Over fourteen hundred guns delivered nearly 3 million shells; the blasts could be heard all the way across the English Channel. The British assumed that this preliminary attack would break the mesh of German wire, destroy Germany's trenches, and clear the way for Allied troops to advance forward and upright, virtually unprotected. They were tragically wrong. The shells the British used were designed for surface combat, not to penetrate the deep, reinforced trenches dug by the Germans. The wire and trenches withstood the bombardment. When the British soldiers were ordered "over the top" toward enemy lines, they found themselves snared in wire and facing fully operational German machine guns. Each man carried sixty pounds of supplies that were to be used during the expected fighting in the German trenches. A few British commanders who had disobeyed orders and brought their men forward before the shelling ended were able to break through German lines. Elsewhere it was hardly a battle; whole British divisions were simply mowed down. Those who made it to the enemy trenches faced bitter hand-to-hand combat with pistols, grenades,

The Lines of Battle on the Western Front. A British reconnaissance photo showing three lines of German trenches (right), No Man's Land (the black strip in the center), and the British trenches (partially visible to the left). The upper right hand quadrant of the photo shows communications trenches linking the front to the safe area.

victories on the Western Front again in 1917. The French general Robert Nivelle (1914–1917) promised to break through the German lines with overwhelming manpower, but the "Nivelle Offensive" (April–May 1917) failed immediately, with first-day casualties like those at the Somme. The British also reprised the Somme at the third battle of Ypres (July–October 1917) where a half million casualties earned Great Britain only insignificant gains—and no breakthrough. The one weapon with the potential to break the stalemate, the tank, was finally introduced into battle in 1916, but with such reluctance by tradition-bound commanders that its half-hearted employment made almost no difference. Other innovations were equally indecisive. Airplanes were used almost exclusively for reconnaissance, though occasional "dogfights" did occur between German and Allied pilots. And though the Germans sent zeppelins to raid London, they did little significant damage.

Off the Western Front, fighting produced further stalemate. The Austrians continued to fend off attacks in Italy and Macedonia, while the Russians mounted a successful offensive against them on the Eastern Front. The initial Russian success brought Romania into the war on Russia's side, but the Central Powers quickly retaliated and knocked the Romanians out of the war within a few months.

The war at sea was equally indecisive, with neither side willing to risk the loss of enormously expensive battleships. The British and German navies fought only one major naval battle early in 1916, which ended in stalemate. Afterward they used their fleets primarily in the economic war of blockades.

As a year of great bloodshed and growing disillusionment, 1916 showed that not even the superbly organized Germans had the mobility or fast-paced communications to win the western ground war. Increasingly, warfare would be turned against entire nations, including civilian populations on the "home front" and in the far reaches of the European empires.

knives, bayonets, and bare hands. On the first day of battle alone, a stunning twenty thousand British soldiers died, and another forty thousand were wounded. The carnage continued from July until mid-November, resulting in massive casualties on both sides: five hundred thousand German, four hundred thousand British, and two hundred thousand French. The losses were unimaginable, and the outcome was equally hard to fathom: for all their sacrifices, neither side made any real gains. The first lesson of the Somme was offered later, by a war veteran: "Neither side had won, nor could win, the War. The War had won, and would go on winning." The futility of offensive war was not lost on the soldiers, yet morale remained surprisingly strong. Although mutinies and desertions occurred on both sides, they were rare, and surrenders became an important factor only in the final months of the war.

With willing armies and fresh recruits, military commanders maintained their strategy and pushed for

WAR OF EMPIRES

What was the role of empire in World War I?

Coming as it did at the height of European imperialism, the Great War quickly became a war of empires, with far-reaching repercussions. As the demands of warfare rose, Europe's colonies provided soldiers and material support. Britain, in particular, benefited from its vast network of colonial dominions and dependencies, bringing in soldiers from Canada, Australia, New Zealand, India, and South Africa. These colonial troops fought with the Allies on the Western Front, as well as in Mesopotamia and Persia against the Turks and in East Africa against Germany. They suffered eight hundred thousand casualties, with one fourth fatalities—losses double those of the United States. Colonial recruits were also employed in industry. In France, where even some French conscripts were put to work in factories, the international labor force numbered over two hundred fifty thousand—including workers from China, Vietnam, Egypt, India, the West Indies, and South Africa.

With the stalemate in Europe, colonial areas also became strategically important theaters for armed engagement. Although the campaign against Turkey began poorly for Britain with the debacle at Gallipoli, beginning in 1916 Allied forces won a series of battles, pushing the Turks out of Egypt and eventually capturing Baghdad, Jerusalem, Beirut, and other cities throughout the Middle East. The British commander in Egypt and Palestine was Edmund Allenby (1919–1925), who led a multinational army against the well-drilled Turks. Allenby was a shrewd general and an excellent manager of men and supplies in desert conditions, but in his campaigns the support of different Arab peoples seeking independence from the Turks proved crucial. Allenby allied himself to the successful Bedouin revolts that split the Ottoman empire; the British officer T. E. Lawrence (1914–1918) popularized the Arabs' guerrilla actions. When one of the senior Bedouin aristocrats, the emir Abdullah, captured the strategic port of Aqaba in July 1917, Lawrence took credit and entered popular mythology as "Lawrence of Arabia."

Britain encouraged Arab nationalism for its own strategic purposes, offering a qualified acknowledgment of Arab political aspirations. At the same time, for similar but conflicting strategic reasons, the British

The War of Empires: Soldiers in Mesopotamia, 1917. France and Britain carved out new spheres of influence in the Middle East during World War I. In this photograph British soldiers gather their Arab allies against the Turks.

declared their support of "the establishment in Palestine of a national home for the Jewish people." Britain's foreign secretary, Arthur Balfour, made the pledge. European Zionists, seeking a Jewish homeland, took the Balfour Declaration very seriously. The conflicting pledges to Bedouin leaders and Zionists sowed the seeds of future Arab-Israeli conflict. The war drew Europe more deeply into the Middle East, where conflicting dependencies and commitments created numerous postwar problems.

IRISH REVOLT

Britain's own empire was also vulnerable, and the demands of war strained precarious bonds to the breaking point. Before the war, long-standing tensions between Irish Catholics and the Protestant British government had reached fever pitch, and civil war was likely. The Sinn Fein ("Ourselves Alone") party had formed in 1900 to fight for Irish independence, and a home rule bill had passed Parliament in 1912. But with the outbreak of war in 1914, national interests took

precedence over domestic politics: the "Irish question" was tabled, and two hundred thousand Irishmen volunteered for the British army. The problem festered, however, and on Easter Sunday, 1916, a group of nationalists revolted in Dublin. The insurgents' plan to smuggle in arms from Germany failed, and they had few delusions of achieving victory. The British army arrived with artillery and machine guns; they shelled parts of Dublin and crushed the uprising within a week.

The revolt was a military disaster, but it was a striking political success. Britain shocked the Irish public by executing the rebel leaders. Even the British prime minister David Lloyd George (1916–1922) thought the military governor in Dublin exceeded his authority with these executions. The martyrdom of the "Easter Rebels" seriously damaged Britain's relationship with its Irish Catholic subjects. The deaths galvanized the cause of Irish nationalism and touched off guerrilla violence that kept Ireland in turmoil for years. Finally, a new home rule bill was enacted in 1920, establishing separate parliaments for the Catholic south of Ireland

Easter Rebellion, Dublin, 1916. British troops line up behind a moveable barricade made up of household furniture during their repression of the brief, ill-fated Irish revolt.

and for Ulster, the northeastern counties where the majority population was Protestant. The leaders of the so-called Dáil Éireann (Irish Assembly), which had proclaimed an Irish Republic in 1918 and therefore been outlawed by Britain, rejected the bill, but accepted a treaty that granted dominion status to Catholic Ireland in 1921. Dominion was followed almost immediately by civil war between those who abided by the treaty and those who wanted to absorb Ulster, but the conflict ended in an uneasy compromise. The Irish Free State was established, and British sovereignty was partially abolished in 1937. Full status as a republic came, with some American pressure and Britain's exhausted indifference, in 1945.

THE HOME FRONT

How did the war change women's lives?

When the war of attrition began in 1915, the belligerent governments were unprepared for the strains of sustained warfare. The costs of war—in both money and manpower—were staggering. In 1914 the war cost Germany 36 million marks per day (five times the cost of the war of 1870), and by 1918 the cost had skyrocketed to 146 million marks per day. Great Britain had estimated it would need one hundred thousand soldiers but ended up mobilizing 3 million. The enormous task of feeding, clothing, and equipping the army became as much of a challenge as breaking through enemy lines; civilian populations were increasingly asked—or forced—to support these efforts. Bureaucrats and industrialists led the effort to mobilize the "home front," focusing all parts of society on the single goal of military victory. The term *total war* was introduced to describe this intense mobilization of society. Government propagandists insisted that civilians were as important to the war effort as soldiers, and in many ways they were. As workers, taxpayers, and consumers, civilians were vital parts of the war economy. They produced munitions, purchased war bonds, and shouldered the burden of tax hikes, inflation, and material privations.

The demands of industrial warfare led first to a transition from general industrial manufacturing to munitions production, and then to increased state control of all aspects of production and distribution. The governments of Britain and France managed to direct the economy politically, without serious detriment to the

Women at Work.
The all-out war effort combined with a manpower shortage at home brought women into factories across Europe in unparalleled numbers. In this photo men and women work side by side in a British shell factory.

standard of living in their countries. Germany, meanwhile, put its economy in the hands of army and industry; under the Hindenburg Plan, named for Paul von Hindenburg (1916–1919), the chief of the imperial staff of the German army, pricing and profit margins were set by individual industrialists.

Largely because of the immediate postwar collapse of the German economy, historians have characterized Germany's wartime economy as a chaotic, ultimately disastrous system governed by personal interest. New research, however, suggests that this was not the case: Germany's systems of war finance and commodity distribution, however flawed, were not decisively worse than those of Britain or France.

WOMEN IN THE WAR

As Europe's adult men left farms and factories to become soldiers, the composition of the work force changed: thousands of women were recruited into fields that had previously excluded them. Young people, foreigners, and unskilled workers were also pressed into newly important tasks; in the case of colonial workers, their experiences had equally critical repercussions. But because they were more visible, it was women who became symbolic of many of the changes brought by the Great War. In Germany, one third of the labor force in heavy industry was female by the end of the war, and in France, 684,000 women worked in the munitions industry alone. In England the "munitionettes," as they were dubbed, numbered nearly a million. Women also entered the clerical and service sectors. In the villages of France, England, and Germany, women became mayors, school principals, and mail carriers. Hundreds of thousands of women worked with the army as nurses and ambulance drivers, jobs that brought them very close to the front lines. With minimal supplies and under squalid conditions, they worked to save lives or patch bodies together.

In some cases, war offered new opportunities. Middle-class women often said that the war broke down the restrictions on their lives; those in nursing learned to drive and acquired rudimentary medical knowledge. At home they could now ride the train, walk the street, or go out to dinner without an older woman present to chaperone them. In terms of gender roles, an enormous gulf sometimes seemed to separate the wartime world from nineteenth-century Victorian society. In one of the most famous autobiographies of the war, Vera Brittain's *Testament of Youth*, Brittain (1896–1970) recorded the dramatic new social norms that she

and others forged during the rapid changes of wartime. "As a generation of women we were now sophisticated to an extent which was revolutionary when compared with the romantic ignorance of 1914. Where we had once spoken with polite evasion of 'a certain condition,' or 'a certain profession,' we now unblushingly used the words 'pregnancy' and 'prostitution.'" For every Vera Brittain who celebrated the changes, however, journalists, novelists, and other observers grumbled that women were now smoking, refusing to wear the corsets that gave Victorian dresses their hourglass shape, or cutting their hair into the new fashionable bobs. The "new woman" became a symbol of profound and disconcerting cultural transformation.

How long lasting were these changes? In the aftermath of the war, governments and employers scurried

German Poster, 1918. "Collect women's hair that has been combed out. Our industry needs it for drive belts." This poster calls on women to donate their hair, which was used to replace leather and hemp, to the war effort.

ONE WOMAN'S WAR

Vera Brittain (1893–1970) was talented, ambitious, and privileged. She was among the few women to attend Oxford University the year before the war. When war broke out, her fiancé enlisted in the British army. Brittain later joined the Voluntary Aid Detachment and served as a nurse in Europe and in the Mediterranean. In the following excerpt from her memoir, Testament of Youth, *Brittain writes home to her family from France in 1917, worrying about morale on the home front. She also reflects on women's different and often conflicting duties, and on what the war meant to her as a sheltered girl from a well-to-do family.*

"Conditions . . . certainly seem very bad," I wrote to my family on January 10th [1917] . . . "But do if you can," I implored, "try to carry on without being too despondent and make other people do the same . . . for the great fear in the Army and all its appurtenances out here is not that it will ever give up itself, but that the civil population at home will fail us by losing heart—and so of course morale—just at the most critical time. . . .

This despondency at home was certainly making many of us in France quite alarmed: because we were women we feared perpetually that, just as our work was reaching its climax, our families would need our youth and vitality for their own support. One of my cousins, the daughter of an aunt, had already been summoned home from her canteen work in Boulogne; she was only one of many, for as the War continued to wear out strength and spirits, the middle-aged generation, having irrevocably yielded up its sons, began to lean with increasing weight upon its daughters. . . .

What exhausts women in wartime is not the strenuous and unfamiliar tasks that fall upon them, nor even the hourly dread of death for husbands or lovers or brothers or sons; it is the incessant conflict between personal and national claims which wears out their energy and breaks their spirit. . . .

When I was a girl . . . I imagined that life was individual, one's own affair; that the events happening in the world outside were important enough in their own way, but were personally quite irrelevant. Now, like the rest of my generation, I have had to learn again and again . . . about the invasion of personal preoccupations by the larger destinies of mankind, and at last to recognise that no life is really private, or isolated, or self-sufficient. People's lives were entirely their own, perhaps . . . when the world seemed enormous, and all its comings and goings were slow and deliberate. But this is so no longer, and never will be again, since man's inventions have eliminated so much of distance and time; for better, for worse, we are now each of us part of the surge and swell of great economic and political movements, and whatever we do, as individuals or as nations, deeply affects everyone else.

Vera Brittain, *Testament of Youth: An Autobiographical Study of the Years 1900–1925* (London, New York: Penguin Books, 1989), pp. 401, 422–423, 471–472.

to send women workers home, in part to give jobs to veterans, in part to deal with male workers' complaints that women were undercutting their wages. Efforts to demobilize women faced real barriers. Many women wage earners—widowed, charged with caring for relatives, or faced with inflation and soaring costs—needed their earnings more than ever. It was also difficult to persuade women workers who had grown accustomed to the relatively higher wages in heavy industry to return to their poorly paid traditional sectors of employment: the textile and garment industries and domestic service. The demobilization of women after the war, in other words, created as many dilemmas as had their mobilization. Governments passed "natalist" policies to encourage women to go home, marry, and most important, have children. These policies did make maternity benefits—time off, medical care, and some allowances for the poor—available to women for the first time. Nonetheless, birth rates had been falling across Europe by the early twentieth century, and they continued to do so after the war. One upshot of the war was the increased availability of birth control—Marie Stopes (1880–1958) opened a birth-control clinic in London in 1921—and a combination of economic hardship, increased knowledge, and the demand for freedom made men and women more likely to use it. Universal suffrage, and the vote for all adult men and women, and for women in particular, had been one of the most controversial issues in European politics before the war. At the end of the fighting it came in a legislative rush. Britain was first off the mark, granting the vote to all men and women over thirty with the Representation of the People Act in 1918; the United States gave women the vote with the Nineteenth Amendment the following year. Germany's new republic and the Soviet Union did likewise. France was much slower to offer woman suffrage (1945), but did provide rewards and incentives for the national effort.

MOBILIZING RESOURCES

Along with mobilizing the labor front, the wartime governments had to mobilize men and money. All the belligerent countries had conscription laws before the war, except for Great Britain. Military service was seen as a duty, not an option. Bolstered by widespread public support for the war, this belief brought millions of young Europeans into recruitment offices in 1914. The French began the war with about 4.5 million trained soldiers, but by the end of 1914—just four months into the war—three hundred thousand were dead and six hundred thousand injured. Conscripting citizens and mustering colonial troops became increasingly important. Eventually, France called up 8 million citizens: almost two thirds of Frenchmen aged 18 to 40. In 1916, the British finally introduced conscription, dealing a serious blow to civilian morale; by the summer of 1918, half its army was under nineteen.

Government propaganda, while part of a larger effort to sustain both soldier and civilian morale, was also important to the recruitment effort. From the outset, the war had been sold to the people on both sides

> In 1916, the British finally introduced conscription, dealing a serious blow to civilian morale; by the summer of 1918, half its army was under nineteen.

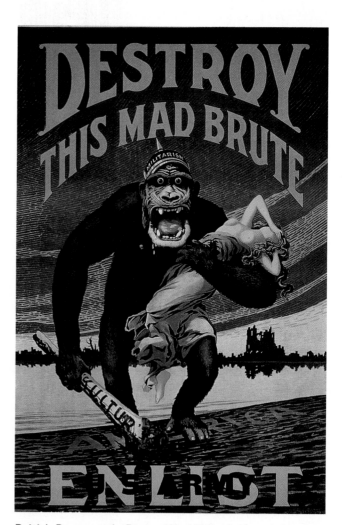

British Propaganda Poster, World War I. The mad beast, meant to represent Germany, with "militarism" on his helmet, threatens British civilization with a club of "Kultur" (culture). All the warring countries produced similar propaganda.

of the conflict as a moral and righteous crusade. In 1914, the French president Raymond Poincaré (1913–1920) assured his fellow citizens that France had no other purpose than to stand "before the universe for Liberty, Justice and Reason." Germans were presented with the task of defending their superior *Kultur* against the wicked encirclement policy of the Allied nations: "May God punish England!" was practically a greeting in 1914. By the middle of the war, massive propaganda campaigns were underway. Film, posters, postcards, newspapers—all forms of media proclaimed the strength of the cause, the evil of the enemy, and the absolute necessity of total victory. The success of these campaigns is difficult to determine, but it is clear that they had at least one painful effect—they made it more difficult for any country to accept a fair, nonpunitive peace settlement.

Financing the war was another heavy obstacle. Military spending accounted for about 3 to 5 percent of government expenditure in the combatant countries before 1914, but soared to perhaps half of each nation's budget during the war. Governments had to borrow money or print more of it. The Allied nations borrowed heavily from the British, who borrowed even more from the United States. American capital flowed across the Atlantic long before the United States entered the war. And though economic aid from the

United States was a decisive factor in the Allies' victory, it left Britain with a $4.2 billion debt and hobbled the United Kingdom as a financial power after the war. The situation was far worse for Germany, which faced a total blockade of money and goods. In an effort to get around this predicament, and lacking an outside source of cash, the German government funded its war effort largely by increasing the money supply. The amount of paper money in circulation increased by over 1,000 percent during the war, triggering a dramatic rise in inflation. During the war, prices in Germany rose about 400 percent, double the inflation in Britain and France. For middle-class people living on pensions or fixed incomes, these price hikes were a push into poverty.

THE STRAINS OF WAR, 1917

The demands of total war worsened as the conflict dragged into 1917. On the front lines, morale fell as war-weary soldiers began to see the futility of their commanders' strategies. After the debacle of the Nivelle Offensive, the French army recorded acts of mutiny in two thirds of its divisions; similar resistance arose in nearly all major armies in 1917. Military leaders portrayed the mutineers as part of a dangerous pacifist movement, but most were nonpolitical. As one soldier put it: "All we wanted was to call the government's attention to us, make it see that we are men, and not beasts for the slaughterhouse." Resistance within the Germany army was never organized or widespread, but existed in subtler forms. Self-mutilation rescued some soldiers from the horror of the trenches; many more were released because of various emotional disorders. Over six hundred thousand cases of "war neuroses" were reported among German troops—an indication, if not of intentional disobedience, of the severe physical and psychological trauma that caused the mutinies.

The war's toll also mounted for civilians, who often suffered from the same shortages of basic supplies that afflicted the men at the front. In 1916–1917, the lack of clothing, food, and fuel was aggravated in central Europe by abnormally cold,

Desperation at Home, 1918. A German photograph of women digging through garbage in search of food. The last year of the war brought starvation to cities in Germany and Austria-Hungary, sending many people into the countryside to forage for provisions.

wet weather. These strains provoked rising discontent on the home front. Although governments attempted to solve the problem with tighter controls on the economy, their policies often provoked further hostilities from civilians. "The population has lost all confidence in promises from the authorities," a German official reported in 1917, "particularly in view of earlier experiences with promises made in the administration of food."

In urban areas, where undernourishment was worst, people stood in lines for hours to get food and fuel rations that scarcely met their most basic needs. The price of bread and potatoes—still the central staples of working-class meals—soared. Prices were even higher in the thriving black market that emerged in cities. Consumers worried aloud that speculators were hoarding supplies and creating artificial shortages, selling tainted goods, and profiting from others' miseries. They decried the government's "reckless inattention" to families. Governments, however, were concentrated on the war effort and faced difficult decisions about who needed supplies the most—soldiers at the front, workers in the munitions industry, or hungry and cold families.

Like other nations, Germany moved from encouraging citizens to restrain themselves—"those who stuff themselves full, those who push out their paunches in all directions, are traitors to the Fatherland"—to direct control, issuing ration cards in 1915. Britain was the last to institute control, rationing bread only in 1917 when Germany's submarines sank an average of 630,000 tons per month and brought British food reserves within two weeks of starvation level. But rations indicated only what was allowed, not what was available. Hunger continued despite mass bureaucratic control. Governments regulated not only food but also working hours and wages, and unhappy workers directed their anger at the state, adding a political dimension to labor disputes and household needs. The bread lines, filled mainly by women, were flash points of political dissent, petty violence, even large-scale riots. Likewise, the class conflicts of prewar Europe had been briefly muffled by the outbreak of war and mobilization along patriotic lines, but as the war ground on, political tensions reemerged with new intensity. Thousands of strikes erupted throughout Europe, involving millions of frustrated workers. In April of 1917, three hundred thousand in Berlin went on strike to protest ration cuts. In May, a strike of Parisian seamstresses touched off a massive work stoppage that included even white-collar employees and munitions workers.

Shipbuilders and steelworkers in Glasgow went on strike as well, and the British government replied by sending armored cars to "Red Glasgow." Stagnation had given way to crisis on both sides. The strains of total war and the resulting social upheavals threatened political regimes throughout Europe. Governments were pushed to their limits. The Russian Revolution, which resulted in the overthrow of the tsar and the rise of Bolshevism, was only the most dramatic response to widespread social problems.

THE RUSSIAN REVOLUTION

How did the Bolsheviks seize power?

The first country to break under the strain of total war was tsarist Russia. The outbreak of war temporarily united Russian society against a common enemy, but Russia's military effort quickly turned sour. All levels of Russian society became disillusioned with Tsar Nicholas II who was unable to provide leadership, but nonetheless unwilling to open government to those who could. The political and social strains of war brought two revolutions in 1917. The first, in February, overthrew the tsar and established a transitional government. The second, in October, was a communist revolution that marked the emergence of the Soviet Union.

WORLD WAR I AND THE FEBRUARY REVOLUTION

Like the other participants in World War I, Russia entered the war with the assumption that it would be over quickly. Autocratic Russia, plagued by internal difficulties before 1914 (see Chapter 25), could not sustain the political strains of extended warfare. In all the warring countries success depended on leaders' ability not only to command, but also to maintain social and political cooperation. Tsar Nicholas II's political authority had been shaky for many years, undermined by his unpopular actions following the October Revolution of 1905 and his efforts to erode the minimal political power he had grudgingly granted to the Duma, Russia's parliament. Corruption in the royal court further tarnished the tsar's image. The best Nicholas's supporters could say about him was that he

Rasputin with his followers. While Tsar Nicholas II was commanding troops at the front, his wife Alexandra was falling under the influence of the charismatic faith healer Rasputin. In this photograph Rasputin is shown (seated at the left) surrounded by his courtly admirers.

was morally upright and devoted to his family. Once war broke out the tsar insisted on personally commanding Russian troops, leaving the government in the hands of his court, especially his wife Alexandra and her eccentric spiritual mentor and faith healer, Grigorii Rasputin (1872?–1916). Rasputin won the tsarina's sympathy by treating her hemophiliac son, and he used his influence to operate corrupt and self-aggrandizing schemes. His presence only added to the image of a court mired in decadence, incompetent to face the modern world.

In 1914 the Russians advanced against the Austrians into Galicia in the south, but during 1915 Russia suffered terrible defeats. All of Poland and substantial territory in the Baltics fell to the Germans at the cost of a million Russian casualties. Although the Russian army was the largest in Europe, it was poorly trained and, at the beginning of the war, undersupplied and inadequately equipped. In the first battles of 1914 generals sent soldiers to the front without rifles or shoes, instructing them to scavenge supplies from fallen comrades. By 1915, to the surprise of many, Russia was producing enough food, clothing, and ammunition, but political problems blocked the supply effort. The tsarist government distrusted public initiatives and tried to direct all provisioning itself. Tsarist officials insisted on making crucial decisions about the allocation of supplies without any consultation. Another major offensive in the summer of 1916 brought hope for success, but turned into a humiliating retreat. Demoralized and poorly supplied, the hastily trained peasants in the Russian armies found their will to fight disappearing fast. When word came that the government

> By 1915, to the surprise of many, Russia was producing enough food, clothing, and ammunition, but political problems blocked the supply effort.

Russian soldiers join the Bolsheviks in front of the Winter Palace, fall 1917.

brought a century-long struggle over Russian autocracy to a sudden end.

After the collapse of the monarchy, two parallel centers of power emerged. Each had its own objectives and policies. The first was the provisional government, organized by leaders in the Duma and composed mainly of middle-class liberals. The new government hoped to establish a democratic system under constitutional rule. Its main task was to set up a national election for a constituent assembly, and it also acted to grant and secure civil liberties, release political prisoners, and redirect power into the hands of local officials. The other center of power lay with the *soviets*, a Russian term for local councils elected by workers and soldiers. Since 1905, socialists had been active in organizing these councils, which claimed to be the true democratic representatives of the people. A Soviet, organized during the 1905 revolution and led by the well-known socialist Leon Trotsky, reemerged after February 1917 and asserted claim to be the legitimate political power in Russia. The increasingly powerful soviets pressed for social reform, the redistribution of land, and a negotiated settlement with Germany and Austria. Yet the provisional government refused to concede military defeat. Continuing the war effort made domestic reform impossible and cost valuable popular support. More fighting during 1917 was just as disastrous as before, and this time the provisional government paid the price. By autumn desertion in the army was rampant, administering the country was nearly impossible, and Russian politics teetered on the edge of chaos.

was requisitioning grain from the countryside to feed the cities, peasants began to desert en masse, returning to their farms to guard their families' holdings. By the end of 1916, a combination of political ineptitude and military defeat brought the Russian state to the verge of collapse.

The same problems that hampered the Russian war effort also crippled the tsar's ability to override domestic discontent and resistance. As the war dragged on, the government faced not only liberal opposition in the Duma, soldiers unwilling to fight, and an increasingly militant labor movement, but also a rebellious urban population. City dwellers were impatient with inflation and shortages of food and fuel. In February 1917, these forces came together in Petrograd (now St. Petersburg). The revolt began on International Women's Day, February 23, an occasion for a loosely organized march of women—workers, mothers, wives, and consumers—demanding food, fuel, and political reform. The march was the latest in a wave of demonstrations and strikes that had swept through the country during the winter months. This time, within a few days the unrest spiraled into a mass strike of three hundred thousand people. Nicholas II sent in police and military forces to quell the disorder. When nearly sixty thousand troops in Petrograd mutinied and joined the revolt, what was left of the tsar's power evaporated. Nicholas II abdicated the throne on March 2. This abrupt decision

THE BOLSHEVIKS AND THE OCTOBER REVOLUTION

The Bolsheviks, a branch of the Russian social democratic movement, had little to do with the events of February 1917. Over the course of the next seven months, however, they became enough of a force to overthrow the provisional government. The chain of events leading to the October revolution surprised most contemporary observers, including the Bolshe-

TOWARD THE OCTOBER REVOLUTION: LENIN TO THE BOLSHEVIKS

In the fall of 1917, Lenin was virtually the only Bolshevik leader who believed that an insurrection should be launched immediately. As the provisional government faltered, he attempted to convince his fellow Bolsheviks that the time for revolution had arrived.

Having obtained a majority in the Soviets of Workers' and Soldiers' Deputies of both capitals, the Bolsheviks can and *must* take power into their hands.

They can do so because the active majority of the revolutionary elements of the people of both capitals is sufficient to attract the masses, to overcome the resistance of the adversary, to vanquish him, to conquer power and to retain it. For, in offering immediately a democratic peace, in giving the land immediately to the peasants, in re-establishing the democratic institutions and liberties which have been mangled and crushed by Kerensky [leader of the provisional government], the Bolsheviks will form a government which *nobody* will overthrow. . . .

The majority of the people is *with* us. . . .[T]he majority in the Soviets of the capitals is the *result of* the people's progress *to our side.* The vacillation of the Socialist-Revolutionaries and Mensheviks . . . is proof of the same thing . . .

To "wait" for the Constituent Assembly would be wrong. . . . Only our party, having assumed power, can secure the convocation of the Constituent Assembly; and, after assuming power, it could blame the other parties for delaying it and could substantiate its accusations. . . .

It would be naive to wait for a "formal" majority on the side of the Bolsheviks; no revolution ever waits for *this.* . . . History will not forgive us if we do not assume power now.

No apparatus? There is an apparatus: the Soviets and democratic organisations. The international situation *just now,* on the *eve* of a separate peace between the English and the Germans, is *in our favour.* It is precisely now that to offer peace to the peoples means to *win.*

Assume power *at once* in Moscow and in Petrograd . . . ; we will win *absolutely and unquestionably.*

Vladimir Ilyich Lenin, *Bol'sheviki dolzhny vzyat'vlast'* (*The Bolsheviks Must Seize Power*), 12–14 (25–7) September 1917, PSS, vol. 34, pp. 239, 240, 241–2. From Richard Sakwa, *The Rise and Fall of the Soviet Union, 1917–1991* (New York and London: Routledge, 1999), p. 45.

viks themselves. Marxism had been quite weak in late-nineteenth-century Russia, although it made small but rapid inroads during the 1880s and 1890s. In 1903 the leadership of the Russian Social Democrats split over revolutionary strategy and the steps to socialism. One group, which won a temporary majority (and chose to call itself the Bolsheviks, or "members of the major-ity"), favored a centralized party of active revolutionar-ies. They believed that revolution alone would lead directly to a socialist regime. The Mensheviks ("members of the minority"), like most European so-cialists, wanted to move toward socialism gradually, supporting "bourgeois" or liberal revolution in the short term. Since peasants constituted 80 to 85% of the population, the Mensheviks also reasoned that a proletarian revolution was premature and that Russia needed to complete its capitalist development first. The Mensheviks regained control of the party, but the Bolshevik splinter party survived under the leadership of the young, dedicated revolutionary Vladimir Ilyich Ulyanov, who adopted the pseudonym Lenin.

Lenin was a member of the middle class; his father had been an inspector of schools and a minor political functionary. Lenin himself had been expelled from university for engaging in radical activity after his elder brother was executed for involvement in a plot to assassinate Tsar Alexander III. Lenin spent three years as a political prisoner in Siberia. After that, from 1900 until 1917, he lived and wrote as an exile in western Europe.

Lenin believed that the development of Russian capitalism made socialist revolution possible. To bring revolution, he argued, the Bolsheviks needed to organize on behalf of the new class of industrial workers. Without the party's disciplined leadership, Russia's factory workers could not accomplish change on the necessary scale. Lenin's Bolsheviks remained a minority among Social Democrats well into 1917 and industrial workers a small part of the population. But the Bolsheviks' dedication to the singular goal of revolution and their tight, almost conspiratorial organization gave them tactical advantages over larger and more loosely organized opposition parties. The Bolsheviks merged a peculiarly Russian tradition of revolutionary zeal with Western Marxism and endowed the mix with a sense that their goals could be achieved immediately. Lenin and his followers created a party capable of seizing the moment that history presented when the tsar left the scene.

Throughout 1917 the Bolsheviks consistently demanded an end to the war, improvement in working and living conditions for workers, and redistribution of aristocratic land to the peasantry. Popular discontent with the provisional government shot up after the government's disastrous military offensives against the Germans. The provisional government tried to enlist a conservative military leader, General Lavr Kornilov, to bring order to Petrograd by military force. While the provisional government struggled to hold together the Russian war effort, Lenin led the Bolsheviks on a bolder course, shunning any collaboration with the "bourgeois" government and condemning its imperialist war policies. Even most Bolsheviks considered Lenin's approach too radical. Yet as conditions in Russia deteriorated, his uncompromising calls for "Peace, Land, and Bread, Now" and "All Power to the Soviets" won the Bolsheviks support from workers, soldiers, and peasants. As many ordinary people saw it, the other

Lenin Speaking to Crowds in Moscow. To the right of the platform, in uniform, is Trotsky.

parties could not govern, win the war, or achieve an honorable peace. While unemployment continued to climb, and starvation and chaos reigned in the cities, the Bolsheviks' power and credibility was rising fast.

In October 1917, Lenin convinced his party to act. He goaded Trotsky, who was better known among workers, into organizing a Bolshevik attack on the provisional government on October 24–25, 1917. On October 25, Lenin appeared from hiding to announce to a stunned meeting of Soviet representatives that "all power had passed to the Soviets." The head of the provisional government fled to rally support at the front lines, and the Bolsheviks took over the Winter Palace, the seat of the provisional government. The initial stage of the revolution was quick and relatively bloodless. In fact, many observers believed they had seen nothing more than a coup d'état, one that might quickly be reversed. Life in Petrograd went on as normal.

> After a long struggle, the regime, weakened by the war, had collapsed with little resistance. By the middle of 1917, Russia was not suffering a crisis of government, but rather an absence of government.

The Bolsheviks took the opportunity to rapidly consolidate their position. First, they moved against all political competition, beginning with the soviets. They immediately expelled parties that disagreed with their actions, creating a new government in the soviets comprised entirely of Bolsheviks. Trotsky, sneering at moderate socialists who walked out to protest what they saw as an illegal seizure of power, scoffed: "You are a mere handful, miserable, bankrupt; your role is finished, and you may go where you belong—to the garbage heap of history." The Bolsheviks did follow through on the provisional government's promise to elect a Constituent Assembly. But when they did not win a majority in the elections, they refused to let the Assembly reconvene. From that point on, Lenin's Bolsheviks ruled socialist Russia, and later the Soviet Union, as a one-party dictatorship.

In the countryside, the new Bolshevik regime did little more than ratify a revolution that had been going on since the summer of 1917. When peasant soldiers at the front heard that a revolution had occurred, they streamed home to take land they had worked for generations and believed was rightfully theirs. The provisional government had set up commissions to deal methodically with the legal issues surrounding the redistribution of land, a process that threatened to become as complex as the emancipation of the serfs in 1861. The Bolsheviks simply approved the spontaneous redistribution of the nobles' land to peasants

without compensation to former owners. They nationalized banks and gave workers control of factories.

Most important, the new government sought to take Russia out of the war. It eventually negotiated a separate treaty with Germany, signed at Brest-Litovsk in March 1918. The Bolsheviks surrendered vast Russian territories: the rich agricultural region of Ukraine, Georgia, Finland, Russia's Polish territories, the Baltic states, and more. However humiliating, the treaty ended Russia's role in the fighting and saved the fledgling communist regime from almost certain military defeat at the hands of the Germans. The treaty enraged Lenin's political enemies, both moderates and reactionaries, who were still a force to be reckoned with—and who were prepared to wage a civil war rather than accept the revolution. Withdrawing from Europe's war only plunged the country into a vicious civil conflict (see Chapter 28).

Russian autocracy had fended off opposition for the better part of a century. After a long struggle, the regime, weakened by the war, had collapsed with little resistance. By the middle of 1917, Russia was not suffering a crisis of government, but rather an absence of government. In June, at the First All-Russian Congress of Soviets a prominent Menshevik declared, "At the present moment, there is not a political party in Russia that would say: Hand the power over to us, resign, and we will take your place. Such a party does not exist in Russia." Lenin shouted back from the audience, "It does exist!" Indeed, seizing power had been easy for the Bolsheviks, but building the new state proved vastly more difficult.

John Reed, an American journalist covering the Russian Revolution, called the events of October "ten days that shook the world." What had been shaken? First, the Allies, for the revolution allowed the Germans to win the war on the Eastern Front. Second, conservative governments, which in the aftermath of the war worried about a wave of revolution sweeping away other regimes. Third, the expectations of many socialists, startled to see a socialist regime gain and hold power in what many considered a backward country. Over the long run, 1917 was to the twentieth century what the French Revolution had been to the nineteenth century. It was a political transformation, it set the agenda for future revolutionary struggles, and it created the frames of mind on the right and the left for the century that followed.

THE ROAD TO GERMAN DEFEAT, 1918

How did the Allies win the war?

Russia's withdrawal dealt an immediate strategic and psychological blow to the Allies. Germany could soothe domestic discontent by claiming victory on the Eastern Front, and it could now concentrate its entire army in the west. The Allies feared that Germany would win the war before the United States, which entered the conflict in April 1917, could make a difference. It almost happened. With striking results, Germany shifted its offensive strategy to infiltration by small groups under flexible command. On March 21, Germany initiated a major assault on the west and quickly broke through the Allied lines. The British were hit hardest. Some units, surrounded, fought to the death with bayonets and grenades, but most recognized their plight and surrendered, putting tens of thousands of prisoners in German hands. The British were in retreat everywhere and their commander, Sir Douglas Haig, issued a famous order warning that British troops "now fight with our backs to the wall." The Germans advanced to within fifty miles of Paris by early April. Yet the British—and especially troops from the overseas empire—did just as they were asked and stemmed the tide. As German forces turned southeast instead, the French, who had refused to participate in the foolish attacks "over the top," showed stubborn courage on the defensive, where they bogged down in heat, mud, and casualties. It had been a last great try by the well-organized German army; exhausted, it now waited for the Allies to mount their own attack.

When it came in July and August, the Allied counterattack was devastating and quickly gathered steam. New offensive techniques had finally materialized. The Allies improved their use of tanks and the "creeping barrage," in which infantry marched close behind a rolling wall of shells to overwhelm their targets. In another of the war's ironies these new tactics were pioneered by the conservative British, who launched a crushing counterattack in July, relying on the survivors of the armies of the Somme reinforced by troops from Australia, Canada, and India. The French made use of the burgeoning numbers of American troops, whose generals attacked the Germans with the same harrow-

Wounded German Soldiers, 1917. Toward the end of the war, morale among German soldiers plummeted in the face of domestic conflict and the Allied blockade.

ing indifference to casualties shown in 1914. Despite their lack of experience the American troops were tough and resilient. When combined with more experienced French and Australian forces, they punched several large holes through German lines, crossing into the "lost provinces" of Alsace and Lorraine by October. At the beginning of November, the sweeping British offensive had joined up with the small Belgian army and was pressing toward Brussels.

The Allies finally brought their material advantage to bear on the Germans, who were suffering acutely by the spring of 1918. This was not only because of the continued effectiveness of the Allied blockade, but also because of growing domestic conflict over war aims. On the front lines, German soldiers were exhausted. Following the lead of their distraught generals, the troops let morale sink, and many surrendered. Facing one shattering blow after another, the German army was pushed deep into Belgium. Popular discontent mounted, and the government, which was now largely in the hands of the military, seemed unable either to win the war or to meet basic household needs.

Germany's network of allies was also coming undone. By the end of September, the Central Powers were headed for defeat. In the Middle East, Allenby's army, which combined Bedouin guerrillas, Indian sepoys, Scottish highlanders, and Australian light cavalry, decisively defeated Ottoman forces in Syria and Iraq. In the Balkans, France's capable battlefield commander, Louis Franchet d'Esperey (1914–1921), completely reorganized the Allied war effort. He transformed the Allied expedition that had been sent to Greece and with the help of sympathetic Greek politicians drew that country into the war. The results were remarkable. In September, a three-week offensive by the Greek and Allied forces knocked Bulgaria out of the war. Franchet d'Esperey's army, which included many exiled Serbs, pushed on to defeat Austrian forces and a number of exhausted German divisions. Austria-Hungary faced disaster on all sides, collapsing in Italy as well as the Balkans. Czech and Polish representatives in the Austrian government began pressing for self-government. Croat and Serb politicians proposed a "kingdom of Southern Slavs" (soon known as Yugoslavia). When Hungary joined the chorus for independence the emperor, Karl I, accepted reality and sued for peace. The empire that had started the conflict surrendered on November 3, 1918, and disintegrated soon after.

Germany was now left with the impossible task of carrying on the struggle alone. By the fall of 1918, the country was starving and on the verge of civil war. German forces in Belgium stemmed the British attack short of Brussels but were still reeling from French and American attacks to the south. A plan to use the German surface fleet to attack the combined British and American navies only produced a mutiny among German sailors at the start of November. Revolutionary tremors swelled into an earthquake. On November 8 a republic was proclaimed in Bavaria, and the next day nearly all of Germany was in the throes of revolution. The kaiser's abdication was announced in Berlin on November 9; he fled to Holland early the next morning. Control of the German government fell to a provisional council headed by Friedrich Ebert (1912–1923), the socialist leader in the Reichstag. Ebert and his colleagues immediately took steps to negotiate an armistice. The Germans could do

nothing but accept the Allies' terms, so at five o'clock in the morning of November 11, 1918, two German delegates met with the Allied army commander in the Compiègne forest and signed papers officially ending the war. Six hours later the order "cease fire" was given across the Western Front. That night thousands of people danced through the streets of London, Paris, and Rome, engulfed in a different delirium from that four years before, a joyous burst of exhausted relief.

THE UNITED STATES AS A WORLD POWER

The final turning point of the war had been the entry of the United States in April 1917. Although America had supported the Allies financially throughout the war, its official intervention undeniably tipped the scales. The United States created a fast and efficient wartime bureaucracy, instituting conscription in May 1917. Ten million men were registered, and by the next year, three hundred thousand soldiers a month were being shipped "over there." Large amounts of food and supplies also crossed the Atlantic, under the armed protection of the U.S. Navy. This system of

Conscription in America. In April 1917 America officially entered the war, and by 1918 hundreds of thousands of soldiers were shipping out to Europe every month. Here Secretary of War Newton D. Baker is seen, blindfolded, drawing the first lots for Selective Service Duty.

convoys effectively neutralized the threat of German submarines to Allied merchant ships: the number of ships sunk fell from 25 to 4 percent. America's entry—though not immediately decisive—gave a quick, colossal boost to British and French morale, while severely undermining Germany's.

The direct cause of America's entry into the war was the German U-boat. Germany had gambled that unrestricted submarine warfare would cripple Britain's supply lines and win the war. But by attacking neutral and unarmed American ships, Germany only provoked an opponent it could not afford to fight. Germany correctly suspected that the British were clandestinely receiving war supplies from U.S. passenger ships, and on February 1, 1917, the kaiser's ministers announced that they would sink all ships on sight, without warning. The American public was further outraged by an intercepted telegram from Germany's foreign minister, Arthur Zimmerman (1916–1917), stating that Germany would support a Mexican attempt to capture American territory if the United States entered the war. The United States cut off diplomatic relations with Berlin, and on April 6 President Woodrow Wilson (1913–1921) requested and received a declaration of war by Congress.

Wilson vowed that America would fight to "make the world safe for democracy," to banish autocracy and militarism, and to establish a league or society of na-

tions in place of the old diplomatic maneuvering. The Americans' primary interest was maintaining the international balance of power. For years, U.S. diplomats and military leaders believed that American security depended on the equilibrium of strength in Europe. As long as Britain could prevent any one nation from achieving supremacy on the Continent, the United States was safe. But now Germany threatened not only the British navy—which had come be seen as the shield of American security—but also the international balance of power. American involvement stemmed those threats in 1918, but the monumental task of establishing peace still lay ahead.

THE PEACE SETTLEMENT

Making peace was a tenuous process, complicated by the conflicting ambitions and interests of the victor nations. Negotiations were held in Paris in 1919 and 1920. In all, five separate treaties were signed, one with each of the defeated nations: Germany, Austria, Hungary, Turkey, and Bulgaria. (The settlement with Germany was called the Treaty of Versailles, after the town in which it was signed.) The peace conference involved representatives from many nations, including small, newly formed states and even non-European ones. Yet both the conference and the treaties were controlled almost entirely by the so-called Big Four: the U.S. president Woodrow Wilson (1913–1921), the British prime minister David Lloyd George (1916–1922), the French premier Georges Clemenceau (1917–1920), and the Italian premier Vittorio Orlando (1917–1919).

The peace progress began in a spirit of idealism, expressed in Wilson's widely publicized Fourteen Points, which he had promoted as the foundation of a permanent peace. Based on the principle of "open covenants of peace, openly arrived at," Wilson's plan called for an end to secret diplomacy, freedom of the seas, removal of international tariffs, and reduction of national armaments "to the lowest point consistent with safety." It also called for the "self-determination of peoples" and for the establishment of a League of Nations to settle international conflicts. Thousands of copies of the Fourteen Points had been scattered by Allied planes over the German trenches and behind the lines in an attempt to convince both soldiers and civilians that the Allied nations were striving for a just and durable peace.

The negotiations, however, followed other dictates. Throughout the war, Allied propaganda led soldiers and

CHRONOLOGY	
MAJOR EVENTS OF WORLD WAR I AND ITS AFTERMATH, 1914–1920	
Battle of the Marne	September 1914
Gallipoli campaign	April–December 1915
Sinking of the *Lusitania*	May 1915
Battle of Verdun	February–July 1916
Battle of the Somme	July–November 1916
Russian Revolution:	
Tsar Nicholas II overthrown	February 1917
Communist Revolution	October 1917
Treaty of Brest-Litovsk	March 1918
Russian Civil War	1918–1920
United States enters the war	April 1917
Final offensives	March–November 1918
Germany surrenders	November 11, 1918
Paris negotiations	1919–1920

civilians to believe that their sacrifices to the war effort would be compensated by payments extracted from the enemy; total war demanded total victory. Lloyd George had campaigned during the British election of 1918 on the slogan "Hang the Kaiser!" Clemenceau had twice in his long lifetime seen France invaded and its existence imperiled. With the tables turned, he believed that the French should take full advantage of their opportunity to place Germany under strict control. The devastation of the war, and the fiction that Germany could be made to pay for it, made compromise impossible. The settlement with Germany reflected this desire for punishment.

The Versailles treaty required Germany to surrender the "lost provinces" of Alsace and Lorraine to France, and to give up territories in the north to Denmark and a large part of Prussia to the new state of Poland. The treaty gave Germany's coal mines in the Saar basin to France for fifteen years, at which point the German government could buy them back. Germany's province of East Prussia was cut off from the rest of its territory. The port of Danzig, with a majority German population, was put under the administrative control of the League of Nations and the economic domination of Poland. Germany was also disarmed. It was forbidden to build an air force, while its navy was reduced to a token force to match an army capped at the strength of one hundred thousand volunteers. To protect France and Belgium, all German soldiers and fortifications were to be removed from the Rhine valley.

The most important part of the Versailles treaty, and the part most at odds with Wilson's original plan, was the "war-guilt" provision in Article 231. Versailles held Germany and its allies responsible for the loss and damage suffered by the Allied governments and their citizens "as a consequence of the war imposed upon them by the aggression of Germany and her allies." Germany would be forced to pay reparations on a crippling scale. The exact amount was left

to a Reparations Commission, which set the total at $33 billion in 1921. The Germans deeply resented these harsh demands, but others outside Germany also warned of the dangers of punitive reparations. In *The Economic Consequences of the Peace*, the noted British economist John Maynard Keynes (1883–1946) argued that reparations would doom Europe's most important task: repairing the world economy.

The treaties signed by the other Central Powers were based partly on the Allies' strategic interests, but also on the principle of national self-determination. The experience of the prewar years convinced leaders that they should draw nations' boundaries to conform to the ethnic, linguistic, and historical traditions of the people they were to contain. This combined with Wilson's idealism about freedom and equal representation, and seemed sensible to most factions at Versailles. It was more difficult to accomplish in practice. National boundaries did not follow ethnic divisions; they were created according to political dictates of the moment. The frustrated expectations of eastern and central European nationalists, combined with other factors, would produce dangerous challenges to European stability during the 1930s.

> Germany would be forced to pay reparations on a crippling scale. The exact amount was left to a Reparations Commission, which set the total at $33 billion in 1921.

Crowds Greet President Wilson in Paris after the War. Despite public demonstrations of this sort, Wilson's attempt to shape the peace was a failure.

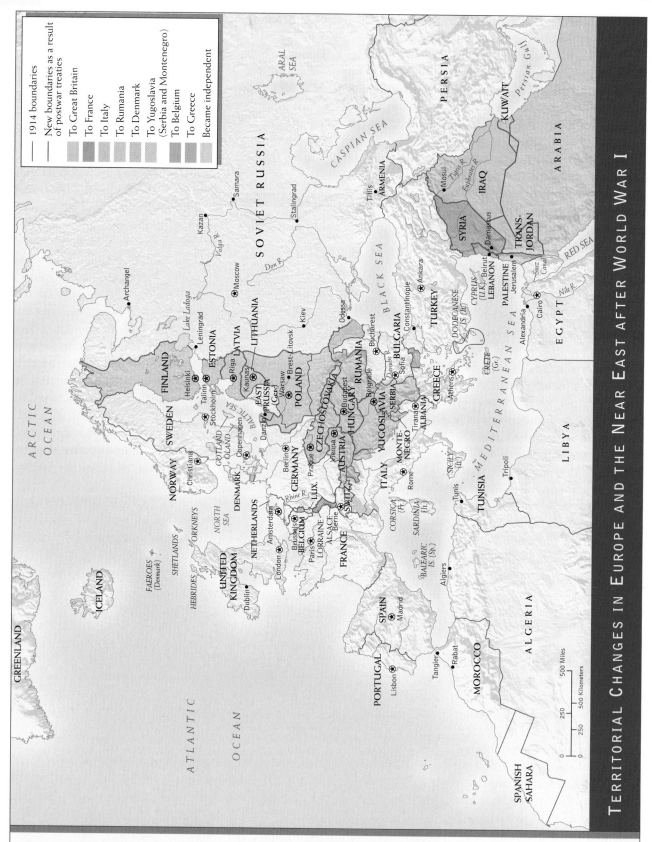

TERRITORIAL CHANGES IN EUROPE AND THE NEAR EAST AFTER WORLD WAR I

Note the changes in geography as a result of World War I. What areas were most affected by the changes within Europe, and why? Can you see any obvious difficulties created by the redrawing of the map of Europe? What historical circumstances and/or new threats guided the victors to create such geopolitical anomalies?

The treaties also reflected European ambitions to shore up, or even expand, their overseas empires. The settlement with Turkey marked the end of the Ottoman empire. It also created an opportunity for Allied leaders to haggle over the spoils of the dismantled state. It did not, however, create the truly independent kingdoms that Bedouin leaders had hoped for during the war. Accompanied by their advocate T. E. Lawrence, the emirs attended the Versailles conference and listened as their independence was circumscribed. Choice pieces of land were divided up as "mandates" held by Britain and France. Lawrence was bitterly disillusioned. The more pragmatic emirs began to turn these new colonial commitments to their advantage by playing Britain and France off one another. The peoples of the Allies' existing colonies were less fortunate. Ho Chi Minh, a young student from Indochina attending a Parisian university, was one of many colonial activists who attended the conference to protest conditions in the colonies and to ask that the rights of nations be extended to their homelands. Well-organized deputations from French West Africa and the Congress Party of India, which favored dominion status in return for the wartime efforts of millions of sepoys who had fought for the British Empire, were also snubbed. Although the European powers spoke about reforming colonial rule, little was done. Many nationalists in the colonies who had favored moderate, legislative change decided that active struggle might be the only answer to the injustices of colonialism.

Although the European powers spoke about reforming colonial rule, little was done. Many nationalists in the colonies who had favored moderate, legislative change decided that active struggle might be the only answer to the injustices of colonialism.

The end of the Ottoman empire also produced two other results: the creation of the modern Turkish state, and a new structure for British and French colonial rule. As territories were taken from the Ottomans, Greece chose to seize some by force. The effort was successful at first but the Turks counterattacked, driving out Greek forces by 1923 and creating the modern state of Turkey under the charismatic leadership of General Mustafa Kemal Attaturk (1923–1938). Ottoman territories placed under French and British control were part of the colonial "mandate system" that legitimized Europe's dominance over territories in the Middle East, Africa, and the Pacific. Territories were officially placed under the supervision of the League of Nations and divided into groups on the basis of their location and level of development.

Incorporated in each of the five peace treaties was the Covenant of the League of Nations, an organization envisioned as the arbiter of world peace but that never achieved the idealistic aims of its founders. The League was handicapped from the start by a number of changes to its original design. The arms-reduction requirement was watered down, and the League's power to enforce it was rendered almost nonexistent. Japan would not join unless it was allowed to keep former German concessions in China. France demanded that both Germany and Russia be excluded from the League, which contradicted Wilson's goals but had already been legitimized by the Paris peace conference, where neither Soviet Russia nor the defeated Central Powers were allowed at the table. The League received an even more debilitating blow when the United States Congress, citing the long-standing national preference for isolation, refused to approve U.S. membership of the League. Hobbled from the start, the international organization had little potential to avert conflicts. Indeed, the League of Nations' failures originated in, and reflected, the larger problems of power politics that emerged after the war.

CONCLUSION

Europe fought the First World War on every front possible—military, political, social, and economic. Consequently, the war's effects extended far beyond the devastated landscapes of the Western Front. Statistics can only hint at the enormous loss of human life: of the 70 million men who were mobilized, nearly 9 million were killed. Russia, Germany, France, and Hungary recorded the highest number of deaths, but the smaller countries of southeast Europe had the highest percentages of soldiers killed. Almost 40 percent of Serbia's soldiers died in battle. With the addition of war-related deaths cause by privation and disease, Serbia lost 15 percent of its population. In comparison, Britain, France, and Germany lost only 2 to 3 percent of their populations. But the percentages are much more telling if we focus on the young men of the war generation. Germany lost one third of men aged nineteen to twenty-two in 1914. France and Britain sustained similar losses, with mortality among young men reaching eight to ten times the normal rate. This was the "lost generation."

The war planted seeds of political and social discontent around the globe. Relations between Russia and western Europe grew sour and suspicious. The Allies had attempted to overthrow the Bolsheviks during the war and had excluded them from the negotiations afterward; these actions instilled in the Soviets a mistrust of the West that lasted for generations. The Allied nations feared that Russia would dominate the new states of eastern Europe, building a "Red Bridge" across the continent. Elsewhere, the conflicting demands of colonialism and nationalism struck only a temporary balance, while the redrawn maps left ethnic and linguistic minorities in every country. The fires of discontent raged most fiercely in Germany, where the Treaty of Versailles was decried as outrageously unjust. Nearly all national governments agreed that it would eventually have to be revised. Neither war nor peace had ended the rivalries that caused the First World War.

The war also had powerful and permanent economic consequences. Beset by inflation, debt, and the difficult task of industrial rebuilding, Europe found itself displaced from the center of the world economy. The war had accelerated the decentralization of money and markets. Many Asian, African, and South American nations benefited financially as their economies became less dependent on Europe, and they were better able to profit from Europe's need for their natural resources. The United States and Japan reaped the biggest gains and emerged as leaders in the new world economy.

Socially, the war's most potent legacy was the death and disfigurement of millions. Its most powerful cultural legacy was disillusionment. A generation of men had been sacrificed to no apparent end. Surviving soldiers—many of them permanently injured, both physi-

cally and psychologically—were sickened by their participation in such useless slaughter. They were disgusted by the greedy abandonment of principles by the politicians at Versailles. In the postwar period many younger men and women mistrusted the "old men" who had dragged the world into the war. These feelings of loss and alienation were voiced in the vastly popular genre of "war literature," memoirs and fiction that commemorated the experience of soldiers on the front lines. The German writer and ex-soldier Erich Maria Remarque captured the disillusion of a generation in his novel *All Quiet on the Western Front:* "Through the years our business has been killing;—it was our first calling in life. Our knowledge of life is limited to death. What will happen afterwards? And what shall come out of us?"

That was the main question facing postwar Europe. The German novelist Thomas Mann recognized that 1918 had brought "an end of an epoch, revolution and the dawn of a new age," and that he and his fellow Germans were "living in a new and unfamiliar world." The struggle to define this new world would increasingly be conceived in terms of rival ideologies—democracy, communism, and fascism—competing for the future of Europe. The eastern autocracies had fallen with the war, but liberal democracy was soon on the decline as well. While militarism and nationalism remained strong, calls for major social reforms gained force during worldwide depression. Entire populations had been mobilized during the war, and they would remain so afterward—active participants in the age of mass politics. Europe was about to embark on two turbulent decades of rejecting and reinventing its social and political institutions. As Tomas Masaryk, the first president of newly formed Czechoslovakia, described it, postwar Europe was "a laboratory atop a graveyard."

KEY TERMS

Allied Powers	trench warfare	Tsar Nicholas II
Central Powers	Lusitania	Vladimir Lenin
Franz Ferdinand	Sinn Fein	Treaty of Versailles
Schlieffen Plan	Testament of Youth	

SELECTED READINGS

Chickering, Roger. *Imperial Germany and the Great War, 1914–1918.* New York, 1998. An excellent new synthesis.

Eksteins, Modris. *Rites of Spring: The Great War and the Birth of the Modern Age.* New York, 1989. Fascinating, though impressionistic, on war, art, and culture.

Ferro, Marc. *The Great War, 1914–1918.* London, 1973. Very concise overview.

Figes, Orlando. *A People's Tragedy: A History of the Russian Revolution.* New York, 1997. Excellent, detailed narrative.

Fischer, Fritz. *War of Illusions.* New York, 1975. Deals with Germany within the context of internal social and economic trends.

Fitzpatrick, Sheila. *The Russian Revolution, 1917–1932.* New York and Oxford, 1982. Concise overview.

Ferguson, Niall. *The Pity of War.* London, 1998. A fresh look at the war, including strategic issues, international relations, and economics.

Fussell, Paul. *The Great War and Modern Memory.* New York, 1975. A brilliant examination of British intellectuals' attitudes toward the war.

Higonnet, Margaret Randolph, et al., eds. *Behind the Lines: Gender and the Two World Wars.* New Haven, 1987.

Hynes, Samuel. *A War Imagined: The First World War and English Culture.* New York, 1991. The war as perceived on the home front.

Jelavich, Barbara. *History of the Balkans: Twentieth Century.* New York, 1983. Useful for an understanding of the continuing conflict in Eastern Europe.

Joll, James. *The Origins of the First World War.* London, 1984. Comprehensive and very useful.

Keegan, John. *The First World War.* London, 1998. The best overall military history.

Mazower, Mark. *Dark Continent: Europe's Twentieth Century.* New York, 1999. An excellent new survey, attentive to the Balkans and Eastern Europe.

Rabinowitch, Alexander. *The Bolsheviks Come to Power.* New York, 1976. A well-researched and carefully documented account.

Roberts, Mary Louise. *Civilization without Sexes: Reconstructing Gender in Postwar France, 1917–1927.* Chicago, 1994. A prize-winning study of the issues raised by the "new woman."

Smith, Leonard. *Between Mutiny and Obedience: The Case of the French Fifth Infantry Division during World War I.* Princeton, N.J., 1994. An account of mutiny and the reasons behind it.

Stites, Richard. *Revolutionary Dreams: Utopian Visions and Experimental Life in the Russian Revolution.* New York, 1989. The influence of utopian thinking on the revolution.

Williams, John. *The Home Fronts: Britain, France and Germany, 1914–1918.* London, 1972. A survey of life away from the battlefield and the impact of the war on domestic life.

Winter, J. M. *The Experience of World War I.* New York, 1989. Comprehensive illustrated history viewing the war from different perspectives.

CHAPTER TWENTY-FIVE

TURMOIL BETWEEN
THE WARS

THE GREAT WAR TOPPLED four empires and left 9 million dead in its wake. Death reached across borders, ideologies, classes, and generations; it touched ancient mansions, industrial cities, towns, and farmsteads across Europe and its overseas dominions. It destroyed lives and futures, shook cherished standards and pillars of stability, and produced haunting revelations of brutality. Coming to terms with the war's incalculable losses produced a wide range of reactions, from dogged efforts to return to prewar "normalcy," to cultural experimentation, repudiation of the past, or the splintering of older political regimes and arrangements. From the perspective of the late 1930s, the most striking development of the interwar period was the near collapse of democracy. At that time, few Western democracies remained. Even in those that did, most notably Great Britain, France, and the United States, regimes were frayed by the same pressures and strains that in other countries wrecked democracy entirely.

The reasons for the decline of democracy varied according to particular national circumstances. We can, however, identify some general causes. The foremost was a series of continuing disruptions in the world economy. These were brought about by dislocations that came in the wake of the First World War and the Versailles reparations settlements, and, later, with the Great Depression of 1929–1933. A second source of the crisis of democracy lay in increased social conflict. Across the West, the strains of war deepened long-standing social rifts, and the disappointments of the postwar period created serious polarization. Many expected the peace to bring change. After the sacrifices of the war years, most citizens had been rewarded with the vote. It was far from clear, however, that their votes counted, or that the traditional elites who dominated the economy and seemed to hold the reins of politics had lost any of their power. Broad swaths of the electorate became increasingly attracted to political parties, many of them extremist, that promised to represent their interests. Finally, nationalism, sharpened by the war, provided a key source of discontent in its aftermath. In Italy and Germany frustrated nationalist sentiment turned against governments. In new countries such as Czechoslovakia,

FOCUS QUESTIONS

• How did the Soviet Union industrialize during the 1930s?

• What were the components of Italian fascism?

• Why did German democracy fail?

 • How did the Nazis come to power?

• How did the Western democracies deal with the Great Depression?

• How did the mass media change everyday life?

and across eastern and southern Europe, friction among national minorities posed enormous problems for relatively fragile democratic regimes.

The most dramatic instance of democracy's decline came with the rise of new authoritarian dictatorships, especially in the Soviet Union, Italy, and Germany. As we shall see, the experiences of those three countries differed significantly as a result of varying historical circumstances and personalities. Yet in each case, many citizens allowed themselves to be persuaded that only drastic measures could bring order from chaos. Those measures, including the elimination of parliamentary government, strict restrictions on political freedom, and increasingly virulent repression of the "enemies" of the state were implemented with a combination of violence, intimidation, and propaganda. That so many citizens seemed willing to sacrifice their freedoms was a measure of their alienation, impatience, or desperation.

THE SOVIET UNION UNDER LENIN AND STALIN

How did the Soviet Union industrialize during the 1930s?

THE RUSSIAN CIVIL WAR

The Bolshevik takeover in October of 1917 was only the beginning of revolutionary events in Russia. After signing a separate peace with Germany in March of 1918, the Bolsheviks, under Lenin's leadership, moved to consolidate their internal political power (see pp. 882–887). But the Bolshevik seizure of power and withdrawal from the war polarized Russian society and ignited a civil war that was far more costly than conflict with Germany. The peace treaty galvanized the enemies of the Bolsheviks, especially those associated with the ousted tsarist regime, who began to attack the new government from the periphery of the old empire. Known collectively as "Whites," the Bolsheviks' opponents were a varied lot, only loosely bound by their common goal of removing the "Reds" from power. Their military force came mainly from supporters of the old regime, including tsarist military officers, reactionary monarchists, the former nobility, and disaffected liberal supporters of the monarchy. The Whites were joined

by groups as diverse as liberal supporters of the provisional government, Mensheviks, Social Revolutionaries, and anarchist peasant bands known as "Greens" who opposed all central state power. The Bolsheviks also faced insurrections from strong nationalist movements in some parts of the former Russian empire, including Ukraine, Georgia, and the north Caucasus regions. Finally, several foreign powers, including the United States, Great Britain, and Japan, launched small but threatening interventions on the periphery of the old empire. Outside support for the Whites proved to be an insignificant threat to the Bolsheviks, but it served as a propaganda device; the Bolsheviks claimed that the Whites were trying to assist foreign powers in invading Russia. The intervention also solidified Bolshevik mistrust of the capitalist world powers, which would, in the Marxist view, naturally oppose the existence of the world's first "socialist" state.

The Bolsheviks eventually won the civil war because they gained greater support—or at least tacit acceptance—from the majority of the population, and because they were better organized for the war effort itself. The Bolsheviks quickly mobilized to fight, foregoing many of their radical concerns about egalitarianism and political self-control in favor of strong bureaucratic and military structures. Leon Trotsky, the revolutionary hero of 1905 and 1917, became the new commissar of war and created a hierarchical, disciplined military machine that grew to some 5 million men by 1920. Trotsky's Red Army triumphed over the White armies by the end of 1920, although fighting continued into 1922. The Bolsheviks also invaded Poland, and nearly reached Warsaw before being thrown back.

When the conflict was over, the country had suffered some one million combat casualties, several million deaths from hunger and disease caused by the war, and one hundred thousand to three hundred thousand executions of noncombatants as part of Red and White terror. The barbarism of the war engendered permanent hatreds within the emerging Soviet nation, especially among ethnic minorities, and it brutalized the fledgling society that came into existence under the new Bolshevik regime.

The civil war also shaped the Bolsheviks' approach to economic aspects of "socialism." On taking power in 1917, Lenin expected to create, for the short term at least, a state-capitalist system that resembled the successful European wartime economies. The new government took control of large-scale industry, banking, and all other major capital concerns while allowing small-scale private economic activity, including agriculture, to continue. The civil war pushed the new government toward a more radical economic stance known as "war communism." The Bolsheviks began to requisition grain from the peasantry, outlawed private trade in consumer goods as "speculation," militarized production facilities, and abolished money. Most of these innovations were improvised responses to deteriorating economic conditions beyond the regime's control. The idea of war communism, however, was attractive to radical Bolsheviks. Indeed, many believed that war communism would replace the capitalist system that had collapsed in 1917.

> In crushing dissent, the Bolshevik regime that emerged from the civil war had made a clear statement that internal competition would not be tolerated.

Such hopes were largely unfounded. War communism, though it sustained the civil war effort, further disrupted the already war-ravaged economy. The civil war devastated Russian industry and emptied major cities. The population of Moscow fell by 50 percent between 1917 and 1920; that of Kiev by 25 percent. The masses of urban workers, who had strongly supported the Bolshevik revolution, melted back into the countryside; only 1.5 million of the 3.5 million workers employed in major industries before 1917 remained on the job by the end of 1920. Industrial output had fallen by 1920–1921 to only 20 percent of prewar levels. Most devastating were the effects of war communism on agriculture. On the one hand, the civil war had solved the "land question" to the benefit of peasants, who spontaneously seized and redistributed noble lands. By 1919 peasants held almost 97 percent of the land in small plots, generally fewer than twenty acres. Nonetheless, the agricultural system was severely disrupted by the civil war, by the grain requisitioning of war communism, and by the outlawing of all private trade in grain. Large-scale famine resulted in 1921 and claimed some 5 million lives.

As the civil war came to a close, urban workers and soldiers became increasingly impatient with the Bolshevik regime, which had promised socialism and workers' control but had delivered something more akin to a military dictatorship. Large-scale strikes and protests broke out in late 1920, but the Bolsheviks moved swiftly and effectively to subdue the "popular revolts." In crushing dissent, the Bolshevik regime that emerged from the civil war had made a clear statement that internal competition would not be tolerated.

THE NEP PERIOD

In response to these political and economic difficulties, the Bolsheviks abandoned war communism and in March 1921 embarked on a radically different course known as the New Economic Policy (NEP). The NEP reverted to the state capitalism that had been tried immediately after the Revolution. The state was to continue to own all major industry and monetary concerns (which Lenin called the "commanding heights" of the economic system), while individuals were to be allowed to own private property, trade freely within limits, and most important, farm their land for their own benefit. Fixed taxes on the peasantry were replaced by grain requisitioning; what peasants grew beyond the tax requirements was theirs to do with as they saw fit. The Bolshevik most identified with the NEP was Nikolai Bukharin (1888–1938), a young and brilliant Marxist theoretician who argued that the Bolsheviks could best industrialize the USSR by taxing private peasant

Lenin and Stalin. Under Stalin this picture was used to show his close relationship with Lenin. In fact, the photograph has been doctored.

Legend

- Area of Russia under Bolshevik (Red) control: 1919
- Area of Russia under anti-Bolshevik (White) control: 1919
- Area lost by Russia, 1914–1921
- → White Russian attacks
- → Non-Russian attacks
- → Movements of Allies

ARCTIC OCEAN

PACIFIC OCEAN

SEA OF OKHOTSK

JAPAN

SEA OF JAPAN

KOREA

SAKHALIN I.

MANCHURIA

CHINA

MONGOLIA

Ulan-Bator

Khabarovsk

Vladivostok

Chita

Lake Baikal

Irkutsk

Krasnoyarsk

Novosibirsk

Yakutsk

Lena R.

Yenisei R.

Ob R.

RUSSIAN SOVIET FEDERATIVE SOCIALIST REPUBLIC

URAL MOUNTAINS

Sverdlovsk

Chelyabinsk

Omsk

Orenburg

Perm

KAZAKH S.S.R.

ARAL SEA

Lake Balkhash

Alma-Ata

Frunze

KIRGIZ S.S.R.

TADZHIK S.S.R.

SINKIANG

INDIA

AFGHANISTAN

Tashkent

UZBEK S.S.R.

Dushanbe

Ashkabad

TURKMEN S.S.R.

IRAN

CASPIAN SEA

Baku

AZERBAIDZHAN S.S.R.

CAUCASUS MTS.

Pyatigorsk

GEORGIAN S.S.R.

Tbilisi

ARMENIAN S.S.R.

Yerevan

TURKEY

SYRIA

IRAQ

Persian Gulf

BLACK SEA

Rostov

Krasnodar

Novorossisk

Stalingrad

Saratov

Kuibyshev

Kazan

Gorki

Volga R.

Ivanovo

Yaroslavl

Moscow

Murmansk

Archangel

NORWAY

SWEDEN

FINLAND

Helsinki

Gulf of Bothnia

BALTIC SEA

Kronstadt

Leningrad

ESTONIAN S.S.R.

LATVIAN S.S.R.

LITHUANIAN S.S.R.

BELORUSSIAN S.S.R.

Minsk

GERMANY

Danzig

POLAND

Warsaw

Brest-Litovsk

CZECHOSLOVAKIA

HUNG.

RUMANIA

MOLDAVIAN S.S.R.

UKRAINIAN S.S.R.

Kiev

Odessa

1000 Miles
1000 Kilometers
500
500

THE SOVIET UNION, 1918–1945

How did the civil war of 1917–1920 affect the new Soviet state? How did the possession of Moscow and Leningrad (St. Petersburg) aid the Bolsheviks in their victory over the "Whites"? How was Stalin's dictatorship instrumental in modernizing and uniting the Soviet Union's vast and diverse landscape?

economic activity. Peasants were encouraged to "enrich themselves" so that their taxes could support urban industrialization and the working class. Lenin himself described the NEP as "one step backward in order to take two steps forward."

The NEP was undeniably successful in allowing Soviet agriculture to recover from the civil war; by 1924 agricultural harvests had returned to prewar levels. It was a prosperous time for peasants—what one historian describes as the "golden age of the Russian peasantry." Peasants were largely left alone to do as they pleased, and they responded by redividing noble lands among themselves to level wealth discrepancies between rich and poor, by reinforcing traditional social structures in the countryside (especially the peasant commune), and by producing enough grain to feed the country, though they continued to use very primitive farming methods to do so. The NEP was less successful, however, in encouraging peasants to participate in markets to benefit urban areas. The Bolsheviks found it difficult during the 1920s to produce manufactured goods cheaply enough to get peasants to trade their grain for them. Peasants responded to these difficulties by simply abstaining from the market and keeping excess grain, their livestock, or their illegal moonshine stills for themselves. The result was a series of shortages in grain deliveries to cities, a situation that prompted many Bolsheviks to call for revival of the radical economic practices of war communism. The fate of these radical proposals, however, was tied to the fate of the man who would, contrary to all expectations, replace Lenin as the leader of the USSR and become one of the most notorious dictators of all time: Joseph Stalin.

CHRONOLOGY

THE EARLY SOVIET UNION, 1917–1929

Bolsheviks seize power	October 1917
Treaty of Brest-Litovsk	March 1918
Russian civil war	1918–1920
Bolsheviks suppress nationalist rebellions	1920–1921
Launch of the NEP	1921
Lenin dies	1924
Stalin, Trotsky, Bukharin vie for power	1924–1928
Stalin seizes full power	1928–1929

STALIN AND THE "REVOLUTION FROM ABOVE"

Stalin's rise was swift and unpredicted. His political success was rooted in intraparty conflicts in the 1920s, but it was also closely tied to the abrupt end of the NEP period in the late 1920s and to the beginning of a massive program of social and economic modernization. This "revolution from above," as it has come to be called, was the most rapid social and economic transformation any nation has seen in modern history. It was carried out, however, at unprecedented human cost.

Stalin (1879–1953) was a Bolshevik from the Caucasus nation of Georgia; his real name was Iosep Jughashvili. The son of a poor shoemaker, Stalin, at his mother's insistence, originally studied at an Orthodox seminary to become a priest. Rejecting the priesthood, he participated in revolutionary activity in the Caucasus and spent many years in Siberian exile before the Revolution. He was an important member of the Bolshevik party before and during the Russian Revolution. Yet Stalin was not one of the central figures of the early Bolshevik party, and he was certainly not a front runner for party leadership. The question of Lenin's successor arose with the leader's poor health after 1922 and his death in 1924, but the civil war hero Leon Trotsky was widely assumed to be the best candidate for Lenin's position. Other top Bolsheviks, however, also aspired to a leading role.

Though not a brilliant orator like Trotsky or a respected Marxist theoretician like Bukharin, Stalin was nonetheless a master political strategist, and he played the game of internal party politics almost without fault after Lenin's death. Stalin sidelined his opponents within the Bolshevik party, many of whom supported the Leninist principle of collective leadership within the top ruling circle, by isolating and expelling each of them successively. Trotsky was the first to go, driven out of top party circles by a coalition of Stalin and others who, ironically, feared Trotsky's desire to take control of the party himself. Stalin then turned on his former allies and removed them in turn, culminating in the removal of Bukharin from the Politburo in 1928–1929.

Stalin's campaign against Bukharin was not just political. It was also connected to Stalin's desire to discard the NEP system and to launch an all-out industrialization drive. By the late 1920s, Stalin had begun to agree with those critics of the NEP who had argued that the USSR could not hope to industrialize by relying on taxes generated from small-scale peasant

STALIN'S INDUSTRIALIZATION OF THE SOVIET UNION

"THE TASKS OF BUSINESS EXECUTIVES"

Stalin gave the following speech at a Conference of Managers of Socialist Industry in 1931. In his usual style, he invoked fears of Soviet backwardness and Russian nationalism while summoning all to take up the task of industrial production.

It is sometimes asked whether it is not possible to slow down the tempo somewhat, to put a check on the movement. No, comrades, it is not possible! The tempo must not be reduced! On the contrary, we must increase it as much as is within our powers and possibilities. This is dictated to us by our obligations to the workers and peasants of the USSR. This is dictated to us by our obligations to the working class of the whole world.

To slacken the tempo would mean falling behind. And those who fall behind get beaten. But we do not want to be beaten. No, we refuse to be beaten! One feature of the history of old Russia was the continual beatings she suffered because of her backwardness. She was beaten by the Mongol khans. She was beaten by the Turkish beys. . . . She was beaten by the British and French capitalists. She was beaten by the Japanese barons. All beat her—for her backwardness: for military backwardness, for cultural backwardness, for political backwardness, for industrial backwardness, for agricultural backwardness. . . .

We are fifty or a hundred years behind the advanced countries. We must make good this distance in ten years. Either we do it, or we shall be crushed. . . .

In ten years at most we must make good the distance which separates us from the advanced capitalist countries. We have all the 'objective' possibilities for this. The only thing lacking is the ability to take proper advantage of these possibilities. And that depends on us. *Only* on us! . . . It is time to put an end to the rotten policy of non-interference in production. It is time to adopt a new policy, a policy adapted to the present times—the policy of interfering in everything. If you are a factory manager, then interfere in all the affairs of the factory, look into everything, let nothing escape you, learn and learn again. Bolsheviks must master technique. It is time Bolsheviks themselves became experts. . . .

There are no fortresses which Bolsheviks cannot capture. We have assumed power. We have built up a huge socialist industry. We have swung the middle peasants to the path of socialism. . . . What remains to be done is not so much: to study technique, to master science. And when we have done that we will develop a tempo of which we dare not even dream at present.

"The Tasks of Business Executives," speech at the First All-Union Conference of Managers of Socialist Industry, February 4, 1931, in Joseph Stalin, *Problems of Leninism* (New York: International Publishers, c. 1934), pp. 350, 354–5, 355–5, 357–8. As found in Richard Sakwa, *The Rise and Fall of the Soviet Union, 1917–1991* (New York and London: Routledge, 1999), pp. 187–188.

Stalin's Industrial Development: The View from Below

How did the Soviet people experience Stalin's industrialization drive? New archives have helped historians glimpse what the common people lived through and how they responded. The following letters come from several hundred that workers and peasants sent to Soviet newspapers and authorities recounting their experiences and offering their opinions. Both were sent to the Soviet paper Pravda.

It should not be forgotten that many millions of workers are participating in the building of socialism. A horse with its own strength can drag seventy-five poods,* but its owner has loaded it with a hundred poods, and in addition he's fed it poorly. No matter how much he uses the whip, it still won't be able to move the cart.

This is also true for the working class. They've loaded it with socialist competition, shock work, overfulfilling the industrial and financial plan, and so forth. A worker toils seven hours, not ever leaving his post, and this is not all he does. Afterward he sits in meetings or else attends classes for an hour and a half or two in order to increase his skill level, and if he doesn't do these things, then he's doing things at home. And what does he live on? One hundred fifty grams of salted mutton, he will make soup without any of the usual additives, neither carrots, beets, flour, nor salt pork. What kind of soup do you get from this? Mere "dishwater."

—B.N. Kniazev, Tula, Sept. 1930.

Comrade Editor, Please give me an answer. Do the local authorities have the right to forcibly take away the only cow of industrial and office workers? What is more, they demand a receipt showing that the cow was handed over voluntarily and they threaten you by saying if you don't do this, they will put you in prison for failure to fulfill the meat procurement. How can you live when the cooperative distributes only black bread, and at the market goods have the prices of 1919 and 1920? Lice have eaten us to death, and soap is given only to railroad workers. From hunger and filth we have a massive outbreak of spotted fever.

—Anonymous, from
Aktybinsk, Kazakhstan

*A pood is a Russian unit of weight, equal to 36.11 pounds.

Lewis Siegelbaum and Andrei Sokolov, *Stalinism as a Way of Life: A Narrative in Documents* (New Haven and London: Yale University Press, 2000), pp. 39–41.

---

agriculture. Stalin began to push for an increase in the tempo of industrialization as early as 1927, prompted by fears of falling behind the West and by the perceived threat of another world war. Almost all of the top-level Bolshevik leaders supported Stalin's plan to step up the tempo of industrialization. But hardly anybody supported what happened next: an abrupt turn toward forced industrialization and collectivization of agriculture.

In 1927 a poor harvest caused yet another crisis in the grain-collection system. Low prices for agricultural goods and high prices for scarce industrial goods led peasants to hoard grain, resulting in food shortages in cities and difficulties in collecting taxes from the peasantry. In early 1928 Stalin ordered local officials in the distant Urals and Siberian areas, which were alleged to have bumper crops but to be behind in tax payments, to begin requisitioning grain. He soon applied this revival of war communism to the entire country. In 1929,

the upper echelons of the party abruptly reversed the course set by NEP, and embarked on the complete collectivization of agriculture, beginning in the major grain-growing areas. Peasants there were to be convinced, by force if necessary, to give up private farmlands. They would either join collective farms, pooling resources and giving a set portion of the harvest to the state, or work on state farms, where they were paid as laborers.

Collectivization

Collectivization was initially expected to be a gradual process, but in late 1929 Stalin embarked on collectivization of agriculture by force. Within a few months, the politburo began to issue orders to use force against peasants who resisted collectivization, though those orders were at first shrouded in secrecy. The process that ensued was brutal and chaotic. Local party and police officials forced peasants to give up their private land, farming implements, and livestock and to join collective farms. Peasants resisted, often violently. There were some sixteen hundred large-scale rebellions in the USSR between 1929 and 1933; some involved several thousand people, and quelling them required military intervention, including the use of artillery. Peasants also resisted collectivization by slaughtering their livestock instead of turning it over to the farms, a loss that hampered agricultural production for years to follow. Sensing a possible crisis, Stalin deftly called the process to a temporary halt in early 1930, but soon thereafter ordered the process to proceed more gradually, and by 1935 collectivization of agriculture was complete in most areas of the USSR.

To facilitate collectivization, Stalin also launched an all-out attack on peasants designated as "kulaks" (a derogatory term for well-to-do farmers, literally meaning "tight-fisted ones"). Most kulaks, though, were not any better off than their neighbors, and the word became one of many terms for peasants hostile to collectivization. Between 1929 and 1933, some 1.5 million peasants were uprooted, dispossessed of their property, and resettled from their farmlands to either inhospitable reaches of the Soviet east and north or to poor farmland closer to their original homes. The land and possessions of these unfortunate peasants were distributed to collective farms or, just as often, to the local officials and peasants participating in the liquidation process. The "liquidation of kulaks as a class" magnified the disruptive effects of agricultural collectivization, and the two together produced one of the most devastating famines in modern European history. Peasants who were forced into collective farms had little incentive to produce extra food, and exiling many of the most productive peasants not surprisingly weakened the agricultural system. In 1932–1933, famine spread across the southern region of the Soviet Union. This was the most productive agricultural area in the country, and the famine that struck there was thus particularly senseless. The 1933 famine cost some 3 to 5 million lives. During the famine, the Bolsheviks maintained substantial grain reserves in other parts of the country, enough to save many hundreds of thousands of lives at a minimum, but they refused to send this grain to the affected areas, preferring instead to seal off famine-stricken regions and allow people to starve. Grain reserves were instead

> Between 1929 and 1933, some 1.5 million peasants were uprooted, dispossessed of their property, and resettled from their farmlands to either inhospitable reaches of the Soviet east and north or to poor farmland closer to their original homes.

sold overseas for hard currency and stockpiled in case of war. After 1935 there would never again be any large-scale resistance to Soviet power in the countryside. Yet resistance had forced the state to cede small private plots of land to peasant families; this land provided as much as 50 percent of the nation's produce from a tiny fraction of the land.

THE FIVE-YEAR PLANS

In Stalin's view, collectivization provided the resources for the other major aspect of his "revolution from above": a rapid campaign of forced industrialization. The roadmap for this industrialization process was the first Five-Year Plan (1928–1932), an ambitious set of goals that Stalin and his cohorts drew up in 1927 and continued to revise upward. The plan called for truly herculean industrialization efforts, and its results rank as one of the most stunning periods of economic growth the modern world has ever seen. The industrial output of the USSR increased by 50 percent in five years; the annual rate of growth during the first Five-Year Plan was between 15 and 22 percent. This rate of growth seemed even more impressive in the context of the economic depression that was shaking the foundations of Western economies in the late 1920s and early 1930s. The Bolsheviks built entirely new industries in entirely new cities. The factory town of Magnitogorsk, for example, emerged from absolutely barren, uninhabited steppes in 1929 to become a steel-producing factory town of some two hundred fifty thousand residents in 1932; at least in scale, it rivaled anything that the West had built. The industrialization drive transformed the nation's landscape and population as well. Cities such as Moscow and Leningrad doubled in size in the early 1930s, while new cities sprang up across the USSR. In 1926, only one fifth of the population lived in towns. Fifteen years later, in 1939, roughly a third did. The urban population had grown from 26 million to 56 million in under fifteen years. The USSR was well on its way to becoming an urban, industrial society.

This rapid industrialization came, however, at enormous human cost. Many large-scale projects were carried out with prison labor, especially in the timber and mining industries. The labor camp system, known as the *gulag*, became a central part of the Stalinist economic system. People were arrested and sent to camps on a bewildering array of charges, ranging from petty criminal infractions to contact with foreigners to having the ill fortune to be born of bourgeois or kulak parents. The camp system spread throughout the USSR in the 1930s: by the end of the decade, roughly 3.6 million people were incarcerated by the regime. This army of prisoners was used to complete the most arduous and dangerous industrialization tasks, such as the construction of the Moscow–White Sea canal. To save money, the canal connecting Moscow to the seaports of the north was constructed without the use of any machinery. It was literally dug by hand, with human labor used to power everything from conveyor belts to pile drivers. Tens of thousands of individuals lost their lives during construction. One of Stalin's pet projects, it never functioned properly, was too shallow, and froze over in winter. It was bombed early in the Second World War.

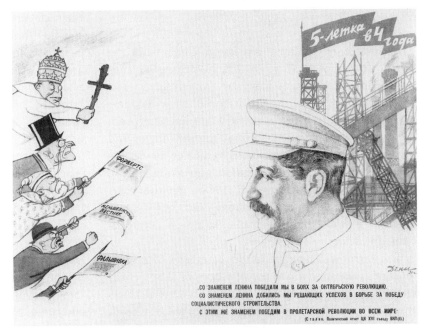

"The Five-Year Plan in Four Years." Stalin faces down capitalist enemies in this Soviet propaganda poster of the 1930s. The caption translates: "Under the banner of Lenin, we triumphed in the battles of the October Revolution. Under the banner of Stalin, we achieved decisive successes in the battle for the victory of socialist construction. Under this banner, we will triumph in the proletarian revolution in all the world."

The economic system created during this "revolution from above" was also fraught with structural problems that would plague the USSR for its entire history. The command economy, with each year's production levels entirely planned in advance in Moscow, never functioned in a rational way. Heavy industry was always favored over light industry, and the emphasis on quantity made quality practically meaningless. A factory that was charged with producing a certain number of pairs of shoes, for example, could cut costs by producing all one style and size. The consumer would be left with useless goods, but the producer would fulfill the plan. Stalin's industrialization drive did transform the USSR from an agrarian nation to a world industrial power in the space of a few short years, but in the longer run, the system would become an economic disaster.

The Stalin revolution also produced fundamental cultural and economic changes. The "revolution from above" altered the face of Soviet cities and the working class populating them. New cities were largely made up of first-generation peasants who brought their rural traditions to the cities with them, changing the fragile urban culture that had existed during the 1920s. Women, too, entered the urban work force in increasing numbers in the 1930s—women went from 20 percent to almost 40 percent of the work force in one decade, and in light industry they made up two thirds of the labor force by 1940.

At the same time, Stalin promoted a sharply conservative shift in all areas of culture and society. In art, the radical modernism of the 1920s was crushed by socialist realism, a deadening aesthetic that celebrated the drive toward socialism and left no room for experimentation. Family policy and gender roles underwent a similar reversal. Early Bolshevik activists had promoted a utopian attempt to rebuild one of the basic structures of pre-Revolutionary society—the family—and to create a genuinely new proletarian social structure. The Bolsheviks in the 1920s legalized divorce, expelled the Orthodox Church from marriage ceremonies, and legalized abortion. Stalin abandoned these ideas of communist familial relations in favor of efforts to strengthen traditional family ties: divorce became more difficult, abortion was outlawed in 1936 except in cases that threatened the life of the mother, and homosexuality was declared a criminal offense. State subsidies and support for mothers, which were progressive for the time, could not change the reality that Soviet women were increasingly forced to carry the double burden of familial and wage labor to support Stalin's version of Soviet society. All areas of Soviet cultural and social policy experienced similar reversals.

THE GREAT TERROR

The apogee of Stalinist repression came with the "Great Terror" of 1937–1938, which left nearly a million people dead and as many as a million and a half more in labor camps. As Stalin consolidated his personal dictatorship over the country, he eliminated enemies—real and imagined—along with individuals and groups he considered superfluous to the new Soviet society. As we have seen, repression was central to the Stalinist system from the early 1930s, yet the years 1937–1938 brought a qualitative and quantitative change—a whirlwind of mass repression unprecedented in scale.

The Terror was aimed at various categories of internal "enemies," from the top to the very bottom of Soviet society. Former and current political elites were perhaps the most visible victims. The top level of the Bolshevik party itself was purged almost completely; some one hundred thousand party members were removed, most facing prison sentences or execution. Many top party officials including Bukharin were condemned at carefully staged show trials and then shot. The purge also struck—with particular ferocity—nonparty elites, industrial managers, and intellectuals. Between 1937 and 1938, Stalin purged the military of people he deemed potential threats, arresting some forty thousand officers and shooting at least ten thousand. These purges disrupted the government and the economy but allowed Stalin to promote a new, young cadre of officials who had no experience in the pre-Stalinist era and who owed their careers, if not their lives, to Stalin personally. Whole ethnic groups were viewed with suspicion, including Poles, Ukrainians, Lithuanians, Latvians, Koreans, and others with supposed cross-border ties that, in Stalin's mind, represented a national security threat. From the "bottom," some two hundred to three hundred thousand "dekulakized" peasants, petty criminals, and other social misfits were arrested, and many shot.

The Great Terror remains one of the most puzzling aspects of Stalin's path to dictatorial power. The Terror succeeded, with a certain twisted kind of logic, in solidifying Stalin's personal control over all aspects of social and political life in the USSR, but it did so by destroying the most talented elements in Soviet society. The Terror was to some extent the result of Stalin's personal paranoia, but it was also a fitting end to the "Stalin revolution" that began in 1927–1928 with the end of the NEP.

The results of the Stalin revolution were profound. No other regime in the history of western Europe had ever attempted to reorder completely the politics, economy, and society of a major nation. The Soviets had done so in a mere ten years. By 1939 private manufacturing and trade had been almost entirely abolished. Factories, mines, railroads, and public utilities were exclusively owned by the state. Stores were either government enterprises or cooperatives in which consumers owned shares. Agriculture had been almost completely socialized. The decade was not entirely grim, however. There were advances, especially in the area of social reform. Illiteracy was reduced from

First Stalinist Purge, 1936. Russian factory workers in Leningrad listen to a report of the trial of several citizens falsely accused of plotting against Stalin. The accused were ultimately executed.

THE STALINIST REVOLUTION, 1927–1938

Launch of collectivization	1927
Launch of the first Five-Year Plan	1928
Stalin breaks with the NEP	1929
Stalin pauses collectivization	1930
Liquidation of the kulaks	1929–1933
The Great Terror	1937–1938

nearly 50 percent to about 20 percent, and higher education was made available to increasingly large numbers. Government assistance for working mothers and free hospitalization did a great deal to raise the national standard of health. The society that emerged from this terrible decade was industrial, more urban than rural, and more modern than traditional. But it was a society badly pummeled in the process, one in which many of the most productive peasants, gifted intellectuals, and experienced economic and social elites were purged from society in the name of total dictatorial power. The USSR that emerged from this tumultuous period would barely be able to withstand the immense strains placed on it when the Germans struck less than three years after the end of the Terror.

THE EMERGENCE OF FASCISM IN ITALY

What were the components of Italian fascism?

Like many European nations, Italy emerged from the First World War as a democracy in distress. Italy was on the winning side and had been among the Big Four nations (with France, Great Britain, and the United States) that put together the postwar settlement. Yet the war had cost Italy nearly seven hundred thousand lives and over $15 billion. These sacrifices were no greater than those of France or Britain but were hard to bear for a much poorer nation. Moreover, Italy had received secret promises of specific territorial gains during the war, only to find those promises withdrawn when they conflicted with principles of self-determination. Italian claims to

the west coast of the Adriatic, for instance, were bitterly disputed and in the end denied by Yugoslavia. Italy received most of the Austrian territories it demanded, but many maintained that these were inadequate rewards for their sacrifices. Groups of militant nationalists seized Fiume, a port city on the Adriatic, and held it for a year before being disbanded by the Italian army. At first the nationalists blamed the "mutilated victory" on President Wilson, but after a short time they turned on their own rulers and what they considered the weaknesses of parliamentary democracy.

Italy had long-standing problems that were made worse by the war. Since unification, the Italian nation had been rent by an unhealthy economic split—divided into a prosperous industrialized north and a poor agrarian south. Social conflict over land, wages, and local power caused friction in the countryside as well as in urban centers. Governments were often seen as corrupt, indecisive, and defeatist. This was the background for the more immediate problems that Italy faced after the war.

Inflation and unemployment were perhaps the most destructive effects of the war. Inflation produced high prices, speculation, and profiteering. And though normally wages would have risen also, the postwar labor market was glutted by returning soldiers. Furthermore, business elites were shaken by strikes, which became increasingly large and frequent, and by the closing of foreign markets. The parliamentary government that was set up after the war failed to ease these dire conditions, and Italians wanted radical reforms. For the working class, this meant socialism. In November of that year, the socialists won about a third of the seats in the Chamber of Deputies. The movement grew increasingly radical: in 1920, the socialist and anarchist workers took over scores of factories, most in the metallurgy sector, and tried to run them for the benefit of the workers themselves. In the countryside, most peasants were land poor, and many had no land at all, but instead worked for wages as rural laborers on large estates. Demands for land reform grew more militant. In some rural areas, so-called Red Leagues tried to break up large estates and force landlords to reduce their rents. In all these actions, the model of the Russian revolution, although it was only vaguely understood, encouraged the development of local radicalism. In large numbers, voters abandoned the poorly organized parties of the center and the moderate left. They supported two more radical groups: the Socialists and the Catholic People's party (newly formed with the pope's blessing) which appealed to the common people,

EUROPE IN 1923

Which countries lost the most territory after World War I? How did those losses affect each nation? What problems were solved by the new national boundaries? What difficulties might the new borders have created?

especially in the countryside. Neither party preached revolution, yet both urged wide-ranging social and economic reforms.

The rising radical tide, especially seen against the backdrop of the Bolshevik revolution, worried other social groups. Industrialists and landowners feared for their property. Small shopkeepers and white-collar workers—social groups that did not think the working-class movement supported their interests—found themselves alienated by business elites on the one hand and by apparently revolutionary radicals on the other. The threat from the left provoked a strong surge to the right. Fascism appeared in the form of vigilante groups breaking up strikes, fighting with workers in the streets, or ousting the Red Leagues from lands occupied in the countryside.

THE RISE OF MUSSOLINI

"I am fascism," said Benito Mussolini, and indeed, the success of the Italian fascist movement depended heavily on his leadership. Mussolini (1883–1945) was the son of a socialist blacksmith. His mother was a schoolteacher, and he deferentially followed in her footsteps. But he was restless and dissatisfied, soon leaving Italy for further study in Switzerland. There he gave part of his time to his books and the rest to writing articles for socialist newspapers. Expelled from the country for fomenting strikes, he returned to Italy, where he became a journalist and eventually the editor of *Avanti*, the leading socialist daily.

Mussolini did not hold to any particular doctrine, and he reversed himself at several points. When war broke out in August 1914, Mussolini insisted that Italy should remain neutral. He had scarcely adopted this position when he began urging participation on the Allied side. Deprived of his position as the editor of *Avanti*, he founded a new paper, *Il Popolo d'Italia,* and dedicated its columns to arousing enthusiasm for war. He regarded the Italian government's decision the following spring to go in on the side of the Allies as a personal victory.

As early as October 1914, Mussolini had organized groups, called *fasci,* to help drum up support for the war. Members of the *fasci* were young idealists, fanatical nationalists. After the war, these groups formed the base of Mussolini's fascist movement. (The word *fascism* derives from the Latin *fasces:* an ax surrounded by a bundle of sticks that represented the authority of the Roman state. The Italian *fascio* means "group" or "band.") In 1919 Mussolini drafted the original platform of the Fascist party. It had several surprising elements, including universal (including woman) suffrage, an eight-hour workday, and a tax on inheritances. A new platform, adopted in 1920, abandoned all references to economic reforms. Neither platform earned the fascists much political success.

What the fascists lacked in political support, they made up for in aggressive determination. They gained the respect of the middle class and landowners, and intimidated many others, by forcefully repressing radical movements of industrial workers and peasants. They attacked socialists, often physically, and succeeded in taking over some local governments. As the national regime weakened, Mussolini's coercive politics made him look like a solution to the absence of leadership. In September 1922, he began to negotiate with other parties and the king for fascist participation in government. On October 28 an army of about fifty thousand fascist militia, in black-shirted uniforms, marched into Rome and occupied the capital. The premier resigned, and the following day the king, Victor Emmanuel III, reluctantly invited Mussolini to form a cabinet. Without firing a shot the Black Shirts had gained control of the Italian government. The explanation of their success is to be found less in the strength of the fascist movement itself than in the Italian disappointments after the war and the weakness of the older governing classes.

The parliamentary system had folded under pressure. And though Mussolini had "legally" been granted his power, he immediately began to establish a one-party dictatorship. The doctrines of Italian fascism had three components. The first was statism. The state was declared to incorporate every interest and every loyalty of its members. There was to be "nothing above

> Members of the *fasci* were young idealists, fanatical nationalists. After the war, these groups formed the base of Mussolini's fascist movement.

Mussolini Reviews a Fascist Youth Parade. Mobilizing youth was central to fascism and Nazism; it demonstrated the vigor of the movements.

the state, nothing outside the state, nothing against the state." The second was nationalism. Nationhood was the highest form of society, with a life and a soul of its own apart from the lives and souls of the individuals who composed it. The third was militarism. Nations that did not expand would eventually wither and die. War ennobled man and regenerated sluggish and decadent peoples.

Mussolini began to rebuild Italy in accordance with these principles. The first step was to change electoral laws so they granted his party solid parliamentary majorities and to intimidate the opposition; he then moved to close down parliamentary government and other parties entirely. He abolished the cabinet system and all but extinguished the powers of the Parliament. He made the Fascist party an integral part of the Italian constitution. Mussolini assumed the dual position of prime minister and party leader (*duce*), and he used the party's militia to eliminate his enemies by violent means. Mussolini's government also controlled the police, muzzled the press, and censored academic activity.

Meanwhile, Mussolini preached the end of class conflict and its replacement by national unity. He began to reorganize the economy and labor, taking away the power of the country's labor movement. The Italian economy was placed under the management of twenty-two corporations, each responsible for a major industrial enterprise. In each corporation were representatives of trade unions, whose members were organized by the Fascist party, the employers, and the government. Together, the members of these corporations were given the task of determining working conditions, wages, and prices. Unsurprisingly, however, the decisions of these bodies were closely supervised by the government and favored the position of management. Indeed, the government quickly aligned with big business, creating more of a corrupt bureaucracy than a revolutionary economy.

Mussolini secured some working-class assent with state-sponsored programs including massive public-works projects, library building, paid vacations for workers, and social security. In 1929, he settled Italy's sixty-year-old conflict with the Roman Catholic Church. He signed a treaty granting independence to the papal residence in the Vatican City and promising restitution for expropriations that occurred during Italian unification. The treaty also established Roman Catholicism as the official religion of the state, guaranteed religious education in the nation's schools, and made religious marriage ceremonies mandatory. The agreement with the church was part of Mussolini's campaign to "normalize" relations with other Italian institutions—army, industry, church, monarchy—in order to maintain stability.

In fact, Mussolini's regime did much to maintain the status quo. Party officers exercised a degree of political supervision over bureaucrats, yet did not infiltrate the bureaucracy in significant numbers. Moreover, Mussolini remained on friendly terms with the elites who had assisted his rise to power, insuring that whatever he might proclaim about the distinctions between fascism and capitalism, the economy of Italy would remain dependent on private enterprise.

The Italian dictator boasted that fascism had pulled the country back from economic chaos. Like other European economies, the Italian economy did improve in the late 1920s. The regime did a great deal to create the appearance of efficiency, and Mussolini's admirers famously claimed that he had at last "made the trains run on time." Fascism, however, did little to lessen Italy's plight during the worldwide depression of the 1930s.

Like Nazism later, fascism had contradictory elements. It sought to restore traditional authority and, at the same time, mobilize all of Italian society for economic and nationalist purposes—a process that inevitably undercut older authorities. It created new authoritarian organizations and activities that comported with these goals such as exercise programs to make the young fit and mobilized, youth camps, awards to mothers of large families, political rallies, and parades in small towns in the countryside. Activities like these offered people a feeling of political involvement though they no longer enjoyed political rights. This mobilized but essentially passive citizenship was a hallmark of fascism.

WEIMAR GERMANY

Why did German democracy fail?

On November 9, 1918—two days before the armistice ending the First World War—thousands of Germans swarmed the streets of Berlin in a nearly bloodless overthrow of the imperial government. A massive and largely unexpected uprising, the demonstration converged on the Reichstag in the city center, where a member of the Social Democratic Party (SPD) announced the birth of the new German republic. The kaiser had abdicated only hours before, turning the government over to the Social Democratic leader Friedrich Ebert. The revolution spread quickly through

The German Election of 1919. Here German women line up to vote for the first time.

1920, creating a lasting bitterness among groups on the left.

More important, the revolutionary aftermath of the war gave rise to bands of militant counterrevolutionaries. Veterans and other young nationalists joined so-called *Freikorps* (free corps). Such groups developed throughout the country, drawing as many as several hundred thousand members. Former army officers who led these militias continued their war experience by fighting against "Bolsheviks," Poles, and communists. The politics of the Freikorps were fiercely right wing. Anti-Marxist, anti-Semitic, and antiliberal, they had scant affection for the new German republic or its parliamentary democracy. Many of the early Nazi leaders had fought in World War I and participated in Freikorps units.

the war-ravaged country; councils of workers and soldiers controlled most major cities within a couple of days, and hundreds of cities by month's end. The "November Revolution" was fast and far reaching, though not as revolutionary as many middle- and upper-class conservatives feared. The majority of socialists steered a cautious, democratic course: they wanted reforms, but were willing to leave much of the existing imperial bureaucracy intact. Above all, they wanted a popularly elected national assembly to draft a constitution for the new republic.

Two months passed, however, before elections could be held— a period of crisis that verged on civil war. Once in control, the Social Democratic leadership made order its top priority. The revolutionary movement that had brought the SPD to power now threatened it. Independent socialists and a nascent Communist party wanted radical reforms, and in December 1918 and January 1919, they staged armed uprisings in the streets of Berlin. Fearful of a Bolshevik-style revolution, the Social Democratic government turned against its former allies and sent militant bands of workers and volunteers to crush the uprisings. During the conflict, the government's fighters murdered Rosa Luxemburg and Karl Liebknecht—two German communist leaders who became instant martyrs. Violence continued into

> The politics of the Freikorps were fiercely right wing. Anti-Marxist, anti-Semitic, and antiliberal, they had scant affection for the new German republic or its parliamentary democracy.

Germany's new government—known as the Weimar Republic for the city where its constitution was drafted—rested on a coalition of socialists, Catholic centrists, and liberal democrats, a necessary compromise since no single party won a majority of the votes in the January 1919 election. The Weimar constitution was based on the values of parliamentary liberalism, and set up an open, pluralistic framework for German democracy. Through a series of compromises, the constitution established universal suffrage (for both women and men) and a bill of rights that guaranteed not only civil liberties but also a range of social entitlements. On paper, at least, the revolutionary movement had succeeded.

Yet the Weimar government lasted just over a decade. By 1930 it was in crisis, and in 1933 it collapsed. What happened? The failure of German democracy was not a foregone conclusion. It resulted from a confluence of social, political, and economic crises that were singly manageable but collectively disastrous.

Many of Weimar's problems were born from Germany's defeat in the First World War, which was not only devastating but also humiliating. The ignominious loss to the Allies shocked many Germans, who soon latched onto rumors that the army hadn't actually been defeated in battle, but instead had been "stabbed in the back" by socialists and Jewish leaders in the German government. Army officers cultivated this story even before the war was over, and though untrue, it helped to salve the wounded pride of German patriots. In the next decade, those in search of a scapegoat also blamed the seemingly lax republican regime, epitomized by what they considered the modern decadence of 1920s Berlin. What was needed, many critics argued, was authoritative leadership to guide the nation and regain the world's respect.

The Treaty of Versailles magnified Germany's sense of dishonor. Germany was forced to cede a tenth of its territory, accept responsibility for the war, and slash the size of its army to a mere one hundred thousand men—a punishment that riled the politically powerful corps of officers. Most important, the treaty saddled Germany with crippling reparations. Negotiating the $33 billion debt created problems for the government and provoked nothing but anger from the public. Some opponents of the reparations settlement urged an obstructionist policy of nonpayment, arguing that the enormous sum would doom Germany's economy for the foreseeable future. Indeed, by one estimate, the debt would not have been paid off until 1987. In 1924 Germany accepted a new schedule of reparations designed by an international committee headed by the American financier Charles G. Dawes. The German chancellor Gustav Stresemann had successfully moved Germany toward a foreign policy of cooperation and rapprochement that lasted throughout the 1920s. Many German people, however, continued to resent reparations, Versailles, and the government that continued to accommodate the treaty.

Major economic crises also played a central role in Weimar's collapse. The first period of emergency occurred in the early twenties. Still reeling from wartime inflation, the government was hard pressed for revenues. Funding postwar demobilization programs, social welfare, and reparations forced the government to continue to print money. Inflation became nearly unstoppable. By 1923, as one historian writes, the economic situation had "acquired an almost surrealistic quality." A pound of potatoes cost about nine marks in January, 40 million marks by October. Beef went for almost 2 trillion marks per pound. The government finally took drastic measures to stabilize the currency in 1924, but millions of Germans had already been ruined. For those on fixed incomes, such as pensioners

and stockholders, savings and security had vanished. Middle-class employees, farmers, and workers were all hard hit by the economic crisis, and many of them abandoned the traditional political parties in protest. In their eyes, the parties that claimed to represent the middle classes had created the problems and proved incapable of fixing them.

Beginning in 1925, however, Germany's economy and government seemed to be recovering. By borrowing money, the country was able to make its scaled-down reparations payments and to earn money by selling cheap exports. In large cities, socialist municipal governments sponsored building projects that included schools, hospitals, and low-cost worker housing. But such economic and political stability was misleading. The economy remained dependent on large infusions of capital from the United States set up by the Dawes plan as part of the effort to settle reparations. That dependence made the German economy especially vulnerable to American economic developments. When the U.S. stock market crashed in 1929, beginning the Great Depression (see below), capital flow to Germany virtually stopped.

The Great Depression pushed Weimar's political system to the breaking point. In 1929, there were 2 million unemployed; in 1932, 6 million. In those three years production dropped by 44 percent. Artisans and small shopkeepers lost both status and income. Farmers fared even worse, having never recovered from the crisis of the early twenties. Peasants staged mass demonstrations against the government's agricultural policies even before the depression hit. For white-collar and civil service employees, the depression meant lower salaries, poor working conditions, and a constant threat of unemployment. The government drifted toward crisis itself, facing opposition from all sides. Burdened with plummeting tax revenues and spiraling numbers of Germans in need of relief, the government repeatedly cut welfare benefits, which further demoralized the electorate. Finally, the crisis created an opportunity for Weimar's opponents. Many leading industrialists supported a return to authoritarian government, and they were allied with equally conservative landowners, united by a desire for protective economic policies to stimulate the sale of domestic goods and foodstuffs. Those conservative forces wielded considerable power in Germany, beyond the control of the government. So too did the army and the civil service, which were staffed with

> The Great Depression pushed Weimar's political system to the breaking point. In 1929, there were 2 million unemployed; in 1932, 6 million. In those three years production dropped by 44 percent.

opponents of the republic—men who rejected the principles of parliamentary democracy and international cooperation that Weimar represented.

HITLER AND THE NATIONAL SOCIALISTS

How did the Nazis come to power?

Adolf Hitler was born in 1889 in Austria, not Germany. The son of a petty customs official in the Austrian civil service, Hitler dropped out of school and went to Vienna in 1909 to become an artist. Rejected from the academy and temporarily homeless, he eked out a dismal existence doing manual labor and painting cheap watercolors in Vienna. Meanwhile he developed the violent political prejudices that would become the guiding principles of the Nazi regime. He ardently admired the Austrian politicians preaching anti-Semitism, anti-Marxism, and Pan-Germanism. When war broke out in 1914, Hitler was among the jubilant crowds in the streets of Munich; and though he was an Austrian citizen, he enlisted in the German army, where he claimed to have finally found meaning in his life. After the war, he joined the newly formed German Workers' Party, whose name changed in 1920 to the National Socialist Workers' Party (abbreviated in popular usage to Nazi). The Nazis were but one among many small, militant groups of disaffected Germans devoted to racial nationalism and to the overthrow of the Weimar Republic. They grew out of the political milieu that refused to accept the defeat or the November Resolution, and that blamed both on socialists and Jews.

Ambitious and outspoken, Hitler quickly moved up the rather short ladder of party leadership as a talented stump orator. By 1921 he was the *Führer*—the leader—to his followers in Bavaria. The wider public saw him as a "vulgar demagogue"—if they noticed him at all. In November of 1923, during the worst days of the inflation crisis, the Nazis made a failed attempt (the Beer Hall Putsch in Munich) at overthrowing the state government of Bavaria. Hitler spent the next seven months in prison, where he wrote his autobiography and political manifesto *Mein Kampf* ("My Struggle") in 1924. Combining anti-Semitism with anticommunism, the book set out at great length the popular theory that Germany had been betrayed by its enemies and that the country needed strong leadership to regain international prominence. The failed 1923 putsch proved an eye-opening experience for Hitler; he recognized that the Nazis would have to play politics if they wanted to gain power. Released from prison in 1924, Hitler resumed leadership of the party. In the next five years, he consolidated his power over a growing membership of ardent supporters. Actively cultivating the image of the Nazi movement as a crusade against (Jewish) Marxism and capitalism, he portrayed himself as the heroic savior of the German people.

CHRONOLOGY

THE RISE OF NAZISM, 1920–1934

National Socialist Workers' Party founded	1920
Beer Hall Putsch in Munich	1923
Hitler writes *Mein Kampf* in prison	1924
Hitler consolidates power	1924–1929
Hitler loses presidential election	1932
Hitler appointed chancellor of Germany	1933
Nazi party rules Germany	1933
Night of Long Knives	1934

Nazism and the Rural Myth. To stress the rural roots of Aryan Germany, Hitler appeared in lederhosen in the 1920s.

An equally important factor in Hitler's rise to power was the Nazis' ambitious and unprecedented campaign program. In the "inflation election" of 1924, the Nazis polled 6.6 percent of the vote as a protest party at the radical fringe. With the economic stabilization of the mid-twenties, their meager share dropped to below 3 percent. But during this time of seeming decline, the Nazis were building an extensive organization of party activists that helped to lay the foundation for the party's electoral gains later.

The 1928 election was a pivotal moment for both Weimar and for the Nazis for two reasons. First, from this point on, politics became polarized between right and left, making it virtually impossible to put together a coalition that would support the continuation of Weimar democracy. Second, it was apparent that alienated voters, especially peasants, were deserting their traditional political parties and voting for other interest-group organizations that would voice their grievances and push their demands. The Nazis quickly learned how to benefit from this splintering of the electorate. Previously they had tried, with little success, to win the large German working-class vote away from the left. Now, guided by its chief propagandist, Joseph Goebbels, the party stepped up its efforts to attract members of the urban and rural middle classes. The party's most consistent message, hammered home in propaganda, speeches, and rallies, was that the Nazis opposed everything about Weimar: the political system, economic organizations, the left and the labor movement, the more liberal moral codes, women wearing "decadent" flapper fashions, and "cosmopolitan" movies such as *All Quiet on the Western Front.* (Nazi gangs started a street riot outside the first showing of the film in Berlin; Goebbels broke up a later showing by tossing stench bombs and mice into the theater.) The answers to Germany's problems, the Nazis argued, could only be found by breaking with Weimar. Presenting itself as young and dynamic, the party built a national profile as an alternative to the parties of middle-class conservatives. In 1930, bolstered by the economic crisis, the Nazis were better funded and better organized than ever, and they won 18.3 percent of the vote.

Who voted for the Nazis? Recent analysis of election results and campaign materials suggests that different groups supported the Nazis at varying times and for varying reasons. The Nazis polled highly with small property holders and the rural middle class long before

the depression. The Nazis offered these voters economic protection and renewed social status. Other segments of the middle class—notably pensioners, the elderly, and war widows—came to support the Nazis during the economic crisis, when they feared reduction of insurance or pension benefits, and when the older conservative parties failed to meet their needs. The Nazis also courted the traditionally elitist civil service. And though they failed to win votes from industrial workers, the Nazis found some of their strongest support among workers in handicrafts and small-scale manufacturing.

In 1930, the Nazi party won 107 of 577 seats in the Reichstag, second only to the Social Democrats, who controlled 143. No party could gain a majority. No governing coalition was possible without Nazi support. And the Nazis refused to join any cabinet that was not headed by Hitler. The chancellor, Heinrich Brüning of the Catholic Center party, continued to govern by emergency decrees, but his deflationary economic policies were disastrous. Industrial production continued to crash and unemployment continued to climb. In 1932, Hitler ran for president and narrowly lost, although he staged an unprecedented campaign by airplane, visiting twenty-one cities in six days. When another parliamentary election was called in July 1932, the Nazis won 37.4 percent of the vote, which, though not a majority, was a significant plurality. The Nazis could claim that they were the party able to draw support across class, geographic, and generational lines. They benefited from their position as outsiders, untainted by involvement in unpopular parliamentary coalitions. Indeed, the failure of the traditional parties was key to the success of the Nazis.

Despite its electoral success in 1932, the Nazi party had not won a majority; Hitler was not in power. He was appointed chancellor in January 1933 by President Hindenburg, who hoped to create a conservative coalition government by bringing the Nazis into line with the less radical parties. But Hindenburg and others in the government had underestimated the Nazis' power and popularity. Legally installed in office, Hitler immediately made the most of it. When a Dutch anarchist with links to the communist party set fire to the Reichstag on the night of February 27, Hitler seized the opportunity to suspend civil rights "as a defensive measure against communist acts of violence." He convinced Hindenburg to dissolve the Reichstag and to order a new election on

> Other segments of the middle class—notably pensioners, the elderly, and war widows—came to support the Nazis during the economic crisis, when they feared reduction of insurance or pension benefits, and when the older conservative parties failed to meet their needs.

NAZI PROPAGANDA

JOSEPH GOEBBELS, "WHY ARE WE ENEMIES OF THE JEWS?"

The Nazis promised many things to many people. As the following document shows, anti-Semitism allowed them to blend their racial nationalism, vaguely defined (and anti-Marxist) socialism, and disgust with the state of German culture and politics. Joseph Goebbels, one of the early members of the party, became director of propaganda for the party in 1928. Later Hitler appointed him head of the National Ministry for Public Enlightenment and Propaganda.

We are NATIONALISTS because we see in the NATION the only possibility for the protection and the furtherance of our existence.

The NATION is the organic bond of a people for the protection and defense of their lives. He is nationally minded who understands this IN WORD AND IN DEED. . . .

Young nationalism has its unconditional demands, BELIEF IN THE NATION is a matter of all the people, not for individuals of rank, a class, or an industrial clique. The eternal must be separated from the contemporary. The maintenance of a rotten industrial system has nothing to do with nationalism. I can love Germany and hate capitalism; not only CAN I do it, I also MUST do it. The germ of the rebirth of our people LIES ONLY IN THE DESTRUCTION OF THE SYSTEM OF PLUNDERING THE HEALTHY POWER OF THE PEOPLE.

WE ARE NATIONALISTS BECAUSE WE, AS GERMANS, LOVE GERMANY. And because we love Germany, we demand the protection of its national spirit and we battle against its destroyers.

WHY ARE WE SOCIALISTS?

We are SOCIALISTS because we see in SOCIALISM the only possibility for maintaining our racial existence and through it the reconquest of our political freedom and the rebirth of the German state. SOCIALISM has its peculiar form first of all through its comradeship in arms with the forward-driving energy of a newly awakened nationalism. Without nationalism it is nothing, a phantom, a theory, a vision of air, a book. With it, it is everything, THE FUTURE, FREEDOM, FATHERLAND! . . .

WHY DO WE OPPOSE THE JEWS?

We are ENEMIES OF THE JEWS, because we are fighters for the freedom of the German people. THE JEW IS THE CAUSE AND THE BENEFICIARY OF OUR MISERY. He has used the social difficulties of the broad masses of our people to deepen the unholy split between Right and Left among our people. He has made two halves of Germany. He is the real cause for our loss of the Great War.

The Jew has no interest in the solution of Germany's fateful problems. He CANNOT have any. FOR HE LIVES ON THE FACT THAT THERE HAS BEEN NO SOLUTION. If we would make the German people a unified community and give them freedom before the world, then the Jew can have no place among us. He has the best trumps in his hands when a people lives in inner and outer slavery. THE JEW IS RESPONSIBLE FOR OUR MISERY AND HE LIVES ON IT.

That is the reason why we, AS NATIONALISTS and AS SOCIALISTS, oppose the Jew. HE HAS CORRUPTED OUR RACE, FOULED OUR MORALS, UNDERMINED OUR CUSTOMS, AND BROKEN OUR POWER. . . .

NATIONAL SOCIALIST CAMPAIGN PAMPHLET, 1932

The Nazis worked hard to win the rural vote, as evidenced by the Nazi campaign pamphlet reprinted below. The Nazis tried to appeal to farmers' economic grievances, their fears of socialism on the one hand and big business on the other, and their more general hostility to urban life and culture.

GERMAN FARMER YOU BELONG TO HITLER! WHY?

The German farmer stands between two great dangers today:

The one danger is the American economic system—Big capitalism!

> it means "world economic crisis"
> it means "eternal interest slavery" . . .
> it means that the world is nothing more than a bag of booty for Jewish finance in Wall Street, New York, and Paris
> it enslaves man under the slogans of progress, technology, rationalization, standardization, etc.
> it knows only profit and dividends
> it wants to make the world into a giant trust
> it puts the machine over man
> it annihilates the independent, earth-rooted farmer, and its final aim is the world dictatorship of Jewry [. . .]
> it achieves this in the political sphere through parliament and the swindle of democracy. In the economic sphere, through the control of credit, the mortgaging of land, the stock exchange and the market principle [. . .]

The farmer's leagues, the Landvolk and the Bavarian Farmers' League all pay homage to this system.

The other danger is the Marxist economic system of bolshevism:

> it knows only the state economy
> it knows only one class, the proletariat
> it brings in the controlled economy
> it doesn't just annihilate the self-sufficient farmer economically—it roots him out [. . .]
> it brings the rule of the tractor
> it nationalizes the land and creates mammoth factory-farms
> it uproots and destroys man's soul, making him the powerless tool of the communist idea—or kills him
> it destroys the family, belief, and customs [. . .]
> it is anti-Christ, it desecrates the churches [. . .]
> its final aim is the world dictatorship of the proletariat, that means ultimately the world dictatorship of Jewry, for the Jew controls this powerless proletariat and uses it for his dark plans

Big capitalism and bolshevism work hand in hand; they are born of Jewish thought and serve the master plan of world Jewry.

Who alone can rescue the farmer from these dangers?

NATIONAL SOCIALISM!

Anton Kaes, Matin Jay, and Edward Dimendberg, *The Weimar Republic Sourcebook* (Los Angeles: University of California Press, 1994), pp. 137–38, 142. (Source for both documents.)

March 5, 1933. Under Hitler's sway, the new parliament legally granted him unlimited powers for the next four years. Hitler proclaimed his new government the Third Reich. (The first Reich was the German empire of the Middle Ages; the second was that of the kaisers.)

NAZI GERMANY

By the fall of 1933, Germany had become a one-party state. The socialist and communist left was crushed by the new regime. Almost all non-Nazi organizations had been either abolished or forced to become part of the Nazi system. Nazi party leaders took over various government departments; party *Gauleiters*, or regional directors, assumed administrative responsibility throughout the country. Party propaganda sought to impress citizens with the regime's "monolithic efficiency." But in fact, the Nazi government was a tangled bureaucratic maze, with both agencies and individuals vying fiercely for Hitler's favor.

Ironically, at the end of the party's first year in power, the most serious challenges to Hitler came from within the party. Hitler's paramilitary Nazi storm troopers (the SA) had been formed to maintain discipline within the party and impose order in society. SA membership soared after 1933, and many in the SA hailed Hitler's appointment as the beginning of a genuinely Nazi revolution. Such radicalism was alarming to the more traditional conservative groups that had helped make Hitler chancellor. If Hitler was to maintain power, then, he needed to tame the SA. On the night of June 30, 1934, more than a thousand high-ranking SA officials, including several of Hitler's oldest associates, were executed in a bloody purge known as the Night of Long Knives. The purge cleared the way for a second paramilitary organization, the *Schutzstaffel* (bodyguard), or SS. Headed by the fanatical Heinrich Himmler, the SS became the most dreaded arm of Nazi terror. As Himmler saw it, the mission of the SS was to fight political and racial enemies of the regime, which included building the system of concentration camps. The first camp, at Dachau, opened in March 1933. The secret state police, known as the Gestapo, were responsible for the arrest, incarceration in camps, and murder of thousands of Germans. But the police force was generally understaffed and deluged with paperwork—as one historian has shown, anything but "omniscient, omnipotent, and omnipresent." In fact, the majority of arrests was based on voluntary denun-

ciations made by ordinary citizens against each other, often as petty personal attacks. It was not lost on the Gestapo leadership that these denunciations created a level of control that the Gestapo itself could never achieve.

Despite—or perhaps because of—these efforts to quash opposition, Hitler and the Nazis enjoyed a sizable amount of popular support. Many Germans approved of Hitler's use of violence against the left. The Nazis could play on deep-seated fears of communism, and they spoke a language of intense national pride and unity that had broad appeal. Many Germans saw Hitler as a symbol of a strong, revitalized Germany. Propagandists fostered a Führer cult, depicting Hitler as a charismatic leader with the magnetic energy to bring people to their knees. Hitler's appeal also rested on his ability to give the German people what they wanted: jobs for workers, a productive economy for industrialists, a bulwark against communism for those who feared the wave of revolution. His appeal lay not so much in the programs he championed, many of which were ill conceived or contradictory, but in his revolt against politics as they had been practiced in Germany. Finally, he promised to lead Germany back to national greatness and to "overthrow" the Versailles settlement, and through the 1930s he seemed to be doing so with a series of bloodless diplomatic triumphs.

Nazi Parade, 1933. The Nazis understood the propaganda value of parades, rituals, and uniforms.

Hitler's plans for national recovery called for full-scale rearmament and economic self-sufficiency. With policies similar to those of other Western nations, the Nazis made massive public investments, set strict market controls to stop inflation and stabilize the currency, and sealed Germany off from the world economy. The regime launched state financed construction projects—highways, public housing, reforestation. Late in the decade, as the Nazis rebuilt the entire German military complex, unemployment dropped from over 6 million to under two hundred thousand. The German economy looked better than any other in Europe. Hitler claimed this as his "economic miracle." Such improvements were significant, especially in the eyes of Germans who had lived through the continual turmoil of war, inflation, political instability, and economic crisis.

Like Mussolini, Hitler moved to abolish class conflict by stripping working-class institutions of their power. He outlawed trade unions and strikes, froze wages, and organized workers and employers into a National Labor Front. At the same time, the Nazis increased workers' welfare benefits, generally in line with the other Western nations. Class distinctions were somewhat blurred by the regime's attempts to infuse a new national "spirit" into the entire society. Popular organizations cut across class lines, especially among the youth. The Hitler Youth, a club modeled on the Boy Scouts, was highly successful at teaching children the values of Hitler's Reich; the National Labor Service drafted students for a term to work on state-sponsored building and reclamation projects. Government policy encouraged women to withdraw from the labor force, both to ease unemployment and to conform to Nazi notions of a woman's proper role. "Can woman," one propagandist asked, "conceive of anything more beautiful than to sit with her husband in her cozy home and listen inwardly to the loom of time weaving the weft and warp of motherhood . . . ?"

NAZI RACISM

At the core of Nazi ideology lay a particularly virulent racism. Much of this racism was not new. Hitler and the Nazis drew on a revived and especially violent form of nineteenth-century social Darwinism, according to which nations and people struggled for survival, with the superior peoples strengthening themselves in the process. By the early twentieth century, the rise of the social sciences had taken nineteenth-century prejudices and racial thinking into new terrain. Just as medical sci-

ence had cured bodily ills, doctors, criminologists, and social workers sought ways to cure social ills. Across the West, scientists and intellectuals worked to purify the body politic, improve the human race, and eliminate the "unfit." Even progressive-minded individuals sometimes subscribed to eugenics, a program of racial engineering to improve either personal or public fitness. Eugenic policies in the Third Reich began with a 1933 law for the compulsory sterilization of "innumerable inferior and hereditarily tainted" people. This "social-hygienic racism" later became the systematic murder of mentally and physically ill patients. Social policy was governed by a basic division between those who possessed "value" and those who did not, with the aim of creating a racial utopia.

The centerpiece of Nazi racism was anti-Semitism. This centuries-old phenomenon was part of Christian society from the Middle Ages on. By the nineteenth

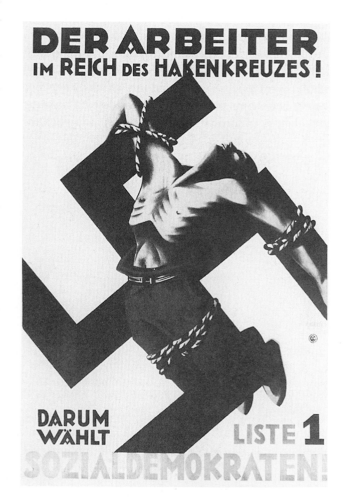

Anti-Nazi Poster, 1932, reads "The worker in the Reich of the Swastika" at top, and "Vote Social Democratic" at bottom.

HOW DID THE WESTERN DEMOCRACIES DEAL WITH THE GREAT DEPRESSION?

THE GREAT DEPRESSION IN THE DEMOCRACIES   919

century, traditional Christian anti-Semitism was joined by a current of nationalist anti-Jewish theory. A great many of the theorists of European nationalism saw the Jewish people as permanent outsiders who could only be assimilated and become citizens if they denied their Jewish identity. At the end of the nineteenth century, during the Dreyfus affair in France (see Chapter 26), French and European anti-Semites launched a barrage of propaganda against Jews—scores of books, pamphlets, and magazines blamed Jews for all the troubles of modernity, from socialism to international banks and mass culture. The late nineteenth century also brought a wave of pogroms—violent assaults on Jewish communities—especially in Russia. Racial anti-Semitism drew the line between Jews and non-Jews on the basis of erroneous biology. Religious conversion, which traditional Christian anti-Semites encouraged, would not change biology. Nor would assimilation, which was counseled by more secular nationalist thinkers.

It is important not to generalize, but anti-Semitism in these different forms was a well-established and open political force in most of the West. By attacking Jews, anti-Semites attacked modern institutions—from socialist parties and the mass press to international banking—as part of a "international Jewish conspiracy" to undermine traditional authority and nationality. Conservative party leaders told shopkeepers and workers that "Jewish capitalists" were responsible for the demise of small businesses, for the rise of giant department stores, and for precarious economic swings that threatened their livelihoods. In Vienna, middle-class voters supported the openly anti-Semitic Christian Democrats. In Germany, in 1893, sixteen avowed anti-Semites were elected to the Reichstag, and the Conservative party made anti-Semitism part of its official program. Hitler gave this anti-Semitism an especially murderous twist by tying it to doctrines of war and social-hygienic racism.

To what extent was the Nazis' virulent anti-Semitism shared? Although the "Jewish Question" was clearly Hitler's primary obsession during the early 1920s, he made the theme less central in campaign appearances as the Nazi movement entered mainstream politics, shifting instead to attacks on Marxism and the Weimar democracy. Moreover, anti-Semitic beliefs would not have distinguished the Nazi from any other party on the political right; it was likely of only secondary importance to people's opinions of the Nazis. Soon after Hitler came to power, though, German Jews faced discrimination, exclusion from rights as citizens, and violence. Racial laws excluded Jews from public office as early as April 1933. The Nazis encouraged a boycott of Jewish merchants,

while the SA created a constant threat of random violence. In 1935, the Nuremberg Decrees deprived Jews (defined by bloodline) of their German citizenship and prohibited marriage between Jews and other Germans. Violence escalated. In November 1938, the SA attacked some seventy-five hundred Jewish stores, burned nearly two hundred synagogues, killed ninety-one Jews, and beat up thousands more in a campaign of terror known as *Kristallnacht*, the Night of Broken Glass. Violence like this did raise some opposition from ordinary Germans. Legal persecution, however, met only silent acquiescence. And from the perspective of Jewish people, *Kristallnacht* made it plain that there was no safe place for them in Germany. Unfortunately, only one year remained before the outbreak of war made it impossible for Jews to escape.

What did national socialism and fascism have in common? Both arose in the interwar period as responses to World War I and the Russian Revolution. Both were violently antisocialist and anticommunist, determined to "rescue" their nations from the threat of Bolshevism. Both were intensely nationalistic; they believed that national solidarity came before all other allegiances and superseded all other rights. Both opposed parliamentary government and democracy as cumbersome and divisive. Both found their power in mass-based authoritarian politics. Similar movements existed in all the countries of the West, but only in a few cases did they actually form regimes. Nazism, however, distinguished itself by making a racially pure state central to its vision, a vision that would lead to global struggle and mass murder.

THE GREAT DEPRESSION IN THE DEMOCRACIES

How did the Western democracies deal with the Great Depression?

The histories of the three major Western democracies—Great Britain, France, and the United States—run roughly parallel during the years after the First World War. In all three countries governments put their trust in prewar policies and assumptions until the Great Depression forced them to make major social reforms, laying the foundations of the modern welfare state. These nations weathered the upheavals of the interwar years, but they did not do so easily.

France continued to fear Germany and took every opportunity to keep the Germans as weak as possible. Under the leadership of the moderate conservative Raymond Poincaré during the 1920s, France tried to keep the price of manufactured goods low by restraining wages. This policy of deflation kept businessmen happy but put a heavy burden on the working class. Édouard Herriot interrupted Poincaré's service as premier, serving for two years in the mid-1920s. A radical socialist by affiliation, Herriot was a spokesman for small-business owners, farmers, and the lower middle class. Herriot said he supported social reform, but refused to raise taxes in order to pay for it. Meanwhile, class conflict simmered just below the surface. As industries prospered, employers refused to bargain with labor unions. A period of major strikes immediately after the war was followed by a sharp decline in union activity. And even though the government passed a modified social insurance program in 1930—insuring against sickness, old age, and death—workers remained dissatisfied.

Social conflict flared in Britain as well. Anxious to regain its position as the major industrial and financial power in the world, Britain also pursued a policy of deflation, hoping to make its manufactured goods cheaper and more attractive on the world market. The result was a reduction in wages that undermined the standard of living of many British workers. Their resentment helped to elect the first Labour party government in 1924, and a second in 1929. The Labour party accomplished little, however, because of its minority position in Parliament. Besides, its leader, Prime Minister J. Ramsay MacDonald, was a rather timid socialist. The Conservative government returned to power in 1925 under Stanley Baldwin and refused to abandon its deflationary policy, which continued to drive down wages. British trade unions grew increasingly militant in response, and in 1926, the unions staged a nationwide general strike. The strike's only appreciable effect was to heighten middle-class antipathy toward workers.

The United States was the bastion of conservatism among the democracies. The presidents elected in the 1920s—Warren G. Harding, Calvin Coolidge, and Herbert Hoover—upheld a social philosophy formulated by the barons of big business in the nineteenth century. The Supreme Court used its power of judicial review to nullify progressive legislation enacted by state governments and occasionally by Congress.

The conservative economic and social policies of the prewar period were dealt their deathblow by the Great Depression of 1929. This worldwide depression peaked during the years 1929–1933, but its effects lasted a decade. For those who went through it, the depression was perhaps the formative experience of their lives and the decisive crisis of the interwar period. It was an important factor in the rise of Nazism, but in fact, it forced every country to forge new economic policies, and to deal with unprecedented economic turmoil.

THE ORIGINS OF THE GREAT DEPRESSION

What caused the Great Depression? Its deepest roots lay in the instability of national currencies, and in the interdependence of national economies. Throughout the 1920s, Europeans had seen a sluggish growth rate. A major drop in world agricultural prices hurt the countries of southern and eastern Europe, where agriculture was small in scale and high in cost. Unable to make a profit on the international market, these agricultural countries bought fewer manufactured goods from the more industrial sectors of northern Europe, causing a widespread drop in industrial productivity. Restrictions on free trade crippled the economy even more. Although debtor nations needed open markets to sell their goods, most nations were raising high trade barriers to protect domestic manufacturers from foreign competition.

Then in October of 1929, prices on the New York Stock Exchange collapsed. On October 24, "Black Thursday," 12 million shares were traded amid unprecedented chaos. Even more surprising, the market kept falling. Black Thursday was followed by Black Monday and then Black Tuesday: falling prices, combined with an enormously high number of trades, made for the worst day in the history of the stock exchange to that point. The rise of the United States as an international creditor during the Great War meant that the crash had immediate, disastrous consequences in Europe. When the value of stocks dropped, banks found themselves short of capital and then, when not rescued by the government, forced to close. International investors called in their debts. A series of banking houses shut their doors, among them Credit Anstalt, the biggest bank in Austria, with significant

> Black Thursday was followed by Black Monday and then Black Tuesday: falling prices, combined with an enormously high number of trades, made for the worst day in the history of the stock exchange to that point.

HOW DID THE WESTERN DEMOCRACIES DEAL WITH THE GREAT DEPRESSION?

THE GREAT DEPRESSION IN THE DEMOCRACIES   921

U.S. Farmers on Their Way West in the 1930s. Forced from their land by depression, debts, and drought, thousands of farmers and their families headed to California, Oregon, and Washington in search of employment.

make money cheaper, and thus more available for economic recovery programs. This action was the forerunner of a broad program of currency management, which became an important element in a general policy of economic nationalism. In another important move, Great Britain abandoned its time-honored policy of free trade in 1932, raising protective tariffs as high as 100 percent. But monetary policy alone could not end the hardships of ordinary families. Governments were increasingly forced to address their concerns with a wide range of social reforms.

Britain was the most cautious in its relief efforts. A national government composed of Conservative, Liberal, and Labour party members came to power in 1931. To underwrite effective programs of public assistance, however, the government would have to spend beyond its income—something it was reluctant to do. France, on the other hand, adopted the most advanced set of policies to combat the effects of the depression. In 1936, responding to a threat from ultraconservatives to overthrow the republic, a Popular Front government under the leadership of the socialist Léon Blum was formed by the Radical, Radical Socialist, and Communist parties, and lasted for two years. The Popular Front nationalized the munitions industry and reorganized the Bank of France to break the largest stockholders' monopolistic control over credit. The government also decreed a forty-hour week for all urban workers and initiated a program of public works. For the benefit of the farmers it established a wheat office to fix the price and regulate the distribution of grain. Although the Popular Front temporarily quelled the threat from the political right, conservatives were generally uncooperative and unimpressed by the attempts to aid the French working class. Both a socialist and Jewish, Blum faced fierce anti-Semitism in France. Fearing that Blum was the forerunner of a French Lenin, conservatives declared, "Better Hitler than Blum." They got their wish before the decade was out.

The most dramatic response to the depression came in the United States for two reasons. First, the United

interests in two thirds of Austrian industry. Workers did not simply lose their jobs, manufacturers laid off virtually entire work forces. In 1930, 4 million Americans were unemployed, in 1933, 13 million—nearly a third of the work force. By then, per capita income in the United States had fallen 48 percent. In Germany, too, the drop was brutal. In 1929, 2 million were unemployed; in 1932, 6 million. Production dropped 44 percent in Germany, 47 percent in the United States. The stock-market collapse led to widespread bank failure and brought the economy virtually to a standstill.

The governments of the West initially responded to the depression with monetary measures. In 1931 Great Britain abandoned the gold standard; the United States followed suit in 1933. By no longer pegging their currencies to the price of gold, these countries hoped to

States had clung longest to nineteenth-century economic philosophy. Prior to the depression, the business classes adhered firmly to the dogma of freedom of contract. The "barons" of industry insisted on their right to form monopolies, and they used the government as a tool to frustrate the demands of both workers and consumers. Second, the depression was more severe in the United States than in the European democracies. America had survived the First World War unscathed—and indeed, had benefited enormously—but now its economy was ravaged even more than Europe's. In 1933, Franklin D. Roosevelt succeeded Herbert Hoover as president and announced the New Deal, a program of reform and reconstruction to rescue the country.

The New Deal aimed to get the country back on its feet without destroying the capitalist system. The government would manage the economy, sponsor relief programs, and fund public-works projects to increase mass purchasing power. These policies were shaped by the theories of the British economist John Maynard Keynes, who had already proved influential during the 1919 treaty meetings at Paris. Keynes argued that capitalism could create a just and efficient society if governments played a part in its management. First, Keynes abandoned the sacred cow of balanced budgets. Without advocating continuous deficit financing, he would have the government deliberately operate in the red whenever private investments weren't enough. Keynes also favored the creation of large amounts of venture capital—money for high-risk, high-reward investments—which he saw as the only socially productive form of capital. Finally, he recommended monetary control to promote prosperity and full employment.

Along with Social Security and other programs, the United States adopted a Keynesian program of "currency management," regulating the value of the dollar according to the needs of the economy. The New Deal helped both individuals and the country to recover, but it left the crucial problem of unemployment unsolved. In 1939, after six years of the New Deal, the United States still had more than 9 million jobless workers—a figure that exceeded the combined unemployment of the rest of the world. Only with the outbreak of a new world war—which required millions of soldiers and armament workers—did the United States reach the full recovery that the New Deal had failed to deliver.

INTERWAR CULTURE: ARTISTS AND INTELLECTUALS

How did the mass media change everyday life?

We have seen how governments and their citizens responded to social, political, and economic crises. The interwar period brought equally dramatic upheavals in the arts and sciences. Revolutionary artistic forms that were pioneered at the turn of the century moved from the margins to the mainstream. Artists, writers, architects, and composers rejected traditional aesthetic values and experimented with new forms of expression. Further affronts to tradition came from scientists and psychologists, whose work challenged deeply held beliefs about the universe and about human nature. Finally, mass culture, in the form of radio, movies, and advertising, sharpened many anxieties, and stood as a stark example of the promise and peril of modern times.

> In his monumental poem *The Waste Land* (1922), Eliot presented a philosophy that was close to despair: life is a living death, to be endured as boredom and frustration.

INTERWAR INTELLECTUALS

Like many other people, novelists, poets, and dramatists were disillusioned by the brute facts of world war and by the failure of victory to fulfill its promises. Much of the literature of the interwar period reflected themes of frustration, cynicism, and disenchantment; but many writers were also fascinated by revolutionary developments in science, including the probing of psychoanalysts into the hidden secrets of the mind. The works of several writers came to represent the mood of the era: the early novels of the American Ernest Hemingway, for example, along with the poetry of the Anglo-American T. S. Eliot and the plays of the German Bertolt Brecht. In *The Sun Also Rises* (1926), Hemingway gave the public a powerful description of the so-called lost generation, a pattern followed by other writers, such as the American F. Scott Fitzgerald. In his monumental poem *The Waste Land* (1922), Eliot presented a philosophy that was close to despair: life is a living death, to be endured as boredom and frustration. Eliot's themes were echoed by William Butler Yeats, an Irish nationalist poet who, like Eliot, deplored the superficiality of modern life. In plays written for the working-class patrons of cabarets, Brecht decried the corruption of the state and the pointlessness of war. Like many artists, he rebelled against high culture and bourgeois values, but he also protested against the pretentious elitism of his contemporaries.

Other writers focused their attention on consciousness and inner life, often experimenting with new forms of prose. The Irish writer James Joyce was much renowned for his experiments with language and literacy forms—especially with the "stream of consciousness" technique, which he perfected in *Ulysses* (1922). The same was true, though to a lesser extent, of the novels of the Frenchman Marcel Proust and the Englishwoman Virginia Woolf (1882–1941). Woolf's essays and novels, among them *Mrs. Dalloway* (1925), *To the Lighthouse* (1927), and *A Room of One's Own* (1929), offered an eloquent and biting critique of Britain's elite institutions, from the universities that isolated women in separate, underfunded colleges to the suffocating decorum of middle-class families and relationships.

The First International Dada-Fair, Berlin, 1920. This gathering of artists features Otto Burchard (standing second from left), George Grosz (standing second from right), Hannah Höch (seated left) and a decor of bizarre juxtapositions that was a trademark of the dada school.

The depression of the 1930s forced many writers to reexamine the style and purpose of their work. Amid threats of economic devastation, totalitarianism, and war, literature became increasingly politicized. Authors felt themselves called to indict injustice and cruelty, and to point the way to a better society. Moreover, they no longer directed their work to fellow intellectuals alone, but to ordinary men and women as well. In *The Grapes of Wrath* (1939), for example, the American writer John Steinbeck depicted the plight of impoverished farmers fleeing from the Dust Bowl to California only to find that all the land had been monopolized by companies that exploited their workers. Young British writers such as W. H. Auden, Stephen Spender, and Christopher Isherwood were communist sympathizers who believed that it was their duty as artists to politicize their work to support the revolution. They rejected the pessimism of their immediate literary forebears in favor of optimistic commitment to their cause.

INTERWAR ARTISTS

Trends in art tended to parallel those in literature. The innovations of the prewar avant-garde thrived in the postwar period, and in fact, continued to dominate art throughout much of the twentieth century. Artists continued to focus on subjective experiences, multiplicities of meaning, and personal expression. Numerous and varied styles emerged, though all were characteristically modern in their rejection of traditional forms and values. Visual art responded to the rapid transformations of twentieth-century society —changes brought about by new technologies, scientific discoveries, the abandonment of traditional beliefs, and the influence of non-Western cultures. Like writers of the period, visual artists pushed the boundaries of aesthetics, moving far from the conventional tastes of average men and women.

Pablo Picasso followed his particular genius as it led him further into cubist variations and inventions. A group known as "expressionists," argued that color and line express inherent psychological qualities all by themselves, and so a painting need not have a representational subject at all. The Russian Wassily Kandinsky carried this position to its logical conclusion by calling his untitled paintings "improvisations" and insisting that they meant nothing. A second group of expressionists rejected these intellectual experiments in favor of what they called "objectivity," by which they meant a candid appraisal of the state of humanity. They were frequent attackers of the greed and decadence of postwar Europe. Chief among this group was the German George Grosz, whose cruel, satiric line has been likened to a "razor lancing a carbuncle." His scathing cartoon-like images became the most popular portraits of the despised Weimar government.

Another school rebelled against the very idea of aesthetic principle. Principles were based on reason, their argument went, and the world had proved beyond all doubt—by fighting itself to death—that reason did not exist. Calling themselves dadaists (allegedly after a name picked at random from the dictionary), these artists were led by the Frenchman Marcel Duchamp, the German Max Ernst, and the Alsatian Jean (Hans) Arp. Rejecting all formal artistic conventions, dadaists concocted haphazard "fabrications" from cutouts and juxtapositions of wood, glass, and metal, and gave them bizarre names, for example, *The Bride Stripped Bare by her Bachelors, Even* (Duchamp). The artists claimed their works were meaningless and playful, but critics thought otherwise, seeing them instead as expressions of the subconscious. Dadaism influenced surrealist artists such as the Italian Giorgio de Chirico and the Spaniard Salvador Dali, who explored the interior of the mind and produced irrational, fantastic, and generally melancholy paintings. Dadaism also took on political undertones, especially in Germany, by offering a nihilistic social critique that bordered on anarchism. Extending their attacks

on rationalism to theater and print, these artists challenged the very basis of national culture.

Some artists responded to the sense of international crisis much as writers did. During the thirties, their paintings expressed pain and outrage directly to a mass audience. The most important members of this new movement were the Mexican muralists Diego Rivera and José Clemente Orozco, and the Americans Thomas Hart Benton and Reginald Marsh. These men sought to depict the social conditions of the modern world, presenting in graphic detail the hopes and struggles of ordinary people. Though they broke with the conventions of the past, there was nothing unintelligible about their work. It was art intended for everyone. Much of it bore the sting of social satire. Orozco, in particular, delighted in pillorying the hypocrisy of the church and the greed and cruelty of plutocrats and plunderers.

Architects, too, rejected sentimentality and tradition. Between 1880 and 1890 designers in Europe and America announced that the prevailing architectural styles were out of harmony with the needs of modern civilization. Modern architects pioneered a style known as "functionalism"; this group included Otto Wagner in Austria, Charles Édouard Jeanneret (known as Le Corbusier) in France, and Louis Sullivan and Frank Lloyd Wright in the United States. The basic principle of functionalism was that the appearance of a building should proclaim its actual use and purpose. "Form ever follows function" was Sullivan's maxim. Ornamentation was designed to reflect an age of science and machines. A leading European practitioner of functionalism was the German Walter Gropius, who in

Architectural Style in Germany between the Wars. The Bauhaus, by Walter Gropius (1883–1969). This school in Dessau, Germany, is a starkly functional prototype of the interwar "international style."

1919 established a school—the Bauhaus—in Dessau to serve as a center for the theory and practice of modern architecture. Gropius and his followers declared that their style of design, which in time came to be called "international," was the only one that permitted an honest application of new materials—chromium, glass, steel, and concrete.

INTERWAR SCIENTIFIC DEVELOPMENTS

One powerful influence on the artists and intellectuals of the day was neither social nor political, but scientific. The pioneering work of the German physicist Albert Einstein revolutionized not only the entire structure of physical science, it also challenged ordinary people's most basic beliefs about the universe. Quickly recognized as one of the greatest intellects of all time, Einstein began to question the very foundations of traditional physics early in the twentieth century. By 1915, he had proposed entirely new ways of thinking about space, matter, time, and gravity. His most famous theory, the principle of relativity, states that space and motion are relative to each other instead of being absolute. To the familiar three dimensions, Einstein added a fourth—time—and represented all four as fused in the space-time continuum. This meant that mass depends on motion, so that bodies in motion (especially at very high velocities) have a different shape and mass than they would at rest.

Einstein's theories paved the way for another revolutionary development in physics—the splitting of the atom. As early as 1905 Einstein became convinced of the equivalence of mass and energy and worked out a formula for the conversion of one into the other. Expressed as $E = mc^2$, the equation states that the amount of energy locked within the atom is equal to the mass multiplied by the square of the velocity of light. The formula had no practical application for years. Then in 1932, when the Englishman Sir James Chadwick discovered the neutron, which carries no electric charge, scientists had an ideal weapon for bombarding the atom—that is, a way to split it. In 1939 two German physicists, Otto Hahn and Fritz Strassman, successfully split atoms of uranium by bombarding them with neutrons. The initial reaction produced a chain of reactions: each atom that was split shot off more neutrons, which split even more atoms. Scientists in Germany, Great Britain, and the United States were spurred on by governments anxious to turn these dis-coveries into weapons during the Second World War. American scientists soon prepared an atomic bomb, the most destructive weapon ever created. The legacy was ironic for Einstein, a man who devoted much of his life to promoting pacifism, liberalism, and social justice.

Another important contribution to physics that quickly entered popular culture was the "uncertainty principle" posited by the German physicist Werner Heisenberg in 1927. Heisenberg, who was strongly influenced by Einstein, showed that it is impossible—even in theory—to measure both the position and the speed of an object at the same time. The theory was of consequence only when dealing with atoms or subatomic particles, because of the interconnected nature of waves and particles on such a small scale. Though the public had little to no understanding of these ground-breaking scientific concepts, metaphorical invocations of "relativity" and the "uncertainty principle" fitted the ambiguities of the modern world. For many people, nothing was definite, everything was changing—and science seemed to be proving it.

MASS CULTURE AND ITS POSSIBILITIES

Cultural change, however, extended far beyond circles of artistic and intellectual elites. The explosive rise of mass media in the interwar years transformed popular culture and the lives of ordinary people. New mass media—especially radio and films—reached audiences of unprecedented size. Political life incorporated many of these new media, setting off worries that the common people, increasingly referred to as the "masses," could be manipulated by demagogues and propaganda. In 1918, mass politics was rapidly becoming a fact of life: that meant nearly universal suffrage (varying by country), well-organized political parties reaching out to voters, and in general, more participation in political life. Mass politics was accompanied by the rise of mass culture: books, newspapers, films, and fashions were produced in large numbers and standardized formats, which were less expensive and more accessible, appealing not only to more, but to more kinds of people. Older forms of "popular culture" were often local and class specific; mass culture, at least in principle, cut across lines of class and ethnicity, and even nationality. The term, however, can easily become misleading. The world of culture did not suddenly become homogenous. No more than half the

> Older forms of "popular culture" were often local and class specific; mass culture, at least in principle, cut across lines of class and ethnicity, and even nationality.

population read newspapers regularly. Not everyone listened to the radio, and those who did certainly did not believe everything they heard. The pace of cultural change, however, did quicken perceptibly. And in the interwar years, mass culture showed that it held both democratic and authoritarian potential.

The expansion of mass culture rested on widespread applications of existing technologies. Wireless communication, for instance, was invented before the turn of the century, and saw limited use in the First World War. With major financial investment in the 1920s, though, the radio industry boomed. Three out of four British families had a radio by the end of the 1930s, and in Germany, the ratio was even higher. In every European country, broadcasting rights were controlled by the government; in the United States, radio was managed by corporations. The radio broadcast soon became the national soapbox for politicians, and it played no small role in creating new kinds of political language. President Franklin Roosevelt's reassuring "fireside chats" took advantage of the way that radio bridged the public world of politics with the private world of the home. Hitler cultivated a different kind of radio personality, barking his fierce invectives; he made some fifty addresses in 1933 alone. In Germany, Nazi propagandists beamed their messages into homes or blared them through loudspeakers in town squares, constant and repetitive. Broadcasting created new rituals of political life—and new means of communication and persuasion.

So did advertising. Advertising was not new, but it was newly prominent. Businesses spent vastly more on advertising than they had before. Hard-hitting visual images replaced older ads that simply announced products, prices, and brand names. Many observers considered advertising the most "modern" of art forms. Why? It was efficient communication, streamlined and standardized, producing images that would appeal to all. It was scientific, drawing on modern psychology; advertising agencies claimed to have a science of selling to people. In a world remade by mass politics, and at a moment when the purchasing power of the common people was beginning to rise, however slowly, the high stakes in advertising (as in much of mass culture) were apparent to many.

The most dramatic changes came on movie screens. The technology of moving pictures came earlier; the 1890s were the era of nickelodeons and short action pictures. And in that period, France and Italy had strong film industries. Further popularized by news shorts during the war, film boomed in the war's after-

math. When sound was added to movies in 1927, costs soared, competition intensified, and audiences grew rapidly. By the 1930s, an estimated 40 percent of British adults went to the movies once a week, a strikingly high figure. Many went more often than that. The United States' film industry gained a competitive edge in Europe, buoyed by the size of its home market, by huge investments in equipment and distribution, by aggressive marketing, and by Hollywood's star system of long-term contracts with well-known actors who, in a sense, standardized the product and guaranteed a film's success.

Germany, too, was home to a particularly talented group of directors, writers, and actors, and to a major production company, UFA (Universum Film AG), which ran the largest and best-equipped studios in Europe. The UFA's history paralleled the country's: it was run by the government during World War I, devastated by the economic crisis of the early twenties, rescued by wealthy German nationalists in the late twenties, and finally taken over by the Nazis. During the Weimar years, UFA produced some of the most remarkable films of the period, including *Der letzte mann* ("*The Last Man*," released as *The Last Laugh* in English), a universally acclaimed film directed by F. W. Murnau, one of the two great masters of German expressionism. Fritz Lang was the other, directing such masterpieces

Scene from *Metropolis*, 1926. In German expressionist-director Fritz Lang's science fiction film, the worker girl Maria attempts to calm the workers of a modernistic city, but a mad scientist creates an evil robot of her to stir up revolt.

CINEMA: FRITZ LANG ON THE FUTURE OF THE FEATURE FILM IN GERMANY, 1926

Fritz Lang (1890–1976) came from Austria to Berlin after World War I and became one of the German Weimar Republic's most brilliant movie directors, best known for Metropolis (1926) *and* M (1931). *In this essay, Lang reflects on the technological, artistic, and human potential of film. Like all European filmmakers he was fascinated by American movies. In 1932 Joseph Goebbels (see p. 915), dazzled by Lang's work, asked him to work on movies for the Nazis. Lang immediately left Germany for Paris, and from there for the United States, where he continued to make films in Hollywood.*

There has perhaps never before been a time so determined as ours in its search for new forms of expression. Fundamental revolutions in painting, sculpture, architecture, and music speak eloquently of the fact that people of today are seeking and finding their own means of lending artistic form to their sentiments. . . .

The speed with which film has developed in the last five years makes all predictions about it appear dangerous, for it will probably exceed each one by leaps and bounds. Film knows no rest. What was invented yesterday is already obsolete today. This uninterrupted drive for new modes of expression, this intellectual experimentation, along with the joy Germans characteristically take in overexertion, appear to me to fortify my contention that film as art will first find its form in Germany. . . .

Germany has never had, and never will have, the gigantic human and financial reserves of the American film industry at its disposal. To its good fortune. For that is exactly what forces us to compensate a purely material imbalance through an intellectual superiority. . . .

The first important gift for which we have film to thank was in a certain sense *the rediscovery of the human face.* Film has revealed to us the human face with unexampled clarity in its tragic as well as grotesque, threatening as well as blessed expression.

The second gift is that of visual empathy: in the purest sense the expressionistic representation of thought processes. No longer will we take part purely externally in the workings of the soul of the characters in film. We will no longer limit ourselves to seeing the effects of feelings, but will experience them in our own souls, from the instant of their inception on, from the first flash of a thought through to the logical last conclusion of the idea. . . .

The internationalism of filmic language will become the strongest instrument available for the mutual understanding of peoples, who otherwise have such difficulty understanding each other in all too many languages. To bestow upon film the double gift of ideas and soul is the task that lies before us. . . .

Anton Kaes, Matin Jay, and Edward Dimendberg, *The Weimar Republic Sourcebook* (Los Angeles: University of California Press, 1994), pp. 622–23.

as the science-fiction film *Metropolis* (1926) and his most famous German film, *M* (1931). After Hitler's rise to power, the Nazis took control of UFA, placing it under the control of Joseph Goebbels and the Ministry of Propaganda. Though production continued unabated during the Third Reich, many of the industry's most talented members fled from the oppressive regime, ending the golden age of German cinema.

Many found the new mass culture disturbing. As they perceived it, the threat came straight from the United States, which deluged Europe with cultural exports after the war. Hollywood westerns, cheap dime novels, and jazz music—which became increasingly popular in the 1920s—introduced Europe to new ways of life. Advertising, comedies, and romances disseminated new and often disconcerting images of femininity. With bobbed haircuts and short dresses, "new women" seemed assertive, flirtatious, capricious, and materialistic. The "Wild West" genre was popular with teenage boys, much to the dismay of their parents and teachers, who saw westerns as an inappropriate, lower-class form of entertainment. In Europe, the cross-class appeal of American popular culture grated against long-standing social hierarchies. Conservative critics abhorred the fact that "the parson's wife sat nearby his maid at Sunday matinees, equally rapt in the gaze of Hollywood stars." American critics expressed many of the same concerns. Yet the United States enjoyed more social and political stability than Europe. War and revolution had shaken Europe's economies and cultures, and in that context "Americanization" seemed a handy shorthand for economic as well as cultural change. One critic expressed a common concern: "America is the source of that terrible wave of uniformity that gives everyone the same [sic]: the same overalls on the skin, the same book in the hand, the same pen between the fingers, the same conversation on the lips, and the same automobile instead of feet."

Authoritarian governments, in particular, decried these developments as decadent threats to national culture. Fascist, communist, and Nazi governments alike tried to control not only popular culture, but also high culture and modernism, which were typically out of line with the designs of the dictators. Stalin much preferred "socialist realism" to the new Soviet avant garde. Mussolini had a penchant for classical kitsch, though he was far more accepting of modern art than Hitler, who despised its "decadence." Nazism had its own cultural aesthetic, promoting "Aryan" art and architecture and rejecting the modern, "international" style they associated with the "international Jewish conspiracy." Modernism, functionalism, and atonality were banned: the hallmarks of Weimar Germany's cultural preeminence were replaced by a state-sponsored revival of an alleged mystical and heroic past. Walter Gropius's acclaimed experiments in modernist architecture, for example, stood as monuments to everything the Nazis hated. The Bauhaus school was closed in 1933, and Hitler hired Albert Speer as his personal architect, commissioning him to design grandiose neo-classical buildings, including an extravagant plan to re-build the entire city of Berlin.

The Nazis, like other authoritarian governments, used mass media as efficient means of indoctrination and control. Movies became part of the Nazis' pioneering use of "spectacular politics." Media campaigns, mass rallies, parades and ceremonies: all were designed to display the strength and glory of the Reich, and to impress and intimidate spectators. In 1934 Hitler commissioned the filmmaker Leni Riefenstahl to record a political rally staged by herself and Albert Speer in Nuremberg. The film, entitled *Triumph of the Will*, was a visual hymn to the Nordic race and the Nazi regime. Everything in the film was on a huge scale: masses of bodies stood in parade formation, flags rose and fell in unison; the film invited viewers to surrender to the power of grand ritual and symbolism. The comedian Charlie Chaplin riposted in his celebrated lampoon *The Great Dictator* (1940), an enormously successful parody of Nazi pomposities.

The Nazis also tried to eliminate the influences of American popular culture, which even before 1933 had been decried as an example of biological and cultural degeneracy. For instance, critics associated American dances and jazz (which were increasingly popular in German cities) with what the Nazis deemed "racially inferior" blacks and Jews. With culture, however, the Nazis were forced to strike a balance between party propaganda and popular entertainment. The regime allowed many cultural imports, including Hollywood films, to continue, while consciously cultivating German alternatives to American cinema, music, fashions, and even dances. Joseph Goebbels, the minister of propaganda who controlled most film production, placed a high value on economic viability. During the Third Reich, the German film industry turned out comedies, escapist fantasies, and sentimental romances. It developed its own star system and tried to keep audiences happy; meanwhile it became a major competitor internationally. For domestic consumption, the industry also produced vicious anti-Semitic films, such as *The Eternal Jew* (1940) and *Jew Süss* (1940), a fictional tale of a Jewish moneylender who brings the city of Württemberg to ruin in the eighteenth century. In the final scene of the film, the town expels the entire Jewish community from its midst, asking that "posterity honor this law." Goebbels reported that the entire Reich cabinet had viewed the film and considered it "an incredible success."

Chapter
TWENTY-SIX

THE SECOND
WORLD WAR

CONCLUSION

The strains of World War I created a world that few recognized—transformed by revolution, mass mobilization, and loss. In retrospect, it is hard not to see the period that followed as a succession of failures. Capitalism foundered in the Great Depression, democracies collapsed in the face of authoritarianism, and the Treaty of Versailles proved hollow. Yet we better understand the experiences and outlooks of ordinary people if we do not treat the failures of the interwar period as inevitable.

By the late 1920s, many were cautiously optimistic that the Great War's legacy could be overcome and that problems were being solved. The Great Depression (1929–1933) wrecked these hopes, bringing economic chaos and political paralysis. Paralysis and chaos, in turn, created new audiences for political leaders who offered authoritarian solutions and more voters for their political parties. Finally, economic troubles and political turmoil made contending with rising international tensions, to which we now turn, vastly more difficult. By the 1930s, even cautious optimism about international relations had given way to apprehension and dread.

KEY TERMS

Bolsheviks
Joseph Stalin
collectivization
"Great Terror"
Benito Mussolini

Weimar Republic
Nazi party
Adolf Hitler
Kristallnacht
Great Depression

New Deal
Albert Einstein
UFA

SELECTED READINGS

Carr, E. H. *The Bolshevik Revolution, 1917–1923.* London and New York, 1950–1953. One of the classics.

Cohen, Stephen F. *Bukharin and the Bolshevik Revolution: A Political Biography, 1888–1938.* New York, 1973.

Conquest, Robert. *The Great Terror: A Reassessment.* New York, 1990.

Crew, David F. *Nazism and German Society, 1933–1945.* New York, 1994. An excellent and accessible collection of essays.

Figes, Orlando. *Peasant Russia, Civil War: The Volga Countryside in Revolution, 1917–1921.* Oxford, 1989.

Friedlander, Saul. *Nazi Germany and the Jews.* New York, 1998. Excellent; the first of a projected two-volume study.

Gay, Peter. *Weimar Culture.* New York, 1968. Concise and elegant overview.

Getty, J. Arch and Oleg V. Naumov. *The Road to Terror: Stalin and the Self-Destruction of the Bolsheviks, 1932–1939.* New Haven, 1999. Combines analysis with many newly discovered documents.

Gilbert, Felix and David C. Large. *The End of the European Era, 1890 to the Present.* New York, 2001.

Goldman, Wendy Z. *Women, the State, and Revolution: Soviet Family Policy and Social Life, 1917–1936.* New York, 1993.

Kershaw, Ian. *Hitler.* 2 vols: *1889–1936 Hubris,* New York, 1999; *1936–1945: Nemesis,* New York, 2001.

———. *The Hitler Myth: Image and Reality in the Third Reich.* New York, 1987.

Klemperer, Victor. *I Will Bear Witness: A Diary of the Nazi Years, 1933–1941.* New York, 1999. *I Will Bear Witness: A Diary of the Nazi Years, 1942–1945.* New York, 2001. Certain to be a classic.

Lewin, Moshe. *The Making of the Soviet System: Essays in the Social History of Interwar Russia.* New York, 1985. One of the best to offer a view from below.

Rentschler, Eric. *The Ministry of Illusion: Nazi Cinema and Its Afterlife.* Cambridge, Mass., 1996. For the more advanced student.

Suny, Ronald Grigor. *The Revenge of the Past: Nationalism, Revolution, and the Collapse of the Soviet Union.* Stanford, Calif., 1993.

Tucker, Robert C. *Stalin as Revolutionary, 1879–1929.* New York, 1973.

———. *Stalin in Power: The Revolution from Above, 1928–1941.* New York, 1990.

IN SEPTEMBER 1939, Europe was consumed by another world war. The Second World War was not simply a continuation of the First. Both were triggered by threats to the European balance of power. Yet even more than the Great War, the Second World War was a conflict among nations, whole peoples, and fiercely opposing ideals. The methods of warfare in the Second World War had little in common with those of the First. In 1914 military firepower had outmatched mobility, resulting in four years of static, mud-sodden slaughter. In 1939, mobility was joined to firepower on a massive scale. The results were terrifying. On the battlefield, the tactics of high-speed armored warfare (*Blitzkrieg*), aircraft carriers sinking ships far below the horizon, and submarines used in vast numbers to dominate shipping lanes changed the scope and the pace of fighting. This was not a war of trenches and barbed wire but a war of motion, dramatic conquests, and terrible destructive power. The devastation of 1914–1918 paled in comparison to this new, global conflict.

The other great change involved not tactics, but targets. Much of the unprecedented killing power now available was aimed directly at civilians. Cities were laid waste by artillery and aerial bombing. Whole regions were put to the torch, while towns and villages were systematically cordoned off and leveled. Whole populations were targeted as well, in ways that continue to appall. The Nazi regime's systematic murder of gypsies, homosexuals, and other "deviants," along with the effort to exterminate the Jewish people completely, made the Second World War a horrifyingly unique event. So did the United States' use of a weapon whose existence would dominate politics and society for the next fifty years: the atomic bomb. The naive enthusiasm that had marked the outbreak of the Great War was absent from the start. Terrible memories of the first conflict lingered. Yet those who fought against the Axis Powers (and many of those who fought for them) found that their determination to fight and win grew as the war went on. Unlike the seemingly meaningless killing of the Great War, the Second World War was cast as a war of absolutes, of good and evil, of national and global survival. Nevertheless the scale of destruction brought with it a profound weariness. It also provoked deep-seated questions about the value of Western "civilization" and the terms on which it, and the rest of the world, might live peaceably in the future.

The Causes of the War: Unsettled Quarrels, Economic Fallout, and Nationalism

What were the long-term causes of World War II?

The causes of the Second World War were rooted in the peace settlement of 1919–1920. The peace had created as many problems as it had solved. The senior Allied heads of state yielded to demands that involved annexing German territory and creating satellite states out of the eastern European empires. In doing so, the peacemakers created fresh bitterness and conflict. The Versailles treaty and its champions, such as President Woodrow Wilson, proclaimed the principle of self-determination for the peoples of eastern and southern Europe. Yet the new states created by the treaty crossed ethnic boundaries, involved political compromises, and frustrated many of the expectations they had raised. The unsteady new boundaries would be redrawn by force in the 1930s. The Allied powers also kept up the naval blockade against Germany after the end of the fighting. This forced the new German government to accept harsh terms that deprived Germany of its political power in Europe, and saddled the German economy with the bill for the conflict in a "war guilt" clause. The blockade and its consequences created grievances that many angry, humiliated Germans considered legitimate.

Power politics persisted after the peace conference, just as it did in the treaties. Although Woodrow Wilson and other sponsors of the League of Nations acclaimed the League as a means to eliminate power struggles, it

did nothing of the sort. The signatures on the peace treaties were hardly dry when the victors began carving out new alliances to maintain their supremacy, interfering in the new central European states and the "mandate" territories added to the British and French empires in the Middle East. Even the League itself was fundamentally an alliance of the victors against the vanquished. Not surprisingly, politicians feared international relations would be undermined by this imbalance of power.

A second cause of World War II was the failure to create lasting, binding standards for peace and security. Diplomats spent the ten years after Versailles trying to restore such standards. Some put their faith in the legal and moral authority of the League. Others saw disarmament as the most promising means of guaranteeing peace. Throughout the 1920s, a number of important European statesmen—the German and French foreign ministers Gustav Stresemann and Aristide Briand, and the British prime ministers Stanley Baldwin and Ramsay MacDonald—tried to reach a set of agreements that would stabilize the peace and prevent rearmament. In 1925 an effort was made to secure the frontiers on the Rhine established at Versailles. In 1928, the Kellogg-Briand Pact attempted to make war an international crime. Despite the good faith of many of the statesmen involved, none of these pacts carried any real weight. Each nation tried to include special provisions and exceptions for "vital interests" and these efforts compromised the treaties from the start. Had the League of Nations been better organized, it might have relieved some of the tensions or at least prevented clashes between nations. But the League was never a league of all nations. Essential members were absent, since Germany and the Soviet Union were excluded for most of the interwar period, and the United States never joined.

Economic conditions were a third important cause of renewed conflict. The huge reparations imposed on the Germans and France's occupation of much of Germany's industrial heartland helped slow Germany's recovery. German and French stubbornness about the pace of repayments combined disastrously to bring on the German inflation of the early 1920s. The spiraling inflation made German money nearly worthless, damaging the stability and credibility of Germany's young republic almost beyond repair.

The depression of the 1930s contributed to the coming of the war in several ways. It intensified economic nationalism. Baffled by problems of unemployment and business stagnation, governments imposed high tariffs in an effort to preserve the home market for their own producers. The collapse of investment and terrible domestic unemployment caused the United States to withdraw even further from world affairs. Although France suffered less than some other countries, the depression still inflamed tensions between management and labor. This conflict exacerbated political battles between left and right, making it difficult for either side to govern France. Britain turned to its empire, raising tariffs for the first time and guarding its financial investments jealously.

These inward-looking policies among the Allies left the door open to more aggressive tactics elsewhere. In Germany, the depression was the last blow to the Weimar Republic. In 1933 power passed to the Nazis, who promised a total program of national renewal. In the fascist states (and, exceptionally, the United States) public works projects of one kind or another were prescribed as an answer to mass unemployment. This produced highways, bridges, and railroads; it also produced a new arms race.

Despite the misgivings of many inside the governments of Britain and France, Germany was allowed to ignore the terms of the peace treaties and rearm. Armaments expansion on a large scale first began in Germany in 1935, with the result that unemployment was reduced and the effects of the depression eased. Other nations followed the German example, not simply as a way to boost their economies but in response to growing Nazi military power. In the Pacific, the decline of Japanese exports meant that the nation did not have enough foreign currency to pay for vital raw materials from overseas. This played into the hands of Japan's military regime. Japanese national ambitions, and Japanese leaders' perception of the political and cultural inferiority of the Chinese, led Japan to fresh imperial adventures in the name of establishing economic stability in East Asia. They began in 1931 with the invasion of Manchuria, and moved from there to create a "Greater Pacific Co-Prosperity Sphere" that involved seizing other territories as Japanese colonies. Raw materials could then be bought with Japanese money, and more of Asia would serve the needs of Japan's empire.

Imperial success could serve as consolation when economic methods failed. As the depression dragged on in fascist Italy, Mussolini tried to distract his public with national conquests overseas, culminating in the invasion of Ethiopia in 1935.

In sum, the tremendous economic hardship of the depression, a contested peace treaty, and political weakness undermined international stability. But the decisive factor in the crises of the 1930s, and the trigger for an-

other world war, lay in a blend of violent nationalism and modern ideologies that glorified the nation and national destiny. This blend, particularly in the forms of fascism and militarism, appeared around the world in many countries. By the middle of the 1930s, recognizing common interests, fascist Italy and Nazi Germany formed an "Axis," an alliance binding their goals of national glory and international power. They were later joined by Japan's military regime. In Spain, the ultranationalist forces that tried to overthrow the Spanish Republic, setting off the Spanish Civil War (see below), believed they were reviving the stability, authority, and morality of the nation. Fascist or semi-fascist regimes spread in Eastern Europe, in Yugoslavia, Hungary, and Romania. One exception to this sobering trend toward authoritarianism was Czechoslovakia. Czechoslovakia boasted no ethnic majority. Although the Czechs practiced an enlightened policy of minority self-government, and though their government was remarkably stable, questions of nationality remained a potential source of friction. Those questions became a key factor as international tensions mounted in the late 1930s.

THE 1930S: CHALLENGES TO THE PEACE, APPEASEMENT, AND THE "DISHONEST DECADE"

What was the policy of "appeasement"?

The 1930s brought the tensions and failures caused by the treaties of 1919–1920 to a head. Fascist and nationalist governments flouted the League of Nations by launching new conquests and efforts at national expansion. With the memories of 1914–1918 still fresh, these new crises created an atmosphere of deepening fear and apprehension. Each new conflict seemed to warn that another, much wider war would follow unless it could somehow be averted. Ordinary people, particularly in Britain, France, and the United States, were divided. Some saw the actions of the aggressors as a direct challenge to civilization, one that had to be met with force if necessary. Others hoped to avoid premature or unnecessary conflict. Their governments tried instead at several points to negotiate with the fascists and keep a tenuous peace. Writers, intellectuals, and politicians on the left vilified these acts of "appeasement." The 1930s were not just a time of renewed warfare and global crisis; many saw the period as a series of missed opportunities to prevent the larger war to come. In 1939, on the first day of the Second World War, the British poet and leftist W. H. Auden condemned the behavior of Western governments, calling the 1930s "a low, dishonest decade."

The object of Auden's venom was the policy of "appeasement" pursued by Western governments in the face of German, Italian, and Japanese aggression. Appeasement was neither simple power politics nor pure cowardice. It was grounded in three deeply held assumptions. The first assumption was that the outbreak of another war was unthinkable. With the memory of the slaughter of 1914–1918 fresh in their minds, many in the West embraced pacifism, or at any rate adopted an attitude that kept them from facing up to the uncompromising aggression of the fascist governments, especially Nazi Germany. Second, many in Britain and the United States argued that Germany had been mistreated by the Versailles treaty and harbored legitimate grievances that should be acknowledged and resolved. Finally, many appeasers were staunch anticommunists. They believed that the fascist states in Germany and Italy were an essential bulwark against the advance of Soviet communism, and that division among the major European states only played into the hands of the USSR. Yet this last point divided the appeasers. All were concerned with maintaining Europe's balance of power. One group, however, believed that the Soviets posed the greater threat, and that accommodating Hitler might create a common interest against a common enemy. The other faction believed that Nazi Germany presented the true threat to European stability; nevertheless, they believed, Hitler would have to be placated until Britain and France finished rearming. At that point, they hoped, their greater military power would deter Hitler or Mussolini from risking a general European war. It took most of the 1930s for the debate between appeasers to come to a head. In the meanwhile, the League of Nations faced more immediate and pressing challenges.

The 1930s brought three crucial tests for the League: crises in China, Ethiopia, and Spain. In China,

> With the memory of the slaughter of 1914–1918 fresh in their minds, many in the West embraced pacifism, or at any rate adopted an attitude that kept them from facing up to the uncompromising aggression of the fascist governments, especially Nazi Germany.

the Japanese invasion of Manchuria in 1931 turned into an invasion of the whole country. Chinese forces were driven before the Japanese advance, and the Japanese deliberately targeted civilians in order to break the Chinese will to fight. In 1937, the Japanese laid siege to the strategic city of Nanjing. Their orders on taking the city were simple: "kill all, burn all, destroy all." More than two hundred thousand Chinese citizens were slaughtered in what came to be known as the "Rape of Nanjing." The League voiced shock and disapproval but did nothing. In 1935 Mussolini began his efforts to make the Mediterranean an Italian empire by returning to Ethiopia to avenge the defeat of 1896. This time the Italians came with tanks, bombers, and poison gas. The Ethiopians fought bravely but hopelessly, and this imperial massacre aroused world opinion. The League attempted to impose sanctions on Italy and condemned Japan. But for two reasons, no enforcement followed. The first was British and French fear of communism, and their hope that Italy and Japan would act as counterweights to the Soviets. The second reason was practical. Enforcing sanctions would involve challenging Japan's powerful fleet or Mussolini's newly built battleships. Britain and France were unwilling, and dangerously close to unable, to use their navies to those ends.

THE SPANISH CIVIL WAR

The third challenge came closer to home. In 1936 civil war broke out in Spain. A series of weak republican governments, committed to large-scale social reforms, could not overcome opposition to those measures and political polarization. War broke out as extreme right-wing military officers rebelled. Although Hitler and Mussolini had signed a pact of nonintervention with the other Western powers, both leaders sent troops and equipment to assist the rebel commander, Francisco Franco (1939–1975). The Soviet Union countered with aid to communist troops serving under the banner of the Spanish Republic. Again, Britain and France failed to act decisively. Thousands of volunteers from England, France, and the United States, including many working-class socialists and writers such as George Orwell and Ernest Hemingway, took up arms as private soldiers for the Republican government. They saw the war as a test of the West's determination to resist fascism and military dictatorships. Their gov-

← Main Nationalist attacks	Nationalist, October 1937
← Main Republican attacks	Nationalist, July 1938
■ "International Brigade" bases	Nationalist, February 1939
Nationalist, July 1936	Republican, February 1939

THE SPANISH CIVIL WAR

Why did thousands of foreign fighters join the war?
How did the strategies and weapons used in the war
anticipate those used in World War II? What were
the consequences of Franco's victory?

each brought in their newest weapons and practiced
their skills in destroying civilian targets from the air. In
April 1937, a raid by German dive bombers utterly destroyed the town of Guernica in northern Spain, in an
effort to cut off Republican supply lines and terrorize
civilians. It shocked public opinion, and was commemorated by Pablo Picasso in one of the most famous
paintings of the twentieth century. Both sides committed atrocities. The Spanish Civil War lasted three years,
ending with a complete victory for Franco in 1939. In
the aftermath, Britain and France proved extremely reluctant to admit Spanish Republicans as refugees, even
though Republicans faced recriminations from Franco's
regime. Franco sent one million of his Republican
enemies to prison or concentration camps. Hitler drew
two lessons from Spain. The first was that if Britain,
France, and the Soviet Union ever tried to contain fascism, they would have a hard time coordinating their
efforts. The second was that Britain and France were
deeply averse to fighting another European war. This
meant that the Nazis could use every means short of
war to achieve their goals.

GERMAN REARMAMENT AND THE POLITICS OF APPEASEMENT

Hitler took advantage of this combination of international tolerance and war weariness to advance his
ambitions. As Germany rearmed, Hitler played on
Germans' sense of shame and betrayal, proclaiming
their right to regain their former power in the world.
In 1933, he removed Germany from the League of
Nations, to which it had finally been admitted in 1926.
In 1935 he defied the disarmament provisions of the
Treaty of Versailles, and revived conscription and universal military training. Hitler's stated goals were the
restoration of Germany's power and dignity inside
Europe, and the unification of all ethnic Germans inside his "Third German Reich." As the first step in this
process, Germany reoccupied the Rhineland in 1936.
It was a risky move, chancing war with the much more
powerful French army. But France and Britain did not
mount a military response. In retrospect, this was an
important turning point; the balance of power tipped
in Germany's favor. While the Rhineland remained
demilitarized and German industry in the Ruhr valley
was unprotected, France held the upper hand. After
1936, it no longer did so.

In March of 1938, Hitler annexed Austria, reaffirm-
ing his intention to bring all Germans into his Reich.
Once more, no official reaction came from the West.

ernments were much more hesitant. For the British,
Franco was anticommunist at least, just like Mussolini
and the Japanese. The French prime minister Léon
Blum, a committed antifascist, stood at the head of a
Popular Front government—an alliance of socialists,
communists, and republicans. The Popular Front had
been elected on a program of social reform and opposition to Hitler abroad and fascism in France. Yet Blum's
margin of support was limited. He feared that intervening in Spain would further polarize his country, bring
down his government, and make it impossible to follow
through on any commitment to the conflict. In Spain,
despite some heroic fighting, the Republican camp degenerated into a hornet's nest of competing factions:
republican, socialist, communist, and anarchist.

The Spanish Civil War was brutal. Both the German
and the Soviet "advisors" saw Spain as a "dress re-
hearsal" for a later war between the two powers. They

Guernica (1937), by Pablo Picasso. One of Picasso's most influential paintings, *Guernica* was painted as a mural for the Spanish republican government as it fought for survival in the Spanish Civil War. The Basque town of Guernica had been bombed by German fighters just a few months earlier, in April 1937. Near the center a horse writhes in agony; to the left a distraught woman holds her dead child.

The Nazis' next target was the Sudetenland in Czechoslovakia, which had a large ethnic German population. With Austria now a part of Germany, Czechoslovakia was almost entirely surrounded by its hostile neighbor. Hitler declared that the Sudetenland was a natural part of the Reich and that he intended to occupy it. The Czechs did not want to give way. Hitler's generals were wary of this gamble. Czechoslovakia had a strong, well-equipped army and a line of fortifications along the border. Many in the French and Polish governments were willing to come to the Czechs' aid. According to plans already being laid for a wider European war, Germany would not be ready for another three to four years. But Hitler did gamble, and the British prime minister, Neville Chamberlain, obliged him. Chamberlain decided to take charge of international talks about the Sudetenland, on Hitler's terms. Chamberlain's logic was that this dispute was about the balance of power in Europe. If Hitler were allowed to unify all Germans in one state, he reasoned, then German ambitions would be satisfied. Chamberlain also believed that his country could not commit to a sustained war. Finally, defending eastern European boundaries against Germany ranked low on Great Britain's list of priorities, at least in comparison to ensuring free trade in western Europe and protecting the strategic centers of the British empire.

On September 29, 1938, Hitler met with Chamberlain, Premier Édouard Daladier (1938–1940) of France,

and Mussolini in a four-power conference in Munich. The result was another capitulation by France and Britain. The four negotiators bargained away a major slice of Czechoslovakia, while Czech representatives were left to await their fate outside the conference room. Chamberlain returned to London proclaiming "peace in our time." Hitler soon proved that boast hollow. In March 1939 Germany invaded what was left of Czechoslovakia and established a puppet regime in its

CHRONOLOGY

THE ROAD TO WORLD WAR II, 1931–1940

Japanese invasion of Manchuria	1931
Germany leaves the League of Nations	1933
Germany begins remilitarization	March 1935
Spanish Civil War	April 1936–April 1939
Germany reoccupies the Rhineland	March 1936
Germany annexes Austria	March 1938
Munich Conference	September 1938
Nazi-Soviet Pact	August 1939
Germany invades Poland	September 1939
Germany invades the Low Countries and France	May 1940

WHAT ACCOUNTS FOR THE EARLY GERMAN SUCCESSES IN WORLD WAR II?

THE OUTBREAK OF HOSTILITIES AND THE FALL OF FRANCE   937

The Munich Conference, 1938. Prime Minister Chamberlain of Britain and Hitler during the Munich conference.

THE OUTBREAK OF HOSTILITIES AND THE FALL OF FRANCE

What accounts for the early German successes in World War II?

After his success in Czechoslovakia, Hitler demanded the abolition of the Polish Corridor. This was a narrow strip of land connecting Poland with the Baltic Sea. The corridor also divided East Prussia from the rest of Germany, separating yet another large German population from union with the Reich. Judging Britain and France by past performance, Hitler believed their pledges to Poland were worthless. With the Soviets now in his camp, he expected that Poland would consent and the Western allies would back down again. When Poland stood firm instead, Hitler attacked. On September 1, 1939, German troops crossed the Polish border. Britain and France sent a joint warning to Germany to withdraw. There was no reply. On September 3, Britain and France declared war.

The conquest of Poland was shockingly quick. It demanded great resources—Germany committed nearly all of its combat troops and planes to the invasion—but the results were remarkable. Well-coordinated attacks by German panzers (tanks) and armored vehicles, supported by devastating air power, cut the large but slow-moving Polish army to pieces. German infantry still moved on foot or via horse-drawn transport, but their disciplined advance followed the devastating work of the panzers. The Poles fought doggedly, but were so stunned and disorganized that they had little hope of mounting an effective defense. The "lightning war" (*Blitzkrieg*) for which the German officer corps had trained so long was a complete success. Within three weeks German troops were laying siege to Warsaw. German terror bombing, designed to destroy the heart of Warsaw from the air and frighten the population into surrender, was successful. Poland, a large country with a large army, was dismembered in four weeks.

In accordance with its agreement with Nazi Germany, the Soviet Union also invaded Poland from the east, taking their share of Polish territory, and using Stalin's signature methods to deal with the enemy: rounding up millions to be deported, imprisoned, or executed. Wary that German aggression would turn on them, the Soviets also hastened to shore up their position to the

capital, Prague. This was Germany's first conquest of non-German territory, and it sent shock waves across Europe. It convinced public and political opinion outside Germany of the futility of appeasement. Chamberlain was forced to shift his policies completely. British and French rearmament sped up dramatically. Together with France, Britain guaranteed the sovereignty of the two states now directly in Hitler's path, Poland and Romania.

Meanwhile, the politics of appeasement had fueled Stalin's fears that the Western democracies might strike a deal with Germany at Soviet expense, thus diverting Nazi expansion eastward. The Soviet Union had not been invited to the Munich conference, and, suspicious that Britain and France were unreliable allies, Stalin became convinced that he should look elsewhere for security. Tempted by the traditional Soviet desire for territory in Poland, Stalin was promised a share of Poland, Finland, the Baltic states, and Bessarabia by Hitler's representatives. In a cynical reversal of their anti-Nazi proclamations, the Soviets signed a nonaggression pact with the Nazis in August 1939. By going to Munich, Britain and France had put their interests first; the Soviet Union would now look after its own.

GERMAN EXPANSION, 1936–1939

What were Hitler's first steps to unify all the ethnic Germans in Europe? How did he use these initial gains to annex territory from the Czechs? What were the official reactions from Britain, France, and the Soviet Union? After winning Czechoslovakia, why did Hitler choose to invade Poland? How were the Germans able to conquer Poland and France so quickly?

WHAT ACCOUNTS FOR THE EARLY GERMAN SUCCESSES IN WORLD WAR II?

THE OUTBREAK OF HOSTILITIES AND THE FALL OF FRANCE   939

north, on the Russo-Finnish border. Since at least 1938 the Soviets had demanded from Finland various arrangements to protect Leningrad, from access to strategic locations and permission to build fortifications in Finland to the outright ceding of territory—all of which the Finns had refused. Shortly after the invasion of Poland, then, the Soviets attacked Finland. Despite the Soviets' overwhelming superiority in numbers and material, the Finns fought back tenaciously. The Soviets faced a very difficult campaign—an alarming demonstration of the damaging effects of Stalin's terror on the Soviet military. Although the USSR concluded the undeclared four-month Winter War with a precarious victory in March of 1940, Hitler and the rest of the world had made note of Stalin's weaknesses.

The the west, after the fall of Poland the conflict became an ominous "phony war" or "sitzkrieg," as it was sometimes called. The fighting in Poland was followed by a winter of anxious nonactivity with occasional headlines about naval skirmishes. In the spring of 1940 that calm was broken by a terrible storm. The Germans struck first in Scandinavia, taking Denmark in a day and invading Norway. Britain and France tried to aid the Norwegian defense and sank a large number of German ships, but the Allied expedition failed. Then the real blow was struck. On May 10, German forces swarmed through Belgium and the Netherlands on their way to France. The two nations were conquered in short order. When the Dutch succeeded in flooding canals that protected their major cities and defended that line with hard-fighting marines, Hitler ordered his air force to bomb the city of Rotterdam. More than eight hundred Dutch civilians died, and the Netherlands surrendered the next day. The Belgians' stubborn and effective defense of their nation was cut short when King Albert suddenly surrendered after two weeks of fighting, fearing similar destruction. In turn Albert stayed on as a figurehead for the Nazis, reviled by Belgians who found other ways to carry on the fight against Germany.

The large French army was carved up by the *Blitzkrieg*. Its divisions were isolated, outflanked, and overwhelmed by German aircraft and armored columns working according to an exacting plan. French units either fought fierce battles until they were hopelessly surrounded, or simply collapsed. French armor and artillery, much of it better built than the German equiv-

> Despite heavy German air attacks, Britain's Royal Navy evacuated more than three hundred thousand British and French troops, with the help of commercial and pleasure boats that had been pressed into emergency service.

alents, were poorly organized and rendered useless in the face of rapid German maneuvers. The defeat turned quickly into a rout. Hundreds of thousands of civilians, each carrying a few precious possessions loaded on carts, fled south. They were joined by thousands of Allied soldiers without weapons, and these columns of refugees were attacked constantly by German dive-bombers. The disorganized British made a desperate retreat to the port of Dunkirk on the English Channel, where many of Britain's best troops were sacrificed holding off the panzers. Despite heavy German air attacks, Britain's Royal Navy evacuated more than three hundred thousand British and French troops, with the help of commercial and pleasure boats that had been pressed into emergency service.

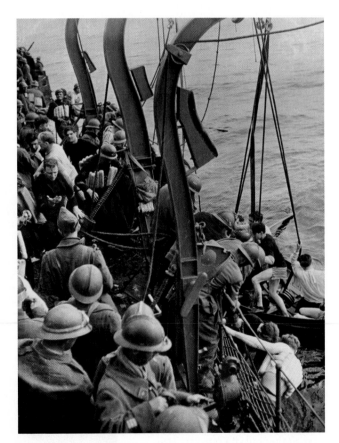

Allied Forces evacuating Dunkirk, France, May and June 1940. In the face of German attacks, refugees and soldiers retreated to the port on the English Channel, frantically seeking to escape from the Continent. Hundreds of thousands of troops were rescued, many in small civilian boats.

After Dunkirk, the conflict was bitter but the outcome inevitable. French reservists fought, as their commanders asked, "to the last cartridge," killing thousands of Germans. Without proper organization and more firepower, however, this bravery was useless. The Germans swept through the northwest and the heart of the country, reaching Paris in mid-June. The political will of France's government collapsed along with its armies. Rather than withdrawing to Britain or French colonies in North Africa, the French surrendered on June 22. The armistice cut France in two. The Germans occupied all of northern France, including Paris and the Channel ports. The south, and French territories in North Africa, lay under the jurisdiction of a deeply conservative government formed at the spa town of Vichy under the leadership of an elderly First World War hero, Marshal Henri Philippe Pétain. France had fallen. One of Germany's historic enemies, the victor of the previous war, an imperial power and nation of almost 60 million citizens, was reduced to chaos and enemy occupation in forty days.

The penalties exacted on France did not end with defeat. Many liberals within France, and most of the "Free French" movement quickly established in London, soon felt they had two enemies to fight: Germany and Pétain's regime. The Vichy government proposed to cooperate with the Germans in return for retaining a small measure of sovereignty. The regime also instituted its own "National Revolution," which came very close to fascism. Vichy repudiated the republic, accusing it of sapping France's strength. The state proceeded to reorganize French life and political institutions, strengthening the authority of the Catholic Church and the family and helping the Germans to crush any resistance. "Work, Family, and Country"—this was Vichy's call to order.

NOT ALONE: THE BATTLE OF BRITAIN AND THE BEGINNINGS OF A GLOBAL WAR

What made World War II a global war?

Before launching an invasion across the Channel, the Nazis attempted to establish superiority in the air. From July 1940 to June 1941, in the Battle of Britain, thousands of planes dropped millions of tons of bombs on British targets: first aircraft and airfields and then, as the focus shifted to breaking Britain's will, civilian targets such as London. More than forty thousand British civilians died. Yet the British stood firm. This was possible in part because of a German mistake. After a daring British bombing raid on Berlin, Hitler angrily told his generals to concentrate on civilian targets. This spared the Royal Air Force, whose bases had been steadily devastated up to that point. Given the chance to keep fighting, the R.A.F. forced a costly stalemate in the air. Hitler scrapped the invasion plans, turning his attention east toward Russia.

Another important reason for the determined British resistance was a change of political leadership. In May

London during the Battle of Britain. German air raids that lasted from August 1940 to June 1941 wrought destruction but did not achieve Hitler's goal of breaking the British. The Holland House Library in London lost its roof, but managed to engage in business as usual.

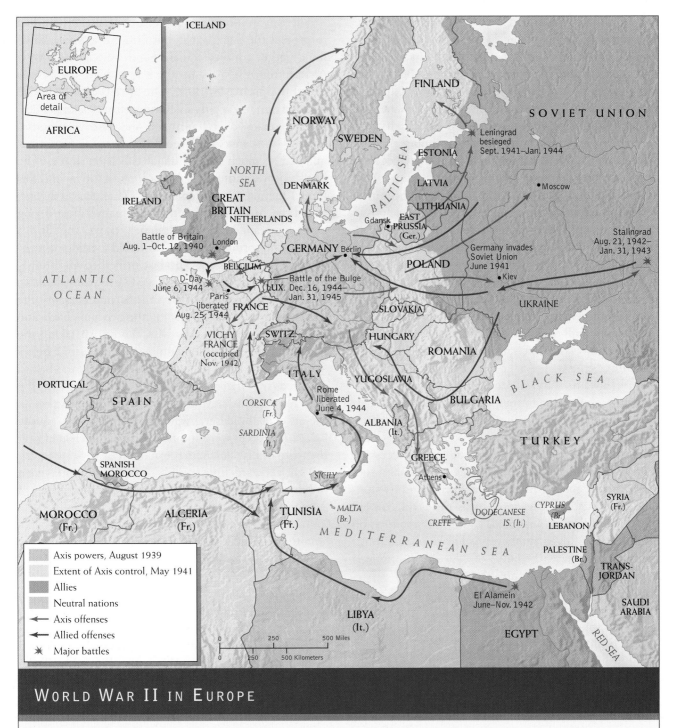

WORLD WAR II IN EUROPE

This map shows the alliance systems and major offensives of the European Theatre in World War II. What explains the rapid expansion of Axis control until May 1941? In what ways did geography both aid and potentially hinder the Axis effort to conquer Europe? How did Adolf Hitler hope to neutralize either the Soviet Union or Great Britain early in the war? How did the sieges at Leningrad and Stalingrad prove instrumental in sustaining the Allied effort?

1940, Chamberlain's catalogue of failures finished his career. He was toppled by a coalition government that brought together Conservative, Liberal, and Labour politicians for the sake of national unity. It was led by

the most unlikely of the choices offered to replace him: Winston Churchill (1940–1945, 1951–1955). Churchill was a political maverick who had changed parties more than once. He was extremely talented, and also arrogant.

He had a sharp temper and sometimes seemed unstable, and before 1939 his political career was judged to be over. As prime minister he was not much of an administrator, constantly proposing wild schemes, but he had two genuine gifts. The first was language. Churchill spoke extraordinary words of courage and defiance just when the British public wanted and needed to hear them. He was utterly committed to winning the war. The second was personal diplomacy. He convinced the American president Franklin Roosevelt (1933–1945), who supported the Allies, to break with American neutrality and send massive amounts of aid and weapons to Britain free of charge, under a program called Lend-Lease. Churchill also allowed the new government coalition to work to best effect. The ablest Conservative ministers stayed, but Labour politicians were also allowed to take positions of genuine power. Most of the Labour representatives turned out to be excellent administrators and were directly in touch with Britain's huge working class, which now felt fully included in the war effort.

With Britain's survival, the European war quickly became a global war in four ways. The first was Germany's submarine campaign to starve out the British. The second came with fighting in North Africa, which threatened the Suez Canal and the Allies' access to Middle Eastern oil. The third came with Japan's successful attack on the Allies in the Pacific and its stunning early success. The fourth was the great conflict Hitler had always imagined, a war of annihilation against Soviet Russia and Europe's Jewish population.

The first of these, the battle of the Atlantic, was a dire threat to the Allies. Learning from World War I, the Germans sent hundreds of submarines (U-boats) out in "wolf packs" to stalk the major sea lanes to Britain. German submarines sank millions of tons of merchant shipping, as far away as the coasts of Brazil and Florida. Britain's supplies of weapons, raw materials, and food hung in the balance. The British devoted a huge naval effort and great technical resourcefulness to saving their convoys. They developed modern sonar and new systems of aerial reconnaissance, and cracked the Germans' codes for communicating with the "wolf packs." These efforts kept supplies coming. When the United States entered the war, the British supplied the experience and technology and the Americans the numbers and firepower to sink many more U-boats. By late 1942 the threat receded.

The war in North Africa began because Britain had to protect the Suez Canal, but Britain was soon drawn into a larger conflict. Indian, South African, and West African troops fighting for the British drove the Italians from Ethiopia in May, 1941. The Soviets and the British invaded Iran to keep its shah (ruler) from making a deal with Germany over Iranian oil and held the country until 1946. A small, well-led British army in Egypt humiliated a much larger Italian invasion force. The British nearly captured Italy's colony of Libya, and this forced Germany to intervene. An elite armored force called the Afrika Korps, led by Germany's most daring tank commander, Erwin Rommel, drove the British back in the spring of 1941 and started a grudging two-year war in the desert. The British fielded an international army that included as many Australians, Indians, and New Zealanders as it did Britons, pitted against the Germans and Italians. The fighting swung back and forth for eighteen months with the British taking the worst of it. Then the momentum shifted. Despite heavy losses from German planes and submarines, the British defeated the Italian navy and took control of the Mediterranean. They also established domination in the air over the desert. When Rommel tried to invade Egypt, his forces were stopped and badly defeated near the town of El Alamein in the autumn of 1942, then driven back toward Tunisia. The United States intervened in November 1942, landing in the French territories of Algeria and Morocco.

A conference was held at Casablanca, Morocco, among the Allied powers to discuss the future course of the war and the fate of French territories in North Africa. French administrators in Algeria and Morocco, who had supported Vichy, at least in public, surrendered peacefully or joined the Allied side. Rommel still defended Tunisia against the Allies for four months, but a joint offensive broke the German lines in March 1943, ending the fighting.

The war became truly global when Japan struck the American naval base at Pearl Harbor, Hawaii, on the morning of December 7, 1941. The Japanese had been involved in a costly war in China since the 1930s. In order to win and to establish a Japanese empire throughout Asia, they would have to destroy America's Pacific fleet and seize the colonies of the British, Dutch, and French empires. Like Germany, Japan began with lightning blows. The attack on Pearl Harbor was a brilliant act of surprise that devastated the American fleet and shocked the American public. It was not, however, the

The war became truly global when Japan struck the American naval base at Pearl Harbor, Hawaii, on the morning of December 7, 1941.

"A date which will live in infamy," December 7, 1941. The *USS West Virginia* was one of eight battleships sunk during the Japanese surprise attack targeting "Battleship Row" at the American naval base at Pearl Harbor. Two thousand people were killed but most of the American fleet, en route to or from other locations in the Pacific, was spared.

success that the Japanese wanted. Eight U.S. battleships were sunk and more than two thousand lives lost, but much of the American fleet, including its aircraft carriers, submarines, and many smaller ships, were safely at sea on the day of the strike. The unprovoked attack galvanized American public opinion in a way the war in Europe had not. When Germany rashly declared war on the United States as well, America declared itself ready to take on all comers and joined the Allies.

Despite the mixed results at Pearl Harbor the Japanese enjoyed other, stunning successes. For the European colonial powers, Japan's entry into the war was a catastrophe. Japanese troops swept through the British protectorate of Malaya in weeks, sinking the Pacific squadrons of both the British and Dutch navies in the swift attacks. Britain's fortified island port at Singapore, the keystone of British defenses in the Pacific, fell at the end of December 1941. The shock of the loss nearly took Churchill's government with it. Thousands of British and Australian troops were captured and sent off to four years of torture, forced labor, and starvation in Japanese prison camps. The Japanese also invaded the Philippines in December, and while American soldiers and marines held out on the island of Corregidor for some time, they too were forced to surrender. Some took to the hills to fight as guerrillas; the rest were forced on a "Death March" to Japanese labor camps. The Dutch East Indies fell next, and it seemed there would be no stopping Japanese ships and soldiers before they reached Australia.

Reeling from Japan's blows, the Allies finally reorganized during 1942. After taking Singapore, Japanese troops pressed on into Burma. Several famous British generals tried and failed to defend Burma, with disastrous losses of men and matériel. After these failures, command fell to an obscure Indian Army officer, William Slim. For a British officer, Slim had quite humble origins. He was a career soldier, a minor hero in the First World War, and perhaps the best strategist in the British Army. Even more important, the millions of non-white imperial troops from India and Africa who were under his command liked and respected him as an honest, unprejudiced man. He reorganized imperial defenses, and a joint force of British and Indian troops defeated an attempted Japanese invasion of India at the border near the end of 1942. After that, with an army drawn from around the world, Slim began to push the Japanese back. In New Guinea, Australian troops fresh from North Africa were first to defeat the Japanese on land in bitter hand-to-hand fighting, and staged a counterattack through the high mountain jungles. At sea, America's navy benefited from a rapidly increased production schedule that turned out new ships and planes to outnumber the Japanese, and two gifted admirals, Chester Nimitz and William Halsey, who outfought them. In 1942 the United States won crucial victories in the Coral Sea and at Midway, a battle fought at sea, but won and lost by aircraft flown from each side's carriers. American marines landed on the island of Guadalcanal in early 1942 and captured this strategic Japanese base

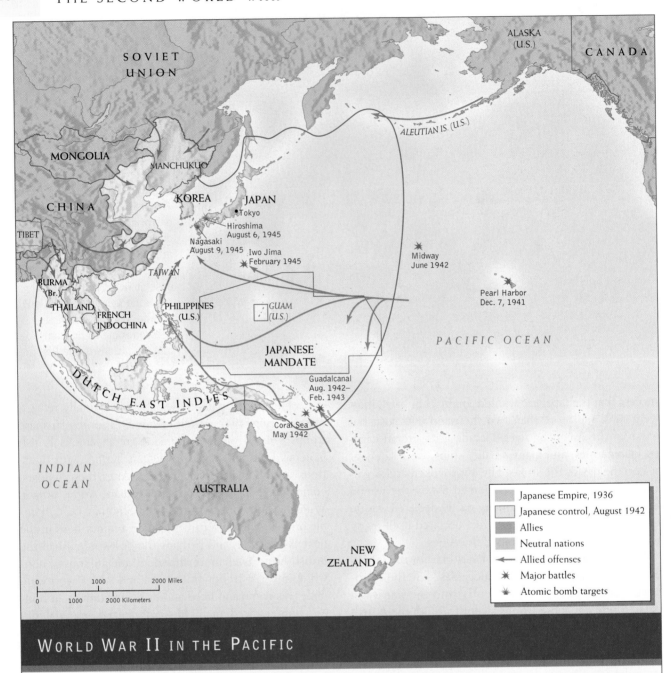

WORLD WAR II IN THE PACIFIC

This map shows the major operations and important geographical features of the Pacific Theater during World War II. Why did the Japanese strategy depend on destroying the American Pacific Fleet at the time Japan attacked the Philippines, Dutch East Indies, and Southeast Asia? How did the fact that American aircraft carriers were not at Pearl Harbor affect the next major battles of the war in the Pacific: Coral Sea and Midway? What factors led the Americans to decide that the dropping of atomic bombs on Hiroshima and Nagasaki was the most expeditious way to end the war?

after months of bitter fighting. Their success began a campaign of "island hopping" as the marines destroyed Japan's network of island bases throughout the Pacific. This was brutal warfare, often settled with grenades and bayonets. Each side considered the other racially in-

ferior. The Japanese often refused to surrender; the Americans and Australians also took few prisoners. By 1943, the Japanese victories had been halted, the Japanese navy had lost most of its capital ships, and the Allies began a slow march to Singapore and the Philippines.

THE RISE AND RUIN OF NATIONS: GERMANY'S WAR IN THE EAST AND THE OCCUPATION OF EUROPE

How were the Nazis able to rule over a continental empire?

While battles ebbed and flowed in the Atlantic and the North African desert, Germany moved south-east into the Balkans. In 1941 Germany took over Yugoslavia almost without a fight. The Germans split Yugoslavia's ethnic patchwork by establishing a Croatian puppet state, pitting Croats against their Serb neighbors who were ruled directly by the Nazis. Romania, Hungary, and Bulgaria joined the Nazis' cause as allies. The Greeks, who had dealt a crushing defeat to an Italian invasion, were suddenly confronted with a massive German force that overran the country. The Greeks stubbornly refused to surrender. An unexpected combination of Greek, British, and New Zealand troops nearly defeated the German paratroopers sent to capture the island of Crete in June of 1941. Many Greeks also took to the mountains as guerrillas, but in the end the country fell. By the summer of 1941, with the exceptions of Sweden and Switzerland, the whole European continent was either allied with the Nazis or subject to their rule. These victories, and the economy of plunder that enriched Germany with forced labor and other nations' money, won Hitler considerable popularity at home. But these were only the first steps in a larger plan.

Hitler's ultimate goals, and his conception of Germany's national destiny, lay to the east. Hitler had always seen the nonaggression pact with the Soviet Union as an act of convenience, to last only until Germany was ready for this final conflict. By the summer of 1941, it seemed Germany was ready. On June 22, 1941, Hitler began Operation Barbarossa, the invasion of the Soviet Union. The elite of the German army led the way, defeating all the forces the Russians could put in front of them. Stalin's purges of the 1930s had exiled or executed many of his most capable army officers, and the effects showed in Russian disorganization and disaffection in the face of the panzers. Hundreds of thousands of prisoners were taken as German forces pressed deep into Byelorussia (modern Belarus), the Baltic states, and the Ukraine. Like Napoleon, the Germans led a multinational army; it included Italians, Hungarians, most of the Romanian army, and freelance soldiers from the Baltics and the Ukraine who bore grudges against Stalin's authoritarian regime. During the fall of 1941, the Nazis destroyed much of the Red Army's fighting strength and vigorously pursued their two goals: the destruction of communism and racial purification.

The war against the Soviets was a war of ideologies and of racial hatred. The advancing Nazi forces left burning fields and towns in their wake and methodically wiped the occupied territories clean of "undesirable elements." When Russian guerrillas counterattacked with sniping and sabotage, German forces shot or hanged hundreds of innocent hostages at a time in reprisal, often torturing their victims first. The Russian guerrillas quickly chose to deliver the same punishment to any captured Germans. By the end of 1941 it was clear that the war in the East was a war of destruction, and that both sides believed that only one side would be allowed to survive. In 1941, it seemed the victors would be German. Their forces were on the march towards the capital at Moscow. On orders from Berlin, however, German forces pushing toward Moscow were diverted south to attack Russia's industrial heartland in an effort to destroy the Soviets' ability to resist before the Russian winter set in. This left the Soviet capital free, and the Russian population, its leaders, and its armies, began to organize a much more determined resistance.

Hitler nonetheless managed to piece together an empire that stretched across the entire continent of Europe. "We come as the heralds of a New Order and a new justice," his regime announced. Hitler specifically compared his rule to a "new Indian empire," and claimed to have studied British imperial techniques. Much of the New Order was improvised and rested on a patchwork of provisional regimes: military government in Poland and the Ukraine, collaborators in France, allied fascists in Hungary, and so on. The clearest principle was German supremacy. "The emphatic German decision to organize Europe hierarchically, like a pyramid with Germany at the top, is known to all," said an Italian diplomat at the time. The empire was meant to feed German citizens, and maintain their morale and support for the war, which would prevent the "stab in the back" that Hitler believed had thwarted a German victory in 1914–1918. Occupied countries paid inflated "occupation costs" in taxes, food, industrial production, and

NORTH SEA

IRELAND

UNITED KINGDOM

NETHLERANDS

London

ATLANTIC OCEAN

BELGIUM

Paris

Occupied

FRANCE

LORRAINE
ALSACE

Vichy

VICHY FRANCE
Unoccupied until
November 1942

PORTUGAL

SPAIN

Toulon

CORSICA
(Vichy)

BALEARIC
ISLANDS

SARDINIA
(It.)

MOROCCO

ALGERIA
(Fr.)

TUNISIA
(Fr.)

NORWAY

SWEDEN

DENMARK

EUPEN
LUX.

SWITZ.

GREATER
GERMANY

Berlin

SUDETEN-
LAND

BOHEMIA

MORAVIA

AUSTRIA

Milan

ITALY

Rome

ADRIATIC SEA

CROATIA

SICILY

FINLAND

Leningrad

ESTONIA

LATVIA

LITHUANIA

MEMELAND
Danzig

EAST
PRUSSIA

BIALYSTOK

POSEN

Warsaw

GOVERNMENT
GENERAL
OF
POLAND

SLOVAKIA

HUNGARY

Budapest

YUGOSLAVIA
Partitioned
April, 1941

Belgrade

SERBIA

CATTARO
(It.)
ALBANIA
(It.)

GREECE

Athens

CRETE

LIBYA
(It.)

BALTIC SEA

Vilna

EASTERN
POLAND

Lemberg

NORTHERN
BUKOVINA

BESSARABIA

ROMANIA

Bucharest

Sofia

BULGARIA

MEDITERRANEAN SEA

MOSCOW

SOVIET
UNION

Kiev

BLACK SEA

Istanbul

TURKEY

Ankara

CYPRUS

LEBANON

PALESTINE

EGYPT

0   250   500 Miles
0   250   500 Kilometers

EUROPE

Area of
detail

AFRICA

Axis states and annexed areas
Axis allies
Axis occupied
Sudetenland

AXIS EUROPE, 1941

How had Hitler and Mussolini come to dominate the bulk of mainland Europe by the eve of the German invasion of the Soviet Union? Why did Hitler choose to annex certain conquests to Germany but settle for occupation in others?

manpower. More than 2 million foreign workers were brought into Germany in 1942–1943 from France, Belgium, Holland, and the Soviet Union. As they conscripted workers, the Nazis spoke of uniting Europe to save it from the "red menace" of communism. That propaganda seems to have had little effect. To the contrary, at least in France, deporting citizens to labor in Germany did more than any other policy to drive individuals into the resistance.

The demands of enemy occupation, and the political and moral questions of "collaboration" and resistance, were issues across occupied Europe. The Nazis set up puppet regimes in a number of occupied territories. Both Norway and the Netherlands were deeply divided by the occupation. In each country a relatively small but dedicated party of Nazis governed in the name of the Germans, while at the same time well-organized and determined resistance movements gathered information for the Allies and carried out acts of sabotage. In Denmark, the population was much more united against their German occupiers, engaging in regular acts of passive resistance that infuriated German administrators. They also banded together as private citizens to smuggle most of the country's Jewish population out to safety in neutral Sweden.

Elsewhere the relationship between collaboration, resistance, and self-interested indifference was more complex. In France, collaboration ranged from simple survival tactics under occupation to active support for Nazi ideals and goals. The worst example of this was the Vichy regime's active anti-Semitism and the aid given by French authorities in isolating, criminalizing, and deporting French Jews to the concentration camps. Living with the German conquerors forced citizens in France (and elsewhere) to make choices. Many chose to protect their own interests by sacrificing those of others, particularly such "undesirables" as Jews and communists. At the same time, communist activists, some members of the military, and ordinary citizens, such as the people of France's central mountains, who had a long tradition of smuggling and resisting government, became active guerrillas (*maquis*) and saboteurs. They established links with the Free French movement in London, led by the charismatic, stiff-necked general Charles de Gaulle, and supplied important intelligence to the Allies. In

French man reacting as Germans march the fallen national flag through the streets of Marseilles, 1941. Split between a German occupation and a pro-German government, French people confronted the choice between collaboration and resistance.

eastern Europe, resistance movements provoked both open warfare against the fascists and civil war within their own countries. The Germans' system of occupation in Yugoslavia pitted a fascist Croat regime against most Serbs; the Croatian fascist guard, the Ustasha, massacred hundreds of thousands of Orthodox Catholic Serbs. Ironically, a Croat, Josip Broz (Tito), emerged as the leader of the most powerful Yugoslavian resistance movement—militarily the most significant resistance in the war. Tito's troops were communists, strong enough to form a guerrilla army. They fought Germans, Italians, and Croat fascists, and they gained support and supplies from the Allies.

Perhaps the most important moral issue facing citizens of occupied Europe was not their national allegiance, but rather their personal attitude to the fate of the Nazis' sworn enemies: Jews, communists, gypsies, homosexuals, and political "undesirables." Some French Jews along the Riviera found the Italian Catholic army officers who occupied the area more willing to save them from deportation than their fellow Frenchmen. This deeply personal dilemma—whether to risk family, friends, and careers to aid the deportees, or simply look the other way and allow mass murder—was one of the most powerful of the war.

> Perhaps the most important moral issue facing citizens of occupied Europe was not their national allegiance, but rather their personal attitude to the fate of the Nazis' sworn enemies: Jews, communists, gypsies, homosexuals, and political "undesirables."

RACIAL WAR, ETHNIC CLEANSING, AND THE HOLOCAUST

In what ways was World War II a "racial war"?

From the beginning, the Nazis had seen the conflict as a racial war. In *Mein Kampf* Hitler had already outlined his view that war against the *Untermenschen*, or "subhuman" Jews, Gypsies, and Slavs, was natural and necessary. Not only would it purify the German people, it would also conquer territory for their expansion. Thus as soon as the war broke out, the Nazis began to implement ambitious plans for redrawing the racial map of the Reich, or what is now called ethnic cleansing. In the fall of 1939, with Poland conquered, Heinrich Himmler directed the SS to begin massive population transfers. Ethnic Germans were moved from elsewhere into the borders of the Reich, while Poles and Jews were deported to specially designated areas in the east. Over two hundred thousand ethnic Germans from the Baltic states were resettled in Western Prussia. Welcoming these ethnic Germans went hand in hand with a brutal campaign of terror against the Poles, especially Polish Jews. The Nazis sought to root out all sources of potential resistance were to be rooted out. Professors at the University of Cracow, considered dangerous intellectuals, were deported to concentration camps, where they died. The SS shot "undesirables," such as the inmates of Polish mental asylums, partly to allow SS troops to occupy the asylums' barracks. Poles were deported to forced labor camps. The Nazis began to transport Jews by the thousands to the region of Lublin, south of Warsaw. Special death squads also began to shoot Jews in the streets and in front of synagogues. These Polish campaigns took one hundred thousand Jewish lives in 1940.

The elimination of European Jewry stood at the center of the Nazis' *Rassenkampf*, or "racial struggle." We have seen the role of anti-Semitism in Hitler's rise to power and the escalating campaign of terror against the Jewish community inside Germany in the 1930s, including the Night of the Broken Glass (see Chapter 25). The war radicalized that campaign. Historians disagree about whether or not the Nazis had a "blueprint" for the extermination of Europe's Jews. Most now emphasize that Nazi priorities shifted according to the war's rhythms and Hitler's wildly changing moods. Between 1938 and 1941 Nazi plans had no single focus. Plans ranged from forcing German Jews to emigrate to deporting all Europe's Jews to Madagascar, a former French colony off the southern coast of Africa. All these schemes took shape against the background of daily terror and frequent massacres, especially in Poland. It is certain, however, that the invasion of the Soviet Union in June 1941 marked a turning point in the deadly path to the Holocaust. Operation Barbarossa, as the invasion was called, brought several changes. First, it was animated by the Nazis' intense ideological and racial hatreds, directed against Slavs, Jews, and Marxists. Goebbels, for example, called the Russians "not a people but an agglomeration of animals." The invasion of Poland had been vicious. The invasion of the USSR was openly a "war of extermination." Second, the invading German army succeeded more quickly than it expected. The huge gains created euphoria in the Nazi hierarchy; Hitler seemed very close to realizing his dreams of an eastern empire. But success also bred fear, or worry at the prospect of controlling the millions of Soviet

Polish Jews, evicted from the Warsaw Ghetto, being deported. Most of their trains led to death camps.

THE HOLOCAUST: MASSACRES IN UKRAINE

The following account of a mass shooting in the Ukraine comes from a German engineer testifying at the Nuremberg trials in 1946. Events like these happened so often that his is but one of many such descriptions. Note that the SS allowed him to witness these events.

From September 1941 until January 1944, I was the manager and chief engineer of a branch of the construction firm, Josef Jung of Solingen with its headquarters in Sdolbunow, Ukraine. In this capacity I had to visit the firm's building sites. The firm was contracted by an Army construction office to build grain silos on the former air field near Dubno in the Ukraine.

When I visited the site office on 5 October 1942 my foreman, Hubert Moennikes of Hamburg–Harburg, Aussenmühlenweg 21, told me that Jews from Dubno had been shot near the site in three large ditches which were about thirty metres long and three metres deep. Approximately 1,500 people a day had been killed. All of the approximately 5,000 Jews who had been living in Dubno up to the action were going to be killed. Since the shootings had taken place in his presence he was still very upset.

Whereupon I accompanied Moennikes to the building site and near it saw large mounds of earth about thirty metres long and two metres high. A few lorries were parked in front of the mounds from which people were being driven by armed Ukrainian militia under the supervision of an SS man. The militia provided the guards on the lorries and drove them to and from the ditch. All these people wore the prescribed yellow patches on the front and back of their clothing so that they were identifiable as Jews.

Moennikes and I went straight to the ditches. We were not prevented from doing so. I could now hear a series of rifle shots from behind the mounds. The peo-ple who had got off the lorries—men, women, and children of all ages—had to undress on the orders of an SS man who was carrying a riding or dog whip in his hand. They had to place their clothing on separate piles for shoes, clothing and underwear. I saw a pile of shoes containing approximately 800–1,000 pairs, and great heaps of underwear and clothing.

Without weeping or crying out these people undressed and stood together in family groups, embracing each other and saying good-bye while waiting for a sign from an-other SS man who stood on the edge of the ditch and also had a whip. During the quar-ter of an hour in which I stood near the ditch, I did not hear a single complaint or a plea for mercy. . . .

I walked round the mound and stood in front of the huge grave. The bodies were lying so tightly packed together that only their heads showed, from al-most all of which blood ran down over their shoulders. Some were still moving. Others raised their hands and turned their heads to show they were still alive. The ditch was already three quarters full. I estimate that it already held about a thousand bodies. I turned my eyes towards the man doing the shooting. He was an SS man; he sat, legs swinging, on the edge of the ditch. He had an automatic rifle resting on his knees and was smoking a cigarette. The people, completely naked, climbed down steps which had been cut into the clay wall of the ditch, stumbled over the heads of those lying there and stopped at the spot indicated by the SS man. They lay down on top of the dead or wounded; some stroked those still living and spoke quietly to them. Then I heard a series of rifle shots. I looked into the ditch and saw the bodies contorting or, the heads already inert, sinking on the corpses beneath. Blood flowed from the nape of their necks. I was surprised not to be ordered away, but I noticed three postmen in uniform standing nearby. Then the next batch came up, climbed down into the ditch, laid themselves next to the previous victims and were shot.

On the way back, as I rounded the mound, I saw another lorry load of people which had just arrived. This one included the sick and infirm. An old and very emaciated woman with frightfully thin legs was being undressed by others, already naked. She was being supported by two people and seemed paralysed. The naked people carried the woman round the mound. I left the place with Moennikes and went back to Dubno by car. . . .

I am making the above statement in Wiesbaden, Germany on 10 November 1945. I swear to God that it is the whole truth.

Fred. Gräbe

J. Noakes and G. Pridham, *Nazism: A History in Document and Eyewitness Accounts, 1919–1945*, Vol. 2 (New York: Schocken, 1988), pp. 1100–1101.

---

prisoners, Soviet civilians, and Soviet Jews who had now fallen into Nazi hands. The combination of elation and anxiety was deadly. It led, quickly, from systematic brutality to atrocities, and then to murder on a scale few could have imagined.

As the Nazi army swept into the Soviet Union in 1941, captured communist officials, political agitators, and any hostile civilians were imprisoned, tortured, or shot. Five and one half million military prisoners were taken and marched to camps. Over half of them died of starvation or were executed. Poles from regions that had been under Soviet rule, Jews, and Russians were deported to Germany to work as slave labor in German factories. On the heels of the army came special battalions of *Einsatzgruppen*, or death squads. Joined by eleven thousand extra SS troops, they stormed through Jewish villages and towns with Russian or Polish populations identified as "difficult". The men of the villages were shot; the women and children either deported to labor camps or massacred along with the men. By September 1941, the *Einsatzgruppen* reported that in their efforts at "pacification" they had killed eighty-five thousand persons, most of them Jews. By April 1942, the number was five hundred thousand. This killing began before the gas chambers had gone into operation and continued through the campaigns on the eastern front. As of 1943, the death squads had killed roughly 2.2 million Jews.

As Operation Barbarossa progressed, German administrations of occupied areas herded local Jewish populations even more tightly into the "ghettos" some Jewish communities had occupied for centuries: Warsaw and Lodz in Poland were the largest. There, Nazi administrators, accusing Jewish people in the ghettos of hoarding supplies, refused to allow food to go in. The ghettos became centers of starvation and disease. Those who left the ghetto were shot rather than returned. A German doctor summarized the regime's logic about killing this way: "One must, I can say it quite openly in this circle, be clear about it. There are only two ways. We sentence the Jews in the ghetto to death by hunger or we shoot them. Even if the end result is the same, the latter is more intimidating." In other words, the point was not simply death, but terror.

Through the late summer and fall of 1941, Nazi officials discussed and put together plans for mass killings in death camps. The ghettos had already been sealed; now orders came down that no Jews were to leave any occupied areas. That summer the Nazis had experimented with vans equipped with poison gas, which could kill thirty to fifty people at a time. Those experiments and the gas chambers were designed with the help of scientists from the T-4 euthanasia program, which had already killed eighty thousand racially, mentally, or physically "unfit" persons in Germany. By October 1941, the SS was building camps with gas chambers and deporting people to them. Auschwitz-Birkenau, which had been built to hold Polish prisoners, was built up to be the largest of the camps. Auschwitz eventually held many different types of prisoners—"undesirables" like Jehovah's Witnesses and

> By September 1941, the *Einsatzgruppen* reported that in their efforts at "pacification" they had killed eighty-five thousand persons, most of them Jews. By April 1942, the number was five hundred thousand.

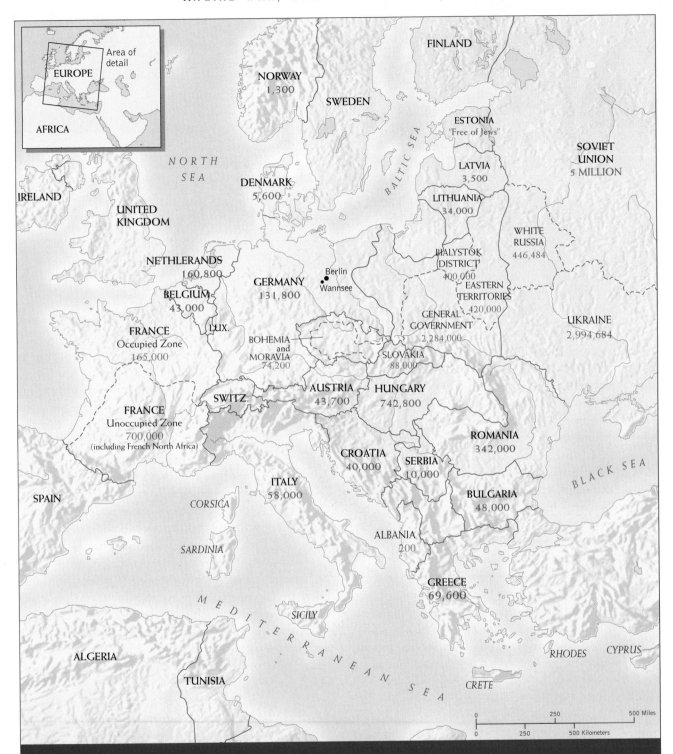

Area of detail

EUROPE

AFRICA

NORTH SEA

IRELAND

UNITED KINGDOM

NORWAY
1,300

SWEDEN

FINLAND

DENMARK
5,600

NETHLERANDS
160,800

BELGIUM
43,000

FRANCE
Occupied Zone
165,000

LUX.

GERMANY
131,800

Berlin
Wannsee

BOHEMIA
and
MORAVIA
74,200

SLOVAKIA
88,000

FRANCE
Unoccupied Zone
700,000
(including French North Africa)

SWITZ.

AUSTRIA
43,700

HUNGARY
742,800

SPAIN

CORSICA

ITALY
58,000

CROATIA
40,000

SERBIA
10,000

ROMANIA
342,000

BULGARIA
48,000

ALBANIA
200

SARDINIA

ALGERIA

TUNISIA

SICILY

MEDITERRANEAN SEA

CRETE

GREECE
69,600

RHODES

CYPRUS

BALTIC SEA

ESTONIA
"Free of Jews"

LATVIA
3,500

LITHUANIA
34,000

BIALYSTOK
DISTRICT
400,000

EASTERN
TERRITORIES
420,000

GENERAL
GOVERNMENT
2,284,000

WHITE
RUSSIA
446,484

SOVIET
UNION
5 MILLION

UKRAINE
2,994,684

BLACK SEA

0   250   500 Miles

0   250   500 Kilometers

HITLER'S "FINAL SOLUTION": JEWS MARKED FOR DEATH

On January 20, 1942, German officials met at Wannsee (just outside Berlin) to discuss the "final solution" to the "Jewish problem." They also discussed what they believed to be the remaining number of Jewish people in territories they controlled or soon hoped to control. Examine these figures closely. How many millions of innocent people did the Nazis propose to slaughter?

THE HOLOCAUST: TWO PERSPECTIVES FROM THE SS

THE DEATH CAMPS

An SS officer charged with inspecting the death camps wrote this account of his visit to Belzec, a camp in occupied Poland, near the former Russian border. He opposed the regime. Shortly after leaving this description, in 1945, he committed suicide.

Next morning, shortly before seven, I was told: 'the first transport will arrive in ten minutes'. And, in fact, after a few minutes, the first train arrived from the direction of Lemberg (Lvov). 45 wagons with 6,700 people, of whom 1,450 were already dead on arrival. Behind the barred hatches stared the horribly pale and frightened faces of children, their eyes full of the fear of death. Men and women were there too. . . .

The chambers fill up. 'Pack them in'—that is what Captain Wirth has ordered. People are treading on each others' toes. 700–800 in an area of twenty-five square metres, in forty-five cubic metres! The SS push them in as far as possible. The doors shut; in the meantime, the others are waiting outside in the open, naked. 'It is the same in winter', I was told. 'But they could catch their death of cold', I say. 'But that's just what they are there for', replied an SS man in dialect.

Now at last I understood why the whole apparatus is called the Heckenholt Foundation. Heckenholt is the driver of the diesel engine, a little technician who constructed the installation. The people are going to be killed by the diesel exhaust gases. But the diesel engine won't start! Captain Wirth arrives. He is clearly embarrassed that this should happen just on the day when I am here. Yes indeed, I can see the whole thing. And I wait. My stop watch faithfully records it all. Fifty minutes, 70 seconds [*sic!*]. Still the diesel won't start. The people wait in their gas chambers. In vain. One can hear them crying, sobbing. . . . Captain Wirth hits the Ukrainian who is responsible for helping *Unterscharführer* Heckenholt with the diesel engine twelve or thirteen times in the face with his riding whip. After two hours forty-nine minutes—the stop watch has recorded it all—the engine starts. Up to this moment,

homosexuals, Poles, Russians, and even some British POWs—but Jews and gypsies were the ones systematically annihilated there. Between the spring of 1942 and the fall of 1944 over a million people were killed at Auschwitz-Birkenau alone. The opening of the death camps set off the greatest wave of slaughter, which came from 1942 to 1943. Freight cars hauled people to the camps, first from the ghettos of Poland, then from

France, Holland, Belgium, Austria, the Balkans, and later from Hungary and Greece. Bodies were buried in pits dug by prisoners or burned in crematoria.

The death camps have come to symbolize the horrors of Nazism as a system of modern mass murder. Yet it is worth emphasizing that much of the slaughter was not anonymous, industrialized, or routine, and that it took place in face-to-face encounters outside the camps.

the people have been living in these four chambers, four times 750 people in four times forty-five cubic metres. A further twenty-five minutes pass. That's right, many are now dead. One can see through the little peepholes when the electric light illuminates the chambers for a moment. After twenty-eight minutes, only a few are still alive. At last, after thirty-two minutes, they are all dead. . . .

HIMMLER'S INSTRUCTIONS TO THE SS

Heinrich Himmler (1900–1945), one of the founding members of the Nazi party and head of the SS, became one of the most powerful members of the Nazi government. He directed the purge of the rebellious SA in 1934, expanded the SS, supervised the network of death camps, and by 1943, when this speech was given, had become minister of the interior for the administration of the Reich. Few represent better the combination of ambition, ideology, and ruthlessness that characterized Nazi leaders. Himmler committed suicide when captured by Allied troops in 1945.

I also want to talk to you quite frankly about a very grave matter. We can talk about it quite frankly among ourselves and yet we will never speak of it publicly. Just as we did not hesitate on 30 June 1934 to do our duty as we were bidden, and to stand comrades who had lapsed up against the wall and shoot them, so we have never spoken about it and will never speak of it. It appalled everyone, and yet everyone was certain that he would do it the next time if such orders should be issued and it should be necessary.

I am referring to the Jewish evacuation programme, the extermination of the Jewish people. It is one of those things which are easy to talk about. 'The Jewish people will be exterminated', says every party comrade, 'It's clear, it's in our programme. Elimination of the Jews, extermination and we'll do it.' And then they come along, the worthy eighty million Germans, and each one of them produces his decent Jew. It's clear the others are swine, but this one is a fine Jew. Not one of those who talk like that has watched it happening, not one of them has been through it. Most of you will know what it means when a hundred corpses are lying side by side, or five hundred or a thousand are lying

there. To have stuck it out and—apart from a few exceptions due to human weakness—to have remained decent, that is what has made us tough. This is a glorious page in our history and one that has never been written and can never be written. For we know how difficult we would have made it for ourselves if, on top of the bombing raids, the burdens and the deprivations of war, we still had Jews today in every town as secret saboteurs, agitators and troublemakers. We would now probably have reached the 1916–17 stage when the Jews were still part of the body of the German nation.

We have taken from them what wealth they had. I have issued a strict order, which SS *Obergruppenführer* Pohl has carried out, that this wealth should, as a matter of course, be handed over to the Reich without reserve. We have taken none of it for ourselves. . . . All in all, we can say that we have fulfilled this most difficult duty for the love of our people. And our spirit, our soul, our character has not suffered injury from it. . . .

J. Noakes and G. Pridham, *Nazism: A History in Document and Eyewitness Accounts, 1919–1945*, Vol. 2 (New York: Schocken, 1988), pp. 1151–1152, 1199–1200.

Jews and other victims were not simply killed. They were tortured, beaten, and executed publicly while soldiers and other onlookers recorded the executions with cameras—and sent photos home to their families. During the last phases of the war, inmates still in the concentration camps were taken on "death marches" whose sole purpose was suffering and death. Nor was the killing done by the specially indoctrinated SS and

Einsatzgruppen. The Nazi regime called up groups of conscripts, such as Reserve Police Battalion 101, from duty in its home city of Hamburg and sent it into occupied territories. Once there, the unit of middle-aged policemen received and obeyed orders to kill, in one day, fifteen hundred Jewish men, women, and children in one village. The commander offered to excuse men who did not feel they could carry out this assignment;

Area of
detail

EUROPE

AFRICA

Bergen

Oslo

Narva

Line of furthest German advance

NORTH
SEA

BALTIC SEA

Kovno

Vilna

Grodno

Hamburg

Sachsenhausen

Berlin

Bialystok

Wolkowysk

Amsterdam

Westerbork

Plonsk

Pruzana

Vught

Brussels

Malines

Buchenwald

Leipzig

Lodz

Radom

Lille

Breslau

Lublin

Rouen

Paris

Theresienstadt

Caen

Auschwitz

Angers

Orléans

Munich

Vienna

Kosice

Munkacs

Beregszasz

Nantes

Tours

Nancy

Eger

Marmarossziget

Bordeaux

Dijon

Budapest

Debrecen

Beszterce

Lyons

Szeged

Cluj

Szasregen

Gurs

Merano

Mako

Turin

Milan

Pecs

Toulouse

Padua

Venice

Trieste

Zagreb

Sepsiszentgyorgy

Avignon

Genoa

Rivesaltes

Marseilles

Pisa

Florence

RAB

ADRIATIC
SEA

BLACK
SEA

Rome

Pristina

Nea Orestea

Skopje

Veles

Xanthi

Florina

Salonica

CORFU

Arta

MEDITERRANEAN SEA

Patras

Athens

0   100   200   300 Miles

0   100   200   300 Kilometers

KOS

RHODES

—— Deportation railroads

DEPORTATION RAILWAYS

Between March 1942 and November 1944, Jews are known to have been deported from every location on this
map—as well as from numerous other locales—to Auschwitz, where most were killed. Note the effort made by the
Nazis to transport Jews from the very frontiers of the empire at the height of a two-front war. Consider what this
says about the Nazi regime in particular, and about other states willing to collaborate with the Nazis.

only a few asked for a different task. In one Polish town, occupied first by the Soviets and then retaken by the Nazis, the Polish villagers themselves, with minimal guidance or help from German soldiers, turned on their Jewish neighbors and killed hundreds in a day.

How many people knew of the extent of the Holocaust? No operation of this scale could be carried out without the cooperation or knowledge of many: the Nazi hierarchy; architects who helped build the camps; engineers who designed the gas chambers and crematoria; municipal officials of cities from which people were deported; train drivers; residents of villages near the camps, who reported the smell of bodies burning; and so on. Not surprisingly, most who suspected the worst were terrified and powerless. Not surprisingly, many people did not want to know, and did their best to ignore evidence and carry on with their lives. Many who continued to support the Nazis did so for other reasons, out of personal opportunism, or because they opposed communism and wanted order restored. Yet mere popular indifference does not provide a satisfactory explanation for the Nazis' ability to accomplish the murder of so many people. Many Europeans—German, French, Dutch, Polish, Swiss, and Russian—had come to believe that there was a "Jewish problem" that had to be "solved." The Nazis tried to conceal the death camps. Yet they knew they could count on vocal support for requiring Jews to be specially identified, for restrictions on marriage and property ownership and for other kinds of discrimination. For reasons that had to do with both traditional Christian anti-Semitism and modern, racialized nationalism, many Europeans had come to see Jewish Europeans as "foreign," no longer members of their national communities.

What of other governments? Their level of cooperation with the Nazis' plans varied. The French Vichy regime, on its own initiative, passed laws that required Jews to wear iden-

> For reasons that had to do with both traditional Christian anti-Semitism and modern, racialized nationalism, many Europeans had come to see Jewish Europeans as "foreign," no longer members of their national communities.

tifying stars and strictly limited their movements and activities. When the German government demanded roundups and deportations of Jews, Vichy cooperated. On the other hand, Italy, though a fascist country, participated less actively. Not until the Germans occupied the north of Italy in 1943 were drastic anti-Semitic measures implemented. The Hungarian government, also fascist and allied with the Nazis, persecuted Jews but dragged its heels about deportations. Thus the Hungarian Jewish community survived—until March 1944, when Germans, disgusted with their Hungarian collaborators, took direct control and immediately began mass deportations. So determined were the Nazis to carry out their "final solution" that they killed up to twelve thousand Hungarian Jews a day at Auschwitz in May of 1944, contributing to a total death toll of six hundred thousand.

In the face of this Nazi determination, little resistance was possible. The concentration camps were designed to numb and incapacitate their inmates, making them acquiesce in their own slow deaths even if they were not killed right away. In his famous account, the survivor Primo Levi writes: "Our language lacks words to express this offence, the demolition of a man. . . . It is

The Holocaust. These German civilians were compelled to view the bodies of concentration camp victims at the Landesburg camp in 1945.

not possible to sink lower than this; no human condition is more miserable than this, nor could it conceivably be so. Nothing belongs to us any more; they have taken away our clothes, our shoes, even our hair; if we speak, they will not listen to us, and if they listen, they will not understand." A few rebellions in Auschwitz and Treblinka were repressed with savage efficiency. In the villages, people rounded up to be deported or shot had to make split-second decisions in order to escape. Saving oneself nearly always meant abandoning one's children or parents, which very few could do. The countryside offered no shelter; local populations were usually either hostile or too terrified to help. Reprisals horrified all. Families of Jews and gypsies were ordinary people whose lives could not have prepared them for the kind of violence that rolled over them. The largest Jewish resistance came in the Warsaw ghetto, in the spring of 1943. The previous summer, the Nazis had deported 80 percent of the ghetto's residents to the camps, making it clear that those left behind had little hope of survival. These people had virtually no resources, yet, when deportations started again, a small Jewish underground movement—a thousand fighters, perhaps, in a community of seventy thousand—took on the Nazis with a tiny arsenal of gasoline bombs, pistols, and ten rifles. The Nazis responded by burning the ghetto to the ground and executing and deporting to the camps nearly everyone who was left. Some fifty-six thousand Jews died. "The Warsaw Ghetto is no more," reported the SS commander at the end. Word of the rising did spread, but the repression made it clear that the targets of Nazi extermination could choose only between death in the streets or death in the camps. Sustained resistance, as one person remarked, would have required "the prospect of victory."

The Holocaust claimed between 4.1 and 5.7 million Jewish lives. Even those numbers do not register the nearly total destruction of some cultures. In the Baltic states (Latvia and Lithuania), Germany, Czechoslovakia, Yugoslavia, and Poland, well over 80 percent of the long-established Jewish communities were annihilated. Elsewhere, the figures were closer to 50 percent. The Holocaust was unique. It was part of a racial war and of an even longer period of ethnically motivated mass murder. Through both world wars and afterward ethnic and religious groups—Armenians, Poles, Serbian

Orthodox, ethnic Germans—were hunted, massacred, and legally deported en masse. Hitler's government had planned to build a "new Europe," safe for ethnic Germans and their allies and secure against communism, on the graveyards of whole cultures.

TOTAL WAR: HOME FRONTS, THE WAR OF PRODUCTION, BOMBING, AND "THE BOMB"

How did the war transform the home fronts?

The Second World War was a "total war." Even more than World War I, it involved the combined efforts of whole populations. Larger armed forces were moving much more swiftly across territory, locked in constant battle with equally well-armed opponents. This demanded massive resources and national commitment to industry, drawing in the whole economies of the combatants. Standards of living changed around the world.

In the neutral nations of Latin America, which supplied vast amounts of raw materials to the Allies, wartime profits led to a wave of prosperity known as the "dance of the millions." In the lands occupied by Germany or Japan, economies of forced extraction robbed local areas of resources, workers, and even food. In East Asia deprivations caused rising resentment of the Japanese, who had been seen initially as liberators ending the rule of the old colonial powers. In the United States, Detroit produced no new models of car or truck between 1940 and 1945. Work schedules were grueling. Women and the elderly, pressed back into wage work or working for the first time, put in long shifts (in Britain and Russia these sometimes ran over twelve hours) before returning home to cook, clean, and care for families and neighbors also affected by enemy bombing and wartime shortages. Diets changed. Though Germany lived comfortably off the farmlands of Europe for several years, and the United States could lean on its huge

> In the Baltic states (Latvia and Lithuania), Germany, Czechoslovakia, Yugoslavia, and Poland, well over 80 percent of the long-established Jewish communities were annihilated.

agricultural base, food, gasoline, and basic household goods were still rationed. In occupied Europe and the Soviet Union rations were just above starvation level, and sometimes fell below in areas near the fighting. Britain, dependent on its empire and other overseas sources for food and raw materials, ran a comprehensive rationing system that kept up production and ensured a drab but consistent diet on the table.

Production—the industrial ability to churn out more tanks, tents, planes, bombs, and uniforms than the other side—was essential to winning the war. Britain, the Soviet Union, and America each launched comprehensive, well-designed propaganda campaigns that encouraged the production of war equipment on an unmatched scale. Appeals to patriotism, to communal interests, and to a common stake in winning the war struck a chord. The Allied societies proved willing to

"Just a Good Afternoon's Work!" A British poster mobilizing women for part-time factory work.

regulate themselves and commit to the effort. Despite strikes and disputes with government officials, the Allied powers devoted more of their economies to war production, more efficiently, than any nations in history. Not only did they build tanks, ships, and planes capable of competing with advanced German and Japanese designs, they built them by the tens of thousands, swamping the enemy with constant reinforcements and superior firepower. Japan nearly reached comparable levels of production but then slowly declined, as Allied advances on land and American submarines cut off overseas sources of vital supplies. Germany, despite its reputation for efficiency and its access to vast supplies of slave labor, was less efficient in its use of workers and materials than the Allied nations. The Germans' ability to produce devastatingly successful weapons led to a damaging side effect—vast amounts of money and time spent developing the pet projects of high-ranking Nazi officials, or trying to make unsuccessful designs work. Rather than losing time and resources pursuing perfection, the Allies developed working, standard designs and produced them in overwhelming numbers.

Since industry was essential to winning the war, centers of industry became vital military targets. The Allies began bombing German ports and factories almost as soon as the Germans started their own campaigns. Over time, American and British planners became equally ruthless on an even larger scale. Both of these Allied nations made a major commitment to "strategic bombing," developing new planes and technology that allowed them to put thousands of bombers in the air both night and day over occupied Europe. As the war wore on and Germany kept fighting, the Allies expanded their campaign. They moved from pinpoint bombing of the military and industry in Germany to striking such targets across all of occupied Europe, and bombing Germany's civilian population in earnest. For the British, despite a public debate about the morality of bombing, it was a war of retribution; for the Americans, it was an effort to grind the Germans down without sacrificing too many Allied lives. That turned out to be a false premise. The Allies killed tens of thousands of German civilians as they struck Berlin, ports such as Hamburg, and the industrial cities of the Ruhr, but German war production persisted. At the same time German fighter planes shot down hundreds of Allied bombers, causing heavy losses. After the Allied invasion of Europe, bombing expanded well beyond targets of military value. The

German city of Dresden, a center of culture and education that lacked heavy industry, was firebombed with a horrifying death toll. This gave Allied generals and politicians pause, but strategic bombing continued. German industry was slowly degraded, but the German will to keep fighting, like Britain's or the Soviet Union's, remained intact.

THE RACE TO BUILD THE BOMB

While the Allies carried out their bombing campaigns over Germany and Japan, Allied scientists in America were at work on the most powerful bomb ever designed. It was an unlikely weapon suggested from an obscure scientific field: atomic physics. British physicists—who, along with German scientists, led the field—believed that it would be possible to split the structure of an atom. The process, called fission, would split the subatomic particles apart in a huge burst of energy. The British scientists believed that, given the resources, they could stage a chain reaction, causing the fission of one atom to trigger splits in others, as though unraveling a thread in the structure of the universe. This would produce an explosion of extraordinary scope and power. British scientists began work on the idea, but lacked the resources and enough radioactive material to stage a controlled chain reaction. The United States had those resources, and as America entered the war the British passed on their theories and technical information to American scientists. A group of physicists, some native-born Americans, many refugees from the fascist regimes of Europe, were set to work creating a chain reaction. Enrico Fermi, an Italian physicist and a dedicated antifascist, was put in charge of designing the world's first nuclear reactor, built on the campus of the University of Chicago. In December 1942 Fermi staged the first controlled chain reaction at the site.

Meanwhile, the governments of the United States and Germany were both racing toward a military application of fission. The Germans were hampered in their efforts from the start. Many of their best specialists were Jewish or anti-Nazi refugees now working for the Americans. The Germans also lacked crucial bits of technical information and had fewer resources. When specially trained Norwegian commandos destroyed the Germans' "heavy water" facility (used to separate out the uranium needed for the bomb) at Telemark, Norway, the German project went with it. Yet American officials feared that it had not been de-

stroyed, and they also sensed the enormous power of the new weapon. A government project, code-named "Manhattan," had already been set up to manage an all-out effort at building an American atomic bomb. The project went on under the tightest security of the war; most of President Roosevelt's cabinet, and the United States Congress, did not know the real purpose of "Manhattan."

In 1943 a laboratory was established at Los Alamos, New Mexico, bringing together the most capable nuclear physicists in the country, citizens and immigrants, old and young, to come up with a working design for a bomb. The physicist J. Robert Oppenheimer was placed in charge of the project, along with a U.S. Army Air Corps supervisor. After nearly two years they came up with a working design whose prototype would be dropped by plane and detonated in midair above the target, for maximum effect. The first test of the device was held on July 16, 1945, near Los Alamos. The wave of heat and the roar of the explosion were indescribable. The test tower was vaporized. The ball of fire that rose in a mushroom shape overhead was the physical expression of a blast equal to twenty thousand tons of dynamite. "Manhattan" was a success. America now possessed the most destructive weapon ever devised. After watching the blast, Oppenheimer was moved to recite a phrase from an ancient Hindu text, a bitter commentary on his own work: "I am become Death, and the destroyer of worlds."

THE ALLIED COUNTERATTACK AND THE DROPPING OF THE ATOMIC BOMB

How did the Soviets defeat the Germans?

Hitler had invaded the Soviet Union in June 1941. Within two years the war in the East had become his undoing; within four years it brought about his destruction.

The early successes of the German-led invasion were crippling. Nearly 90 percent of the Soviets' tanks, most of their aircraft, and huge stores of supplies were destroyed or captured. Nazi forces penetrated deep into European Russia. The Soviets fought regardless. By late 1941 German and Finnish forces had cut off and besieged Leningrad (St. Petersburg). Yet the city held out for 844 days—through three winters, massive destruction by artillery and aircraft, and periods of starvation—until a large relief force broke the siege. Russian partisans stepped up their campaigns of ambush and terrorism, and many of the Germans' former allies in the Ukraine and elsewhere turned against them in reaction to Nazi "pacification" efforts.

THE EASTERN FRONT

Most important, the character of the war on the Eastern Front changed. What had begun as a struggle between Nazi invaders and Stalin's regime became a war to save the *rodina*, the Russian motherland, as Russians fought for their own homes and families. Stalin, a shrewd politician, understood this; the message of Soviet propaganda changed to include a healthy dose of praise for Mother Russia. After surviving the winter of 1941–1942, the Russian public became convinced that they could indeed survive the war and became committed to driving the Germans from their homeland, whatever the cost. The second change in the war was a Russian victory won by what Stalin called "General Winter." Successive winters, followed by hot, muddy summers, took a steady toll in Nazi lives and supplies, sapping German morale. The third change was the astonishing recovery of Soviet industry. The Soviets received some American and British aid, delivered at great risk over Arctic routes, but most of their achievement was self-sufficient. Whole industries were rebuilt behind the safety of the Ural Mountains, and entire populations of cities were displaced to work in them, turning out tanks, fighter planes, machine guns, and ammunition. Once the Russians achieved the same aerial stalemate that existed over Britain, their seemingly endless labor reserves were backed with boundless reserves of equipment. The fourth change in the war had to do with the Germans, who became victims of their own success. The *Blitzkrieg*, at first a brilliantly inventive way of fighting a war, became a predictable set of maneuvers run

according to a checklist. The Russians were eager students of that routine. They learned each stage of the process well, exploited its weaknesses, and became particularly good at lulling the Germans into a false sense of success before overwhelming them from unexpected angles.

The crucial year on the Russian Front came in 1943, as German efforts to break the back of Soviet industry resulted in the largest, most destructive battles the world has ever seen. The first of these began in 1942, with a massive German-led offensive in the Volga River valley, aimed at the city of Stalingrad. The Germans hoped to split Soviet forces and destroy valuable factories. But once German, Romanian, and Italian troops entered the suburbs of the city they were drawn into bitter house-to-house fighting by Russian defenders. The outnumbered Soviet forces fought beyond the "last cartridge," using rocks and knives when they had to. Germany's panzers were rendered useless with grenades and firebombs in the narrow streets. The city was reduced to rubble, which sometimes gave the Russians cover to surprise German and Romanian units. Russian forces were pushed back to the Volga River as winter came on, but the Nazis' supplies began to run low. In November 1942 large Russian armies encircled the enemy forces inside the city itself. The attackers were now besieged, in a battle that went on through a cruel winter.

Infuriated, Hitler demanded that his commanders relieve the embattled troops. Every attempt to break through was defeated, and at the end of January 1943 the German commander in Stalingrad defied orders

> The crucial year on the Russian Front came in 1943, as German efforts to break the back of Soviet industry resulted in the largest, most destructive battles the world has ever seen.

CHRONOLOGY

THE EASTERN FRONT

Germans invade Soviet Union	June 1941
Siege of Leningrad	Sept. 1941–Jan. 1942
Battle of Stalingrad	Sept. 1942–Jan. 1943
Battle of Kursk	July 1943
Soviet forces reach Berlin	April 1945
Germany surrenders	May 1945

and surrendered the haggard survivors of his army. More than a quarter of a million German, Romanian, and Italian bodies were dragged from the wrecked city. Two times that many German troops died in the whole course of the battle. The Russians suffered up to a million casualties, including 100,000 civilians. Despite the unparalleled casualties—the battle dwarfed even Verdun in the Great War, or the fighting between China and Japan—the Russians had won a crucial victory. After Stalingrad Hitler appeared less and less often in public, and his worst tendencies to gloom and paranoia grew as the Russian front turned against his dreams.

Following Stalingrad, the Soviets mounted a series of offensives that turned German forces back from the heart of Russia. In the summer of 1943 German tank commanders launched a massive counterattack near the city of Kursk in the center of the front lines. Their early victories were a baited trap; several Russian armies were waiting, with masses of men and the newest Russian tanks, specially designed to destroy the panzers. The result may have been the largest battle ever fought, lasting six weeks and involving over six thousand tanks and more than 2 million men between the two sides. Bogged down amid snipers and minefields and raked by Russian artillery and rocket launchers, the German army group, nearly a million strong, was crushed. The Russians, led by their commander at Stalingrad and the shrewdest opponent of the *Blitzkrieg*, Grigorii Zhukov, then launched a major offensive into Ukraine. By the spring of 1944 Ukraine was back in Soviet hands. With the relief of Leningrad and attacks into Byelorussia that reached the Polish border, the Russians turned the tables. Romania was knocked out of the war during 1944, and Soviet armies poured into the Balkans, eventually meeting up with Tito's victorious partisans in Yugoslavia. Zhukov, who had taken charge of most of the Soviet armies, ground down German resistance in Poland during the winter of 1944. Several German armies collapsed, and Soviet forces, joined by communist partisans from the eastern European countries, retook large parts of Czechoslovakia. It was these battles, along with the fighting in Italy and Yugoslavia, that destroyed the German army. Hitler's most ambitious goal had brought the downfall of the Nazi regime and death to a generation of German soldiers.

THE WESTERN FRONT

During the campaigns in the East, Stalin continually pressured his allies to open a second front in the West. The American-led attack on Italy was a response to that pressure. Allied forces first invaded Sicily and then the Italian mainland. Italy's government deposed Mussolini and surrendered in the summer of 1943. A civil war ensued, for most Italians, especially communist partisans, sided with the Allies, while dedicated fascists continued to fight for their exiled leader. Italy was invaded by both sides; large Allied armies and more than a dozen elite German divisions occupied the country. The result was eighteen months of bitter fighting on Italy's muddy hillsides, in high mountains and bombed-out towns, consuming vast resources and tens of thousands of lives on each side. Nevertheless, the fighting in Italy cost Germany much more than it did the Allies, who liberated all the major Italian cities and entered Austria by the spring of 1945.

The major "second front" was opened on June 6, 1944, with the massive Allied landings in Normandy. Though deadly in places, the landings were a masterpiece of planning and deception. The Germans fiercely defended the dense hedgerows of Normandy, but Allied air superiority and a vast buildup of men and matériel led to a breakthrough. An American landing on the Riviera in August had much more immediate success, aided by the French resistance. In late July and August the Allies swept through France, liberating Paris on August 14 and pushing into Belgium. After that it was rough going. Allied commanders in the

> The major "second front" was opened on June 6, 1944, with the massive Allied landings in Normandy.

CHRONOLOGY

THE WESTERN FRONT

Germany invades the Low Countries	May 1940
French surrender	June 1940
Battle of Britain	July 1940–June 1941
D-Day invasion	June 1944
Liberation of Paris	August 1944
Battle of the Bulge	December 1944
Allies invade Germany	April 1945
Germany surrenders	May 1945

D-Day. Cargo ships are seen pouring supplies ashore during the invasion of France on June 6, 1944. Barrage balloons float overhead to protect the ships from low-flying enemy planes.

West were gifted organizers, but their skills as strategists were mixed. A British airborne invasion of the Netherlands and an American thrust into the forests of the Rhineland were bloody failures. The Germans mounted their own devastating attack in December 1944, under cover of winter storms, in the Battle of the Bulge. It was a last effort with their best men and equipment; they captured thousands of prisoners and nearly broke through Allied lines. Nevertheless, several elite American units beat off much larger German forces at key points until the snow cleared and the Allies mounted a crushing counterattack. Over the winter they destroyed German forces in the Rhineland and Holland. In April 1945, the Allies crossed the Rhine—in one of the war's ironies, French troops were the first to do so. The Germans collapsed. American tanks swept south, British and Canadian forces north. The Allies had learned the tactics of the *Blitzkrieg* on the re-

ceiving end, and now the Americans used them to overwhelm resistance. This genuine military success was helped by the fact that most Germans preferred to surrender to Americans or Britons than face the Russians to the east.

At the same time, those Soviet troops were approaching fast. By late April they had taken Prague and Vienna. On April 21, 1945, Zhukov's forces hammered their way into the suburbs of Berlin. During the next ten days a savage battle raged amid the ruins and heaps of rubble. More than a hundred thousand Russians and Germans died. Adolf Hitler killed himself in a bombproof shelter beneath the Chancellery on April 30. On May 2 the heart of the city was captured, and the Soviets' red banner flew from the Brandenburg Gate. On May 7 the German high command signed a document of unconditional surrender. By the next day the war in Europe was over.

May 1945. A Soviet soldier raises the flag over the Reichstag in Berlin after the Germans are defeated.

THE WAR IN THE PACIFIC

The war in the Pacific came to an end four months later. The Japanese were rolled back on all fronts. Slim's international army in Burma had waged a wily campaign to drive out the Japanese. British, Indian, and Nepalese troops liberated the Burmese capital, Rangoon, at the same time the Germans were surrendering in the West. That same spring, Australian forces recaptured the Dutch East Indies, while an Anglo-Australian attack on Singapore was planned for the autumn. The United States Navy had won one of its greatest victories the previous fall, when William Halsey's task force destroyed most of Japan's surviving surface ships in the gulfs of the Philippine islands. American forces landed and within weeks the Philippine capital of Manila fell, taken house by house in bloody fighting. The remaining battles, amphibious assaults on a series of islands running toward the Japanese mainland, were just as brutal. Japanese pilots, hopelessly outnumbered in the air, mounted suicide attacks on American ships, while American marines and Japanese soldiers fought over every inch of the shell-blasted rocks in the middle of the Pacific. In June 1945, the Japanese island of Okinawa fell to American forces after eighty-two days of desperate fighting. American forces now had a foothold less than five hundred miles from the Japanese home

islands. Chinese forces, Nationalist and communist alike, combined to force the Japanese back on Hong Kong. The Soviets chose this moment to enter the fray. Their forces marched rapidly through Manchuria and into the colonial territory of Korea. The government in Tokyo awaited an invasion and called on its citizens for supreme endeavors to meet the crisis.

On July 26 the heads of the United States, British, and Chinese governments issued a joint proclamation calling on Japan to surrender or be destroyed. The United States had already begun that process of destruction by using its most advanced bomber, the B-29, which could fly above Japanese efforts to shoot it down, in the systematic bombing of Japanese cities. Many of the wooden Japanese cities were hit with firebombs, which created storms of flame and killed hundreds of thousands of civilians. Yet the Japanese refused to surrender. In the absence of that surrender the United States planned to increase the pace of destruction. They chose to use the atomic bomb.

Many senior military and naval officers argued that use of the bomb was not necessary, on the assumption that Japan was already beaten. Some of the scientists

CHRONOLOGY	
THE WAR IN THE PACIFIC	
Japanese bomb Pearl Harbor	December 1941
Singapore falls to Japan	December 1941
Battles of Midway, Coral Sea, and Guadalcanal	1942
Invasion of the Philippines	Fall 1944
Battle of Okinawa	June 1945
Soviets invade Manchuria and Korea	June–July 1945
Atomic bombs dropped on Hiroshima and Nagasaki	August 6 and 9, 1945
Japan surrenders	August 14, 1945

THE ATOMIC BOMB AND ITS IMPLICATIONS

A PETITION TO THE PRESIDENT OF THE UNITED STATES

In July 1945, scientists associated with the Manhattan Project became involved in debates about how the atomic bomb could be deployed. Members of the Scientific Panel of the Secretary of War's Interim Advisory Committee agreed that a bomb could be used militarily, but disagreed about whether it could be used without prior warning and demonstration. Other groups of scientists secretly began to circulate petitions, such as the one below, in which they set out their views. The petitions never reached the president, but they raised issues that did emerge in the postwar period.

July 17, 1945

A PETITION TO THE PRESIDENT OF THE UNITED STATES

We, the undersigned scientists, have been working in the field of atomic power. Until recently we have had to fear that the United States might be attacked by atomic bombs during this war and that her only defense might lie in a counterattack by the same means. Today, with the defeat of Germany, this danger is averted and we feel impelled to say what follows:

The war has to be brought speedily to a successful conclusion and attacks by atomic bombs may very well be an effective method of warfare. We feel, however, that such attacks on Japan could not be justified, at least not unless the terms which will be imposed after the war on Japan were made public in detail and Japan were given an opportunity to surrender. . . .

[I]f Japan still refused to surrender our nation might then, in certain circumstances, find itself forced to resort to the use of atomic bombs. Such a step, however, ought not to be made at any time without seriously considering the moral responsibilities which are involved.

The development of atomic power will provide the nations with new means of destruction. The atomic bombs at our disposal represent only the first step in this direction, and there is almost no limit to the destructive power which will become available in the course of their future development. Thus a nation which sets the precedent of using these newly liberated forces of nature for purposes of destruction may have to bear the responsibility of opening the door to an era of devastation on an unimaginable scale.

If after this war a situation is allowed to develop in the world which permits rival powers to be in uncontrolled possession of these new means of destruction, the cities of the United States as well as the cities of other nations will be in continuous danger of sudden annihilation. . . .

The added material strength which this lead [in the field of atomic power] gives to the United States brings with it the obligation of restraint and if we were to violate this obligation our moral position would be weakened in the eyes of the world and in our own eyes. It would then be more difficult for us to live up to our responsibility of bringing the unloosened forces of destruction under control.

In view of the foregoing, we, the undersigned, respectfully petition: first, that you exercise your power as Commander-in-Chief, to rule that the United States shall not resort to the use of atomic bombs in this war unless the terms which will be imposed upon Japan have been made public in detail and Japan knowing these terms has refused to surrender; second, that in such an event the question of whether or not to use atomic bombs be decided by you in the light of the considerations presented in this petition as well as all the other moral responsibilities which are involved.

Michael B. Stoff, Jonathan F. Fanton, and R. Hal Williams, eds., *The Manhattan Project: A Documentary Introduction to the Atomic Age* (New York: McGraw-Hill, 2000), p. 173.

President Truman's Memoirs

In this section of his memoirs, President Harry S Truman sets out the views of other scientists on the Secretary of War's Advisory Committee. He explains the logic of his decision to use the atomic bomb against Hiroshima (August 6, 1945) and Nagasaki (August 9, 1945) and the events as they unfolded.

I had realized, of course, that an atomic bomb explosion would inflict damage and casualties beyond imagination. On the other hand, the scientific advisers of the committee reported, "We can propose no technical demonstration likely to bring an end to the war; we see no acceptable alternative to direct military use." It was their conclusion that no technical demonstration they might propose, such as over a deserted island, would be likely to bring the war to an end. It had to be used against an enemy target.

The final decision of where and when to use the atomic bomb was up to me. Let there be no mistake about it. I regarded the bomb as a military weapon and never had any doubt that it should be used. The top military advisers to the President recommended its use, and when I talked to Churchill he unhesitatingly told me that he favored the use of the atomic bomb if it might aid to end the war.

In deciding to use this bomb I wanted to make sure that it would be used as a weapon of war in the manner prescribed by the laws of war. That meant that I wanted it dropped on a military target. I had told Stimson that the bomb should be dropped as nearly as possibly upon a war production center of prime military importance.

Stimson's staff had prepared a list of cities in Japan that might serve as targets. Kyoto, though favored by General Arnold as a center of military activity, was eliminated when Secretary Stimson pointed out that it was a cultural and religious shrine of the Japanese.

Four cities were finally recommended as targets: Hiroshima, Kokura, Niigata, and Nagasaki. They were listed in that order as targets for the first attack. The order of selection was in accordance with the military importance of these cities, but allowance would be given for weather conditions at the time of the bombing. Before the selected targets were approved as proper for military purposes, I personally went over them in detail with Stimson, Marshall, and Arnold, and we discussed the matter of timing and the final choice of the first target. . . .

On August 6, the fourth day of the journey home from Potsdam, came the historic news that shook the world. I was eating lunch with members of the *Augusta's* crew when Captain Frank Graham, White House Map Room watch officer, handed me the following message:

To the President
from the Secretary of War

Big bomb dropped on Hiroshima August 5 at 7:15 P.M. Washington time. First reports indicate complete success which was even more conspicuous than earlier test.

I was greatly moved. I telephoned Byrnes aboard ship to give him the news and then said to the group of sailors around me, "This is the greatest thing in history. It's time for us to get home."

Harry S Truman, *Memoirs*, Vol. 1 (Garden City, NY: Doubleday, 1955), pp. 419–21.

involved, who had done their part hoping to counter the Nazis, believed that using the bomb for political ends would set a deadly precedent. Harry Truman, who had succeeded Roosevelt following the latter's death in April 1945, decided otherwise. On August 6, a single atomic bomb was dropped on Hiroshima, obliterating about 60 percent of the city. Three days later a second bomb was dropped on Nagasaki. President Truman warned that the United States would use as many atom bombs as necessary to bring Japan to its knees. On August 14, Japan surrendered unconditionally.

The decision to drop the bomb, and its consequences, was extraordinary. It did not greatly alter the scope of or the plans for the American destruction of Japan. Many more Japanese died in the earlier fire bombings than in the two atomic blasts. Yet the bomb

View of Hiroshima after the First Atom Bomb Was Dropped. This photo, taken one month after the bomb was dropped, shows the utter devastation of the city. Only a few steel and concrete buildings remained intact.

was an entirely new kind of weapon, built with untried technology; some of its designers feared that the test blast might split *every* atom in the universe. It was one of the most terrifying results of the new relationship between science and political power. The nature of the bomb mattered as well. The instant, total devastation of the blasts, along with the cancerous radiation that lingered for years and claimed victims decades later, was something terribly new. The world now had a weapon that could destroy not just cities and peoples, but humanity itself.

 CONCLUSION

After World War I, many Europeans awoke to find a world they no longer recognized. In 1945 many Europeans came out from shelters or began the long trips

back to their homes, faced with a world that hardly existed at all. The products of industry—tanks, submarines, strategic bombing—had destroyed the structures of industrial society—factories, ports, and railroads. The tools of mass culture—fascist and communist appeals, patriotism proclaimed via radios and movie screens, mobilization of mass armies and industry—had been put to full use. In the aftermath, much of Europe lay destroyed and, as we will see, vulnerable to the rivalry of the postwar superpowers: the United States and the Soviet Union.

The two world wars profoundly affected Western empires. Nineteenth-century imperialism had made twentieth-century war a global matter. In both conflicts the warring nations had used the resources of empire to their fullest. Key campaigns, in North Africa, Burma, Ethiopia, the Pacific, were fought in and over colonial territories. Hundreds of thousands of colonial troops—sepoys and Gurkhas from India and Nepal,

Britain's King's African Rifles, French from Algeria and West Africa—served in armies on both sides of the conflict. After two massive mobilizations, many anticolonial leaders found renewed confidence in their own peoples' courage and resourcefulness, and they seized the opportunity of European weakness to press for independence. In many areas that had been under European or Japanese imperial control, from sections of China, to Korea, Indochina, Indonesia, and Palestine—the end of World War II only paved the way for a new round of conflict. This time, the issue was when imperial control would be ended, and by whom.

The Second World War also carried on the Great War's legacy of massive killing. Historians estimate that nearly 50 million people died. The killing fields of the East took the highest tolls: 25 million Soviet lives. Of those, 8.5 million were in the military, and the rest civilians; 20 percent of the Polish population and nearly 90 percent of the Polish Jewish community; 1 million Yugoslavs, including militias of all sides; 4 million German soldiers and five hundred thousand German civilians, not including the hundreds of thousands of ethnic Germans who died while being deported west at the end of the war, in one of the many acts of ethnic cleansing that ran through the period. Even the United States, shielded from the full horrors of total war by two vast oceans, lost 292,000 soldiers in battle and more to accidents or disease.

Why was the war so murderous? The advanced technology of modern industrial war and the openly genocidal ambitions of the Nazis offer part of the answer. The global reach of the conflict offers another. Finally World War II overlapped with, and eventually devolved into, a series of smaller, no less bitter conflicts: a civil war in Greece; conflicts between Orthodox, Catholics, and Muslims in Yugoslavia; and political battles for control of the French resistance. Even when those struggles claimed fewer lives, they left deep political scars. So did memories of the war. Hitler's empire could not have lasted as long as it did without active collaboration or passive acquiescence from many, a fact that produced bitterness and recrimination for years.

In this and many other ways, the war haunted the second half of the century. Fifty years after the battle of Stalingrad, the journalist Timothy Rybeck discovered that hundreds of skeletons still lay, in the open, on the fields outside the city. Many bodies had never been buried. Others had been left in shallow, mass graves. As wind and water eroded the soil, farmers plowed the fields, and teenagers dug for medals and helmets to sell as curiosities, more bones kept rising to the surface. One of the supervisors charged with finding permanent graves and building memorials responded to the task by voicing more than simple weariness. "This job of reburying the dead," he said, "will never be done."

KEY TERMS

Blitzkreig

appeasement

Guernica

Dunkirk

Winston Churchill

Pearl Harbor

Operation Barbarossa

Auschwitz-Birkenau

Manhattan Project

Hiroshima

SELECTED READINGS

Bartov, Omer. *Hitler's Army: Soldiers, Nazis, and War in the Third Reich.* New York, 1991.

Burrin, Philippe. *France under the Germans: Collaboration and Compromise.* New York, 1996.

Browning, Christopher R. *The Path to Genocide: Essays on Launching the Final Solution.* Cambridge, 1992.

Carr, Raymond. *The Spanish Tragedy: The Civil War in Perspective.* London, 1977. A thoughtful introduction to the Spanish Civil War and the evolution of Franco's Spain.

Dawidowicz, Lucy S. *The War against the Jews, 1933–1945.* New York, 1975. A full account of the Holocaust.

Divine, Robert A. *Roosevelt and World War II.* Baltimore, 1969. A diplomatic history.

Gilbert, Martin. *The Appeasers.* Boston, 1963. Excellent study of British pro-German sentiment in the 1930s.

———. *The Second World War: A Complete History.* Rev. ed. New York, 1991. An up-to-date general account.

Hilberg, Raul. *The Destruction of the European Jews,* 2d ed. 3 vols. New York, 1985. Another excellent treatment of the Holocaust, its origins, and its consequences.

Kedward, Roderick. *In Search of the Maquis: Rural Resistance in Southern France, 1942–1944.* Oxford, 1993.

Keegan, John. *The Second World War.* New York, 1990. A classic.

Marrus, Michael R. *The Holocaust in History.* Hanover, N.H., 1987. Thoughtful analysis of central issues.

Michel, Henri. *The Shadow War: The European Resistance, 1939–1945.* New York, 1972. Compelling reading.

Milward, Alan S. *War, Economy, and Society, 1939–1945.* Berkeley, 1977. Analyzes the impact of the war on the world economy and the ways in which the economic resources of the belligerents determined strategies.

Noakes, Jeremy, and Geoffrey Pridham. *Nazism: A History in Documents and Eyewitness Accounts, 1919–1945.* New York, 1975. An excellent combination of analysis and documentation.

Overy, Richard. *Russia's War.* New York, 1998.

Paxton, Robert O. *Vichy France: Old Guard and New Order, 1940–1944.* New York, 1982.

Stoff, Michael B. *The Manhattan Project: A Documentary Introduction to the Atomic Age.* New York, 1991.

Weinberg, Gerhard L. *A Global History of World War II.* New York, 1995. Now the most comprehensive history.

Wilkinson, James D. *The Intellectual Resistance in Europe.* Cambridge, Mass., 1981. A comparative study of the movement throughout Europe.

Wright, Gordon. *The Ordeal of Total War, 1939–1945.* New York, 1968. Particularly good on the domestic response to war and the mobilization of the resources of the modern state.

DIGITAL HISTORY

COLD WAR

It is quite clear from Soviet theory and practice that the Kremlin seeks to bring the free world under its dominion by the methods of the cold war. The preferred technique is to subvert by infiltration and intimidation. Every institution of our society is an instrument which it is sought to stultify and turn against our purposes. Those that touch most closely our material and moral strength are obviously the prime targets, labor unions, civic enterprises, schools, churches, and all media for influencing opinion.

NSC 68: United States Objectives and Programs for National Security

Although the United States and Soviet Union became allies during World War II, there seemed to be little doubt that their opposing ideologies would ultimately produce a cold war. And overshadowing such a war was the atomic bomb. Before the war had even ended, the Soviets were convinced that Eastern European buffer states had to be created to protect the Soviet Union from future invasion. The United States saw these same nations as buffer states against the Soviet Union. The Truman Doctrine, Marshall Plan, and NATO were all intended to keep Russian ideology within its own borders. This notion of containment was first voiced by George Kennan's "Long Telegram" of 1946. Throughout the 1950s and into the 1960s and 1970s, the United States clung to this policy—indeed, containment conditioned our cold war.

The cold war was a global phenomenon and was clearly conditioned by the political, economic, and social aspirations of the two superpowers. Between 1945 and 1989 Europe became a testing ground for the cold war itself. The 1956 uprising in Hungary and the Prague Spring of 1968 are two examples of the form in which these battles would be fought. Ultimately the cold war came to an end following the collapse of the Berlin Wall in November 1989. Soviet-style communism was considered a spent force in Eastern Europe, and on October 3, 1990, East and West Germany were reunited.

The images and documents in the "Cold War" Digital History Feature at www.wwnorton.com/wciv reveal how the new Soviet and American superpowers shaped foreign policy, politics, and everyday life after 1945. As you explore the feature on the *Western Civilizations* Web site, consider the following:

• What events led to the control of the world by two heavily armed nations, each with the capability of initiating a nuclear holocaust?

• Why did the Soviet Union find it essential to intervene in Hungary in 1956 and in Czechoslovakia in 1968?

• What is the significance of the cold war? How have historians shaped the way that the cold war is understood?

• In any war there are winners and losers. What does it mean to have won or lost the cold war?

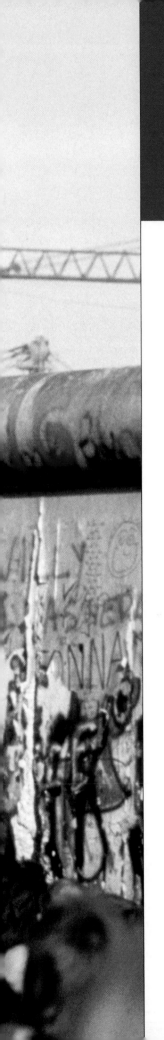

PART VIII

THE WEST AND THE WORLD

THE SECOND WORLD WAR was perhaps the great watershed of the twentieth century. Its legacies were many and pervasive. The "hot war" between the Allies and the Axis was superseded by a rivalry between the most powerful of the Allies: the United States and the Soviet Union. The superpowers possessed nuclear weapons, global reach, and networks of alliances that gave them the authority of empires. The "cold war" between these powers dominated the recovery from the world war, and global politics in general, for four decades. The rise and fall of cold-war politics is a fundamental theme in twentieth-century history; it is one of the two historical trends followed here.

While the cold war seemed to centralize the political, cultural, and economic life of the world around the twin poles of the superpowers, the other key theme of the later twentieth century involves the decentralizing effects of globalization. This began with the breaking apart of Europe's old colonial empires and the emergence of new nations. New forms of politics and protest emerged as well, based on social movements of women, ethnic "minorities," and peoples denied a political voice in the age of imperialism. The Western European empires were not the only ones to collapse. With the end of the cold war, the unofficial empire of the Soviet Union collapsed as well, producing new nations and new hopes. These events seemed to leave the United States as the world's leading power, yet the rest of the world would not simply become an American empire by default or consent to being "Americanized" on the United States' terms. As the twentieth century came to and end, it was clear that the west operated in a much tighter network of world civilizations. The circumstances in which this "globalized" world emerged are the focus of this last section.

	POLITICS	SOCIETY AND CULTURE	ECONOMY	INTERNATIONAL RELATIONS
				Mohandas Gandhi (1869–1948)
	Malcolm X (1925–1965)	Alexander Fleming discovers first antibiotic, penicillin (1928)		
	Martin Luther King Jr. (1929–1968)			
1940		Albert Camus, *The Stranger* (1942)		Gandhi leads independence movement in India (1940s)
				Soviet Union draws Iron Curtain over eastern Europe (1945–1948)
				Chinese Communist Revolution (1945–1949)
				India gains independence; formation of Pakistan (1947)
				Truman Doctrine (1947)
				Vietnam War, French phase (1947–1954)
	Germany divided; Berlin airlift (1948–1949)		Marshall Plan (1948)	Civil war in Greece (1948)
				Josip Tito declares Yugoslavia independent of Soviet Union (1948)
				State of Israel formed (1948)
	Konrad Adenauer, chancellor of West Germany (1949–1963)	George Orwell, *1984* (1949)		Formation of NATO (1949)
1950	Mao Zedong's Great Leap Forward (1950s)	Simone de Beauvoir, *The Second Sex* (1949)	European Coal and Steel Community created (1951)	Korean War (1950–1953)
				Abdel Nasser becomes president of Egypt (1952)
	Joseph Stalin dies (1953)	Samuel Beckett, *Waiting for Godot* (1953)		United States and Soviet Union test hydrogen bombs (1953)
	Khrushchev's regime (1953–1964)	Francis Crick and James Watson discover structure of DNA (1953)		Algerian war ends with Algerian independence (1954–1962)
		Jonas Salk develops polio vaccine (1953)		Formation of Warsaw Pact (1955)
				Vietnam War, U.S. phase (1955–1975)
	Nikita Khrushchev begins de-Stalinization (1956)	Boris Pasternak, *Dr. Zhivago* (1957)		Suez Crisis (1956)
				Hungarian rebellion repressed by Soviets (1956)
	Charles de Gaulle forms Fifth Republic in France (1958)		European Economic Community (EEC, Common Market) formed (1958)	
1960	Cultural Revolution in China (1960s)	Günter Grass, *The Tin Drum* (1959)	Inflation rates rise across western Europe (late 1960s–1970s)	Castro to power in Cuba (1959)
	John F. Kennedy, president (1961–1963)	Joseph Heller, *Catch-22* (1961)		
	Berlin Wall built (1961)	Frantz Fanon, *The Wretched of the Earth* (1961)		Cuban Missile Crisis (1962)
		Rachel Carson, *Silent Spring* (1962)		Vietnam War (1963–1975)
	Martin Luther King Jr. leads March on Washington (1963)	Betty Friedan, *The Feminine Mystique* (1963)		
	Leonid Brezhnev leads Soviet Union (1964–1982)	Herbert Marcuse, *One-Dimensional Man* (1964)		
		The Beatles play in New York (1964)		
		Birth control pill becomes available (mid-1960s)		Six-Day War between Israel and Arab nations (1967)
	Student protests and worker strikes in Paris (1968)			
	Czech revolt; Prague Spring (1968)			
1970	Willy Brandt, chancellor of West Germany (1970–1974)			SALT treaties (1970s and early 1980s)
				Gradual détente between Soviet Union and Western powers (1970s)
	Watergate scandal (1972–1974); President Richard Nixon resigns		Western European citizens elect representatives to EEC parliament (1972)	Nixon visits China (1972)

POLITICS	SOCIETY AND CULTURE	ECONOMY	INTERNATIONAL RELATIONS	
		Oil prices rise steadily, worsening widespread recession (1973–1980s)	OPEC embargo against Western powers (1973) Arab-Israeli War (1973) Camp David Accords (1978) Soviet military intervention in Afghanistan (1979–1989)	1973
Margaret Thatcher prime minister of England (1979–1990) Polish Solidarity workers movement organizes strikes (1980) Ronald Reagan, president (1980–1988) Helmut Kohl becomes chancellor of West Germany (1982) Mikhail Gorbachev, leader of Communist party (1985–1991) Renewed Solidarity strikes in Poland, demonstrations across Eastern bloc (1988) Break-up of Soviet power in eastern Europe (1989) Berlin Wall falls (1989) Tiananmen Square massacre (1989) Germany reunifies (1990) Boris Yeltsin elected president of Russian Federation (1990) Soviet Union dissolved (1992)	Asian population reaches 3 billion (1986) Nuclear reactor accident at Chernobyl (1986)	Computer revolution begins (1980s)		1980
Nelson Mandela elected president of South Africa; end of apartheid (1994)		Eastern European economies in crisis (1990s) Internet revolution begins (1990s) NAFTA signed by Canada, Mexico, and United States (1993)	Persian Gulf War (1991) Yugoslavian civil wars (1991–1992, 1992–1995) Genocide in Rwanda (1994) Russia's war with Chechnya begins (1994) Pakistan and India test nuclear weapons (late 1990s) War in Kosovo (1999)	1990
	Scientists in Scotland clone a sheep (1997) Global population exceeds 6 billion (2001)		United States declares war on terrorism (2001)	2001

CHAPTER TWENTY-SEVEN

THE COLD WAR WORLD: GLOBAL POLITICS, ECONOMIC RECOVERY, AND CULTURAL CHANGE

The war ended the way a passage through a tunnel ends," wrote Heda Kovály, a Czech woman who survived the concentration camps. "From far away you could see the light ahead, a gleam that kept growing, and its brilliance seemed ever more dazzling to you huddled there in the dark the longer it took to reach it. But when at last the train burst out into the glorious sunshine, all you saw was a wasteland." The war left Europe a land of wreckage and confusion. Millions of refugees trekked hundreds or thousands of miles on foot to return to their homes while others were forcibly displaced from their lands. In some areas housing was practically nonexistent, with no available means to build anew. Food remained in dangerously short supply; a year after the war, roughly 100 million people in Europe still lived on less than 1,500 calories per day. Families scraped vegetables from their gardens or traded smuggled goods on the black market. Governments continued to ration food, and without rationing a large portion of the Continent's population would have starved. During the winter of 1945–1946, many regions had little or no fuel for heat. What coal there was—less than half the prewar supply— could not be transported to the areas that needed it most. The brutality of international war, civil war, and occupation had divided countries against themselves, shredding relations among ethnic groups and fellow citizens. Ordinary people's intense relief at liberation often went hand in hand with recriminations over their neighbors' wartime betrayal, collaboration, or simple opportunism.

How does a nation, a region, or a civilization recover from a catastrophe on the scale of World War II? Nations had to do much more than deliver food and rebuild economic infrastructures. They had to restore—or create—government authority, functioning bureaucracies, and legitimate legal systems. They had to rebuild bonds of trust and civility between citizens, steering a course between demands for justice on the one hand and the overwhelming desire to bury memories of the past on the other. On the contrary, rebuilding entailed a commitment to renewing democracy— to creating democratic institutions that could withstand threats such as those the West had experienced in the 1930s. Some aspects of this process were extraordinarily successful, more so than even the most optimistic forecaster might have thought possible in 1945. Others failed or were deferred until later in the century.

FOCUS QUESTIONS

- What were the causes of the cold war?
- How did Western Europe recover from World War II?

- What were the links between decolonization, World War II, and the cold war?
- What themes defined postwar culture?

Berlin, 1945.

The war's devastating effects brought two dramatic changes in the international balance of power. The first change was the emergence of the so-called superpowers, the United States and the Soviet Union, and the swift development of a "cold war" between them. The cold war divided Europe, with Eastern Europe occupied by Soviet troops, and Western Europe dominated by the military and economic presence of the United States. The second great change came with the dismantling of the European empires that had once stretched worldwide. The collapse of empires and the creation of newly emancipated nations raised the stakes in the cold war and brought superpower rivalry to far-flung sections of the globe. Those events, which shaped the postwar recovery and necessarily created a new understanding of what "the West" meant, are the subject of this chapter.

THE COLD WAR AND A DIVIDED CONTINENT

What were the causes of the cold war?

No peace treaty ended World War II. Instead, as the war drew to a close, relations between the Allied powers began to fray over issues of power and influence in Central and Eastern Europe. After the war, they de-

scended from mistrust to open conflict. The United States and Soviet Union rapidly formed the centers of two imperial blocs. Their rivalry, which came to be known as the cold war, pitted against each other two military powers, two sets of state interests, and two ideologies: capitalism and communism. The cold war's manifold repercussions reached well beyond Europe, for anticolonial movements, sensing the weakness of European colonial powers, turned to the Soviets for help in their struggles for independence. The cold war thus structured the peace, shaped international relations for four decades, and affected governments and peoples across the globe who depended on either of the superpowers.

THE IRON CURTAIN

The Soviet Union had insisted during the wartime negotiations at Tehran (1943) and Yalta (1945) that it had a legitimate claim to control Eastern Europe, a claim that some Western leaders accepted as the price of defeating Hitler and others ignored so as to avoid a dangerous confrontation. When visiting Moscow in 1944, Churchill and Stalin quietly bargained over their respective spheres of influence, offering each other "percentages" of the countries that were being liberated. The Declaration of Principles of Liberated Europe issued at Yalta in 1945 guaranteed free elections, but Stalin believed that the framework of allied cooperation gave him a free hand in Eastern Europe. Stalin's siege mentality pervaded his authoritarian regime and cast nearly everyone at home or abroad as a potential threat or enemy of the state. Yet Soviet policy did not rest on personal paranoia alone. The country's catastrophic wartime losses made the Soviets determined to maintain political, economic, and military control of the lands they had liberated from Nazi rule. For the Soviets, Eastern Europe served as both "a sphere and a shield." When their former allies resisted their demands, the Soviets became suspicious, defensive, and aggressive.

In Eastern Europe, the Soviet Union used a combination of diplomatic pressure, political infiltration, and

Legend:
- Allied occupation of Germany and Austria, 1945–1955
- Territory lost by Germany
- Territory gained by Soviet Union
- Postwar national boundaries, to 1989
- "Iron Curtain" to 1989
- **1945** Year Communist control of government was gained

East Germany inset:
EAST GERMANY

French Sector
WEST
EAST

British Sector
Soviet Sector

BERLIN
U.S. Sector
BERLIN

Potsdam

— Berlin Wall (1961–1989)

0 · 10 Miles
0 · 10 Kilometers

Map labels:

From Finland, 1940–1956

FINLAND

NORWAY

Oslo

SWEDEN

Helsinki

Leningrad

Stockholm

ESTONIA
To U.S.S.R. 1940

LATVIA
To U.S.S.R., 1940

NORTH SEA

DENMARK

Copenhagen

Incorporated into U.S.S.R., 1945

LITHUANIA
To U.S.S.R. 1940

BALTIC SEA

NETHERLANDS

U.S. Zone

Gdansk (Danzig)

WHITE RUSSIA

Amsterdam

Bremen

British Zone

Soviet Zone

Berlin

Incorporated into Poland, 1945

Warsaw

Brest

BELGIUM

Elbe R.

EAST GERMANY (1949)

POLAND (1947)

From Poland, 1940–1947

Brussels

Bonn

Rhine R.

Oder R.

UKRAINE

SOVIET UNION (1917)

French Zone

WEST GERMANY

U.S. Zone

Prague

CZECHOSLOVAKIA (1948)

From Czechoslovakia, 1945–1947

From Romania, 1940–1947

LUXEMBOURG

Munich

U.S. Zone

Vienna

Soviet Zone

Budapest

BESSARABIA

Bern

French Zone

AUSTRIA

British Zone

HUNGARY (1949)

CRIMEA

SWITZERLAND

Milan

From Italy, 1945

ROMANIA (1947)

Yalta

Po R.

Bucharest

BLACK SEA

YUGOSLAVIA (1945)

CORSICA (Fr.)

ITALY

ADRIATIC SEA

Danube R.

From Romania, 1940–1947

Rome

BULGARIA

Tirane

Sofia (1946)

Istanbul

SARDINIA (It.)

ALBANIA (1944)

GREECE

TURKEY

Area of detail

EUROPE

AFRICA

SICILY (It.)

Athens

CRETE

CYPRUS

MEDITERRANEAN

SEA

0 · 200 · 400 Miles
0 · 200 · 400 Kilometers

TERRITORIAL CHANGES IN EUROPE AFTER WORLD WAR II

At the end of World War II, the Soviet Union annexed territory in Eastern Europe to create a buffer between it and Western Europe. At the same time, the United States established a series of military alliances in Western Europe to stifle the spread of communism in Europe. How did these new territorial boundaries aggravate tensions between Soviet Union and the United States?

military power to create "people's republics" sympathetic to Moscow. In country after country, the same process unfolded: first, states set up coalition governments that excluded former Nazi sympathizers; next came coalitions dominated by communists; finally, one party took hold of all the key positions of power. This was the process that prompted Winston Churchill, speaking at a college graduation in Fulton, Missouri, in 1946, to say that "an Iron Curtain" had "descended across Europe." In 1948, the Soviets crushed a Czechoslovakian coalition government headed by the liberal leaders Eduard Beneš and Jan Masaryk—a break with Yalta's guarantee of democratic elections that shocked many. By that year, governments dependent on Moscow had also been established in Poland, Hungary, Romania, and Bulgaria. Together these states were referred to as the Eastern bloc.

The Soviet campaign to control Eastern Europe did not go unchallenged. The Yugoslavian communist and resistance leader Marshal Tito (Josip Broz, 1892–1980) fought to keep his government independent of Moscow. Unlike most Eastern European communist leaders, Tito came to power on his own during the war. He drew on support from Serbs, Croats, and Muslims in Yugoslavia—thanks to his wartime record, which gave him political authority rooted in his own country. Moscow charged that Yugoslavia had "taken the road to nationalism," or become a "colony of the imperialist nations" and expelled the country from the communist countries' economic and military pacts. Determined to reassert control elsewhere, the Soviets demanded purges in the parties and administrations of various satellite governments. These began in the Balkans and extended through Czechoslovakia, East Germany, and Poland. The fact that democratic institutions had been shattered before the war made it easier to establish dictatorships in its aftermath. The purges succeeded by playing on fears and festering hatreds; in several areas those purging the governments attacked their opponents as Jewish. Anti-Semitism, far from being crushed, remained a potent political force—as Heda Kovály explained, it became common to blame Jews for bringing the horrors of war.

The end of war did not mean peace. In Greece, as in Yugoslavia and through much of the Balkans, war's end brought a local communist-led resistance to the verge of seizing power. The British and the United States, however, were determined to keep Greece in their sphere of influence, as per informal agreements with the Soviets. Only large infusions of aid to the anticommunist monarchy allowed them to do so. The bloody

civil war that lasted until 1949 took a higher toll than the wartime occupation. Greece's bloodletting became one of the first crises of the cold war and a touchstone for the United States' escalating fear of communist expansion. "Like apples in a barrel infected by the corruption of one rotten one, the corruption of Greece would infect Iran and all to the East . . . Africa . . . Italy and France," warned Dean Acheson in 1947, then

GERMANY DIVIDED AND THE BERLIN AIRLIFT

In the summer of 1948, the Soviet Union blocked routes through the German Democratic Republic to the Western Allies zone of Berlin. The blockade exacerbated tensions between the Soviet Union and the United States and forced the Allies to airlift supplies to West Berlin. At one point, planes landed in Berlin every three minutes.

deputy head of America's State Department. "[N]ot since Rome and Carthage had there been such a polarization of power on this earth."

Defeated Germany lay at the heart of these two polarizing power blocs and soon became the front line of their conflict. The Allies had divided Germany into four zones of occupation. Although the city of Berlin was deep in Soviet territory, it too was divided. The occupation zones were intended to be temporary, pending an official peace settlement. But the Soviets and the French, British, and Americans quarreled over reparations and policies for the economic development of Germany. Administrative conflicts among the Western powers were almost as intense as their disagreements with the Soviets; Britain and the United States nearly had a serious falling out over food supply and trade in their zones. Yet the quickening cold war put those arguments on hold, and in 1948 the three Western allies began to create a single government for their territories. They passed reforms to ease the economic crisis and introduced a new currency—a powerful symbol of economic unity. The Soviets retaliated by cutting all road, train, and river access from the western zone to West Berlin, but the Western allies refused to cede control over the capital. For eleven months they airlifted supplies over Soviet territory to the besieged western zone of Berlin, a total of 12,000 tons of supplies carried by hundreds of flights every day. The Berlin blockade lasted nearly a year, from June 1948 to May 1949. It ended with the creation of two Germanies, the Federal Republic in the West and the German Democratic Republic in the former Soviet zone. Within a few short years both countries looked strikingly like armed camps.

THE MARSHALL PLAN

The United States countered the expansion of Soviet power and locally based communist movements with massive programs of economic and military aid to Western Europe. In a 1947 speech to Congress arguing for military assistance to anticommunists in Greece, President Harry Truman set out what would come to be called the Truman Doctrine, a pledge to support the resistance of "free peoples" to communism. The Truman Doctrine, however, also tied the contest for political power to economics. The American president declared the Soviet-American conflict to be a choice between "two ways of life." A few months later, Secretary of State George Marshall outlined an ambitious plan of economic aid to Europe including, initially, the Eastern European states: the European Recovery Program. The Marshall Plan provided $13 billion of aid over four years (beginning in 1948), targeted to industrial redevelopment. The plan supplied American tractors, locomotive engines, food, technical equipment, and capital to participating states. Unlike a relief plan, however, the Marshall Plan encouraged the participating states to diagnose their own economic problems and to develop their own solutions. The Marshall Plan also encouraged coordination between European countries, partly out of idealism (some spoke of a "United States of Europe") and partly to dissuade France from asking for reparations and trying to dismantle the German economy. With a series of other economic agreements the Marshall Plan became one of the building blocks of European economic unity.

The American program, however, required measures such as decontrol of prices, restraints on wages, and balanced budgets. The Americans encouraged opposition to left-leaning politicians and movements that might be sympathetic to communism.

The United States also hastened to shore up military defenses. In April 1949, Canada, the United States, and representatives of Western European states signed an agreement establishing the North Atlantic Treaty Organization (NATO). Greece, Turkey, and West Germany were later added as members. An armed attack against any one of the NATO members would now be regarded as an attack against all and bring a united military response. NATO established a joint military command in 1950, with Dwight Eisenhower, the wartime commander of Allied forces in the West, as its senior military officer. NATO's ground forces began with thirty divisions in 1950, and by 1953 had nearly sixty—including, perhaps most surprisingly, a dozen divisions from the young state of West Germany. West German rearmament had been the subject of agonizing debate, particularly in Britain and France, but American pressure and a sense of strategic necessity led to its acceptance within Western Europe. Among the most striking aspects of World War II's aftermath was how rapidly Germany was reintegrated into Europe. In the new cold war world, "the West" quickly came to mean anticommunism. Potentially reliable allies, whatever their past, were not to be punished or excluded.

> In the new cold war world, "the West" quickly came to mean anticommunism. Potentially reliable allies, whatever their past, were not to be punished or excluded.

NATO's preparations for another European war depended heavily on air power, a new generation of jet bombers that would field the ultimate weapon of the age, the atomic bomb. Thus any conflict that broke out along the new German frontier threatened to dwarf the slaughter that had so recently passed.

TWO WORLDS AND THE RACE FOR THE BOMB

The Soviets viewed NATO, the Marshall Plan, and especially the United States' surprising involvement in Europe's affairs with mounting alarm. Rejecting an original offer of Marshall Plan aid, they established an Eastern European version of the plan, the Council for Mutual Economic Assistance, or Comecon. In 1947 the Soviets organized an international political arm, the Cominform (Communist Information Bureau), responsible for coordinating worldwide communist policy and programs. They responded to NATO with the establishment of their own military alliances, confirmed by the Warsaw Pact of 1955. This agreement set up a joint command among the states of Albania, Bulgaria, Czechoslovakia, Hungary, Poland, Romania, and East Germany, and guaranteed the continued presence of Soviet troops in all those countries.

All these conflicts were darkened by the shadow of the nuclear arms race. In 1949, the USSR surprised American intelligence by testing its first atom bomb (modeled on the plutonium bomb that Americans had tested in 1945). In 1953 both superpowers demonstrated a new weapon, the hydrogen or "super" bomb, which was one thousand times more powerful than the bomb dropped on Hiroshima. Within a few years both countries developed smaller bombs and systems of delivery that made them usable. Intercontinental missiles were built that could field first one and then several nuclear warheads, fired from land or from a new generation of atomic-powered submarines that roamed the seas at all times ready to act. J. Robert Oppenheimer warned that the H-bomb so dramatically raised the ability to make war against civilians that it could become a "weapon of genocide." Beyond the grim warnings that nuclear war would wipe out human civilization, "the bomb" had more specific strategic consequences. The "nuclearization of warfare" fed into the polarizing effect of the cold war, for countries without nuclear arms found it difficult to avoid joining either the Soviet or American pact. Over the long term, it encouraged a disparity between two groups of nations: on the one hand, the superpowers, with their enormous military budgets, and on the other nations that came to rely on agreements and international law. It changed the nature of face-to-face warfare as well, encouraging "proxy wars" between clients of the superpowers and raising fears that local conflicts might trigger general war. The hydrogen bomb quickly took on enormous cultural significance as the single most compelling symbol of the age. It seemed to confirm both humanity's power and its vulnerability. The leaps in knowledge that it represented boosted contemporaries' confidence in science and progress. At the same time, weapons of mass destruction and humanity's

The Cold War: A Soviet View. "Nyet!" or "No!" and an arm raised in protest and fear.

emerging power to obliterate itself raised gnawing questions about whether that confidence was misplaced.

Was the cold war inevitable? Could the Americans and the Soviets have negotiated their disagreements? On the Soviet side, Stalin's personal suspiciousness, ruthlessness, and autocratic ambitions combined with genuine security concerns to fuel the cold war mentality. U.S. leaders, for their part, believed that the devastation of the continent gave the Soviets an opportunity to establish communist regimes in Western as well as Eastern Europe. Western Europeans alone could not respond effectively to multiplying postwar crises in Germany, Greece, and elsewhere. The United States, too, was unwilling to give up the military, economic, and political power it had acquired during the war. As it turned away from its traditional isolationism, the U.S. thus articulated new strategic interests with global consequences, including access to European industry and far-flung military bases. These interests played into Soviet fears. In this context, trust became all but impossible.

A new international balance of power quickly produced new international policies. In 1946 George Kennan argued that the United States needed to make containing the Soviet threat a priority. The Soviets had not embarked on world revolution, Kennan said. Thus the United States needed to respond, not with "histrionics: with threats or blustering or superfluous gestures of outward toughness" but rather "by the adroit and vigilant application of counter-force at a series of constantly shifting geographical and political points." Containment became the point of reference for U.S. foreign policy for the next forty years.

At its height, the cold war had a chilling effect on domestic politics in both countries. In the Soviet Union writers and artists were attacked for deviation from the party line. The party disciplined economists for suggesting that Western European industry might recover from the damage it had sustained. The radio blared news that Czech or Hungarian leaders had been exposed as traitors. In the United States, congressional committees launched campaigns to root out "communists" everywhere. On both sides of the Iron Curtain, the cold war intensified everyday anxiety, bringing air-raid drills, spy trials, a belief that a way of life was at stake, and appeals to defend family and home against the menacing "other."

> On both sides of the Iron Curtain, the cold war intensified everyday anxiety, bringing air-raid drills, spy trials, a belief that a way of life was at stake, and appeals to defend family and home against the menacing "other."

KHRUSHCHEV AND THE "THAW"

Stalin died in 1953. Nikita Khrushchev's slow accession to power, not secure until 1956, signaled a change of direction. Khrushchev possessed a kind of earthy directness that, despite his hostility to the West, helped for a time to ease tensions. Stalin had secluded himself in the Kremlin; Khrushchev traveled throughout the world. On a visit to the United States in 1959, he traded quips with Iowa farmers and was entertained at Disneyland. Khrushchev was a shrewd politician, switching quickly between angry anti-American rhetoric and diplomatic reconciliation. Showing his desire to reduce international conflict, Khrushchev soon agreed to a summit meeting with the leaders of Britain, France, and the United States. This summit led to a series of understandings that eased the frictions in heavily armed Europe and produced a ban on testing nuclear weapons above ground in the early 1960s.

Khrushchev's other change of direction came with his famous "secret speech" of 1956, in which he acknowledged (behind the closed doors of the Twentieth Party Congress) the "excesses" of Stalin's era. Though the speech was secret, Khrushchev's accusations were widely discussed. The harshness of Stalin's regime had

CHRONOLOGY

THE EARLY COLD WAR IN EUROPE, 1946–1961

Churchill's "Iron Curtain" speech	1946
Truman Doctrine	1947
Soviets launch Cominform and COMECON	1947
Eastern bloc established	1948
Marshall Plan	1948
Berlin blockade	1948–1949
Formation of NATO	1949
Stalin dies	1953
Formation of the Warsaw Pact	1955
Revolts in East Germany, Poland, and Hungary	1953–1956
Khrushchev visits the U.S.	1959
Building of the Berlin Wall	1961

THE COLD WAR: SOVIET AND AMERICAN VIEWS

The excerpt below is from a speech titled "The Sinews of Peace" that was delivered by Winston Churchill at Westminster College in Fulton, Missouri, in early 1946. In it, he coined the phrase "Iron Curtain," warning of the rising power of the Soviet Union in Eastern Europe.

The next excerpt is from an address by Nikita Khrushchev, who became first secretary of the Communist party in 1953. Three years later, his power secure, he began publicly to repudiate the crimes of Joseph Stalin. Khrushchev presided over a short-lived thaw in Soviet-American relations. Yet, as can be seen in his address, Khrushchev shared Winston Churchill's conception of the world divided into two mutually antagonistic camps.

WINSTON CHURCHILL'S "IRON CURTAIN" SPEECH

A shadow has fallen upon the scenes so lately lighted by the Allied victory. Nobody knows what Soviet Russia and its Communist international organization intend to do in the immediate future, or what are the limits, if any, to their expansive and proselytizing tendencies. I have a strong admiration and regard for the valiant Russian people and for my wartime comrade, Marshal Stalin. There is deep sympathy and goodwill in Britain . . . towards the people of all the Russias and a resolve to persevere through many differences and rebuffs in establishing lasting friendships. We understand the Russian need to be secure on her western frontiers by the removal of all possibility of German aggression. We welcome Russia to her rightful place among the leading nations of the world. We welcome her flag upon the seas. Above all, we welcome constant, frequent and growing contacts between the Russian people and our own people on both sides of the Atlantic. It is my duty however . . . to place before you certain facts about the present position in Europe.

From Stettin in the Baltic to Trieste in the Adriatic, an iron curtain has descended across the Continent. Behind that line lie all the capitals of the ancient states of Central and Eastern Europe. Warsaw, Berlin, Prague, Vienna, Budapest, Belgrade, Bucharest and Sofia, all these famous cities and the populations around them lie in what I must call the Soviet sphere, and all are subject in one form or another, not only to Soviet influence but to a very high and, in many cases, increasing measure of control from Moscow. . . .

From what I have seen of our Russian friends and Allies during the war, I am convinced that there is nothing they admire so much as strength, and there is nothing for which they have less respect than for weakness, especially military weakness. For that reason the old doctrine of a balance of power is unsound. We cannot afford, if we can help it, to work on narrow margins, offering temptations to a triad of strength. If the Western Democracies stand together in strict adherence to the principles of the United Nations Charter, their influences for furthering those principles will be immense and no one is likely to molest them. If however they become divided or falter in their duty and if these all-important years are allowed to slip away then indeed catastrophe may overwhelm us all.

Winston Churchill, *Winston S. Churchill: His Complete Speeches, 1897–1963*, vol. 7, 1943–1949, edited by Robert Rhodes James (New York: Chelsea House Publishers, 1983), pp. 7290–7291.

Nikita Khrushchev, "Report to the Communist Party Congress (1961)"

Comrades! The competition of the two world social systems, the socialist and the capitalist, has been the chief content of the period since the 20th party Congress. It has become the pivot, the foundation of world development at the present historical stage. Two lines, two historical trends, have manifested themselves more and more clearly in social development. One is the line of social progress, peace and constructive activity. The other is the line of reaction, oppression and war.

In the course of the peaceful competition of the two systems capitalism has suffered a profound moral defeat in the eyes of all peoples. The common people are daily convinced that capitalism is incapable of solving a single one of the urgent problems confronting mankind. It becomes more and more obvious that only on the paths to socialism can a solution to these problems be found. Faith in the capitalist system and the capitalist path of development is dwindling. Monopoly capital, losing its influence, resorts more and more to intimidating and suppressing the masses of the people, to methods of open dictatorship in carrying out its domestic policy and to aggressive acts against other countries. But the masses of the people offer increasing resistance to reaction's acts.

It is no secret to anyone that the methods of intimidation and threat are not a sign of strength but evidence of the weakening of capitalism, the deepening of its general crisis. As the saying goes, if you can't hang on by the mane, you won't hang on by the tail! Reaction is still capable of dissolving parliaments in some countries in violation of their constitutions, of casting the best representatives of the people into prison, of sending cruisers and marines to subdue the "unruly." All this can put off for a time the approach of the fatal hour for the rule of capitalism. The imperialists are sawing away at the branch on which they sit. There is no force in the world capable of stopping man's advance along the road of progress.

Current Soviet Policies IV, edited by Charlotte Saikowski and Leo Gruliow, from the translations of the Current Digest of the Soviet Press. Joint Committee on Slavic Studies, 1962, pp. 42–45.

generated popular discontent and demands for a shift from the production of heavy machinery and armaments to the manufacture of consumer goods, for a measure of freedom in the arts, for an end to police repression. How, under these circumstance, could the regime keep de-Stalinization within safe limits? The thaw did unleash forces that proved difficult to control. Between 1956 and 1958, the Soviet prison camps released thousands of prisoners. Soviet citizens besieged the regime with requests to rehabilitate relatives who had been executed or imprisoned under Stalin, partly to make themselves again eligible for certain privileges of citizenship, such as housing. In the new cultural climate, private life—family issues, the shortage of men after the war, and the problem of orphans—became a legitimate subject of concern and discussion.

The thaw provided a brief window of opportunity for some of the Soviet Union's most important writers. In 1957, Boris Pasternak's novel *Doctor Zhivago* could not be published in the Soviet Union, and Pasternak was barred from receiving his Nobel Prize. That Aleksandr Solzhenitsyn's first novel, *One Day in the Life of Ivan Denisovich*, could be published in 1962 marked the relative cultural freedom of the thaw. *Ivan Denisovich* was based on Solzhenitsyn's own experiences in the camps, where he had spent eight years for criticizing Stalin in a letter, and was a powerful literary testimony to the repression Khrushchev had acknowledged. By 1964, however, Khrushchev had fallen and the thaw ended, driving criticism and writers such as Solzhenitsyn underground. *The First Circle* (1968), also autobiographical, told the story of a group of imprisoned scientists doing research for the secret police. Solzhenitsyn kept working on what would become *The Gulag Archipelago*, the first massive historical and literary study of the Stalinist camps (gulags). He secretly collected memoirs and personal testimony from prisoners, kept notes on cigarette rolling papers, and buried drafts of chapters behind his house. The Soviet secret

Nikita Khrushchev. Premier (1958–1964) and First Secretary of the Communist party (1953–1964) of the Soviet Union, Khrushchev visited the United States in 1959. Here he is shown joking with an Iowan farmer.

police found a copy of the manuscript in a taxicab just when Solzhenitsyn had finished it. *The Gulag Archipelago* was published nonetheless in 1973 in Paris, but one year later the regime arrested Solzhenitsyn on charges of treason and sent him into exile. The most celebrated Soviet dissident was neither a democrat nor pro-Western. He was an idealist and a moralist, with roots among nineteenth-century Russian authors and philosophers. From exile Solzhenitsyn attacked the corruptions of American commercialism as well as Soviet repressiveness.

REPRESSION IN EASTERN EUROPE

The year of Stalin's death, tensions had exploded in Eastern Europe. The East German government, burdened by reparations payments to the Soviet Union, faced an economic crisis. The government's awareness of West German economic success made matters worse. The illegal exodus of East German citizens to the West rose sharply: fifty-eight thousand left in March 1953 alone. In June, when the government demanded hefty increases in industrial productivity, strikes broke out in East Berlin. Unrest spread through-

out the country. The Soviet army put down the uprising, and hundreds were executed in the subsequent purge. In the aftermath, the East German government, under the leadership of Walter Ulbricht, used fears of disorder to solidify one-party rule.

In 1956, emboldened by Khrushchev's de-Stalinization, Poland and Hungary rebelled, demanding more independence in the management of their domestic affairs. Striking workers led the opposition in Poland. The government wavered, responding first with military repression and then with a promise of liberalization. Eventually the anti-Stalinist Polish leader Wladyslaw Gomulka won Soviet permission for his country to pursue its own "ways of Socialist development" by pledging Poland's loyalty to the terms of the Warsaw Pact.

Events in Hungary turned out very differently. The charismatic leader of Hungary's communist government, Imre Nagy, was as much a Hungarian nationalist as a communist. Under his government, protests against Moscow's policies developed into a much broader anticommunist struggle and, even more important, attempted secession from the Warsaw Pact. Khrushchev might contemplate looser ties between Eastern Europe and Moscow, but he would not tolerate an end to the pact. On November 4, 1956, Soviet troops occupied Budapest, arresting and executing leaders of the Hungarian rebellion. The Hungarians took up arms, and street fighting continued for several weeks. The Hungarians had hoped for Western aid, but Dwight Eisenhower, newly elected to a second term as president, steered clear of giving support. Soviet forces installed a new government under the staunchly communist Janos Kadar, the repression continued, and tens of thousands of Hungarian refugees fled for the West. Khrushchev's efforts at presenting a gentler, more conciliatory Soviet Union to the West had been shattered by revolt and repression.

Khrushchev's policy of "peaceful coexistence" with the West did not reduce his determination to stave off any military threat to Eastern Europe. By the mid-1950s, NATO's policy of putting battlefield nuclear weapons in West Germany seemed evidence of just such a threat. What was more, East Germans continued to flee the country via West Berlin. Between 1949 and 1961, 2.7 million East Germans left, blunt evidence of the unpopularity of the regime. Attempting to stem the tide, Khrushchev demanded that the West recognize the permanent division of Germany with a free city in Berlin. When that demand was refused, in 1961 the East German government built a ten-foot

The Berlin Wall, 1961. Thirteen years after the blockade, the East German government built a wall between East and West Berlin to stop the flow of escapees to the West. This manifestation of the "Iron Curtain" was dismantled in 1989.

in peacetime: improved communications (the invention of radar, for example), the development of synthetic materials, the increasing use of aluminum and alloy steels, and advances in the techniques of prefabrication. Wartime manufacturing had added significantly to nations' productive capacity. The Marshall Plan seems to have been less central than many claimed at the time, but it solved immediate problems having to do with the balance of payments and a shortage of American dollars to buy American goods. This boom was fueled by a third set of factors: high consumer demand and, consequently, very high levels of employment throughout the 1950s and 1960s. Brisk domestic and foreign consumption encouraged expansion, continued capital investment, and technological innovation. Rising demand for Europe's goods hastened agreements that encouraged the free flow of international trade and currencies (see below).

wall separating the two sectors of the city. The wall brought a dangerous show of force on both sides, as the Soviets and Americans mobilized reservists for war. The newly elected American president, John F. Kennedy, marked Berlin's contested status with a visit when he proclaimed that "all free men" were fellow citizens of noncommunist West Berlin. For almost thirty years, until 1989, the Berlin Wall remained a monument to how the "hot" war had gone "cold," and mirrored, darkly, the division of Germany and Europe as a whole.

It was now assumed that states would do much more economic management—directing investment, making decisions about what to modernize, coordinating policies between industries and countries—than before. This, too, was a legacy of wartime. As one British official observed, "We are all planners now." Government tactics for steering the economy varied. West Germany provided tax breaks to encourage business investment; Britain and Italy offered investment allowances to their steel and petroleum industries. France, Britain, Italy, and Austria led the way in experiments with nationalizing industry and services in an effort to raise productivity. The result was a series of "mixed" economies combining public and private ownership. In France, where public ownership was already well advanced in the 1930s, railways, electricity and gas, banking, radio and television, and a large segment of the automobile industry were brought under state management. In Britain, the list was equally long: coal and utilities; road, railroad, and air transport; and banking. Though nationalization was less common in West Germany, the railway system (state owned since the late nineteenth century); some electrical, chemical, and metallurgical concerns; and the Volkswagen company—the remnant of Hitler's attempt to produce a "people's car"—were all

ECONOMIC RENAISSANCE

How did Western Europe recover from World War II?

Despite the ongoing tensions of a global superpower rivalry, the postwar period brought a remarkable recovery in Western Europe: the economic "miracle." Economists still debate its causes. Some factors resulted directly from the war, which encouraged a variety of technological innovations that could be applied in state hands, though the latter was largely returned to the private sector in 1963.

These government policies and programs contributed to astonishing growth rates. Between 1945 and 1963 the average yearly growth of West Germany's gross domestic product (gross national product minus income received from abroad) was 7.6 percent; in Austria, 5.8 percent; in Italy, 6 percent; in the Netherlands, 4.7 percent; and so on. Not only did the economies recover from the war, they reversed prewar economic patterns of slack demand, overproduction, and insufficient investment. Production facilities were hard pressed to keep up with soaring demand.

West Germany's recovery was particularly spectacular, and particularly important to the rest of Europe. Production increased sixfold between 1948 and 1964. Unemployment fell to record lows, reaching 0.4 percent in 1965, when there were six jobs for every unemployed person. The contrast with the catastrophic unemployment of the Great Depression heightened the impression of a "miracle." Prices rose but then leveled off, and many citizens could plunge into a domestic buying spree that caused production to soar. In the 1950s, the state and private industry built half a million new housing units each year, to accommodate citizens whose homes had been destroyed, new resident refugees from East Germany and Eastern Europe, and transient workers from Italy, Spain, Greece, and elsewhere drawn by West Germany's high demand for labor. German cars, specialized mechanical goods, optics, and chemicals returned to their former role leading world markets. West German women were included in the process: during the 1950s, German politicians encouraged women to take up a role as "citizen consumers," as active but prudent buyers of goods that would keep the German economy humming.

Under the direction of a minister for planning, Jean Monnet, the French government played a direct role in industrial reform, contributing not only capital but expert advice, and facilitating shifts in the national labor pool to place workers where they were most needed. The plan gave priority to basic industries; the production of electricity doubled, the steel industry was thoroughly modernized, and the French railway system became the fastest and most efficient on the Continent. Italy's industrial "miracle" came later but was even more impressive. Stimulated by infusions of capital

from the government and from the Marshall Plan, Italian companies soon began to compete with other European international giants. The products of Olivetti, Fiat, and Pirelli became familiar in households around the world to an extent that no Italian goods had in the past. Electric power production doubled between 1938 and 1953. By 1954 real wages were 50 percent higher than they had been in 1938.

European nations with little in common in terms of political traditions or industrial patterns all shared in the general prosperity. Rising GNPs, however, did not level the differences among and within states. In southern Italy, illiteracy remained high and land continued to be held by a few rich families; the per capita GNP in Sweden was almost ten times that of Turkey. Britain remained a special case. The Conservative prime minister, Harold Macmillan, campaigned successfully for reelection in 1959 with the slogan "You've never had it so good"—an accurate enough boast. British growth was respectable when compared with past performance. Yet the British economy remained sluggish. The country was burdened with obsolete factories and methods, the legacy of its early industrialization, and by an unwillingness to adopt new techniques in old industries or invest in more successful new ones. It was plagued as well by a series of balance-of-payments crises precipitated by an inability to sell more goods abroad than it imported.

> Not only did the economies recover from the war, they reversed prewar economic patterns of slack demand, overproduction, and insufficient investment. Production facilities were hard pressed to keep up with soaring demand.

EUROPEAN ECONOMIC INTEGRATION

The Western European renaissance was a collective effort. From the Marshall Plan on, a series of international economic organizations began to bind the Western European countries together. The first of these was the European Coal and Steel Community (ECSC), founded in 1951 to coordinate trade in, and the management of, Europe's most crucial resources. Coal was still king in mid-twentieth century Europe; it fueled everything from steel manufacturing and trains to household heating, and counted for 82 percent of Europe's primary energy consumption. It was also key to relations between West Germany, with abundant coal mines, and France, with its coal-hungry steel mills. The ECSC joint High Authority, which consisted of experts from each of the participating countries, had power to regulate prices, to increase or limit production, and to

Heating Fuel Shortage in Great Britain. This scene of British householders lining up for coal during the bitterly cold winter of 1948 shows that "winners" as well as "losers" suffered in the immediate aftermath of the Second World War.

impose administrative fees. In 1957, the Treaty of Rome transformed France, West Germany, Italy, Belgium, Holland, and Luxembourg—into the European Economic Community (EEC), or Common Market. The EEC aimed to abolish trade barriers among its members. Moreover, the organization pledged itself to common external tariffs, to the free movement of labor and capital among the member nations, and to building uniform wage structures and social security systems in order to create similar working conditions throughout the Common Market. A commission headquartered in Brussels administered the program; by 1962, Brussels had more than three thousand "Eurocrats."

Integration did not proceed smoothly. Great Britain stayed away, fearing the effects of the ECSC on its declining coal industry and on its long-time trading relationship with Australia, New Zealand, and Canada.

Britain did not share France's need for raw materials and the others' need for markets; it continued to rely on its economic relations with the empire and Commonwealth. One of the few victors in World War II, Britain assumed that it could hold its global economic position in the postwar world. In the other countries, domestic opposition to EEC provisions on wages or agricultural prices often threatened to scuttle agreements. The French and other countries insisted on protecting agriculture, remembering the importance of the peasantry to political stability and invested in the countryside's place in national identity.

The seismic shifts that began to make oil and atomic power more important than coal (see Chapter 28) made the ECSC less effective. Still, the European Economic Community was a remarkable success. By 1963, it had become the world's largest importer. Its steel production was second only to that of the United States, and total industrial production was over 70 percent higher than it had been in 1950. Last, it established a new long-term political trend: individual countries sought to "Europeanize" solutions to their problems.

Likewise, crucial agreements reached in Bretton Woods, New Hampshire, in July 1944 aimed to coordinate the movements of the global economy and to "internationalize" solutions to economic crises, avoiding catastrophes such as those that plagued the 1930s. Bretton Woods created the International Monetary Fund and the World Bank, both designed to establish predictable and stable exchange rates, prevent speculation, and enable currencies—and consequently trade—to move freely. All other currencies were pegged to the dollar, which both reflected and enhanced the United States' role as the foremost financial power. The new international system was formed with the American-European sphere in mind, but these organizations soon began to play a role in economic development in what came to be known as the Third World. The postwar period, then, quickened global economic integration, largely on American terms.

ECONOMIC DEVELOPMENT IN THE EAST

Although economic development in Eastern Europe was not nearly so dramatic as that in the West, significant advances occurred there as well. National incomes rose and output increased. Poland and Hungary, in particular, strengthened their economic connections with the West, primarily with France and West Germany. By the late 1970s, about 30 percent of Eastern Europe's trade was conducted outside the Soviet bloc. Nevertheless, the Soviet Union required its satellites to design their economic policies to serve more than their own national interests. Regulations governing COMECON, the Eastern European equivalent of the Common Market, ensured that the Soviet Union could sell its exports at prices well above the world level and compelled other members to trade with the Soviet Union to their disadvantage. Emphasis initially was on heavy industry and collectivized agriculture, though political tension in countries such as Hungary and Poland forced the Soviets eventually to moderate their policies so as to permit the manufacture of more consumer goods and the development of a modest trade with the West.

> Although the British Labour party and continental socialist parties pressed these measures, welfare was a consensus issue, backed by the moderate coalitions that governed most postwar Western European states.

THE WELFARE STATE

Economic growth became one of the watchwords of the postwar era. Social welfare was another. The roots of the new legislation extended back to the insurance plans for old age, sickness, and disability introduced by Bismarck in Germany in the late 1880s. But economic expansion allowed postwar European states to fund more comprehensive social programs, and commitments to putting democracy on a stronger footing provided the political motivation. Clement Atlee, a socialist and the leader of the British Labour party, coined the term "welfare state"; his government, in power until 1951, led the way in enacting legislation that provided free medical care to all through the National Health Service, assistance to families, and guaranteed secondary education of some kind. The welfare state also rested on the assumption that governments could and should try to support popular purchasing power, generate demand, and provide either employment or unemployment insurance, assumptions spelled out earlier by John Maynard Keynes (*General Theory*, 1936) or William Beveridge's important 1943 report on full employment. Although the British Labour party and continental socialist parties pressed these measures, welfare was a consensus issue, backed by the moderate coalitions that governed most postwar Western European states.

Understood in this way, welfare was not poor relief, but an entitlement. Thus it marked a break with centuries-old ways of thinking about poverty and citizenship. In 1950, the British sociologist T. H. Marshall outlined a short but influential history of states, citizenship, and rights. The late seventeenth and eighteenth centuries had brought civil rights, Marshall argued—the Lockean freedoms of religion, property, and contract. The nineteenth century brought political rights. The twentieth century would bring the "whole range [of social rights] from the right to a modicum of economic welfare and security to the right to share to the full in the social heritage and to live the life of a civilized being according to the standards prevailing in the society." It is worth noting that Marshall's short history did not explain why the history of women's rights was so different; not only did they get civil and political rights late, but they gained social rights only insofar as they were family members or mothers. Still, Marshall's theory best expressed the new political current of social democracy: the growing conviction that democracy and social welfare went hand in hand, that all deserved the same "social heritage," and that diminishing the sharp inequalities of class society and giving all the would strengthen democratic culture.

EUROPEAN POLITICS

Postwar political leaders were overwhelmingly pragmatic. Konrad Adenauer, the West German chancellor from 1949 to 1963, despised German militarism and blamed that tradition for Hitler's rise to power. Still, he was apprehensive about German parliamentary democracy and governed in a paternalistic, sometimes authoritarian, manner. His determination to end the centuries-old hostility between France and Germany contributed significantly to the movement toward economic union. Alcide De Gasperi, the Italian premier from 1948 to 1953, was also centrist. Among postwar French leaders, the most colorful was the Resistance hero General Charles de Gaulle. De Gaulle had retired from politics in 1946 when French voters refused to accept his proposals for strengthening the executive branch of the government. In 1958, faced with civil turmoil caused by the Algerian war (see p. 990) and an abortive coup attempt by a group of right-wing army

EUROPE DURING THE COLD WAR

Examine the membership of NATO and the Warsaw Pact, respectively. What type of government characterized the member states of each? Why did the membership of each alliance stay relatively stable for nearly half a century? Why did certain socialist governments (Sweden, Finland) and federal democracies (Switzerland) remain neutral rather than join either pact? Why did Yugoslavia, under a communist government, not join the Warsaw Pact?

officers, France's government collapsed and de Gaulle was invited to return. De Gaulle accepted, but insisted on a new constitution. That constitution, which created the Fifth Republic in 1958, strengthened the executive branch of the government in an effort to avoid the parliamentary deadlocks that had weakened the country earlier. De Gaulle used his new authority to restore France's power and prestige. "France is not really herself unless in the front rank," he wrote in his memoirs. "France cannot be France without greatness." Greatness, for de Gaulle, involved reorienting foreign policy, which included an end to France's grip on Algeria. Resisting U.S. influence in Europe, he pulled French forces out of NATO in 1966. He cultivated better relations with the Soviet Union and with West Germany. Finally, he accelerated French economic and

Charles de Gaulle Presenting His Plan to Strengthen the Executive Branch of the Government in 1946. When voters rejected his ideas, he retired, only to return in 1958 to outline a new constitution.

industrial expansion by building a modern military establishment, complete with atomic weapons. Like his counterparts, de Gaulle was not, by nature, a democrat. He steered a centrist course, working hard to produce "practical" solutions to political problems and thereby undermine radicalism in any form. Most other Western European nations did the same.

REVOLUTION, ANTICOLONIALISM, AND THE COLD WAR

What were the links between decolonization, World War II, and the cold war?

In the colonial world as in Europe, the end of war unleashed new conflicts. Those conflicts became closely bound up with Europe's political and economic recovery, they had an enormous if delayed effect on Western culture, and they complicated the cold war. The cold war, as we have seen, created two powerful centers of

gravity for world politics. But the wave of anticolonial independence movements that swept through postwar Asia and Africa created a new group of nations that would attempt to avoid aligning with one or the other bloc, and would call itself the "Third World."

THE CHINESE REVOLUTION

The first in this wave of movements was also the single most radical change in the developing world after World War II: the Chinese Revolution. A civil war had raged in China since 1926, when Nationalist forces under Jiang Jeishi (Chiang Kai-shek, 1887–1975) had fought first in the south, then in the north, against communist insurgents under the leadership of Mao Zedong (1893–1976). A truce in 1937 brought the warring sides together to face the Japanese. When Japan was defeated and the occupation ended, the communists, still led by Mao, refused to surrender the northern provinces they controlled. Civil war broke out again. The United States intervened, first to mediate and then with massive military support for the Nationalists. But the Nationalists, corrupt and unrepresentative, were defeated in the field and surrendered in 1949.

Even more than the Russian Revolution, the Chinese Revolution was the act of a nation of peasants. With a

WHAT WERE THE LINKS BETWEEN DECOLONIZATION, WORLD WAR II, AND THE COLD WAR?

REVOLUTION, ANTICOLONIALISM, AND THE COLD WAR   991

program that emphasized radical reform in the countryside (reducing rents, providing health care and education, and reforming marriage) peasant mobilization, and autonomy from Western colonial powers, Mao adapted Marxism to conditions very different from those imagined by its founders. And as in Russia, communism in China provided a model—not necessarily successful—for economic development. The new leaders of the "great people's revolution" set about turning the country into a modern, industrial nation within a generation, at huge human cost and with very mixed results.

As a successful peasant revolt, the Chinese Revolution stood as a model to anticolonial activists the world over. To colonial powers, it represented a dangerous possible outcome of decolonization. The "loss of China" provoked fear and consternation in the West, particularly in the United States. Although Mao and Stalin distrusted each other, and relations between the two largest communist countries were extremely difficult, the United States considered these two nations a "communist bloc" until the early 1970s. In its immediate aftermath, the Chinese Revolution seemed to tip the balance in a standoff between communism and capital-

ism and it intensified Western military and diplomatic anxiety about governments throughout Asia.

THE KOREAN WAR

This anxiety helped make Korea into one of the "hot spots" of the cold war. Effectively a Japanese colony since the 1890s, Korea suffered as its Japanese occupiers subjected the country to horrendous violence and exploited its resources for generations. At the end of World War II the Soviet Union's eastern offensive forced the Japanese out; Korea was then divided between those Russian troops in the north and their American counterparts in the south. As in Germany, two new states were established: communist North Korea, run by the Soviet client Kim Jong Il, and South Korea, run by the anticommunist autocrat Syngman Rhee. North Korea's government soon decided that this arrangement should not last. In June 1950, communist North Korean troops attacked across the border, crushing resistance in the south and forcing noncommunist forces and a small American garrison to retreat to the far end of the peninsula. The United States took advantage of a temporary Russian boycott of the

A Red Guard Demonstration. Middle-school students display their solidarity with Mao Zedong's revolution by waving copies of a book of his quotations. The slogan proclaims, "Not only are we able to destroy the old world, we are able to build a new world instead—Mao Zedong."

United Nations and brought the invasion before the Security Council. The council passed a resolution permitting an American-led "police action" to defend South Korea and counter the communists.

That action fell to General Douglas MacArthur, a hero of the Second World War and the military governor of occupied Japan. He mounted an audacious amphibious attack behind North Korean lines and cut northern forces to pieces. MacArthur drove the Korean communists to the Chinese border and pressed for the authority to attack them as they retreated into China, hoping to punish China and help reverse the Chinese Revolution. President Harry S. Truman (1945–1953) denied this rash request and relieved MacArthur of command for exceeding his authority. The price had already been paid, however; more than a million Chinese troops flooded across the border in support of the North Koreans. The international troops aiding South Korea were forced into a bloody, headlong retreat in the dead of winter. During that difficult winter the able and patient American general Matthew Ridgeway took over from MacArthur and stemmed the retreat. The war, however, became a stalemate. Chinese and North Korean troops dug in against the United Nations force, composed largely of American and South Korean troops but drawn from around the world—small contingents from Britain, Australia, Ethiopia, the Netherlands, and Turkey distinguished themselves in the fighting. The conflict dragged on for two years as peace talks began. It was a bitter war of artillery battles, hand-to-hand fighting, attacks up well-defended hillsides, and punishing cold. The end, decreed in June of 1953, was inconclusive. Korea remained divided roughly along the original line drawn in 1945, no longer at war but not at peace. With fifty-three thousand Americans and over a million Koreans and Chinese dead, South Korea had not been "lost," but neither had China or the United States won a decisive victory. As in Germany, the inability of major powers to achieve their ultimate goals resulted in a divisive settlement and a divided nation.

DECOLONIZATION

The Chinese Revolution proved the start of a larger wave. Between 1947 and 1960 the sprawling European empires built during the nineteenth century disintegrated. Imperialism had always provoked resistance. Opposition to colonial rule had stiffened after World War I, forcing war-weakened European states to renegotiate the terms of empire. After World War II, older

CHRONOLOGY

MAJOR DEVELOPMENTS IN ASIA, 1947–PRESENT

India gains independence	1947
Chinese Communist Revolution	1949
Korean War	1950–1953
Vietnamese defeat the French	1954
Chinese Cultural Revolution	1960s
Vietnam war (U.S.)	1964–1975
United States recognizes Communist China	1972
Tiananmen Square	1989
Hong Kong reverts to Chinese control	1997

forms of empire quickly became untenable. In some regions, European states simply sought to cut their losses and withdraw, their financial, political, and human resources depleted. In others, well-organized and tenacious nationalist movements successfully demanded new constitutional arrangements and independence. In a third set of cases, European powers were drawn into complicated, multifaceted, and extremely violent struggles between different movements of indigenous peoples and European settler communities—conflicts the European states had helped create.

THE BRITISH EMPIRE UNRAVELS

India was the first and largest of the colonies to win self-government following the war. As we have seen, rebellions such as the Sepoy Mutiny challenged the representatives of Britain in India throughout the nineteenth century (see Chapter 25). During the early stages of the Second World War, the Indian National Congress (founded 1885), the umbrella party for the independence movement, called on Britain to "quit India." The extraordinary Indian nationalist Mohandas K. (Mahatma) Gandhi (1869–1948) had been at work in India since the 1920s, and had pioneered anticolonial ideas and tactics that echoed the world over. In the face of colonial domination, Gandhi advocated not violence but *swaraj*, or self-rule, urging Indians individually and collectively to develop their own resources and to withdraw from the imperial economy—by going on strike, refusing to pay taxes, or boycotting imported textiles and wearing homespun. By 1947 Gandhi and his fellow nationalist Jawaharlal Nehru (1889–1964, prime minister 1947–1964), the leader of the proindependence Congress party, had gained such

MOHANDAS GANDHI AND NONVIOLENT ANTICOLONIALISM

After leading a campaign for Indian rights in South Africa between 1894 and 1914, Mohandas K. Gandhi (1869–1948), known as Mahatma ("great-souled") Gandhi, became a leader in the long battle for home rule in India. This battle was finally won in 1947 and brought with it the partition of India and the creation of Pakistan. Gandhi's insistence on the power of nonviolent noncooperation brought him to the forefront of Indian politics and provided a model for many later liberation struggles, including the American civil rights movement. Gandhi argued that only nonviolent resistance, which dramatized the injustice of colonial rule and colonial law, had the spiritual force to unite a community and end colonialism.

Passive resistance is a method of securing rights by personal suffering; it is the reverse of resistance by arms. When I refuse to do a thing that is repugnant to my conscience, I use soul-force. For instance, the Government of the day has passed a law which is applicable to me. I do not like it. If by using violence I force the Government to repeal the law, I am employing what may be termed body-force. If I do not obey the law and accept the penalty for its breach, I use soul-force. It involves sacrifice of self.

Everybody admits that sacrifice of self is infinitely superior to sacrifice of others. Moreover, if this kind of force is used in a cause that is unjust, only the person using it suffers. He does not make others suffer for his mistakes. Men have before now done many things which were subsequently found to have been wrong. . . . It is therefore meet that he should not do that which he knows to be wrong, and suffer the consequence whatever it may be. This is the key to the use of soul-force. . . .

It is contrary to our manhood if we obey laws repugnant to our conscience. Such teaching is opposed to religion and means slavery. If the Government were to ask us to go about without any clothing, should we do so? If I were a passive resister, I would say to them that I would have nothing to do with their law. But we have so forgotten ourselves and become so compliant that we do not mind any degrading law.

A man who has realized his manhood, who fears only God, will fear no one else. Man-made laws are not necessarily binding on him. Even the Government does not expect any such thing from us. They do not say: "You must do such and such a thing." But they say: "If you do not do it, we will punish you." We are sunk so low that we fancy that it is our duty and our religion to do what the law lays down. If man will only realize that it is unmanly to obey laws that are unjust, no man's tyranny will enslave him. This is the key to self-rule or home-rule.

M. K. Gandhi, "Indian Home Rule (1909)," in *The Gandhi Reader: A Source Book of His Life and Writings*, edited by Homer A. Jack (Bloomington: Indiana University Press, 1956), pp. 104–121.

widespread support that the British found it impossible to continue in power. The Labour party government elected in Britain in 1945 had always favored Indian independence. Now that independence became a British political necessity.

While talks established the procedures for independence, however, India was torn by ethnic and religious conflict. A Muslim League, led by Mohammed Ali Jinnah (1876–1948), wanted autonomy in largely Muslim areas and feared the predominantly Hindu Congress party's authority in a single united state. Cycles of riot-

ing broke out between the two religious communities. In June 1947, British India was "partitioned" into the nations of India (majority Hindu) and Pakistan (majority Muslim). The process of partition brought brutal religious and ethnic warfare. More than a million Hindus and Muslims died, and an estimated 12 million became refugees, evicted from their lands or fleeing the fighting. Throughout the chaos Gandhi, now eighty, continued to protest violence and to focus attention on overcoming the legacy of colonialism. He argued that "[R]eal freedom will come when we free ourselves of

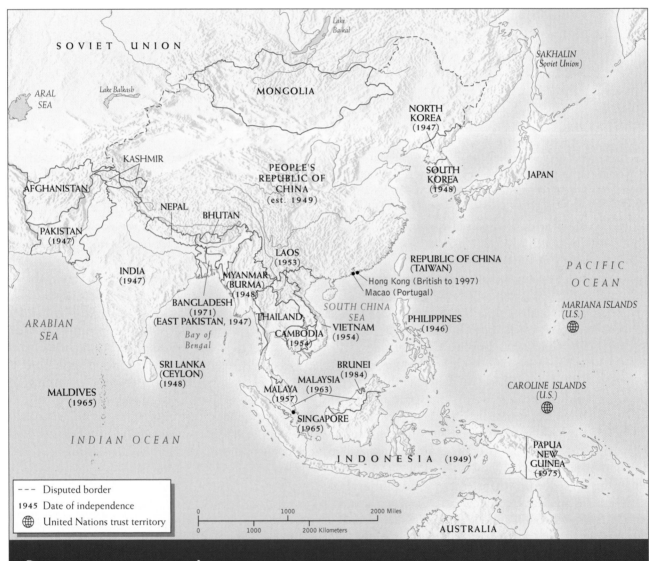

DECOLONIZATION IN ASIA

Britain and the United States facilitated relatively peaceful transitions to independence for their possessions in Asia. France fought hard to hold Indochina but left after major military defeats. Cold war tensions in Asia led to both the Korean War and the Vietnam War.

WHAT WERE THE LINKS BETWEEN DECOLONIZATION, WORLD WAR II, AND THE COLD WAR?

REVOLUTION, ANTICOLONIALISM, AND THE COLD WAR   995

Leaders of Indian Nationalism—Nehru and Gandhi. Mohandas Gandhi was assassinated in 1948. Jawaharlal Nehru served as prime minister of India from 1947 to his death in 1964.

the dominance of western education, western culture, and western way of living which have been ingrained in us." In January 1948, he was assassinated by a Hindu zealot. Conflict continued between the independent states of India and Pakistan. Nehru, who became first prime minister of India, embarked on a program of industrialization and modernization—not at all what Gandhi would have counseled. Nehru proved particularly adept at maneuvering in the cold war world, steering a course of nonalignment with either of the blocs, getting aid for industry from the USSR and food imports from the United States.

PALESTINE

The year 1948 brought more crises for the British empire, including an end to the British mandate in Palestine. During WWI, British diplomats had encouraged Arab nationalist revolts against the Ottoman empire. With the 1917 Balfour Declaration, they had also promised a "Jewish homeland" in Palestine for European Zionists. Contradictory promises and the flight of European Jews from Nazi Germany contributed to rising conflict between Jewish settlers and Arabs in Palestine during the 1930s and provoked an Arab revolt bloodily suppressed by the British. At the same time, the newly important oil concessions in the Middle East were multiplying Britain's strategic interests in the Suez Canal, Egypt, and the Arab nations generally.

Mediating local conflicts and balancing their own interests proved an impossible task. In 1939, in the name of regional stability, the British strictly limited further Jewish immigration. They tried to maintain that limit after the war, but now they faced pressure from tens of thousands of Jewish refugees from Europe. The conflict quickly became a three-way war: among Palestinian Arabs fighting for what they considered their land and their independence, Jewish settlers and Zionist militants determined to defy British restrictions, and British administrators with divided sympathies, embarrassed and shocked by the plight of Jewish refugees and committed to maintaining good Anglo-Arab relations. The British responded militarily. By 1947, there was one British soldier for every eighteen inhabitants of the Mandate. The years of fighting, however, with terrorist tactics on all sides, persuaded the British to leave. The United Nations voted (by a narrow margin) to partition the territory into two states. Neither Jewish settlers nor

Mob of Jewish Children in Tel Aviv, 1948. On the day the new state of Israel is declared in Palestine, a street vendor is overrun in the demand to purchase the new flag.

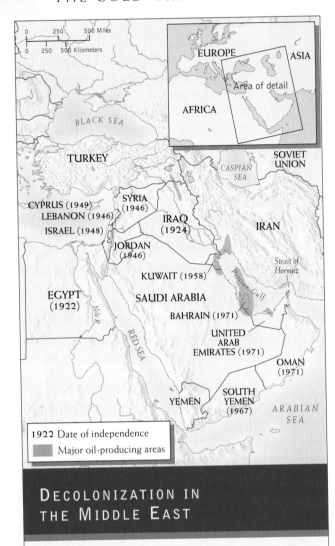

DECOLONIZATION IN THE MIDDLE EAST

Under the control of the Ottoman Empire prior to World War I, much of the Middle East was ruled directly or indirectly by the British and French after the war. Britain, the main colonial power, granted independence to most of its holdings in the first years after World War II, although it did maintain control of small states in the Persian Gulf and Arabian Sea region until 1971.

of Jordan. Remarkably enough, the conflict did not become a cold war confrontation at the start. For their own reasons, both Soviets and Americans recognized Israel. The new nation, however, marked a permanent change to the culture and balance of power in the region.

AFRICA

A number of West African colonies established assertive independence movements before and during the 1950s, and the British government moved hesitantly to meet their demands. By the middle of the 1950s, Britain agreed to a variety of terms for independence in these territories, leaving them with written constitutions and a British legal system, but little else in terms of modern infrastructure or economic support. Defenders of British colonialism claimed that these formal institutions would give advantages to the independent states, but without other resources even the most promising foundered. Ghana, known formerly as the Gold Coast and the first of these colonies to gain independence, was seen in the early 1960s as a model for free African nations. Its politics soon degenerated, however, and its president, Kwame Nkrumah, became the first of several African leaders driven from office for corruption and autocratic behavior.

Belgium and France also withdrew from their holdings. By 1965 virtually all of the former African colonies had become independent, and virtually none of them possessed the means to redress losses from colonialism to make that independence work. As Belgian authorities raced out of the Congo in 1960, they left crumbling railways and fewer than two dozen indigenous persons with college educations.

The process of decolonization was relatively peaceful—except where large populations of European settlers complicated European withdrawal. In the north, settler resistance made the French exit from Algeria wrenching and complex (see below). In the east, in Kenya, the majority Kikuyu population revolted against British rule and against a small group of settlers. The uprising, which came to be known as the Mau Mau rebellion, soon turned bloody. British troops fired freely at targets in rebel-occupied areas, sometimes killing civilians. Internment camps set up by colonial security forces became sites of atrocities that drew public investigations and condemnation by even the most conservative British politicians and army officers. In 1963, a decade after the rebellion began, the British conceded Kenyan independence.

Palestinian Arabs found the partition satisfactory and both began to fight for territory even before British troops withdrew. No sooner did Israel declare its independence in May 1948 than five neighboring states invaded. The new but well-organized Israeli nation survived the war and extended its boundaries. On the losing side a million Palestinian Arabs who fled or were expelled found themselves clustered in refugee camps in the Gaza strip and on the West Bank of the Jordan river, which the armistice granted to an enlarged state

WHAT WERE THE LINKS BETWEEN DECOLONIZATION, WORLD WAR II, AND THE COLD WAR?

REVOLUTION, ANTICOLONIALISM, AND THE COLD WAR   997

Legend:
- Date of independence
- Former colonial power
  - British
  - French
  - Portuguese
  - Spanish
  - Belgian
  - Italian
  - Former German colony, mandate of League of Nations after WWI
  - Independent state
- ✳ Anti-colonial revolt or war since 1945

Map labels:
TUNISIA 1956
MEDITERRANEAN SEA
MOROCCO 1956
ATLAS MOUNTAINS
ALGERIA 1962 ✳1954–1962
LIBYA 1951
Suez crisis ✳ 1956
EGYPT 1922 with severe restrictions 1954 British withdraw troops
WESTERN SAHARA 1975
SAHARA DESERT
RED SEA
NUBIAN DESERT
Nile R.
MAURITANIA 1960
MALI 1960
NIGER 1960
CHAD 1960
SUDAN 1956
ERITREA 1993
Senegal R.
SENEGAL 1960
GAMBIA 1965
Gambia
Niger R.
UPPER VOLTA (BURKINA FASO) 1960
Lake Chad
DJIBOUTI 1977
GUINEA BISSAU 1974 ✳1961–1974
GUINEA 1958
DAHOMEY (BENIN) 1960
NIGERIA 1960
CENTRAL AFRICAN REPUBLIC 1960
ETHIOPIAN HIGHLANDS
ETHIOPIA
IVORY COAST 1960
SIERRA LEONE 1961
LIBERIA
GHANA 1957
TOGO 1960
CAMEROON 1960
SOMALIA 1960 ✳1950–1960
EQUATORIAL GUINEA 1968
GABON 1960
CONGO R.
RWANDA 1962
UGANDA 1962
KENYA 1963 ✳1952–1957
SÃO TOMÉ & PRINCIPE 1975
CONGO 1960
CONGO BASIN
CONGO (ZAIRE) 1960
BURUNDI 1962
Lake Victoria
ATLANTIC OCEAN
Lake Tanganyika
TANZANIA (TANGANYIKA) 1961
Lake Nyasa
ANGOLA 1975 ✳1961–1974
ZAMBIA 1964
Zambezi
MALAWI 1964
RHODESIA 1965
ZIMBABWE 1980 ✳1965–1980
MADAGASCAR 1960 ✳1947–1948
SOUTH-WEST AFRICA (NAMIBIA) (controlled by South Africa) 1990 ✳1966–1990
BOTSWANA 1966
KALAHARI DESERT
MOZAMBIQUE 1975 ✳1964–1974
INDIAN OCEAN
SOUTH AFRICA 1910–1961 1994 whole population votes ✳1948–1994
SWAZILAND 1968
LESOTHO 1966

Scale: 0 500 1000 Miles
0 500 1000 Kilometers

DECOLONIZATION OF AFRICA

African decolonization, like such developments elsewhere, occurred after World War II, largely in the 1950s, 1960s, and 1970s.

In the late 1950s, the British prime minister Harold Macmillan endorsed independence for a number of Britain's African colonies as a response to powerful "winds of change." In southern Africa, the exceptionally large and wealthy population of European settlers set their sails against those winds, a resistance that continued on for decades. These settlers, a mixture of English migrants and the Franco-Dutch Afrikaners who traced their arrival to the eighteenth century, controlled huge tracts of fertile farmland along with some of the most lucrative gold and diamond mines on earth. This was especially true in South Africa. There, during the late 1940s, Britain's Labour government set aside its deep dislike of Afrikaner racism in a fateful political bargain. In return for guarantees that South African gold would be used carefully to support Britain's global financial power, Britain tolerated the introduction of apartheid in South Africa. Even by other standards of segregation, apartheid was especially harsh. Under its terms, Africans, Indians, and colored persons of mixed descent lost all political rights. All the institutions of social life, including marriage and schools, were segregated. What was more, the government tried to block the dramatic social consequences of the expansion of mining and industrialization in general, especially African migration to cities and a new wave of labor militancy in the mines. Apartheid required Africans to live in designated "homelands," forbade them to travel without specific permits, and created elaborate government bureaus to manage the labor essential to the economy. The government also banned any political protest. These measures made Western powers uncomfortable with the segregationist regime, but white South Africans held on to American support by presenting themselves as a bulwark against communism.

To the north, in the territories of Rhodesia, the British government encouraged a large federation, controlled by white settlers but with the opportunity for majority rule in the future. By the early 1960s, however, the federation was on the verge of collapse; the majority-rule state of Malawi was allowed to exit the federation in 1964, and Rhodesia split on northern and southern lines. In the north, the premier relented and accepted majority government under the black populist Kenneth Kaunda. In the south, angry Afrikaners backed by two hundred thousand right-wing English migrants who had arrived since 1945 refused to accept majority rule. When the British government attempted to force their hand, the settlers unilaterally declared independence in 1965 and began a bloody civil war against Southern Rhodesia's black population that lasted half a generation.

CRISIS IN SUEZ AND THE END OF AN ERA

For postwar Britain, empire was not only politically complicated, it cost too much. Britain began to withdraw from naval and air bases around the world because they had become too expensive to maintain. The Labour government did try to maintain British power and prestige in the postwar world. In Malaya, British forces repressed a revolt by ethnic Chinese communists and then helped support the independent states of Singapore and Malaysia, maintaining British companies' and banks' ties with Malaysia's lucrative rubber and oil reserves. Labour also launched carefully targeted efforts at "colonial development" to tap local natural resources Britain hoped to sell on world markets. "Development," however, was underfunded and largely disregarded in favor of fulfilling cold war commitments elsewhere. In the Middle East, the British government protected several oil-rich states with its military and helped overthrow a nationalist government in Iran to ensure that the oil states invested their money in British financial markets.

In Egypt, however, the British refused to yield a traditional point of imperial pride. In 1951 nationalists compelled the British to agree to withdraw their troops from Egyptian territory within three years. In 1952 a group of nationalist army officers deposed Egypt's King Farouk, who had close ties to Britain, and proclaimed a republic. Shortly after the final British withdrawal an Egyptian colonel, Gamal Abdel Nasser (1918–1970), became president of the country (1956–1970). His first major public act as president was to nationalize the Suez Canal Company. So doing would help finance the construction of the Aswan Dam on the Nile, and both the dam and nationalizing the canal represented economic independence and Egyptian national pride. Nasser also helped to develop the anticolonial ideology of pan-Arabism, proposing that Arab nationalists throughout the Islamic world should create an alliance of modern nations, no longer beholden to the West. Finally, Nasser was also willing to take aid and support from the Soviets

> Nasser also helped to develop the anticolonial ideology of pan-Arabism, proposing that Arab nationalists throughout the Islamic world should create an alliance of modern nations, no longer beholden to the West.

WHAT WERE THE LINKS BETWEEN DECOLONIZATION, WORLD WAR II, AND THE COLD WAR?

REVOLUTION, ANTICOLONIALISM, AND THE COLD WAR   999

CHRONOLOGY

MAJOR DEVELOPMENTS IN AFRICA, 1952–PRESENT

Egypt gains independence	1952
Congo gains independence	1960
Algeria gains independence	1962
Rhodesia gains independence	1965
Ethnic and tribal conflicts throughout Africa	1960s–present
Massive economic decline	1970s–1990s
Apartheid ends in South Africa	1992–1994
AIDS epidemic in sub-Saharan Africa	1980s–present

in order to achieve that goal, which made the canal into a cold war issue.

Three nations found Nasser and his pan-Arab ideals threatening. Israel, surrounded on all sides by unfriendly neighbors, was looking for an opportunity to seize the strategic Sinai Peninsula and create a buffer against Egypt. France, already fighting a war against Algerian nationalists, hoped to destroy what it considered the Egyptian source of Arab nationalism. Britain depended on the canal as a route to its strategic bases and was stung by this blow to imperial dignity. Though the British were reluctant to intervene, they were urged on by their prime minister, Sir Anthony Eden; Eden had developed a deep personal hatred of Nasser. In the autumn of 1956, the three nations colluded in an attack on Egypt. Israel occupied the Sinai while British and French jets destroyed Egypt's air force on the ground. The former colonial powers landed troops at the mouth of the canal but lacked the resources to push on in strength toward Cairo. As a result the war left Nasser in power and made him a hero to the Egyptian public for holding the imperialists at bay. The attack was condemned around the world. The United States angrily called its allies' bluff, inflicting severe financial penalties on Britain and France. Both countries were forced to withdraw their expeditions. For policy makers in Great Britain and France, the failure at Suez marked the end of an era.

FRENCH DECOLONIZATION

In two particular cases, France's experience of decolonization was bloodier, more difficult, and more damaging to French prestige and domestic politics than any in Britain's experience, with the possible exception of Northern Ireland. The first was Indochina, where

French efforts to restore imperial authority after losing it in World War II only resulted in military defeat and further humiliation. The second case, Algeria, became not only a violent colonial war but also a struggle with serious political ramifications at home.

THE FIRST VIETNAM WAR, 1946–1954

Indochina was one of France's last major imperial acquisitions in the nineteenth century. Here, as elsewhere, the two world wars had helped galvanize first nationalist and then, also, communist independence movements. In Indonesia, nationalist forces rebelled against Dutch efforts to restore colonialism, and the country became independent in 1949. In Indochina, the communist resistance became particularly effective under the leadership of Ho Chi Minh. Ho was French educated and, his expectations raised by the Wilsonian principles of self-determination, had hoped his country might win independence at Versailles in 1919 (see Chapter 24). He read Marx and Lenin, and absorbed the Chinese communists' lessons about organizing peasants around social and agrarian as well as national issues. During World War II, Ho's movement fought first the Vichy government of the colony and later Japanese occupiers, and provided intelligence reports for the Allies. In 1945, however, the United States and Britain repudiated their relationship with Ho's independence movement and allowed the French to reclaim their colonies throughout Southeast Asia. The Vietnamese communists, who were fierce nationalists as well as Marxists, renewed their guerrilla war against the French.

The fighting was protracted and bloody; France saw in it a chance to redeem its national pride. After one of France's most capable generals, Jean de Lattre de Tassigny, finally achieved a military advantage against the rebels in 1951, the French government might have decolonized on favorable terms. Instead, it decided to press on for total victory, sending troops deep into Vietnamese territory to root out the rebels. One major base was established in a valley bordering modern Laos, at a hamlet called Dien Bien Phu. Ringed by high mountains, this vulnerable spot became a base for thousands of elite French paratroopers and colonial soldiers from Algeria and West Africa—the best of France's troops. The rebels besieged the base. Tens of thousands of Vietnamese nationalist fighters hauled heavy artillery by hand up the mountainsides and bombarded the network of forts set up by the French. The siege lasted for months, becoming a protracted national crisis in France.

THE VIETNAM WAR: AMERICAN ANALYSIS OF THE FRENCH SITUATION

At the end of World War II, the French government sought to recoup its prestige and empire by reasserting control of the former colony of Indochina. The French faced fierce resistance from nationalist forces under the French-educated leader Ho Chi Minh. Within a few years, American advisors were beginning to shore up the faltering French army. Cold war ideology, anxiety about China and Korea, and a conviction that they could do what the French could not combined to draw the Americans more deeply into the war. In 1950, the Central Intelligence Agency drew up this analysis of the strategic situation.

For more than three years, an intense conflict has been in progress in Indochina in which nationalistic Vietnamese forces under the leadership of the Moscow-trained revolutionist, Ho Chi Minh, have opposed the reimposition of French authority. Within Vietnam . . . a precarious military balance exists between the French and their Vietnamese followers on the one hand and Ho's resistance forces on the other. Thus far, French progress toward both political and military objectives has been substantially less than is necessary to eliminate the threat to French tenure posed by the resistance.

The French position and Bao Dai's [emperor of Vietnam since 1926] prospects have recently been further weakened: politically by Chinese Communist and Soviet recognition of Ho Chi Minh, and militarily by the ability of the Chinese Communist forces to make military supplies available to Ho's forces. Unless the French and Bao Dai receive substantial outside assistance, this combined political and military pressure may accelerate a French withdrawal from all or most of Indochina which, previous to the Chinese Communist and Soviet recognition of Ho, had been estimated as probably occurring within two years. . . .

The fighting in Indochina constitutes a progressive drain on French military resources which is weakening France as a partner in the Western alliance. If France is driven from Indochina, the resulting emergence of an indigenous Communist-oriented regime in Vietnam, in combination with the pressures which will be exerted by the new government of China and the Soviet Union, can be expected to cause adjacent Thailand and Burma to yield to this Communist advance. Under these conditions Malaya and Indonesia would also become highly vulnerable.

The French are trying to halt the present unfavorable trend by according certain aspects of sovereignty to Emperor Bao Dai. . . . The French political aim is to attract non-Communist nationalists from the leadership of Ho Chi Minh to that of Bao Dai.

Meanwhile, Soviet and Chinese Communist recognition of Ho's regime has made it clear that the Kremlin is now prepared to exert greater pressure to achieve its objective of installing a Communist regime in Indochina. France alone is incapable of preventing such a development and can turn only to the US for assistance in thwarting this Communist strategy. Having already publicly proclaimed support of Bao Dai, the US is now faced with the choice of bolstering his weak and vulnerable position or of abandoning him and accepting the far-reaching consequences of Communist control of Indochina.

From the National Archives, College Park, Md. Record Group 263 (Records of the Central Intelligence Agency), *Estimates of the Office of Research Evaluation, 1946–1950*, box 4.

WHAT WERE THE LINKS BETWEEN DECOLONIZATION, WORLD WAR II, AND THE COLD WAR?

REVOLUTION, ANTICOLONIALISM, AND THE COLD WAR   1001

"Dien-Bien-Phu: . . . they sacrificed themselves for liberty."
The sentiments expressed in this poster, which was intended
to commemorate the French soldiers who died at Dien
Bien Phu in May 1954, helped to deepen French commitments to colonial control in Algeria.

When Dien Bien Phu fell in May 1954, the French
government began peace talks in Geneva. The Geneva
Accords, drawn up by the French, Vietnamese politicians including the communists, the British, and the
Americans, divided Indochina three countries: Laos,
Cambodia, and Vietnam, partitioned into two states.
North Vietnam was taken over by Ho Chi Minh's party;
South Vietnam by a succession of Western-supported
politicians. Corruption, repression, and instability in
the south, coupled with Ho Chi Minh's nationalist desire to unite Vietnam, guaranteed that the war would
continue. The United States government, which had
provided military and financial aid to the French, began
to send aid to the South Vietnamese regime. The
Americans saw the conflict through the prism of the
cold war: their project was not to restore colonialism,
but to contain communism and prevent it from spreading through Southeast Asia. The limits of this policy
would not become clear until the mid-1960s.

ALGERIA

Still reeling from the humiliation of Dien Bien Phu,
France faced a complex colonial problem closer to
home, in Algeria. Since the 1830s, the colony had
evolved into a settler society of three social groups.
First, in addition to a small class of French soldiers and
administrators, there were also one million European
settlers. They typically owned farms and vineyards
near the major cities, or formed the working-class and
merchant communities inside those cities. All of them
were citizens of the three administrative districts of
Algeria, which were legally part of France. The community produced some of France's best-known writers
and intellectuals: Albert Camus, Jacques Derrida, and
Pierre Bourdieu among others. In the small towns and
villages of Algeria lived a second group of (largely
Muslim) Berbers, whose long history of service in the
French army entitled them to certain formal and informal privileges within the colony. Finally, there were
millions of Muslim Arabs, some living in the desert
south but most crowded into impoverished neighborhoods in the cities. The Arabs were the largest and
most deprived group in Algerian society. Between the
world wars the French government had offered small
reforms to increase their rights and representation, and
it had hoped to meld the three groups into a common
Algerian society. Reforms came too late, and were also
undercut by European settlers anxious to maintain
their privileges.

At the end of the Second World War, Algerian nationalists called on the Allies to recognize Algeria's independence in return for good service during the war.
Public demonstrations became frequent, and in several
cases turned into attacks on settler-landowners. In one
rural town, Setif, celebrations of the defeat of Germany flared into violence against settlers. French repression was harsh and immediate: security forces
killed several thousand Arabs. After the war the French
government approved a provincial assembly for all of
Algeria, elected by two pools of voters, one made up of
settlers and mostly Berber Muslims, the other of Arabs.
This very limited enfranchisement gave Arab Algerians
no political power. The more important changes were
economic. All of Algeria suffered in the difficulties
after the war. Many Arab Algerians felt they had to
emigrate; several hundred thousand went to work in
France. While citizens of mainland France read their
papers and frowned over the war in Indochina, the situation in Algeria grew more serious. By the middle of
the 1950s, a younger generation of Arab activists, unhappy with the leadership of the moderates, had taken

charge of a movement dedicated to independence by force. The National Liberation Front (FLN) was organized, which leaned toward socialism and demanded equal citizenship for all.

The war in Algeria became a war on three fronts. The first was a guerrilla war between the regular French Army and the FLN, fought in the mountains and deserts of the country. This war continued for years, a clear military defeat for the FLN but never a clear-cut victory for the French. The second war, fought out in Algeria's cities, began with an FLN campaign of bombing and terrorism. European civilians were killed, and the French administration retaliated with its own campaign. French paratroopers hunted down and destroyed the networks of FLN bombers. The information that allowed the French to break the FLN network was extracted through systematic torture conducted by French security forces. The torture became an international scandal, bringing waves of protest in France. This third front of the Algerian war divided France, brought down the government, and ushered de Gaulle back into power.

De Gaulle visited Algiers to wild cheering from settlers and declared that Algeria would always be French. After another year of violence, he and his advisors had changed their minds. By 1962 talks had produced a formula for independence: a referendum would be held, voted on by the whole population of Algeria. On July 1, 1962, the referendum passed by a landslide vote. Arab political groups and guerrillas from the FLN entered Algiers in triumph. Settlers and Berbers who had fought for the French army fled Algeria for France by the hundreds of thousands. Later, these refugees were joined in France by another influx of Arab economic migrants.

Algeria illustrated the dramatic domestic impact of decolonization. The war cut deep divides through French society, largely because the very identity of France seemed at stake. Withdrawing from Algeria meant reorienting French views of what it meant to be a modern power. De Gaulle summed up the trade-off in his memoirs: to stay in Algeria would "keep France politically, financially, and militarily bogged down in a bottomless quagmire when, in fact, she needed her hands free to bring about the domestic transformation necessitated by the twentieth century and to exercise her influence abroad unencumbered." In France and other imperial powers, the conclusions seemed clear. Traditional forms of colonial rule could not withstand the demands of postwar politics and culture; the leading European nations, once distinguished by their empires, would have to look for new forms of influence. The domestic transformation of which de Gaulle spoke—recovery from the war, economic restructuring, and political renewal—had to take place on a radically changed global stage.

POSTWAR CULTURE AND THOUGHT

What themes defined postwar culture?

The postwar period brought a remarkable burst of cultural production. Writers and artists did not hesitate to take up big issues: freedom, civilization, and the human condition itself. The search for democratic renewal gave this literature urgency; the moral dilemmas of war, occupation, and resistance gave it resonance and popular appeal. The process of decolonization, too, forced the issues of race, culture, and colonialism to center stage in Western debates.

THE BLACK PRESENCE

The journal *Présence Africaine* ("African Presence"), founded in Paris in 1947, was only one in a chorus of new cultural voices. *Présence Africaine* published such writers as Aimé Césaire (b. 1913), the surrealist poet from Martinique, and Léopold Senghor of Senegal (1906–2001). Césaire and Senghor were brilliant students, educated in the most elite French universities, and elected to the French National Assembly. Césaire became an important political figure in the former French Caribbean colony and (after 1946) Department of Martinique; in 1960 Senghor was elected the first president of Senegal. Both men, in important respects models of Frenchness, became the most influential exponents of *Négritude*, which could be translated as "black consciousness" or "black pride." Senghor wrote:

> Assimilation was a failure. We could assimilate mathematics of the French language, but we could never strip off our black skins or root out black souls. And so we set out on a fervent quest for . . . our collective soul. Negritude is the whole complex of civilized values—cultural, economic, social and political—which characterize the black people.

ANTICOLONIALISM AND VIOLENCE

Born in the French Caribbean colony of Martinique, Frantz Fanon (1925–1961) studied psychiatry in France before moving on to work in Algeria in the early 1950s. Fanon became a member of the Algerian revolutionary National Liberation Front (FLN) and an ardent advocate of decolonization. Black Skin, White Masks, *published in 1952 with a preface by Jean-Paul Sartre, was a study of the psychological effects of colonialism and racism on black culture and individuals.* The Wretched of the Earth *(1961) was a revolutionary manifesto, one of the most influential of the period. Unlike Gandhi, Fanon believed that violence lay at the heart of both the colonial relationship and anticolonial movements. Fanon attacked nationalist leaders for their ambition and corruption. He believed that revolutionary change could come only from poor peasants, those who "have found no bone to gnaw in the colonial system." Diagnosed with leukemia, Fanon sought treatment in the Soviet Union and then in Washington, D.C., where he died.*

In decolonization, there is therefore the need of a complete calling in question of the colonial situation. If we wish to describe it precisely, we might find it in the well-known words: "The last shall be first and the first last." Decolonization is the putting into practice of this sentence. . . .

The naked truth of decolonization evokes for us the searing bullets and blood-stained knives which emanate from it. For if the last shall be first, this will only come to pass after a murderous and decisive struggle between the two protagonists. That affirmed intention to place the last at the head of things, and to make them climb at a pace (too quickly, some say) the well-known steps which characterize an organized society, can only triumph if we use all means to turn the scale, including, of course, that of violence.

You do not turn any society, however primitive it may be, upside down with such a program if you have not decided from the very beginning, that is to say from the actual formation of that program, to overcome all the obstacles that you will come across in so doing. The native who decides to put the program into practice, and to become its moving force, is ready for violence at all time.

From birth it is clear to him that this narrow world, strewn with prohibitions, can only be called in question by absolute violence.

Frantz Fanon, *The Wretched of the Earth,* translated by Constance Farrington (New York: Grove Press, 1963), pp. 35–37.

Césaire's early work took its lead from surrealism and the exploration of consciousness. Later, his work became more political. *Discourse on Colonialism* (1950) was a powerful indictment of the material and spiritual squalor of colonialism, which, he argued, not only dehumanized colonial subjects, but degraded the colonizers themselves.

Césaire's student Frantz Fanon (1925–1961), also from Martinique, went further. He argued that withdrawing into an insular black culture (as he interpreted Negritude) was not an effective response to racism. People of color, he believed, needed a theory of radical social change. Fanon trained in psychiatry and worked in Algeria, where he became a member of the National

Liberation Front. In *Black Skin, White Masks* (1952) he examined the effects of colonialism and racism from the point of view of a radical psychiatrist. *The Wretched of the Earth* (1961) became one of the most influential revolutionary manifestos of the period. More than Césaire, and bluntly rejecting Gandhi's theories and practice, Fanon argued that violence was rooted in colonialism and, therefore, in anticolonial movements. But he also believed that many anticolonial leaders would be corrupted by their ambition and by collaboration with former colonial powers. Revolutionary change, he believed, could only come from poor peasants, or those who "have found no bone to gnaw in the colonial system."

How did these writers fit into postwar culture? Western intellectuals sought to revive humanism and democratic values after the atrocities of World War II. Fanon and others pointed out that the struggles over colonialism made that project more difficult; the violent repression of anticolonial movements in places such as Algeria seemed to be a relapse into brutality. They pointed to the ironies of Europe's "civilizing mission" and demanded a reevaluation of blackness as a central concept in Western culture. The West's postwar recovery would entail eventually facing this challenge to the universal claims of its culture.

EXISTENTIALISM

The French existentialist writers, most prominently Jean-Paul Sartre (1905–1980) and Albert Camus (1913–1960), put the themes of individuality, commitment, and choice at center stage. The existentialists took themes from Nietzsche, Heidegger, and Kierkegaard, reworking them in the new context of war-torn Europe. Their starting point was that "existence precedes essence." In other words, meaning in life is not given, but created. Thus individuals were "condemned to be free," and to give their lives meaning by making choices and accepting responsibility. To deny one's freedom or responsibility was to act in "bad faith." War, collaboration and resistance, genocide, and the development of weapons of mass destruction all provided specific points of reference and gave these abstractions new meaning. The existentialists' writing was also clear and accessible, which contributed to their enormous popularity. Although Sartre wrote philosophical treatises, he also published plays and short stories. Camus's own experience in the resistance gave him tremendous moral authority—he became the symbol of a new genera-

Simone de Beauvoir.

tion. His novels—including *The Stranger* (1942), *The Plague* (1947), and *The Fall* (1956)—often revolved around metaphors for the war, showing that people were responsible for their own dilemmas and, through a series of antiheroes, exploring the limited ability of men and women to help each other.

Existentialist insights opened other doors. The existentialist approach to race, for instance, emphasized that no meaning inhered in skin color; instead race derived meaning from a lived experience or situation. As Franz Fanon wrote, white and black exist "only insofar as they create one another." The same approach could be applied to gender. In her famous introduction to *The Second Sex* (1949), Simone de Beauvoir (1908–1986) argued that "One is not born a woman, one becomes one." Women, like men, were condemned to be free. Beauvoir went on to ask why women seemed to accept their secondary status or why, in her words, they "dreamed the dreams of men." The scope and ambition of *The Second Sex* helped make it enormously influential; it was virtually encyclopedic, analyzing history, myth, biology and psychology, bringing the insights of Marx and Freud to bear on the "woman question." Beauvoir's life also contributed to the book's high profile. A brilliant student from a strict middle-class background, she had a lifelong affair with Sartre, but did not marry him, leading many to romanticize her as a "liberated" and accomplished woman intellectual. She had little to do with feminism, however, until the late 1960s. When *The Second Sex* was published, it was associated with existentialism; only later would it become a key text of the women's movement (see Chapter 28).

MEMORY AND AMNESIA: THE AFTERMATH OF WAR

The theme of individual helplessness in the face of state power ran through countless works of the period, beginning, most famously, with George Orwell's *Animal Farm* (1946) and *1984* (1949). The American Joseph Heller's wildly popular *Catch-22* (1961) represented a form of popular existentialism, concerned with the absurdity of war and offering a biting commentary on regimentation and its toll on individual freedom. The Czech author Milan Kundera, who fled the repressive Czech government to live in Paris, eloquently captured the bittersweet efforts to resist senseless bureaucracy. Some writers expressed their despair by escaping into the absurd and fantastic. In Samuel Beckett's deeply pessimistic *Waiting for Godot* (1953, by an Irishman in French) and in the Briton Harold Pinter's *Caretaker* (1960) and *Homecoming* (1965) nothing happens. Characters speak in banalities, paralyzed by the absurdity of modern times.

Other authors ventured into the realms of hallucination, science fiction, and fantasy. The novels of the Americans William Burroughs and Kurt Vonnegut carry readers from interior fantasies to outer space. One of the most popular books of the period was *The Lord of the Rings* (1954–1955), written before and during the Second World War by the Briton J. R. R. Tolkien. Set in the fantasy world of Middle Earth, Professor Tolkien's tribute to the ancient Celtic and Scandinavian languages he studied and the power of human myths was seized on by a generation of young romantics who rebelled against postwar Western culture for their own reasons.

Questions of terror and dictatorship haunted social and political thought of the postwar era, and especially the work of émigrés from Europe. Representatives of the "Frankfurt school" of German Marxism, by wartime refugees in the United States, sought to understand how fascism and Nazism had taken root in Western culture and politics. Theodor Adorno joined Max Horkheimer in a series of essays, *Dialectic of Enlightenment* (1947), the best known of which indicted the "culture industry" for depoliticizing the masses and crippling democracy. Adorno also co-authored *The Authoritarian Personality* (1950), which used social surveys in an effort to discover how people become receptive to racism, prejudice, and dictatorship. Whatever the specific roots of German Nazism, the Frankfurt school suggested, there were also more general tendencies in modern societies that should give cause for concern.

Hannah Arendt (1906–1975), a Jewish refugee from Germany, was the first to propose that both Nazism and Stalinism should be understood as forms of a novel, twentieth-century form of government: totalitarianism (*The Origins of Totalitarianism*, 1951). Unlike earlier forms of tyranny or despotism, totalitarianism worked by mobilizing mass support. It used terror to crush resistance, break down political and social institutions, and atomize the public. Totalitarianism, Arendt argued, also forged new ideologies. Totalitarian regimes did not concern themselves with whether killing was justified by law; they justified camps and extermination by pointing to the objective laws of history or racial struggle. By unleashing destruction and eliminating entire populations, totalitarian politics made collective resistance virtually impossible. Arendt returned to the same theme in a provocative and disturbing essay on the trial of a Nazi leader, *Eichmann in Jerusalem* (1963). To many readers' distress, she pointedly refused to demonize Nazism. Instead she explored what she termed "the banality of evil": how the rise of new forms of state power and terror had created in a world in which Nazis such as Adolf Eichmann could implement genocide as simply one more policy. The crisis of totalitarianism, Arendt argued, was the moral collapse of society, for it destroyed human feeling and the power of resistance in executioners and victims—"tormentors and the tormented"—alike.

Discussions of the war and its legacy, however, were limited. Some memoirs and novels dealing directly with the war and its brutal aftermath did reach a large international public: Jerzy Kosinski's novel about a boy in wartime Poland, *The Painted Bird*; Czeslaw Milosz's memoir of intellectual collaboration in Eastern Europe, *The Captive Mind* (1951); the German Günter Grass's *Tin Drum* (1959), which portrayed the Nazi and war experience in a semi-autobiographical genre and earned Grass recognition as "the conscience of his

> Questions of terror and dictatorship haunted social and political thought of the postwar era, and especially the work of émigrés from Europe.

THE WAR THAT REFUSES
TO BE FORGOTTEN

Heda Margolis Kovály was born in Prague and returned to her city after surviving the concentration camps. Like many refugees and survivors, she received an uncertain welcome home. In Czechoslovakia and elsewhere, the Nazi occupation left a legacy of bitterness and division that persisted for decades. Survivors reminded other Europeans of the war and made them defensive. Paradoxically, as Kovály shows, it was common to blame the victims for the war's troubles.

And so ended that horrible long war that refuses to be forgotten. Life went on. It went on despite both the dead and the living, because this was a war that no one had quite survived. Something very important and precious had been killed by it or, perhaps, it had just died of horror, of starvation, or simply of disgust—who knows? We tried to bury it quickly, the earth settled over it, and we turned our backs on it impatiently. After all, our real life was now beginning and what to make of it was up to us.

People came crawling out of their hide-outs. They came back from the forests, from the prisons, and from the concentration camps, and all they could think was, "It's over; it's all over." . . . Some people came back silent, and some talked incessantly as though talking about a thing would make it vanish. . . . While some voices spoke of death and flames, of blood and gallows, in the background, a chorus of thousands repeated tirelessly, "You know, we also suffered. . . . [N]othing but skimmed milk. . . . No butter on our bread. . . ."

Sometimes a bedraggled and barefoot concentration camp survivor plucked up his courage and knocked on the door of prewar friends to ask, "Excuse me, do you by any chance still have some of the stuff we left with you for safekeeping?" And the friends would say, "You must be mistaken, you didn't leave anything with us,

but come in anyway!" And they would seat him in their parlor where his carpet lay on the floor and pour herb tea into antique cups that had belonged to his grandmother. . . . He would say to himself, "What does it matter? As long as we're alive? What does it matter?". . .

It would also happen that a survivor might need a lawyer to retrieve lost documents and he would remember the name of one who had once represented large Jewish companies. He would go to see him and sit in an empire chair in a corner of an elegant waiting room, enjoying all that good taste and luxury, watching pretty secretaries rushing about. Until one of the pretty girls forgot to close a door behind her, and the lawyer's sonorous voice would boom through the crack, "You would have thought we'd be rid of them finally, but no, they're impossible to kill off—not even Hitler could manage it. Every day there're more of them crawling back, like rats. . . ." And the survivor would quietly get up from his chair and slip out of the waiting room, this time not laughing. On his way down the stairs his eyes would mist over as if with the smoke of the furnaces at Auschwitz.

Heda Margolis Kovály, *Under a Cruel Star: A Life in Prague 1941–1968*, translated from the Czech by Franci Epstein and Helen Epstein with the author (Cambridge, Mass.: Plunkett Lake Press, 1986), pp. 45–46.

generation." Of all the memoirs, *The Diary of a Young Girl* by Anne Frank, published in 1947, was undoubtedly the most widely read. Yet the main current in postwar culture ran in a different direction, toward repressing painful issues and bad memories. Postwar governments could not or would not purge all those implicated in war crimes. In France, the courts sentenced 2,640 to death and executed 791; in Austria 13,000 were convicted of war crimes and 30 executed. Those who called for justice grew demoralized and cynical. Others responded by mythologizing the Resistance and exaggerating participation in it, and by avoiding discussion of collaboration. For ten years French television considered *The Sorrow and the Pity* (1969), Marcel Ophüls's brilliant and unsparing documentary on a French town under Vichy, too "controversial" for broadcast. Most Jewish survivors, wherever they lived, found that few editors were interested in publishing their stories. In 1947, only a small publishing house would take on the Italian survivor Primo Levi's *Survival in Auschwitz*; the book and Levi's other writings did not find a wide audience until later.

The cold war was an important factor in burying and distorting memories. West of the Iron Curtain, the eagerness to embrace West Germany as an ally, the single-minded emphasis on economic development, and ardent anticommunism blurred views of the past. One example involved Klaus Barbie, an agent for the Gestapo in occupied France who among other things arrested and personally tortured members of the Resistance and deported thousands, including Jewish children, to concentration camps. After the war American intelligence services recruited Barbie for his anticommunist skills and paid to smuggle him out of Europe, beyond the reach of those who wanted to prosecute him for war crimes. He was finally extradited from Bolivia in 1983, tried in France for crimes against humanity, and convicted. In the Eastern bloc, regimes declared fascism to be a thing of the past, and did not scrutinize that past or seek out the many who collaborated with the Nazis. Thus, reckoning with history was postponed until the fall of the Soviet Union.

On both sides of the Iron Curtain, the vast majority of people turned inward, cherishing their domestic lives, relieved to have privacy.

CONCLUSION

One of the last serious and most dramatic confrontations of the cold war came in 1962, in Cuba. A revolution in 1958 had brought the charismatic communist Fidel Castro to power. Immediately after, the United States began to work with exiled Cubans, supporting among other ventures a bungled attempt to invade via the Bay of Pigs in 1961. Castro not only aligned himself with the Soviets, he invited them to base nuclear missiles on Cuban soil, only a few minutes' flying time from Florida. When American spy planes identified the missiles and related military equipment in 1962, Kennedy confronted Khrushchev. After three nerve-wracking weeks, the Soviets agreed to withdraw and to remove the bombers and missiles already on Cuban soil. But citizens of both countries had spent many anxious hours in their bomb shelters, and onlookers the world over wrestled with their rising fears that a nuclear Armageddon was upon them.

The Cuban missile crisis provided one inspiration for Stanley Kubrick's classic *Dr. Strangelove* (1964), a devastating and dark comedy with many cold war

Bay of Pigs, 1961. American President John F. Kennedy brandishes the combat flag of the Cuban landing brigade.

themes. The story concerns an "accidental" nuclear attack and the demented characters responsible for it. It also concerns the repression of memory and the sudden reversals of alliances brought about by the cold war. The wildly eccentric German scientist Dr. Strangelove shuttles between his present life working for the Americans and his barely repressed past as an enthusiastic follower of Hitler. The screenplay was based on the British writer Peter Bryant's *Two Hours to Doom* (1958), one of many 1950s novels with an apocalyptic scenario. The Cuban missile crisis brought the plot so close to home that when the film came out Columbia Pictures felt compelled to issue a disclaimer: "It is the stated position of the United States Air Force that their safeguards would prevent the occurrence of such events as are depicted in this film."

In sum, the cold war dominated postwar culture and politics. It decisively shaped the development of both the Soviet and American states. In his farewell address, President Eisenhower warned that a "military-industrial complex" had taken shape and that its "total influence—economic, political, even spiritual—is felt in every city, every statehouse, every office of the federal government." Yet other, equally important developments marked the period. The nation-state expanded in nonmilitary realms, taking on new roles in economic planning and management, in educating citizens, and in ensuring social welfare. Those changes were driven by a search for democracy and stability. Former colonies became nations. In the long run the formation of the Third World mattered as much, if not more, than the bipolar divisions established by the cold war. Global and regional economic integration quickened. Economic growth helped all the Western nations (in different measures) recover from the devastation of war, though whether Europe would regain its former global power was doubtful. Finally, economic growth had unintended consequences. By the 1960s, social and cultural changes were beginning to undermine the cold war settlement.

KEY TERMS

Marshall Plan	Mohandas K. (Mahatma) Gandhi	Berlin blockade
NATO	Ho Chi Minh	ECSC
Khrushchev	Algerian war	social democracy
Aleksandr Solzhenitsyn	Berlin wall	existentialism
Mao Zedong		

SELECTED READINGS

Aron, Raymond. *The Imperial Republic: The United States and the World, 1945–1973.* Lanham, Md., 1974. An early analysis by a leading French political theorist.

Carter, Erica. *How German Is She? Postwar West German Reconstruction and the Consuming Woman.* Ann Arbor, 1997. A thoughtful examination of gender and the reconstruction of the family in West Germany during the 1950s.

Clayton, Anthony. *The Wars of French Decolonization.* London, 1994. Good survey.

Connelly, Matthew. *A Diplomatic Revolution: Algeria's Fight for Independence and the Origins of the Post–Cold War Era.* New York and Oxford, 2003. An international history.

Cooper, Frederick, and Ann Laura Stoler, eds. *Tensions of Empire: Colonial Cultures in a Bourgeois World.* Berkeley, 1997. Collection of new essays, among the best.

Darwin, John. *Britain and Decolonization: The Retreat from Empire in the Postwar World.* New York, 1988. Best overall survey.

Deák, István, Jan T. Gross, and Tony Judt, eds. *The Politics of Retribution in Europe: World War II and Its Aftermath.* Princeton, N.J., 2000. Collection focusing on the attempt to come to terms with the Second World War in Eastern and Western Europe.

Farmer, Sarah. *Martyred Village: Commemorating the 1944 Massacre at Oradour-sur-Glane.* Berkeley, 1999. Gripping story of French attempts to come to terms with collaboration and complicity in atrocities.

Fulbrook, Mary, ed. *Europe Since 1945* (The Short Oxford History of Europe). Oxford, 2001. A recent and excellent collection of essays.

Gilbert, Felix, and David Clay Large. *The End of the European Era, 1890 to the Present.* 5th ed. New York, 2002. Comprehensive overview of political developments.

Herf, Jeffrey. *Divided Memory: The Nazi Past in the Two Germanys.* Cambridge, Mass., 1997.

Holland, R. F. *European Decolonization 1918–1981: An Introductory Survey.* New York, 1985. Sprightly narrative and analysis.

Jarausch, Konrad Hugo, ed. *Dictatorship as Experience: Towards a Socio-Cultural History of the GDR.* Translated by Eve Duffy. New York, 1999. Surveys recent research on the former East Germany.

Judt, Tony. *Past Imperfect: French Intellectuals, 1944–1956.* Berkeley, 1992. Very readable, on French intellectuals, who loomed large during this period.

———. *A Grand Illusion? An Essay on Europe.* New York, 1996. Short and brilliant.

———. *The Burden of Responsibility: Blum, Camus, and the French Twentieth Century.* Chicago and London, 1998. Also on French intellectuals.

Kolko, Gabriel. *The Politics of War: The World and United States Foreign Policy, 1943–1945.* New York, 1990. Argues that the blame for the cold war rests with the Western Allies.

Koven, Seth, and Sonya Michel. *Mothers of a New World: Maternalist Politics and the Origins of Welfare States.* New York, 1993. Excellent essays on the long history of welfare politics.

LaFeber, Walter. *America, Russia, and The Cold War.* New York, 1967. A classic, now in its ninth edition.

Laqueur, Walter. *Europe In Our Time: A History, 1945–1992.* New York, 1992. A useful, thorough survey.

Large, David Clay. *Berlin.* New York, 2000.

Leffler, Melvyn P. *A Preponderance of Power: National Security, the Truman Administration, and the Cold War.* Stanford, 1992.

Macey, David. *Frantz Fanon.* New York, 2000. Comprehensive recent biography.

Medvedev, Roy. *Khrushchev.* New York, 1983. A perceptive biography of the Soviet leader by a Soviet historian.

Milward, Alan S. *The Reconstruction of Western Europe, 1945–1951.* Berkeley, 1984. A good discussion of the "economic miracle."

Moeller, Robert G. *Protecting Motherhood: Women and the Family in the Politics of Postwar West Germany.* Berkeley, 1993.

———. *War Stories: The Search for a Usable Past in the Federal Republic of Germany.* Berkeley, 2001. Revealing analyses of postwar culture and politics.

Reynolds, David. *One World Divisible: A Global History Since 1945.* New York, 2000. Fresh approach, comprehensive, and very readable survey.

Rousso, Henri. *The Vichy Syndrome: History and Memory in France since 1944.* Cambridge, Mass., 1991. First in a series of books by one of the preeminent French historians.

Schissler, Hanna, ed. *The Miracle Years: A Cultural History of West Germany, 1949–1968.* Princeton, N.J., 2001. The cultural effects of the "economic miracle."

Schneider, Peter. *The Wall Jumper: A Berlin Story.* Chicago, 1998. A fascinating novel about life in divided Berlin.

Trachtenberg, Mark. *A Constructed Peace: The Making of the European Settlement, 1945–1963.* Princeton, N.J., 1999.

Yergin, Daniel. *Shattered Peace: The Origins of the Cold War.* New York, 1977.

Young, Marilyn B. *The Vietnam Wars, 1945–1990.* New York, 1991. Excellent account of the different stages of the war and its repercussions.

CHAPTER
TWENTY-EIGHT

RED FLAGS
AND VELVET
REVOLUTIONS:
THE END OF
THE COLD WAR,
1960–1990

THE YEAR 1960 SEEMED GOLDEN and full of promise. Despite nearly constant international tension, everyday life in Europe and North America seemed to be improving. Economies recovered, many standards of living rose, and new forms of culture flourished. The economic horizon looked bright. By 1990, most of that familiar landscape had been dramatically transformed. Western Europeans could no longer be so certain of their prosperity or of their leaders' ability to provide the sort of life they took for granted. Societies had fragmented in unexpected ways. The startlingly sudden dissolution of the Soviet bloc brought down the foundation of the cold war world, which raised both hopes for peace and fears of conflict from unexpected quarters.

How can we explain this transformation? By the middle of the 1960s, social and economic tensions were undermining the consensus that postwar prosperity had created in the West. The economic expansion after 1945 ushered in dramatic changes: new industries, new economic values, new social classes, and a newly acute sense of generational difference. Governments faced demands from new social groups and were frequently baffled in their efforts to respond. Tensions exploded in the late 1960s. In 1968 uprisings and strikes broke out across the West, from Czechoslovakia to Germany, France, the United States, and Mexico. Problems were compounded after 1975 by a continuing economic crisis that threatened the security a generation had labored so hard to achieve. As the economy stalled, social protest continued in Europe and the United States for at least a decade after "the Sixties" technically ended.

The challenges of these decades proved even more fundamental in the Soviet sphere. Economic decay combined with political and social stagnation to produce another wave of revolt. The year 1989 marked the beginning of an extraordinarily rapid and surprising series of events. Communist rule collapsed in Eastern Europe, and the Soviet Union itself disintegrated. The cold war no longer seemed to matter. What these changes meant for the future of democracy, and the political stability of a vast region stretching from the borders of China in the east to the borders of Poland in the west, remained an open question.

FOCUS QUESTIONS

- How was daily life transformed during this period?

- What spurred the social movements of the 1960s?

- What caused the economic stagnation of the 1970s and 1980s?

- What caused the collapse of communism?

SOCIETY AND CLASS, 1945–1968

How was daily life transformed during this period?

The "boom" of the 1950s, made especially striking by contrast with the bleak years immediately after World War II, had profound and far-reaching effects on social life. To begin with, the population expanded, though unevenly. It shifted across the Continent. Both West Germany and France found it necessary to import workers in order to sustain their production booms. By the mid-1960s, there were 1.3 million foreign workers in West Germany and 1.8 million in France as wages rose and unemployment fell. Most came from the south, particularly from the agrarian areas of southern Italy, where unemployment remained high. Workers from former colonies emigrated to Britain, often to take low-paid, menial jobs and encounter pervasive discrimination at work and in the community. Migrations of this sort, in addition to the vast movement of political and ethnic refugees that occurred during and immediately after the war, contributed to the breakdown of national barriers that was accelerated by the creation of the Common Market.

The most dramatic changes were encapsulated in the transformation of the land and agriculture. Agricultural productivity had barely changed over the first half of the century. After mid-century it soared. To take one example, West German farm land (and labor) sufficient to feed five people in 1900 would feed six in 1950 and thirty-five in 1980. In West Germany and France, Common Market policy, state-sponsored programs of modernization, new agricultural machinery, and new kinds of fertilizer, seed, and animal feed helped to produce the transformation. In Poland and the Eastern bloc, socialist regimes replaced small peasant holdings with large-scale agriculture. The effects reached across the economic and social landscape. Abundance meant lower food prices. Families spent a smaller proportion of their budgets on food, freeing up money for other forms of consumption and fueling economic growth. The percentage of the labor force

employed in agriculture fell, fueling an expansion in industry and, especially, the service sector. Peasants with large holdings or valuable specialized crops (dairy products or wine), who could withstand debt, adjusted. Others lost ground. The French spoke of an "end of the peasantry;" in the 1960s one hundred thousand moved from the countryside each year. These changes sparked continuous protest as farmers tried to protect their standard of living. The Common Market agreed to policies of shoring up agricultural prices, but the dynamics remained the same.

Change came in the workplace, eroding traditional social distinctions. Many commentators noted the striking growth in the number of middle-class, white-collar employees—the result, in part, of the dramatic bureaucratic expansion of the state. By 1964, the total number of men and women employed in government service in most European states exceeded 40 percent of the labor force, significantly higher than the number in the 1920s and 1930s. In business and industry, the number of "middle-management" employees grew as well. In industry, even within the factory work force, salaried employees—supervisors, inspectors, technicians, and drafters—multiplied. In West Germany, for example, the number of such workers increased by 95 percent between 1950 and 1961. Industrial labor meant something far different from what it had meant in the nineteenth century. Skills were more specialized, based on technological expertise rather than custom and routine. "Skill" meant the ability to monitor automatic controls, to interpret abstract signals, and to make precise, mathematically calculated adjustments. More women entered the work force, meeting less resistance than they had in the past, and their jobs were less starkly differentiated from men's.

Nineteenth-century society had been marked by clearly defined class cultures. The working class lived "a life apart," with easily identifiable patterns of consumption, dress, leisure, notions of respectability, gender relations, and so on. In 1900, no one would have mistaken a peasant for a worker, and middle-class people had their own schools, recreations, and stores. But economic changes after 1950 chipped away at those distinctive cultures. Trade unions remained powerful institutions: the largest of the French general unions had a membership of 1.5 million; of the Italian, 3.5 million; of the German, 6.5 million. Britain's Trades

> By 1964, the total number of men and women employed in government service in most European states exceeded 40 percent of the labor force, significantly higher than the number in the 1920s and 1930s.

Morning Calisthenics at Russian Factory, 1961. The growing number of industrial workers and women in the work force in the latter half of the twentieth century was reflected in this Soviet factory. The "worker state" still bestowed little status on its workers, however, a factor that contributed to the weakened Russian economy.

the product of persistent labor shortages and the accompanying fear of labor unrest. As far as the middle classes were concerned, two wars and state socialism devastated traditional, insular "bourgeois" culture throughout eastern Europe, though the regimes also created new ways of gaining privilege and status and commentators spoke of a "new class" of bureaucrats and party members. Educational reforms instituted by Nikita Khrushchev in 1958 encouraged bright children to pursue a course of study leading eventually to managerial positions. Soviet education also aimed to unify a nation that remained culturally heterogeneous. Turkish Muslims, for instance, constituted a sizable minority in the Soviet Union. Concern lest the pull of ethnic "nationality" tear at the none-too-solid fabric of the Soviet "union" increased the government's desire to impose one unifying culture by means of education, not always with success.

Union Congress, an affiliation of separate unions, boasted close to 8 million members—including many more women than in the past. Communist parties had powerful electoral clout. But new social movements also grew. Workers still identified themselves as such, but class had a less rigidly defined meaning.

The expansion of education helped shift social hierarchies. All Western nations passed laws providing for the extension of compulsory secondary education—up to the age of sixteen in France, West Germany, and Britain. New legislation combined with rising birthrates to boost school populations dramatically. Between 1950 and 1960, secondary school enrollment in France, Holland, and Belgium doubled. In Britain and West Germany it grew by more than 50 percent. Education did not automatically produce social mobility, but when combined with economic prosperity, new structures of labor, and the consumerist boom, it began to lay the foundation for what would be called "post-industrial" society.

How did patterns differ in the Eastern bloc? Soviet workers were not noted for their specialized skills—in fact, a major factor in the slowdown of the Soviet economy was its failure to innovate. Workers in the "workers' state" commonly enjoyed higher wages than people in middle-class positions (with the exception of managers), but they had far less status. Their relatively high wages owed little to independent trade unions, which had been effectively abolished under Stalin; they were

MASS CONSUMPTION

Rising employment, higher earnings, and lower agricultural prices combined to give households and individuals more purchasing power. They had more to spend on newspapers, cigarettes, tickets to sporting events, movies, and health and hygiene (which registered the largest increase). Families put money into their homes. Household appliances and cars were the most striking emblems of what was virtually a new world of everyday objects. In 1956, 8 percent of British households had refrigerators. By 1979 that figure had skyrocketed to 69 percent. Vacuum cleaners, washing machines, and telephones all became common features of everyday life. They did not simply save labor or create free time, for household appliances came packaged with more demanding standards of housekeeping and new investments in domesticity—"more work for mother," in the words of one historian. We should not exaggerate the transformation. In 1962, only 40 percent of French households had a refrigerator; in 1975, only 35 percent had a telephone; but even this was still vastly more than the poorer nations of Europe or elsewhere in the world.

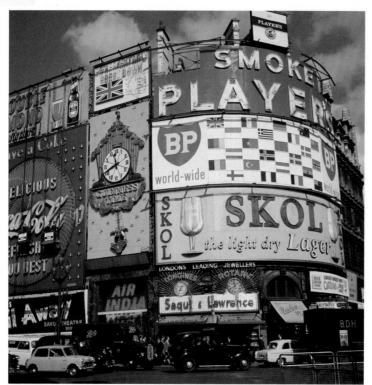

Piccadilly Square, London. In the 1960s and 1970s, a growing consumer culture encountered an influx of automobiles and the expansion of the marketing and advertising industries.

In 1948, 5 million Western Europeans had cars; in 1965, 40 million. In 1950, Italian workers rode bicycles to work; ten years later the factories were building parking lots for their employees' automobiles. Cars captured imaginations throughout the world; in magazines, advertisements, and countless films, the car was central to new images of romance, movement, freedom, and vacation. Of course automobiles alone did not allow workers to take inexpensive holidays; reducing the work week from forty-eight hours to about forty-two was more important, as was the institution of annual vacations—in most countries workers received over thirty days of paid vacation per year.

These changes marked a new culture of mass consumption. They were boosted by new industries devoted to marketing, advertising, and credit payment. They also entailed shifts in values. In the nineteenth century, a responsible middle-class family did not go into debt; discipline and thrift were hallmarks of "respectability." By the second half of the twentieth century, banks and retailers, in the name of mass consumption and economic growth, were persuading middle- and working-class people alike not to be ashamed of debt. Abundance, credit, consumer spending, and standards of living—all these terms became

part of the vocabulary of everyday economic life. Most important, the new vocabulary gradually came to reshape how citizens thought about their needs, desires, and entitlements. Standards of living, for instance, created a yardstick for measuring—and protesting—glaring social inequalities. Politicians, economists, and marketing experts paid much closer attention to the spending habits of ordinary people.

In Eastern Europe and the Soviet Union, consumption was organized differently. Governments rather than markets determined how consumer goods would be distributed. Economic policy channeled resources into heavy industry at the expense of consumer durables. This resulted in general scarcity, erratic shortages of even basic necessities, and often poor-quality goods. Women in particular often waited for hours in store lines after finishing a full day of wage work. Though household appliances increased dramatically in the Soviet Union and in Eastern Europe, the inefficiencies of Soviet consumption made women's double burden of work and housework especially heavy. Citizens' growing unhappiness with scarcities and seemingly irrational policies posed serious problems. As one historian puts it, the failure of policies on consumption was "one of the major dead ends of communism," and it contributed to the downfall of communist regimes.

MASS CULTURE

New patterns of consumption spurred wide-ranging changes in mass culture. The origins of "mass" culture lay in the 1890s, in the expansion of the popular press, music halls, organized sports, and "Nickelodeons," all of which started the long process of displacing traditional, class-based forms of entertainment: village dances, boulevard theater, middle-class concerts, and so on. Mass culture quickened in the 1920s, its importance heightened by mass politics (see Chapter 25). The social transformations of the 1950s, which we have traced above, meant that families had both more spending money and more leisure time. The combination created a golden opportunity for the growing culture industry. The postwar desire to break with the past created further impetus for change. The result can fairly be called a cultural revolution: a transformation of culture, of its role in the lives of ordinary men and women, and of the power wielded by the media.

MUSIC AND YOUTH CULTURE

Much of the new "mass culture" of the 1960s depended on the spending habits and desires of the new generation. That new generation stayed in school longer, prolonging the adolescent years. Young people had more distance from their parents and the work force and more time to be with each other. In the countryside especially, schooling began to break down the barriers that had separated the activities of boys and girls, creating one factor in the "sexual revolution" (see below). From the late 1950s on, music became *the* cultural expression of this new generation. The transistor radio came out at the time of the Berlin airlift; by the mid-1950s these portable radios began to sell in the United States and Europe. Radio sets gave birth to new radio programs and, later, to magazines reporting on popular singers and movie stars. All of these helped create new communities of interest. As one historian puts it, these radio programs were the "capillaries of youth culture." Social changes also affected the content of music: its themes and lyrics aimed to reach the young. Technological changes made records more than twice as long as the old 78s, and less expensive. The price of record players fell, multiplying the number of potential buyers. Combined, these developments changed how music was produced, distributed, and consumed. It was no longer confined to the concert hall or café but instead reverberated through people's homes or cars and teenagers' rooms—providing a soundtrack for everyday life.

Postwar youth culture owed much to the hybrid musical style known as rock and roll. During the 1930s and 1940s, the synthesis of music produced by whites and African Americans in the American South found its way into northern cities. After World War II, black rhythm and blues musicians and white Southern rockabilly performers found much wider audiences through the use of new technology—electric guitars, better equipment for studio recording, and wide-band radio stations in large cities. The blend of styles and sounds and the cultural daring of white teenagers who listened to what recording studios at the time called "race music" came together to create rock and roll. The music was exciting, sometimes aggressive, and full of energy—all qualities that galvanized young listeners, eager to buy the latest records by their favorite performers.

In Europe, rock and roll found its way into working-class neighborhoods, particularly in Britain and Ireland. There, local youths took American sounds, echoed the

The Beatles performing in Munich, Germany, 1966.
The "British invasion" hit Germany and the rest of Europe as well as the United States. Sixties music was only one reflection of important but less visible social and cultural changes.

inflections of poverty and defiance, and added touches of music-hall showmanship to produce successful artists and bands, collectively referred to as the "British invasion." During the 1960s, British sounds and stars had blended with their American counterparts. As the music's popularity spread, music culture came lose from its national moorings. In France before the 1960s, trendy American songs had been covered by the performer Johnny Hallyday, who sang French popular music as well. The Beatles, though, managed to get their own music on the hit lists in France, Germany, and the United States. By the time of Woodstock (1969), youth music culture was international. Rock became the sound of worldwide youth culture, absorbing Eastern influences such as the Indian sitar and the rebellious energy of a folk-music revival. It provided a bridge across the cold war divide: despite Eastern bloc limits on importing "capitalist" music, pirated songs circulated—sometimes on X-ray plates salvaged from hospitals. Recording studios latched on to the earning potential of the music, and became corporations as powerful as car manufacturers or steel companies.

ART AND PAINTING

The cultural revolution we have been tracing changed "high" as well as "popular" art. Record companies' influence reached well beyond rock. New recording techniques made it possible to reissue favorites in classical music, and companies marketed them more aggressively. Record companies buoyed the careers of internationally acclaimed stars, such as the soprano Maria Callas and (much later) the tenor Luciano Pavarotti,

staging concerts, using their influence on orchestras, and offering new recordings of their art.

Painting and art, too, were changed by the rise of mass and consumer culture. The art market boomed. The power of the dollar was one factor in the rise of New York as a center of modern art, one of the most striking developments of the period. Immigration was another: a slow stream of immigrants from Europe nourished American art as well as social and political thought (see Chapter 27) and New York proved hospitable to European artists. The creative work of the school of abstract expressionism sealed New York's postwar reputation. The abstract expressionists— William de Kooning (from the Netherlands), Mark Rothko (from Russia), Franz Kline, Jackson Pollock, Helen Frankenthaler, and Robert Motherwell—followed trends established by the cubists and surrealists, experimenting with color, texture, and technique to find new forms of expression. Many of them emphasized the physical aspects of paint and the act of painting. Pollock is a good example. He poured and even threw paint on the canvas, creating powerful images of personal and physical expressiveness. Some dubbed the process "action painting." His huge-scale canvases, which defied conventional artistic structures, gained immediate attention. Critics called the drip paintings "unpredictable, undisciplined, and explosive," and saw in them the youthful exuberance of postwar American culture. Mark Rothko created a series of remote yet extraordinarily compelling abstractions with glowing or somber rectangles of color imposed on other rectangles, saying they represented "no associations, only sensation." The enormous influence of abstract expressionism moved one critic to declare in grandiose fashion that "the main premises of Western art" had moved to the United States, along with "industrial production and political power."

But abstract expressionism also produced its opposite, sometimes called pop art. Pop artists distanced themselves from the moody and elusive meditations of abstract expressionism. They refused to distinguish between "avant garde" and "popular" art, or between the "artistic" and the "commercial." They lavished attention on commonplace, instantly recognizable, often commercial

Abstract Expressionism. *Sea Change,* by Jackson Pollock (1912–1956). Pollock, one of the new American "moderns," improvised with new techniques to express gesture, movement, and feeling.

images; they borrowed techniques from graphic design; they were interested in the immediacy of everyday art and ordinary people's visual experience. Jasper Johns's paintings of the American flag formed part of this trend. So did the work of Andy Warhol and Roy Lichtenstein, who took objects such as soup cans and images of comic-strip heroes as their subjects. Warhol did not see his work as a protest against the banality of commercial culture. Instead, he argued that he was continuing to experiment with abstractions. Treating popular culture with this tongue-in-cheek seriousness became one of the central themes of 1960s art.

FILM

Mass culture made its most powerful impact in the visual world, especially through film. Film flourished after World War II, developing along several different lines. The Italian neorealists of the late 1940s and 1950s, antifascists and socialists, set out to capture authenticity, or "life as it was lived," by which they usually meant working-class existence. They dealt with the same themes that marked the literature of the period: loneliness, war, and corruption. They shot on location, using natural light and little-known actors, deliberately steering away from the artifice and high production values they associated with the tainted cinema of fascist and wartime Europe. Not strictly realists, they played with nonlinear plots, unpredictable characters and motivations. Roberto Rossellini's *Rome: Open City* (1945) was a loving portrait of Rome under Nazi occupation. Vittorio de Sica's *Bicycle Thief* (1948) tells a story of a man struggling against unemployment and poverty, who desperately needs his bicycle to keep his job as a poster hanger. The film highlighted the contrast between rich and poor—the man's son enviously watches another's family enjoying huge plates of pasta—and between American glamour, represented by movie stars on the posters, and Italy's war-scarred poverty. Federico Fellini came out of the neorealist school and began his career writing for Rossellini. Fellini's break-out film *La Dolce Vita* (1959) (starring Marcello Mastroianni) took Italian film to screens throughout Europe and the United States, and it also marked Fellini's transition to his signature surrealist and carnivalesque style, developed in 8½ (1963).

The French directors of the "new wave" continued to develop this unsentimental, naturalistic, and enigmatic

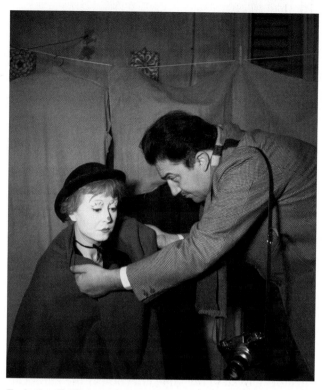

Federico Fellini on the set of *La Strada,* 1954. Fellini was an Italian neorealist filmmaker who sought to depict "life as it was lived."

Mass culture made its most powerful impact in the visual world, especially through film.

social vision. New wave directors worked closely with each other, casting each other (and their wives and lovers) in their films, encouraged improvisation, and experimented with disjointed narrative. François Truffaut (1932–1984), *400 Blows* (1959) and *The Wild Child* (1969), and Jean-Luc Godard (1930–), *Breathless* (1959) and *Contempt* (1963, with Brigitte Bardot), are leading examples. *Closely Watched Trains* (1966) was the Czech director Jiří Menzel's (1938–) contribution to the new wave. The new wave raised the status of the director, insisting that the film's camera work and vision (rather than the writing) constituted the real art—part, again, of the new value accorded to the visual. France made other contributions to international film by sponsoring the Cannes Film Festival. The first Cannes festival was held before World War II, but the city opened its gates again in 1946 under the banner of artistic internationalism. As one commentator put it, "There are many ways to advance the cause of peace. But the power . . . of cinema is greater than other forms of expression, for it directly and simultaneously touches the masses of the world." Placing itself at the center of an international film industry became part of France's ongoing recovery from the war, and Cannes became one of the world's largest markets for film.

HOLLYWOOD AND THE AMERICANIZATION OF CULTURE

The American film industry, however, had considerable advantages, and the devastating after-effects of World War II in Europe allowed Hollywood to consolidate its earlier gains (see Chapter 27). The United States' huge domestic market gave Hollywood its biggest advantage. In 1946 an estimated 100 million Americans went to the movies every week. By the 1950s Hollywood was making five hundred films a year and counted for between 40 and 75 percent of films shown in Europe. The same period brought important innovations in filmmaking: the conversion to color and new optical formats, including widescreen. As far as their themes were concerned, some American directors moved in the same direction as the European neorealists. As one critic put it, they tried to "base fictional pictures on fact and, more importantly, to shoot them not in painted studio sets but in actual places."

The domestic politics of the cold war weighed heavily on filmmaking in the United States. Between 1947 and 1951, the infamous House Un-American Activities Committee called before it hundreds of persons, investigating alleged sympathies with communism or association with any left-wing organization. Hundreds of actors, directors, and writers were blacklisted by the studios. At the same time, paradoxically, American censorship was breaking down, with dramatic consequences on screen. Since the early 1930s, the Motion Picture Production Code had refused to approve "scenes of passion" (including married couples sharing a bed), immorality and profanity (the Code banned "virgin" and "cripes"), depictions of guns, details of crimes, suicide, or murder. Foreign films, however, came into the United States without the Code's seal of approval. The State of New York tried to ban a film (*The Miracle*, directed by Rossellini and written by Fellini) as "sacrilegious," but in 1952 the Supreme Court ruled that film was protected by the First Amendment. A 1955 Otto Preminger movie in which Frank Sinatra played a heroin addict (*The Man with the Golden Arm*) was released despite the disapproval of the Production Code and went on to become a box-office success—a sign of changing mores. *Rebel without a Cause* (1955) made juvenile delinquency a legitimate subject

for film. By the 1960s, the Production Code had been scuttled. The extremely graphic violence at the end of Arthur Penn's *Bonnie and Clyde* (1967) marked the scope of the transformation.

Hollywood's expanding influence was but one instance of the "Americanization" of Western culture. Europeans had worried about the United States as a model since at least the 1920s; the U.S. seemed to be the center for the "production and organization of mass civilization." American films in the 1950s multiplied these worries. So did television, which by 1965 had found its way into 62 million homes in the United States, 13 million in Britain, 10 million in West Germany, and 5 million each in France and Italy and had an even more important impact on everyday life and sociability. The issues were not simply cultural; they included the power of American corporations, American business techniques, aggressive marketing, and American domination of global trade networks. Many concerns were raised, and sometimes they contradicted each other. Some observers believed that the United States and its cultural exports were materialistic, conformist, and complacent. Others considered Americans to be rebellious, lonely, and sexually unhappy. *Rebel without a Cause* (1955), for instance, with James Dean as an alienated teenager in a dysfunctional family and with its scenes of knife fights and car races,

James Dean in *Rebel Without a Cause*. While some argued that American movies exported notions of juvenile delinquency, films from the 1950s and 1960s did contribute to the romanticization of automobiles, sexuality, and youthful rebellion.

provoked cries of outrage from German critics who deplored the permissiveness of American parents and expressed shock that middle-class children behaved like "hoodlums."

Is it helpful, though, to speak of the "Americanization" of culture? First, the term refers to many different processes. United States industrialists openly sought greater economic influence and economic integration: opening markets to American goods, industry to American production techniques, and so on. The United States government also aimed to export American political values, above all anticommunism, via organizations such as Radio Free Europe. Yet the farthest-reaching American influences were conveyed, unintentionally, by music and film: images of rebellious teenagers, a society of abundance, cars and the romance of the road, tangled race relations, flirting working girls (who seemed less identifiably working-class than their European counterparts), or bantering couples. These images could not be completely controlled, and they had no single effect. Movies about young Americans might represent the romance of American power, they might represent a rebellion against that power. Second, American goods were put to different use in local cultures. Third, journalists, critics, and ordinary men and women tended to use "American" as an all-purpose label for various modern or mass culture developments that were more properly global, such as inexpensive electronics from Asia. As one historian puts it, America was less of a reality than an idea—and a contradictory one at that.

GENDER ROLES AND SEXUAL REVOLUTION

What some called the "sexual revolution" of the 1960s had several aspects. The first was less censorship, which we have already seen in film, and fewer taboos regarding discussion of sexuality in public. In the United States, the notorious "Kinsey reports" on male and female sexuality (in 1948 and 1953 respectively) made morality and sexual behavior front-page news. Alfred Kinsey was a zoologist turned social scientist, and the way in which he applied science and statistics to sex attracted considerable attention. An enthusiastic journalist in Europe reported that the massive numbers

Kinsey compiled would, finally, reveal the "truth of sex." The truth, though, was elusive. At the very least Kinsey showed that moral codes and private behaviors did not line up neatly. For instance, 80 to 90 percent of the women he interviewed disapproved of premarital sex, but 50 percent of the women he interviewed had had it. *Time* magazine warned that publicizing disparities between beliefs and behavior might prove subversive—that women and men would decide there was "morality in numbers."

Across Europe and North America, however, young men and women seemed to be reaching rebellious conclusions on their own. As one Italian teenager said, defending her moral codes, "It is our elders who behave scandalously. . . . [W]omen were kept under lock and key, girls married to men who were twice their age. . . . [B]oys, even the very youngest, had total freedom and so queued up at the brothels." Teenage girls in Italy and France told researchers and reporters that taboos were not just old fashioned but damaging, that their mothers had kept them in the dark about matters as rudimentary as menstruation, leaving them unprepared for life.

Was the family crumbling? Transformations in agriculture and life in the countryside did mean that the peasant family was no longer the institution that governed birth, work, courtship, marriage, and death. Yet the family became newly important as the center of consumption, spending, and leisure time, for television took people (usually men) out of bars, cafés, and music halls. It became the focus of government attention in the form of family allowances, health care, and cold war appeals to family values. People brought higher expectations to marriage, which raised rates of divorce, and they paid more attention to children, which brought smaller families. Despite a post-war spike in the birth rate which produced the "baby boom," over the long term fertility declined, even in countries that outlawed contraception. The family assumed new meanings as its traditional structures of authority—namely paternal control over wives and children—were eroding under the pressure of social change.

A second aspect of the "revolution" was the centrality of sex and eroticism to mass consumer culture. Magazines, which flourished in this period, offered advice on how to succeed in love and be attractive. Cultivating one's looks, including sexiness, fit with the

> The family assumed new meanings as its traditional structures of authority—namely paternal control over wives and children—were eroding under the pressure of social change.

new accent on consumption; indeed health and personal hygiene was the fastest rising category of family spending. Advertising, advice columns, TV, and film blurred boundaries between buying consumer goods, seeking personal fulfillment, and sexual desire. There was nothing new about appeals to eroticism. But the fact that sexuality was now widely considered a form of self-expression—perhaps even the core of oneself—was new to the twentieth century. These developments helped to propel change, and they also made the "sexual revolution" prominent in the politics of the time.

The third aspect of the "revolution" came with legal and medical or scientific changes in contraception. Oral contraceptives, first approved for development in 1959, became mainstream in the next decade. The pill did not have revolutionary effects on the birth rate, which was already falling. It marked dramatic change, however, because it was simple (though expensive), and could be used by women themselves. By 1975, two thirds of British women between fifteen and forty-four said they were taking the pill. Numbers like these marked a long, drawn-out end to centuries-old views that to discuss birth control was pornographic, an affront to religion, and an invitation to indulgence and promiscuity. By and large, Western countries legalized contraception in the 1960s and abortion in the 1970s. In 1965, for instance, the U.S. Supreme Court struck down laws banning the use of contraception, though selling contraceptives remained illegal in Massachusetts until 1972. The Soviet Union legalized abortion in 1950, after banning it during most of Stalin's regime. Throughout Eastern Europe, abortion rates were extremely high, for contraceptives proved as difficult to obtain as other consumer goods, men often refused to use them, and women, doubly burdened with long hours of work and housework and facing, in addition, chronic housing shortages, had little choice but to resort to abortion.

Legal changes would not have occurred without the women's movements of the time. For nineteenth-century feminists, winning the right to vote was the most difficult practical and symbolic struggle (see Chapter 23). For the revived feminism of the 1960s and 1970s, the family, work, and sexuality—all put on the agenda by the social changes of the period—were central. Since World War II the assumption that middle-class women belonged in the home had been challenged by the steadily rising demand for workers, especially in education and the service sector. Thus many more married women and many more mothers were part of the labor force. Moreover, across the West young middle-class women, like men, were part of the rising number of university students. But in the United States, to take just one example, only 37 percent of women who enrolled in college in the 1950s finished their degrees, believing they should marry instead. As one of them explained, "We married what we wanted to be": doctor, professor, manager, and so on. Women found it difficult to get nonsecretarial jobs, received less pay for the same work, and, even when employed, had to rely on their husbands to establish credit.

The tension between rising expectations that stemmed from abundance, growth, and the emphasis on self-expression on the one hand and the reality of narrow horizons on the other created quiet waves of discontent. Betty Friedan's *Feminine Mystique* (1963) brought much of this discontent into the open, contrasting the cultural myths of the fulfilled and happy housewife with the realities of economic inequality, hard work, and narrowed horizons. In 1949, Simone de Beauvoir had asked how Western culture (myth, literature, and psychology) had created an image of woman as the second, and lesser sex; Friedan, using a more journalistic style and writing at a time when social change had made readers more receptive to her ideas, showed how the media, the social sciences, and advertising at once exalted femininity and lowered women's expectations and possibilities. Friedan founded NOW (National Organization of Women) in 1966; smaller and often more radical women's movements multiplied across Europe in the following decades. For this generation of feminists, reproductive freedom was both a private matter and a basic right—a key to women's control over their lives. Outlawing contraception and abortion made women alone bear responsibility for the consequences of sweeping changes in Western sexual life. Such measures were ineffective as well as unjust, they argued. French feminists dramatized the point by publishing the names of 343 well-known women, including Beauvoir, who admitted to having had illegal abortions. A similar petition came out in Germany the following year, and was followed by petitions from doctors and tens of thousands of supporters. In sum, the legal changes followed from political demands, and those in turn reflected a quiet or subterranean rebellion of many women (and men)—one with longer-term causes. Mass consumption, mass culture, and startlingly rapid transformations in public and private life were all intimately related.

THE "WOMAN QUESTION" ON BOTH SIDES OF THE ATLANTIC

How did Western culture define "femininity" and did women internalize those definitions? These questions were central to postwar feminist thought, and they were sharply posed in two classic texts: Simone de Beauvoir's The Second Sex *(1949) and Betty Friedan's* The Feminine Mystique *(1963). Beauvoir (1908–1986) started from the existentialist premise that humans were "condemned to be free" and to give their own lives meaning. Why, then, did women accept the limitations imposed on them and, in Beauvoir's words, "dream the dreams of men"? Although dense and philosophical,* The Second Sex *sent shock waves through Catholic France and was published throughout the world. Betty Friedan's equally influential bestseller took up much the same issue, trying to find the origins of the "feminine mystique," Friedan's term for the model of femininity promoted by experts, advertised in women's magazines, and seemingly accepted by middle-class housewives in the postwar United States. As Friedan points out in the excerpt below, the new postwar "mystique" was in many ways more conservative than prewar ideals had been, despite continuing social change, a greater range of careers opening up to women, the expansion of women's education, and so on. Friedan (1921–) co-founded the National Organization for Women in 1966 and served as its president until 1970.*

SIMONE DE BEAUVOIR, *THE SECOND SEX*

But first we must ask: what is a woman? . . .

All agree in recognizing the fact that females exist in the human species; today as always they make up about one half of humanity. And yet we are told that femininity is in danger; we are exhorted to be women, remain women, become women. . . . Although some women try zealously to incarnate this essence, it is hardly penetrable. It is frequently described in vague and dazzling terms that seem to have been borrowed from the vocabulary of the seers. . . .

If her functioning as a female is not enough to define woman, if we decline also to explain her through "the eternal feminine," and if nevertheless we admit, provisionally, that women do exist, then we must face the question: what is a woman?

To state the question is, to me, to suggest, at once, a preliminary answer. The fact that I ask it is in itself significant. A man would never get the notion of writing a book on the peculiar situation of the human male. But if I wish to define myself, I must first of all say: "I am a woman"; on this truth must be based all further discussion. A man never begins by presenting himself as an individual of a certain sex; it goes without saying that he is a man. The terms *masculine* and *feminine* are used symmetrically only as a matter of form, as on legal papers. In actuality the relation of the two sexes is not quite like that of two electrical poles, for man represents both the positive and the neutral . . . whereas woman represents only the negative, defined by limiting criteria, without reciprocity. . . .

A man is in the right in being a man; it is the woman who is in the wrong. Woman has ovaries, a uterus; these peculiarities imprison her in her subjectivity, circumscribe her within the limits of her own nature. . . .

For him she is sex—absolute sex, no less. She is defined and differentiated with reference to man and not he with reference to her; she is the incidental, the inessential as opposed to the essential. He is the subject, he is the Absolute—she is the Other.

Simone de Beauvoir, *The Second Sex*, translated and edited by H. M. Parshley (New York: Random House, 1974), p. xix.

Betty Friedan, *The Feminine Mystique*

In 1939, the heroines of women's magazine stories were not always young, but in a certain sense they were younger than their fictional counterparts today. They were young in the same way that the American hero has always been young: they were New Women, creating with a gay determined spirit a new identity for women—a life of their own. There was an aura about them of becoming, of moving into a future that was going to be different from the past. . . .

These stories may not have been great literature. But the identity of their heroines seemed to say something about the housewives who, then as now, read the women's magazines. These magazines were not written for career women. The New Woman heroines were the ideal of yesterday's housewives; they reflected the dreams, mirrored the yearning for identity and the sense of possibility that existed for women then. . . .

In 1949 . . . the feminine mystique began to spread through the land. . . .

The feminine mystique says that the highest value and the only commitment for women is the fulfillment of their own femininity. It says that the great mistake of Western culture, through most of its history, has been the undervaluation of this femininity. . . . The mistake, says the mystique, the root of women's troubles in the past, is that women envied men, women

tried to be like men, instead of accepting their own nature, which can find fulfillment only in sexual passivity, male domination, and nurturing maternal love.

But the new image this mystique gives to American women is the old image: "Occupation: housewife." The new mystique makes the housewife-mothers, who never had a chance to be anything else, the model for all women; it presupposes that history has reached a final and glorious end in the here and now, as far as women are concerned. . . .

It is more than a strange paradox that as all professions are finally open to women in America, "career woman" has become a dirty word; that as higher education becomes available to any woman with the capacity for it, education for women has become so suspect that more and more drop out of high school and college to marry and have babies; that as so many roles in modern society become theirs for the taking, women so insistently confine themselves to one role. Why . . . should she accept this new image which insists she is not a person but a "woman," by definition barred from the freedom of human existence and a voice in human destiny?

Betty Friedan, *The Feminine Mystique* (New York: W. W. Norton & Company, Inc., 2001), pp. 38, 40, 42–43, 67–68.

Social Movements During the 1960s

> What spurred the social movements of the 1960s?

The social unrest of the sixties was international. Its roots lay in the political struggles and social transformations of the postwar period. Of these, the most important were anticolonial and civil rights movements. The successful anticolonial movements (see Chapter 27) reflected a growing racial consciousness and also helped to encourage that consciousness. Newly independent African and Caribbean nations remained wary about revivals of colonialism and the continuing economic hegemony of Western Europe and America. Black and

Asian immigration into those nations produced tension and frequent violence. In the West, particularly in the United States, people of color identified with these social and economic grievances.

The Civil Rights Movement

The emergence of new black nations in Africa and the Caribbean was paralleled by growing African American insurgency. World War II increased African American migration from the American South to northern cities, intensifying a drive for rights, dignity, and independence that began in the prewar era with organizations such as the National Association for the Advancement of Colored People (NAACP) and the National Urban League. By 1960, various civil rights groups, led by the Congress of Racial Equality (CORE), had started to organize boycotts and demonstrations directed at private businesses and public services that discriminated against blacks in the South. The preeminent figure in the civil rights movement in the United States during the 1960s was Martin Luther King, Jr. (1929–1968). A Baptist minister, King embraced the philosophy of nonviolence promoted by the Indian social and political activist Mohandas K. Gandhi. King's personal participation in countless demonstrations, his willingness to go to jail for a cause that he believed to be just, and his ability as an orator to arouse both blacks and whites with his message led to his position as the most highly regarded—and most widely feared—defender of black rights. His inspiring career was tragically ended by assassination in 1968.

Martin Luther King, Jr., and organizations such as CORE aspired to a fully integrated nation. Other charismatic and important black leaders sought complete independence from white society, fearing that integration would leave African Americans without the spiritual or material resources necessary for a community's pride, dignity, and autonomy. The most influential of the black nationalists was Malcolm X (1925–1965), who assumed the "X" after having discarded his "white" surname (Little). For most of his adult life a spokesman for the Black Muslim movement, Malcolm X urged blacks to renew their commitment to their own heritage, to establish black businesses for economic autonomy, and to fortify economic, political, and psychological defenses against white domination. Like King he was assassinated, in 1965 while addressing a rally in Harlem.

Civil rights laws passed under President Lyndon B. Johnson in the 1960s did bring African Americans some measure of equality with regard to voting rights—and, to a much lesser degree, school desegregation. In other areas, such as housing and job opportunities, white racism continued. Economic development passed by many African American communities and subsequent administrations pulled back from the innovative programs of the Johnson era.

These problems were not confined to the United States. West Indian, Indian, and Pakistani immigrants in Britain met with discrimination in jobs, housing, and everyday interaction with the authorities—producing frequent racial disturbances in major British cities. France witnessed hostility toward Algerian immigra-

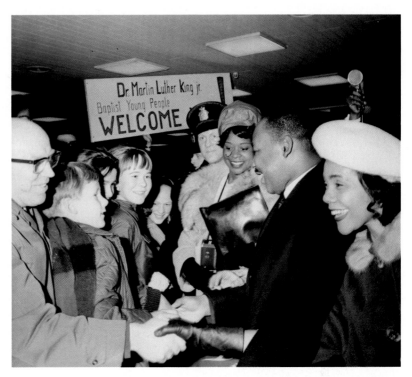

Martin Luther King, Jr., 1964. The African American civil rights leader is welcomed in Oslo, Norway, on a trip to accept the Nobel Peace Prize. He would be assassinated four years later.

tion, Germany toward the importation of Turkish labor. In Western Europe, as in the United States, struggles for racial and ethnic integration became central to the postcolonial world.

The civil rights movement had enormous significance for the twentieth century, and it galvanized other movements as well. It dramatized as perhaps no other movement could the chasm between the egalitarian promises of American democracy and the real inequalities at the core of the American social and political life—a chasm that could be found in other Western nations as well. African American claims were morally as well as politically compelling, and the civil rights movement sharpened others' criticisms of what they saw as a complacent, narrowly individualistic, materialist culture.

THE ANTIWAR MOVEMENT

The United States' escalating war in Vietnam became a lightning rod for discontent. In 1961, President John F. Kennedy (1917–1963) promised to "bear any burden" necessary to fight communism and to ensure the victory of American models of representative government and free-market economics in the developing nations. Kennedy's plan entailed massive increases in foreign

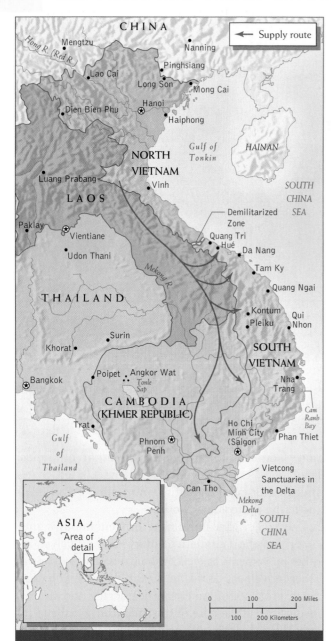

THE WAR IN VIETNAM AND SOUTHEAST ASIA

The 1954 Geneva Accords divided Vietnam at the seventeenth parallel. The north went to Ho Chi Minh, the communist leader, and the south was controlled by Ngo Dinh Diem, an ally of the United States. In 1956, South Vietnam refused to hold the elections mandated in the Geneva Accords. Ho Chi Minh mobilized a guerrilla army, the Viet Cong, and the Vietnam War began. How did the Viet Cong use the proximity of Cambodia and Laos to their strategic advantage? Why did the United States choose to get involved?

aid, much of it in weapons. It provided the impetus for humanitarian institutions such as the Peace Corps, intended to improve local conditions and show Americans' benevolence and good intentions. Bearing burdens, however, also meant fighting guerrillas who turned to the Soviets for aid. This involved covert interventions in Latin America, the Congo, and, most important, Vietnam.

By the time of Kennedy's death in 1963, nearly fifteen thousand American "advisors" were on the ground alongside South Vietnamese troops. Kennedy's successor, Lyndon B. Johnson, began the strategic bombing of North Vietnam and rapidly drew hundreds of thousands of American troops into combat in South Vietnam. The rebels in the South, known as the Viet Cong, were solidly entrenched, highly experienced guerrilla fighters, and were backed by the professional, well-equipped North Vietnamese army under Ho Chi Minh. The South Vietnamese government resisted efforts at reform, losing popular support. Massive efforts by the United States produced only stalemate, mounting American casualties, and rising discontent.

Vietnam did much to cause the political turmoil of the 1960s in the United States. As Martin Luther King, Jr., pointed out, the war—which relied on a disproportionate number of black soldiers to conduct a war against a small nation of color—echoed and magnified racial inequality at home. Exasperated by troubles in the field, American planners continued to escalate military commitments, with no effect. Peace talks in Paris stalled while the death toll on all sides increased. The involuntary draft of young American men expanded and polarized the public. In 1968 criticism forced President Johnson to abandon his plans to run for a second term. Johnson's successor, Richard M. Nixon, who won a narrow victory on the basis of promises to end the war, expanded it instead. Student protests against the war frequently ended in violence. The government brought criminal conspiracy charges against Benjamin Spock, the nation's leading pediatrician, and William Sloane Coffin, the chaplain of Yale University, for encouraging young people to resist the draft. Avoiding the draft became so widespread that the system was changed in 1970. And from other countries' points of view, the Vietnam War became a spectacle: one in which the most powerful, wealthiest nation of the world seemed intent on destroying a land of poor peasants in the name of anticommunism, democracy, and freedom. The tarnished image of Western values stood at the center of 1960s protest movements in the United States and Western Europe.

THE STUDENT MOVEMENT

The student movement itself can be seen as a consequence of postwar developments: a growing cohort of young people with more time and wealth than in the past, generational consciousness heightened, in part, by the marketing of mass youth culture, and educational institutions unable to deal with rising numbers or expectations. In France, the number of students in high school rose from four hundred thousand in 1949 to 2 million in 1969; in universities, over the same period, enrollments skyrocketed, from one hundred thousand to six hundred thousand. The same was true in Italy, Britain, and West Germany. Universities, which had been created to educate a small elite, found both their teaching staffs and their facilities overwhelmed. Lecture halls were packed, university bureaucracies did not respond to requests, and thousands of students took exams at the same time. More philosophically, students raised questions about the role and meaning of elite education in a democratic society, and about the relationships between the university as a "knowledge factory," consumer culture, and neocolonial ventures such as the Vietnam War and, for the French, the Algerian wars. Conservative traditions made intellectual reform difficult. In addition, student demands for fewer restrictions on personal life—for instance, permission to have a member of the opposite sex in a dormitory room—provoked authoritarian reactions from university representatives. Waves of student protest were not confined to the United States and Western Europe. They swept across Poland and Czechoslovakia where students protested one-party bureaucratic rule, stifling intellectual life, and authoritarianism, and helped sustain networks of dissidents. By the mid 1960s, simmering anger in Eastern Europe had once again reached a dangerous point.

> The student movement itself can be seen as a consequence of postwar developments: a growing cohort of young people with more time and wealth than in the past, generational consciousness heightened, in part, by the marketing of mass youth culture, and educational institutions unable to deal with rising numbers or expectations.

1968

Nineteen sixty-eight was an extraordinary year, quite similar to 1848 with its wave of revolution (see Chapter 20). It was even more intensely international, a reflection of tightening global ties. International youth culture fostered a sense of collective identity. The new media relayed images of civil rights protest in the United States to Europe, and broadcast news footage of the Vietnam War on television screens from West Virginia to West Germany. The wave of unrest shook both the Eastern and Western blocs. Protest movements assailed bureaucracy and the human costs of the cold war: on the Soviet side, bureaucracy, authoritarianism, and indifference to civilians; on the Western side, bias and monopolies in the news media, the "military-industrial complex," and American imperialism. The Soviet regime, as we have seen, responded with repression. In the United States and Western Europe, traditional political parties had little idea what to make of these new movements and those who participated in them. In both cases, events rapidly overwhelmed political systems.

PARIS

The most serious outbreak of student unrest in Europe came in Paris in the spring of 1968. The French Republic had been shaken by conflicts over the Algerian war in the early 1960s. Even more important, the economic boom had undermined the foundations of the regime and de Gaulle's traditional style of rule. French students at the University of Paris demanded reforms that would modernize their university. Protest first peaked at Nanterre, a new branch of the university built on a former air force depot, in a poor and poorly served neighborhood, and starved for funds and overcrowded with students. Petitions, demonstrations, and confrontations with university authorities traveled quickly from Nanterre to the Sorbonne, in central Paris and in the face of growing disorder, the University of Paris shut down—sending students into the streets and into uglier confrontations with the police. The police reacted with repression and violence, which startled onlookers and television audiences and backfired on the regime. Sympathy with the students' cause expanded rapidly, bringing in other opponents of President de Gaulle's regime. Massive trade-union strikes broke out. Workers in the automobile industry, technical workers, and public-sector employees—from gas and electricity utilities, the mail system, to radio and television—went on strike. By mid-May, an astonishing 10 million French workers had walked off their jobs. De Gaulle had no sympathy for the students: "Reform, yes—bed wetting, no," he reportedly declared at

1960s POLITICS:
THE SITUATIONISTS

In 1957, a small group of European artists and writers formed a group called the Situationist International. The movement combined the artistic traditions of dada and surrealism with anarchism and Marxism. Unlike traditional Marxists, the situationists did not focus on the workplace. Instead they developed a broad critique of everyday life, protesting the stifling of art, creativity, and imagination in contemporary society. They denounced the "tyranny" of consumer culture, which constantly invented new needs and desires in order to fuel consumption. Capitalism, they said, had "colonized" everyday life. The situationists' ideas and especially their unorthodox, surrealist style, became influential during the events of May 1968 in France. All around Paris students painted situationist slogans such as those printed below.

The social movements of 1968 cut across cold war boundaries, attacking Western consumerism as well as Soviet authoritarianism. A group of students and situationists sent a telegram (second excerpt below) to the Politburo of the Communist Party of the USSR in May 1968.

SITUATIONIST ANTICAPITALISM, 1968

OCCUPY THE FACTORIES

POWER TO THE WORKERS COUNCILS

ABOLISH CLASS SOCIETY

DOWN WITH THE
SPECTACLE-COMMODITY SOCIETY

ABOLISH ALIENATION

ABOLISH THE UNIVERSITY

HUMANITY WON'T BE HAPPY TILL THE
LAST BUREAUCRAT IS HUNG WITH THE GUTS
OF THE LAST CAPITALIST

DEATH TO THE COPS

FREE ALSO THE 4 GUYS CONVICTED FOR
LOOTING DURING THE 6 MAY RIOT

—OCCUPATION COMMITTEE OF THE
AUTONOMOUS AND POPULAR
SORBONNE UNIVERSITY

SITUATIONIST ANTICOMMUNIST SLOGANS, 1968

17 MAY 1968 / To the Politburo of the Communist party of the USSR the Kremlin Moscow / Shake in your shoes bureaucrats. The international power of the workers councils will soon wipe you out. Humanity won't be happy till the last bureaucrat is hung with the guts of the last capitalist. Long live the struggle of the Kronstadt sailors and of the Makhnovshchina against Trostky and Lenin. Long live the 1956 Councilist insurrection of Budapest • Down with the state • Long live revolutionary Marxism. Occupation committee of the Autonomous and Popular Sorbonne

"Slogans to be Spread Now by Every Means," in *Situationist International Anthology*, edited and translated by Ken Knabb (Berkeley: Bureau of Public Secrets, 1981), pp. 334–345.

the height of the confrontation. At one point, it looked as if the government would fall. The regime, however, was able to satisfy the strikers with wage increases and to appeal to public demand for order. The student movements, isolated, gradually petered out and students agreed to resume university life. The regime did recover, but the events of 1968 helped weaken de Gaulle's position as president and contributed to his retirement from office the following year.

There had been protest and rebelliousness in the 1950s, but the scale of events in 1968 was astonishing. Paris was not the only city to explode in 1968. Student protest broke out in West Berlin, targeting the government's close ties to the autocratic shah of Iran and the power of media corporations. Clashes with the police turned violent. In Italian cities, undergraduates staged several demonstrations to draw attention to university overcrowding. Twenty-six universities were closed. The London School of Economics was nearly shut down by protest. In Mexico City a confrontation with the police ended with the deaths of hundreds of protesters, most of them students—on the eve of the 1968 Olympics, hosted by the Mexican government. Those Olympics reflected the political contests of the period: African nations threatened to boycott if South Africa, with its apartheid regime, participated. Two African American medalists raised their hands in a black power salute during an awards ceremony— and the Olympic Committee promptly sent them home. In Vietnam, the Viet Cong defied American claims to have turned the tide by launching a new offensive. The Tet offensive, named for the Vietnamese new year, brought the highest casualty rates to date in the Vietnam War and an explosion of protest. Antiwar demonstrations and student rebellions spread across the country. President Lyndon Johnson, battered by the effects of Tet and already worn down by the war, chose not to run for reelection. Nineteen sixty-eight also saw damage and trauma for the country's political future, because of the assassinations of Martin Luther King, Jr. (April 4, 1968) and presidential candidate Robert F. Kennedy (June 5, 1968). King's assassination was followed by a wave of rioting in more than fifty cities across the United States, followed in late summer by street battles between police and student protesters at the Democratic National Convention in Chicago. Some saw the flowering of protest as another "springtime of peoples." Others saw it as a long nightmare.

> When Dubček attempted to democratize the Communist party and did not attend a meeting of members of the Warsaw Pact, the Soviets sent tanks and troops into Prague in August of 1968.

PRAGUE

The student movement in the United States and Western Europe also took inspiration from one of the most significant challenges to Soviet authority since the Hungarian revolt of 1956 (see Chapter 27): the "Prague spring" of 1968. The events began with the emergence of a liberal communist government in Czechoslovakia, led by the Slovak Alexander Dubček. Dubček had outmaneuvered the more traditional, authoritarian party leaders. He advocated "socialism with a human face"; he encouraged debate within the party, academic and artistic freedom, and less censorship. As was often the case, party members were divided between proponents of reform and those fearful that reform would unleash revolution. The reformers, however, also gained support from outside the party, from student organizations, the press, and networks of dissidents. As in Western Europe and the United States, the protest movement overflowed traditional party politics.

In the Soviet Union, Khrushchev had fallen in 1964, and the reins of Soviet power passed to Leonid Brezhnev as secretary of the Communist party. Brezhnev was more conservative than Khrushchev, less inclined to bargain with the West, and prone to defensive actions to safeguard the Soviet sphere of influence. Initially, the Soviets tolerated Dubček as a political eccentric. The events of 1968 raised their fears. Most Eastern European communist leaders denounced Czech reformism, but student demonstrations of support broke out in Poland and Yugoslavia, calling for an end to one-party rule, less censorship, and reform of the judicial system. In addition, Josip Broz Tito of Yugoslavia and Nicolae Ceausescu of Romania—two of the more stubbornly independent communists in Eastern Europe—visited Dubček. To Soviet eyes these activities looked as if they were directed against the Warsaw Pact and Soviet security; they also saw American intervention in Vietnam as evidence of heightened anticommunist activities around the world. When Dubček attempted to democratize the Communist party and did not attend a meeting of members of the Warsaw Pact, the Soviets sent tanks and troops into Prague in August of 1968. Again the world watched as streams of Czech refugees left the country and a repressive government, picked by Soviet security forces, took charge. Dubček and his allies were subjected to imprisonment or "internal exile." Twenty percent of the members of

LUDVÍK VACULÍK,
"TWO THOUSAND WORDS"

During the Prague spring of 1968, a group of Czech intellectuals published a document titled "Two Thousand Words that Belong to Workers, Farmers, Officials, Scientists, Artists, and Everybody" that has become known simply as the "Two Thousand Words." This manifesto called for further reform, including increased freedom of the press. Seen as a direct affront by Moscow, the manifesto heightened Soviet-Czech tensions. In August 1968, Warsaw Pact tanks rolled into Prague, overthrowing the reformist government of Alexander Dubček.

Most of the nation welcomed the socialist program with high hopes. But it fell into the hands of the wrong people. It would not have mattered so much that they lacked adequate experience in affairs of state, factual knowledge, or philosophical education, if only they had enough common prudence and decency to listen to the opinion of others and agree to being gradually replaced by more able people. . . .

The chief sin and deception of these rulers was to have explained their own whims as the "will of the workers." Were we to accept this pretense, we would have to blame the workers today for the decline of our economy, for crimes committed against the innocent, and for the introduction of censorship to prevent anyone writing about these things. The workers would be to blame for misconceived investments, for losses suffered in foreign trade, and for the housing shortage. Obviously no sensible person will hold the working class responsible for such things. We all know, and every worker knows especially, that they had virtually no say in deciding anything. . . .

Since the beginning of this year we have been experiencing a regenerative process of democratization. . . .

Let us demand the departure of people who abused their power, damaged public property, and acted dishonorably or brutally. Ways must be found to compel them to resign. To mention a few: public criticism, resolutions, demonstrations, demonstrative work brigades, collections to buy presents for them on their retirement, strikes, and picketing at their front doors. But we should reject any illegal, indecent, or boorish methods. . . .

Let us convert the district and local newspapers, which have mostly degenerated to the level of official mouthpieces, into a platform for all the forward-looking elements in politics; let us demand that editorial boards be formed of National Front representatives, or else let us start new papers. Let us form committees for the defense of free speech. . . .

There has been great alarm recently over the possibility that foreign forces will intervene in our development. Whatever superior forces may face us, all we can do is stick to our own positions, behave decently, and initiate nothing ourselves. We can show our government that we will stand by it, with weapons if need be, if it will do what we give it a mandate to do. . . .

The spring is over and will never return. By winter we will know all.

Originally published as "Dva Tisice Slov," *Literarny Listy* (Prague) June 27, 1968. Translated by Mark Kramer, Joy Moss, and Ruth Tosek. From Jaromir Navratil, *The Prague Spring 1968* (Budapest: Central European Press, 1998), pp. 177–181.

the Czech Communist party were expelled in a series of purges. After the destruction of the "Prague spring," Soviet diplomats consolidated their position according to the new "Brezhnev doctrine." The doctrine stated that no socialist state could adopt policies endangering the interests of international socialism, and that the Soviet Union could intervene in the domestic affairs of any Soviet-bloc nation if communist rule was threatened. In other words, the repressive rules applied to Hungary in 1956 would not change.

What were the effects of 1968? De Gaulle's government recovered. The Republican Richard M. Nixon won the U.S. election of 1968. From 1972 to 1975 the United States withdrew from Vietnam; in the wake of that war came a refugee crisis and a new series of horrific regional conflicts. In Prague, Warsaw Pact tanks put down the uprising, and in the Brezhnev Doctrine the Soviet regime reasserted its right to control its satellites. Serious cold war confrontations rippled along Czechoslovakia's western border as refugees fled west, and in the Korean peninsula after North Korea's seizure of an eavesdropping ship from the United States Navy. Over the long term, however, the protesters' and dissidents' demands proved more difficult to contain. In Eastern Europe and the Soviet Union, dissent was defeated but not eliminated. The crushing of the Czech rebellion proved thoroughly disillusioning, and in important respects the events of 1968 prefigured the collapse of Soviet control in 1989. In Western Europe and the United States, the student movement subsided but its issues and the kinds of politics that it pioneered proved more enduring. Feminism (or, more accurately, second-wave feminism) really came into its own after 1968, its numbers expanded by women a generation younger than Simone de Beauvoir and Betty Friedan. They had been in student political organizations in the 1960s and their impatience with traditional political parties and, often, their male student allies, sent them into separate groups, where they championed equality in sexual relationships and in the family. In a phrase that captured some of the changes of the 1950s and 1960s, they insisted that "the personal is political." As one English woman said, "We wanted to redefine the meaning of politics to include an analysis of our daily lives," which meant sexuality, health, child care, cultural images of women, and so on. The antiwar movement took up the issue of nuclear weapons—a particularly volatile issue in Europe. Finally, the environmental movement took hold—concerned not only with pollution and the world's dwin-

dling resources, but also with mushrooming urbanization and the kind of unrestrained economic growth that had given rise to the 1960s. Over the long term, in both Europe and the United States, voters' loyalties to traditional political parties became less reliable and smaller parties multiplied; in this way, new social movements eventually became part of a very different political landscape.

ECONOMIC STAGNATION: THE PRICE OF SUCCESS

What caused the economic stagnation of the 1970s and 1980s?

Economic as well as social problems plagued Europe during the 1970s and 1980s, but these problems had begun earlier. By the middle of the 1960s, for example, the West German growth rate had slowed. Demand for manufactured goods fell, and in 1966 the country suffered its first postwar recession. Volkswagen, the symbol of the German "miracle," introduced a shortened work week; almost seven hundred thousand West Germans were thrown out of work altogether. In France a persistent housing shortage increased the cost of living. Though new industries continued to prosper, the basic industries—coal, steel, and railways—began to run up deficits. Unemployment was rising in tandem with prices. Prime Minister Harold Wilson's pledge to revive Britain's economy by introducing new technology foundered on crises in the foreign-exchange value of the pound, which were compounded by continued low levels of growth. The Common Market—expanded in 1973 to include Britain, Ireland, and Denmark, and again in the early 1980s to admit Greece, Spain, and Portugal—struggled to overcome problems stemming from the conflict between the domestic economic regulations characteristic of many European states and the free-market policies that prevailed within what would become the European Economic Community (EEC) countries.

Oil prices spiked for the first time in the early 1970s, compounding these difficulties. In 1973, the Arab-dominated Organization of Petroleum Exporting Countries (OPEC) instituted an oil embargo against the Western powers. In 1973, a barrel of oil cost $1.73; in 1975, it cost $10.46; by the early 1980s, the price had risen to over $30. This increase produced an infla-tionary spiral; interest rates rose and with them the price of almost everything else Western consumers were used to buying. Rising costs produced wage de-mands and strikes. The calm industrial relations of the 1950s and early 1960s were a thing of the past. At the same time, European manufacturers encountered seri-ous competition, not only from such highly developed countries as Japan but also from the increasingly active economies of Asia and Africa, in which the West had invested capital eagerly in the previous decades. By 1980 Japan had captured 10 percent of the automobile market in West Germany and 25 percent in Belgium. In 1984, unemployment in Western Europe reached about 19 million. The lean years had arrived.

Economies in the Soviet bloc also stalled. The ex-pansion of heavy industry had helped recovery in the postwar period, but by the 1970s, those sectors no longer provided growth or innovation. The Soviet Communist party proclaimed in 1961 that by 1970 the USSR would exceed the United States in per capita production. By the end of the 1970s, however, Soviet per capita production was not much higher than in the less industrialized countries of southern Europe. The Soviets were also overcommitted to military defense industries that had become inefficient, though lucra-

tive for the party members who ran them. The Soviet economy did get a boost from the OPEC oil price hikes of 1973 and 1979. (The Organization of Petro-leum Exporting Countries was founded in 1961; the USSR did not belong but as the world's largest pro-ducer of oil, it benefited from rising prices.) Without this boost, the situation would have been far grimmer.

Following an impressive economic performance dur-ing the early 1970s, the Eastern European nations en-countered serious financial difficulties. Their success had rested in part on capital borrowed from the West. By 1980 those debts weighed heavily on their national economies. Poland's hard-currency indebtedness to Western countries, for example, was almost four times greater than its annual exports. The solution to this problem, attempted in Poland and elsewhere, was to cut back on production for domestic consumption in order to increase exports. Yet this policy encountered strong popular opposition. Although there was virtu-ally no unemployment in Eastern Europe, men and women were by no means happy with their economic situation. Working hours were longer than in Western Europe, and goods and services, even in prosperous times, were scarce.

Western governments struggled for effective reac-tions to the abrupt change in their economic circum-

Unemployment Demonstration, 1974. A crowd of workers in Rome, Italy, gathered to protest in-flation and unemployment, in a strike that lasted 24 hours.

CHRONOLOGY

DEVELOPMENT OF THE EUROPEAN ECONOMIC COMMUNITY

European coal and steel community founded	1951
Rome treaty forms EEC	1957
European community expanded	1985
Treaty of Maastricht creates European union	1991

stances. The new conservative leader of the British Conservative party, Margaret Thatcher, was elected prime minister in 1979—and reelected in 1983 and 1987—on a program of curbing trade-union power, cutting taxes to stimulate the economy, and privatizing publicly owned enterprises. The economy remained weak, with close to 15 percent of the work force unemployed by 1986. In West Germany, a series of Social Democratic governments attempted to combat economic recession with job-training programs and tax incentives, both financed by higher taxes. These programs did little to assist economic recovery, and the country shifted to the right.

The fact that governments of right and left were unable to recreate Europe's unprecedented postwar prosperity suggests the degree to which economic forces remain outside the control of individual states. The continuing economic malaise renewed efforts to "Europeanize" common problems. By the end of the 1980s, the EEC embarked on an ambitious program of integration. Long-term goals, agreed on when the EU (European Union) was formed in 1991, included a monetary union, with a central European bank and a single currency, and unified social policies to reduce poverty and unemployment. As the twenty-first century opened, the European member states had begun to institute several of these steps. It remained unclear whether that new European "federal" state would overcome its members' claims of national sovereignty or whether it would develop the economic and political strength to counter the global domination of the United States.

SOLIDARITY IN POLAND

In 1980, unrest again peaked in Eastern Europe, this time with the Polish labor movement Solidarity. Polish workers organized strikes that brought the govern-

ment of the country to a standstill. The workers formulated several key demands. First, they objected to working conditions imposed by the government to combat a severe economic crisis. Second, they protested high prices and, especially shortages, both of which had roots in government policy and priorities. Above all, though, the Polish workers in Solidarity demanded truly independent labor unions instead of labor organizations sponsored by the government. Their belief that society had the right to organize itself and, by implication, create its own government, stood at the core of the movement. The strikers were led by an electrician from the Gdansk shipyards, Lech Walesa. Walesa's charismatic personality appealed not only to the Polish citizenry but to sympathizers in the West. Again, however, the Soviets assisted a military regime in reimposing authoritarian rule. The Polish president, General Wojciech Jaruzelski, had learned from Hungary and Czechoslovakia and played a delicate game of diplomacy to maintain the Polish government's freedom of action while repressing Solidarity itself. But the implied Soviet threat remained.

EUROPE RECAST: THE COLLAPSE OF COMMUNISM AND THE END OF THE SOVIET UNION

What caused the collapse of communism?

One of history's fascinations is its unpredictability. There has been no more telling example of this in recent times than the sudden collapse of the Eastern European communist regimes in 1989, the dramatic end to the cold war, and the subsequent disintegration of the once-powerful Soviet Union.

GORBACHEV AND SOVIET REFORM

This sudden collapse flowed, unintended, from a new wave of reform begun in the mid-1980s. In 1985 a new generation of officials began taking charge of the Soviet Communist party, a change heralded by Mikhail Gorbachev's appointment to the party leadership. In his mid-fifties, Gorbachev was significantly younger than his immediate predecessors and less prey to the habits of mind that had shaped Soviet domestic and foreign affairs. He was frankly critical of the repressive aspects of communist society as well as its sluggish economy, and he did not hesitate to voice those criticisms openly. His twin policies of *glasnost* (intellectual openness) and *perestroika* (economic restructuring) held out hope for a freer, more prosperous Soviet Union. Under Gorbachev, a number of imprisoned dissidents were freed, among them Andrei Sakharov, the scientist known as the "father of the Soviet hydrogen bomb," and later a fierce critic of the cold war arms race.

Gorbachev and the Old Guard. Gorbachev is pictured here at the height of his power in 1986, with KGB chief Victor Chebrikov, President Andrei Gromyko, and Premier Nikolai Rzyhkov. Perestroika aimed at the privileges of the political elite and would eventually lead to the fall from power of all these men.

The policies of perestroika took aim at the privileges of the political elite and the immobility of the state bureaucracy by instituting competitive elections to official positions and limiting terms of office. Gorbachev's program of perestroika called for a shift from the centrally planned economy instituted by Stalin to a mixed economy combining planning with the operation of market forces. In agriculture, perestroika accelerated the move away from cooperative production and instituted incentives for the achievement of production targets. Gorbachev planned to integrate the Soviet Union into the international economy by participating in organizations such as the International Monetary Fund.

Even these dramatic reforms, however, were too little too late. Ethnic unrest, a legacy of Russia's nineteenth-century imperialism, threatened to split the Soviet Union apart, while secession movements gathered steam in the Baltic republics and elsewhere. From 1988 onward, fighting between Armenians and Azerbaijanis over an ethnically Azerbaijani region located inside Armenia threatened to escalate into a border dispute with Iran. Only Soviet troops patrolling the border and Gorbachev's willingness to suppress a separatist revolt in Azerbaijan by force temporarily quelled the conflict.

Spurred on by these events in the Soviet Union, the countries of Eastern Europe began to agitate for independence from Moscow. Gorbachev encouraged open discussion—glasnost—not only in his own country but also in the satellite nations. He revoked the Brezhnev Doctrine's insistence on single-party socialist governments and made frequent and inspiring trips to the capitals of neighboring satellites.

Glasnost rekindled the flame of opposition in Poland, where Solidarity had been defeated but not destroyed by the government in 1981. In 1988 the union launched a new series of strikes. These disturbances culminated in an agreement between the government and Solidarity that legalized the union and promised open elections. The results, in June 1989, astonished the world: virtually all of the government's candidates lost; the Citizen's Committee, affiliated with Solidarity, won a sizable majority in the Polish parliament.

In Hungary and Czechoslovakia, events followed a similar course during 1988 and 1989. Janos Kadar, the Hungarian leader since the Soviet crackdown of 1956, resigned in the face of continuing demonstrations in May 1988 and was replaced by the reformist government of the Hungarian Socialist Workers' party. By the spring of 1989 the Hungarian regime had been purged of Communist party supporters. The government also began to dismantle its security fences along the Austrian border. A year later the Hungarian Democratic Forum, pledging it would reinstate full civil rights and restructure the economy, secured a plurality of seats in the National Assembly.

The Czechs, too, staged demonstrations against Soviet domination in late 1988. Brutal beatings of student demonstrators by the police in 1989 radicalized the nations' workers and provoked mass demonstrations. Civic Forum, an opposition coalition, called for the installation of a coalition government to include non-communists, for free elections, and for the resignation of the country's communist leadership. It reinforced its demands with continuing mass demonstrations and threats of a general strike that resulted in the toppling of the old regime and the election of the playwright and Civic Forum leader Václav Havel as president.

FALL OF THE BERLIN WALL

The most significant political change in Eastern Europe during the late 1980s was the collapse of communism in East Germany and the unification of East and West Germany. Although long considered the most prosperous of the Soviet satellite countries, East Germany suffered from severe economic stagnation and environmental degradation. Waves of East Germans registered their discontent with worsening conditions by massive illegal emigration to the West. This exodus combined with evidence of widespread official corruption to force the resignation of East Germany's long-time, hard-line premier, Erich Honecker. His successor, Egon Krenz, promised reforms, but he was nevertheless faced with continuing protests and continuing mass emigration.

On November 4, 1989, the government, in a move that acknowledged its powerlessness to hold its citizens captive, opened its border with Czechoslovakia. This move effectively freed East Germans to travel to the West. In a matter of days, the Berlin wall—the embodiment of the cold war, the Iron Curtain, and the division of East from West—was demolished by groups of ordinary citizens. Jubilant throngs from both sides walked through the gaping holes that now permitted men, women, and children to take the few steps that symbolized the return to freedom and a chance for national unity. Free elections were held throughout Germany in March 1990, resulting in a victory for the Alliance for Germany, a coalition allied with the West German chancellor Helmut Kohl's Christian Democratic Union. With heavy emigration continuing, reunification talks quickly culminated in the formal proclamation of a united Germany on October 3, 1990.

The public mood, in Eastern Europe and perhaps worldwide, was swept up with the jubilation of these

The Fall of the Berlin Wall, 1989. When East German officials announced that citizens could leave the country through any border crossing, rendering the Berlin wall obsolete, people gathered at the wall to celebrate and to tear it down with picks, axes, and small hammers.

peaceful "velvet revolutions" during the autumn of 1989. Yet the end of one-party rule in Eastern Europe was not accomplished without violence. The single most repressive government in the old Eastern bloc, Nicolae Ceaucescu's outright dictatorship in Romania, came apart with much more bloodshed. By December, faced with the wave of popular revolts in surrounding countries and riots by the ethnic Hungarian minority in Transylvania, a number of party officials and army officers in Romania tried to hold on to their own positions by deposing Ceaucescu. His extensive secret police, however, organized resistance to the coup; the result was nearly two weeks of bloody street fighting in the capital Bucharest. Individual snipers loyal to Ceaucescu were still killing passing civilians from rooftops, forcing dangerous efforts to root them out, while the rest of Eastern Europe celebrated Christmas and the new year with new political systems. Ceaucescu himself and his wife were seized by populist army units and executed; images of their bloodstained bodies flashed worldwide by satellite television.

Throughout the rest of Eastern Europe, single-party governments in the countries behind what was left of the tattered Iron Curtain—Albania, Bulgaria, and Yugoslavia—collapsed in the face of democratic pressure for change. Meanwhile, in the Soviet Union itself, inspired by events in Eastern Europe, the Balkan republics of Lithuania and Latvia strained to free themselves from Soviet rule. In 1990 they unilaterally proclaimed their independence from the Soviet Union, throwing into sharp relief the tension between "union" and "republics." Gorbachev reacted with an uncertain mixture of armed intervention and promises of greater local autonomy. In the fall of 1991 Lithuania and Latvia, along with the third Baltic state of Estonia, won international recognition as independent republics.

THE COLLAPSE OF THE SOVIET UNION

While Soviet influence eroded in Eastern Europe, at home the unproductive Soviet economy continued to fuel widespread ire. With the failure of perestroika—largely the result of a lack of resources and an inability to increase production—came the rise of a powerful political rival to Gorbachev, his erstwhile ally Boris Yeltsin. The reforming mayor of Moscow, Yeltsin was elected president of the Russian Federation—the largest Soviet republic—on an anti-Gorbachev platform in 1990. Pressure from the Yeltsin camp weakened Gorbachev's ability to maneuver independent of reactionary factions in the Politburo and the military, undermining his reform program and his ability to remain in power.

The Soviet Union's increasingly severe domestic problems led to mounting protests in 1991, when Gorbachev's policies failed to improve—indeed diminished—the living standard of the Soviet people. Demands increased that the bloated government bureaucracy respond with a dramatic cure for the country's continuing economic stagnation. Gorbachev appeared to lose his political nerve, having first ordered and then canceled a radical "five-hundred-day" economic reform plan, at the same time agreeing to negotiations with the increasingly disaffected republics within the union, now clamoring for independence. Sensing their political lives to be in jeopardy, a group of highly placed hard-line Communist party officials staged an abortive coup in August 1991. They made Gorbachev and his wife prisoners in their summer villa, then declared a return to party-line orthodoxy in an effort to salvage what remained of the Soviet Union's global leverage and the Communist party's domestic power. The Soviet citizenry, especially in large cities like Moscow and Leningrad, defied their self-proclaimed saviors. Led by Boris Yeltsin, who at one point mounted a tank in a Moscow street to rally the people, they rallied support among the Soviet republics and the military, and successfully called the plotters' bluff. Within two weeks, Gorbachev was back in power and the coup leaders were in prison.

Ironically, this people's counterrevolution returned Gorbachev to office while destroying the power of the Soviet state he led. Throughout the fall of 1991, as Gorbachev struggled to hold the Union together, Yeltsin joined the presidents of the other large republics to capitalize on the discontent. On December 8, 1991, the presidents of the republics of Russia, Ukraine, and Byelorussia (now called Belarus) declared that the Soviet Union was no more: "The USSR as a subject of international law and geopolitical reality is ceasing to exist." Though the prose was flat, the message was momentous. The once-mighty Soviet Union, founded seventy-five years before in a burst of revolutionary fervor and violence, had evaporated nearly overnight, leaving in its wake a collection of eleven far from powerful nations loosely joined together as the Commonwealth of Independent States. On December 25, 1991, Gorbachev resigned and left political life, not pushed from office in the usual way but made irrelevant as other actors dismantled the state. The Soviet flag—the hammer and sickle symbolizing the nation that for fifty years had kept half of Europe in thrall—was lowered for the last time over the Kremlin.

The mighty fall left mighty problems in its wake. Food shortages worsened during the winter of 1992. The value of the ruble plummeted. The republics could not agree on common military policies or resolve diffi-

> Throughout the fall of 1991, as Gorbachev struggled to hold the Union together, Yeltsin joined the presidents of the other large republics to capitalize on the discontent.

Boris Yeltsin Faces Down the Coup, August 1991. Russian president Boris Yeltsin stood his ground at the Russian parliament building against the hard-liners who attempted to overthrow Mikhail Gorbachev. Here Yeltsin is encouraging the people to fight the takeover of the central government.

a notable bloc of the vote thanks to the steady blame he heaped on the West for Russia's troubles.

Meanwhile, ethnic and religious conflict plagued the republics. In the first years following the dissolution of the Soviet Union, warfare flared in Georgia, Armenia, and Azerbaijan. The most serious conflict arose in the predominantly Muslim area of Chechnya, bordering Georgia in the Caucasus, which had declared its independence from Russia in late 1991. The Chechen rebels were heirs to a tradition of banditry and separatism against Russian authority that stretched into the nineteenth century. In 1994 the Russian government, weary of this continuing challenge to its authority, launched a concerted effort to quash resistance. As Russian forces moved into the Chechen capital, Grozny, they were ambushed with firepower largely stolen from disused Russian armories. The result was a massacre of the invading Russians, followed by a long and bloody siege to take the city. This in turn fueled a long and particularly bloody guerrilla war between Russian and Chechen forces, marked by repeated atrocities on both sides. After brief pauses in 1995 and 1997, this Chechen war dragged on into the new century, echoing Russia's conflict in Afghanistan (see Chapter 27) on a scale that was both bloodier and closer to home.

The Iron Curtain had established one of the most rigid borders in European history. The collapse of the Soviet Union opened up both Russia and its former imperial dominions. That transformation brought the cold war to an end. It also created a host of unforeseen problems throughout Eastern Europe and the advanced industrial world: ethnic conflict, diplomatic uncertainty about the new Russian government, and single superpower domination, sometimes called American "unilateralism." Within the Russian and several of the former Soviet republics there emerged a new era that some called the Russian "Wild West." Capitalist market relations began to develop without clearly defined property relations or a stable legal framework. Former government officials profited from their positions of power to take over whole sectors of the economy.

cult and dangerous questions concerning the control of nuclear warheads. Yeltsin's pleas for economic assistance from the West resulted in massive infusions of private and public capital, which nevertheless failed to prevent serious economic hardship and dislocation. Free enterprise brought with it unemployment and encouraged profiteering through crime. Yeltsin's determination to press ahead with his economic program met with stiff resistance from a parliament and citizenry alarmed by the ruthlessness and rapidity of the change they were experiencing. When the parliament balked at Yeltsin's proposals in September 1993, he dissolved it. This helped provoke an attempted coup two months later, staged by conservative politicians and army officers. Officials loyal to Yeltsin put the revolt down with far more force than the 1991 coup attempt—television viewers worldwide watched artillery shells slam into the rebel-occupied parliament building in Moscow during a bloody shootout. When the parliament was restored, elections in 1995 served as a benchmark of discontent: the resurgent communists claimed roughly one third of the seats, while xenophobic nationalists led by Vladimir Zhirinovsky also took

Corruption ran rampant. Organized crime controlled industries, stock exchanges, a thriving trade in illegal drugs, and even some local governments. Even the most energetic central governments in the large republics such as Russia, Ukraine, and Kazakhstan found themselves faced with enormous problems. Post-Soviet "openness" could lay the groundwork for a new democratic Russia; it could also set in motion the resurgence of older forms of tyranny.

POSTREVOLUTIONARY TROUBLES: EASTERN EUROPE AFTER 1989

The "velvet revolutions" of Central and Eastern Europe raised high hopes: local hopes that an end to authoritarian government would produce economic prosperity and cultural pluralism, and Western hopes that these countries would join them as capitalist partners in an enlarged European Community. The reality was slower and harder than the optimists of 1989 foresaw. The largest struggle, one with continuing implications for the European continent, has been the reunification of Germany. The euphoria of reunification masked uncertainty even among Germans themselves. The foundering East German economy has remained a problem. Piled onto other economic difficulties in the former West Germany during the 1990s, it has produced much resentment of the need to "rescue" the East. What the writer Günter Grass described as the "wall in the mind" long divided the countries. Though there has been great progress in integrating elections and the bureaucracies of the two German states, economic and cultural unity has been much harder to come by.

Adapting to change has been difficult throughout Eastern Europe. Attempts to create free-market economies have brought inflation, unemployment, and—in their wake—anticapitalist demonstrations. Inefficient industries, a work force resistant to change, energy shortages, lack of venture capital, and a severely polluted environment have combined to hinder progress and dash hopes. Uprisings in Bulgaria and Albania in early 1997 were fueled by the inability of those governments to resolve basic economic and social problems. In addition, racial and ethnic conflicts have continued to divide newly liberated democracies, recalling the divisions that led to the First World War and that have plagued Eastern Europe throughout its history. Minorities waged campaigns for autonomous rights or outright secession that often descended into violence.

Czechoslovakia's "velvet revolution" collapsed into a "velvet divorce," as Slovakia declared itself independent from the Czechs, forcing Havel's resignation and slowing down the promising cultural and economic reforms begun in 1989. Poland enjoyed an upswing in its economy during the 1990s, after many years of hardship, but most of the rest of Eastern Europe continues to find transformation rough going. These difficulties have been accompanied by revived ethnic tensions formerly suppressed by centralized communist governments. There has been violence against non-European immigrants throughout Eastern Europe, against gypsies (Romani) in the Czech Republic and Hungary, and against ethnic Hungarians in Romania.

The most extreme example of these conflicts came with the implosion of the state of Yugoslavia. After the death of Tito in 1980 the government that had held Yugoslavia's federalist ethnic patchwork together came undone. The 1960s and 1970s brought uneven economic growth, benefiting the capital, Belgrade, and the provinces of Croatia and Slovenia the most, but heavy industrial areas in Serbia, Bosnia-Hercegovina, and the tiny district of Kosovo began to lag far behind. A number of Serb politicians, most notably Slobodan Milosevic, began to redirect Serbs' frustration with economic hardship toward subjects of national pride and sovereignty.

Nationalism, particularly Serb and Croat nationalism, had long dogged Yugoslavia's firmly federal political system. Feelings ran especially deep among Serbs. Serbian national myths reach back to the Middle Ages; the country also has more recent traditions of political separatism on ethnic grounds. Milosevic and the Serb nationalists who gathered around him ignited those political flashpoints in ways that caught the fears and frustrations of his times. More important for Milosevic, it catapulted him into crucial positions of authority. In these posts, he alienated representatives from the non-Serb republics. Inspired by the peaceful transformations of 1989, representatives of the small province of Slovenia declared they had been denied adequate representation and economic support inside the republic. In 1991, on a tide of nationalism and reform, the Slovenes seceded from Yugoslavia. After a brief attempt to hold the union together by force, the Yugoslav government relented and let Slovenia claim its independence. Ethnic nationalists in the other republics followed suit. A much deeper, bloodier process of disintegration had begun.

The large republic of Croatia, once part of the Habsburg empire and briefly an independent state allied with the Nazis during World War II, cited injustices by

EASTERN EUROPE IN 1989

What political changes in the Soviet Union allowed for the spread of demonstrations throughout Eastern Europe? Why did the first political upheavals of 1989 occur in Poland and East Germany?

Serb officials in the Yugoslav government and declared independence as a free, capitalist state. War broke out between federal Yugoslav forces and the well-armed militias of independent Croatia, a conflict that ended in arbitration by the United Nations. The religious nature of the conflict—between Catholic Croats and Orthodox Serbs—and the legacies of fighting in the Second World War produced violence on both sides. Towns and villages where Serbs and Croats had lived together since the 1940s were torn apart as each ethnic group rounded up and massacred members of the other.

The next conflict came in the same place that in 1914 had sparked a much larger war: the province of Bosnia-Hercegovina. Bosnia was the most ethnically diverse republic in Yugoslavia. Its capital, Sarajevo, was home to several major ethnic groups and had often been praised as an example of peaceful coexistence. When Bosnia joined the round of secessions from Yugoslavia in 1992, ethnic coexistence came apart. Bosnia began the war with no formal army: armed bands equipped by the governments of Serbian Yugoslavia, Croatia, and Bosnia battled each other throughout the new country. The Serbs and Croats, both of whom disliked the Muslim Bosnians, were especially well equipped and organized. They rained shells and bullets on towns and villages, burned houses with families inside, imprisoned Muslim men in detention camps and starved them to death, and raped thousands of Bosnian women. All sides committed atrocities. The Serbs, however, orchestrated and carried out the worst crimes. These included what came to be called "ethnic cleansing." This involved sending irregular troops on campaigns of murder and terror through Muslim or Croat territories in order to encourage much larger populations to flee the area. During the first eighteen months of the fighting as many as one hundred thousand people were killed, including eighty thousand civilians, mostly Bosnian Muslims. Although the campaigns appalled Western governments, those countries worried that intervention would only result in another Vietnam or Afghanistan with no clear resolution of the horrific ethnic slaughter itself. The outside forces, mostly European troops in United Nations "blue helmets," concentrated on humanitarian relief, separating combatants, and creating "safe areas" for persecuted ethnic populations from all parties.

The crisis came to a head in the autumn of 1995. Sarajevo had been under siege for three years, but a series of mortar attacks on public marketplaces in Sarajevo produced fresh Western outrage and moved the

When Bosnia joined the round of secessions from Yugoslavia in 1992, ethnic coexistence came apart.

United States to act. Already Croat forces and the Bosnian army had turned the war on the ground against the Serb militias, and now they were supported by a rolling wave of American air strikes. The American bombing, combined with a Croat-Bosnian offensive, forced the Bosnian Serbs to negotiate. Elite French troops supported by British artillery broke the siege of Sarajevo. Peace talks were held at Dayton, Ohio. The agreement divided Bosnia, with the majority of land in the hands of Muslims and Croats, and a small, autonomous "Serb Republic" in areas that included land "ethnically cleansed" in 1992. Stability was restored, but three years of war had killed over two hundred thousand people.

The legacy of Bosnia flared into conflict again over Kosovo, the medieval homeland of the Orthodox Christian Serbs, now occupied by a largely Albanian, Muslim population. Milosevic accused the Albanians of plotting secession and of challenging the Serb presence in Kosovo. In the name of a "greater Serbia," Serb soldiers fought Albanian separatists rallying under the banner of "greater Albania,"with both sides using terrorist tactics. Western nations were anxious lest the conflict might spread to the strategic, ethnically divided country of Macedonia and touch off a general Balkan conflict. Western political opinion was outraged, however, as Serbian forces used many of the same murderous tactics in Kosovo that they had employed earlier in Bosnia. Talks between Milosevic's government and the Albanian rebels were sponsored by the NATO powers but fell apart in early 1999. That failure was followed by a fresh wave of American-led bombing against Serbia itself, as well as against Serbian forces in Kosovo. A new round of ethnic cleansing drove hundreds of thousands of Albanians from their homes. Unwilling to fight a war on the ground in the mountainous, unforgiving terrain of the southern Balkans, the United States and its European allies concentrated on strategic attacks on bridges, power plants, factories, and Serbian military bases. The Russian government, bothered by this unilateral attack on fellow Slavs, nonetheless played an important part in brokering a cease-fire. Milosevic was forced to withdraw from Kosovo, leaving it in the hands of another force of armed NATO peacekeepers.

Finally, Serb-dominated Yugoslavia, worn by ten years of war and economic sanctions, turned against Milosevic's regime. Wars and corruption had destroyed Milosevic's credentials as a nationalist and populist. After he attempted to reject the results of a democratic

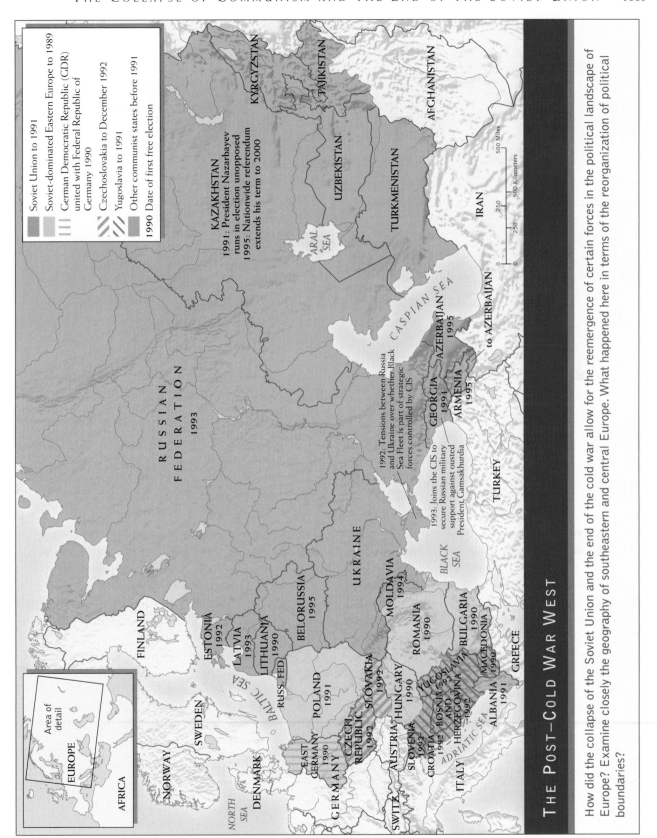

Soviet Union to 1991

Soviet-dominated Eastern Europe to 1989

German Democratic Republic (GDR) united with Federal Republic of Germany 1990

Czechoslovakia to December 1992

Yugoslavia to 1991

Other communist states before 1991

1990 Date of first free election

Area of detail

EUROPE

AFRICA

KYRGYZSTAN

TAJIKISTAN

AFGHANISTAN

UZBEKISTAN

TURKMENISTAN

KAZAKHSTAN
1991: President Nazarbayev runs in election unopposed
1995: Nationwide referendum extends his term to 2000

ARAL SEA

IRAN

CASPIAN SEA

AZERBAIJAN 1995

to AZERBAIJAN

GEORGIA 1991

ARMENIA 1995

TURKEY

1992: Tensions between Russia and Ukraine over whether Black Sea Fleet is part of strategic forces controlled by CIS

1993: Joins the CIS to secure Russian military support against ousted President Gamsakhurdia

RUSSIAN FEDERATION 1993

BLACK SEA

UKRAINE

BELORUSSIA 1995

MOLDAVIA 1994

ROMANIA 1990

BULGARIA 1990

MACEDONIA 1990

GREECE

FINLAND

ESTONIA 1992

LATVIA 1993

LITHUANIA 1990

RUSS. FED.

POLAND 1991

SLOVAKIA 1992

HUNGARY 1990

YUGOSLAVIA 1992

ALBANIA 1991

SWEDEN

NORWAY

BALTIC SEA

DENMARK

EAST GERMANY 1990

CZECH REPUBLIC 1992

AUSTRIA

SLOVENIA 1992

CROATIA 1992

BOSNIA AND HERZEGOVINA 1992

ITALY

ADRIATIC SEA

SWITZ.

GERMANY

NORTH SEA

500 Miles

500 Kilometers

250

250

THE POST–COLD WAR WEST

How did the collapse of the Soviet Union and the end of the cold war allow for the reemergence of certain forces in the political landscape of Europe? Examine closely the geography of southeastern and central Europe. What happened here in terms of the reorganization of political boundaries?

Mass Funeral in Kosovo, 1999. Ethnic Albanians bury victims of a Serbian massacre toward the end of Yugoslavia's ten years of fighting.

election in 2000, his government fell to popular protests.

As we gain perspective on the twentieth century, it is clear that the Yugoslavian wars of the 1990s were not an isolated instance of "Balkan" violence. The issues are thoroughly Western. The Balkans form one of the West's borderlands, where cultures influenced by Roman Catholicism, Eastern Orthodoxy, and Islam meet, overlap, and contend for political domination and influence. Since the nineteenth century, this region of enormous religious, cultural, and ethnic diversity has struggled with the implications of nationalism. We have seen how conflicts over the creation of new national states drawn mostly on ethnic lines were worked out in central Europe, with many instances of tragic violence. The Yugoslav wars fit into some of the same patterns.

CONCLUSION

The Eastern European revolutions of 1989 and the subsequent collapse of the Soviet Union were a revolutionary turning point. Like the French Revolution of 1789, they brought down not only a regime, but an empire. Like the French Revolution, they gave way to violence. And again like the French Revolution, they had sweeping international consequences. These revolutions and the fall of the Soviet Union marked the end of the cold war, which had structured international politics and shaped the everyday lives of millions of people since the end of World War II. In the last chapter of this book, we consider how the cold war itself has given way to more complex global relations.

KEY TERMS

abstract expressionism

French "new wave"

The Feminine Mystique

NAACP

Prague spring

perestroika

"velvet revolutions"

Slobodan Milosevic

Boris Yeltsin

SELECTED READINGS

Bailey, Beth. *From Front Porch to Back Seat: Courtship in Twentieth-Century America.* Baltimore, 1988. Good historical perspective on the "sexual revolution."

Beschloss, Michael, and Strobe Talbott. *At the Highest Levels: The Inside Story of the End of the Cold War.* Boston, 1993. An analysis of the relationship between presidents Gorbachev and Bush, and their determination to ignore hard-liners.

Brown, Archie. *The Gorbachev Factor.* Oxford and New York, 1996.

Caute, David. *The Year of the Barricades: A Journey through 1968.* New York, 1988. A well-written global history of 1968.

Charney, Leo, and Vanessa R. Schwartz, eds. *Cinema and the Invention of Modern Life.* Berkeley, 1995. Collection of essays.

Dallin, Alexander, and Gail Lapidus. *The Soviet System: From Crisis to Collapse.* Boulder, 1995.

Echols, Alice. *Daring to be Bad: Radical Feminism in America, 1967–1975.* Minneapolis, 1989. Good narrative and analysis.

Eley, Geoff. *Forging Democracy: The History of the Left in Europe, 1850–2000.* Oxford and New York, 2002. Among its other qualities, one of the best historical perspectives on the 1960s.

Fink, Carole, Phillipp Gassert, and Detlef Junker, eds. *1968: The World Transformed.* Cambridge, 1998. A transatlantic history of 1968.

Fulbrook, Mary, ed. *Europe Since 1945* (The Short Oxford History of Europe). Oxford, 2001. Particularly good articles on economics and political economy. Structural analysis.

Garton Ash, Timothy. *In Europe's Name: Germany and the Divided Continent.* New York, 1993. An analysis of the effect of German reunification on the future of Europe.

Glenny, Misha. *The Balkans, 1804–1999: Nationalism, War and the Great Powers.* London, 1999. Good account by a journalist who covered the fighting.

Horowitz, Daniel. *Betty Friedan and the Making of the Feminine Mystique: The American Left, the Cold War, and Modern Feminism.* Amherst, 1998. An excellent new account.

Hosking, Geoffrey. *The Awakening of the Soviet Union.* Cambridge, Mass., 1990. The factors that led to the end of the Soviet era.

Hughes, H. Stuart. *Sophisticated Rebels: The Political Culture of European Dissent, 1968–1987.* Cambridge, Mass., 1990. The nature of dissent on both sides of the disintegrating Iron Curtain in the years 1988–1989.

Hulsberg, Werner. *The German Greens: A Social and Political Profile.* New York, 1988. The origins, politics, and impact of environmental politics.

Jarausch, Konrad. *The Rush to German Unity.* New York, 1994. The problems of reunification analyzed.

Judah, Tim. *The Serbs: History, Myth, and the Destruction of Yugoslavia.* New Haven, 1997.

Kaplan, Robert D. *Balkan Ghosts: A Journey through History.* New York, 1993.

Kotkin, Stephen. *Armegeddon Averted: The Soviet Collapse, 1970–2000.* Oxford, 2001.

Lewin, Moshe. *The Gorbachev Phenomenon,* expanded ed., Berkeley, 1991. Written as a firsthand account, tracing the roots of Gorbachev's successes and failures.

Lieven, Anatol. *Chechnya, Tomb of Russia Power.* New Haven and London, 1998.

Maier, Charles S. *Dissolution: The Crisis of Communism and the End of East Germany.* Princeton, N.J., 1997.

Marwick, Arthur. *The Sixties.* Oxford and New York, 1998.

Pells, Richard. *Not Like Us: How Europeans Have Loved, Hated, and Transformed American Culture since World War II.* New York, 1997.

Poiger, Uta G. *Jazz, Rock, and Rebels: Cold War Politics and American Culture in a Divided Germany.* Berkeley, 2000. Pioneering cultural history.

Sheehan, Neil. *A Bright Shining Lie: John Paul Vann and America in Vietnam.* New York, 1988.

Strayer, Robert. *Why Did the Soviet Union Collapse? Understanding Historical Change.* Armonk, N.Y., and London, 1998. A good introduction, with bibliography.

Wright, Patrick. *On Living in an Old Country: The National Past in Contemporary Britain.* New York, 1986. The culture of Britain in the 1980s.

WAR AND TECHNOLOGY

No mockeries now for them; no prayers nor bells;

Nor any voice of mourning save the choirs, —

The shrill, demented choirs of wailing shells;

And bugles calling for them from sad shires.

What candles may be held to speed them all?

Not in the hands of boys but in their eyes

Shall shine the holy glimmers of goodbyes.

—Wilfred Owen, *Anthem for a Dammed Youth* (1917)

The four battles covered in this Digital History Feature all serve as "snapshots of a cultural tradition of war making."

In the battle at Rorke's Drift in 1879, the supply station manned by 139 British soldiers with Martini-Henry rifles, was attacked by four thousand Zulus. When the battle ended, 15 British soldiers had been killed and the bodies of 600 Zulu warriors lay scattered over the terrain.

Although Hitler and the Soviets had signed a nonaggression pact, by 1941 Hitler had invaded the Soviet Union. Late in 1942, Hitler diverted his forces to Stalingrad in order to slow Soviet war production and destroy Stalin's city. The German 6th Army seemed to have the upper hand until the end of 1943, when Soviet sniper fire combined with a will to fight led to the defeat of the German army.

In mid-November 1965, Lt. Col. Hal Moore took 400 men of the 7th Cavalry into the Ia Drang Valley near the Cambodian border of South Vietnam. Completely outnumbered by PAVN (People's Army of Vietnam) forces, Moore's men fought for four days and nights until finally subduing the PAVN army. Both sides claimed victory at Ia Drang, the first major battle between the American army and the PAVN.

On March 19, 2003, the United States and coalition forces began military operations to disarm Iraq and bring down President Saddam Hussein. With the invasion of Iraq, the United States moved away from policies of deterrence and containment and toward the idea of the preemptive strike. The invasion, named "Operation Iraqi Freedom," was swift, and the Iraqi government and military collapsed in about three weeks. On December 13, 2003, Saddam Hussein was captured in a "spider hole"; however, the future of Iraq still hangs in the balance.

The images and documents in the War and Technology Digital History Feature at www.wwnorton.com/wciv show how new tactics and technologies determined the outcomes of four landmark battles. As you explore this feature on the *Western Civilizations* Web site, consider the following:

• What lessons might have been learned from each of these battles?

• Does technology—spears, shields, arrows, guns, tanks, aircraft, and bombs, among other things—always determine the outcome of a battle?

• Why is the "Bush Doctrine," as outlined by President George W. Bush in 2002, such a radical departure from previous American foreign policy initiatives?

• How has the face of war changed over the past century?

CHAPTER
TWENTY-NINE

A WORLD
WITHOUT WALLS:
GLOBALIZATION
AND THE WEST

IN THE TWENTY-FIRST CENTURY, the world has reentered a period in which basic assumptions about the role of nation-states, the roots of prosperity, and the boundaries of cultures are changing fast. We say "reentered" because, as we have seen, a disconcerting sense of seismic and little-understood change has been central to Western culture during several different historical periods. The Industrial Revolution of the nineteenth century is an example, and just as "industrial revolution," a term coined in the early nineteenth century, seemed to capture contemporaries' perceptions of changes in their own time, so "globalization" seems to capture ours.

We know, intuitively, what globalization means: the Internet, protests against the WTO, outsourcing of jobs and services, Wal-Mart in Mexico, the dismantling of the Berlin wall. All of these are powerful images of larger, enormously significant developments. The Internet represents the stunning transformation of global communication, the media, and forms of knowledge. The Berlin wall once stood for a divided cold war world; its fall marked a dramatic reconfiguration of international relations, an end to the ideological battle over communism, the creation of new alliances, markets, and communities. The attack on the World Trade Center in 2001 gave the term "globalization" a new and frightening meaning as well. It shattered many Americans' sense of relative isolation and security. "Globalization," then, conjures up new possibilities but also new vulnerabilities.

What, precisely, does the term mean? What causes or drives globalization, and what are its effects? Is it new? To begin simply, globalization means integration. It is the process of creating a rising number of networks—political, social, economic, and cultural—that span the globe. New technologies, new economic imperatives, and changing laws have combined to make global exchange faster and, by the same token, to intensify economic, social, and cultural relationships. Information, ideas, goods, and people now move rapidly and easily across national boundaries. Yet "globalization" is not synonymous with "internationalization," and the distinction is important. International relations are established between nation-states. Global exchange can be quite independent of national control: today trade, politics, and

• What is globalization?

• Why did postcolonial development unfold differently in different regions?

• How did the global demand for oil reshape politics, religion, and society in the Middle East?

• How has globalization changed the politics of terrorism?

cultural exchange often happen "underneath the radar of the nation-state," in the words of one historian.

Globalization has radically altered the distribution of industry and patterns of trade around the world, as Asian nations in particular emerge as industrial giants and Western powers become increasingly dependent on energy resources drawn from former colonies. Globalization has forced the reorganization of economic enterprises from banking and commerce to manufacturing. Supranational economic institutions such as the International Monetary Fund are examples of globalization and also work to quicken its pace. Likewise, the International Criminal Court represents an important trend in law: the globalization of judicial power. New, rapid, and surprisingly intimate forms of mass communication (Web logs, Internet-based political campaigns, and so on) have spawned new forms of politics whose long-term effects are hard to predict. International human-rights campaigns, for instance, owe an enormous debt to global communications and the communities they create. Perhaps most interesting, the sovereignty of nation-states and the clear boundaries of national communities seem to be eroded by many globalizing trends.

Although globalization means integration, it does not necessarily produce peace, equality, or homogeneity. Its effects are hard to predict. During the early 1900s many Europeans firmly believed that the world, at least the part of the world dominated by Western empires, would become harmonious, that Western culture would be exported, that Western standards were universal, and so on. History defied those expectations. The term *globalization* can be misleading, for it suggests a uniform, leveling process, one that operates similarly everywhere. Globalization has very different and disparate effects, effects shaped by vast asymmetries of power and wealth between nations or regions, and in the last several decades, worldwide inequality has increased. Global processes meet with obstacles and resistance; they sow division as well as unity. At the level of everyday human contact, globalization has hastened new kinds of cultural blending and new forms of sociability, but it has also produced a backlash against that blending. The heady word *global* can distort our analyses or point us in the wrong direction. As one historian argues, although it is crucial to be able to think outside of "national or continental containers," it would be misleading to believe "that there is no container at all, except the planetary one." Finally, globalization is not new. It is at a new stage. As we have seen, empires, religion, trade, and commerce have all had globalizing

impulses and effects. The East India Company, to take one example, was certainly a global enterprise; how it differs from Microsoft is a fascinating question. Historians are only beginning to write that story.

In this chapter, then, we explore three subjects crucial to our early efforts to understand globalization, especially as it relates to the post–cold war world of the twenty-first century. The first subject is the set of global changes that have accelerated the free flow of money, people, products, and ideas. The second subject is what we have come to call "postcolonial" politics—the varied trajectories that mark the contemporary experience of former colonies. Finally, we will consider in greater depth the complex and important role of Middle Eastern politics in contemporary global affairs. Throughout, we hope to suggest ways in which recent developments relate to familiar historical issues we have already examined in other contexts.

LIQUID MODERNITY? THE FLOW OF MONEY, IDEAS, AND PEOPLES

What is globalization?

A key feature of globalization has been the transformation of the world economy, highlighted by the rapid integration of markets since 1970. In a series of historic changes, the international agreements that had regulated the movement of people, goods, and money since the Second World War were overturned. To begin with, the postwar economic arrangements sealed at Bretton Woods (see Chapter 27) steadily eroded in the late 1960s, as Western industrial nations faced a double burden of inflation and economic stagnation. A crucial shift in monetary policy occurred in 1971, when the United States abandoned the postwar gold standard and allowed the dollar—the keystone of the system—to range freely. As a result, formal regulations on currencies, international banking, and lending among states faded away. They were replaced with an informal network of arrangements managed autonomously by large private lenders, their political friends in leading Western states, and independent financial agencies such as the International Monetary Fund and the World Bank. The economists and administrators who dominated these new networks steered away from the interventionist policies that shaped postwar planning and recovery. Instead they relied on a broad range of market-driven models dubbed "neoliberalism." In a variation on classic liberal economics, neoliberal economists stressed the value of free markets, profit incentives, and sharp restraints on both budget deficits and social welfare programs, whether run by governments or corporations. The new systems of lending they backed had mixed results, funding breakneck growth in some cases and bringing catastrophic default in others. Industrial development in the globalized economy has created jarring juxtapositions of development and deterioration across entire continents and even within single cities—a phenomenon described as a "checkerboard of poverty and affluence."

> Industrial development in the globalized economy has created jarring juxtapositions of development and deterioration across entire continents and even within single cities—a phenomenon described as a "checkerboard of poverty and affluence."

At the same time, the world's local, national, and regional economies became far more connected and interdependent. Export trade flourished and, with the technological advances of the 1960s and 1980s, came to include an increasing proportion of high-technology goods. The boom in export commerce was tied to important changes in the division of labor worldwide. More industrial jobs emerged in the postcolonial world, not just among the Asian "tigers" but also in India, Latin America, and elsewhere. Although such steady, skilled manual employment started to disappear in Western nations—often replaced by lower-paying menial work—financial and service sector employment leaped ahead. The exchange and use of goods became much more complex. Goods were designed by companies in one country, manufactured in another, and tied into a broader interchange of cultures. Taken together, these global economic changes had

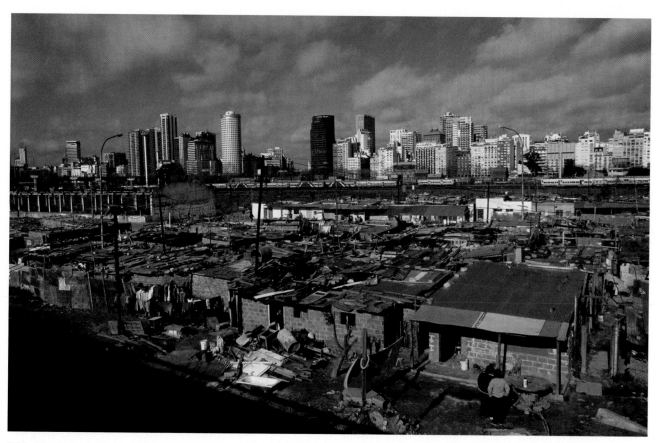

"Checkerboard of poverty and affluence." Scenes of slums confronting towering skylines, such as this one from Argentina in 2000, were visible around the world as one of the side effects of development and deterioration.

deep political effects, forcing painful debates over the nature of citizenship and entitlement inside national borders, about the power and accountability of transnational corporations, and about the human and environmental costs of global capitalism.

Another crucial change involved not only the widespread flow of information but also the new commercial and cultural importance attached to information itself. Electronic systems and devices designed to create, store, and share information multiplied, becoming staggeringly more powerful and accessible—none with so great an impact on the everyday lives of men and women around the world as the personal computer. By the early 1990s increasingly sophisticated computers brought people into instant communication with each other across continents, not only by new means, but also in new cultural and political settings. Electronic communications over the Internet gave a compelling new meaning to the term *global village*. The Internet revolution shared features of earlier print revolutions: entrepreneurs with utopian ambitions; a fascination with culturally illicit and politically scandalous materials published easily and informally; the new social settings made available to specific groups; and the eager efforts of large, established corporate interests to cash in on new channels of culture and business.

However common their use seems, the Internet and similar technologies have had wide-ranging effects on political struggles around the globe. Embattled ethnic minorities have found worldwide audiences through on-line campaign sites. Satellite television arguably sped the sequence of popular revolts in Eastern Europe in 1989. That same year, fax machines brought Chinese demonstrators at Tiananmen Square news of international support for their efforts. Meanwhile, leaps forward in electronic technologies provided new worldwide platforms for commercial interests. Companies such as Sony, RCA, and others produced entertainment content, including music, motion pictures, and television shows, as well as the electronic equipment to play that content. Bill Gates's Microsoft emerged as the world's major producer of computer software—with a corporate profit margin that surpassed Spain's gross domestic product. At the level of production, marketing, and management, information industries are global, spread widely across the United States, India, Western Europe, and parts of the developing world. Their corporate headquarters, however,

typically remain in the West and support neoliberal politics. The international media, news, and entertainment conglomerates run by the Australian Rupert Murdoch or by Time Warner, for example, are firmly allied to Western institutions and world views, edging aside state-run companies and providing local venues with a particular version of the free market.

Like the fluid movement of money, goods, and ideas, the free flow of labor has become a central aspect of globalization. Since 1945, the widespread migration of peoples, particularly between former colonies and imperial powers, has changed everyday life around the world. Groups of immigrant workers have filled the lower rungs of thriving economies not only in Europe but also in oil-rich Arab states that attracted Asian and Filipino laborers, and in the United States, where both permanent and seasonal migrations from Mexico and other Latin American nations have spread across the continent. This fusion of peoples and cultures has produced novel multicultural encounters, including striking new blends of music, food, language, and other forms of popular culture and sociability. It has also raised tensions over the definition of citizenship and the boundaries of political and cultural communities—familiar themes from modern history. As a result, cycles of violent xenophobic backlash, bigotry, and political extremism have appeared in host countries and regions, but so too have new conceptions of civil rights and cultural belonging.

> Since 1945, the widespread migration of peoples, particularly between former colonies and imperial powers, has changed everyday life around the world.

As suggested above, sharp divides exist between the most successful global players and the poorer, disadvantaged, sometimes embattled states and cultures. In one particular area of manufacture, however, poorer postcolonial regions have been able to respond to a steady and immensely profitable market in the West. The production of illegal drugs such as opium, heroin, and cocaine is a thriving industry in countries such as Colombia, Myanmar (formerly Burma), and Malaysia. Though the trade in such substances is banned, the fragile economies of the countries where they are produced have encouraged public and private powers to turn a blind eye to their production—or even to intervene for their own profit. Other, similar forms of illegal commerce have also grown far beyond the old label of "organized crime" in their structure and political importance. Trafficking in illegal immigrants, the management of corrupt financial dealings, trade in illicit animal products, or "conflict" diamonds from several brutal postcolonial civil wars are all indicative of

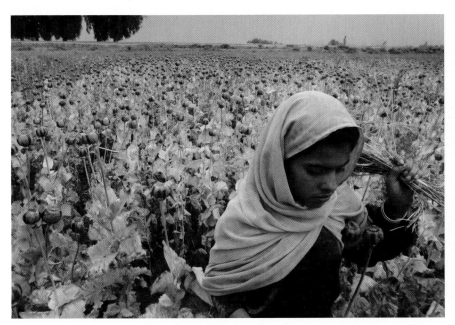

An Afghan girl weeds a poppy field, 2004. Though Afghanistan was historically a center for the silk trade, opium is its most important cash crop today.

this trend. The organizations behind these criminal trades grew out of the political violence and economic breakdown of failing postcolonial states, or from the human and commercial traffic between these parts of the world and leading Western economic powers. They have exploited cracks, loopholes, and unsupervised opportunities in the less regulated system of global trade and carved out centers of power not directly subject to the laws of any single state.

DEMOGRAPHICS AND GLOBAL HEALTH

The developments of globalization are tied in complex ways to the evolving size and health of the world's population. Between 1800 and the middle of the twentieth century, the worldwide population roughly tripled, rising from 1 to 3 billion. Between 1960 and 2000, however, population doubled again, to 6 billion or more. Haphazard but huge improvements in basic standards of health, particularly for young children and childbearing women, contributed to the increase—as did localized efforts to improve the urban-industrial environment in postcolonial regions. For instance, parts of eastern and southern Africa, South and Southeast Asia, and the cities of Latin America have made tremendous improvements. Asia's population as a whole has increased nearly four times over since 1900, to nearly two thirds of the world's present population. Such growth has strained underdeveloped social services, public-health facilities, and urban infrastructures—increasing the potential for epidemic dis-

ease, as well as for cycles of ethnic and ideological violence nursed by poverty and dislocation.

A different type of demographic crisis confronts parts of the West, where steadily shrinking populations erode social welfare systems. Longer life spans, broadened welfare programs, rising health-care costs, and simpler, more socially acceptable opportunities for divorce have contributed to the challenge, but most important has been the availability of reliable birth control methods and a new sense of choice in family planning. While such nations as the United States and Great Britain have kept stable populations or seen mild growth thanks to immigration, other locales such as Italy and Scandinavia have faced sharp declines in the birth rate, leading to population decline. During the 1990s Russia also took a sudden and potentially disastrous lurch in this direction, spurred by post-Soviet poverty, emigration, and dislocation. Declining birth rates have been accompanied by growing populations of older adults, whose health and vitality resulted from decades of improved medical standards and state-run entitlement programs. Maintaining the long-term solvency of such programs poses difficult choices for European countries in particular, as they struggle to balance guarantees of social well-being with fiscal and political realities.

Globalization has also changed the arena of public health and medicine, creating dangerous new threats as well as promising new treatments. Better and more comprehensive health care has generally accompanied other kinds of prosperity, and has thus been more accessible in the West. In Africa, Latin America, and elsewhere, political chaos, imbalances of trade, and the practices of some large pharmaceutical companies have often resulted in shortages of medicine and a rickety medical infrastructure, making it difficult to combat deadly new waves of disease. Indeed, the worldwide risk of exposure to epidemic diseases is a new reality of globalization—a product of increased cultural interaction, exposure of new ecosystems to human development, and the speed of intercontinental transportation. By the 1970s the acceleration of airplane travel led to fears that an epidemic would leapfrog the globe much faster than the pandemics of the Middle Ages. Such

Government efforts to curtail the spread of Severe Acute Respiratory Syndrome.
In May 2003, migrant workers at a Beijing railway station line up to have their temperatures checked before boarding the trains.

a clone (an exact genetic copy) of a sheep. Genome research also broadened and deepened medical understanding of biological "defects" and diversions from the genetic norms of human development. As a new form of knowledge in an age of global interconnection, genetic engineering leaped across the legal and moral boundaries of human societies. The question of who would govern these advances—nations, inter national bodies, or local cultural and religious communities—was opened to passionate debate. So were fresh arguments about where to draw lines between lifesaving intervention and cultural preference, between individual agency and biological determinism. Like past scientific investigations directed at humankind, genetics raised fundamental questions about ethics, citizenship, and the measure of humanity.

fears were confirmed by the worldwide spread of human immunodeficiency virus disease (HIV), whose final stage is acquired immune deficiency syndrome (AIDS), which first appeared at the end of the 1970s. As HIV-AIDS became a global health crisis—particularly in Africa, where the disease spread catastrophically—international organizations recognized the need for an early, swift, and comprehensive response to future outbreaks of disease, as evidenced by the successful global containment of severe acute respiratory syndrome (SARS) in 2003.

Meanwhile, the work of multinational medical research firms continued to extend the ability to prevent and treat disease. One of the most powerful tools in this endeavor was the development of genetic engineering, which stemmed from the monumental discovery of DNA in the 1950s. By the 1990s, several laboratories were engaged in the most ambitious medical research ever attempted: the mapping of the human genome—that is, the entire architecture of chromosomes and genes contained in basic human DNA. Through this process and alongside it, genetic engineers developed methods to alter the biology of living things. Infertile couples, for instance, could now conceive through out-of-body medical procedures. Genetic engineers developed—and patented—strains of mice and other laboratory animals that carried chemical markers, cells, even organs, of other species. By 1997 British researchers succeeded in producing

AFTER EMPIRE: POSTCOLONIAL POLITICS IN THE GLOBAL ERA

Why did postcolonial development unfold differently in different regions?

Even after the superpower rivalry of the cold war collapsed, another legacy of the postwar era continued to shape international relations into the twenty-first century. The so-called postcolonial relationships between former colonies and Western powers emerged from the decolonization struggles detailed in Chapter 27. Former colonies, as well as other nations that had fallen under the political and economic sway of imperial powers, gained formal independence at the least, along with new kinds of cultural and political authority. In other respects, however, very little changed for people in the former colonies. The very term *postcolonial* underlines the fact that colonialism's legacies endured even after independence. Within these regions, political communities new and old handled the legacies of empire and the postcolonial future in a variety of ways. In some cases the former colonizers or their local allies retained so much power that formal independence actually meant very little. In others, bloody independence struggles poisoned the political culture. The emergence of new states and new kinds of politics was sometimes propelled by economic goals, sometimes by the revival of cultural identities that preceded colonization, and in other cases by ethnic conflict. The results ranged from breakneck industrial success to ethnic slaughter, from democratization to new local models of absolutism. During the cold war, these postcolonial regions were often the turf on which the superpower struggle was waged. They benefited from superpower patronage, but also became the staging ground for proxy wars funded by the West in the fight against communism. Their various trajectories since 1989 point to the complex legacy of the imperial past in the post–cold war world of globalization.

> The emergence of new states and new kinds of politics was sometimes propelled by economic goals, sometimes by the revival of cultural identities that preceded colonization, and in other cases by ethnic conflict.

EMANCIPATION AND ETHNIC CONFLICT IN AFRICA

The legacies of colonialism weighed heavily on sub-Saharan Africa. Most of the continent's former colonies came into their independence after World War II with their basic infrastructures deteriorating after decades of imperial negligence. The cold war decades brought scant improvement, as governments across the continent were plagued by both homegrown and externally imposed corruption, poverty, and civil war. In sub-Saharan Africa, two very different trends began to emerge around 1989, each shaped by a combination of the end of the cold war and volatile local conditions.

The first trend can be seen in South Africa, where politics had revolved for decades around the brutal racial policies of apartheid, sponsored by the white minority government. The most prominent opponent of apartheid, Nelson Mandela, who led the African National Congress (ANC), had been imprisoned since 1962. Intense repression and violent conflict continued into the 1980s and reached a dangerous impasse by the end of the decade. Then the South African government chose a daring new tack: in early 1990 it released Mandela from prison. He resumed leadership

of the ANC and turned the party toward a combination of renewed public demonstrations and plans for negotiation. Politics changed within the Afrikaner-dominated white regime as well when F. W. de Klerk succeeded the reactionary P. W. Botha as prime minister. A pragmatist who feared civil war and national collapse over apartheid, de Klerk was well matched to Mandela. In March 1992 the two men began direct talks to establish majority rule. Legal and constitutional reforms followed, and in May 1994, during elections in which all South Africans took part, Nelson Mandela was chosen the country's first black president. Although many of his government's efforts to reform housing, the economy, and public health foundered, Mandela defused the climate of organized racial violence. He also gained and kept tremendous personal popularity among black and white South Africans alike as a living symbol of a new political culture. Mandela's popularity extended abroad, within sub-Saharan Africa and worldwide. In a number of smaller postcolonial states such as Benin, Malawi, and Mozambique, the early 1990s brought political reforms that ended one-party or one-man rule in favor of parliamentary democracy and economic reform.

The other major trend ran in a different, less encouraging direction. Some former autocracies gave way to calls for pluralism, but other states across the continent collapsed into ruthless ethnic conflict. In Rwanda, a former Belgian colony, conflicts between the Hutu and Tutsi populations erupted into a highly organized campaign of genocide against the Tutsi after the country's president was assassinated. Carried out by ordinary Hutus of all backgrounds, the ethnic slaughter left over eight hundred thousand Tutsi dead in a matter of weeks. International pressure eventually turned local Rwandan politics against the perpetrators. Many of them fled to neighboring Zaire and became hired mercenaries in the many-sided civil war that followed the collapse of Mobutu Sese Seko, the country's long-time dictator, infamous for diverting billions of dollars in foreign aid into his personal bank accounts. A number of ambitious, neighboring countries intervened in Zaire, hoping not only to secure its valuable resources but also to settle conflicts with their own ethnic minorities that spilled over the border. Fighting continued through the late 1990s into the new century, dubbed "Africa's world war" by many observers. Public services, normal trade,

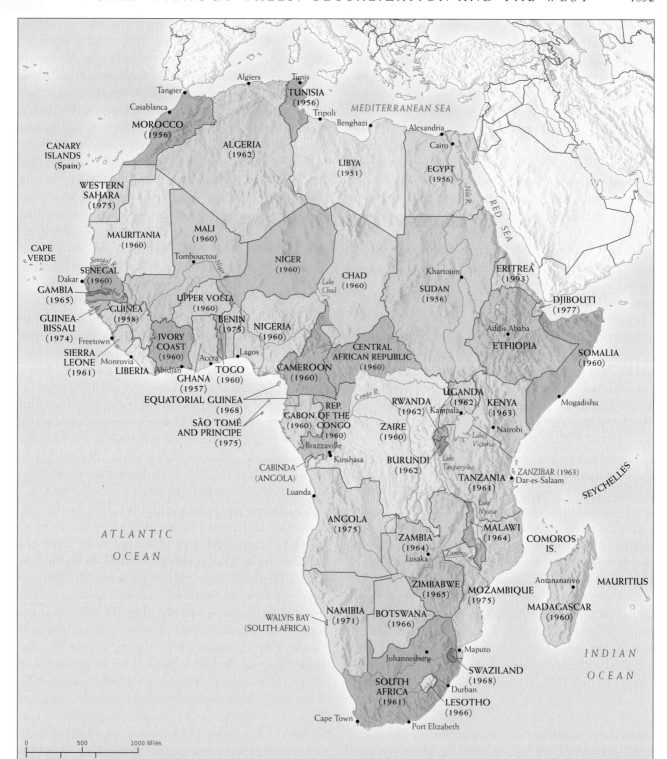

DECOLONIZATION IN AFRICA TO 1980

How do the modern borders of African nations still bear the stamp of European colonization? What effect do you suspect this has had on ethnic tensions within these nations?

even basic health and safety inside Zaire—renamed the Democratic Republic of Congo by an ineffective government in Kinshasa—collapsed. With a death toll that reached into the millions from combat, massacre, and disease, the fighting remained unresolved in the next decade.

ECONOMIC POWER ON THE PACIFIC RIM

By the end of the twentieth century, East Asia had become a center of industrial and manufacturing production. China, whose communist government began to establish commercial ties with the West in the 1970s, was the world's leading heavy industrial producer by the year 2000. Its state-owned companies acquired contracts from Western firms to produce products cheaply and in bulk, for sale back to home markets in the United States and Europe. In a deliberate reversal of Europe's nineteenth-century intrusions on the "China trade," Beijing established semicapitalist commercial

zones around major port cities like Shanghai, a policy whose centerpiece was the reclamation of Hong Kong from Britain in 1997. The commercial zones were intended to encourage massive foreign investment on terms that left China a favorable balance of trade for its huge volume of cheap exports. In practice, they enjoyed only mixed success. Downturns in farming and a looming energy crisis hampered prosperity and economic growth inland, but Hong Kong worked to maintain its economic and cultural middle ground with the rest of the world as it had since the days of the opium trade (see Chapter 22).

Other Asian nations emerged as global commercial powers as well. Industry flourished in a string of countries, starting with Japan and extending along Asia's Pacific coastline into Southeast Asia and Oceania, during the decades after World War II. By the 1980s their robust industrial expansion and their apparent staying power earned them the collective nickname of "the tigers," taken from the ambitious, forward-looking tiger in Chinese mythology. These "Pacific rim" states collectively formed the most important industrial region in

Industrialization in China, 2002. The Three Gorges Dam on the Yan River in Yichang will be the largest hydroelectric dam in the world when completed. It has been called the largest construction project in China since the Great Wall.

the world outside the United States and Europe. Among them, Japan not only led the way but also became the most influential model of success, with a postwar revival that eventually surpassed West Germany's "economic miracle" (see Chapter 28). Japanese firms concentrated on the efficiency and technical reliability of their products: fuel-efficient cars, specialty steel, small electronic goods, and so on. Japanese diplomacy and large state subsidies supported the success of Japanese firms, while a well-funded program of technical education hastened research and development of new goods. Japanese firms also appeared to benefit from collective loyalty among civil servants and corporate managers, attitudes that were encouraged by Japan's long experience of trade guilds and feudal politics. Other East Asian nations, newer or less stable than Japan, tried to mimic its success. Some, such as South Korea and the Chinese Nationalist stronghold of Taiwan, treated the creation of prosperity as a fundamental patriotic duty. In postcolonial nations such as Malaysia and Indonesia, governments parlayed their natural resources and expansive local labor pools (which had made them attractive to imperial powers in earlier times) into investment for industrialization. As in China, the factories that emerged were either subsidiaries of Western companies or operated on their behalf in new multinational versions of the putting-out system of early industrialization

The Pacific rim's boom, however, also contained the makings of a first "bust." During the 1990s a confluence of factors resulted in an enormous slowdown of growth and the near collapse of several currencies. Japan experienced rising production costs, overvalued stocks, rampant speculation on its high-priced real estate market, and the customary kickbacks that rewarded staunch corporate loyalty. In Southeast Asia, states such as Indonesia found they had to pay the difference on overvalued industrial capital to Western lenders who set rigid debt repayment schedules. Responses to the economic downturn varied widely. In South Korea an older generation that remembered economic catastrophe after the Korean War responded to national calls for sacrifice, frequently by investing their own savings to prop up ailing companies. Japan launched programs of monetary austerity to cope with its first serious spike in unemployment in two generations. In Indonesia, inflation and unemployment reignited sharp ethnic conflicts that prosperity and violent state repression had dampened in earlier times. This predominantly Muslim country, with a long tradition of tolerance and pluralism inside the faith, also saw outbursts of violent religious fundamentalism popularly associated with another region—the Middle East.

A NEW CENTER OF GRAVITY: ISRAEL, OIL, AND POLITICAL ISLAM IN THE MIDDLE EAST

How did the global demand for oil reshape politics, religion, and society in the Middle East?

Perhaps no other region has drawn more attention from the West in the age of globalization than the Middle East, where a volatile combination of Western military, political, and economic interests converged with deep-seated regional conflicts and transnational Islamic politics. The results of this ongoing confrontation promise to shape the twenty-first century. Here we consider three of the most important aspects of recent history in the region. First is the unfolding of the Arab-Israeli conflict. Second is the region's vital development as the global center of oil production. The third emerges from inside the Arab world, largely as a reaction against the recent relations with the West. This is the development of a specific, modern brand of Islamic radicalism that challenges the legacies of imperialism and promises revolutionary and sometimes apocalyptic change in postcolonial nations, and whose most violent elements generate a cycle of fear, anger, and ultimately direct conflict with Western governments.

THE ARAB-ISRAELI CONFLICT

As we saw in Chapter 27, Israel's existence was a battleground from the start. The national aspirations of Jewish immigrants from Europe, determined to survive and transcend the Holocaust and violent postwar anti-Semitism, clashed directly with the motives of pan-Arabists—secular, anticolonial nationalists who urged Arab pride and self-reliance against European domination. By the late 1970s, in the aftermath of two Arab-Israeli wars, it appeared that a generation of fighting might come to an end. American mediators began sponsoring talks to prevent further, sudden outbursts of conflict, while Soviet leaders remained neutral but supportive of peace efforts. Most notably, the Egyptian president Anwar Sadat, who authorized and directed the 1973 war against Israel, decided that coexistence rather than the destruction of Israel was the long-term

HOW DID THE GLOBAL DEMAND FOR OIL RESHAPE POLITICS, RELIGION, AND SOCIETY IN THE MIDDLE EAST?

ISRAEL, OIL, AND POLITICAL ISLAM IN THE MIDDLE EAST   1055

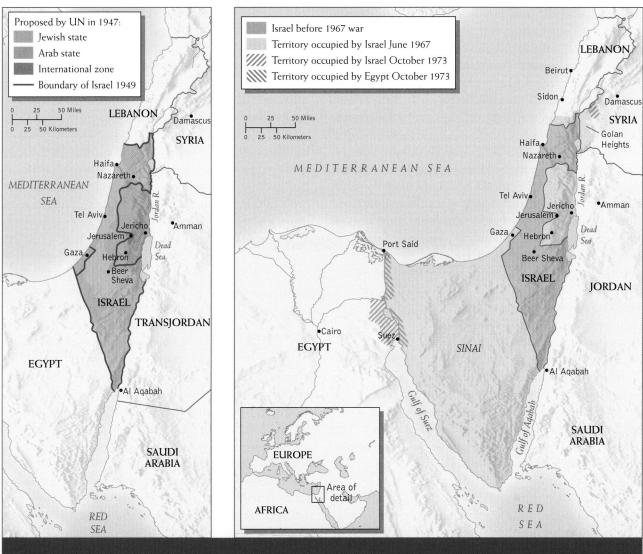

Proposed by UN in 1947:
- Jewish state
- Arab state
- International zone
- Boundary of Israel 1949

- Israel before 1967 war
- Territory occupied by Israel June 1967
- Territory occupied by Israel October 1973
- Territory occupied by Egypt October 1973

THE ARAB-ISRAELI WARS OF 1967 AND 1973

This map shows the changes in the political geography of the Middle East as a result of the Arab-Israeli conflicts of 1967 and 1973. What factors led to the Arab attacks on Israel in these two wars? Why did the Israelis wish to occupy the Sinai and West Bank regions at the end of the 1967 war? What problems did this create, and how might it have led to the conflict in 1973? Study the distribution of Israeli-occupied and Egyptian-occupied territory at the end of the 1973 war. Why was the resolution of the Sinai problem considered a top priority by many political figures in the West?

answer to regional conflict. Aided by the American president Jimmy Carter, Sadat brokered a peace between Egypt and Israel's staunchly conservative leader, Menachem Begin, in 1978. Leaders on both sides of the conflict believed the potential rewards were greater than the obvious risks.

But hopes for a lasting peace were soon dashed. Hostilities escalated between Israel and the Palestinian Arabs displaced by Arab-Israeli warfare, a confronta-

tion that increasingly polarized a much larger group of people. On each side of the Israeli-Palestinian conflict, a potent blend of ethnic and religious nationalism began to control both debate and action. Conservatives in Israel played to a public sentiment that put security ahead of other priorities, particularly among the most recent Jewish immigrants, often from the former Soviet Union. On the other side, younger Palestinians, angered by their elders' failures to provoke revolution, turned against the secular radicalism of the Palestinian Liberation Organization and toward radical Islam.

In this combustible political environment, the desperately overcrowded Palestinians living on the West Bank and in the Gaza Strip revolted in an outburst of street rioting in 1987. This rebellion—called the *intifada* (literally, a "throwing off" or uprising)—continued for years in daily battles between stone-throwing Palestinian youths and armed Israeli security forces. The street fights escalated into cycles of Palestinian terrorism, particularly suicide bombings of civilian targets, and reprisals from the Israeli military. International efforts to broker a peace produced some results, including the official autonomy of a Palestinian "authority" led by the PLO chief, Yasser Arafat. Yet the peace was always fragile at best—suffering perhaps fatal damage from the assassination of Israel's reformist prime minister Yitzhak Rabin in 1995 by a reactionary Israeli and from continued attacks by Islamist terrorists. By the turn of the twenty-first century the cycle of violence flared again, with a "second *intifada*" launched by Palestinians in late 2000. Thus continued the war of riots and bombings fought by next-door neighbors.

> With the pan-Arab nationalists fading from the scene, the rising revolutionary force gathered instead around modern readings of Islamic fundamentalism, now tied to postcolonial politics.

OIL, POWER, AND ECONOMICS

The struggles between the state of Israel and its neighbors have been important in their own right. Yet one of the most compelling reasons that this conflict mattered to outside powers was material—oil. The global demand for oil skyrocketed during the postwar era and has accelerated since. Starting with the consumer boom in the cold war West, ordinary citizens bought cars and other petroleum-powered consumer durables, while industrial plastics made from petroleum by-products were used to manufacture a wealth of basic household items. Those needs, and the desires for profit and power that went with them, drew Western corporations and governments steadily toward the oil-rich states of the Middle East, whose vast reserves were discovered in the 1930s and 1940s. Large corporations conducted joint diplomacy with Middle Eastern states and their own home governments to design concessions for drilling, refining, and shipping the oil. Pipelines were laid by contractors based around the world, from California to Rome to Russia.

The enormous long-term economic value of the Middle Eastern oil reserves made oil a fundamental tool in new struggles over political power, and many producer states sought to turn their resources into leverage with the West's former imperial powers. In 1960, the leading Middle Eastern, African, and Latin American producers banded together in a cartel to take advantage of this vital resource, forming the Organization of the Petroleum Exporting Countries (OPEC) to regulate the production and pricing of crude oil. During the 1970s, OPEC played a leading role in the global economy. Its policies reflected not only the desire to draw maximum profits out of bottlenecks in oil production but also the militant politics of some OPEC leaders who wanted to use oil as a weapon against the West in the Arab-Israeli conflict. After the 1973 Arab-Israeli war, an embargo inspired by the hardliners sparked spiraling inflation and economic troubles in Western nations, triggering a cycle of dangerous recession that lasted nearly a decade.

In response, Western governments treated the Middle Eastern oil regions as a vital strategic center of gravity, the subject of constant Great Power diplomacy. If conflict directly threatened the stability of oil production or friendly governments, Western powers were prepared to intervene by force, as the 1991 Gulf War demonstrated. By the 1990s another new front of competition and potential conflict emerged as the energy demands of postcolonial nations also grew. In particular, the new industrial giants China and India eyed the Middle Eastern oil reserves with the same nervousness as the West. The oil boom also generated violent conflict inside Middle Eastern producer states. Oil revenue produced an uneven form of economic development. The huge gaps between or inside Middle Eastern societies that divided oil's "haves" and "have-nots" caused deep resentments, continued official corruption, and spurred a new wave of radical politics. With the pan-Arab nationalists fading from the scene, the rising revolutionary force gathered instead around modern readings of Islamic fundamentalism, now tied to postcolonial politics.

THE RISE OF POLITICAL ISLAM

In North Africa and the Middle East, processes of modernization and globalization produced tremendous discontents. The new nations that emerged from decolonization often shared the characteristics of the "kleptocracies" south of the Sahara: corrupt state agencies, cronyism based on ethnic or family kinship,

HOW DID THE GLOBAL DEMAND FOR OIL RESHAPE POLITICS, RELIGION, AND SOCIETY IN THE MIDDLE EAST?

ISRAEL, OIL, AND POLITICAL ISLAM IN THE MIDDLE EAST   1057

decaying public services, rapid increases in population, and constant state repression of dissent. Disappointment with these conditions ran deep, perhaps nowhere more so than in the seat of pan-Arabism, Nasser's Egypt. During the 1960s, Egyptian academics and cultural critics leveled charges against Nasser's regime that became the core of a powerful new political movement. Their critique offered modern interpretations of certain legal and political currents in Islamic thought, ideas linked loosely across centuries by their association with revolt against foreign interference and official corruption. They denounced Egypt's nationalist government as greedy, brutal, and corrupt.

There was a twist to their claims, however: that the roots of the Arab world's moral failure lay in centuries of colonial contact with the West. The most influential of these Islamist critics, Sayyid Qutb (1906–1966), presented these ideas in a series of essays for which he was arrested several times by Egyptian authorities and ultimately executed. His argument ran as follows. As a result of corrupting outside influences, the ruling elites of the new Arab states pursued policies that frayed local and family bonds, deepening economic divides while abandoning the government's responsibility for charity and stability. What was more, the nation's elites were morally bankrupt—their lives defied codes of morality, self-discipline, and communal responsibility rooted in Islamic faith. To maintain power, the elites lived in the pockets of Western imperial and corporate powers. From Qutb's point of view, this collaboration not only caused cultural impurity, it also eroded authentic Muslim faith. This dire judgment of Arab societies—that they were poisoned from without and within—required an equally drastic solution. Arab societies should reject not only oppressive postcolonial governments but also all the political and cultural ideas that traveled with them, especially those that could be labeled "Western." After popular revolts, the Arab autocracies would be replaced by an idealized form of conservative Islamic government—a system in which a rigid form of Islam would link law, government, and culture.

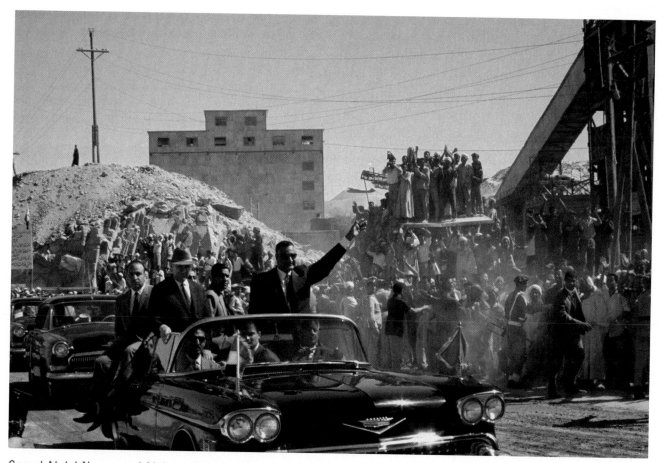

Gamal Abdel Nasser and Aleksey Kosygin, 1966. As the most prominent spokesman for Secular Pan-Arabism, Nassar became a target for Islamist critics, such as Sayyid Qutb and the Muslim Brotherhood, angered by the Western-influenced policies of his regime.

In a formula familiar to historians of European politics throughout the nineteenth and twentieth centuries, this particular brand of Islamist politics combined popular anger, intellectual opposition to "foreign" influences, and a highly idealized vision of the past. By the 1970s it began to express itself openly in regional politics. Qutb's ideas were put into practice by Egypt's Muslim Brotherhood, a secretive but widespread society rooted in anticolonial politics, local charity, and violently fundamentalist Islam. The same ideas spread among similar organizations in other urbanized Arab countries and leading Islamic universities, which were historically centers of debate about political theory and religious law. Radical Islam emerged as a driving force in criticism and defiance of autocratic Arab regimes. Secular critics and more liberal Islamists, who called for open elections and a free press, were more fragmented and thus easier to silence, whereas the new wave of fundamentalists gained concessions that allowed them to preach and publish in public so long as they did not launch actual revolts. Despite the movement's steady rise, the most dramatic turn still managed to surprise observers. Like Protestantism's emergence in the fractious German states, for example, or communism's successful revolution in Russia, radical Islam's defining moment as a political force came in an unexpected place: Iran.

IRAN'S ISLAMIC REVOLUTION

Iran offered one of the most dramatic examples of "modernization" gone sour in the Middle East. Despite tremendous economic growth in the 1960s and 1970s, Iranians labored with legacies of foreign intervention and corrupt rule at the hands of the shah, Reza Pahlavi, a Western-friendly leader installed during a 1953 military coup supported by Britain and the United States. In exchange for the shah's role as a friend to the West during the cold war and for providing a steady source of reasonably priced oil, the Iranian government received vast sums in oil contracts, weapons, and development aid. Thousands of Westerners, especially Americans, came to Iran, introducing foreign influences that not only challenged traditional values but also offered economic and political alternatives. The shah, however, kept these alternatives out of reach, consistently denying democratic representation to "westernizing" middle-class Iranian workers and deeply religious university students alike. He governed through a small aristocracy divided by constant infighting. His army and secret police conducted regular and brutal campaigns of repression. Despite all this, and the public protests it spurred

in the West, governments such as the conservative Nixon administration embraced the shah as a strategically vital ally: an important cold war ally, a key to anti-Soviet alliances, and a safe source of oil.

Twenty-five years after the 1953 coup, the shah's autocratic route to an industrial state ended. After a lengthy economic downturn, public unrest, and personal illness, the shah realized he could not continue in power. He retired from public life under popular pressure in February 1979. Eight months of uncertainty followed, most Westerners fled the country, and the provisional government appointed by the shah collapsed. The strongest political coalition among Iran's revolutionaries surged into the vacuum—a broad Islamic movement centered on the ayatollah Ruhollah Khomeini (1902–1989), Iran's senior cleric and theologian, returned from exile in France. Other senior clerics and the country's large population of unemployed, deeply religious university students provided the movement's energy. Disenfranchised secular protestors joined the radical Islamists in condemning decades of Western indifference and the shah's oppression. Under the new regime, some limited economic and political populism combined with strict constructions of Islamic law, restrictions on women's public life, and the prohibition of many ideas or activities linked to Western influence.

The new Iranian government also defined itself against its enemies: against the Sunni religious establishment of neighboring states, against "atheistic" So-

CHRONOLOGY

MAJOR DEVELOPMENTS IN THE MIDDLE EAST, 1948–PRESENT

Israeli state formed	1948
First Arab-Israeli War	1948–1949
Egypt gains independence	1952
Israeli-Egyptian War	1956
Formation of OPEC	1960
Six-Day War; Israel occupies West Bank	1967
Second Arab-Israeli War	1973
Camp David peace accords	1978
Iran-Iraq War	1980–1988
Persian Gulf war	1991
Palestinians granted self-rule	1995
9/11 terrorist attacks; U.S. action against al Qaeda and the Taliban in Afghanistan	2001
U.S. invasion of Iraq; fall of Saddam Hussein	2003
Israeli-Palestinian conflict continues	present

HOW DID THE GLOBAL DEMAND FOR OIL RESHAPE POLITICS, RELIGION, AND SOCIETY IN THE MIDDLE EAST?

ISRAEL, OIL, AND POLITICAL ISLAM IN THE MIDDLE EAST   1059

viet communism, but especially against Israel and the United States. Iranians feared the United States would try to overthrow Khomeini as it had other leaders. Violence in the streets of Tehran reached a peak when militant students stormed the American embassy in November 1979 and seized fifty-two hostages. The act quickly became an international crisis that heralded a new kind of confrontation between Western powers and postcolonial Islamic radicals. President Jimmy Carter's administration ultimately gained the hostages' release, but not before the catalog of earlier failures led to the election of the conservative Ronald Reagan.

IRAN, IRAQ, AND UNINTENDED CONSEQUENCES OF THE COLD WAR

Iran's victory in the hostage crisis was fleeting. During the later part of 1980, Iran's Arab neighbor and traditional rival Iraq invaded, hoping to seize Iran's southern oil fields during the revolutionary confusion. Iran counterattacked. The result was a murderous eight-year conflict marked by the use of chemical weapons

and human waves of young Iranian radicals fighting the Soviet-armed Iraqis. The war ended with Iran's defeat, but not the collapse of its theocratic regime. In the short term, their long defense of Iranian nationalism left the clerics more entrenched at home, while abroad they used oil revenues to back grass-roots radicals in Lebanon and elsewhere who engaged in anti-Western terrorism. The strongest threats to the Iranian regime ultimately came from within, from a new generation of young students and disenfranchised service workers who found their prospects for prosperity and active citizenship had not changed much since the days of the shah.

The Iran-Iraq conflict created another problem for Western interests and the governments of leading OPEC states: Iraq. Various governments—including an unlikely alliance of France, Saudi Arabia, the Soviet Union, and the United States—supported Iraq during the war in an effort to bring down Iran's clerics. Their patronage went to one of the most violent governments in the region, Saddam Hussein's dictatorship. Iraq exhausted itself in the war, politically and economically. In order to shore up his regime and restore

The Iraqi Threat to Stability in the Middle East: The Case of Jordan. Left: In the wake of the Iraqi invasion and occupation of Kuwait, thousands of refugees fled from Kuwait to Jordan, where they were stranded in tent cities. Added to the existing Palestinian refugee problem, this latest wave of displaced people placed an enormous burden on Jordan's fragile economy. Right: Large numbers of Jordanians and Palestinians rallied to Saddam Hussein's call for a "holy war" to free Arab soil of Western imperialists and their agents. Caught between Iraq and an international force led by a U.S. army of over four hundred thousand men and women, the government of King Hussein of Jordan faced the specter of revolution.

Smoke rises from burning oil refineries in Abadan, Iran. Due to the high concentrations of oil fields in Abadan, it was heavily attacked and largely destroyed during the Iran-Iraq War.

Iraq's influence, Hussein looked elsewhere in the region. In 1990 Iraq invaded its small, oil-rich neighbor Kuwait. With the cold war on the wane, Iraq's Soviet supporters would not condone Iraqi aggression. A number of Western nations led by the United States reacted forcefully. Within months Iraq faced the full weight of the United States military—trained intensively since Vietnam to rout much more capable Soviet-armed forces than Iraq's—along with forces from several OPEC states, French troops, and armored divisions from Britain, Egypt, and Syria. This coalition pummeled Iraqi troops from the air for six weeks, then routed them and retook Kuwait in a brief, well-executed ground campaign. This changed the tenor of relations between the United States and Arab oil producers, encouraging not only closeness between governments but also anti-American radicals angry at a new Western presence. It was also the beginning rather than the end of a Western confrontation with Iraq, centered on Hussein's efforts to develop nuclear and biological weapons.

Elsewhere in the region, the proxy conflicts of the cold war snared both superpowers in the new and growing networks of Islamic radicalism. In 1979 the socialist government of Afghanistan turned against its Soviet patrons. Fearing a result like Iran, with a spread of fundamentalism into the Muslim regions of Soviet Central Asia, Moscow responded by overthrowing the Afghan president and installing a pro-Soviet faction. The new government, backed by more than one hundred thousand Soviet troops, found itself immediately at war with fighters who combined local conservatism with militant Islam, and who attracted volunteers from radical Islamic movements in Egypt, Lebanon, Saudi Arabia, and elsewhere. These fighters, who called themselves *mujahidin*, viewed the conflict as a holy war. The *mujahidin* benefited from advanced weapons and training, given by Western powers led by the United States. Those who provided the aid saw the conflict in cold war terms, as a chance to sap Soviet resources in a fruitless imperial war. On those terms the aid worked; the war dragged on for nearly ten years, taking thousands of Russian lives and damaging the Soviet government's credibility at home. Soviet troops withdrew in 1989. After five years of clan warfare, hard-line Islamic factions tied to the foreign elements in the *mujahidin* took over the country. Their experiment in theocracy made Iran's seem mild by comparison.

VIOLENCE BEYOND BOUNDS: WAR AND TERRORISM IN THE TWENTY-FIRST CENTURY

How has globalization changed the politics of terrorism?

The global networks of communication, finance, and mobility discussed at the beginning of this chapter gave radical political violence a disturbing new character at the end of the twentieth century. In the 1960s, organized, sectarian terrorist tactics had become an important part of political conflict in the Middle East, Europe, and Latin America. Most of these early terrorist organizations (including the Irish Republican Army, the Italian Red Brigades, and the different Palestinian revolutionary organizations) had specific goals, such as ethnic separatism or the establishment of revolutionary governments. By the 1980s and increasingly during the 1990s, such groups were complemented and then supplanted by a different brand of terrorist organization, one that ranged freely across territory and local legal systems. These newer, apocalyptic terrorist groups called for decisive conflict to eliminate their enemies and grant themselves martyrdom. Some such groups emerged from the social dislocations of the postwar boom, others were linked directly to brands of radical religion. They often divorced themselves from the local crises that first spurred their anger, roaming widely among countries in search of recruits to their cause.

A leading example of such groups, and soon the most famous, was the radical Islamist umbrella organization al Qaeda. It was created by leaders of the foreign *mujahidin* who had fought against the Soviet Union in Afghanistan. Its official leader and financial supporter was the Saudi-born multimillionaire Osama bin Laden. Among its operational chiefs was the famous Egyptian radical Ayman al-Zawahiri, whose political career linked him directly to Sayyid Qutb and other founding thinkers in modern revolutionary Islam. These leaders organized broad networks of largely self-contained terrorist cells around the world, from the Islamic regions of Southeast Asia to Europe, East Africa, and the United States, funded by myriad private accounts, front companies, illegal trades, and corporate kickbacks throughout the global economy. Their organization defied borders, and so did their goals. They did not seek to negotiate for territory, or to change the government of a specific state. Instead, they spoke of the destruction of the state of Israel and American, European, and other non-Islamic systems of government worldwide, and called for a united, apocalyptic revolt by fundamentalist Muslims to create an Islamic community bounded only by faith. During the 1990s they involved themselves in a variety of local terrorist campaigns in Islamic countries and organized

large-scale suicide attacks against American targets, notably the American embassies in Kenya and Tanzania in 1998.

At the beginning of the twenty-first century, al Qaeda's organizers struck again at their most obvious political enemy, the symbolic seat of "globalization": the United States. Small teams of suicidal radicals, aided by al Qaeda's organization, planned to hijack airliners and use them as flying bombs to strike the most strategically important symbols of America's global power. On September 11, 2001, they carried out this mission in the deadliest series of terrorist attacks ever to occur on American soil. In the space of an hour, hijacked planes struck the Pentagon, the headquarters of the U.S. military, and the World Trade Center towers in New York City. A fourth plane, possibly aimed at the U.S. Capitol, crashed in open farmland in Pennsylvania, its attack compromised when the passengers fought back against their captors. The World Trade Center towers, among the tallest buildings in the world, crumbled into ash and wreckage in front of hundreds of millions of viewers on satellite television and the Internet. In these several simultaneous attacks roughly three thousand people died.

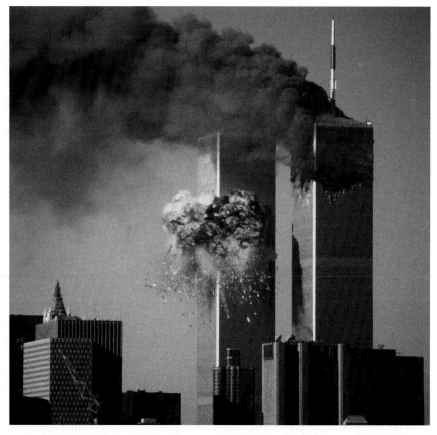

New York's World Trade Center towers, September 11, 2001.

The attacks were at once a new brand of terror, deeply indebted to globalization in both its outlook and its method, and something older: the extreme, opportunistic violence of marginal groups against national cultures during a period of general dislocation and uncertainty. The immediate American response was action against al Qaeda's central haven in Afghanistan, a state in total collapse after the warfare of the previous thirty years. The United States' combination of versatile professional soldiers, unmatched equipment, and armed Afghan militias angry at the country's disarray quickly routed al Qaeda's Taliban sponsors and scattered the terrorists themselves. That effort, however, failed to pinpoint and eliminate the hidden networks of leadership, finance, and information that propel apocalyptic terrorism. The rebuilding and rehabilitation of Afghanistan, a necessary consequence of American and European action, began from almost nothing in terms of administration and infrastructure. Pressing crises elsewhere and the changeable nature of Western popular concerns made a recovery difficult.

One reason for the persistent fears about such groups as al Qaida has to do with the increasing power and availability of weapons they might use: chemical substances, biological agents that could kill millions, even portable nuclear weapons. With the end of the cold war, methods and technologies that the superpowers employed to maintain their nuclear "balance of terror" became more available on the margins to displaced groups with the financial or political leverage to seek them out. Other major arms races, centered, for example, around Israel or the conflicts between India and Pakistan, helped spread the availability of production sites and resources for weapons of horrific power, no longer governed absolutely by the legal conventions and deterrent strength of superpowers. Fear that the Iraqi government of Saddam Hussein was reaching for biological and nuclear capabilities helped propel the Gulf War of 1991 and active international efforts to disarm Iraq thereafter. Anxiety that states such as Iraq might transfer such weapons to apocalyptic terrorists, a fear given new life after the attacks on New York and Washington, provided the rationale for an American-led invasion of Iraq in the spring of 2003. The campaign, which used a remarkably small force both on the ground and in the air, quickly took Iraq over and deposed Hussein. No immediate evidence of recent, active weapons development programs was found, however, and in the process the United States inherited the complex reconstruction of a broken state, punctuated by guerilla violence and anti-Western terrorism.

A similar threat remained present in North Korea. After the loss of Soviet patronage in 1991, the isolated North Korean state careened from one economic disaster to another, with verified reports of local starvation in some regions of the country and a breakdown of government into military and political fiefdoms. The North Korean government pursued the development of a nuclear arsenal as a bargaining chip against the other major states of northeast Asia and the United States. Those neighbors each understood the grim chance that North Korea might break the last and perhaps most crucial nuclear threshold, providing nuclear weapons not to hard-pressed states but instead to stateless organizations. In short, by the early twenty-first century, warfare and the terrifying killing power of modern technology threatened to elude the control of national states and clearly defined political communities.

CONCLUSION

In such a complex world, the loss of familiar moorings makes fundamental questions about human behavior and political community difficult to answer. History offers no quick solutions. Historians are loath to offer what historian Peter Novick calls "pithy lessons that fit on a bumper sticker." As Novick puts it:

> If there is, to use a pretentious word, any wisdom to be acquired from contemplating an historical event, I would think it would derive from confronting it in all its complexity and its contradictions; the ways in which it resembles other events to which it might be compared as well as the way it differs from them. . . . If there are lessons to be extracted from encountering the past, that encounter has to be with the past in all its messiness; they're not likely to come from an encounter with a past that's been shaped so that inspiring lessons will emerge.

The untidy and contradictory evidence that historians discover in the archives rarely yields unblemished heroes or unvarnished villains. Instead, good history reveals to us the complex processes and dynamics of change over time. It does help us understand the many layers of the past that have formed and constrain us in our present world. At the same time, it shows again and again that these constraints do not preordain what happens next or how we can make the history of the future.

KEY TERMS

globalization	Rwanda	Sayyid Qutb
AIDS	intifada	Saddam Hussein
DNA	OPEC	al Qaeda
Nelson Mandela		

SELECTED READINGS

Achebe, Chinua. *Things Fall Apart.* Expanded edition with notes. Portsmouth, N.H., 1996. An annotated edition of the now classic novel about postcolonial Africa.

Bates, Robert H. *Essays on the Political Economy of Rural Africa.* Cambridge, 1983. Still an important study of debt, food production, and postcolonial Africa, written at the leading edge of the sub-Saharan debt crisis.

Coetzee, J. M. *Waiting for the Barbarians.* London, 1980. A searing critique of apartheid-era South Africa by a leading Afrikaner novelist.

Cooper, Frederick. *Colonialism in Question: Theory, Knowledge, History.* Los Angeles and Berkeley, 2005.

Cooper, Frederick. "What is the Concept of Globalization Good For? An African Historian's Perspective." *African Affairs* (2001). Helpful critical analysis, and a useful antidote to loose use of the term.

Geyer, Michael, and Charles Bright. "World History in a Global Age." *American Historical Review* (October 1995). An excellent short discussion.

Held, David, et al. *Global Transformations: Politics, Economics, and Culture.* Stanford, 1999. Major survey of the globalization of culture, finance, criminality, and politics.

Hopkins, A. G., ed. *Globalization in World History.* New York, 2002. Written by one of the first historians to engage social scientific debates on globalization. Excellent introduction and articles on different stages of globalization.

Keddie, Nikki. *Modern Iran: Roots and Results of Revolution.* New Haven, 2003. A revised edition of her major study of Iran's 1979 revolution, with added perspective on Iran's Islamic government.

Lacqueur, Walter. *The Age of Terrorism.* Boston, 1987. An important study of the first wave of post-1960s terrorism.

Landes, David. *The Wealth and Poverty of Nations: Why Some Are So Rich and Some So Poor.* New York, 1998. Leading economic historian's account of globalization's effects on the international economy.

Lewis, Bernard. *The Crisis of Islam: Holy War and Unholy Terror.* New York, 2003. Conservative scholar of the Arab world discussing the political crises that fueled terrorism.

McNeill, J. R. *Something New Under the Sun: An Environmental History of the Twentieth-Century World.* New York and London, 2000. Fascinating new approach to environmental history.

Ngugi wa Thiong'o. *Petals of Blood.* New York, 1977. A scathing critique of neocolonialism in Kenya by Africa's best-known novelist.

Novick, Peter. *The Holocaust in American Life.* Boston, 1999.

Power, Samantha. *The Problem from Hell: America in the Age of Genocide.* A prize-winning survey of the entire twentieth century, its genocides, and the different human rights movements that responded to them.

Reynolds, David. *One World Divisible: A Global History since 1945.* New York and London, 2000. Excellent study of the different dimensions of globalization.

Shlaim, Avi. *The Iron Wall: Israel and the Arab World.* New York, 2000. Leading Israeli historian on the evolution of Israel's defensive foreign policy.

Stiglitz, Joseph E. *Globalization and Its Discontents.* New York, 2002. A recent and important consideration of contemporary globalization's character and the conflicts it creates, particularly over commerce and culture.

Shilts, Randy. *And the Band Played On: Politics, People, and the AIDS Epidemic.* New York, 1987. An impassioned attack on the individuals and governments that failed to come to grips with the early spread of the disease.

Turkle, Sherry. *Life on the Screen: Identity in the Age of the Internet.* New York, 1995. An important early study of "Web culture" and the fluid possibilities of electronic communication.

RULERS OF PRINCIPAL STATES

THE CAROLINGIAN DYNASTY

Pepin of Heristal, Mayor of the Palace, 687–714
Charles Martel, Mayor of the Palace, 715–741
Pepin III, Mayor of the Palace, 741–751; King, 751–768
Charlemagne, King, 768–814; Emperor, 800–814
Louis the Pious, Emperor, 814–840

WEST FRANCIA
Charles the Bald, King, 840–877; Emperor, 875–877
Louis II, King, 877–879
Louis III, King, 879–882
Carloman, King, 879–884

MIDDLE KINGDOMS
Lothair, Emperor, 840–855
Louis (Italy), Emperor, 855–875
Charles (Provence), King, 855–863
Lothair II (Lorraine), King, 855–869

EAST FRANCIA
Ludwig, King, 840–876
Carloman, King, 876–880
Ludwig, King, 876–882
Charles the Fat, Emperor, 876–887

HOLY ROMAN EMPERORS

SAXON DYNASTY
Otto I, 962–973
Otto II, 973–983
Otto III, 983–1002
Henry II, 1002–1024

FRANCONIAN DYNASTY
Conrad II, 1024–1039
Henry III, 1039–1056
Henry IV, 1056–1106
Henry V, 1106–1125
Lothair II (Saxony), 1125–1137

HOHENSTAUFEN DYNASTY
Conrad III, 1138–1152
Frederick I (Barbarossa), 1152–1190
Henry VI, 1190–1197
Philip of Swabia, 1198–1208 ⎱ Rivals
Otto IV (Welf), 1198–1215 ⎰
Frederick II, 1220–1250
Conrad IV, 1250–1254

INTERREGNUM, 1254–1273

EMPERORS FROM VARIOUS DYNASTIES
Rudolf I (Habsburg), 1273–1291
Adolf (Nassau), 1292–1298
Albert I (Habsburg), 1298–1308
Henry VII (Luxemburg), 1308–1313
Ludwig IV (Wittelsbach), 1314–1347
Charles IV (Luxemburg), 1347–1378
Wenceslas (Luxemburg), 1378–1400
Rupert (Wittelsbach), 1400–1410
Sigismund (Luxemburg), 1410–1437

HABSBURG DYNASTY
Albert II, 1438–1439
Frederick III, 1440–1493
Maximilian I, 1493–1519
Charles V, 1519–1556
Ferdinand I, 1556–1564
Maximilian II, 1564–1576
Rudolf II, 1576–1612

Matthias, 1612–1619
Ferdinand II, 1619–1637
Ferdinand III, 1637–1657
Leopold I, 1658–1705
Joseph I, 1705–1711
Charles VI, 1711–1740

Charles VII (not a Habsburg), 1742–1745
Francis I, 1745–1765
Joseph II, 1765–1790
Leopold II, 1790–1792
Francis II, 1792–1806

RULERS OF FRANCE FROM HUGH CAPET

CAPETIAN DYNASTY
Hugh Capet, 987–996
Robert II, 996–1031
Henry I, 1031–1060
Philip I, 1060–1108
Louis VI, 1108–1137
Louis VII, 1137–1180
Philip II (Augustus), 1180–1223
Louis VIII, 1223–1226
Louis IX (St. Louis), 1226–1270
Philip III, 1270–1285
Philip IV, 1285–1314
Louis X, 1314–1316
Philip V, 1316–1322
Charles IV, 1322–1328

VALOIS DYNASTY
Philip VI, 1328–1350
John, 1350–1364
Charles V, 1364–1380
Charles VI, 1380–1422
Charles VII, 1422–1461
Louis XI, 1461–1483
Charles VIII, 1483–1498
Louis XII, 1498–1515
Francis I, 1515–1547

Henry II, 1547–1559
Francis II, 1559–1560
Charles IX, 1560–1574
Henry III, 1574–1589

BOURBON DYNASTY
Henry IV, 1589–1610
Louis XIII, 1610–1643
Louis XIV, 1643–1715
Louis XV, 1715–1774
Louis XVI, 1774–1792

AFTER 1792
First Republic, 1792–1799
Napoleon Bonaparte, First Consul, 1799–1804
Napoleon I, Emperor, 1804–1814
Louis XVIII (Bourbon dynasty), 1814–1824
Charles X (Bourbon dynasty), 1824–1830
Louis Philippe, 1830–1848
Second Republic, 1848–1852
Napoleon III, Emperor, 1852–1870
Third Republic, 1870–1940
Péain regime, 1940–1944
Provisional government, 1944–1946
Fourth Republic, 1946–1958
Fifth Republic, 1958–

RULERS OF ENGLAND

ANGLO-SAXON DYNASTY
Alfred the Great, 871–899
Edward the Elder, 899–924
Ethelstan, 924–939
Edmund I, 939–946
Edred, 946–955
Edwy, 955–959
Edgar, 959–975
Edward the Martyr, 975–978
Ethelred the Unready, 978–1016

Canute, 1016–1035 (Danish Nationality)
Harold I, 1035–1040
Hardicanute, 1040–1042
Edward the Confessor, 1042–1066
Harold II, 1066

HOUSE OF NORMANDY
William I (the Conqueror), 1066–1087
William II, 1087–1100

Henry I, 1100–1135
Stephen, 1135–1154

HOUSE OF PLANTAGENET
Henry II, 1154–1189
Richard I, 1189–1199
John, 1199–1216
Henry III, 1216–1272
Edward I, 1272–1307
Edward II, 1307–1327
Edward III, 1327–1377
Richard II, 1377–1399

HOUSE OF LANCASTER
Henry IV, 1399–1413
Henry V, 1413–1422
Henry VI, 1422–1461

HOUSE OF YORK
Edward IV, 1461–1483
Edward V, 1483
Richard III, 1483–1485

HOUSE OF TUDOR
Henry VII, 1485–1509
Henry VIII, 1509–1547
Edward VI, 1547–1553
Mary, 1553–1558
Elizabeth I, 1558–1603

HOUSE OF STUART
James I, 1603–1625
Charles I, 1625–1649

COMMONWEALTH AND PROTECTORATE, 1649–1659

HOUSE OF STUART RESTORED
Charles II, 1660–1685
James II, 1685–1688
William III and Mary II, 1689–1694
William III alone, 1694–1702
Anne, 1702–1714

HOUSE OF HANOVER
George I, 1714–1727
George II, 1727–1760
George III, 1760–1820
George IV, 1820–1830
William IV, 1830–1837
Victoria, 1837–1901

HOUSE OF SAXE-COBURG-GOTHA
Edward VII, 1901–1910
George V, 1910–1917

HOUSE OF WINDSOR
George V, 1917–1936
Edward VIII, 1936
George VI, 1936–1952
Elizabeth II, 1952–

RULERS OF AUSTRIA AND AUSTRIA-HUNGARY

*Maximilian I (Archduke), 1493–1519
*Charles V, 1519–1556
*Ferdinand I, 1556–1564
*Maximilian II, 1564–1576
*Rudolf II, 1576–1612
*Matthias, 1612–1619
*Ferdinand II, 1619–1637
*Ferdinand III, 1637–1657
*Leopold I, 1658–1705
*Joseph I, 1705–1711
*Charles VI, 1711–1740
Maria Theresa, 1740–1780

*also bore title of Holy Roman Emperor

*Joseph II, 1780–1790
*Leopold II, 1790–1792
*Francis II, 1792–1835 (Emperor of Austria as Francis I after 1804)
Ferdinand I, 1835–1848
Francis Joseph, 1848–1916 (after 1867 Emperor of Austria and King of Hungary)
Charles I, 1916–1918 (Emperor of Austria and King of Hungary)
Republic of Austria, 1918–1938 (dictatorship after 1934)
Republic restored, under Allied occupation, 1945–1956
Free Republic, 1956–
*Frederick I, 1701–1713
*Frederick William I, 1713–1740
*Frederick II (the Great), 1740–1786

RULERS OF PRUSSIA AND GERMANY

*Frederick William II, 1786–1797
*Frederick William III,1797–1840
*Frederick William IV, 1840–1861
*William I, 1861–1888 (German Emperor after 1871)
Frederick III, 1888
*William II, 1888–1918
Weimar Republic, 1918–1933
Third Reich (Nazi Dictatorship), 1933–1945

*Kings of Prussia

Allied occupation, 1945–1952
Division into Federal Republic of Germany in west and
    German Democratic Republic in east, 1949–1991
Federal Republic of Germany (united), 1991–

RULERS OF RUSSIA

Ivan III, 1462–1505
Vasily III, 1505–1533
Ivan IV, 1533–1584
Theodore I, 1534–1598
Boris Godunov, 1598–1605
Theodore II,1605
Vasily IV, 1606–1610
Michael, 1613–1645
Alexius, 1645–1676
Theodore III, 1676–1682
Ivan V and Peter I, 1682–1689
Peter I (the Great), 1689–1725
Catherine I, 1725–1727
Peter II, 1727–1730

Anna, 1730–1740
Ivan VI, 1740–1741
Ellzabeth, 1741–1762
Peter III, 1762
Catherine II (the Great), 1762–1796
Paul, 1796–1801
Alexander I,1801–1825
Nicholas I, 1825–1855
Alexander II,1855–1881
Alexander III, 1881–1894
Nicholas II, 1894–1917
Soviet Republic, 1917–1991
Russian Federation, 1991–

RULERS OF SPAIN

Ferdinand { and Isabella, 1479–1504
            and Philip I, 1504–1506
            and Charles I, 1506–1516
Charles I (Holy Roman Emperor Charles V), 1516–1556
Philip II, 1556–1598
Philip III, 1598–1621
Philip IV, 1621–1665
Charles II, 1665–1700
Philip V, 1700–1746
Ferdinand VI, 1746–1759
Charles III, 1759–1788
Charles IV, 1788–1808

Ferdinand VII, 1808
Joseph Bonaparte, 1808–1813
Ferdinand VII (restored), 1814–1833
Isabella II, 1833–1868
Republic, 1868–1870
Amadeo, 1870–1873
Republic, 1873–1874
Alfonso XII, 1874–1885
Alfonso XIII, 1886–1931
Republic, 1931–1939
Fascist Dictatorship, 1939–1975
Juan Carlos I, 1975–

Rulers of Italy

Victor Emmanuel II, 1861–1878
Humbert I, 1878–1900
Victor Emmanuel III, 1900–1946

Fascist Dictatorship, 1922-1943 (maintained in northern
   Italy until 1945)
Humbert II, May 9–June 13, 1946
Republic, 1946–

Prominent Popes

Silvester I, 314–335
Leo I, 440–461
Gelasius I, 492–496
Gregory I, 590–604
Nicholas I, 858–867
Silvester II, 999–1003
Leo IX, 1049–1054
Nicholas II, 1058–1061
Gregory VII, 1073–1085
Urban II, 1088–1099
Paschal II, 1099–1118
Alexander III, 1159–1181
Innocent III, 1198–1216
Gregory IX, 1227–1241
Innocent IV, 1243–1254
Boniface VIII, 1294–1303
John XXII, 1316–1334
Nicholas V, 1447–1455
Pius II, 1458–1464

Alexander VI, 1492–1503
Julius II, 1503–1513
Leo X, 1513–1521
Paul III, 1534–1549
Paul IV, 1555–1559
Sixtus V, 1585–1590
Urban VIII, 1623–1644
Gregory XVI, 1831–1846
Pius IX, 1846–1878
Leo XIII, 1878–1903
Pius X, 1903–1914
Benedict XV, 1914–1922
Pius XI, 1922–1939
Pius XII, 1939–1958
John XXIII, 1958–1963
Paul VI, 1963–1978
John Paul I, 1978
John Paul II, 1978–

GLOSSARY

Peter Abelard (1079–1142) Famed French theologian, logician, and university lecturer.

Absolutism Form of government in which one body, usually the monarch, controls the right to make war, tax, judge, and coin money. The term was often used to refer to the state monarchies in seventeenth- and eighteenth-century Europe.

Abstract Expressionism The mid-twentieth-century school of art based in New York that included Jackson Pollock, Willem de Kooning, and Franz Kline. It emphasized form, color, gesture, and feeling instead of figurative subjects.

acid rain Precipitation laced with heavy doses of sulfur, mainly from coal-fired plants.

African National Congress (ANC) Multiracial organization founded in 1912 whose goal was to end racial discrimination in South Africa.

Afrikaners Descendants of the original Dutch settlers of South Africa; formerly referred to as Boers.

AIDS Acquired immune deficiency syndrome. AIDS first appeared in the 1970s and has developed into a global health catastrophe; it is spreading most quickly in developing nations in Africa and Asia.

Akhenaten The fourteenth-century B.C.E. pharaoh who developed a sun-oriented religion and ultimately damaged Egypt's position in the ancient world.

Alexander (356–323 B.C.E.) The Macedonian general who conquered northwest Asia Minor, and Persia, and built an empire that stretched as far east as the Indus River.

Allied Powers The World War I coalition of Great Britain, Ireland, Belgium, France, Italy, Russia, Portugal, Greece, Serbia, Montenegro, Albania, and Romania.

al-Qaeda The radical Islamic organization founded in the late 1980s by former *mujahedin* who had fought against the Soviet Union in Afghanistan. Al-Qaeda carried out the 9/11 terrorist attacks and is responsible as well for attacks in Africa, Southeast Asia, Europe, and the Middle East.

Amnesty International Nongovernmental organization formed in 1961 to defend "prisoners of conscience"—those detained for their beliefs, color, sex, ethnic origin, language, or religion.

Anabaptists Swiss Protestant movement that began in 1521 and insisted that only adults could be baptized Christians. The movement's first generation, who had been baptized as infants according to Catholic practice, was "re-baptized," hence the name.

Anarchism The social and political movement that began in the mid-nineteenth century and advocated the destruction of the state through violence and terrorism.

Apartheid The racial segregation policy of the Afrikaner-dominated South African government. Legislated in 1948 by the Afrikaner National Party, it existed in South Africa for many years.

aqueducts Engineering system that brought water from the mountains down to Roman cities.

Saint Thomas Aquinas (1225–1274) Italian Dominican monk and theologian whose intellectual style encouraged the study of ancient philosophers and science as complementary to theology.

Arians The fourth-century followers of a priest named Arius, who rejected the idea that Christ could be equal with God.

Asiatic Society A cultural organization founded in 1784 by British Orientalists who lauded native culture but believed in colonial rule.

Assyrians A Semitic-speaking people that emerged around 2400 B.C.E. in northern Mesopotamia. Their highly militarized empire dominated Near-Eastern politics for close to two thousands years.

astrolabe An ancient navigational instrument, thought to have been invented in 150 B.C.E., that was used to find latitude while at sea.

Atlantic system A system of trade and expansion that linked Europe, Africa, and the Americas. It emerged in the sixteenth century in the wake of European voyages across the Atlantic Ocean.

Saint Augustine (c. 354–397) One of the most influential Christian theologians of all time, Saint Augustine described his conversion in his autobiographical *Confessions* and formulated new aspects of Christian theology in *On the City of God*.

Augustus (63 B.C.E.–14 C.E.) The grandnephew and adopted son of Julius Caesar and first emperor of the Roman empire.

Auschwitz-Birkenau The Nazi concentration camp in Poland that was designed to systematically murder Jews and gypsies. Between 1942 and 1944 over one million people were killed in Auschwitz-Birkenau.

Austro-Hungarian empire   The dual monarchy established by the Habsburg family in 1867; it collapsed at the end of World War I.

authoritarianism   A centralized and dictatorial form of government, proclaimed by its adherents to be superior to parliamentary democracy and especially effective at mobilizing the masses. Authoritarianism was prominent in the 1930s.

Avignon   City on the southeastern border of France. Between 305 and 378 it was the seat of the papacy.

Aztecs   Native American people of central Mexico; their empire was conquered by the Spanish in the sixteenth century.

baby boom (1950s)   The post–World War II upswing in U.S. birth rates; it reversed a century of decline.

Baghdad Pact (1955)   The Middle Eastern military alliance among countries friendly with America who were also willing to align themselves with the Western countries against the Soviet Union.

Balfour Declaration   A letter dated November 2, 1917, by Lord Arthur J. Balfour, British Foreign Secretary, that promised a homeland for the Jews in Palestine.

Baroque   An ornate style of art and music associated with the Counter Reformation (from the French word for "irregularly shaped pearl").

Bay of Pigs (1961)   The unsuccessful invasion of Cuba by Cuban exiles, supported by the U.S. government. The rebels intended to incite an insurrection in Cuba and overthrow the Communist regime of Fidel Castro.

Beer Hall Putsch (1923)   The Nazi invasion of a meeting of Bavarian leaders and supporters in a Munich beer hall; Adolf Hitler was imprisoned for a year after the incident.

Saint Benedict of Nursia (c. 480–c. 547)   Considered the father of western monasticism, Saint Benedict created the Benedictine rule that became the guide for nearly all western monks. Monks were required to follow the rules laid down by Saint Benedict: poverty, sexual chastity, obedience, labor, and religious devotion.

Berlin Airlift (1948)   The supply of vital necessities to West Berlin by air transport primarily under U.S. auspices. It was initiated in response to a blockade of the city that had been instituted by the Soviet Union to force the Allies to abandon West Berlin.

Berlin Wall   The wall built in 1961 by East German Communists to prevent citizens of East Germany from fleeing to West Germany; it was torn down in 1989.

Bill of Rights   The first ten amendments to the U.S. Constitution; it was ratified in 1791.

Otto von Bismarck (1815–1890)   The prime minister of Prussia and later the first chancellor of Germany, Bismarck helped consolidate the German people's economic and military power.

Black Death   The epidemic of bubonic plague that ravaged Europe, East Asia, and North Africa in the fourteenth century, killing one-third of the European population.

Black Jacobins   A nickname for the rebels in Saint Domingue, including Toussaint L'Ouverture, a former slave who in 1791 led the slaves of this French colony in the largest and most successful slave insurrection.

Black Panthers   A radical African American group that came together in the 1960s; the Black Panthers advocated black separatism and pan-Africanism.

Blackshirts   The troops of Mussolini's fascist regime; the squads received money from Italian landowners to attack socialist leaders.

Black Tuesday (October 24, 1929)   The day on which the U.S. stock market crashed, plunging the U.S. and international trading systems into crisis and leading the world into the "Great Depression."

Blitzkreig   The German "lightning war" strategy used during World War II; the Germans invaded Poland, France, Russia, and other countries with fast-moving well-coordinated attacks using aircraft, tanks and other armored vehicles, followed by infantry.

Bloody Sunday   On Sunday, January 22, 1905, the Russian tsar's guards killed 130 demonstrators who were protesting the tsar's mistreatment of workers and the middle class.

Giovanni Boccaccio (1313–1375)   Italian prose writer famed for his *Decameron*, one hundred short stories about the human condition, mostly from a comic or cynical point of view.

Boer War   Conflict between British and ethnically European Afrikaners in South Africa, 1898–1902, with terrible casualties on both sides.

Simon de Bolivar (1783–1830)   Venezuelan-born general called "The Liberator" for his assistance in helping Bolivia, Panama, Colombia, Ecuador, Peru, and Venezuela win independence from Spain.

Bolsheviks   Former members of the Russian Social Democratic Party who advocated the destruction of capitalist political and economic institutions and started the Russian Revolution. In 1918 the Bolsheviks changed their name to the Russian Communist Party.

Napoleon Bonaparte (1769–1821)   Corsican-born French general who seized power and ruled as dictator 1799–1814. After successful conquest of much of Europe, he was defeated by Russian and Prussian forces and died in exile.

Bourgeoisie   The French term for the middle class, which emerged in Europe during the Middle Ages. The Bourgeoisie sought to be recognized not by birth or title, but by capital and property.

Boxer Uprising (1899–1900)   Chinese peasant movement that opposed foreign influence, especially that of Christian missionaries; it was finally put down after the Boxers were defeated by a foreign army comprised mostly of Japanese, Russian, British, French, and American soldiers.

British Commonwealth of Nations   Formed in 1926, the Commonwealth conferred "dominion status" on Britain's white settler colonies in Canada, Australia, and New Zealand.

Brownshirts   Troops of young German men who dedicated themselves to the Nazi cause in the early 1930s by holding street marches, mass rallies, and confrontations. They engaged in beatings of Jews and anyone who opposed the Nazis.

bubonic plague   An acute infectious disease caused by a bacterium that is transmitted to humans by fleas from infected rats. It ravaged Europe and parts of Asia in the fourteenth century. Sometimes referred to as the "black death."

Julius Caesar (100–44 B.C.E.) The Roman general who conquered the Gauls, invaded Britain, and expanded Rome's territory in Asia Minor. He became the dictator of Rome in 46 B.C.E. and was murdered by Brutus and Cassius, which led to the rise of Augustus and the end of the Roman republic.

caliphs Rulers of the Islamic community who claimed descent from Muhammad.

John Calvin (1509–1564) French-born Protestant theologian who stressed the predestination of all human beings according to God's will.

Canary Islands Islands off the western coast of Africa conquered by Portugal and Spain in the mid-1400s. Used to supply expeditions around the African coast and across the Atlantic.

Canterbury Tales Middle English verse stories by Geoffrey Chaucer (c.1340–1400) that reflect different classes and experiences in late medieval England.

caravans Companies of men who transported and traded goods along overland routes in North Africa and central Asia; large caravans consisted of 600 to 1,000 camels and as many as 400 men.

caravel Sailing vessel suited for nosing in and out of estuaries and navigating in waters with unpredictable currents and winds.

Carthage A great maritime empire that rivaled Rome; at its height, it stretched across the northern coast of Africa from modern-day Tunisia to the Strait of Gibraltar. Carthage fought against Rome in the Punic Wars that began in 264 B.C.E. The wars ended with the destruction of Carthage in 146 B.C.E.

Cassiodorus (490–583) Author of the *Institutes*, which instructed medieval readers on the essential works of literature a monk should know before moving on to more intensive study of theology and the Bible.

caste system A hierarchical system of organizing people and distributing labor, often based on heredity or regional origin.

Baldassare Castiglione (1478–1529) Author of *The Book of the Courtier*, a popular treatise on upper-class social graces.

Catherine the Great (1729–1796) German-born empress of Russia who maintained an absolutist feudal system but encouraged Enlightenment philosophy and the arts at court.

Catholicism Branch of Christianity headed by the pope.

Camillo Benso di Cavour (1810–1861) Anti-papist Italian leader who led the initial stages of revolution against the Habsburgs.

Central Powers The World War I alliance between Germany, Austro-Hungary, Bulgaria, and Turkey.

Charlemagne (742–814) Frankish ruler 767–813 who consolidated much of western Europe by adding Lombardy and Saxony to the Frankish kingdoms. With a strong sense of divine purpose, he forced the Christian conversion of pagan peoples and sponsored arts and learning at court. In 800 he became the first Roman emperor in the west since the 5th century.

Chartism (1834–1848) Mass democratic movement to pass the Peoples' Charter in Britain, granting male suffrage, secret ballot, equal electoral districts, and annual Parliaments, and absolving the requirement of property ownership for members of Parliament.

Chernobyl (1986) Site of the world's worst nuclear power accident; in Ukraine, formerly part of the Soviet Union.

chivalry From the word for "horsemanship"; an aristocratic ideology originating with the knights of eleventh-century Europe that encouraged military prowess and social graces.

Winston Churchill (1874–1965) The British prime minister who led the country during World War II. He also coined the phrase "Iron Curtain" in a speech at Westminster College in 1946.

Church of England Founded by Henry VIII in the 1530s after his excommunication from the Catholic Church by Pope Clement VII, it is the established form of Christianity in England.

Cicero (106–43 B.C.E.) The most famous Stoic philosopher and orator of Rome.

Civil Rights Act (1964) U.S. legislation that banned segregation in public facilities, outlawed racial discrimination in employment, and marked an important step in correcting legal inequality.

Civil War (1861–1865) Conflict between the northern and southern states of America that cost over 600,000 lives; this struggle led to the abolition of slavery in the United States.

Cluny A Benedictine monastery, founded in 910, whose reform ideology tried to separate its network of religious houses from control by lay people.

Cold War (1945–1990) Ideological conflict in which the U.S.S.R. and Eastern Europe opposed the United States and Western Europe.

collectivization The process under Stalin in the 1920s and 1930s where peasants were forced to give up private farmland and join collective farms, which were supported by the state.

Colons French settler population in Algeria that ran the colonial government between 1830 and 1962.

Committee of Public Safety Political body during the French Revolution that was controlled by the Jacobins, who enforced party rule by executing thousands during the Reign of Terror, September 1793–July 1794.

The Communist Manifesto (1818–1883) Radical pamphlet by Karl Marx that predicted the downfall of the capitalist system and its replacement by a system that operated in the interests of the working class (proletariat).

Compromise of 1867 Agreement between the Habsburgs and the peoples living in Hungarian parts of the empire that the Habsburg state would be officially known as the Austro-Hungarian Empire.

concession areas Territories, usually ports, established by the 1842 Treaty of Nanjing, where Chinese emperors allowed European merchants to trade and European people to settle.

Congo Independent State Large colonial state in Africa created by Leopold II, king of Belgium, during the 1880s, and ruled by him alone. After reports of mass slaughter and enslavement, the Belgian parliament took the land and formed a Belgian colony.

Congress of Vienna (1814–1815) International conference to reorganize Europe after the downfall of Napoleon. European monarchies agreed to respect each other's borders and to cooperate in guarding against future revolutions and war.

Conquistador Spanish term for "conqueror," applied to European leaders of campaigns against indigenous peoples in central and southern America.

conservativism   Reactionary mode of thinking that held that tradition, including hereditary monarchy, would dispel the divisive ideas of the Enlightenment.

Constantinople   Former capital of the Byzantine empire, eventually renamed Istanbul after its conquest by the Ottomans in 1453.

Constitutional Convention (1787)   Meeting to formulate the Constitution of the United States of America.

Nicholas Copernicus (1473–1543)   Polish astronomer who advanced the radical idea that the earth moved around the sun in *De Revolutionibus*.

Corn Laws   Laws that imposed tariffs on grain imported to Great Britain, intended to protect British farming interests. The Corn Laws were abolished in 1846 as part of a British movement in favor of free trade.

Council of Trent   Intermittent meeting of Catholic leaders (1545–1563) that reaffirmed Catholic doctrine against Protestant criticisms while also reforming the church.

Counter Reformation Movement   To counter the spread of the Reformation, the Counter Reformation was initiated by the Catholic Church at the Council of Trent in 1545.

coup d'état   Overthrow of established state by a group of conspirators, usually from the military.

courtly love   Codes of refined romantic behavior between men and women of high station.

courtly romances   Long narrative poems written in vernacular languages based on myths and legends but expressing ideals of medieval aristocratic conduct.

creoles   Persons of European descent who were born in the West Indies or Spanish America.

Crimean War (1854–1856)   War waged by Russia against Great Britain and France. Spurred by Russia's encroachment on Ottoman territories, the conflict revealed Russia's military weakness when Russian forces fell to British and French troops.

Oliver Cromwell (1599–1658)   Puritan leader of the Parliamentary army that defeated the royalist forces in the English Civil War. After the 1649 execution of King Charles I and dispersion of Parliament, Cromwell ruled as self-styled Lord Protector from 1653 until his death.

Crusades (1096 to 1291)   Series of wars undertaken to free Jerusalem and the Holy Lands from Muslim control.

Cuban Missile Crisis (1962)   Diplomatic standoff between the United States and the Soviet Union that was provoked by the Soviet Union's attempt to base nuclear missiles in Cuba; it brought the world closer to nuclear war than ever before or since.

"Cult of domesticity"   Concept associated with Victorian England that idealized women as nurturing wives and mothers.

Cult of the Virgin Mary   A surge in veneration of the mother of Jesus beginning in the twelfth century that seemed to portend a change in how women were regarded as religious and moral beings.

cuneiform   One of the earliest writing systems, beginning around 3500 B.C.E., it was the Mesopotamian form of writing on clay tablets using a stylus.

Cyrus (c.585–529 B.C.E.)   The ruler of the Persians from circa 559 B.C.E. until 529 B.C.E.

Charles Darwin (1809–1882)   British naturalist who wrote *Origin of the Species* and developed the theory of natural selection to explain the evolution of organisms.

David   King of the Hebrews from around 1000 B.C.E. to 973 B.C.E. David united Israel and made Jerusalem his capital.

Leonardo da Vinci (1452–1519)   Florentine painter, architect, musician, and inventor whose breadth of interests typifies Renaissance ideals.

D-Day (June 6, 1944)   Date of the Allied invasion of Normandy under General Dwight Eisenhower to liberate Western Europe from German occupation.

Decembrists   Russian army officers who were influenced by events in France and formed secret societies that espoused liberal governance. They were put down by Nicholas I in December 1825.

Declaration of Independence   Historic U.S. document stating the principles of government on which America was founded.

Declaration of the Rights of Man and Citizen (1789)   French charter of liberties formulated by the National Assembly that marked the end of dynastic and aristocratic rule. The seventeen articles later became the preamble to the new constitution, which the Assembly finished in 1791.

Olympe de Gouges (1745–1793)   French political radical and feminist whose *Declaration of the Rights of Women* demanded an equal place for women in the new French republic.

Dhimmis   "Peoples of the Book"; i.e., Jews and Christians, who were given a protected but subordinate place in Muslim society.

Charles Dickens (1812–1870)   Hugely popular English novelist whose fiction exposed urban crime, poverty, and injustice but maintained Victorian domestic ideals.

Dien Bien Phu (1954)   Defining battle in the war between French colonialists and the Viet Minh that secured North Vietnam for Ho Chi Minh and his army and left the south to form its own government to be supported by France and the United States.

The Diet of Worms   Examination of Luther by a church council in 1521. The council condemned him, and Luther was rescued by Frederick of Saxony.

Directory   Temporary military committee that took over the affairs of the state of France in 1795 from the radicals and held control until the coup of Napoleon Bonaparte.

Discourse on Method   Philosophical treatise by René Descartes (1596–1650) proposing that the path to knowledge was through logical speculation, beginning with one's own self: "I think, therefore I am."

Divine Comedy   Italian verse narrative by Dante Alighieri (1265–1321); its complex themes exemplify the concerns of medieval learning.

DNA (deoxyribonucleic acid)   Discovered by James Watson and Francis Crick in 1953, DNA contains an organism's genetic information and hereditary characteristics.

Dominion in the British Commonwealth   Canadian promise to keep up their fealty to the British crown, even after their independence in 1867. Later applied to Australia and New Zealand.

Don Quixote   Comical adventure by Spanish writer Miguel de Cervantes (1547–1616) that mocks chivalric ideas.

Dreyfus Affair   The 1894 French scandal surrounding accusations that a Jewish captain, Alfred Dreyfus, sold military secrets to the Germans. Convicted, Dreyfus was sentenced to life in prison. However, after public outcry, it was revealed that the trial documents were forgeries and Dreyfus was released.

Il Duce   Term designating the fascist Italian leader Benito Mussolini.

Duma   The Russian parliament.

Dunkirk   The French port on the English Channel where the British and French forces retreated after sustaining heavy losses against the German military. Between May 27 and June 4, 1940, the Royal Navy evacuated over three hundred thousand troops using commercial and pleasure boats.

Earth Summit (1992)   Meeting in Rio de Janeiro between many of the world's governments in an effort to address international environmental problems.

Eastern Front   Battlefront between Berlin and Moscow during World War I and World War II.

East India Company (1600–1858)   British charter company created to outperform Portuguese and Spanish traders in the Far East; in the eighteenth century the company became, in effect, the ruler of a large part of India. There was also a Dutch East India Company.

Edict of Nantes (1598)   Edict issued by Henry IV to end the French Wars of Religion. The edict declared France a Catholic country, but tolerated some Protestant worship.

Eiffel Tower   Named after its creator, Gustave Eiffel, the tower was completed in 1889 for the Paris Exposition. This steel monument was twice the height of any other building at the time.

Albert Einstein (1879–1955)   German physicist who developed the theory of relativity, which states that space and motion are relative to each other instead of being absolute.

Elizabeth I (1533–1603)   Protestant daughter of Henry VIII, Queen of England 1558–1603. During her long reign, the doctrines and services of the Church of England were defined and the Spanish Armada was defeated.

Enabling Act (1933)   Emergency act passed by the *Reichstag* (German parliament) that helped transform Hitler from Germany's chancellor, or prime minister, into a dictator, following the suspicious burning of the *Reichstag* building and a suspension of civil liberties.

enclosure   Long process of privatizing what had been public agricultural land in the eighteenth century that changed the nature of economic activity in England.

The Encyclopedia   Joint venture of French *philosophe* writers, helmed by Denis Diderot (1713–1784), which proposed to summarize all modern knowledge.

Endeavor   Ship of Captain James Cook, whose widely celebrated voyages to the South Pacific at the end of the eighteenth century supplied Europe with information about the plants, birds, landscapes, and people of this uncharted territory.

Friedrich Engels (1820–1895)   German social and political philosopher who collaborated with Karl Marx on many publications.

English Navigation Act of 1651   Act stipulating that only English ships could carry goods between the mother country and its colonies.

Enlightenment   Intellectual movement stressing natural laws and classifications in nature, in eighteenth-century Europe.

Epicureanism   Greek philosophy that emphasized the individual, denied the existence of spiritual forces, and proposed that the highest good is pleasure.

Desiderius Erasmus (c. 1469–1536)   Dutch-born scholar and social commentator who proclaimed his humanist views in lively treatises like *In Praise of Folly* and the *Colloquies*.

Estates-General   French quasi-parliamentary body called in 1789 to deal with the financial problems that afflicted France at the time. It had not met since 1614.

Etruscans   Non-Indo-European-speaking settlers of the Italian peninsula who dominated the region from the late Bronze Age until the rise of the Romans in the sixth century B.C.E.

Euclid   Hellenistic mathematician whose book *Elements of Geometry* was the basis of modern geometry.

eugenics   Term, meaning "good birth," referring to the project of "breeding" a superior human race. It was popularly championed by scientists, politicians, and social critics in the late nineteenth and early twentieth centuries.

Eurasia   The combined area of Europe and Asia.

European Union (EU)   An international political body that was organized after World War II to reconcile Germany and the rest of Europe as well as to forge closer industrial cooperation. Over time, member states of the EU have relinquished some of their sovereignty, and cooperation has evolved into a community with a single currency, the euro, and a common European parliament.

Exclusion Act of 1882   U.S. congressional act prohibiting nearly all immigration from China to the United States; fueled by animosity toward Chinese workers in the American West.

Existentialism   The philosophy that arose out of World War II and emphasized the human condition. Led by Jean Paul Sartre and Albert Camus, existentialists encouraged humans to take responsibility for their own decisions and dilemmas.

Fascists   Radical right-wing group of the disaffected that formed around Mussolini in 1919 and a few years later came to power in Italy.

February Revolution (1917)   The first of two uprisings of the Russian Revolution, which led to the end of the Romanov dynasty.

Federal Deposit Insurance Corporation (FDIC)   Created in 1933 to guarantee all bank deposits up to $2,000 as part of the New Deal in the United States.

Federalists   Supporters of the ratification of the U.S. Constitution, which was written to replace the Articles of Confederation.

Federal Republic of Germany (1949–1990)   Country formed of the areas occupied by the Allies after World War II. Also known as West Germany, this country experienced rapid demilitarization, democratization, and integration into the world economy.

Federal Reserve Act (1913)   U.S. legislation that created a series of boards to monitor the supply and demand of the nation's money.

Feminine Mystique Groundbreaking book by feminist Betty Friedan (b. 1921), which tried to define "femininity" and explored how women internalized those definitions.

Fertile Crescent An area of fertile land in what is now Syria, Israel, Turkey, eastern Iraq, and western Iran that was able to sustain settlements due to its wetter climate and abundant natural food resources. Some of the earliest known civilizations emerged there between 9000 and 4500 B.C.E.

feudalism A loose term reflecting the political and economic situation in eleventh- and twelfth-century Europe. In this system, lords were owed agricultural labor and military service by their serfs, and in turn owed allegiance to more powerful lords and kings.

First Crusade (1095–1099) Forces were sent by Pope Urban II to assist Byzantine emperor Alexius Comnenus in fighting Turkish forces in Anatolia. The struggle to recapture Jerusalem for western Christianity was eventually successful. This crusade prompted attacks against Jews throughout Europe and resulted in six subsequent military campaigns to the Holy Land.

First World War A total war from August 1914 to November 1918, involving the armies of Britain, France, and Russia (the Allies) against Germany, Austria-Hungary, and the Ottoman empire (the Central Powers). Italy joined the Allies in 1915, and the United States joined them in 1917, helping to tip the balance in favor of the Allies, who also drew upon the populations and material of their colonial possessions. Also known as the Great War.

Five-Year Plan Soviet effort launched under Stalin in 1928 to replace the market with a state-owned and state-managed economy in order to promote rapid economic development over a five-year period and thereby "catch and overtake" the leading capitalist countries. The First Five-Year Plan was followed by the Second Five-Year Plan (1933–1937), and so on, until the collapse of the Soviet Union in 1991.

Flagellants European social group that came into existence during the bubonic plague in the fourteenth century; they believed that the plague was caused by the wrath of God and chose to beat and mutilate themselves as a form of religious penance.

Franciscan order Order of monks established in 1209 by Saint Francis of Assisi (1182–1226); its members strove to imitate the life and example of Jesus.

Frankfurt Assembly An 1848 gathering of delegates from all German states that attempted to unify them into one nation. The liberal agenda and squabbling over whose plan for the nation was best led to the failure of the gathering.

Franz Ferdinand (1863–1914) Archduke of Austria and heir to the Austro-Hungarian empire; his assassination led to the beginning of World War I.

Frederick the Great (1740–1786) Prussian ruler who engaged the nobility in maintaining a strong military and bureaucracy, and led Prussian armies to notable military victories. He also encouraged Enlightenment rationalism and artistic endeavors.

French New Wave A group of filmmakers in the 1950s and 1960s that emphasized naturalistic and unsentimental portrayals of ordinary life. Famous New Wave directors included Francois Truffaut (1932–1984), Jean-Luc Godard (b. 1930), and Eric Rohmer (b. 1920).

French Revolution of 1848 Brief uprising caused by economic grievances; it was violently quelled by the government.

Sigmund Freud (1865–1939) The Austrian physician who founded the discipline of psychoanalysis and suggested that human behavior was largely motivated by unconscious and irrational forces.

Front de Libération Nationale (FLN)/Algerian Revolutionary National Liberation Front An anti-colonial, nationalist party that waged an eight-year war, beginning in 1954, against French troops for Algerian independence; the war forced nearly all of the 1 million French colonists to leave.

Galileo Galilei (1564–1642) Italian physicist and inventor. The implications of his ideas raised the ire of the Catholic Church, and he was forced to retract most of his findings.

Mohandas K. (Mahatma) Gandhi (1869–1948) The Indian leader who advocated nonviolent noncooperation and helped win home rule for India in 1947.

Giuseppe Garibaldi (1807–1882) Italian revolutionary leader who led the fight to free Sicily and Naples from the Habsburg empire; the lands were then peaceably annexed by Sardinia.

garrisons Military bases inside cities that were often used for political purposes, such as protecting the rulers and putting down domestic revolt or enforcing colonial rule.

Gaul The region of the Roman empire that is modern Belgium, Germany west of the Rhine, and France.

Gdansk shipyard Site of mass strikes in Poland that led to the formation in 1980 of the first independent trade union, Solidarity, in the Communist bloc.

Geneva Peace Conference (1954) International conference to restore peace in Korea and Indochina. The chief participants were the United States, the Soviet Union, Great Britain, France, the People's Republic of China, North Korea, South Korea, Vietnam, the Viet Minh party, Laos, and Cambodia. The conference resulted in the division of North and South Vietnam.

German Democratic Republic Nation founded from the Soviet zone of occupation of Germany after World War II; also known as East Germany.

German Social Democratic Party Founded in 1875, it was the most powerful Socialist party in Europe before 1917.

Gilgamesh The hero of the Sumerian epic, which was recorded in written form around 2000 B.C.E. Gilgamesh was a powerful ruler who, along with his friend Enkidu, battled monsters and gods and searched for immortality.

Girondins Liberal revolutionary group that supported the creation of a constitutional monarchy during the early stages of the French Revolution.

globalization The term used to describe political, social, and economic networks that span the globe. These global exchanges are not limited by nation states and often rely on new technologies, international laws, and economic imperatives.

Arthur de Gobineau (1816–1882) French writer whose pseudoscientific, racist ideology provided a rationale for European imperialism.

Gold Coast   Name that European mariners and merchants gave to that part of West Equatorial Africa from which gold and slaves were exported. Originally controlled by the Portuguese, this area later became the British colony of the Gold Coast.

Gothic style   Period of graceful architecture emerging after the Romanesque style in twelfth- and thirteenth-century France. The style is characterized by pointed arches, delicate decoration, and large windows.

Great Depression   Period following the U.S. stock market crash on October 29, 1929, and ending in 1941 with America's entry into World War II.

great divide   Refers to the division between economically developed nations and less developed nations.

Great East Asia Co-Prosperity Sphere   Term used by the Japanese during the 1930s and 1940s to refer to Hong Kong, Singapore, Malaya, Burma, and other states that they seized during their run for expansion.

The "Great Terror"   The systematic murder of nearly a million people and the deportation of another million and a half to labor camps by Stalin's regime during 1937 in an attempt to consolidate power and remove perceived enemies.

The Great War (1914–1918)   World War I.

Greek Civil War (1821–1827)   Conflict between Greek Christians and Muslim Ottomans.

Pope Gregory I (540?–604)   Roman Catholic Pope 590–604. Used his political influence and theological teachings to separate the western Latin from the eastern Greek church. He also encouraged the Benedictine monastic movement and missionary expeditions.

Guerillas   Portuguese and Spanish peasant bands who resisted the revolutionary and expansion efforts of Napoléon; after the French word for war, *guerre.*

Guernica   The Basque town bombed by German planes in April 1937 during the Spanish Civil War. It is also the subject of Pablo Picasso's famous painting from the same year.

guest workers   Migrants looking for temporary employment.

guilds   Professional organizations in commercial towns that regulated the business conditions and privileges of those practicing a particular craft.

gulag   The vast system of forced labor camps under the Soviet regime; it originated in 1919 in a small monastery near the Arctic Circle and spread throughout the Soviet Union and to other Soviet-style socialist countries. Penal labor was required of both ordinary criminals and those accused of political crimes (counterrevolution, anti-Soviet agitation).

Gulf War (1991)   Armed conflict between Iraq and a coalition of thirty-two nations, including the United States, Britain, Egypt, France, and Saudi Arabia. The seeds of the war were planted with Iraq's invasion of Kuwait on August 2, 1990.

Habsburg empire   Ruling house of Austria, which once ruled the Netherlands, Spain, and Central Europe but came to settle in lands along the Danube River. It played a prominent role in European affairs for many centuries. In 1867, the Habsburg empire was reorga-nized into the Austro-Hungarian Dual Monarchy, and in 1918 it collapsed.

Hadith   Sayings attributed to the Prophet Muhammad and his early converts. Used to guide the behavior of Muslim peoples.

Hagia Sophia   The largest house of worship in all of Christendom, located in Constantinople and built by the emperor Justinian. When Constantinople fell to Ottoman forces in 1453, it was turned into a mosque.

Hajj   The pilgrimage to Mecca; an obligation for Muslims.

Hammurabi   The ruler of Babylon from 1792 to 1750 B.C.E. Hammurabi issued a collection of laws that were greatly influential in the Near East for centuries.

harem   Secluded women's quarters in Muslim households.

Harlem Renaissance   Cultural movement in the 1920s that was based in Harlem, a part of New York City where a large African American population resided. The movement gave voice to black novelists, poets, painters, and musicians, many of whom used their art to protest racial subordination; also referred to as the "New Negro Movement."

Henry VIII (1491–1547)   Oft-married English monarch who broke with the Roman Catholic church when the pope refused to grant him an annulment. The resulting modified version of Christianity became the Church of England, or Anglicanism.

Henry of Navarre (1553–1610)   Crowned King Henry IV of France, he renounced his Protestantism but granted limited toleration to Huguenots (French Protestants) with the 1598 Edict of Nantes.

Prince Henry the Navigator (1394–1460)   Portuguese noble who encouraged conquest of western Africa and trade in gold and slaves.

hero cults   Important ancient Greek families would claim that an impressive Mycenean tomb was that of their own famous ancestor and would practice sacrifices and other observances to strengthen their claim. This devotion could extend to their followers, and eventually whole communities would identify with such local heroes.

Hiroshima   Japanese port devastated by an atomic bomb on August 6, 1945.

Adolf Hitler (1889–1945)   The author of *Mein Kampf* and leader of the Nazis. Hitler and his Nazi regime started World War II and orchestrated the systematic murder of over five million Jews.

Hittites   An Indo-European-speaking people that migrated into Anatolia (now Turkey) around the beginning of the second millennium B.C.E.

Ho Chi Minh (1890–1969)   The Vietnamese communist resistance leader who drove the French out of Vietnam and controlled North Vietnam after the Geneva Accords divided the region into four countries.

Holy Roman Empire   The collection of lands in central and western Europe ruled over by the kings of Germany (and later Austria) from the twelfth century until 1806.

Holy Russia   Name applied to Muscovy, and then to the Russian empire, by Slavic Eastern Orthodox clerics who were appalled by the Muslim conquest in 1453 of Constantinople (the capital of

Byzantium and of Eastern Christianity), and who were hopeful that Russia would become the new protector of the faith.

home charges   Fees India was forced to pay to Britain as its colonial master; these fees included interest on railroad loans, salaries to colonial officers, and the maintenance of imperial troops outside India.

Homo sapiens   Term defined by Linnaeus in 1737 and commonly used to refer to fully modern human beings.

hoplite   A Greek foot soldier armed with a spear or short sword and protected by a large round shield (a hopla). In battle, hoplites stood shoulder to shoulder in a close formation called a phalanx.

Huguenots   French Protestants who endured severe persecution in the sixteenth and seventeenth centuries.

Human Comedy   Masterpiece of French novelist Honoré de Balzac (1799–1850) that criticized materialist values.

humanism   Medieval program of study built around the seven liberal arts: grammer, logic, rhetoric, arithmetic, music, geometry, and astronomy.

Hundred Years' War (1337–1453)   Long conflict, fought mostly on French soil, between England and France, centering on English claims to the throne of France.

Saddam Hussein (b. 1937)   The former dictator of Iraq who invaded Iran in 1980 and started the eight-year-long Iran-Iraq War; invaded Kuwait in 1990, which caused the Gulf War of 1991; and was overthrown when the United States invaded Iraq in 2003. Involved in Iraqi politics since the mid-1960s, Hussein became the official head of state in 1979.

Il-khanate   Mongol-founded dynasty in thirteenth-century Persia.

Imam   Muslim religious leader and also a politico-religious descendant of Ali; believed by some to have a special relationship with Allah.

Imhotep   The chief adviser to the Pharaoh Djoser, who ruled in the 27th century B.C.E. Often considered to be the first architect, Imhotep designed tombs and other structures to express the power of the Egyptian pharaohs.

Indian National Congress   Formed in 1885, this political party was deeply committed to constitutional methods, industrialization, and cultural nationalism.

Indo-Europeans   A group of people that spoke variations of the same language and moved into the Near East and Mediterranean shortly after 2000 B.C.E.

indulgences   Remissions of the penances owed by Catholics as part of the process by which their sins are forgiven.

Inquisition   Tribunal of the Roman Catholic Church that aimed to enforce religious orthodoxy and conformity.

International Monetary Fund (IMF)   Established in 1945 to promote the health of the world economy, the IMF is a specialized agency of the United Nations.

Intifada   Uprising in the Palestinian occupied territories from 1987 to 1993, in protest against the Israeli occupation and politics. The Oslo Agreement (1993) helped to reduce the tension between the two sides and the Intifada all but ceased by the end of 1993. In early 2000, the Intifada resumed.

Investiture Conflict   A disagreement between Pope Gregory VII and Emperor Henry IV of Germany that tested the power of kings over church matters. After years of diplomatic and military hostility, it was settled by the Concordat of Worms in 1122.

invisible hand   Described in Adam Smith's *The Wealth of Nations*, the idea that the operations of a free market would produce economic efficiency and economic benefits for all.

Irish Home Rule   The late-nineteenth- and early-twentieth-century movement, led by Sinn Fein (established 1905), for Irish self-government.

Irish potato famine   Period of agricultural blight from 1845 to 1849 whose devastating results prompted a mass emigration to America.

Iron Curtain   Term coined by Winston Churchill in 1946 to refer to the division of Western Europe, under American influence, from Eastern Europe, under the domination of the Soviet Union.

Ivan the Great (1440–1505)   Emperor of Russia who annexed neighboring territories and began Russia's career as a European power.

Jacobins   Radical French political group that came into existence during the French Revolution, executed the French king, and sought to remake French culture.

Jacquerie   Violent 1358 peasant uprising in northern France, incited by disease, war, and taxes.

James I (1566–1625)   Monarch of Scotland and England from 1603 to 1625. He oversaw the English vernacular translation of the Bible known by his name.

Janissaries   Corps of enslaved soldiers recruited as children from the Christian provinces of the Ottoman empire and brought up with intense loyalty to the Ottoman state and its sultan. The sultan used these forces to curb local autonomy and to serve as his personal bodyguards.

Jesuits   Religious order founded in 1540 by Ignatius Loyola to counter the inroads of the Protestant Reformation; the Jesuits were active in politics, education, and missionary work.

Jihad   A struggle and, if need be, a holy war toward the advancement of the cause of Islam.

Joan of Arc (c. 1412–1431)   French teenager, supposedly divinely inspired, who led forces against the English during the Hundred Years' War. Burned at the stake for heresy by the English and later made a Catholic saint.

Justinian (527–565)   Emperor of eastern Rome. Justinian codified Roman law in the Corpus Juris Civilis and tried to reunify the eastern and western halves of the old Roman empire.

Das Kapital **(Capital)**   The 1867 book by Karl Marx that outlined the theory behind historical materialism and attacked the socioeconomic inequities of capitalism. Mixing economic theory and revolutionary politics, the book became the preeminent socialist critique of capitalism.

Johannes Kepler (1571–1601)   Mathematician and astronomer who elaborated on and corrected Copernicus's theory and is chiefly remembered for his discovery of the three laws of planetary motion that bear his name.

GLOSSARY

Keynesian Revolution Post-Depression economic ideas developed by the British economist John Maynard Keynes, wherein the state took a greater role in managing the economy, stimulating it by increasing the money supply and creating jobs.

KGB Soviet political police and spy agency, first formed as the Cheka not long after the Bolshevik coup in October 1917. It grew to more than 750,000 operatives with military rank by the 1980s.

Chingiz Khan (c. 1167–1227) Title taken by Mongol chief Temujin meaning "The Oceanic Ruler." Began dynasty that conquered much of southern Asia.

Khanate Major political unit of the vast Mongol empire. There were four Khanates, including the Yuan empire in China, forged by Chingiz Khan's grandson Kubilai in the 13th century.

Nikita Khrushchev (1894–1971) Leader of the Soviet Union during the Cuban Missile Crisis, Khrushchev had quickly reached power soon after Stalin's death in 1953. His reforms and criticisms of the excesses of the Stalin regime led to his fall from power in 1964.

Kremlin Once synonymous with the Soviet government, it refers to Moscow's walled city center.

Kristallnacht The Nazi destruction of seventy-five hundred Jewish stores and two hundred synagogues on November 9, 1938.

kulaks Originally a pejorative term used to designate better-off peasants, it was used in the late 1920s and early 1930s to refer to any peasant, rich or poor, perceived as an opponent of the Soviet regime. Russian for "fist."

Labour Party Founded in Britain in 1900, this party represented workers and was based on socialist principles.

League of Nations International organization founded after World War I to solve international disputes through arbitration; it was dissolved in 1946 and transferred its assets to the United Nations.

Nikolai Lenin (1870–1924) Leader of the Bolshevik Revolution in Russia (1917) and the first leader of the Soviet Union.

Leopold II (1835–1909) Belgian king who sponsored colonizing expeditions into Africa.

Leviathan A book by Thomas Hobbes (1588–1679) that recommended a ruler have unrestricted power.

liberalism Political and social theory that advocates representative government, free trade, and freedom of speech and religion.

lithograph Art form that involves putting writing or design on stone and producing printed impressions.

Long March (1934–1935) Trek of over 10,000 kilometers by Mao Zedong and his Communist followers to establish a new base of operations.

lord Privileged landowner who exercised authority over the people who lived on his land.

lost generation Refers to the 17 million former members of the Red Guard and other Chinese youth who were denied education from the late 1960s to the mid-1970s as part of the Chinese government's attempt to forestall political disruptions.

Louis XIV (1638–1715) The "Sun King," known for his opulent court and absolutist political style.

Louis XVI (1754–1793) Well-meaning but ineffectual king of France, finally deposed and executed with his family by revolutionaries.

Luftwaffe Literally "air weapon," this is the name of the German air force, which was founded during World War I, disbanded in 1945, and reestablished when West Germany joined NATO in 1950.

Lusitania The passenger liner that was secretly carrying war supplies and was sunk by a German U-boat (submarine) on May 7, 1915.

Lutheranism Branch of Protestantism that followed Martin Luther's (1483–1546) rejection of the Roman Catholic "doctrine of works."

lycées System of high schools instituted by Napoleon as part of his domestic reform campaign.

madrassas Muslim schools devoted to the study of the Quran and Islam.

Magna Carta "Great Charter" of 1215 signed by King John of England, which limited the king's fiscal powers and is seen as a landmark in the political evolution of the West.

Moses Maimonides (1135–1204) Spanish-born Jewish scholar, physician, and scriptural commentator.

Nelson Mandela (b. 1918) The South African opponent of *apartheid* who led the African National Congress and was imprisoned from 1962 until 1990. After his release from prison, he worked with Prime Minister Frederik Willem De Klerk to establish majority rule. Mandela became the first black president of South Africa in 1994.

Manhattan Project The secret U.S. government research project in Los Alamos, New Mexico, to develop the first nuclear bomb. The first test of a nuclear bomb was near Los Alamos on July 16, 1945.

manorialism System common to England, northern France, and Germany in the Middle Ages of communal peasant farming under the protection of a landholding lord.

Mao Zedong (1893–1976) The leader of the Chinese Revolution who defeated the Nationalists in 1949 and established the Communist regime in China.

Marshall Plan Economic aid package given to Europe after World War II in hopes of a rapid period of reconstruction and economic gain and to secure the countries from a Communist takeover.

Master Eckhart (c. 1260–1327) Dominican monk who preached an introspective and charismatic version of Christian piety.

Karl Marx (1818–1883) German philosopher and economist who believed that a revolution of the working classes would overthrow the capitalist order and create a classless society. Author of *Das Kapital* and *The Communist Manifesto*.

Maxim gun Invented in 1885 by an American, Hiram Maxim, the Maxim gun was the first portable machine gun. Quickly adopted by the majority of European armies and capable of firing 500 rounds per minute, it played a major role in the imperial conquests of the African continent.

Mayans Native American peoples whose culturally and politically sophisticated empire encompassed lands in present-day Mexico and Guatemala.

Giuseppe Mazzini (1805–1872) Founder of Young Italy and an ideological leader of the Italian Nationalist movement.

Mecca Major commercial city of the Arabian peninsula in the sixth century C.E., at which time the founder of Islam, Muhammad, was born and achieved prominence. From the earliest days of the spread of Islam, the city was the destination of the chief religious pilgrimage for Muslims, and it is now considered the holiest site in the Islamic world.

Medici Dynasty of Florentine bankers and politicians known for their patronage of the arts.

Meiji empire Empire created under the leadership of Mutsuhito, emperor of Japan from 1868 until 1912. During the Meiji period Japan became a world industrial and naval power.

Menander (342 B.C.E.?–292 B.C.E.) Ancient Greek dramatist who wrote over 100 plays, many of which were standards of Western literature for hundreds of years. Only one complete surviving play is known, *The Grouch*, which was rediscovered in 1957.

mercantilism A popular Western belief between 1600 and 1800 that a country's wealth and power was based on a favorable balance of trade (more exports and fewer imports) and the accumulation of precious metals.

Michelangelo (1475–1564) Virtuoso artist, best known for the Sistine Chapel ceiling in Rome and his sculptures *David* and *Pieta*.

John Stuart Mill (1806–1873) English radical philosopher whose writings advocated aspects of socialism and civil liberties.

Slobodan Milosevic (b. 1941) The Serbian nationalist politician who took control of the Serb government and orchestrated the genocide of thousands of Croatians, Bosnian Muslims, Albanians, and Kosovars. After ten years of war, he was ousted by a popular revolt in 2000.

Minoans A sea empire that flourished on Crete and in the Aegean Basin from 1900 B.C.E. until the middle of the second millennium B.C.E.

Modernism The series of artistic movements, manifestos, innovations, and experiments that redefined art in the first half of the twentieth century. Modernism rejected history and tradition in favor of expressive and experimental freedom.

Michel de Montaigne (1533–1592) French philosopher known for his *Essays*.

mosque Place of worship for the people of Islam.

Wolfgang Amadeus Mozart (1756–1791) Austrian child prodigy and composer of instrumental music and operas.

Muhammad (570–632 C.E.) The founder of Islam, he claimed to be the prophet whom God (Allah) had chosen for his final revelation to mankind.

Mullahs Iranian religious leaders who led the opposition movement against the shah and denounced the depravity of late-twentieth-century American materialism and secularism.

multinational corporations Corporations based in many different countries that have global investment, trading, and distribution goals.

Muslim Brotherhood Egyptian organization founded in 1938 by Hassan al-Banna. It attacked liberal democracy as a façade for middle-class, business, and landowning interests and fought for a return to a purified form of Islam.

Muslim League National Muslim party of India.

Benito Mussolini (1883–1945) The Italian founder of the Fascist party who came to power in Italy in 1922 and allied himself with Hitler and the Nazis during World War II.

Mutiny of 1857 Uprising of Indian soldiers against the ruling British, sometimes called the Sepoy Rebellion.

Mycenaens The ancient Greek civilization that settled in Greece during the second millennium B.C.E. and organized around powerful citadels.

Nagasaki Second Japanese city on which the United States dropped an atomic bomb. The attack took place on August 9, 1945; the Japanese surrendered shortly thereafter, ending World War II.

Napoleonic Code Legal code drafted by Napoleon in 1804; it distilled different legal traditions to create one uniform law. The code confirmed the abolition of feudal privileges of all kinds and set the conditions for exercising property rights.

National Assembly of France Governing body of France that succeeded the Estates-General in 1789 during the French Revolution. It was composed of, and defined by, the delegates of the Third Estate.

National Association for the Advancement of Colored People (NAACP) Founded in 1910, this U.S. civil rights organization was dedicated to ending inequality and segregation for black Americans.

Nationalism Movement to unify a country based on a people's common history and social traditions.

NATO The North Atlantic Treaty Organization, which was a 1949 agreement between the United States, Canada, Great Britain, and 8 European countries that declared that an armed attack against any one of the members would be regarded as an attack against all. Other European countries have since joined.

"navvies" Slang for laborers who built railroads and canals.

Nazi Party Founded in the early 1920s, the National Socialist German Workers' Party (NDSAP) gained control over Germany under the leadership of Adolf Hitler in 1933 and continued in power until Germany was defeated in 1945.

Nefertiti The wife of Akhenaten, the fourteenth-century B.C.E. Egyptian pharaoh.

Neolithic The "New" Stone Age, which began around 11,000 B.C.E., saw new technological and social developments, including managed food production, the beginnings of semipermanent and permanent settlements, and the rapid intensification of trade.

New Deal President Franklin Delano Roosevelt's package of government reforms that were enacted during the 1930s to provide jobs for the unemployed, social welfare programs for the poor, and security to the financial markets.

new imperialism Expansion of colonial power by Western European nations, especially in Asia, in the last three decades of the nineteenth century.

Isaac Newton (1642–1727) One of the foremost scientists of all time, Newton was an English mathematician and physicist; he is noted for his development of calculus, work on the properties of light, and theory of gravitation.

Nicholas I (1796–1855) Russian tsar who executed the leaders of the 1825 December Revolution and pursued an absolutist reign.

Tsar Nicholas II (1868–1918) The last Russian tsar, who abdicated the throne in 1917. He and his family were executed by the Bolsheviks on July 17, 1918.

Nicomachean Ethics The treatise on moral philosophy by Aristotle, which teaches that the highest good consists of the harmonious functioning of the individual human mind and body.

Friedrich Nietzsche (1844–1900) The German philosopher who denied the possibility of knowing absolute "truth" or "reality," since all knowledge comes filtered through linguistic, scientific, or artistic systems of representation. He also criticized Judeo-Christian morality for instilling a repressive conformity that drained civilization of its vitality.

Non-governmental organizations (NGOs) Private organizations like the Red Cross that play a large role in international affairs.

North American Free Trade Agreement (NAFTA) Treaty negotiated in the early 1990s to promote free trade among Canada, the United States, and Mexico.

Novum Organum Work by English statesman and scientist Francis Bacon (1561–1626) that advanced a philosophy of study through observation.

OPEC (Organization of Petroleum Exporting Countries) Organization created in 1960 by oil-producing countries in the Middle East, South America, and Africa to regulate the production and pricing of crude oil.

Operation Barbarossa The codename for Hitler's invasion of the Soviet Union.

Opium War (1839–1842) War fought between the British and Qing China to protect British trade in opium; resulted in the ceding of Hong Kong to the British.

Oracle at Delphi Dating to 1400 B.C.E., the oracle was the most important shrine in ancient Greece. A priestess of Apollo who attended the shrine was believed to be able to predict the future. The shrine ceased to function in the fourth century C.E.

Ottoman slavery Social system of using slave labor for domestic, administrative, and military work that permitted social advancement and religious diversity within the Muslim empire.

Pan-African Conference 1900 assembly in London which sought to draw attention to the sovereignty of African people and their mistreatment by colonial powers.

Pan-Slavism Cultural movement that sought to unite native Slavic peoples within the Russian and Habsburg empires.

papal Of, relating to, or issued by a pope.

Patria Latin, meaning "fatherland."

patricians The uppermost elite class of ancient Rome.

Paul One of the twelve apostles of Jesus, Paul spread Christianity throughout the Near East and Greece.

Pearl Harbor The American Navy base in Hawaii that was bombed by the Japanese on December 7, 1941, which brought the United States into World War II.

Peloponnesian War The ancient Greek war between Sparta and Athens that began in 431 B.C.E. and ended with the destruction of the Athenian fleet in 404 B.C.E.

People's Charter An action of the Chartist Movement (1839–1848); between 1839 and 1842 over 3 million British signed this document calling for universal suffrage for adult males, the secret ballot, electoral districts, and annual parliamentary elections.

Perestroika Introduced by Soviet leader Mikhail Gorbachev in June 1987, Perestroika was the name given to economic and political reforms begun earlier in his tenure. It restructured the state bureaucracy, reduced the privileges of the political elite, and instituted a shift from the centrally planned economy to a mixed economy, combining planning with the operation of market forces.

Pericles The fifth-century B.C.E. Athenian leader who served as strategos for thirty years and pushed through reforms to make Athens more democratic by giving every citizen the right to propose and amend legislation and making it easier for citizens to participate in the assembly and the great appeals court of Athens by paying an average day's wage for attendance.

Peterloo Massacre (1819) The killing of 11 and wounding of 460 following a peaceful demonstration for political reform by workers in Manchester, England.

Peter the Great (1672–1725) Energetic tsar who transformed Russia into a leading European country by centralizing government, modernizing the army, creating a navy, and reforming education and the economy.

Francesco Petrarch (1304–1374) Italian scholar and writer who revived interest in classical writing styles and was famed for his love sonnets.

Pharisees A group of Jewish teachers and preachers that emerged in the third century B.C.E. and insisted that all of Yahweh's (God's) commandments were binding on all Jews.

Philip II (382–336 B.C.E.) The Macedonian king who consolidated the southern Balkans and the Greek city-states; he was the father of Alexander.

Phoenicians The semitic-speaking residents of present-day Lebanon from around 1200 to 800 B.C.E. The Phoenician cities were centers for trade throughout the Mediterranean.

Plato's Republic The first systematic treatment of political philosophy ever written, it argued for an elitist state in which most people would be governed by intellectually superior "philosopher-kings."

plebians The citizen population of ancient Rome that included farmers, merchants, and the urban poor; plebians comprised the majority of the population.

Plotinus (204–270 C.E.) The neo-Platonist philosopher who taught that everything that exists proceeds from the divine and that the highest goal of life should be the mystic reunion of the soul with the divine, which can be achieved through contemplation and asceticism.

Polis One of the major political innovations of the ancient Greeks was the Polis, or city-state. They were independent social

---

and political structures, organized around an urban center, containing markets, meeting places, and a temple; they controlled a limited amount of the surrounding territory.

Marco Polo (1254–1324) Venetian merchant who traveled through Asia for twenty years and published his observations in a widely read memoir, *Travels*.

Populists Members of a political movement that supported U.S. farmers in late nineteenth-century America. The term is often used generically to refer to political groups who appeal to the mass of the population.

potato famine (1845–1850) Severe famine in Ireland that led to the migration of large numbers of Irish to the United States.

Prague Spring A period of political liberalization in Czechoslovakia between January and August 1968 that was initiated by Alexander Dubček, the Czech leader. This period of expanding freedom and openness in this Eastern bloc nation ended on August 20, when the USSR and Warsaw Pact countries invaded with 200,000 troops and 5,000 tanks.

The Praise of Folly 1511 satire by Erasmus that attacked the corruption of the papacy.

Pre-Socratics A group of philosophers on the Greek island of Miletus, including Thales, Anaximander, and Anaximenes, who raised questions about the relationship between the natural world, the gods, and humans, and formulated rational theories to explain the physical universe they observed.

Primitivism Movement in Western art forms in the late nineteenth and early twentieth centuries that used the so-called primitive art forms of Africa, Oceania, and pre-Columbian America to inspire a break with the established art world.

The Prince Influential treatise by Niccolo Machiavelli (1469–1527) that attempts to lay out methods to secure and maintain political power.

Protestantism Division of Christianity that emerged in sixteenth-century western Europe at the time of the Reformation. It focused on individual spiritual needs and rejected the social authority of the papacy and the Catholic clergy.

Ptolemy (c. 85–165 C.E.) One of the most influential ancient Greeks; he was a leading astronomer, mathematician, and geographer who lived his entire life in Alexandria and helped to transform that city into a center of scientific study and scholarship.

puppet states Governments that have little power in the international arena and follow the dictates of their more powerful neighbors or patrons.

Puritans Seventeenth-century reform group of the Church of England; also known as dissenters or nonconformists.

Quran (often Koran) Islam's holy book, comprised of Allah's revelations.

Sayyid Qutb (1906–1966) The Egyptian critic who became one of the most important intellectual leaders of the Muslim Brotherhood and whose writings are often cited as philosophical inspiration for Osama bin Laden and other Islamic radicals.

François Rabelais (c. 1494?–1553) French humanist satirist best known for his crudely comic *Gargantua and Pantagruel*, in which he espouses the "eat, drink, and be merry" lifestyle. Originally a novice in the Franciscan order, later a Benedictine monk who left the order to study medicine, Rabelais spent time in hiding for fear of being labeled a heretic, and some of his books were banned.

radicals Widely used term in nineteenth-century Europe that referred to those individuals and political organizations that favored the total reconfiguration of Europe's old state system.

Raj Term referring to the British crown's administration of India following the end of the East India Company's rule after the Indian Mutiny of 1857.

Ramadan Ninth month of the Muslim year, during which all Muslims must fast during daylight hours.

Raphael (1483–1520) Italian painter noted for his warmly human treatment of religious subjects, particularly his Madonnas and large-figure compositions in the Vatican in Rome.

Realism Artistic and literary style which sought to portray common situations as they would appear in reality.

Realpolitik Political strategy advancing power for its own sake.

Rebellion of 1857 Indian rebellion against the English East India Company to bring religious purification, an egalitarian society, and local and communal solidarity without the interference of British rule.

Reds The Bolsheviks.

Reformation Religious and political movement in sixteenth-century Europe that led to the breakaway of Protestant groups from the Catholic Church; notable figures include Martin Luther and John Calvin.

Reich A term for the German state. The first Reich corresponded to the Holy Roman Empire (9th century to 1806), the second Reich was from 1871 to 1919, and the third Reich lasted from 1933 through May 1945.

Reign of Terror Campaign at the height of the French Revolution (1793–1794) in which violence, including systematic executions of opponents of the Revolution, was used to purge France of its "enemies" and to extend the Revolution beyond its borders; radicals executed as many as 40,000 persons who were judged enemies of the state.

Religious Peace of Augsburg 1555 settlement between factions within the Holy Roman Empire that stated a territory would follow the religion of its ruler, whether Catholic or Protestant.

Renaissance Term meaning "rebirth" that historians use to refer to the expanded cultural production of European nations between 1300 and 1600.

Restoration period (1815–1848) European movement after the defeat of Napoleon to restore Europe to its pre-French revolutionary status and to prevent radical movements from arising.

Richard II (1367–1400) King of England (r. 1377–1399), chiefly remembered for his successful resolution of the Peasants' Rebellion (1381) and as a vacillating, yet tyrannical monarch. He was deposed by his cousin Henry Bolingbroke (Henry IV) and assassinated.

Cardinal Richelieu (1585–1642) First minister to French King Louis XIII, who centralized political power and deprived the Huguenots of many rights.

Romanticism Beginning in Germany and England in the late 18th century and continuing up to the end of the 19th century, a movement in art, music, and literature that countered the rationalism of the Enlightenment by stressing a highly emotional response to nature.

Jean-Jacques Rousseau (1718–1778) Philosopher and radical political theorist whose *Social Contract* attacked privilege and inequality. One of the primary principles of Rousseau's political philosophy is that politics and morality should not be separated.

Russification Programs designed to assimilate people of over 146 dialects into the Russian empire by the tsars in the late 19th century.

Rwanda A former Belgian colony in central Africa that has been torn by ethnic violence between the Hutus and the Tutsis since before the country's independence in 1962.

Saint Bartholomew's Day Massacre Massacre of French Protestants (Huguenots) by Catholic crowds that began in Paris on August 24, 1572, spreading to other parts of France and continuing into October of that year. More than 70,000 were killed.

St. Domingue Former French Caribbean colony and site of a slave rebellion in 1791, which embroiled English and French forces until 1804, when St. Domingue was declared the independent nation of Haiti.

salons Informal gatherings of intellectuals and aristocrats that allowed discourse about Enlightenment ideas.

Santa Sophia The Byzantine church in Constantinople, constructed by emperor Justinian I in the sixth century, and famous for its dome, which rested on the keystones of four great arches.

Sappho (c. 620–c. 550 B.C.E.) One of the most famous Greek lyric poets, she wrote beautiful poetry about romantic longing and sexual lust, sometimes about men, but more often about women.

Sargon (r. 2334–2279 B.C.E.) The Akkadian leader who unified Mesopotamia.

Schlieffen Plan Devised by Count Alfred von Schlieffen in 1905 and put into operation on August 2, 1914, the Schlieffen Plan required France to be attacked first through Belgium and a quick victory to be secured so that the German army could fight Russia on the Eastern Front.

Scramble for Africa European rush to colonize parts of Africa at the end of the nineteenth century.

Second Industrial Revolution The technological developments in the last third of the nineteenth century, which that included new techniques for refining and producing steel; increased availability of electricity for industrial, commercial, and domestic use; advances in chemical manufacturing; and the creation of the internal combustion engine.

Second World Term invented during the cold war to refer to the Communist countries, as opposed to the West (or First World) and the former colonies (or Third World).

Second World War Worldwide war that began in September 1939 in Europe, and even earlier in Asia (1930s), and that pitted Britain, the United States, and especially the Soviet Union (the Allies) against Nazi Germany, Italy, and Japan (the Axis).

Seleucus (d. 280 B.C.E.) The Macedonian general who ruled the Asian territory of Alexander the Great's empire and founded Greek colonies such as Antioch and Selsucia.

Semitic The Semitic language family has the longest recorded history of any linguistic group and is the root language for most of the languages of the Middle and Near East. Ancient Semitic languages include the language of the ancient Babylonians and Assyrians, Phoenician, the classical form of Hebrew, early dialects of Aramaic, and the classical Arabic of the *Quran*.

sepoys Hindu and Muslim recruits of the East India Company's military force.

serfdom Slavery-like system of customs and laws whereby peasants were kept poor and stationary by their manor lords; it had spread throughout the West by the 10th century and its peak was the Middle Ages.

Seven Years War (1756–1763) Worldwide war that ended when Prussia defeated Austria, establishing itself as a European power, and when Britain gained control of India and many of France's colonies through the Treaty of Paris. It is known as the French and Indian War in the United States.

Shah Traditional title of Persian rulers.

Shiism One of the two main branches of Islam. Shiites recognize Ali, the fourth caliph, and his descendants as rightful rulers of the Islamic world; practiced in the Safavid empire.

Shiites An often-persecuted minority religious party within Islam that insists only descendants of Ali can have any authority over the Muslim community. Today, Shiites rule Iran and are numerous in Iraq but make up only 10 percent of the worldwide population of Islam.

Silicon Valley Valley between California's San Francisco and San Jose, known for its innovative computer and high-technology industry.

Sinn Fein The Irish revolutionary organization that formed in 1900 to fight for Irish independence.

Sino-Japanese War (1894–1895) Conflict over the control of Korea in which China was forced to cede the province of Taiwan to Japan.

Adam Smith (1723–1790) Scottish economist and philosopher who proposed that individual self-interest naturally promoted a healthy national economy. He became famous for his influential book, *The Wealth of Nations* (1776).

Social Darwinism Belief that Charles Darwin's theory of natural selection (evolution) was applicable to human societies and justified the right of the ruling classes or countries to dominate the weak.

socialism Political ideology that calls for a classless society with collective ownership of all property.

Social Security Act (1935) New Deal act that instituted old-age pensions and insurance for the unemployed in the United States.

Society of Jesus Also called the Jesuit order, a group of priests influenced by military discipline. The society was founded by Saint Ignatius of Loyola (1491–1556) and is still very active in the field of education.

Socrates (469–399 B.C.E.) The ancient Greek philosopher who emphasized the reexamination of all inherited assumptions and tried to base his philosophical speculations on sound definitions of words. He also wished to advance to a new system of truth by examining ethics rather than by studying the physical world.

Solidarity The communist bloc's first independent trade union; it was established in Poland at the Gdansk shipyard in 1980.

Solon (d. 559 B.C.E.) Elected archon in 594 B.C.E., this ancient Greek aristocrat enacted a series of political and economic reforms that made Athenian democracy possible.

Aleksandr Solzhenitsyn (b. 1918) This Soviet novelist was a critic of the Soviet regime and wrote *The Gulag Archipelago*, which was published in 1974.

Sophists Ancient Greek professional teachers who taught that sense perception was the source of all knowledge and that only particular truths could be valid for the individual knower.

South African War (1899–1902) Often called the Boer War, this conflict between the British and Dutch colonists of South Africa resulted in bringing two Afrikaner republics under the control of the British.

Soviet bloc International alliance that included the East European countries of the Warsaw Pact as well as the Soviet Union, but also came to include Cuba.

Spanish-American War (1898) War between the United States and Spain in Cuba, Puerto Rico, and the Philippines. It ended with a treaty in which the United States took over the Philippines, Guam, and Puerto Rico; Cuba won partial independence.

Spanish Armada Supposedly invincible fleet of warships sent against England by Philip II of Spain in 1588, but routed by the English and bad weather in the English Channel.

Spartiate A full citizen of Sparta who was a professional soldier of the hoplite phalanx.

spinning jenny Invention of James Hargreaves (c. 1720–1774) that revolutionized the British textile industry.

S.S. (*Schutzstaffel*) Formed in 1925 to serve as Hitler's personal security force and to guard Nazi party (NDSAP) meetings, the SS were notorious for their participation in carrying out Nazi policies.

Joseph Stalin (1879–1953) The Bolshevik leader who succeeded Lenin as the leader of the Soviet Union in 1924 and ruled until his death.

Strategic Defense Initiative (Stars Wars) Master plan initiated by President Ronald Reagan that envisioned the deployment of satellites and space missiles to insulate the United States from nuclear bombs missiles.

Stoicism The ancient Greek and Roman philosophy that held that the cosmos is an ordered whole in which all contradictions are resolved for ultimate good. Everything that happens is rigidly determined in accordance with rational purpose, and no individual is master of his or her fate. Founded in the fourth century B.C.E. and still popular well into the fifth century C.E.

Suez Canal Built in 1869 across the Isthmus of Suez to connect the Mediterranean Sea with the Red Sea and to lower the costs of international trade.

Sufism Emotional and mystical form of Islam that appealed to the common people.

sultan An Islamic political leader. In the Ottoman empire, the sultan combined a warrior ethos with an unwavering devotion to Islam.

Sumerians The civilization and people that arose in southern Mesopotamia (modern Iraq and Kuwait) around 4000 B.C.E. and developed one of the first written languages.

Sunnism Orthodox Islam, as opposed to Shiite Islam.

supranational organizations International organizations such as NGOs, the World Bank, and the IMF.

survival of the fittest A main concept of Charles Darwin's theory of natural selection (evolution), which holds that as animal populations grow and resources become scarce, a struggle for existence arises, the outcome of which is that only the "fittest" survive.

sweatshops Textile factories with poor pay and work conditions.

Syndicalism Late-nineteenth-century organization of workplace associations that included unskilled labor.

tabula rasa Term used by John Locke (1632–1704) to describe man's mind before he acquired ideas as a result of experience; Latin for "clean slate."

Testament of Youth The memoir by Vera Brittain about the home front and the changing social norms during World War I.

Tetrarchy Diocletian's political reform, which divided the Roman empire into two halves ruled by two rulers and two lieutenants.

Third Estate Delegates from the common class to the Estates General, the French legislature, whose refusal to capitulate to the nobility and clergy in 1789 led to the Revolution.

Third Reich The German state from 1933 to 1945 under Adolf Hitler and the Nazi party.

Third World Nations—mostly in Asia, Latin America, and Africa—that are not highly industrialized and developed.

Thirty Years' War (1618–1648) Beginning as a conflict between Protestants and Catholics in Germany, it escalated into a general European war fought in Germany by Sweden, France, and the Holy Roman Empire.

Tiananmen Square Largest public square in the world, located in Beijing, the site of the Chinese pro-democracy movement in 1989 that resulted in the killing of as many as 1,000 protesters by the Chinese army.

Timur the Lame (1336–1405) Mongol ruler who was the last leader of the Khans' south Asian empire. Also known as Tamerlane.

total war All-out war involving civilian populations as well as military forces, often used in reference to World War II.

Treaty of Brest-Litovsk (1918) Separate peace between imperial Germany and the new Bolshevik regime in Russia. The treaty acknowledged the German victory on the Eastern Front and withdrew Russia from the war.

Treaty of Nanjing (1842) Treaty between China and Britain following the Opium War; it called for indemnities, the opening of new ports, and the cession of Hong Kong to the British.

Treaty of Utrecht (1713) Resolution to the War of Spanish Succession that redistributed territory among the warring nations of Europe and encouraged England's colonial conquests.

Treaty of Versailles Signed on June 28, 1919, this peace settlement ended World War I and required Germany to surrender a large part of its most valuable territories and to pay huge reparations to the Allies.

trench warfare The twenty-five thousand miles of holes and ditches that stretched across the Western Front during World War I and where most of the fighting took place.

"triangular" trade   The eighteenth-century commercial Atlantic shipping pattern that took rum from New England to Africa, traded it for slaves taken to the West Indies, and brought sugar back to New England to be processed into rum.

Tripartite Pact (1940)   A pact that stated that the countries of Germany, Italy, and Japan would act together in all future military ventures.

Triple Entente   Alliance developed before World War I that eventually included Britain, France, and Russia.

Truman Doctrine (1947)   Declaration promising U.S. economic and military intervention, whenever and wherever needed, for the sake of preventing further communist expansion.

Truth and Reconciliation Commission   Quasi-judicial body established after the overthrow of the apartheid system in South Africa and the election of Nelson Mandela as the country's first black president in 1994. The commission was to take evidence about the crimes committed during the apartheid years. Those who showed remorse could appeal for clemency. The South African leaders believed that an airing of the grievances from this period would promote racial harmony and reconciliation.

tsar   Russian translation, similar to the German *kaiser*, of the Roman title "caesar" (emperor), a title claimed by the rulers of medieval Muscovy and then the Russian empire.

Mary Tudor (1516–1558)   Catholic daughter of Henry VIII who reinstituted Catholicism in England when she acceded to the throne; she was called "Bloody Mary" for her violent suppression of Protestants during her five-year reign.

Two Treatises on Government   Published in 1690, this work by John Locke (1632–1704) defended humans' right to freedom against absolutist ideas and served as one of the underpinnings of the U.S. Constitution.

Ubaid   This cultured flourished in Mesopotamia between 5500 and 4000 B.C.E., characterized by large village settlements and the first temples built in that area. A precursor to the Sumerians and the development of "urban" civilizations.

UFA   The German film company that produced films by expressionist directors like F. W. Murnau and Fritz Lang during the 1920s. Under Hitler, it was controlled by the state and began turning out Nazi propaganda.

Universal Declaration of Human Rights (1948)   United Nations declaration that laid out the rights to which all human beings were entitled.

Utopia   Humanist social critique by English statesman Thomas More (1478–1535).

utopian socialism   The most visionary of all Restoration-era movements, Utopian socialists, like Charles Fourier, dreamt of transforming states, workplaces, and human relations, and proposed actual plans to do so.

"velvet revolutions"   The peaceful political revolutions throughout Eastern Europe in 1989.

Versailles   Splendid palace outside Paris where Louis XIV and his nobles resided.

Versailles Conference (1919)   Peace conference between the victors of World War I; resulted in the Treaty of Versailles, which forced Germany to pay reparations and to give up its colonies to the victors.

Queen Victoria (1819–1901)   Influential monarch who reigned from 1837 to her death; she presided over the expansion of the British empire as well as the evolution of English politics and social and economic reforms.

Viet Cong   Vietnamese communist group formed in 1954; committed to overthrowing the government of South Vietnam and reunifying North and South Vietnam.

A Vindication of the Rights of Woman   Noted work of Mary Wollstonecraft (1759–1797), English republican who applied Enlightenment political ideas to issues of gender.

Virgil (70–19 B.C.E.)   One of the most influential Roman authors, his surviving works include the Eclogues and the Roman epic poem, the *Aeneid*.

Visigoths   The German "barbarians" who sacked Rome in 410.

Voltaire   Pseudonym of French philosopher and satirist Francois Marie Arouet (1694–1797), who championed the cause of human dignity against state and church oppression. Noted Deist and author of *Candide*.

Voting Rights Act (1965)   Law that granted universal suffrage in the United States.

War of the Roses   Fifteenth-century conflict between the English dynastic houses of Lancaster and York (each symbolized in heraldry by the rose), ultimately won by Lancastrian Henry VII.

Warsaw Pact (1955–1991)   Military alliance between the U.S.S.R. and other Communist states that was established as a response to the creation of the NATO alliance.

James Watt (1736–1819)   Scottish inventor and scientist who developed the steam engine.

Wealth of Nations   1776 treatise by Adam Smith, whose *laissez-faire* ideas predicted the economic boom of the Industrial Revolution.

Weimar Republic   The government of Germany between 1919 and the rise of Hitler and the Nazi party.

Western Front   Military front that stretched from the English Channel through Belgium and France to the Alps during World War I.

Whites   Refers to the "counterrevolutionaries" of the Bolshevik Revolution (1918–1921) who fought the Bolsheviks (the "Reds"); included former supporters of the tsar, Social Democrats, and large independent peasant armies.

William and Mary (1650–1702 and 1662–1694)   Dutch noble couple who supplanted the deposed Catholic King James II in 1688 as monarchs of England.

William the Conqueror (1027–1087)   Duke of French Normandy who crossed the English Channel and defeated Harold for the English throne in 1066. Imposed a centralized feudal system on England and introduced French as the official language.

women's suffrage   The movement to win legal and political rights, including the right to vote for all women.

Works Progress Administration (WPA)   New Deal program instituted in 1935 that put nearly 3 million people to work building roads, bridges, airports, and post offices.

World Bank   International agency established in 1944 to provide economic assistance to war-torn and poor countries. Its formal title is the International Bank for Reconstruction and Development.

Yalta Accords   Meeting between President Franklin D. Roosevelt, Prime Minister Winston Churchill, and Premier Josef Stalin that occurred in the Crimea in 1945 to to prepare for the postwar order.

yellow press   Newspapers that sought increased circulation by featuring sensationalist reporting that appealed to the masses.

"Young Turks"   The 1908 Turkish nationalist movement to depose Sultan Abdul Hamid II.

Zionism   Formally founded in 1897, a political movement holding that the Jewish people constitute a nation and are entitled to a national homeland, originally advocating the reestablishment of a Jewish homeland in Palestine

Zoroastrians   Founded by Zoroaster around 600 B.C.E., this Persian religion urged people to be truthful, to help each other, and to practice hospitality. Those who did would be rewarded in an afterlife after a "judgment day."

Zulus   African tribe that, under Shaka, created a ruthless warrior state in southern Africa in the early 1800s.

TEXT CREDITS

ILLUSTRATION CREDITS

de Police de la Ville de Paris); **829:** The Hulton Deutsch Collection/ Corbis; **830 (top):** Library of Congress; **(bottom):** Corbis; **831:** The Hulton Deutsch Collection/Corbis; **832:** Bettman/Corbis; **836:** Bildarchiv Preussischer Kulturbesitz, Berlin; **839:** Schefler Collection/Corbis; **842:** Staatliche Museen zu Berlin—Preußisher Kulturbesitz; **848:** Michael Nicholson/Corbis; **849:** Library of Congress/Corbis; **853:** Erich Lessing/Art Resource, NY, © 2005 Artists Rights Society (ARS), New York/ADAGP, Paris; **854:** © The Art Institute of Chicago; **855:** The Metropolitan Museum of Art, H. O. Havemeyer Collection, Bequest of Mrs. H. O. Havemeyer, 1929. (29.100.64) Photograph © 1984 The Metropolitan Museum of Art. **Digital History, 858:** © Hulton-Deutsch Collection/CORBIS; **859 (top):** © Leonard de Selva/CORBIS; **859 (bottom):** © Reuters NewMedia Inc./CORBIS.

Chapter 24: 860: The Art Archive/Imperial War Museum; **862:** Staatliche Museen zu Berlin—Preußischer Kulturbesitz; **866, 879, 885:** French soldiers (Imperial War Museum); **871:** © Bettmann/ CORBIS; **873:** Getty Images, Inc; **874:** Trustees of the Imperial War Museum, London; **875:** © Hulton-Deutsch Archives/CORBIS; **876:** Bettmann/CORBIS; **877:** The Imperial War Museum, London; **878:** Hoover Institution Archives, Stanford University; **880:** Hoover Institution Archives, Stanford University; **881:** Bildarchiv Preussischer Kulturbesitz; **883:** © Hulton-Deutsch Collection/Corbis; **884:** The Warder Collection, NY; **886:** The Warder Collection, NY; **888:** © Bettmann/CORBIS; **889:** © Bettmann/ CORBIS; **891:** The National Archives.

Chapter 25: 896: *The Funeral Procession,* by George Grosz (VAGA/ Art Resource, NY); **899:** Staatliche Museen zu Berlin—Preußischer Kulturbesitz; **902, 915, 927:** *Detroit Industry,* by Diego Rivera (Gift of Edsel B. Ford. © 1998 Institute Nacional de Bellas Artes, Mexico City. Photograph © The Detroit Institute of Arts); **905:** The Fotomas Index, London/The Warder Collection, NY; **906:** © Hulton-Deutsch Collection/Corbis; **909:** Brown Brothers; **911:** Stefan Lorant/The Warder Collection, NY; **913:** Stefan Lorant/ The Warder Collection, NY; **917:** The Hulton Deutsch Collection; **918:** The New York Public Library: Astor, Lenox, and Tilden Foundations; **921:** © Arthur Rothstein/CORBIS; **923:** © Bildarchiv Preussischer Kulturbesitz/Art Resource, NY; **924:** The Museum of Modern Art, New York. Photograph Courtesy The Museum of Modern Art, New York; **926:** © Bettmann/Corbis.

Chapter 26: 930: Winston Churchill, Franklin Roosevelt, and Joseph Stalin at the Yalta Conference, 1945 (Snark/Art Resource, NY); **936, 949, 952, 963:** *Guernica,* by Pablo Picasso (Giraudon/Art Resource, NY. © 2005 Estate of Pablo Picasso/ Artists Rights Society (ARS), New York); **937:** The National Archives/Corbis; **393:** © Hulton-Deutsch Collection/Corbis; **940:** © Hulton Deutsch Collection/Corbis; **943:** © Corbis; **947:** © Bettmann/Corbis; **948:** The Warder Collection, NY; **955:** AP/ World Wide Photos; **957:** Public Record Office Image Library; **961:** The National Archives/Corbis; **962:** The Imperial War Museum, London; **965:** © Hulton Deutsch Collection/Corbis. **Digital History, 968:** © Bettmann/CORBIS; **969 (top):** © Bettmann/ CORBIS; **969 (bottom):** © Bettmann/CORBIS.

Part VIII: 970–971: A scene from the fall of the Berlin Wall (© David and Peter Tumley/Corbis)

Chapter 27: 974: The Berlin airlift (UPI/Corbis-Bettman); **976:** UPI/Corbis-Bettmann; **980:** Yerevan, Armgosizdat, 1958; **982, 993, 1000, 1003, 1006:** A scene from the Soviet occupation of Czechoslovakia (Hulton Deutsch Collection/Corbis); **984:** AP/ Wide World Photos; **985:** German Information Center/The Warder Collection, NY; **987:** AP/Wide World Photos; **990:** © Bettmann/ CORBIS; **991:** Sovfoto/Eastfoto; **995 (top):** The Warder Collection, NY; **995 (bottom):** Associated Press; **1001:** Corbis; **1004:** Hulton Deutsch Collection/Corbis; **1007:** Corbis.

Chapter 28: 1010: © Bettmann/Corbis; **1013:** © Bettmann/Corbis; **1014:** © Paul Almasy/Corbis; **1015:** © Bettmann/Corbis; **1016:** Seattle Art Museum/Corbis. © 2005 Pollock-Krasner Foundation/Artists Rights Society (ARS), New York; **1017:** © Studio Patellani/Corbis; **1018:** © Bettmann/Corbis; **1021, 1026, 1028:** A scene from the student uprisings in Paris, May, 1968. (Bettman/ Corbis); **1023:** Associated Press; **1030:** © Bettmann/Corbis; **1032:** AP/World Wide Photos; **1033:** © Alexandra Avakian/ Woodfin Camp; **1035:** AP/Wide World Photos; **1040:** Patrick Robert/Corbis Sygma. **Digital History, 1042:** © Tim Page/CORBIS; **1043 (top):** © Olivier Coret/In Visu/CORBIS; **1043 (bottom):** © Olivier Coret/In Visu/CORBIS.

Chapter 29: 1044: © Antoine Serra/In Visu/Corbis; **1047:** © Michale Brennan/Corbis; **1049:** © Shaul Schwaz/Corbis; **1050:** © Reuters/Corbis; **1053:** © Reuters/Corbis; **1057:** © Bettmann/Corbis; **1059 (left):** Reuters/Corbis-Bettmann;

Every effort has been made to contact the copyright holders of the selections. Any corrections should be forwarded to W. W. Norton & Company, Inc., 500 Fifth Avenue, New York, NY 10110.

INDEX